Communicating through letters and reports

[You learn more by thinking about what you're doing than by simply thinking or simply doing.]

Communicating through letters and reports

J. H. MENNING

Professor of Marketing
in Charge of Business Writing Courses
School of Commerce and Business Administration
University of Alabama

and

C. W. WILKINSON

Professor of English, and Chairman,
Business and Technical Communications Courses
University of Florida

With the assistance of

DOROTHY COLBY MENNING

FIFTH EDITION · 1972

RICHARD D. IRWIN, INC.   *Homewood, Illinois 60430*
Irwin-Dorsey International   *London, England WC2H 9NJ*
Irwin-Dorsey Limited   *Georgetown, Ontario L7G 4B3*

Fifth Edition

First Printing, April 1972
Second Printing, March 1974

Library of Congress Catalog Card No. 70–180494
Printed in the United States of America

Preface

To teachers and students:

THIS FIFTH EDITION of a popular book retains the basic content, spirit, and special teaching and learning aids which met with wide approval in the first four editions.

As before, the central purpose of the book is to help you improve your written business communications.

As our main improvements for this fifth edition, therefore, we have:

1. Revised and supplemented the case materials with many new problems for greater variety and currency.
2. Updated the text, illustrations, and assignments in line with current products, policies, and practices.
3. Made numerous editorial changes, primarily for reasons of conciseness and readability.
4. Improved the checklists, making them more broadly applicable yet more pointed and concise.

Students and teachers of college courses in correspondence, in reports, and in combinations of the two will find the book easily adaptable to varying standards and student abilities. By attention to only the major principles and the easier problems, freshmen and sophomores of average ability can use the book effectively. By attention to all the refinements and the more difficult problems, upperclassmen who are Beta Gamma Sigmas and Phi Beta Kappas in our best universities will find it among their most challenging texts.

To students (in and out of school):

In learning anything as complex as writing superior letters and reports, you need instruction in PRINCIPLE, then ILLUSTRATION, and finally PRACTICE in applying the principles. Accordingly, the first four chapters present what we consider to be the basic tests applicable to all business letters. If you go no further, you will have a fundamental concept of the appearance, language and style, tone, and psychology of effective business letters.

v

For more detailed analysis and application, the next eight chapters show you how to handle your business letters functionally according to three basic plans: good-news, disappointing, and persuasive messages. Though the book presents analyses and examples of inquiries, replies, orders, acknowledgments, credits, collections, sales, and applications, the presentation is not in that order nor is the emphasis on specific letter types. As you read through the book, you will see the fundamentals applied in the many illustrations.

Some of the illustrations are modifications of good letters and reports written by businessmen. As most businessmen and teachers of business writing know, however, even comparatively good business letters that go through the mail do not serve well as textbook illustrations. Along with their good points, they usually contain defects attributable to pressure of time or the writers' temporary lapses, carelessness, or lack of training. For illustrations, therefore, we have carefully selected actual business letters and then edited them beyond merely changing names of companies, products, and individuals. In many instances we have written our own. We are fully aware, however, that the perfect letter never has been and never will be written.

Writing *perfect* letters or reports is next to impossible for all of us. Writing even *good* ones does not just come naturally to most. If you are content to write them as many *are* written, instead of as they *should* be, you will gain little or nothing from studying this book (or any other book or course on writing). But with a concentrated effort to improve, you probably can learn to write superior ones.

Having studied the principles and seen them illustrated, you can then make the principles stick in your mind (and thus make their application habitual) by putting them to use in working out selected problems from the many given at the ends of sections. The ample number and the variety of problems (many of them in a new, more succinct style) allow selection to fit your interests, abilities, and desired emphasis.

Please remember, however, that this book is not a dictionary, formula book, or cookbook to be followed blindly. Your aim should be thoughtful consideration of principles for use in the creation of your own original writing rather than slavish imitation of textbook models. You should learn and follow the *principles* illustrated, *not the wording* of the illustrations.

Likewise, the checklists (a special feature of this book) are thought starters rather than thought-stopping rules to be followed blindly. They are summary reminders of points about the particular kind of letter under discussion, not formulas for writing or straitjackets on it. They do *not* mean that all the points discussed earlier about a kind of letter and summarized in a checklist are applicable to every letter of that general class. Thoughtful consideration of a point in a checklist will quickly tell you whether the point is applicable to your particular letter problem, but ignoring the lists will frequently lead to omission of important points; and slavish following of a list will often lead to inappropriate contents in a letter. Hence, when used properly, the checklists can help you produce better letters, help teachers to mark student shortcomings quickly, and thus help you to see where you went wrong.

Besides the special feature of the checklists, you'll notice throughout the book that we have thrown overboard much conventional thinking about textbook writing. For example, we have chosen to address you directly instead of writing impersonally. This you-and-we style is better because (1) this is a book of instruction from us to you, and the natural way to write it is to talk with you; (2) through reading such style you will absorb better stylistic practices to apply in your own writing.

As another example, we have used contractions where they're natural and where they increase readability.

And for still another example, we have not stressed "correctness" as one of the requirements of letter and report style. For one reason, before using this book you should have learned spelling, grammar, punctuation, and sentence structure pretty well; to repeat much of your former instruction would only kill interest in the functional writing discussed here. For those who need some review, however, we have provided Appendix D, which affords ample material on the most likely shortcomings.

Our main reason, however, is that we think "inconspicuousness" is a more appropriate term than "correctness." We know that errors in punctuation, spelling, sentence structure, grammar, and word choice are undesirable because they distract the reader, slow him up, cause him to lose respect for the writer, and sometimes confuse him. On the other hand, we know that language scholars and wide-awake teachers of writing have discarded many old grammar-book rules of so-called correctness. Clearness, naturalness, appropriateness, and simplicity are more important than a purist's "correctness" in getting your message across to your reader.

From the many businessmen we have talked and worked with, from thousands of articles in business magazines, from the many textbooks on the subject, from associating with many other teachers on the job, through long and active membership in the American Business Communication Association (including terms as president), and from college students and business people we have taught, we have learned much about letters and reports and effective ways for teaching people to write better ones. We have brought together and modified what we have learned from a combined 60 years of experience. And we have contributed our own ideas.

In studying this one book, then, you learn what we think is the best that has been thought and said about letter and report writing through the years. By learning its suggestions, you can improve your letters and reports.

J. H. Menning
C. W. Wilkinson

March 1972

Contents

Checklists

The letter cases in this book are disguised and sometimes slightly modified real situations. Mostly they are from among the more difficult letter-writing situations of business. All names of firms and individuals are fictitious for obvious reasons. Purposely, ZIP code numbers are incorrect.

We have tried to give you the basic information needed without complicating details. You are expected to fill in details from your own imagination. But you are not to go contrary to the statements or implications in the cases, and your imaginary details must be reasonably likely.

The writing in the problems is intentionally not good—nor is the order of points the best— because you would learn nothing from copying from us. So beware of copying sentences and clauses in your letters. Put your ideas in your own words.

Why study
letter writing?

ALMOST ANYONE *can* (and everyone does) write letters, but are they good ones? Unless the writer has had some training in letter writing and gives some thought and planning to his letters, they are not likely to be good.

The main reason you should study letter writing depends on two facts:

1. You are almost certain to write many business letters during the rest of your life, regardless of the kind of work you do.
2. By studying the principles and practicing the skills and arts of letter writing, you can learn to write letters that will more frequently bring the desired results.

The letter is the most common form of written communication for managing business affairs, and everybody has business affairs to manage. Whether you fail or succeed in managing many of these affairs will depend on whether you send an ordinary letter or a really good one. Through systematic study and practice you can learn to write good ones.

Other things you learn

In learning to write better letters, you will also learn some principles of practical psychology that will enable you to get along better professionally and socially with other people.

When you improve your ability to write clear, concise, persuasive, and natural English (which *is* the desirable language of business), you gain accuracy and naturalness in phrasing anything else you have to write or speak.

Through your study of letters you will get further insight into the ways of the business world: practices used in getting people to buy; handling orders; gaining and refusing credit; making collections; adjusting claims; and selecting employees.

You will learn how to save time and money on letter writing. As a good letter writer, you can often write one letter to settle a business transaction that would require two or three from an untrained writer. By using form letters and form paragraphs, you can cut down on letter costs when the form message will do the job. When, however, you have situations requiring individual letters, you will recognize them and know better than to waste money on forms. You will also be able to dictate or write the necessary individualized letters more rapidly because you will have gained the self-confidence that comes from knowing how to tackle a job. You will write freely and effectively the letters you *have* to write and the many others you *should* write.

Perhaps most important of all, you will realize that every letter you write is an item in your overall public relations—and you will try to make each letter win, instead of lose, friends.

Letter volume and costs

Editors of *The Reporter of Direct Mail Advertising* (June, 1962, pp. 22 ff.) predicted that 62 billion pieces of mail would be handled by the U.S. Post Office for 1962, 70 billion for 1963, and 90 billion for 1970. Some pessimists questioned this in view of increasing postal rates and use of the telephone. But *Time* (January 7, 1966, p. 44) reported 72 billion pieces of mail ZIPing through the hands of postal sorters (both human and mechanical) in 1965.

Time editors (March 30, 1971, p. 14) also reported that there were 82 billion pieces a year (270 million pieces a day, 35 million daily in New York alone). Mr. Winton M. Blount, Postmaster General of the new United States Postal Service (*Parade*, June 27, 1971, p. 16) says, "It will involve more than 86 billion pieces of mail a year—soon to be over 100 billion pieces."

If we accept the ratio of 2:1 for first- and third-class mailings that has appeared in U.S. Post Office annual reports in recent years, this means, for 1971, 58 billion first-class letters that went through the mail—an average of over 280 for every person in the United States. This average includes children, housewives, day laborers, and many other groups who write fewer than the average number of letters. Business and professional men write many more than the average. And remember that they also send out billions of third-class mailings (roughly 29 billion if the foregoing estimates are correct), practically all of which are business letters.

All these letters cost money, too. A businessman can send processed third-class mailings in large quantities, enjoying the advantages of reduced postage rates, for costs varying from 10 cents on up (the sky really is the limit here; for illustrations, color, gadgets, and the like can increase mailing costs materially). But for first-class letters, when he figures the dictator's and transcriber's time, the stationery, the stamps, and the allocation of equipment, storage, and space expenses, he must admit that the $3.05 IBM estimate is about right. If the letters are written by executives or department heads, the cost can soar to $4 or $6 or more per letter.

These estimates have climbed from 75 cents in the late 1930s to 91 cents in 1953 to $1.70 in 1957 to $1.83 in 1961 to $2 or over in 1965, and $3.05 in 1969. Even if you assume that only half the first-class letters are business letters, you're forced to admit that a $58-billion cost figure is not far off. And if you further assume even the minimum estimate of 10 cents for mass third-class mailings, you have to add another $2.5 billion to that impressive figure. Business letter writing is big business—big enough to justify considerable attention to its efficiency!

Most important, isn't it likely that you will be one in a business or professional group that writes more than the average number of letters? And that you will be at least partially responsible for effective control of this high-cost, but often necessary, way of doing business?

Letter advantages

When you consider the advantages of doing business by letter, you see why businessmen write so many letters and spend so much money on them. Despite the cost of a letter, it is often the most economical way to transact business. You can't go far (not even across town, if you figure your time and traveling expense) or talk far by long distance or say much in a telegram for the cost of a letter. But for that money you can put your message in a letter and send it anywhere in the country or almost anywhere in the world.

Even if you do talk to the other fellow, you do not have a written record, as you do if you follow the almost universal business practice of making a copy of your letter. The fact that a letter and its answer can make a written contract is one reason why letters often replace personal calls and telephone calls even when the two parties are in the same city.

Still another advantage is that both the writer and reader can handle a letter at their most convenient times. Therefore, it can get by receptionists and secretaries many times when a telephone call or a personal call cannot. Moreover, the reader usually gives it his full attention without raising partially considered objections and without interruption. This is a decided psychological advantage.

Emphasis in business

When executives began to realize how much letters cost, how important letters and reports are to the smooth operation of their firms, and how few of their employees were capable writers, many of them started training programs and correspondence control programs. At General Electric, Westinghouse, Southern Pacific, Marshall Field's, the New York Life Insurance Company, and the big mail-order houses (Montgomery Ward, Spiegel's, and Sears Roebuck), to mention only a few of the leaders, such programs have demonstrated the economy and efficiency resulting from improved correspondence. Even these firms, however, prefer to hire people who can already write rather than train them on company time.

A frequent question in employment interviews and in inquiry letters to professors, therefore, concerns the ability of college graduates to do such writing. An applicant who presents evidence that he can write good letters and reports becomes a favored applicant for nearly any job.

Emphasis in schools

Many of the executives who are aware of the importance of good letters are graduates of the few schools where instruction in business writing has been given since early in the 1900s. These business leaders are the main reason why today in the majority of respectable colleges and universities literally thousands of students are studying and practicing how to write more effectively for business. Without exception, surveys by such organizations as Delta Sigma Pi, the American Association of Collegiate Schools of Business, and the American Business Communication Association have confirmed the high regard of former students for the work.

Business letter-writing instructors frequently hear student comments such as "I learned more English in letter writing than in any other course I ever had!" or "*Everybody* should be required to take a course in letter writing!" or "This course is good preparation for living in general."

Common misconceptions

Yet some people—mostly for lack of information—do not respect even university work in business writing. They sometimes think courses in letter writing are merely about letter forms. Although this is a part of the course, it is only a small part (less than 5 percent of this book).

You may even hear the mistaken idea that students of letter writing learn the trite, wordy, and nearly meaningless expressions so common at the beginnings and endings of letters written by some untrained businessmen. Actually, you learn to write naturally, concisely, and clearly, to take care of the business without beating about the bush, and to end letters when you are through—without wasting first and last sentences saying nothing.

Still others think that in the study of letter writing the emphasis is on high-pressure techniques and tricks and gadgets. Just the opposite is true. In drawing on the findings of psychologists, we are *not* advocating that you attempt to *manipulate* or outsmart your reader in sly, unethical fashion. Use of the findings of psychology is good or bad depending on the intent of the user. The intent of the writer toward his reader should always be morally and ethically proper. Our intent is to help you write acceptable things (determined by you) in an acceptable way (determined by your reader) more likely to convince your reader of the legitimacy and the attractiveness (or soundness) of your proposal or position.

You may hear that letter writing is "just a practical study." It certainly is practical, for the ability to write good business letters is useful. But it is also a cultural study because its primary purposes are the development of (1) your ability to maintain pleasant relations with your fellow men and (2) your language effectiveness.

Why the high regard for letter writing?

One of the reasons why courses in business letter writing have found increasing favor with students—as well as with executives and college administrators—is that it is a blend of the cultural and the practical.

The business correspondent writes to an individual for a definite, practical purpose. Emphatically, he must write with the same exactness as other good writers. Unlike them, however, he does not seek to entertain his reader (or to please himself with his purple passages and "deathless prose"). He wants to arrange an interview for a job or a sales demonstration, to secure the appropriate signatures on a contract, to get prospects to visit a showroom, or to secure the agreement of a customer to a delay or a substitution. *Action* is usually his goal. Letter writing is partially a study of probable or estimated human *reaction* as the basis for securing the desired *action*. Since the quality of persuasion is more important to the letter writer than to most writers, a good knowledge of practical psychology is essential in his work.

The good correspondent must learn to do more than just sell goods and services. In his handling of claim, adjustment, credit, and collection letters, he learns tact, patience, consideration of the other fellow, a necessarily optimistic attitude, and the value of saying things pleasantly and positively instead of negatively. These are the reasons why you can expect more successful social and business relations with other people after a thorough, conscientious, and repeated analysis and application of the principles of good letter writing.

Furthermore, the good letter writer must learn to be concise, interesting, and easy to follow if he is to hold his reader. For reasons of courtesy a listener will bear with a long-winded, dull, or unclear conversation. He will even ask for explanations. But the reader of a letter feels no such courtesy toward it. The good letter writer therefore edits his work carefully so that he will phrase ideas more effectively in writing than he can in talking. In conversation one can cushion the effect or shade the meaning of his words with the twinkle of his eye, the inflection of his voice, or the gesture of his hand. As he proceeds, he can adjust and adapt his presentation according to the reaction he observes in his listener. With far less chance of failure he can get along by "doin' what comes naturally." The letter writer has no such chance to observe the effects of the first part of his presentation and adapt the last part accordingly. He must therefore learn to *foresee* the reader's reaction all the way through. This requires more thorough knowledge of practical psychology, more preliminary analysis of what his reader is like, more careful planning of his message, and more careful phrasing of his thoughts than in oral communications.

Such planning and editing establishes good habits of expression—habits which carry over to the spoken message. This is the reason we say that you will learn to talk better if you learn to write better. It is also the reason we say that, in learning to write effective letters, you will learn to do a better job of writing anything else you have to write.

Art, science, or skill?

The use of the language—in clear, concise adaptation to one's readers so that they can absorb the message with the least amount of effort and the greatest amount of pleasant reaction—is an art. Several generations of business writers have shown that the proper language for business in general and for letters in particular is just plain good English. Though it is more concise and more precise, it is neither more nor less formal than the conversational language of people for whom letters are intended.

Good business letters are also the result of a conscious use of principles which have evolved since the turn of the century. It would be an exaggeration to claim that business letter writing is a science, but it would be folly to ignore the experiences of prominent business writers who have experimented with letters for over 60 years. As a result of their experiences, they have given us a near-scientific framework of principles as a starting point. Though many of these principles have not been demonstrated with scientific exactness, they have taken a great deal of the speculative out of letter writing. We can therefore approach the writing of business letters with considerable knowledge of what good letter-writing principles are and *when, where,* and *how* to apply them.

Writing good business letters, then, is neither exclusively an art nor exclusively a science. Yet it is certainly more than what we frequently call a skill. It involves thinking of a very complex kind: analyzing both a situation and a reader, and then using good judgment in applying knowledge of English, business, and psychology.

Summary

In studying letter writing, you not only learn how to get the desired results from the many letters you will have to write. You will also get a greater understanding of people and how to influence them, an increased facility in the use of language (both oral and written), a more thorough knowledge of business practices and ethics, and a resultant confidence in yourself.

You may want to make a career of business letters. Correspondence supervisors, letter consultants, and direct-mail specialists have found it highly rewarding. But in *any* business, industry, or profession—as well as in your private life—your ability to write a good letter will be a vital tool and a powerful factor in your eventual success.

Why study
report writing?

A BASIC FACT about report writing, as about letter writing, is that most people who have not studied it do it rather poorly.

The basic language of good reports differs little from the standard English used in any good functional writing, but good report writing requires the use of certain supplementary communication devices rarely learned except in report-writing courses. The forms of reports deserve some attention, but they are easily learned. Putting the words on paper, however, is only a part of the problem.

If you consider the meaning of *communicating through reports,* you'll realize that *preparation* is involved. And preparation means making a plan, getting the material or evidence (research), organizing for meaning and coherence, analyzing this material to arrive at a solution to the problem, and *then* writing up your analysis clearly and concisely.

You realize, too, that improving your ability to do all these things is an important education. Study and practice in writing reports *can* therefore help you when you're a student. They *will* help you when you're a job candidate and when you're on the job.

Help when you're a student

Learning to write a good report can help you to earn better grades. The increased familiarity with sources of information—not just published sources and how to find them in the libraries, but also methods of securing original data—enables you to do research more efficiently for papers required in other courses. (Reports are certainly not like term papers in objective or in some phases of treatment, but the research behind them is similar.) Documenting is also similar in the two. And certainly you'll profit from the carry-over of organization principles and improved language ability. For these reasons students who have studied and applied report-writing principles usually earn better grades on term papers in advanced courses and hence better grades in the courses.

If you go on to graduate school, you will find that your work in report writing has been your best preparation. When you have to write the many long research papers and a thesis, you will already know how to collect, organize, and interpret data and to document your writing. Indeed, you will probably join the many graduate students we have heard make comments to the effect that "Thanks to my course in report writing, I know how to go about writing course papers and my thesis."

Help when you're a job candidate

If you apply for a job, you'll find that employers put a premium on the services of people who can write well. Because reports play such a prominent role in most businesses (for reasons explained early in Chapter 13), prospective employers often give preference to those applicants who have had training in report writing. They prefer to hire people who can already write reports rather than to spend vast sums of money on company-sponsored report-writing courses (as hundreds of companies find it necessary to do for people who have not had such preparation).

One director of a collegiate employment bureau reports that an increasing number of employee recruiters ask, as one of the first questions, what grade a prospective employee earned in report writing. (Note that they assume students have had such training.) These men apparently regard the report-writing performance of the student in his college course as an indication of his ability to do something that is important to their organizations.

Help when you're on the job

If you are surprised by the interest of *prospective* employers in your ability to write reports, you may be even more surprised by their interest as *employers*. The reports a trainee on a new job is usually required to submit not only help to determine the division of the company where he will be assigned; but they also often determine whether he will be retained at the end of the training period. Even after a man is a full-fledged employee, management studies his reports not only for information and ideas in the solution of problems but also for evidence of the employee's ability to communicate clearly, quickly, and easily. To his immediate superior, an employee will often report orally, but the immediate superior is not usually the one who makes the final decisions about an employee's salary increases and promotions. Those who do may consider the immediate superior's evaluation, but they often consider equally important the *written* reports of the employee being evaluated. Employers often regard the reports he writes as the best—and sometimes they are the only—indication of how well he is doing his job.

Your study of report writing, as you see, can help your grades in school, your chances at a desirable job, and your effectiveness and status in your career.

PART ONE

How a reader
reacts to a letter

*[Through your letters you quickly reveal the kind
of gentleman or stinker you are.]*

<table>
<tr><td>chapter 1</td><td>

Appearance:
What the reader sees

[Appropriate dress is usually the first indication of competence.]

Stationery
Letterhead
Forms of indention and punctuation
Placement on the page
    Picture-frame plan
    Standard-line plan
Position and spacing of letter parts
    Standard parts
    Special parts
Addressing the envelope; folding and inserting the letter

</td></tr>
</table>

JUST ABOUT EVERYBODY has to write business letters. Most people consider themselves "pretty fair" letter writers, too. Actually, however, the statement "Anything done by everybody is seldom done well" is as true of business letter writing as it is of any other activity.

If you do write good business letters, you can answer yes to the following questions:

1. Is the appearance of your letters pleasant and unobtrusive?
2. Is the style of your letters interesting, clear, and inconspicuous?
3. Do your letters follow good persuasion principles?
4. Do your letters reflect basic goodwill?

You and any other business letter writer should apply these four tests because

—A pleasant and unobtrusive (undistracting) appearance is important; it is the first impression the reader has of your letter. If the appearance is bad, you start off with one strike against you.

11

—Your letter may establish a favorable first impression because its appearance is pleasant and unobtrusive, yet fail completely because its language is dull, vague, inaccurate, difficult to follow, unnatural, or full of errors.

—Its appearance may be good, and it may be written in natural, clear style, yet fail because it does not stress benefits to the reader (that is, it does not follow good psychology).

—Even with good looks, appropriate style, and persuasive presentation, your letter can fail if it reflects poor tone and/or fails to reflect a desire to be of service to the reader.

—With all four desirable qualities—goodwill, appropriate persuasion, good style, and good looks—it will accomplish its purpose in most instances.

To explain and illustrate these four essentials of any good letter is the function of Part One of this book. To show how the principles apply in all kinds of letters is the main function of the other chapters on letters.

We do not believe you can write the good letters you are capable of writing without understanding each of these four essentials. For that reason we ask you to read extensively before you start writing; hence no letter cases appear until the end of Part One.

The appearance of an individualized letter is like the appearance of a person: Since it is not the most important thing, the less it attracts attention to itself, the better. The wording, the persuasive qualities, and a desirable tone reflecting goodwill are more influential than the looks of the letter in determining its success or failure. But just as some listeners will reject the messages of speakers who do not come up to expected standards of favorable appearance, so will many readers reject the written message that calls attention to the format and distracts from the ideas.

A personalized (individualized) letter sent by first-class mail will nearly always get a reading. Flashy designs and lavish colors in it are like yelling at a person whose attention you already have. Even worse, if your letter is either too messy or too gaudy, or if it violates the conventions of letter form, the appearance distracts the reader's attention from the important feature—your message.

Sales letters are sometimes justifiable exceptions. Because they are usually unpersonalized mass mailings, they sometimes struggle to get read at all. In striving to capture attention, their writers may wisely use cartoons, gadgets, and lavish colors *if* the unusual appearance is a symbol of the key idea and *if* the message quickly takes over the hold on the reader's attention. In general, however, the physical letter should serve only as a vehicle for your message and should not be noticed.

STATIONERY

The first thing noticed if it is inappropriate is your stationery. The most common business stationery—and therefore the least noticed—is 20-pound bond with some rag content in 8½- by 11-inch sheets. Variations acceptable under appropriate circumstances include heavier and lighter paper, different sizes, and various colors and shades.

Paper heavier than 20-pound is more expensive, too stiff for easy folding, and too thick for clear carbons; and lighter than 16-pound is too flimsy and transparent for letters. (If used, carbon copies are usually on lighter paper, both because it is cheaper and because you can make a greater number of clear copies with it.)

The main off-standard sizes are Executive or Monarch letterheads (7½ by 10½ or 11 inches), used mainly by top executives, and half sheets (8½ by 5½ inches), used most frequently in intracompany notes but also often for short replies. A common objection to any odd size is that it does not fit standard files and envelopes.

Though white is the standard, only the rainbow and your sense of appropriateness to your kind of business set the limits for color variations. Numerous tests have shown that colored papers sometimes produce better results in sales mailings. But existing test results do not prove that any one color will always work best for any one kind of letter. If you are sending out large mailings, you may be wise to run your own test on a small sample to see what color works best for that particular situation.

Paper with some rag content is more expensive than all-pulp paper, but it gives the advantages of easier and neater erasures, pleasant feel, durability, and resistance to yellowing. The new plasticized papers have all these advantages plus easier erasing.

Whatever your choice of paper for the letter sheets, you should use the same quality for envelopes and second pages.

The acceptable variations in stationery allow you to reflect the personality of your business, just as you select clothes appropriate to your personality. A back-alley repair shop would not use pink-tinted 24-pound bond in the Monarch size. Nor would a bank president select paper that looks and feels cheap. The big points are appropriateness and inconspicuousness. In selecting the paper for your letterheads, then, you should have a good reason before choosing something other than 20-pound bond, 8½ by 11 inches. Anything else is more likely to distract the reader's attention from the message of the letter.

LETTERHEAD

Designing letterheads has become a job for specialists who know paper stocks, color, and design; so most paper suppliers provide such specialists, at least as consultants. Any business writer, however, should know something of the main principles and trends.

The main trend for some years has been toward simplicity. Letterheads used to take up a good part of the sheet with slogans, names of officers, and pictures of the firm's plant and products. The good modern letterhead usually takes no more than 2 inches at the top. It uses wording and design

RICHARD   D. *R* I R W I N · I N C.

1818 RIDGE ROAD · HOMEWOOD, ILLINOIS · A SUBURB OF CHICAGO

CHICAGO TELEPHONE: INTEROCEAN 8-9200   LONG DISTANCE TELEPHONE: SYCAMORE 8-6000

ZIP CODE 60430

PUBLISHERS OF BOOKS IN ECONOMICS AND BUSINESS

to convey the necessary information and an atmosphere symbolic of the business firm it represents. The minimum content is the name and address of the firm, including the ZIP code. An added trademark or slogan indicates the nature of the business unless the name makes it clear. Telephone numbers (with area codes) and departmental designations are other common additions. Firms doing much international business frequently give a code address for cablegrams. On the theory that age suggests stability, many firms also give their starting dates. Though two or more colors sometimes appear, modern designers are careful to avoid garish combinations, elaborate designs, and usually any color unless it signifies something about the nature of the business. The letterheads for all the letters in this chapter are typical modern forms.

FORMS OF INDENTION AND PUNCTUATION

Letters 1 through 4 in this chapter illustrate the main letter forms in use today. They discuss decisions you will have to make in choosing an acceptable form for your letters. They are integral parts of the explanation; so you should read them thoroughly as well as look at them. Some of the important points to note are:

1. The two big trends are toward simplicity and time-saving.

2. All consistent forms are "correct," but either the outmoded or the ultramodern does tend to call attention to itself and characterize its user.

3. In studying letter writing, you should learn all widely used current forms, with their advantages, disadvantages, and dangers; but you should realize that if you go to work for a company, you should use the company's established form unless and until you can persuade responsible personnel to change.

You should also realize that you can mix forms (with blocked parts and indented paragraphs, for example) and be in perfectly good company. Hanging indention (the first line of the paragraph extending out five or more spaces to the left beyond the other lines) is also an accepted form, though not common.

PLACEMENT ON THE PAGE

Even with appropriate paper and a well-designed letterhead, you can still spoil the appearance (and thus distract from the message) unless you place the letter on the page properly. Two methods are in common use: the picture-frame and the standard-line plans.

Picture-frame plan

Typing a letter so that it looks like a picture framed by the white space around it, as in Letter 1, is still the more widely used plan. It takes a little more time than the standard-line method because you have to set the marginal stops according to your estimate of each letter's length, but it enables you to fit long and short letters to the page in more conventional fashion. Also, you can sometimes save time by increasing the line length and thus

LETTER 1   Picture-frame layout, semiblock with mixed punctuation, elite type.

UNIVERSITY OF FLORIDA

COLLEGE OF ARTS AND SCIENCES

GAINESVILLE

32601

DEPARTMENT OF ENGLISH   February 7, 19--

Miss Elizabeth Diller
1328 Waukegan Street
Grand Rapids, Michigan 49504

Dear Miss Diller:

Both you and your employer are right. Indented form with closed punctuation is "correct"; but so are several others, including the much more popular semiblock with mixed punctuation I'm using here.

Since the boss has the right to establish policy, however, you'll have to type his letters the way he wants them. Of course if he welcomes suggestions, you can tell him that indented form with closed punctuation strikes most modern readers as behind the times; and you can show him that it costs him money by slowing you up.

That form was the style before typewriters came into use. Then one day a bright secretary decided to quit wasting time indenting and punctuating the lines in headings and inside addresses. That started a continuing trend toward efficiency and simplicity in letter form.

Since she still indented for paragraphs, the form she used is called semiblock; and since she continued to use a colon after the salutation and a comma after the complimentary close, she used what is now called mixed punctuation. Later dropping of the paragraph indention, and omitting the useless colon and comma, produced block form with open punctuation.

Semiblock and block are certainly more widely used today than the other forms; and the order of frequency in punctuation style is mixed, open, and closed. But all are correct.

You may show your employer this letter as the most widely used form if you want to; but don't lose your job over such a small matter as which form to use for his letters.

Cordially yours,

C. W. Wilkinson, Professor

---

getting on one page material that would require two pages by the standard-line plan.

The idea is that a rectangle drawn around the letter (not including a printed letterhead) should look like a picture framed in the marginal white space. You determine the width of side margins according to your letter length and make the top margin the same. The bottom margin will take care of itself automatically. It should be about one and a half times as long (deep) as the other margins.

In gaining experience, a typist soon learns where to set a typewriter's marginal stops for letters of varied lengths. If you're just starting to gain the experience, however, you might well try this general plan. For short letters (100 words or less) leave about 2-inch margins at the top and sides. For long letters (over 200 words) leave at least 1-inch margins. Split the difference for middle-length letters.

Standard-line plan

As illustrated by Letter 2, the standard-line plan of placing a letter on the page saves time because the typist does not have to reset marginal stops for letters of varied length. Typewriters are set to the company's standard line (usually six inches); thus all letters have the same side margins. The top margin is about the same as the side margins, and the bottom margin is about one and a half times as wide. By varying from the standard spacing between letter parts (more or less between the date and inside address, for example, or three spaces instead of two between paragraphs), the typist can adjust letters of differing lengths for proper height.

POSITION AND SPACING OF LETTER PARTS

Standard parts

The usual business letter has six standard parts. As a general rule, single space within parts and double space between parts. But note exceptions as they come up in the explanation.

The *heading* or first part of a letter on plain paper must include the sender's address (but usually not his name) and the date. It establishes both top and side margins because it is the first thing on the page, and the end of the line going farthest to the right sets the margin. It may appear on the left, too, in a pure block form. Such a heading is usually three lines but often more. Thus it affects the number of words you can fit into a given typewriter setting.

On printed stationery you can write the dateline as a unit with the letter-head (to complete the heading, as in Letter 1) or as a separate part. As a unit with the letterhead, place the typed-in date for best appearance according to the design of the printed part. Usually it retains the balance by appearing directly under the center of a symmetrical letterhead; often it rounds out one that is off balance. Frequently it is a separate part because of the difference between print and type. As a separate part, it fixes the upper right corner of the letter or, in full block, the left corner (as in Letter 2). That is, it leaves the top margin (equal to the side margins)

LETTER 2   Standard-line layout, block with mixed punctuation, pica type.

UNIVERSITY OF ALABAMA
SCHOOL OF COMMERCE AND BUSINESS ADMINISTRATION
UNIVERSITY, ALABAMA 35486

DEPARTMENT OF MARKETING

February 7, 19--

Miss Elizabeth Diller
1328 Waukegan Street
Grand Rapids, Michigan   49504

Dear Miss Diller:

Though most letters are written according to the Picture-Frame plan, certain outstanding firms for years have saved time with what is called the Standard Line.

Following this system, the secretary never resets the margin stops on her typewriter and begins all letters at the same top position on the page.

If the letter is short, she makes the black material extend over the greater part of the white space by increasing spaces between paragraphs and/or between the standard letter parts.

Thus she saves time consumed in calculating and in resetting margin stops to place extra-short letters on the page.

Some folks might be a little startled the first time they see a Standard-Line letter. But if your letters really have something to say, readers won't pay much attention to an appearance which is a little unorthodox but is certainly justifiable. Some readers won't even be aware of the difference.

Show this one to your employer, too; you may be surprised at his agreeableness.

Cordially yours,

J. H. Menning

J. H. Menning
Professor

---

between itself and the letterhead, and its end sets the right margin (or its beginning the left margin). Thus it is the first exception to the general rule of double spacing between letter parts.

The *inside address* includes the title, name, and address of the person to receive the letter, including the ZIP code. The beginning of the address establishes the upper left corner of the letter if the date is a unit with a printed letterhead. Otherwise, it begins at the left margin, two to six spaces lower than the dateline. So it is the second exception to double spacing between letter parts. (*Warning:* Be careful to spell names right and to use the proper title; nobody likes to have his name misspelled or to be given the wrong title. And *always* put some form of title—professional, honorary, or courtesy—in *front* of *other* people's names.)

The *salutation* or friendly greeting, the third standard part, begins at the left margin a double space below the inside address and ends with a colon (:) or no punctuation whatsoever. The wording must match up with the first line of the address. That is, if you address an individual, the salutation must fit (usually *Dear* plus title and name); if you address a firm or other group, you must choose an appropriate salutation.

Since a salutation is the first indication of the formality of the letter, you should give some thought to the implications of how you greet your reader and how you match the tone of your salutation in the complimentary close. The main forms listed below are for letters addressed to persons, in ascending order of formality with appropriate complimentary closes:

Dear (given name, nickname, or such more familiar term as originality can produce and good taste will allow)	Cordially yours or some more familiar phrasing, as long as it remains in good taste
Dear (surname or given name)	Sincerely yours or Cordially yours
Dear (appropriate title plus surname)	Sincerely yours or Yours truly
My dear Mr. (or Mrs.) White	Yours truly or Sincerely yours
My dear Sir (or Madam)	Respectfully yours or Yours truly

"Gentlemen" is the proper salutation for letters addressed to a company, regardless of formality and regardless of an attention line (even when some of the "gentlemen" are ladies). In line with the trend toward informal friendliness of business letters, most business writers use the person's name in the salutation when they can and match the friendly tone with some form of *sincerely* or *cordially*.

The *body* or message of the letter begins a double space below the salutation. Usually single-space within paragraphs and double-space between, though in very short letters you may use double spacing within and triple spacing between paragraphs. Since the body is all one part, regardless of the number of paragraphs, the standard double spacing between paragraphs is a third exception to the general rule of spacing. The number of paragraphs therefore affects the fit of a letter to a given typewriter setting. A letter of 250 words in seven paragraphs, for example, will take at least four more lines than the same number of words in three paragraphs. Yet you should not overlook the chance to improve readability by keeping paragraphs short and itemizing points.

LETTER 3 Picture-frame layout, simplified form with open punctuation, elite type.

UNIVERSITY OF FLORIDA

COLLEGE OF ARTS AND SCIENCES

GAINESVILLE

32601

DEPARTMENT OF ENGLISH

February 7, 19--

Miss Elizabeth Diller
1328 Waukegan Street
Grand Rapids, Michigan 49504

SIMPLIFIED LETTER FORM

Both you and your employer are right, Miss Diller. Indented form with closed punctuation is "correct." But so are semiblock and block forms with open punctuation. Both are more widely used than indented form is.

The further simplified form which I am using here, with all parts beginning at the left margin to save time, is fast gaining favor. This form was first introduced during World War I but did not take hold well until the National Office Management Association (NOMA) sponsored it after World War II. It is based on the ideas that

-- no parts need labels. (The subject line in this letter is clear without a label, isn't it?)

-- if you use the reader's name in the first line or two and write your letters sincerely or cordially, you do not need salutations or complimentary closes.

-- by beginning all parts flush with the left margin and omitting end punctuation, you can turn out more letters at lower cost.

True simplification of letters means more than that, of course; but as far as form is concerned, those are the most important considerations.

Though many outstanding firms have adopted the form, and though it may be almost universal in American business sometime in the future, it may yet distract the attention of readers who aren't used to it.

Perhaps after seeing the advantages of this simplified form, you'll want to change your mind. If your boss asks for your suggestions, or if he welcomes them, you can show him the advantages. He's sure to be impressed by the argument that you can turn out more letters this way.

The *complimentary close* (worded appropriately according to the ascending scale of formality illustrated above) goes a double space below the last line of the body. It may begin at the center of the page, or in line with the beginning of a typed heading, or in line with the dateline used as a separate part, or at a point to space it evenly between the center

Miss Elizabeth Diller, February 7, 19--, page 2

But since your employer has the right to establish policy, you should
set up his letters the way he wants them. If he wants to pay you to
take the time to type more conservative-appearing letters--which are
just as "correct"--don't give the matter a second thought. Save your
patience and energy for more significant considerations.

C. W. Wilkinson

C. W. Wilkinson, Professor

and right margin of the letter. As you've seen, the most common forms employ one of four key words—*cordially, sincerely, truly,* and *respectfully* —each ordinarily used with *yours.* Juggling the order of the key word and *yours* or adding *very*—as *Yours truly, Yours very truly, Very truly yours*— makes little difference. The key word is the main consideration.

LETTER 4   Nonletterhead layout, block form, pica type, on plain paper.

---

46 Guilds Woods
Tuscaloosa, Alabama 35401
February 7, 19--

Miss Elizabeth Diller
1328 Waukegan Street
Grand Rapids, Michigan 49504

Dear Miss Diller:

Your preference for blocked form with open
punctuation is certainly justified; it is definitely more popular and is more economical
than the indented form with closed punctuation
which you used to show what your boss prefers.

That form is not "incorrect" by any standard
(though it is practically outlawed by correspondence supervisors and office managers). It is
the preferred form of many executives associated
with prominent firms of impeccable standing.
Such fine men often got their training in letter
writing in the early 1900's.

If your employer is willing to pay for your
extra time in following that form and chooses
to be "old school," that is his decision.

Sincerely yours,

J. H. Menning

J. H. Menning
Professor

The proper form of the *signature block* depends on whether the letter
is about your private affairs or your company business. In writing about
your own business, you space four times below the complimentary close
and type your name. The typed name is important for legibility—and consideration for the reader. You then pen your signature above it.

But if you're writing about company business and the company is to be legally responsible for the letter, the company name should appear above the signature. The fact that the letter is on company stationery makes no difference. So if you want to protect yourself against legal involvement, type the company name in solid capitals (that's the way most firms do) a double space below the complimentary close; then make the quadruple space for your signature before your typed name. You also give your title on the next line below the typed name or, if there is room, put a comma and your title on the same line with your name. Thus you indicate that you are an agent of the company legally authorized to transact business.

```
Very truly yours,                    Sincerely yours,
ACME PRODUCTS, INC.                  LOVEJOY AND LOEB




John Y. Bowen               (Miss) Phyllis Bentley, Treasurer
Comptroller
```

Because the possibility of legal involvement is usually remote, many writers prefer to omit the company name from the signature block in the hope of gaining a more personal effect through a letter from an individual instead of from a company. If you feel that way and are willing to take the legal risk, you can set up the signature block as follows:

```
Cordially yours,                                  Sincerely yours,




H. P. Worthington               (Mrs.) Phyllis B. Hudson
Assistant Public Relations              Treasurer
    Manager
```

Before you do, however, we suggest that you

1) get official agreement to bail you out of any legal involvement and
2) remember that some readers will feel greater security in dealing with a company instead of an individual.

Women's signatures bring up a special problem. Note that in all the men's signatures illustrated, no title precedes the names. Without some indication, however, the person who answers a woman's letter does not know whether to address her as Miss or Mrs. Some writers dodge the question by using Ms., but this is far from standard practice. As a matter of consideration for the other fellow, a woman should indicate whether she is Miss or Mrs.—the way Miss Bentley, who became Mrs. Hudson, did in the preceding examples.

Special parts

Besides the six standard parts of a business letter, you will often find good use for one or more of seven widely used special parts.

You can use an *attention line* in a letter addressed to a company if you want a certain individual in the company to read it. If you don't know the person's name, you may refer to him by title. For example, in a sales letter you may ask for the attention of the purchasing agent like this:

```
Black, Decker, and Smith
1223 South Congress Avenue
Minneapolis, Minnesota
Attention of the Purchasing Agent
Gentlemen:
```

It's equally good form to write "Attention: Purchasing Agent" or "Attention, Purchasing Agent." Don't be surprised to see "The Purchasing Agent, Please"; it gets the job done perfectly well and without offense. You may center the attention line, if you prefer, and underscore it for increased emphasis. In either position, flush with the left margin or centered, double space above and below. Remember, however, that the salutation remains the same as for any letter to a company—"Gentlemen"—even when you use an individual's name in the attention line:

```
Black, Decker, and Smith
1223 South Congress Avenue
Minneapolis, Minnesota
Mr. C. R. Smith, please
Gentlemen:
```

The *subject line* may save words and help you get off to a fast start by telling your reader quickly what the letter is about or referring him to former correspondence for necessary background which he may have forgotten. It usually appears a double space below the salutation; it often appears a double space above the salutation; and when space is at a premium, it may appear on the same line as the salutation. To make it stand out, either underscore it or use solid capitals. In centered position or flush with the left margin it is equally acceptable. You can save some time by starting it at the left margin and typing it in solid capitals, as illustrated in Letter 3. The legal forms "Re" and "In re" are gradually disappearing. The informal "About" is increasing in use. And more and more correspondents omit the word *Subject* or its equivalent. The position and wording make clear what the subject line is.

Initials of the dictator and the typist often appear at the left margin a double space below the last line of the signature block. The trend is toward omitting the dictator's initials because of repetition from the signature block; but if used, they come first (usually in unspaced capitals), separated from the typist's by a colon, a diagonal, a dash, or an asterisk. A good method that saves time is to lock the shift and type all as CRA:MF or just write all in lower case as cra/mf. Some writers place the typed name here and omit from the signature block, as in the following:

Very truly yours,

[quadruple space for a signature]

Comptroller

J. H. Jennings:dp

An *enclosure notation,* a single or double space below the identifying initials (or in their place), is a reminder to the person putting up the mail that he must actually make the enclosure. It is especially important in large offices. Sometimes it is reinforced by an asterisk in the left margin at the line in the body referring to the enclosure. The word *Enclosure* may be spelled out or abbreviated *Encl.* or *Enc.,* followed by a number indicating how many enclosures or by a colon and words indicating what the enclosures are.

Carbon-copy designations are useful when persons other than the addressee should be informed of the contents of the letter. The names of people to receive carbons are usually listed after *CC* (or *Cc* or *cc* or just *Copy to*) at the left margin, a single or double space below either the initials or the enclosure notation if it is used.

Postscripts are rarely used in business today in the original sense of afterthoughts. Rather than arouse his reader's resentment by his poor planning, the modern business writer would have the letter typed over, or in informal correspondence he might add a penwritten note when signing. (Incidentally, some research evidence suggests that such notes actually increase the pulling power of letters—probably because they give the letter a more personal touch.)

The main use of postscripts now is as punch lines. Since they have the advantage of the emphatic end position, writers often plan them from the beginning to emphasize an important point. The well-planned postscript that ties in with the development of the whole letter and stresses an important point is effective.

When you do decide to use a postscript, it should be the last thing on the page, a double space below the last of the preceding parts. The "P.S." is optional; position and wording clearly indicate that it is a postscript.

Second-page headings are helpful for filing and for reassembling multipage letters that become separated (especially true when a letter runs to three or more pages). Since pages after the first should be on plain paper, even when the first page has a printed letterhead, for identification they should carry something like one of the following, typed down from the top the distance of the side margins:

Mr. C. R. Jeans   -2-   March 21, 19—

or

```
Mr. C. R. Jeans
March 21, 19—
Page 2
```

or (for speed and equal acceptability)

```
Mr. C. R. Jeans, March 21, 19—, page 2
```

The body of the letter continues a quadruple space below this.

ADDRESSING THE ENVELOPE; FOLDING AND INSERTING THE LETTER

For those people who open their own mail, the envelope makes the first impression. The envelope should be of the same quality as the letterhead stationery, with the return address printed in the upper left corner in the same design as the printed letterhead. For unprinted envelopes the return address should be typed in the same place in the style of indention and punctuation used for the letter (including ZIP code, of course).

Proper form for the main address on envelopes has changed considerably in recent years. In trying to speed up and economize on mail handling, our postal services are working on some new equipment and new regulations for addressing to enable the new electronic machines to sort and route the mail. Until the Postal Service completes its plans and issues the new information, we can only advise you to keep on the alert for the new directions on addressing. Meanwhile, the best you can do about addressing your letters for good service is to continue what has long been preferred practice.

The main address—the same as the inside address, except double-spaced if it is less than four lines—should be placed in the lower half of the envelope and balanced between the ends. That is, the beginning point should be the same distance from the left edge of the envelope as the ending point from the right edge. Since most addresses are blocked, it usually boils down to centering the longest line in the address.

If you elect to enjoy the economies of window envelopes, you have no problem of addressing the envelope. Just remember to fold the sheet so that the inside address will show through without revealing any other part of the letter. When you crease the upper part of the letter so that the window will reveal nothing but the inside address, you usually have creases that divide the letter into approximately equal thirds. Most window envelopes used for letters are the No. 10.

When you're not using a window envelope, you fold and insert the letter according to the size of the envelope you are using. Two sizes are in common use: the No. 6¾ or commercial size, 3⅝ by 6½ inches; and the No. 10 or official size, 4⅛ by 9½ inches. For the first, fold the bottom up to within a half to a quarter inch of the top; fold from right to left about one third the width; then fold from left to right about one third, so that the last fold just fails to meet the other edge. For the No. 10 envelope, fold up from the bottom about one third the distance, then down from the top about one third, so that the last fold just fails to meet the other edge. In each method you divide your letter into approximately equal thirds. Then insert the letter in the envelope with the last fold to the back of the envelope and the open edge of the letter up. Thus the letter will avoid annoying and distracting the reader because it will unfold easily, quickly, and naturally.

(*All the letter cases for the first four chapters are at the end of Part One because we think you should cover all four basic tests of a good business letter before trying to write any kind of letter. We urge you to read the first four chapters quickly but thoroughly so that you can put all the basic principles to use even in your first letter.*)

chapter 2

Style:
What the reader reads

[Transmission of ideas and enthusiasm is essential to great accomplishment.]

How to write interestingly
    Depend mainly on content
    Put the emphasis where it belongs
    Write concisely but completely
        Ideas which don't deserve to be put into words
        Deadwood phrases
    Write vividly: Avoid indefiniteness
        People in action
        Active rather than passive voice
        Concrete rather than abstract language
        Specific rather than general words
        Enough details to make the picture clear
    Write naturally to avoid triteness and pomposity
    Vary sentence pattern, type, and length to avoid monotony
How to make your writing clear
    Make it easy to read
        Words your reader understands
        Reasonably short and direct sentences
        Adjustment of paragraph pattern and length
        Frequent personal references
        Itemizations and tabulations
    Plan for unity, coherence, progress, and proper emphasis
    Use accurate wording, punctuation, grammar, and sentence structure
How to keep your style inconspicuous
    Choose the right level of usage for the situation
        Informal English
        Formal English
        The illiterate level of usage
    Follow the conventions
        Spelling
        Word choice
        Standard punctuation
        Grammar and sentence structure
Exercises

15593
G

HAVING SURVIVED your reader's test of appearance, your letter must pass the test of readability.

For the second test of a good letter (or any other piece of writing), ask yourself: *Is it written in an interesting, clear, and inconspicuous style?*

If your letter is so uninteresting that it isn't read, you've obviously wasted your time.

If your letter is interesting enough to be read but is not clear, you've probably annoyed your reader because you've confused him. If he doesn't drop the matter, he has to write again to find out just what you mean.

And if your style is conspicuous because of something unexpected, inappropriate, or incorrect, it distracts the reader from *what* you've said (by calling attention to how you've said it) and causes him to doubt that your facts and reasoning are any more reliable than your writing. Both weaken the impact of your message, which is the important thing in letters.

Though poets, story writers, and essayists may sometimes write for the beauty of their style, a letter writer's language is only a means of communicating facts and ideas—without distorting or otherwise damaging them in transit.

To be effective, then, your letter style should be—to the reader—interesting enough to be read, clear when read, and inconspicuous. The *effect on the reader* is the test!

HOW TO WRITE INTERESTINGLY

Depend mainly on content

In writing most letters, you should depend on the message, not the style, to arouse and hold your reader's interest. Usually you have an inquiry or some other indication that your reader is interested in your general subject. A first-class letter addressed to him will therefore nearly always get a reading. Tricks of style are unnecessary and even distracting to him.

If the bare facts have insufficient appeal to gain the attention of your reader, you can make them both interesting and persuasive if you *show him how they affect his life by benefiting him* (YA in Appendix D). In writing about a product, for example, a description that merely gives the physical facts (size, shape, color, and/or material) may be pretty dull. But if you interpret the facts as providing reader benefits, the content is much more interesting (psychological description): "Made of aluminum, the Gizmo is light and rust-free; you don't need to paint." And if you write so that the reader visualizes himself actually using and enjoying the benefits of the product (dramatized copy), the content is even more interesting.

If you have no inquiry or other indication that the reader is already interested, you may be right occasionally to forget about keeping your style inconspicuous and to work for temporary attention by means of gadgets, tricks of style, and other artificial means at the beginning of your letter. Even then, however, you will have accomplished nothing unless your stunt leads into the message naturally and yields the stage to it promptly.

But just as many a good story or joke is ruined in the telling, a perfectly good message can become dull if poorly presented. Wordiness, indefiniteness, triteness and pompousness, monotony, and difficult reading are the most common offenders. By replacing these with their opposites, you will have a style that will speed up your message rather than slow it down or lose it completely—and that's all you can expect style to contribute to making your letters interesting.

Put the emphasis where it belongs (**Emp** and **Sub** in Appendix D)

Since the content of your letter is the greatest means of gaining interest, the big ideas of your message deserve the major emphasis.

Though you may use minor mechanical means of emphasis (underscoring, capitalizing, itemizing, using two colors), your four primary means of emphasizing an idea are (1) position, (2) space, (3) phrasing, and (4) sentence structure.

The most significant ideas you depend on to hold your reader's interest need to be placed in the emphatic beginning and ending positions of the letter, of your paragraphs—even of your sentences.

In addition, you write more about those points you think need stressing. If you write 10 lines about the efficiency of a dishwasher and only two lines about the convenience of it, you have emphasized efficiency more than convenience.

As a third major means of emphasis, you select concrete, specific words and phrases to etch the welcome or important idea in your reader's mind. When the idea is unwelcome or insignificant, you choose general words that merely identify, not stress. *Specific:* "Your versatile IBM Selectric typewriter will . . . ." *General:* "The typewriter needs several new parts and . . . ."

Because an independent clause carries more emphasis than a dependent one, you can also stress or subordinate ideas through your choice of sentence structure. An important idea calls for statement in one independent clause (a simple sentence). Sometimes, however, you have two equally important and closely related ideas; so you should put two independent clauses together in a compound sentence. If you have two related ideas of different importance, a complex sentence of one independent and one dependent clause shows the real relationship. You may have noticed, for example, that the minor mechanical means of stressing ideas were merely named parenthetically in a dependent clause. The four primary means, however, were first itemized; then each was given a separate paragraph of discussion and thereby emphasized by independent-clause statement and by means of space.

In messages carrying ideas which the reader will welcome, then, use those ideas to begin and end letters. They usually should begin and end paragraphs. They should take up most of the space of the letter. They should be phrased specifically. And they should enjoy the benefits of independent instead of dependent construction. Conversely, unwelcome or unimportant ideas should be embedded in a middle paragraph, covered just enough to establish their true meaning, and stripped of the emphasis of concrete, specific words.

The letter samples throughout this book make use of these principles for appropriate emphasis and its opposite—subordination. Two special points, however, deserve your attention right here:

1. You may be inclined to write something the reader already knows. If it serves no purpose, of course you should omit it. But if you need to say it (for emphasis or as a basis for something else you want to say), put it subordinately. That is, do *not* put it in an independent clause: *not* "Summer will soon be here . . ." but "Since summer will soon be here. . . ."

2. When you need to refer the reader to an enclosure for more information, word your reference to emphasize what he should look for or get from it. *Don't* emphasize that it is enclosed: *not* "Enclosed is (or please find) . . ." but something like "You'll find further details of construction and users' satisfaction in the enclosed pamphlet."

Write concisely but completely (Conc and Dev in Appendix D)

Every word you can spare without reducing the effectiveness of your writing is wasteful if it remains. If you use too many words for the ideas you express, you stretch interest to the breaking point. But if you leave out necessary information and vivid details in trying to achieve brevity, you frequently fail to develop enough interesting ideas to hold or persuade your reader. You therefore face the dilemma of length.

A first step in the solution of that dilemma is a clear distinction between brevity and conciseness. Brevity is mere shortness—which is often overstressed. A common mistake in letter writing is that of sacrificing completeness because of a mistaken notion about the importance of brevity. Writing a letter lacking necessary information (and therefore lacking interest and persuasion) is poor economy. Either the letter is pure waste because it produces no result, or both you and your reader have to write additional letters to fill in the missing links of information. Even those people who say a business letter should be brief do not mean that they are so illogical as to want to make decisions without all the pertinent information.

What these people who are overly conscious of brevity want—what you want—is consiseness, making every word contribute to your purpose. A 50-word letter is brief; but if you can write the message in 25 words, the 50-word letter is not concise. A 400-word letter is not short; but if all the words contribute to the purpose, it is concise. So if you need three pages to cover all your points adequately and make your letter do what you want it to do, you should use that much space. Conciseness, then, comes not from omitting necessary information or details that contribute to clearness, persuasiveness, or interest but from writing all you should say in as few words as possible.

Experience may teach you to compose first drafts of letters that are both complete and concise; but while you are gaining that experience, you need to

1. Avoid expressing ideas that don't deserve to be put into words.
2. Revise first drafts to eliminate deadwood.

Besides obviously irrelevant material, *ideas which don't deserve to be put into words are*

Things the reader already knows which you do not wish to emphasize.
Ideas which can be implied with sufficient emphasis.

Because it is often insulting as well as wasteful and dull, avoid using an emphatic independent clause for things the reader already knows. For example, a heating engineer's letter to an office manager about the discomfort of workers began as follows:

```
Three days ago you asked us to investigate the problem of
discomfort among your office workers.  [Assumes that the reader
has a short memory.]  We have made our study.  [Obviously, or
he couldn't be reporting.]  Too low humidity is apparently the
main cause of your trouble.  Your building is steam-heated.
[Doesn't the reader know?]  Therefore your solution is
to. . . .
```

The following revision says or implies everything in that paragraph, avoids the insults, saves most of the words, and is more interesting:

```
Too low humidity is apparently the main cause of your workers'
discomfort.  Since your building is steam-heated, your
solution is to. . . .
```

To show the reasoning behind your suggestion, you do need to mention the fact that the building is heated by steam; but the subordinating *since* implies "Of course you and I know this, but it has to go in for the record and for completeness of logic." When you *have* to establish something the reader knows, or when the reader probably knows but you can't risk his not knowing or remembering, inform him *subordinately*.

As a general principle, in answering a recent letter from an individual, don't waste words to say "I have your letter of . . ." or to tell what it said.

Obviously, you got the letter or you wouldn't be answering it; and he will remember what it said—at least when you start talking about the same subject. Instead of

```
You asked us to let you know when the new model of the Clarion
radio came on the market.  It is obtainable now.
```

you can say the same thing with

```
The new model of the Clarion is now available.
```

The fact that you got his letter and the idea of "You asked us to let you know" are clearly implied.

Of course, if the inquiry is not recent, or if somebody other than the original inquirer may read the answer (as often happens in big companies), you may need to make specific reference (by topic and date) to the letter you are answering. But even then you can often use a subject line to save words and allow the emphatic first sentence to say something important. Rather than

```
On February 20 you inquired about our experience with Mr.
James H. Johnson.  We are glad to tell you about his work for
us.

Johnson was a steady, conscientious worker during the 18
months he kept books for us.
```

you might better write:

```
Mr. James H. Johnson, about whom you inquired on February 20,
was a steady, conscientious bookkeeper here for 18 months.
```

Under no circumstances do you need to waste words as in the following paragraph:

```
Permit me to take this opportunity to thank you for your
letter which I have just received.  In reply I wish to state
that we shall be very glad to exchange the electric water
heater in question for a similar one in a larger size in
accordance with your request.
```

Through implication you can reduce that wordy beginning to

```
We shall be glad to exchange your water heater for a similar
one in a larger size.
```

In most refusals you can save words and your reader's feelings by eliminating the negative statement of what you won't do and concentrating on what you will do. You thus *imply* the negative idea, for economy as well as interest. For illustrations, see "Positive Statement" (p. 65).

If your first draft contains any of the foregoing wasteful expressions, revision should eliminate them and *deadwood phrases* (those which take the long way around or contribute nothing to the ideas expressed).

Consider the following suggestive but far from complete list of offenders, in which the deadwood is blocked out or the concise statement follows in parentheses:

long ~~period of~~ time

at ~~a distance of~~ 100 ft.

is ~~at this time~~

at ~~a price of~~ $50

~~important~~ essentials

enclosed ~~herewith~~

remember ~~the fact~~ that

held a meeting (met)

main problem is ~~a matter of~~ cost

your ~~order for a~~ cultivator was shipped

~~in the opinion of~~ Mr. Johnson (thinks)

that is the situation ~~at this time~~ (now)

the X plow is quite different ~~in character~~

made the announcement that (announced)

for the purpose of providing (to provide)

all the people who are interested in (interested people)

at an early date (soon, if you have to be indefinite)

decide at a meeting ~~which will be held~~ Monday

eliminate needless words ~~that may be present~~

~~there is~~ only one point ~~that~~ is clear, ~~and that is~~

the price was higher than I expected ~~it to be~~

the workers ~~are in a position to~~ (can) accept or reject

would like to (want to)

during ~~the course of~~ the

~~engaged in~~ making a survey

~~the color of~~ the X is blue

until ~~such time as~~ you can

in regard to (about or regarding)

in the development of (developing)

in this day and age (today or now)

the soldering process proved ~~to be of an~~ unsatisfactory ~~nature~~

the general consensus of opinion among most businessmen is that (most businessmen think that)

~~the trouble with~~ the light was ~~that it was~~ too dim

in ~~the state of~~ Texas

neat ~~in appearance~~

at ~~the hour of~~ 4

eight ~~in number~~

circular ~~in shape~~

throughout the ~~entire~~ week

~~at a~~ later ~~date~~

during ~~the year of~~ 1972

costs ~~the sum of~~ $10

came ~~at a time~~ when

at all times (always)

in the event that (if)

put in an appearance (came)

during the time that (while)

these facts ~~serve to~~ give an idea

made stronger ~~with a view to~~

if ~~it is~~ possible, let me have

~~according to~~ Mr. Johnson (says)

arrived at the conclusion (concluded)

Sometimes you can save several words by changing a whole clause to one word. For example:

buying new machines which are expensive—buying expensive new machines

using processes that are outmoded—using outmoded processes

saving work that does not need to be done—saving unnecessary work

Write vividly: Avoid indefiniteness (Spec in Appendix D)

Even good content concisely stated can be uninteresting if your reader gets only an inactive or fuzzy mental picture. The sharper you can make that picture, the better it will be. You will write vividly if you apply these five techniques:

1. Write about people in action. Make people the subject or object of many sentences.
2. Use active rather than passive voice most of the time.
3. Use concrete rather than abstract language.
4. Use specific rather than general words.
5. Give enough details to make the picture clear.

The most interesting thing in the world is *people in action.* Things happen because people make them happen. The most interesting, the most natural, and the clearest way to write about those happenings is to talk about those people who are the principal actors. That is why we suggest that you make people the subject or object of your sentences.

And since the reader of a letter is most interested in himself, his interest will be influenced by how you put him into the picture as the main actor. "You can save 30 minutes at dinner time with a Pronto pressure cooker" is more vivid than "A Pronto pressure cooker saves 30 minutes at dinner time." (For psychological reasons, if a point is a criticism and hence unpleasant, however, make your actor a third person or your message impersonal.)

Consistent use of people as subjects will help you to write in *active rather than passive voice.* The passive "30 minutes at dinner time can be saved" lacks the vividness of the original illustration because it omits the all-important *who.* Besides, passive constructions are usually longer, weaker, and fuzzier than active ones. Excessive use of "to be" verbs (*be, is, am, are, was, were, been, being*) usually produces flat writing, partly because it leads to a passive style. If the basic verb in more than half your sentences derives from "to be," your style will seem flat instead of lively. "There are" and "It was" beginnings (expletives) delay the real idea of the sentence and frequently force a writer to use the unemphatic passive voice. The sentence "There are 1 million people in Cincinnati" is not so vivid as "One million people live in Cincinnati." "It was felt that . . ." becomes more vivid when the writer rephrases with "We felt . . . ."

You can eliminate most passives and expletives if you will conscientiously try to use action verbs. People live, run, eat, buy—in short, act. They do not just exist, as indicated by *is, was, were, have been.* The price of a stock *creeps up, rises, jumps, zooms*—or *plummets.* For vividness (and for economy) good writers make their verbs do a big share of the work. Far be it from us to encourage you to needless and frivolous word coinage; but *dip, curve, skyrocket, phone, wire,* and many other original nouns are now commonly accepted verbs because people recognized the vividness of their use as verbs. The more action you can pack into your verbs, the more specific and concrete you can make your writing.

When you *use concrete rather than abstract language,* you give your reader sharper mental pictures. When you write *superiority, efficiency,* and *durability* in telling about a product, your words are abstract; they give your reader only hazy ideas. To make the picture sharp and lively, give the evidence back of the abstraction rather than naming the abstraction itself. If you think your product is of highest quality, you must have reasons for thinking so. To establish the idea of superiority in cloth, for instance: Thread count? Number of washings before fraying? Tensile strength? Resistance to shrinkage and fading? Note that answers to these questions also show durability.

In job applications you need to put across the ideas of your sociability, initiative, and dependability, which you can concretize by citing activities and organizational memberships, ideas and plans you have originated, attendance records, and completed projects. Thus you give evidence of these qualities and let your reader draw the abstract conclusions.

You further eliminate haziness and dullness when you use *specific rather than general words.* An investment, for instance, may be a stock certificate, a bond, or a piece of real estate. To illustrate further, stock may be common or preferred. The closer you can come to making your reader visualize the special type of thing named rather than just its general class, the more specific and hence the more vivid your writing is.

Take the verb *walk* as another example. Does a person amble, trudge, skip, or one of the 50 or more other possible ways of walking? When you are inclined to write *contact,* do you mean write, go see, telephone, telegraph? You will present a sharper picture if you name the specific action.

Comparisons help you to explain the unknown or variable in terms of the known. *Slowly* becomes sharper if you say "about as fast as you normally walk." "A saving of 2 percent when paid within 10 days" becomes more vivid if you add "$2.80, or two free boxes of Lane's choice chocolates, on your present invoice of $140."

You *can* be specific and concrete in the kind of information you give your reader, but unless you *give enough details to make the picture clear,* you will fail to attain vividness. Specifications for a house may indicate that the house is to be painted. But unless they tell the kind of paint, how many coats, and what colors, the painter does not have a clear picture of what he is to do until he comes back and asks. You need to flesh out the skeletons to bring them to life, even if it means some loss of brevity.

Write naturally to avoid triteness and pomposity (Nat in Appendix D)

All kinds of trite expressions and jargon—usually the result of hazy thinking, or not thinking, by the writer—are inclined to dull interest and put the reader to sleep instead of stimulating his mind to action. They are even called "bromides" ("flat, commonplace statements," Webster says) because of the use of bromides as sleep-inducing medicines.

A businessman meeting another on the street would not say, "I beg to report receipt of your favor of the 29th ult." And if he is a good letter writer he would not write it either. He would more likely say or write, "Those tonnage figures for April were just what I needed," or "Your suggestions about the committee memberships helped a lot in my decision. Thanks." The first is slow, vague, roundabout, and stilted; the others are clear, direct, and natural.

Bromidic style goes back to the times when businessmen first began to have social status enough to write to kings, princes, and others at court. Feeling inferior, they developed a slavish, stilted, and elaborately polite style to flatter the nobility. They "begged to advise" the nobleman that his "kind favor of recent date" was "at hand" and "wished to state" that "this matter" would "receive our prompt attention" and "begged to remain your humble, obedient servant." Today businessmen need not be so meek. Unfortunately, too many sheepishly follow somebody else, learn all they know about letter writing from the letters they receive, and thus continue an outmoded, inappropriate, and unnatural style. Like parrots, they use expressions unthinkingly.

Pompous writing (puffed-up, roundabout, and using big words) is as dull and confusing as the use of bromides. Why many businessmen write, "We will ascertain the facts and advise accordingly," when in conversation they would say quite naturally, "We'll find out and let you know," is a mystery. A Washington blackout order during wartime originally read: "Obscure fenestration with opaque coverings or terminate the illumination." A high official who wanted the message understood revised it to read: "Pull down the shades or turn out the lights."

A young lawyer was certainly pompous when he wrote as follows about a husband being sued for divorce:

```
The defendant is renowned as a person of intemperate habits.
He is known to partake heavily of intoxicating beverages.
Further, he cultivates the company of others of the distaff
side, and wholly, regularly, and consistently refuses, demurs,
and abstains from earnest endeavor to gain remuneration.
```

The judge summed up that "Mrs. Rigoni's husband drinks, chases other women, and refuses to work."

Stuffed-shirt writers frequently use a phrase or a whole clause when a well-chosen verb would express the idea better. For example: "Smith raises the objection that . . ." instead of "Smith objects that (or objects to). . . ." One writer stretched a simple "Thank you" to "I wish to assure you that it has been a great pleasure to have been the recipient of your gracious generosity."

The good letter writer avoids both bromides and pompous wording to make his letters natural. The advice to "write as you talk" can be taken too literally, however. You would have an extremely hard job trying to write just as you talk; and even if you could, the informal style appropriate to letters is more precise and concise than good conversation. What the advisers really mean is that you should not stiffen up, use big words and trite expressions, or get involved in complicated and formal sentences when you write letters. Rather, let the words flow out naturally and informally in phrases and sentences with the general tone and rhythm of the language actually used by men rather than stuffed shirts.

Write like this—	*Not like this—*
Many people	A substantial segment of the population
Know well	Fully cognizant of
Object	Interpose an objection
Wait	Hold in abeyance
Carry out the policy	Effectuate (or implement) the policy
As you requested	Pursuant to your request
Before, after	Prior to, subsequent to
Get the facts	Ascertain (secure) the data
Ask him	Interrogate him
Find it hard to	Encounter difficulty in
Big difference	Marked discrepancy
Begin (or start)	Initiate (or institute)
Complete (or finish)	Consummate
In the first place	In the initial instance
Haste makes waste	Precipitation entails negation of economy
Make unnecessary	Obviate the necessity of

Vary sentence pattern, type, and length to avoid monotony

Unvaried sentence pattern, type, length, or rhythm causes many a reader's mind to wander. Though the necessary variety should come naturally from writing well, revision can sometimes enliven your style by removing a dull sameness.

The normal English sentence pattern is subject-verb-complement (or object). Most of your sentences should follow that sequence; but if all of them do, they produce monotony. Particularly noticeable are series of sentences all beginning the same way. The following list suggests possible variations of sentence beginnings:

With a subject: A simple way of keying returns is the use of different return envelopes with the several different letters being tested.

With a clause: Because human beings are unpredictable, the sales process cannot be riveted to a formula.

With a phrase: For this reason, no large mailing should be made until tests have proved which letter is best.

With a verb: Should you find that all pull about the same, you have the usual direct-mail dilemma!

With correlative conjunctions: Not only the lack of funds but also the results of continual overcrowding and busing in secondary schools for the past few years will continue to lower the caliber of work in American colleges.

With an adverb: Ordinarily, students like courses in business letter writing.

With a verbal: Allowing plenty of time, the student started his report early in the semester.

With an infinitve: To be a successful business letter writer, a student must be able to lose himself in contemplation of his reader's problem.

With adjectives: Congenial and cooperative, he worked many nights until midnight when we faced a deadline.

Proper emphasis of ideas (p. 30) is the main reason for varying sentence type, but the variation also avoids monotony and retains interest. Choosing sentence patterns in terms of needed emphasis will nearly always result in enough variety to prevent monotony.

Sameness of sentence length (and to some extent, paragraph length) can be just as monotonous as unvarying sentence pattern and type. Together they produce an interest-killing rhythm characteristic of a childish style. Children's books put both listener and reader to sleep—but business letters are not intended to.

Although readability specialists have done much good by inducing some people to keep their sentences down to reasonable length, they have done some harm by leading others who have misunderstood them to write too mechanically in trying to average about 16–20 words a sentence. That is an *average*, remember. Nothing could be more monotonous than a series of 14-word sentences—or of 6-word sentences or of 26-word sentences. Lack of variety in sentence length can be just as monotonous as lack of variety in sentence pattern or type.

HOW TO MAKE YOUR WRITING CLEAR

The strongest rebuke a reader can give a writer is "I don't understand; what do you mean?"

Obviously, your message must be clear to your reader, or the interest which induced him to read it accounts for nothing. Conciseness helps clarity as well as interest by relieving your reader of the job of separating the important from the unessential, and vividness helps by giving a sharp, clear picture. But other more important aids to clearness are

1. Making your writing easy to read.
2. Planning for unity, coherence, progress, and proper emphasis.
3. Using accurate wording, punctuation, grammar, and sentence structure.

Make it easy to read

Readability is a factor affecting interest, but it is more intimately related to clarity. You have the responsibility as a writer to present ideas so that the reader understands with the least possible effort. As the difficulty of understanding an idea increases, people are more inclined to skip it. Any time your reader has to back up and reread or has to slow down to understand you thoroughly, you are risking the chance that he will go on and misunderstand, or make the effort and get the point but become disgusted with you, or lose interest and toss your letter aside.

Using only those *words which your reader will understand* immediately and sharply is a first step in making letters easy to read. You will usually be wise to choose the more commonly known of two words; an uneducated person will understand you, and an educated reader will appreciate your making his reading job easy. Although some short words are not well known and some long ones are common knowledge, your letters will be easier to read if you use one-syllable words most of the time. If you have more than 50 percent more syllables than words, your writing requires more reader effort than it should. And the greater number of polysyllabic profundities you use, the greater the likelihood that you'll strike your reader as pompous.

Keeping your sentences reasonably short and direct will also help to make your letters easy to read and hence clear. An average of 16–20 words is a healthy one for readability. But you need not avoid sentences of 4 or 5 words—or 40, if necessary for presenting an idea exactly. If the average length is not too much above 20, smooth sequence of thought and directness are more important than the word count. To avoid involved, indirect sentences, look at the punctuation. It cannot make a basically bad sentence into a good one. If you have to punctuate a sentence heavily, you will be wise to rephrase it more directly. Sometimes the best solution is to break it up into two or three sentences.

Paragraph pattern and length influence readability, too. The usual pattern of letter paragraphs is a topic sentence followed by supporting or developing details. But if you write one sentence which says all you need to on that topic, start another paragraph rather than pad one with needless stuff or cover two topics in it because some composition books ban single-sentence paragraphs.

Frequently a single-sentence paragraph is highly desirable to give an idea the emphasis you want!

Especially in letters, long paragraphs are uninviting and hard to read. First and last paragraphs of more than four lines and others of more than eight should be reconsidered for breaking up.

Frequent personal references (names of people and pronouns referring to them) also make your letters more interesting and readable. Since you and your reader are the two persons most directly involved in the action, desires, and benefits you write about in letters, most of your pronouns will be "you" (or "you" understood) and "I" (or "we").

Itemizations and tabulations may help to make your whole letter or a paragraph clear and easy to read. For instance, if your topic sentence mentions three big advantages in using XYZ wafers, the three will stand out more clearly if you number them and list them on separate lines.

Plan for unity, coherence, progress, and proper emphasis

Later you will study planning for psychological effect as a principle of persuasion, but planning also affects clarity. If you are answering a letter, underscore points in it to be covered. In any case think your answer through before you start to write; you can't plan anything more than a simple letter by just thinking as you write. Clear letters are usually the product of a three-step process which stresses organization and coherence:

1. Preliminary planning for completeness, unity, progress, and proper emphasis.
2. Continuous fast writing or dictating for the natural coherence that comes from following a chain of thought straight through.
3. Revision for tone (see pp. 71 ff.), conciseness (pp. 31 ff.), coherence, and correctness (pp. 42 ff. and 44 ff.).

The preliminary planning step requires specific answers to four questions:

1. *What effect do I want the letter to produce?* Decide specifically what you want to happen as a result of your letter, and make this central purpose clear to your reader. Without keeping the central purpose in mind, you cannot achieve one of the main objectives of organizing—unity. That is, good organization should result in a oneness by showing how every part is related to the general theme or idea.
2. *Who is the reader?* Until you make a clear estimate of what your reader is like, you cannot hope to apply the principles of adaptation (p. 62).
3. *What facts and ideas must I present to produce the desired effect on this kind of reader?* You should list not only points of positive interest but probable reader objections to be overcome.
4. *What is the best order of presenting the items listed in answer to Question 3?* You will be prepared to answer generally as plan A, B, or C (from your study of "Planned Presentation," pp. 55 ff.). But that is only a general plan for the whole letter. Organization includes much more than that.

You can organize well only by answering all four of the questions in preliminary planning. Good organization is the marshaling of statements and supporting details, the orderly procession of paragraphs, the disposition of parts so that each finds its proper place.

Fundamentally, organization is the process of grouping things according to likeness and then putting the groups into an appropriate sequence. For example, if you explain in your letter or report how something is made, you should treat that part fully before going on to explain how it operates. Either of these topics may be just one paragraph, or it may be several. But you do want to group together all the details about how it is made before proceeding. Thus you achieve unity of that topic.

Having grouped according to likenesses, you have several choices of sequence for either a whole letter or a paragraph. Common paragraph sequences are (1) general to specific, (2) cause to effect, (3) order of importance, (4) nearest to farthest (space relations), and (5) order of happening (time relations). All of these may be reversed.

In the second step of writing well-organized letters—continuous fast writing—you merely follow your preliminary plan and *keep going*. Write the entire letter without stopping.

In the third step—revising—you may need to reorganize a bit by shifting words, sentences, or whole paragraphs into better position. But usually the main work on organization through revision will be a few changes in wording for better coherence. You may find that some transitional words are unnecessary because of the natural, logical sequence of the sentence and paragraph; or you may need to strengthen coherence by inserting more transitional words like *and, but, for,* and the variants of each (See **Coh 3** in Appendix D, the "Concise Writer's Handbook"). Although you do not leave out any necessary bridges between parts, the fewer you can use and still make the sequence of thought clear, the better. Try especially to avoid overformal references like *the latter, the above-mentioned,* and *namely.*

Use accurate wording, punctuation, grammar, and sentence structure

Proper usage of words, punctuation, and grammar is established by convention, not rules. The important thing is that you use them in writing with the exact significance the reader attaches to them. Words, for example, are mere labels we apply to actions and things. In Great Britain such simple words as *ton* and *gallon* do not mean the same as they do in the United States.

Moreover, words and sentences sometimes change meanings according to what precedes and succeeds them. For instance, a would-be secretary brought laughs when the last two sentences of her ad for a job read: "No bad habits. Willing to learn." Similarly, the last two sentences in an ad of a big dog for sale read: "Will eat anything. Loves children." For proper word relations, guard particularly against the errors discussed in **Mod 1** and **2** in Appendix D, the "Concise Writer's Handbook."

The difficulties of accurate expression stem partly from the fact that words pick up related meanings and personal significance from everyday use (connotations, in addition to their denotations or dictionary meanings). Consider the difference between *cheap* and *inexpensive* or between *house* and *home.* And note that *hope, trust* and *if* all suggest doubt. "You claim" or "you say" even suggests doubt of the reader's truthfulness. The accurate user of words will be alert to connotations and implications—if not to avoid confusion, at least to produce effectiveness.

Exceptional cases of failure to follow the conventions have led to readers' getting a completely wrong idea. But rarely does such failure *leave* a reader confused; usually he can figure out approximately what the meaning is. Of course, if you say *profit* for what is generally spoken of as the selling price, you will mislead your reader.

Much more frequently, unconventional usage of words confuses a reader temporarily, causes him to back up and reread, or leaves him uncertain of the writer's intention. The words you use should give him not only the general idea but the precise idea quickly. If you say *soon* or *later,* your reader doesn't know just when you mean. If you say *checks, notes, stocks, etc.,* nobody can tell whether you mean to include bonds. (In most business letters *etc.* should be used only if its meaning is perfectly clear, as in "I am particularly interested in the odd-numbered questions, 1, 3, 5, etc." But it then becomes unnecessary, as it usually does when it is clear.) If you are inclined to write *actuarially,* most readers will get the meaning more quickly if you write *statistically.* The advantage of an extensive vocabularly is that you can choose the precise word to give the exact idea. But if you don't use judgment with a big vocabulary, you sometimes use words that leave the reader in the dark or slow him up.

Punctuation marks, like words, mean only what a reader takes them to mean. They can be helpful to him by breaking your sentences into thought groups if you follow the conventions and use them as they are generally used. But if you use a system of your own which your reader does not understand, you mislead him just as if you used words in unfamiliar senses.

For instance, if you put up a sign on a parking lot to mean

No Parking: Reserved for Our Customers

you will certainly mislead people if you write:

No Parking Reserved for Our Customers

Like faulty wording, however, faulty punctuation often confuses only temporarily, if at all, but distracts the reader's mind from the key idea. You've surely seen the laughable sign "Slow Men Working."

Fortunately, the system of English punctuation is pretty well established (by convention, not by rules), and most readers know at least the main parts of the conventions. Unfortunately many people who know how to *read* punctuation marks correctly do not know the conventions well enough to use them precisely *in writing.* If you have any doubts about the following main troublesome areas of punctuation, see the symbol **P** in Appendix D, the "Concise Writer's Handbook," for explanation and illustration:

—Semicolon between independent clauses except with strong conjunction (**P** 2).

—Comma after all dependent clauses at the beginnings of sentences and with nonessential ones elsewhere (**P** 3).

—Comma to separate coordinate adjectives (**P** 5).

—Pair of commas around a parenthetical expression unless you want to de-emphasize by parentheses, emphasize by dashes, or avoid confusion with other commas by using parentheses or dashes (**P** 4, 7).

—Hyphen between words used as a single modifier of a following noun or pronoun (**P** 8).

So-called "errors" in grammar and sentence structure probably mislead readers even less frequently than unconventional uses of words and punctuation; but they, too, slow up reading and produce indefiniteness. Of course, the statement "Strawberries should not be planted where tomatoes have been grown for several years" will mislead readers if you mean "Wait several years before planting strawberries where tomatoes have been grown." And the dangling participle in "Smelling of liquor, the officer arrested the reckless driver" might cause a policeman to be asked why he was drinking on duty. But these are exceptional cases of bad sentence structure. Faulty pronoun references can confuse too, but usually they don't. Most readers will understand perfectly, despite shifts in number like "The Acme Company is located in Chicago. They manufacture. . . ." Wrong verb forms like "He come to my house at 10 P.M." or the wrong choice between *lie* and *lay* are usually definite, quick, and clear. Even this ungrammatical question asked at a state-line roadblock is perfectly clear: "You-all ain't a-totin' no cottonseeds, is ya?"

Indeed, poor grammar and sentence structure so infrequently cause confusion that they hardly need be discussed in connection with clarity. The other factors already discussed are more important influences on clarity; and grammar and sentence structure are more important as factors of the third requirement of good letter style—that it be inconspicuous.

HOW TO KEEP YOUR STYLE INCONSPICUOUS

An obvious striving for "style" is a sign of immaturity. When a reader starts your letter, he is looking for what you say, not to see how you say it. He will notice your style only if you do something unexpected with it. In reading a well-ordered sentence, he will receive no jolt. But if he consciously responds to an expression as an artificiality, he is distracted and you lose his attention to your message. Simplicity and naturalness are good guides on the right road.

If you make your style too flowery, formal, or stiff for the situation, or if you make it too flippant and familiar, it will distract the reader from your message and cause him to question your sense of appropriateness. If you violate any of the conventions of word choice, spelling, punctuation, sentence structure, or grammar, the unconventional practice will both distract him and cause him to doubt your general knowledge and ability. For instance, if you cause the reader to say, "Why, he can't even spell," the *even* strongly implies "So of course he can't be depended on to know anything else either."

The two main ways a writer does something unexpected with style and thus draws undue attention to it, then, are

1. Choosing the wrong level of usage for the situation.
2. Violating any of the more common conventions of word choice, spelling, punctuation, grammar, and sentence structure.

Both weaken the impact of your message—the important thing.

Choose the right level of usage for the situation

Language appropriateness, like proper dress, is a highly variable thing. What is effective in one situation may not be suitable in another. Formal dress is no better for a day in the office or a weiner roast than a business suit or sports clothing is for a formal party, or beach togs for anywhere except on the beach.

The first step in choosing the right level of usage is to analyze the situation in the light of the five communication factors (sometimes called the "communication formula"):

1. A writer (or speaker) who has
2. A particular message to communicate through
3. A medium (letter, report, advertisement) to
4. A definite readership (or audience) for
5. A definite purpose.

If any of the factors of communication change, the situation shifts so that a formerly good sentence may become bad, or vice versa. Still, many thoughtless writers almost ignore the last two factors. Only in view of all of them can you classify the situation and choose the appropriate level of usage.

Having classified the communication situation, you can take the second step in choosing the appropriate level of usage by considering the nature of the different levels. Whole books have been written naming and describing them. More concise treatments also appear in some modern college composition books. Some linguists distinguish as many as seven levels, but a more usual classification names three: formal, informal, and illiterate.

Informal English is much the most useful level for letters and for most other kinds of speaking and writing today. In it, the writer's interest is more on content than on style. The emphasis is more on being functional than on being elegant. Its general tone is that of the natural speech of educated people in their usual business and social affairs. In its written form it is more concise and more precise than normal conversation; but its vocabulary, phrasing, sentence structure, grammar, and hence its natural rhythm and tone are essentially the same as in good conversation among educated people. This—rather than a literal interpretation of the words—is the meaning of the often-heard advice that you should write as you talk.

But informal English is a broad category, ranging all the way from a style which verges on formal English to that which verges on the illiterate. When informal English approaches the formal, it does not allow slang, shoptalk, contractions, or omission of relative pronouns and other connecting words. It may use generally understood allusions, figures of speech a little more complex than similes, and words and sentences that are somewhat long. Some writers insist on the highly questionable requirement of impersonal style (no pronouns referring to writer or reader) for reports and research papers at this dignified-informal level of usage.

Near the deep end of the informal level of usage is what we call "familiar-informal." Its whole attention should be on content, to the disregard of style. It's OK if you're writing to a guy you know pretty well or if you have a lot in common with him. It is used where there is no need to establish your dignity or your knowledge of the language. Even Churchill and Roosevelt sometimes joshed each other quite a bit in their messages. As in this paragraph, it uses contractions, a light touch, and rather simple sentence structure and words, including some slang and shoptalk. Its value is its freshness, vividness, emphasis, and naturalness. The danger point, which this paragraph flirts with, is that it will be abused in an attempt to be clever and thus will call attention to itself.

Formal English is characterized by precision and elegance of diction, sentence structure, and grammar. Like the man dressed in formal clothes, it often appears stiff and unnatural, more to be admired for its appearance than for any function it may perform. It admits of no contractions, ellipses, or indignities of any kind. Of necessity, it uses many everyday words, but by design it includes many that are not commonly heard. Like the man of high society, it sometimes chooses its associates with more attention to their paternity than to what they are. As a consequence, its words are frequently somewhat rare and long, with histories traceable back to the first word families of Old French or Latin. It is often fraught with abstruse literary and historical allusions. Instead of concerning itself with facilitating the reader's comprehension, it often uses long and involved sentences that are more elegant and rhythmical than functional. Following an unsound belief that they are thereby being more objective, its writers usually strive for an impersonal style. Its worst misguided practitioners— some lawyers, doctors, engineers, and politicians, apparently hoping to achieve dignity (and defending their practices by claiming that they achieve precision)—frequently abuse acceptable formal English by carrying it to the ridiculous extremes of the too technical, the pompous, and the flatulent (now commonly called "gobbledygook" or "bafflegab").

Abused formal English has no reason for being. Even in its best sense, formal English is nearly always unsuitable for business letters. It would be noticed as inappropriate in all but the most formal occasions.

The illiterate level of usage is the third one of them three we dun named. It ain't got no bizness in letters. Ya see, folks who reads letters spects you ta right right. If'n ya writes wrong, he shore sees ya errors and knows ya ain't eddicated so he thinks ya don't know nuthin else neither if ya cain't get yer rightin right.

An easy way to choose the appropriate level of usage for a situation you have analyzed is to ask yourself which type of dress would be most suitable if you were going to see your reader and talk your message to him. If the answer is formal dress, choose formal English or dignified-informal. If the answer is an everyday business suit, use the broad middle ground of informal English. If the answer is sporty clothes, use familiar-informal. Only if you are the kind of person who goes to church in dirty work clothes should you feel comfortable while revealing your illiteracy by violating the writing conventions expected of educated people.

Follow the conventions

You have already seen how following the conventions of wording, punctuation, sentence structure, and grammar affects clarity. But violations of those and other conventions have an even more important bearing on keeping your style inconspicuous. If you go contrary to the conventions, you do something your reader doesn't expect of an educated writer. You therefore distract his attention from your message and lose his respect and his faith in you.

Even the following first paragraph in a letter from a hotelman to an association president is clear. You know what the writer means, despite his poor sentence, but you are distracted and you can't respect him:

```
Your recent convention over with and successful, we are
wondering if since then you have decided on the next year's
meeting city, and you jotting down on the margin of this
letter the city and dates selected, this will be indeed
appreciated.
```

From this, don't you get the impression that if he is so sloppy about his language, his hotel might not be a very well run, clean place to stay?

Spelling is probably the most exactly established convention in the English language. A few words are spelled two ways, but most of them are listed only one way in the dictionary. Because of this definiteness, spelling has acquired much more importance in the minds of most people than it deserves. Although a misspelled word almost never leads to confusion and therefore makes little difference in terms of real communication, most readers (even relatively uneducated ones) will notice your errors and look down on you for them. So unless you prefer to write in other languages (nearly all of which have more systematic and easier-to-learn spelling), you had better accept your fate and learn English spelling.

Because it is so unsystematic, there is no easy way. Consider yourself fortunate if you have learned to spell by observing the words you read and by listening closely to how words are pronounced. If you have not used these methods, you should start now; but don't assume that pronunciation is always a safe guide. (See **Sp** in Appendix D.)

Poor *word choice* that is close enough to meet the basic requirement of clarity is usually not so noticeable as misspelling, but it may be distracting and even degrading. Among the thousands of possible bad choices, the pairs listed under Diction in Appendix D give the most trouble. If you are unsure of any of the distinctions, look up the words; any educated reader will notice if you confuse them.

Unconventional punctuation may lead to misunderstanding, but more frequently it distracts and retards the reader. If you have trouble with punctuation, study the material under **P** in Appendix D.

Grammar and sentence structure are so closely related that they should be considered together. They have a definite bearing on clarity (see discussion on p. 42), but they have more significance in terms of making your style inconspicuous. Most of the troubles come from:

—A writer's having heard uneducated people speak unconventionally, particularly his family and fellow workers. (Solution: Observe the skill of other writers and speakers, study writing, practice.)

—Simple carelessness (Solution: Revise).

—Trying to use big words and complicated sentence structures before mastering them. (Solution: Remember that they are unnecessary to dignity; write simply, at least until you can use more involved structures precisely and clearly.)

In trying to keep your style unnoticed by avoiding violations of the conventions of good English, you would have an easier job if all your readers were modern linguists.

Language scholars know that many of the so-called "rules" of English are

—Latin rules foisted off on English by early writers who knew Latin and thought English should follow the same system.

—Rules concocted to systematize English by people who ignored the true nature and history of the language.

Here is a realistic interpretation of some points that language scholars make in contradiction to statements of some less well-informed people:

—A split infinitive is undesirable only if it is awkward or unclear.

—*And, but,* and *so* are good sentence beginnings if they deserve the emphasis they get there. The same applies to *however* and other transitional words, but some people object only to *and, but,* and *so.*

—Prepositions are perfectly good at the ends of sentences if you want them to have that much emphasis.

—One-sentence paragraphs are perfectly good. The ban on them is nonsense. Often a one-sentence paragraph, especially the first or last in a letter, is just what is needed.

—Passive voice is usually undesirable because it is weak, wordy, and awkward; but it has been retained in the language because it is useful in some situations (to avoid direct accusations, for example). To ban it completely is high-handed.

—Colloquial expressions and slang are important and useful parts of the language; when the situation calls for the informal level of usage, they can improve language effectiveness.

—Many a word has several possible meanings when used alone; but if the context makes the interpretation readily clear and definite, to ban use of these words or to limit them (*while* or *since*, for example) to one use is unrealistic and lordly.

—The distinctions between *shall* and *will* are almost completely gone except in formal English; *will* is much more widely used.

Unfortunately, not all your readers will have studied courses on the history of the language and modern English usage or have read books on those subjects. Many of them will have been misled by linguistically unsound books and teachers. But they will *think* they know what is right and wrong. If you don't do what they think is right, you will distract them and lose their respect.

If you are writing to someone likely to be linguistically misinformed, we advise you to adhere to the widespread, though unsound "rules" when you can do so easily. Otherwise, we suggest that you forget unjustifiable restrictions on the language and give your attention to the more important aspects of good style—interest, clarity, and inconspicuousness.

Appendix D covers some common violations of these conventions and gives suggestions for avoiding criticism.

(*All letter cases for the first four chapters are at the end of Part One because we think you should cover all four basic tests of a good business letter before trying to write any kind of letter. We urge you to read the first four chapters quickly but thoroughly so that you can put all the basic principles to use even in your first letter.*)

(*Since you will remember the principles of good style better if you practice them while concentrating on them alone, however, you may profit by working through at least some of the following exercises.*)

EXERCISES

Determine what is not good about the sentences and rewrite them or be prepared to discuss them, as your teacher directs. You may also benefit by finding (in Appendix D) the appropriate symbol(s) for criticism of each sentence and reading the discussion of the symbol(s).

1. We should take steps to eliminate the one sixth of our population which is now in poverty.
2. The dinner is to honor residents and interns who are leaving the hospital and their wives.
3. Gadgets can be bought to tell the temperatures and relative humidity at hardware and department stores.
4. (*From an ad.*) Solid oak posture chairs for secretaries with built-in padding.
5. No lawyer ever learned all the law he practices in the college in which he studied.
6. (*From a report on rainmaking.*) The responsible scientists of the project interpret the long series of experiments to mean that recently proposed artificial weather modification processes are of relatively little economic importance.
7. According to the trade journal *Trusts and Estates,* a greater percentage of common stocks are now included in the investment portfolios of more than 3,000 banks in the United States.
8. To me, this trend toward greater holding of common stocks in banks' portfolios is very surprising and confirms my opinion that the Dow-Jones averages, Barron's Business Gauge, and the Security Exchange Commission, which all predict bear-market conditions, overstate the extent of our present business recession.
9. There are some milling machine manufacturers that I was unable to contact or that did not answer my letter, however, the figures here cover all the major producers in this area.
10. My own evaluation of Honeywells is the same as that of the authors and should be installed in our plant.
11. It was found that there are 12 main reasons why goods are returned. The most significant of these being entirely or almost entirely customer faults. The 12 reasons are: . . . .
12. When buying from an equipment supplier the prices might be a bit higher than these but would include shipping charges.
13. The size of the plant and the nature of its hazards determines the fire brigade setup necessary.
14. While the clothing field has a large number of returns and is a good place to start it is not at all representative of the whole retailing world.
15. The channel of distribution being utilized most is the use of a traveling sales force.
16. Mr. Johnson insists on neat accurate work.

17. Because of its greater tensil, tear, and bursting strength, it assures less shutdowns in the packaging line.

18. In order to understand how this method of distribution would achieve its purpose an analysis of it is necessary.

19. While I worked with the fire crew I was only involved in one run.

20. Unless the Office of Price Administration or an authorized representative thereof shall, by letter mailed to the applicant within 21 days from the date of filing application, disapprove the requested increase in the maximum price, such price increase shall be deemed to have been approved, subject to nonretroactive written disapproval or adjustment at any later time by the Office of Price Administration.

21. Common stock can be classified under three main types. These types are: (a) income stocks, (b) cyclical stocks, and (c) growth stocks.

22. The report describes the method of operation of the hydrogen plant and a brief discussion of the Girbotol process.

23. The weight of the machines range from 6,000–6,400 pounds.

24. Costs of cleaning materials, Windex and rags were considered negligible and not computed.

25. Seasonal resort investments may often lay idle for as many as eight months out of the year.

26. The consensus of opinion from members of the committee was that polyethylene had a high probability of meeting the requirements.

27. This gives the company that choses the paper bag more versatility in their packaging line.

28. Not only is this welder useful in the manufacture of products but also in repairing of equipment where replacement of the damaged parts is expensive.

29. By adjusting the screws, the spirit bubble may be centered in its tube.

30. "Nonconference" groups are those comprised of individuals that are brought together as a result of their association or relationship to the university (i.e., football team).

31. It has been enjoyable making this study for you, as it is a subject I've wanted to learn more about.

32. Arc welding has some advantages over other methods: easier wedge preparation, faster welding speed and it eliminates the use of flux.

33. I am of the opinion that before investing funds in personnel and equipment for such a center, certain pilot projects ought to be undertaken to determine the value of such a project.

34. The report is designed primarily to show the particular need existing in Latin America and recommending a possible solution for it.

35. Included in the shipment are three small one ounce packages and one big 16 ounce package of Alpha bits.

36. Mr. Rich's recommendation for this versatile work was the Brown & Sharpe because he felt it required the least upkeep of the two machines.

37. A complete cost, both initial and operational, estimate will be presented.

38. The varied kinds of work we can perform includes: property surveys, staking out of substations, taking elevations for contours, and steel inventories.

39. The observers were very interested in large projectiles, especially the 4-inch model for aircraft that weighed about 18 pounds.

40. There are three types of meters used. There is the ammeter which measures current, the wattmeter which measures power and the voltmeter which measures the voltage or electrical pressure.

41. After the grain leaves the seperator it falls to a screw conveyor, and then this conveyor carries it to one of eight bins for storage.

42. The purpose of the program was set up for the improvement of reading rate and the improvement of reading comprehension.

43. The subcontractors draw the final detailed plans which are called shop drawings for their men in the field.

44. An attempt to explain each individual type would be a long tiring thing both from the standpoint of the reader and myself.

45. After the concrete has hardened the forms are removed from the walls.

46. According to population studies by the Bureau of Social Studies which were published in 1955 the population of Latin America will reach 321 million persons by 1980 if it continues at the present rate of increase.

47. The other type uses the hot escaping exhaust fumes to turn a turbine.

48. Inside the tube is also placed a tiny drop of mercury and a small amount of argon gas.

49. Information on the subject was only available in technical journals.

50. While working in Plant 4, fireproof coveralls and protective glasses are issued as a safety measure.

51. The business district in that area is El Cajon and it has its own police force in it.

52. This highly satisfactory garbage can is made by the Jordan Company who have been known for years for their outstanding products.

53. The polyethylene derives two advantages here which are:
    a) Heat sealing made possible by its use speeds up the process.
    b) Economy of eliminating excess material.

54. A report is a communication of fact-supported ideas; if you do not communicate the ideas are of little worth.

55. The problems selected for study were chosen through personal interviews with the workers, manager and my own personal experience with the company.

56. The legislators are expected to vote bigger outlays for highways, schools, water, power, and flood-control projects, hospitals, defense, and medical research.

57. Approximately 66 percent had made their most recent hardware purchase in Tulsa. This is an increase over previous findings of 4 percent.

58. Thank you for your order and let us know if we can be of service again.

59. Minimum and average costs for various items are listed and the individual costs may vary according to taste, budget and needs.

60. At the first registration, all students must pay a $5 deposit to the bursar which will be returned to the student upon leaving the university.

61. In order to satisfy you completely, will you check your preference on the enclosed card?

62. In conformance with our conversation on March 30, the *Report of the Uranium Corporation* has been reviewed, to determine wherein the operations of the corporation may have been presented inadequately; further, suggested changes in format, illustrations, and treatment of text have been developed, for consideration in the preparation of subsequent reports.

63. Simply check your choice on the return card and immediately upon receiving your preference, the typewriter will be on the way to you.

64. You might also show accounts receivable, long-term accounts, and discuss the future outlook.

65. The evaluation of these problems were made by the department of market research.

66. The high pressure air then rushes into the cylinder carrying the oil charge with it.

| # Persuasion: What the reader does

[Knowledge or skill without justice is cunning, not wisdom.]

Planned presentation
    Good-news or neutral messages
    Disappointing messages
    Persuasive messages
You-viewpoint
Adaptation
    Adapting talking points
    Adapting language and style
    Referring to common experiences
    Personalizing
Positive statement
Success consciousness

BECAUSE IN MOST business letters you are trying to produce an action or a reaction which may lead presently to an action, many correspondents maintain that every letter is a sales letter. In the broad sense that you are usually trying to persuade someone that your suggestion (whether it's a product, a service, or an idea) is a good one and/or that yours is a good firm to deal with, that's right.

If you are going to be successful in that mission, you'll want to make conscious use of five principles of persuasion which have proved helpful in getting the desired positive response:

1. Planned presentation in the light of your objective

2. You-viewpoint interpretation

3. Adaptation—even personalization when possible

4. Positive statement

5. Success consciousness

PLANNED PRESENTATION

You can make your job of beginning fairly simple if you will classify your letter according to one of the following three probable reactions of your reader:

A. Does it contain information which will please the reader? Does it take action the reader has requested? Does it request action the reader is prepared to take?

B. Does it contain bad news?

C. Or does it request action the reader is probably not already willing to take?

According to subject matter, you can list hundreds of different kinds of business letters; but for predetermining its beginning and the subsequent development of points, all you need to decide upon is whether your letter contains good news or neutral information (A–plan), disappointing information (B–plan), or persuasion leading to action (C–plan).

Good-news or neutral messages

Most A–plan letters say or imply yes, as in favorable replies to requests, acknowledgments in which you can ship goods as ordered, adjustments fully complying with the reader's request, and credit approvals. Since you are doing what the reader wants you to do, the first sentence should contain the big idea of the letter; that is what the reader most wants to know. Then you follow up with necessary details in an order of relative importance or natural sequence. Frequently letters of this kind end with a short punch line recalling the benefits of the good news in the beginning, as suggested by Figure 1.

FIGURE 1   Good-news and routine letters.

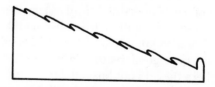

Letters which merely seek or transmit business information follow the same basic order: inquiries and replies about personnel applicants and explanations or identifications of something about an organization, its personnel, or its products. All these are situations in which your reader is neutral (neither pleased nor displeased), and so the letters are taken for granted. They should be characterized by the same directness and dispatch in their handling as in the following "Yes" letter (replacing a clock ordered for a birthday gift and damaged in transit):

Your new Admiral desk clock was mailed by insured parcel post this morning and should be at your door about January 23.

The same kind of heavy padding carefully protecting your new Admiral in the large corrugated box will be used for all future shipments of fragile articles so that they will arrive in the same perfect condition in which they leave the store.

And now will you take a moment to assist us in recovering for the clock from the Postal Service? Just sign the enclosed notification forms and return them to us with the original clock.

The recipient of the new Admiral on January 26 will no doubt be pleased with its beauty and practicality. It is an appropriate birthday surprise.

Disappointing messages

B–plan letters, those that say "No" or "Yes, but . . ." (that is, modified refusals), should not be direct. If you have to tell a reader that you can't give him the booklet he wants, that you can't fill his order as he has specified, that you can't extend credit to him, or that you can't make the adjustment he has requested, you have a situation which is potentially good-will-killing—especially if you blurt out the disappointing information immediately.

We assume throughout this book that you are a fair-minded person who does not act high-handedly or arbitrarily and that you therefore have good reasons when you refuse anything. We know, too, that in most cases you can show that some of your reasons are beneficial to the other person—as when a mother refuses her child something for the child's good as well as (sometimes even *rather than*) her own. The following psychology of refusing therefore depends on your having good reasons, as does any satisfactory refusal.

You know that when you refuse anybody anything to which he thinks he's entitled, he becomes frustrated unless he receives justifying reasons (not just excuses or no explanation at all). You know further that if you begin with the refusal, you will at least disappoint your reader, and you may anger him. You also know that an angry person is not a logical one. So even if you do give good reasons *after* the refusal, they fall on an illogical mind, where they do not take effect.

But if you start pleasantly and give justifying reasons *before* a refusal, your reader is much more likely to accept your refusal without irritation because you lead him to see the justice of it. Thus your logical reasons fall on a logical mind, and the reasons which caused you to feel justified in refusing convince your reader that you *are* justified. This psychology directs you to a rather specific plan for all refusals.

To soften the effect, you try to catch the reader's favorable interest in the opening remarks with something from the situation on which both reader and writer can agree. This is commonly called a "buffer." Writers use it for two reasons: (1) to suggest that the writer is a reasonable person who can see two sides of the question and (2) to set the stage for a review of the facts in the case. A good buffer will therefore be

—Pleasant, usually agreeing with something the reader has said
—Relevant, thus quickly showing the subject of the letter
—Equivocal, avoiding any implication that the answer is yes or no
—Carefully worded for a natural transition to the explanation

After you establish compatibility, you analyze the circumstances sympathetically and understandingly, giving the reasons why you can't do what the reader wants you to do. Not until you have tactfully prepared the way with these justifying reasons do you want to reveal the disappointing news. You further attempt to soften the blow by embedding the refusal, by giving it minimum space, and by positive statement when you have to state it; but better, when possible, you may be able to make the refusal clear by implication. Certainly you do not want to stress it.

Nor do you want to end your letter on a note of disappointment; to close, select some point of favorable interest to your reader which demonstrates your desire to retain him as a friend and customer.

Graphically, your procedure looks like the line in Figure 2. The following positive refusal illustrates the strategy:

FIGURE 2   Bad-news letters.

Your comments, Professor McGinnis, on the effectiveness of the "More Business" series are helpful to those of us at Read's who worked on these practical guides for users of direct mail.

When we first planned the booklets for our customers, we had in mind a checklist for a business using direct mail extensively rather than a thoroughgoing treatment suitable for a textbook. Accordingly, our quota for noncommercial users was set at a low figure—partly because we did not anticipate many requests.

Since the series has proved so popular with our customers, we have for over a month been distributing copies only to commercial users, although we are glad to make available what we can to training institutions.

Perhaps you may be able to use the extra copy—sent to you this morning by parcel post—as a circulating library for your correspondence students. Two or three days' use should be ample for most of them, and they're perfectly welcome to copy anything they care to.

Will you give us the benefit of your suggestions for making
the series more extensive after you have had an opportunity to
test its teachability more thoroughly?

Persuasive messages

The third basic letter situation, the C–plan, if graphed, shows three
areas of interest, as in Figure 3. You start off with something that you can
be reasonably sure your reader wants or is interested in, preferably a
promised or implied benefit, thus catching his attentive interest from the
start. Develop your letter in concrete pictures of what will benefit him. If
you can start off with his agreeing with you and maintain this agreement
as you try to convince him of the worth of your proposition, you can wind
up with his agreeing that he wants to do what you want him to do.

FIGURE 3   Selling letters.

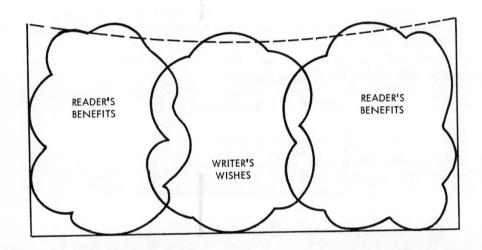

Starting a letter of this kind need not be difficult if you will make your
most honest and concrete attempt to figure out what it is the reader wants
(or needs) that you can give him. When you have developed the benefits
he will derive from complying with your suggestion and have supplied
enough evidence for him to believe that your claims are true, you are in a
psychological position to ask him to do what you want him to do.

Prospecting (cold-turkey) sales and application letters, persuasive
requests, and some collections follow this pattern, as in the following
persuasive request for a confidential manual:

How often have you received—from well-educated people—
letters that are not worth your attention?

You, as a public relations director and an employer, are of course interested in this problem. And I, as a teacher of business communication, am too. Here at Harwood we're turning out a thousand students each year who are better trained in writing effective letters than the usual college graduate. We'd like to be sure that we're giving them what business wants.

It's quite likely, you know, that some of these students will some day be writing letters for companies like yours. Wouldn't they be better prepared if we instructors could stress the ideas that you have given special emphasis to in your recent correspondence manual? Both the students and business firms would benefit from your letting us have a copy for our teaching files. Of course, we'd handle the material with whatever confidence you specify. And I assure you we'd be most grateful for this practical teaching aid.

But the ones especially benefiting from your sending a copy would be the students and business firms like Southern Atlantic.

Will you send us a copy today?

The planned steps in all selling are here. Whether you want to call them four steps (Attention, Interest, Conviction, and Action, or Promise, Picture, Prove, and Push) or three steps (Attentive Interest, Conviction or Evidence, and Action) or more doesn't matter. But it does matter that you get attentive interest quickly by promising a reader benefit, give evidence backing up that promised benefit, and confidently ask the reader to do what you want him to do.

YOU-VIEWPOINT
[People wrapped up in themselves are usually small packages.]

The you-viewpoint or you-attitude is a state of mind: always ferreting out and emphasizing the benefits to the reader resulting from your suggestion or decision and subordinating or eliminating (but not denying) your own.

Of course, it isn't pure unselfishness. All businesses must be motivated by the profit motive. When you try to sell something, obviously you are trying to make some money, but you don't need to put that idea into words. When you attempt to collect, obviously you want—maybe even need—the money; you don't need to put that idea into words. When you apply for a job, obviously you either want or need work to earn some money; you don't need to put that idea into words. Both reader and writer *assume* all these ideas. Putting them into words merely sounds selfish, wastes words, and helps your cause not one bit.

Nor is the you-attitude a question merely of politeness, courtesy, or good manners. The hard business reason for you-viewpoint presentation is that when you show you are aware of and are doing something about your reader's needs or problems, he will react more favorably to your suggestion. In other words, he will do what you want him to if—and only if—you show him that he gets something worth the cost and trouble.

Nothing else is so important to your reader as himself (and when he's writing to you so that you're the reader, he'll take the same stand if he's smart). So by central theme and wording you show that you are thinking of him and his welfare as you write.

The you-viewpoint requires imagination, certainly. The old story of the village half-wit's answer to how he found the mule ("Why, I just thought, If I was a mule, where would I go?") is apt. The ability to visualize the reader's desires, circumstances, and probable reactions and write in those terms is the answer. When you write to secretaries, you *are* a secretary; when you write to doctors, you *are* a doctor; when you write to merchants, you *are* a merchant. It requires that you be able to play many roles. Without this basic outlook and attitude, you-viewpoint presentation may be superficial.

Phrasing helps, it is true. You are more likely to write in terms of the reader if you use more *you's* and *your's* than the first-person pronouns *I, me, mine, we, us, our.* But if you apply that test, the sentence "We want your check" has more you-viewpoint than "We want our check," when obviously neither has any. "Please send your check" is neutral. The reader-dominated sentence might well read, "To keep your account in the preferred-customer class, send your check for $142.63 today," or "Get your account in shape for the heavy Christmas buying coming up by sending your check for $142.63 today." Whether you say "sending *us* your check" or not is immaterial, except that it wastes a word; the *us* is clearly understood. But what is much more significant, the reader-benefit reason —the you-viewpoint—is there.

WE-VIEWPOINT	YOU-VIEWPOINT
We are shipping your order of June 2 this afternoon.	You should receive the Jurgin crosscut saw you ordered June 2 no later than Saturday, June 7.
We have spent 27 years making the Jurgin the finest of its kind.	Back of your Jurgin blade are 27 years of successful testing and remodeling. Because it is taper-ground alloy steel, it slides through the wood more freely than other models.

Making your reader the subject or object of your sentences will help you keep you-viewpoint interpretation. As you've already seen in the discussion of writing interestingly (p. 29), psychological description and dramatized copy are effective because they keep the reader involved and show that you have the you-viewpoint. The only way to get it in the first place, however, is to subordinate your own reactions to those you estimate are your reader's probable reactions and then to write in a manner which clearly shows that your reader's interests dominate.

An example of well-intentioned writing that is fundamentally writer-dominated is the conventional thank-you beginning: "Thank you for your order of June 2 for one Jurgin crosscut saw blade" and "We are grateful for . . . ." Even worse is the selfish "We are glad to have your order for . . . ." All three variations have this strike against them: They emphasize the personal reaction of the writer rather than something the reader is interested in knowing.

If you can (or will) make shipment, an opening like the following has more you-viewpoint than any of the three foregoing:

```
Your Jurgin crosscut saw blade should arrive by prepaid
railway express no later than Friday, June 7.
```

This is something your reader wants to know! If you can't make shipment, a resale comment is a better example of you-viewpoint than the selfish statement of pleasure upon the receipt of another order or the disappointing statement that the reader is not now getting what he wants. If shipment will be delayed only a few days, this is a possibility for retaining positiveness and you-viewpoint:

```
The Jurgin crosscut saw blade you ordered will give you long
and faithful service.
```

When the reader has done you a favor, some form of thank you may be one of the best beginnings you could use. In place of the conventional "Dear Mr. Miller," the salutation—

```
Thank you, Mr. Miller!
```

—has directness and enthusiasm which are heartwarming. The first paragraph may then concentrate on a more significant point:

```
Those articles about palletization which you suggested contain
some of the best information I've been able to uncover.
```

But doesn't the statement of the significance you attach to your reader's contribution adequately establish your appreciation?

We do not mean to imply that an expression of gratitude is out of place. No one ever offended a reader with a genuine, appropriate thank you. But we do want to stress to you that you can accomplish the same function with some statement which will place more emphasis on your reader—where it should be!

The preceding remarks concerning planned presentation and you-viewpoint apply whether you're writing a special or a form letter—a sales, credit, collection, application, or simple reply. The closer you can come to making your reader nod his head in agreement and think, "That's what I want to hear," the greater your possibilities for favorable reception of your letter.

ADAPTATION

When you can make him also think "That sure fits me," you have an additional advantage. Successful adaptation makes your reader feel that your letter has been written with him in mind.

Even in a mailing to a large number of people, you will have identifiable common characteristics (of geography, age, educational level, vocation, or income status, for example) that will enable you to adapt the talking points, language, and style of your letter and to make references to commonplace circumstances and events.

Adapting talking points

In adapting talking points (or theme), you simply seek out and emphasize those reasons you believe will be most influential in causing your reader to act or react as you want him to. Specifically, you would try to sell a typewriter to a secretary on the basis of ease of operation, to an office manager on ease of maintenance and durability, but to a purchasing agent on the basis of long-range cost. The lawn mower which you would sell to a homeowner because of its ease of handling and maintenance, you would sell to a hardware dealer because of its salability and his profit margin. A car is more likely to appeal to a man on the basis of economy and dependability of operation; to a woman the appeals of appearance and comfort are stronger. When a man buys a shirt, he is interested in appearance and fit; his wife is more interested in launderability and long wear.

Accordingly, you adapt your talking points to your reader(s) for increased persuasiveness. This is a fairly simple procedure when you are writing a single letter and is entirely possible in a mass mailing if you study the characteristics common to all people on your mailing list.

Adapting language and style

You adapt language and style, in general, in the light of your reader's age, educational level, and vocation (which influence his social and economic position). As your reader's years, professional and social prestige, and financial status increase, you are safer in using longer sentences, uncommon words, and more formal language. Sometimes you will want to use the specialized terms of vocational classes, such as doctors, lawyers, and insurance men, for instance. Although some of these terms are more technical than you would use in writing to a general audience, to the specialized reader they convey the impression that you, the writer, understand his problems. The application of this suggestion means that when you write to doctors, references to patients, laboratories, diagnoses, and the like help; to an insurance man, prospects, premiums, and expirations are likely referents.

Referring to common experiences

Better adaptation than language and style, however, are references to common experiences in the reader's life. A reference to vocation, to a geographical factor, to some home and family status—in fact, to any activity or reaction you can be reasonably sure your reader has experienced—rings the bell of recognition and makes the reader feel that very definitely you are writing to and about him.

In a letter to college students, for instance, the following reference would almost universally bring positive (and in most cases humorous) recognition:

```
When your teacher talks on . . . and on . . . and on . . .
(even when it's two minutes past the bell!). . . .
```

To parents:

```
When your child yawns, turns over, and finally goes to sleep.
```

To doctors:

```
. . . for the elimination of dust, smoke, and antiseptic odors
from your reception room.
```

To school superintendents:

```
. . . to reduce the necessary and healthy noise of active
adolescents when they're changing classes.
```

To almost any businessman:

```
. . . when your files simply won't reveal an important carbon.
```

To anyone who is or has been a secretary:

```
An hour's transcription to get in the night's mail—and at 5
minutes to 5!
```

Any of the preceding phrases could go into a form letter or an individual letter. The more specifically you can phrase these references to make them pinpoint your one reader, the more effective your adaptation will be.

Personalizing

To further the impression that the letter has been prepared for the reader and to heighten the feeling of friendliness, correspondents sometimes use the reader's name or other references so specific as to be individualizing, not only in the inside address and the salutation but also in the letter copy. At about the middle of the letter, much as one uses a friend's name in talking with him, or near the end of the letter in the same way you frequently use a person's name in ending a conversation, such references as the following help to give the impression that the letter is for one person rather than a group:

You'll also appreciate the lightness of the Multimower, Mr. Bowen.

--

Your Atlanta Luminall representative, Mr. Paul Owen, will be glad to call on you and answer any other questions you may have, Mr. Bowen.

Just check a convenient time on the enclosed card and drop it in the mail today.

In individually typed letters the placement of the name presents no problem; in form letters, try to put the name at the end of a line (as in the first of the preceding examples) so that typing in the reader's name is easy, regardless of length. Unless you can match type and print perfectly, however, you may do more harm than good. (Computerized letters enable a writer to insert special phrasing at any point in a letter. But because of costs this is a process available only to those firms sending out mailings in the thousands, even millions.) In any case use of the reader's name is a more or less mechanical process; it is probably the least effective means of adapting.

You can also increase the feeling of friendliness by the wording of your salutation and complimentary close. *Dear Sir* and *Very truly yours,* although appropriate many times, are somewhat formal and do not reflect the warmth of *Dear Mr. Bowen* and *Sincerely yours* or some other less formal phrasing. The main forms and their order of formality are discussed in detail on page 19.

Of far greater significance are adaptation of talking points and lifelike references to the reader's activities. The following letter answers the lady's questions in salesmanlike presentation and enhances the persuasiveness of the message with special references (such as to the servant and the power failure mentioned in her inquiry) that could apply to no one but the reader:

Dear Mrs. Jackson:

The Stair-Traveler you saw in the June <u>Home and Yard</u> will certainly make daily living easier for you and your faithful old servant. You can make as many trips upstairs and downstairs as you care to <u>every day</u> and still follow your doctor's advice.

Simply sit down on the bench (about the same size as a dressing-table stool) and press the button. Gently and smoothly your Stair-Traveler takes you upstairs at a rate just a little faster than ordinary walking. Should the electricity fail in Greenbriar while you're using your Stair-Traveler, automatic brakes bring it to a gentle stop and hold it in place until the current comes on. Then you just press the button to start it again.

Folded back against the wall when not in use, the Stair-Traveler's simple, straight lines of mahogany will blend in well with your antiques. Your Stair-Traveler will be right at home on your front straight stairway, Mrs. Jackson. It will be more convenient for you there, and as it is designed only for straight stairways, the installation is simple and economical. Notice the folded Stair-Traveler on page 3 of the booklet I'm sending; it looks somewhat like a console table.

To explain how simply and economically your Stair-Traveler can be installed, Mr. J. B. Nickle, our Memphis representative, will be glad to call at a time convenient for you. Will you use the enclosed postcard to let him know when that will be?

Such specialized references do increase letter costs when they mean writing a personal letter rather than using a form. But many times a personal letter must be used if the letter is to get the job done. Even in form paragraphs and entire form letters, however, you usually can make some adaptation to the reader's situation.

You can find out a great deal about your reader through his letters to you, your credit records (including credit reports), salesmen's reports, and the like. Even a bought or rented mailing list contains the names of people with some common characteristics of vocation, location, age, sex, finances, and buying and living habits. You won't make your letter do all it could do if you don't use your knowledge of these common characteristics to adapt your letter according to talking points and endow it with the marginal pulling power of known references to familiar events, activities, places, or persons.

A word of caution is appropriate here, however: Don't try to be specific beyond the point of likelihood. For example, you may have a mailing list of parents, but you don't know how many children these people have or what the sex is. A reference to "your child" is safe (even if the reader has more than one); a reference to "your children" is not—and certainly not to "your boy" or "your girl." Obviously, you cannot safely use such tags as "Junior" and "Sister" and certainly not individual names like "Bobby" and "Janie" unless you *know* your reader does have a Bobby or a Janie.

POSITIVE STATEMENT

Your letters have greater prospects for success if you focus on positive ideas because people—most of them, at any rate— respond more favorably to a positive prospect than to a negative one.

Saying the cheerful, positive thing that people want to hear rather than the unpleasant or unhappy, negative thing they do not want to hear is really just an extension of you-viewpoint presentation and tact. It requires, first of all, staying optimistic yourself so that you can see the rosier side of any picture. It comes from constantly superimposing a positive picture on a negative one, thus completely eliminating, or at least subordinating, the negative idea. Translated into letter-writing procedures, it is the result of stressing what something is rather than what it is not, emphasizing what the firm or product can and will do rather than what it cannot, leading with action rather than apology or explanation, and avoiding words that convey basically unpleasant ideas.

Test after test of both advertising copy and letter copy has demonstrated the wisdom of positive statement. That is why nearly 40 years ago successful copywriters warned against the denied negative (and today's writers still issue the same warning). That is why the effective writer will make the following positive statements rather than their negative counterparts:

NEGATIVE	POSITIVE
Penquot sheets are not the skimpy, loosely woven sheets ordinarily in this price class.	Penquot sheets are woven 186 threads to the square inch for durability and, even after 3-inch hems, measure a generous 72 by 108 inches.
We are sorry that we cannot furnish the club chairs by August 16.	After checking with the Production Department, we can definitely assure you your club chairs by August 29.
We cannot ship in lots of less than 12.	To keep down packaging costs and to help customers save on shipping costs, we ship in lots of 12 or more.
I have no experience other than clerking in my father's grocery store.	Clerking in my father's grocery store for three summers taught me the value of serving people courteously and promptly.
If we can help, please do not hesitate to get in touch with us.	Can we help further?

A special form of negativism is the challenging question which invites a negative answer. Although it contains no negative wording, the question "Wouldn't you rather drink Old Judge?" is more likely to bring forth the reply "No, I'd rather drink Colonel Dalton" or maybe "Make mine Dipsi-Cola!" than it is to get a yes answer. "Who wouldn't want a Kreisler Regal?" will bring something like a bristling "Not me, brother; I want a Cabriolet!" from most readers, who will resent the presumptuousness of such a question. "What could be finer than an XYZ dishwasher?" will elicit, among other answers, "A full-time maid!" Such questions, along with the apparently harmless "Why not try a Blank product?" get your reader out of step with you and, because they invite a negative response, are a deterrent to the success of your suggestion.

Keeping your messages positive also means deliberately excluding negative words. You can't be "sorry" about something without recalling the initial unhappy experience. You can't write "unfortunately" without restating some gloomy aspect of a situation. Nor can you write in terms of "delay," "broken," "damages," "unable to," "cannot," "inconvenience," "difficulty," "disappointment," and other negatives without stressing some element of the situation which makes your reader react against you rather than with you.

For all these reasons the effective writer will write "ABC Dog Biscuit will help keep your dog healthy" instead of "ABC Dog Biscuit will help keep your dog from getting sick." It's just a question of accentuating the positive.

SUCCESS CONSCIOUSNESS

Success consciousness is the confident attitude that your reader will do what you ask him to do or accept the decision your letter announces. To reflect this attitude in your letters, guard against any phrasing which suggests that the reader may not take the action you want him to.

Success consciousness is based on your own conviction that your explanation is adequate, your suggestion legitimate and valuable to your reader, your decision the result of adequate evidence and logical, businesslike reasoning. Thus assured yourself, you are not likely to write something which suggests or even implies that you are unsure of your ground. The sales correspondent who writes

> If you'd like to take advantage of this timesaving piece of equipment, put your check and completed order blank in the enclosed envelope and drop it in the mail today.

would be better off if he did not remind the reader of his option to reject the proposal. Simply omitting the phrase *if you'd like* establishes a tone of greater confidence. The one word *if* is the most frequent destroyer of success consciousness.

Likewise, when tempted to write

> Why not try a sample order?

the correspondent should remember that the suggestion is stronger with the elimination of *why not*. It has not only the disadvantage of suggesting that the writer is not sure of his own case but also the distinct disadvantage of inviting the reader to think of reasons why he should not do what the letter suggests. When he puts his mind to it, he can probably come up with several reasons.

Hope and its synonym *trust* are second only to *if* as destroyers of success consciousness. In a letter granting an adjustment, the sentence

> We hope you'll approve of our decision.

has greater success consciousness (and thus more reader response) when revised to read:

> With this extension of your subscription to Vacation you can continue to read each month about the world's most interesting places.

By assumption (implication)—by definitely omitting the doubtful-sounding expression—the writer seems to say, "Of course, you and I realize that this is what you want."

In refusals the following sentence sometimes appears in an otherwise well-written letter:

```
We trust you will understand our position.
```

Usually, however, it appears in a poorly written letter. And it is most frequently the result of inadequate explanation. The writer seems to despair of giving an adequate explanation and to hope that the reader will figure out one for himself. If you find yourself writing or wanting to write such a sentence, go back and see whether your explanation is ample. If it is, omit such a sentence; if it is not, revise your explanation so that it is convincing—and substitute some positive, confident statement for the weak-kneed expression.

Even in simple replies the problem arises with such a sentence as

```
We hope this is the information you wanted.
```

The implications of doubt can be removed quickly and easily with

```
We're glad to send you this information.
```

This principle of success consciousness applies in all types of letters, but it is most significant in selling letters.

A word of caution against high-pressure presumptuousness should be injected here, however. To omit a reference to a reader's alternative is one thing; to imply that the reader has no alternative is quite another! The application letter writer who so boldly and confidently asks

```
When may I come in to see you?
```

gives the impression that he thinks his reader has no alternative but to see him. With such presumptuousness he may irritate his reader. Rephrased like the following, his request for an interview would strike most readers favorably:

```
Will you write me a convenient time when I may come in and
tell you more about why I believe I am the aggressive salesman
you're looking for?
```

The proper degree of success consciousness requires careful wording, particularly at the end. Basically, you need to consider what the purpose of the letter is.

Sometimes you want the reader to take no overt action on the topic of the letter—as in most B–plan letters and some A's. In that case you may end with a pleasant comment or further support for something said earlier (thanks or resale, for example), with an off-the-subject comment (usually a pleasant look to the future, perhaps sales promotion material), or with something else pleasant. Certainly you want to avoid suggesting inade-quacy of treatment and such jargon as "Please do not hesitate . . ." or "Feel free to . . . ." And in B–plan letters, guard particularly against referring back to the trouble you've supposedly cleared up.

At other times you are asking for action that is simple, easy, and likely

—as in most A–plan letters (no strong reader resistance). Here a subtle reference to or suggestion of that action is most appropriate:

—I shall appreciate your answers to. . . .

—You are cordially invited to. . . .

—When you send in your check for the $27.50 now due. . . .

In C–plan letters, you are asking for action the reader is reluctant to take. The force of your push for action—to overcome reader resistance—must continue to the end. Here particularly, such words as *if, trust,* and *hope* will show a lack of success consciousness that will be self-defeating.

As you see, each of the three situations requires an ending quite different from what is appropriate for the others. You will do well, therefore, to keep in mind the principle of success consciousness as you study the discussions, illustrations, and checklists for different classes of letters throughout this book.

One important general point should be established here, however: Even though the earlier part of the letter may have indicated a desired action, you need to refer to, suggest, ask for, or push for that action *at the end.*

(All the cases for the first four chapters are at the end of Part One because we think you should cover all four basic tests of a good business letter before trying to write any kind of letter. We urge you to read the first four chapters quickly but thoroughly so that you can put all the basic principles to use even in your first letter.)

chapter 4 | # Goodwill:
How the reader feels

[Disagreements come from lost accord.]

Tone
    Acceptable balance of personalities
        Undue humility
        Flattery
        Condescension
        Preachiness
        Bragging
    Courtesy
        Anger
        Accusations
        Unflattering implications
        Sarcasm
        Curtness
        Stereotyped language
        Physical appearance
    Sincerity
        Effusiveness
        Exaggeration
        Undue familiarity
Service attitude
    Resale material
    Sales promotion material
    Special goodwill letters

MOST BUSINESS PEOPLE define goodwill as "the disposition of customers to return to the place where they have been treated well." Look it up in your dictionary, however, and you'll find friendly, positive words like *kindly feeling, benevolence, cheerful consent, heartiness,* and *cordiality.* A business letter helps to produce that positive disposition in the reader by developing his friendly, confident feeling toward the writer.

No business firm or individual would intentionally drive away present or possible future customers or friends by creating ill will or by seeming indifferent. For lack of conscious effort to build goodwill, however, many letter writers do drive customers away. Proper *tone* and the *service attitude* are the methods of winning the reader's friendliness and confidence —that is, his goodwill or disposition to return to you because you have treated him well.

TONE

[Beware of those who fall at your feet; they may be reaching for the rug.]

No doubt you have heard someone complain, "It isn't *what* he said— it's the *way* he said it!" Inflections and modulations of the voice, facial expressions, hand gestures—all affect the tone or overall impression of a spoken remark almost as much as the words do, sometimes even more. The point applies in writing too—especially in writing letters, the most personal, me-to-you kind of writing. If you want your letters to build goodwill, you *will make a conscious effort to control the tone.*

Basic to a desirable tone in letters is a balance of personalities (writer's and reader's) acceptable to both. Without an attitude of mutual respect, you will have difficulty achieving in your letters the other two qualities necessary for good tone—courtesy and sincerity.

Acceptable balance of personalities

As a writer of good business letters you will need to subordinate your own wishes, reactions, and opinions; the suggestion "Make it *big you* and little me" can be overdone, however. Anything you say that looks up to or down on the reader will throw the relationship off balance.

Undue humility usually backfires. Such a fawning, servile tone as in the following is unwise because it is obviously insincere-sounding; no reader expects a writer to have such a humble opinion of himself:

```
I'm sorry to ask a busy man like you to take his valuable time
to help me, but without your help I do not know how to
proceed.  Since you are a world authority on . . . , and I
know nothing about it. . . .
```

In addition to the insincere implications, it also suggests an incompetent person whose request for advice is hardly worth considering.

Flattery is another reason why readers question the sincerity or integrity of some writers, especially when it is obvious flattery in connection with the writer's attempt to get the reader to do something or to keep buying. The reader, sure that the writer has an ax to grind, discounts such passages as the following:

```
Your keen discrimination in the matter of footwear is
evidenced in your order of the ninth.
```
--
```
You and you alone can give us the information we need about
Gullett razors.
```
--

```
Your eminent position in commercial aviation, Mr. Pogue, is
the subject of much admiration.
                            --
Your meteorlike rise in the field of retailing, Mr.
Bowen, . . .
                            --
When an Atlanta girl marries, she immediately thinks of
Rich's, the merchandising cynosure of the South!
```

Flattery also embarrasses many readers and makes them uncomfortable even in the privacy of reading a letter. Instead of gaining favor, the writer loses face and the reader's faith. Passing deserved compliments or giving credit where credit is due is something else; it is expected of anybody except a boor. When you want to indicate your awareness of the reader's position or accomplishment, handle the reference subordinately. The writer who began his letter with

```
You are receiving this questionnaire because you are an
authority in the retailing field.
```

got off to a bad start because of the obviousness of his flattery. He might well have revised his sentence this way:

```
As an authority in retailing, how do you think the passage of
HR-818 will affect co-ops?
```

Before this reader has time to feel irritation or embarrassment over the initial phrase (it's so short and touched so lightly that he may experience a faint glow of satisfaction), he is forced into consideration of an impersonal point.

Handling a compliment subtly is frequently a question of inserting a complimentary phrase in a statement intended primarily to accomplish something else. The indirect compliments in the following openings imply that the reader's opinion is worth seeking but have no obvious flattery:

```
How, in your opinion, will passage of HR-818 affect co-ops?
                            --
After successful experience in the field, would you say that
there is any single area of preparation more important than
others for effective public relations work?
```

More frequent than undesirable humility and flattery, however, is a writer's implication of too much respect for himself and too little for his reader. Lack of respect usually reflects itself in (1) condescension ("talking down" to the other person), (2) preachiness (*didacticism* is another word for it), and (3) bragging.

Condescension is quick evidence that the writer considers himself superior to his reader and maybe does not even respect him. Almost everybody has a good share of self-respect. No one wants to be considered a nobody and looked down on or talked down to.

Yet, in attempting to be bighearted, a businessman insulted his reader when he wrote, "It is unlikely that the machine is defective, but a firm of our size and standing can afford to take it back and give you a new one." In the same category go the sentences "I am surprised that you would question the adjustment procedure of a firm like Blank's" or "You are apparently unaware of the long history of satisfactory customer relations at Blank's." The statement "We shall allow you to" has condescending connotations that are not present in "We shall be glad to" or "Certainly you may."

A particular danger lies in writing to children, who are not lacking in respect for their own ways of looking at things. When the secretary of a boys' club requested that a department store manager contribute some boxing gloves to the club, the manager answered: "When you grow up to have the heavy business responsibilities I have and you're asked for contributions by all kinds of charitable organizations, you'll understand why I cannot make a donation to your club." The boy's vocabulary failed him, but what he tried to express was "That pompous man!" And to make matters worse, the manager began his next sentence with "You are probably unaware. . . ."

A slightly different form of condescending attitude crops up in application letters in a statement like "You may call me at 743-4601." The implication is that the writer is permitting the reader a privilege when just the opposite is true. An applicant is in no position to appear so aloof.

Repeated use of such phrases as "we think," "we believe," and "we suggest" often are interpreted as condescension. The writer who reflects such a sense of superiority is almost certain to erect a barrier of incompatibility between himself and his reader. Far from attracting a reader, such egocentric talk causes him to sputter, "Well, who does he think he is?" When this happens, the goodwill of the reader is affected in varying degrees.

Preachiness (didacticism), which is an extension of condescension, is undesirable because

1. Most people (especially residents of the United States) do not like to be bossed.
2. When you tell your reader what he ought to do, you imply that he does not know and thus you suggest your superiority and his incapability.

The juvenile-sounding marketing lecture some sales writers put into letters to retailers is one of the most frequent offenders (because it is so elementary). The following are typical:

```
The only way for you to make money is by offering your
customers merchandise that has utility, good quality, and an
attractive price.

                              --

It's time for all dealers to get in their Christmas stock!
```

A retailer would not remain a retailer very long if he did not realize the truth of such statements and act accordingly. Whether he is an old-timer or a beginner, when he reads such preachy statements as the foregoing, his usual reaction is an emphatic negative one like "Who is he to be telling me how to run my business?" or a vigorous "Let me make my own decisions!"

When a statement is flat and obvious, it is frequently irritating to the reader, even though the intent of the writer is good, as in the following:

```
Satisfaction of your customers means turnover and profits to
you.
                              --
You need something new and different to show your customers.
```

You, as a business letter writer, will do well to examine carefully the expressions "you want," "you need," "you should," and their variations, seeking to eliminate them whenever you can without altering the meaning. The following illustration from an application letter is preachy:

```
The business cycle is changing from a seller's market to a
buyer's market.  You are going to need a strong force of good
salesmen.
```

Here is one way it could be improved for the reader's acceptance of the idea without irritation:

```
Now that business is shifting from a seller's market to a
buyer's market, you're probably thinking about the strong
force of good salesmen with which you'll meet competition.
```

The sales writer in the following example is vague, flat, and preachy:

```
Spring will soon be here . . . rain in the morning, cold and
clear in the afternoon.  To be safe, you should carry both a
topcoat and a raincoat with you every day.  But that's a
bother.
```

He could have improved his presentation this way (among others):

```
For these early spring days when it's raining in the morning
but clearer and colder in the afternoon, a topcoat which is
also a raincoat will give you protection to and from work—

—and without your having to worry each morning over "Which
shall I take today?"
```

One of the worst kinds of intellectual and psychological browbeating is this:

```
Do you want Davison's to keep growing and keep getting better?

Of course you do!

Then you should employ only those individuals who want to
move steadily forward and push Davison's on to greater heights.
```

Far more likely to win the reader's approval is the following version, with positive phrasing and a studied attempt not to tell the reader how he should be running his business:

```
Good merchandise at the right prices is not the only reason
Davison's has grown as it has in the last five years:  The
team of Davison men and women has been equally influential.
```

Careful phrasing can eliminate most of the irritation due to preachiness. Often the key is to subordinate—that is, put in a phrase or dependent clause—the obvious or known.

Bragging is another undesirable extension of the writer's ego. And as advertising and public relations improve, as well as the general educational level, bragging brings to the minds of more and more readers the sometimes comical, sometimes pitiful, sometimes disgusting, chest-pounding would-be caveman. Conscious use of superlative wording ("latest and greatest," "outstandingly superior," "final word") is a flagrant and obvious way to make your reader not believe you. Most thoughtful writers will eliminate such references mentally before words get on paper. But even experienced writers annoy readers with undesirable—and almost always unsupported—references to size of company, efficiency of operations, or quality of product. The following are examples:

```
In a business as large as ours—with literally thousands of
retailers selling our products— . . . .
```

```
In a firm as large as Bowen and Bowen, such incidents are
bound to happen.
```

```
You are unfortunately a victim of routine made necessary by
the vastness of an institution so well operated as the White
Sands Hotel.
```

```
You will understand, I'm sure, that it takes longer than usual
when orders are handled as exactingly as we do.
```

All business writers will do well to remind themselves that

—Silver notes never come from brass horns

and

—An ounce of fact is worth a ton of ballyhoo.

The desirable adjustment to both reader and writer (through elimination of servility, flattery, condescension, preachiness, and bragging) will help to improve the tone of your letters; but it will not assure courtesy, the second element in desirable letter tone.

Courtesy

[Kindness is the oil that reduces friction between people.]

A dictionary definition of courtesy is "excellent manners or behavior; politeness." Being courteous is being considerate of the other person's feelings through exercising patience and tact. These come only from conscious and determined effort in many cases, because often one's instantaneous, emotional, or unthinking reaction is an impatient or tactless expression. For that reason, one famous lecturer regularly suggests the use of a "soaking drawer"—a special drawer in the desk to put nasty-toned letters overnight, for revision the next day.

Contrary to an oft stated phrase, people are not "born courteous." (If you doubt this, spend an hour talking with almost any child.) Courtesy often requires a conscious effort to be understanding and forgiving, to anticipate the reader's likely reaction, and to avoid offense.

For that reason correspondents need to keep in mind the major causes of discourtesy. An old French proverb applies here: To speak kindly does not hurt the tongue.

Anger displayed is almost certain to cause loss of the reader's friendliness toward you and confidence in you. The average business reader has a good deal of self-respect and confidence in the wisdom of his own decisions. When they are attacked, he too feels a wave of anger and a consequent necessity to defend himself. The result is two people seriously estranged. Such sentences as the following are almost sure to produce that result:

```
We cannot understand why you are so negligent about paying
bills.
                            --
What's going on in the office at your place?
                            --
We certainly have no intention of letting you get away with
that!
```

Crude slang or profanity, especially if used in connection with a display of heightened feeling, is likely to be interpreted as anger, whether or not it is intended as such. Don't use either. (And don't try to be coy and cute with quotation marks for questionable slang or dashes in words that are obviously profanity.)

Petulance (peevishness or fretfulness) is simply anger in a modified degree. It is comparable to the scoldings children often must receive from parents (and unfortunately from teachers too!). Here is how a woman scolded an interior decorator: "When do you expect to return my furniture? You've had it now for more than two weeks. That ought to be long enough to do a little upholstering job." A calm request that the work be finished as soon as possible because of the need for the furniture would probably bring just as quick action, and it would leave the upholsterer in a better mood to do a good job.

Business readers have usually graduated from sandpile psychology too. When they read "We have played fair with you; why don't you play fair with us?" they are likely to regard the writer's whining as unnecessarily and undesirably juvenile.

Both anger and petulance are the result of impatience and unwillingness to accept the responsibilities of successful human relations.

Accusations, on the other hand, are usually the result of insensitivity to how another person will react to a remark. One cannot cultivate tact (skill in dealing with others without giving offense) without a deep and almost constant concern for the feelings of others. The sensitive, thoughtful person knows that people do not like to be reminded of their care-lessness or ignorance; he also knows that they will develop an unfriend-liness toward the person who insists upon reminding them of their errors. The customer may not always be right, but if you are going to keep his greatest friendliness (goodwill), you will remember not to call attention to the error if you can avoid doing so, or to do it with the least likely offense (impersonal style or by implication). The writer of the following letter displayed an almost completely insensitive attitude toward his reader:

> Much as we dislike doing so, we shall have to delay your order of May 12.
>
> <u>You neglected</u> to specify which shade of sweater you desire.
>
> Kindly check your catalog and <u>this time</u> let us know whether you want navy, midnight, or powder blue.
>
> We have enclosed an envelope for your convenience.

The following revised version has much better tone and is thus more likely to retain the goodwill of the reader. It eliminates the accusation and the unfavorable reminder in the underlined words of the preceding example, the sarcasm the reader would probably read into *kindly,* and the pompous-sounding reference to the enclosure.

> Since we want you to be entirely satisfied with the blue sweater you ordered on May 12, will you please let us know which shade you prefer?
>
> You may obtain the cardigan style in navy, midnight, or powder blue. All are popular this spring.
>
> Just check the appropriate blank on the enclosed reply card. As soon as we receive it, we will mail your sweater.

In this revision the reader infers his own carelessness, but he will feel more friendly toward the writer and his firm for the gentlemanlike way of asking for additional information without accusing.

Unflattering implications are usually the result of tactlessness combined with suspicion or distrust. The collection correspondent who wrote, "When we sold you these goods, we thought you were honest," implied an idea of much greater impact than the literal statement, an implication which is distinctly unflattering and thus destructive of goodwill.

The adjustment correspondent who writes, "We are investigating ship-ment of the goods *you claim* you did not receive," need not be surprised to receive a sharp reply. When he writes, *"We are surprised* to receive your report," or *"We cannot understand* why you have had trouble with the Kold-Hold when other people like it so well," he is establishing by implication his doubts of the reader's reasonableness, honesty, or intelligence.

And the sales correspondent who begins his message implying that he doubts his reader's alertness can expect few returns to his letter:

```
Alert hardware dealers everywhere are stocking No-Flame, the
fire-resistant liquid which more and more home builders are
including in their specifications.

Are you prepared to meet the demands of your home-building
customers?
```

In similar vein the phrases "Do you realize . . . ?" and "Surely you are . . ." immediately suggest the writer's doubts that the reader measures up on either score.

Such lack of tact is frequently unintentional. Most readers, however, do not question whether it is intentional; the result is ill will for the writer and the firm.

Sarcasm, on the other hand, is generally deliberate. And it is usually dangerous in business correspondence. The smile which accompanies friendly sarcastic banter cannot find its way onto paper; unfriendly sarcasm is sheer malice. It is the direct opposite of the attitude necessary for a tone of goodwill because it shows a lack of respect for the other fellow and a deliberate attempt to belittle him. The sales manager sending the following message to a group of salesmen falling short of their quotas would build no goodwill:

```
Congratulations on your magnificent showing!

We're only $50,000 short this week.

How do you do it?
```

The United Fund leader of a community fund drive who included the following in his public report could hardly expect future cooperation from the division indicated:

```
The ABC employees, with an assigned goal of $800, magnificently
responded with $452.  Such generosity should not go
unmentioned.
```

Sarcasm should never be used in business correspondence except between people of equal intelligence, of equal station in life, and with highly similar senses of humor. To be on the safe side, do not use it at all. The moment of triumph is short-lived; the loss of the friendship of the reader may be permanent.

Curtness, born of impatience and a false sense of what constitutes desirable business brevity, reflects indifference and thus seems discourteous. The manufacturer sending the following letter was promptly labeled a boor by the woman who received it:

```
We have your request for our booklet and are enclosing same.
Thanking you for your interest, we are. . . .
```

Better to send no letter than this. Booklets usually do a good job. And experiment after experiment has shown that a good letter accompanying a booklet increases the pulling power. On the other hand, a poor letter like this, reflecting such lack of interest, destroys some of the favorable impression made by the booklet.

This correspondent might very well have helped to convert a casual inquiry into a sale if he had taken the time to show interest in serving the customer with a letter like the following, which is superior because of the service attitude reflected, the positive and specific resale material, and the action ending (all of which are discussed later):

We're glad to send you Siesta's booklet <u>Color at Mealtime</u>.

When you read it, you'll understand why we say that in Siesta you can now have handsome dinnerware that is sturdy enough for everyday use, yet surprisingly inexpensive.

No photography, however, can do justice to the delicacy of some Siesta shades or to the brilliance of the others.

Your friendly local dealer will be glad to show you his selection of Siesta. Unless his stock is complete, he'll be glad to order additional colors for your examination.

See him soon and start enjoying Siesta's color at mealtime.

You can find Siesta in Omaha at (name and address of dealer).[1]

Stereotyped language is another mark of discourtesy because it suggests indifference. And nobody likes to have his business treated in an indifferent, routine way. Writers of letters like the following can expect little feeling of friendliness from the reader:

We have your favor of the 19th and in reply beg to state that the interest on your mortgage is now $361.66.

We trust this is the information you desired, and if there is any other way we can oblige, please do not hesitate to call upon us.

Since stereotyped language is primarily a question of style, see p. 36 for fuller discussion.

Physical appearance is one other factor affecting the apparent courtesy of letters, in the eyes of most readers. Sleazy paper, poor placement, strikeovers, messy erasures, dim or clogged type, poorly matched type and processed material, and penciled signatures are like trying to gain admission to the 21 Club when you're dressed in sweat shirt, dungarees, and sneakers (see Chapter 1).

In putting his best foot forward through courtesy, however, a correspondent must be careful not to trip himself; overdone attempts to be courteous may seem insincere and thus destroy the third element in desirable letter tone.

Sincerity
[Don't stretch the truth; it snaps back.]

When a reader feels his first flashes of doubt, with a resultant reaction of "Well, I'll take that with a grain of salt," he has lost confidence in the writer—most likely because of apparent insincerity.

---

[1] This letter can easily be set up as a form letter with only this one line and the inside address and salutation individually typed.

Sincere cordiality is entirely free of hypocrisy. It is unwillingness to exaggerate or fictionalize upon the true state of a situation. Inappropriate cordiality (usually unbelievable and sometimes distasteful) is commonly the result of effusiveness, exaggeration, and undue familiarity. (Flattery and undue humility, it is true, often sound insincere. But in our opinion they are more intimately linked with the desirable balance of personalities discussed in a preceding section.)

Effusiveness means gushiness. It is excessive politeness which often *is* insincere and always *sounds* insincere. "Overdone" means the same thing. Your letters can sound effusive simply because you've used too many adjectives and adverbs, as in the following examples:

```
We are extremely happy to place your name on our list of
highly valued charge customers, and we sincerely want you to
know that we have hundreds of loyal employees all very eager
and anxious to serve.
                          --
Your excellent choice of our fine store for the opening of a
charge account we consider a distinct compliment to the superb
quality of our merchandise and outstanding service.  And we're
genuinely happy about it.
                          --
I was exceptionally pleased to note your name on this
morning's list of much-appreciated new charge customers.
                          --
It is indeed a pleasure for the house of Le Roi to serve you,
and you may feel sure that we shall do everything possible to
keep you happy.
```

The plain fact is that in a business relationship such highly charged personal reactions as those suggested in the foregoing examples do not exist— and any reader knows it. No writer and no firm are going to "do everything possible to keep you happy." Rarely will a credit man be "extremely happy" or "exceptionally pleased" to add a name to a charge list. Phrases like "do all we can" and simply "happy" or "pleased" are appropriate because they are believable.

Furthermore, the coy quality of the following endings is unrealistic in a business situation—and therefore unbelievable:

```
We do hope you'll come in soon.  We can hardly wait!
                          --
Don't forget to come in soon.  We'll be looking for you!
                          --
Simply note your color choice on the enclosed card, mail it to
us—and then sit back with an air of expectancy.
```

The usual cause of effusiveness is a writer's choosing too strong and too many adjectives and adverbs in an attempt to please the reader by making him feel important. You'll do well to watch especially overused words ilke *very, indeed, genuinely, extremely, really,* and *truly*—all of which begin to gush in a very short time.

Exaggeration is stronger, and therefore more destructive of sincerity, than effusiveness. The correspondent who wrote, "Work is a pleasure when you use these precision-made tools," appears to be overstating his case to his carpenter-reader. And the writer of the following, if he could overhear, should be prepared for an unrestrained, emphatic *"Bosh!"* when his dealer-customer opens the letter and reads:

> New customers, happy and eager to buy, will surely applaud
> your recent selection of 4 dozen Tropical Holiday playsuits for
> women.

> Especially made for the humidity of Macon, these garments will
> lead girls and women for miles around to tell their friends
> that "Thompson's has them!"

Superlatives and other forms of strong wording are among the most frequent reasons why so many letters sound exaggerated, unbelievable, and therefore insincere. The trite "more than glad" is nearly always an insincere attempt to exaggerate a simple "glad." And "more than happy," if translated literally, could mean only slaphappy. The classic illustration is the misguided "What could be finer than . . . ?" Any reader can supply at least one quick answer of something which in his opinion is finer than the product or service mentioned. What's more, he usually does.

Exaggerated wording is nearly always challenging. Few things are actually *amazing, sensational, revolutionary, ideal, best, finest,* or *perfect.* Simple, accurate, specific statements of quality and value not only avoid the impression of insincerity; they are often more forceful than the general superlatives made nearly meaningless by 70 years of American advertising. If you describe products or services in terms like the following, you are inviting negative responses toward yourself and your firm:

> You'll find that Loomoleum is truly the ideal low-priced floor
> covering.
>
> --
>
> Are you looking for something that will sell like wildfire and
> give your customers the greatest possible satisfaction?
>
> --
>
> Want Amazing Protection
> That Can <u>Never</u> Be Canceled?
>
> Here is a really magnificent opportunity. Imagine a health
> and accident policy that can never be canceled.
>
> --
>
> This new mower is revolutionary in build, style, performance,
> and customer appeal. Amazing, of course! Here is your golden
> opportunity!

Whether the reader of such statements feels irritation or disgust is relatively immaterial. What counts is that he does not believe them. His confidence in the writer and the house, and therefore his goodwill, take a sharp downturn.

Undue familiarity also causes a writer to lose favor with his reader in many instances. Sometimes it crops out merely because the writer is uncouth. The reader may feel sympathy for the poor fellow who does not know how to act with people, but he will not have the disposition to return for more uncouthness.

Undue familiarity results from (1) calling the reader by name too frequently or writing in too informal language to a stranger and (2) making references to subjects which are entirely too personal for business discussions. For an obvious purpose the writer pretends a closeness of friendship or an overweening interest which does not exist. It is characteristic of the shyster. Like other forms of pretense, it is resented. In the following letter giving information on home insulation to a college professor, the jocularity doesn't just fall flat; it boomerangs!

> Just set the thermostat and relax. That's all you have to do, Professor Eckberg. Pick up your book and settle down in a cozy chair. The Mrs. won't be continually warning you to get your old sweater, or nagging you to shovel more coal on the fire, or to put another blanket on the cherubs.
>
> Yes, Professor Eckberg, Isotemp will guard over your household. Take a gander at the statistical table in the folder, <u>Modern Insulation for Older Homes</u>. This table shows that out of every 8 million cases of respiratory diseases, 6,536,042 occurred in uninsulated homes—over 75 percent from the very type of home you're now living in!
>
> Didn't you say you spent over $300 for coal last year, Professor Eckberg? That's a lot of money out of a professor's salary; and as you said, "Even then the place wasn't always warm."
>
> If you fill in and return the enclosed card, we will send Mr. Don Diller, our Milwaukee representative, to answer any of your questions. Incidentally, Professor Eckberg, Mr. Diller is a graduate of the University of Wisconsin with a degree in heating engineering. He may be the guy who slept through half your classes six years ago, but somewhere he learned how to make your home more comfortable and reduce those high coal bills. Then the Mrs. can buy that fur coat she's been nagging you about for when she goes outside, where it <u>is</u> cold!

Such diction as *cherubs, gander,* and *nagging* might be used in breezy conversation with an old friend and perhaps in a letter to the old friend but certainly not in a letter to someone the writer does not know. Using the reader's name four times in such short space gives the impression of fawning. And the assumptions and references to family relations and activities are typical of familiarity that breeds contempt. These spring from insincerity, but they are discourteous in the truest sense and thus destructive of goodwill.

SERVICE ATTITUDE

In addition to a desirable tone as a means of maintaining goodwill, good letter writers show that their concern extends beyond making a profit or other purely selfish interests. A business organization obviously must make profits if it is to exist; both reader and writer accept that premise. To deny it is trying to fly under false colors. The answer is neither to deny nor to affirm; just don't talk about it! Instead, let your letters remind readers of your thoughtfulness and genuine desire to be of service, through

1. Resale material on the goods and/or the house
2. Sales promotional material on other goods (in some letters)
3. Special-occasion letters

Resale material

Often a writer needs to assure a reader of the wisdom of his choice of goods or of the house he has chosen to do business with and thus stress satisfaction. In *keeping the goods sold,* resale material fosters repeat orders and forestalls complaints. It is an effective device in meeting competition.

As the phrase is most frequently applied by correspondents to goods and services, "resale" means favorable talk about something the reader has already bought, although he may not yet have received it. Most buyers would feel better about the product upon reading the following resale idea woven into an acknowledgment letter:

```
The Henshaw electric boudoir clocks (eight at $12) you ordered
on March 1 are our fastest-selling models in this price range.
Because they are accurate as well as beautiful, they make
excellent gifts.
```

The woman receiving the following would most likely feel much more secure in her choice of a suit—and thus happier with the suit as well as the company that sold it to her:

```
Your new suit is one of the Fashion-Tone line by Andreena.
With its simple, slenderizing skirt and tuxedo jacket (both
Coleman 100 percent wool), it will give you equal pleasure and
comfort at church, at a football game, or at an informal
luncheon.
```

Such material is *most effective when it is relatively short and when it is specific.* Tell a reader buying a white shirt, for instance, that

```
It will launder rapidly and easily because the collars and
cuffs are permanently starched.
```

or

```
It will retain its comfortable shape because it's preshrunk
and guaranteed to shrink no more than 1 percent.
```

or

```
The buttons will stay on because they are double-lockstitched.
```

or

```
Made from long-staple California cotton, your Pallcraft shirt
will give you the wear you expect from a shirt of this
quality.
```

But don't try to tell your reader *all* these points in a resale passage. And for your own greatest effectiveness as a writer, don't try just to get by with a lame "Pallcraft shirts are a good buy."

Used most frequently in acknowledgments, resale material on the goods may also appear in certain credit, collection, and adjustment letters.

Resale material on the house consists of pointing out reader-oriented policies, procedures, guarantees, and special services sometimes called "the little extras" the firm renders its customers. Especially in the beginning of a business relationship, you want to tell your reader about services you render—sales assistance, advertising aids, and the like to dealers. Retail stores often talk of lounges, lunchrooms, and personal shoppers, to mention only a few.

The following excerpt from a letter to a dealer is typical:

```
Along with your shipment of Lane candies are some display
cards and window stickers which you'll find valuable aids in
bringing these delicious candies to the attention of your
customers.  Our Advertising Department will regularly furnish
you with seasonal displays and will be glad to help you on any
special display problem in connection with the sale of Lane's.
```

And this—from a retail store to a new charge customer—is also a good sample of resale on the house:

```
You are welcome to use Rosen's air-conditioned lounging and
rest rooms on the mezzanine, the fountain luncheonette on the
first floor, or the spacious parking lot right behind the
store.  It is absolutely free to customers shopping at
Rosen's, even if your purchase amounts to only a spool of
thread.
```

Also from a retail department store to a new customer:

```
When you cannot come to the store, call or write Lola Lane,
our personal shopper, who will gladly do your shopping for
you.  Most of the time she can have your merchandise on the
delivery truck or in the mail the same day she receives your
order.
```

Resale material on the house need not—indeed, should not—be confined solely to letters to new customers. Any time a new service is added, an old one improved, or a line expanded is an appropriate occasion to tell customers about the firm's continued attempt to give satisfaction.

Resale passages are the writer's attempts to confirm or increase the faith of the reader in goods, services, or the firm he is already interested in. Sales promotion material on new and different goods or services seeks to promote interest in something else the firm can supply.

Sales promotion material

For a number of reasons, sales material about related products is desirable in some acknowledgment, credit, collection, and even adjustment letters. The most obvious business reason is that regardless of what you try to market, you must constantly seek to sell more of it to more customers all the time. In letters, however, *the most significant reason is the concrete demonstration that the firm desires to be of further service.* A third function of sales promotion material is that it can end a letter naturally and easily, with emphasis on further service. The following example illustrates the point:

> Your carpenter's tools, as itemized on the enclosed invoice, were shipped this morning by parcel post; they should reach you by October 15. Thank you for your check, which covers all charges.

Resale
> The Crossman level with aluminum frame is stronger and weighs less than wooden ones, and it will remain bright and true. The true-tempered steel used in the Flex-Line tape is permanently oiled, so you can be sure it will easily and rapidly unwind and rewind every time you use it.

Sales
> When you receive the fall and winter catalog we're sending separately, turn to page 126 and read the description of the Bradford 6½-inch electric handsaw. This is the lowest price at which it has ever been offered. To enjoy the savings in time and energy this efficient piece of equipment offers, use the handy order blank at the back of the catalog.

You'll need to observe a few precautions in the use of sales material. Above all, it should reflect *the desire to be of service* rather than the desire to sell more goods. It is low-pressure sales effort, comparable to the way a salesman, after selling a woman a pair of shoes, will casually pick up a matching or complementary purse and say, "Perhaps you'd like to examine this purse, which goes with your shoes so well." Only after the customer displays an interest in the suggested item does the salesman begin a real sales talk. If he makes another sale, that's good. But if he doesn't, it's still good: most customers are pleased because of the demonstrated interest in their welfare or happiness.

If, however, the insatiable sales appetite of "I want to sell you more" shows through selfish, greedy terminology, you neither promote sales nor please the customer. When emphasis is on *what we want* rather than *what you get,* the effect is unfavorable, maybe even repellent, as in the following:

> More than 8,000 of these Multimowers have been sold through our factory!

> And now that a large demand has been built up for our product, we want to sell it through dealers.

When emphasis is on *order* instead of *service,* Greedy Gus overtones are almost inevitable:

> We also sell attractive summer purses, silk and nylon hosiery, and costume jewelry to complete your excellent line of goods. We are sending you our catalog. And we hope to fill many more orders for you.

In terms of customer goodwill, this correspondent would have made a better impression had he rephrased the foregoing passage somewhat like this:

The summer purses and costume jewelry shown on pages 29 to 32
of the accompanying catalog have also sold well for many of
our other customers. We'll be glad to handle your order for
these items on the same terms as this one. Use the handy
order blank and reply envelope, in the back of the catalog.

Appropriateness is also a factor. When a woman buys a suit, a natural item to call to her attention is a blouse; a man buying a suit may be interested in matching or blending shirts, ties, hats, or shoes. But to tell a purchaser of heavy-duty truck tires about the good buy you now have in refrigerators or the buyer of a washing machine about your special on tires would be questionable most of the time because such suggestions appear to be dictated by the greedy desire to further sales rather than by an eagerness to render service. Almost always, sales material should be on items related to those under consideration.

Before using sales material, consider also the kind of letter you are writing and what it is supposed to do. A letter requiring further action on the reader's part needs final emphasis on that action, not on sales material. In acknowledgment letters, for example, you can use sales material endings to good purpose when you are sending the goods as requested, but not when additional action by the customer is necessary. Also, although you might use sales material in an early collection letter to a good customer, it is decidedly inappropriate as soon as your letter reflects concern over the account. And in adjustments you may safely use sales material to end a letter making full reparation, because you can be fairly sure the customer is going to be pleased with the results, but its use in a compromise or a refusal is usually questionable.

Both resale and sales material help to sell more merchandise, but they are even more effective as goodwill builders because they imply positively and emphatically the general statement "We are eager to serve you well."

Special goodwill letters

Also, to demonstrate continuing interest in the customer and the desire to serve, special goodwill letters subtly use resale material on the goods and the house, and sales material. They have often been called the "letters you don't have to write—but should." Since the customer does not expect them, since they usually bring something pleasant, and since your reader knows you do not have to write them, they are doubly welcome and thus greater builders of goodwill than some other types. Because they are of great variety in function and occasion, and because you can write them with greater understanding and skill after studying some other kinds of letters, they are treated in greater detail in Chapter 6.

Suffice it to say here—before we take up some other kinds of letters— that your study of special goodwill letters will reinforce the central theme of the preceding four chapters: consideration for the other fellow.

Letter cases for part one

1. Set up *any one* of the four following letters in acceptable format as directed by your instructor:

(*a*) *Letterhead:* Henry Spelling, 1342 Avenue A, Worcester, Massachusetts 01605. *Inside address:* L. M. Grant, 7 Berry Hill Road, Decatur, Maryland 20781. *Signature block:* Sincerely yours, Nelson J. Adams, Adjustment Manager. Use the current date. *Body:* The enclosed check is proof of our "Money back if not entirely satisfied" guarantee on all goods—and especially on the economy Pack Tent (6 F 801) you ordered on April 20. Thank you for writing us. Two weeks ago we sent out a tracer and found that your tent went to Decatur, Illinois, instead of Decatur, Maryland, probably because of the wrong ZIP code. It was then redirected to Maryland. As you know, freight delivered express charges collect is returned to the sender if no one is present to pay the charges. Consequently, your tent found its way back to Worcester. Two weeks ago we also sent you a postcard notification in response to your letter. It has not been returned to us; perhaps it too was misdirected. Will you please reconfirm your address for both your and our convenience? Mr. Grant, camping weather has just begun, and the tent you ordered (6½ x 8½-ft. base, yet folds to 10 x 36 in.) is excellent for camping. The tent is strongly built for many years of rough use and is water-repellent. It is made of 2-ounce nylon and has a vinyl-coated floor. Besides the 20 x 21-inch window, there is a nylon zip screen door. The price is only $54.50, much less than the price in a sporting-goods store. So that your boys can be enjoying this tent soon, just initial and return this letter along with the enclosed check, and we will rush the tent to you. You could insure safe arrival of your tent by sending us the $3.05 shipping charges. We have already paid previous shipping charges, and we are glad to absorb them. Just use the enclosed envelope. I am sure the Pack Tent will be a treasure for you and your boys.

(*b*) *Letterhead:* Shawnee Pre-Fabricates, Paducah, Kentucky 40227. *Inside address:* Lester P. Mullins, Lowell Brick Company, Louisville, Kentucky 40522. *Signature block:* Sincerely yours, Mason Lowell, Jr., President. *Subject:* Requested confidential information about Steven Rose. *Body:* Rose has worked for me for a year and a half. He came here as an accountant and assistant business manager in 19—. Since then, he has advanced until he is now plant manager. Steven is a hard worker and very eager to succeed in everything he attempts. Sometimes he drives himself into a tense condition, but he always seems to thrive on the challenge his job offers him, and I am sure that in a larger plant like Lowell he will be confronted with enough challenge to satisfy him. Also, Steven and his wife want to live in a larger city where they can enjoy all the cultural opportunities a city has to offer. Although at Pre-Fabricates Steven has no opportunity to sell, saleswork probably wouldn't be hard for him because he does enjoy people, is impressive looking, and is persistent. All of our employees like Steven—even our truck drivers, for whom he has to plan very strict budgets. In many ways I'll hate to lose Steven, but I know he wants larger horizons.

(*c*) *Letterhead:* Bonham Department Store, 2531 Main Street, Savannah, Georgia 31406. *Inside address:* Mrs. J. M. Ball, 1106 South Alpine Drive, Dalton, Georgia 30620. *Signature block:* Sincerely yours, James P. Landers, Adjustment Manager. *Body:* You are right, Mrs. Ball, in thinking that any Bonham sweater should last for more than a month—even one marked down as a second. We are continually testing our fabrics to determine the strongest weave possible. The seam in the left sleeve of the sweater should have been joined more carefully, and if it is not mended, it is likely to be torn even more. A tear like the one in the elbow of the sweater came from a tear on a sharp object. We have yarn that matches your boy's sweater, and one of our expert alterations women in the service department is mending the elbow and rejoining the seam at no cost to you. The sweater will be returned in two or three days, and you will have to look very closely to distinguish it from a new one. Mrs. Ball, with summer rapidly approaching, I am sure you and your family will be enjoying many outdoor activities. Next time you are in town, come in and let us show you our attractive variety of the latest summer fashions.

(*d*) *Letterhead:* Bowman Brothers, Main and Lamar, Houston, Texas 77052. *Inside address:* L & M Hardware Company, Cedar Lane, Bay City, Texas 77414. *Signature Block:* Cordially yours, James Leverton, Credit Manager. Use a spring date. *Body:* The garden equipment you ordered will be shipped today, freight charges collect, and should be in your store in two days. With the planting and gardening season rapidly drawing near, I am sure your sprayers and spreader carts will be in great demand. The $152 itemized on the enclosed invoice has been debited to your newly opened account. You have earned this credit because of your willingness to pay and the rapidly increasing volume of business you are developing. Probably you will want to take advantage of our regular terms of 3/10, n/60. The 3 percent discount you will receive by paying within 10 days after the date of your invoice ($4.56 on this one order—enough to pay your cost on one sprayer) will soon add up to a nice sum which you may use to purchase other merchandise. Otherwise, payment of the net amount within 60 days will keep you in the preferred-customer class. You may purchase as much as $500 worth of merchandise in any one 60-day period. New merchandise is no more than a few hours away from you because of the good transportation between Houston and Bay City. This gives you the advantage of keeping your inventory down to a minimum. Your Bowman representative, William Bailey, will be glad to offer any advice and assistance to you that he can. He will be bringing attractive display cards and other merchandising aids as he calls on you. Should you need any Bowman gardening equipment between his visits, a letter or a phone call will have your stock on the way to you within 24 hours after we hear from you.

2. For your teacher, type the following letter in the form he prefers for his letters. *Inside address:* Professor Harry B. Smitherman, Division of Business, University of Arizona, Tucson, Arizona 21857. *Salutation:* Dear Professor Smitherman. *Body:* Yes, I'll be glad to work on your problems committee. When you have your committee and your plan set, just let me know what you want me to do. Though I am on another committee of the Untied Communication Association and am revising a book, I'll find time to do my fair share of work on your committee because I am interested.

3. For your teacher, type the following letter in the form he prefers for his letters. *Inside address:* Professor John Bennett, College of Business, Eastern Michigan University, Ypsilanti, Michigan 48506. *Salutation:* Dear John. *Body:* Just back from Texas for a hectic registration of 40,000 students—most of whom seem to want the courses in communications—I'm somewhat slow in answering your letter of August 15. Your plan for the American Communication Association program looks good, and I'm flattered by your wanting me on the international communication panel. Before I could do justice to that topic, I would have to do a lot of research, for which I do not have time while trying to finish a manuscript for a revised edition of my book by December 1. Moreover, I have already accepted jobs on two ACA committees. Though I expect to be in Atlanta and to enjoy the program, even my department head insists I must reduce the activities I undertake. Good luck, John, in your big and important job of arranging the program. I shall look forward to seeing you and hearing it.

4. For the head of the department in which your course in business communication is offered, type the following letter in the form suggested by your instructor. *Inside address:* Richard D. Irwin, Inc. 1818 Ridge Road, Homewood, Illinois 60430. *Salutation:* Gentlemen. *Body:* Please send three desk copies of Menning and Wilkinson, *Communicating through Letters and Reports* (with Teachers Guide)—for use by our three new teachers, Dr. M. L. Meir, Dr. James Daly, and Mr. Clark Peters. Also, please send two desk copies of Lesikar, *Report Writing for Business,* for me and Dr.

K. K. Kendall. You may send the books directly to the individuals—same address as mine—or send all to me for distribution.

5. Two weeks ago you employed Universal Moving Vans to move you from a rented house to your new home. The service was entirely satisfactory. Today you received the following letter. Rewrite it for the company, making every change a really good letter writer would have made.

This letter is to express our thanks to you. We sincerely appreciate the fact you called upon our company to serve you—and we want you to know it.

We also want to be certain that our service was exactly as you wished it—for we know our business can grow only through satisfied customers.

Will you take a moment to fill out the enclosed card and drop it in the mail? It may seem like a minor thing, but it's very important to us, and will be appreciated.

We are looking forward to the opportunity of serving you and your friends in the future.

6. Improve the following letter in any way you can, but particularly by removing the insincerity and exaggeration. Assume that it is addressed to Professor M. W. Felts, secretary of the United Communications Association (an association of teachers and practitioners of business writing interested in improving the quality of letters and reports).

Our XXXX Hotel has over the years built its fabulous international reputation on the best precepts of service—service from the time that a convention agreement is inked until the last delegate has departed after the most successful meeting in your group's history.

To implement the service for which our XXXX has become world famous, we now plan personal contact with our clientele and we are looking forward to having the opportunity to call on you in your office in the near future.

In the meantime, I would appreciate it if you would be kind enough to peruse the enclosed brochure outlining the new and vast facilities of this magnificent edifice, whereby, you may become acquainted with its outstanding features as it relates to your particular meeting.

Our XXXX is outstanding in every way—we have a wide selection of meeting rooms that can comfortably accommodate 10 to 1,000 at a meeting and banquet in excess of 750 in one room. All of our rooms are beautiful in decor and, of course, have the very latest in sound and lighting equipment; chalkboards, easels, podiums, etc., are all part of our meeting room setup.

Dining is an adventure at the XXXX that is unequaled anywhere across the nation. And, of course, our East Gate Room for your evening's pleasure, featuring outstanding musical entertainment.

I am fully cognizant that you are an extremely busy person. However, I would greatly appreciate it if you would be kind enough to take time out of your busy day to advise me of your future meeting plans, as I shall be awaiting with keen interest your favorable response.

Kindest regards.

7. Clear up the following letter to Mrs. James T. Trotter, 810 Adobe Road, Anderson, Indiana 46016, from Flyntwood Brothers, Evansville, Indiana 47713.

We are indeed sorry that we failed to send the casters for your bed with your furniture. We were happy to send it to you.

Thank you for your order and we shall be looking forward to serving you often.

Rewrite the letter for greater clarity and positiveness as well as effective use of resale on the modern maple bed, nightstand, and chair the store delivered to Mrs. Trotter. The casters have been sent express charges prepaid, after having been omitted from the first shipment.

8. Correct the following letter for spelling, punctuation, and economy of phrasing. Set up in acceptable form as directed by your instructor. It is to go to Wilson P. Lutz, 5 Crystal Lake, Barrington, Illinois 60010, and is signed by the sales manager of Instantfold, Inc., 1108 Nolan Avenue, Indianapolis, Indiana 46219.

Dear Mr. Lutz:

The woodmaster Instantfold door you wrote about comes in heights of nine feet and eight feet with tracts 1½″ by 1½″. These doors come in a variety of colors as illustrated in the enclosed pamphlet. All doors are coated with convursion clear finish—the finest available today. These Instantfold doors are mar resistent, as shown in tests conducted by *Good Housekeeping* magazine. The eight foot doors cost $165 while the nine foot doors cost $205. Since your ceiling is nine feet high, you would need an eight-foot door. An attached pertition to the eciling would have to be instaled. All instantfold doors are not completely soundproof, but they do reduce the noise by one fifth. Out of the 1,200 doors we have installed in the last four years, not one of these doors has warpped. If you would like to know more about these doors and see some samples; simply fill out the enclosed reply card and place it in the nearest mail box.

9. *From:* United Encyclopedia, Merchandise Mart, Chicago 60621. *To:* Mrs. Sally Moore, 646 Cornwell Street, Boca Raton, Florida 33432. Eliminate the cliches, and incorporate resale passages to enhance the goodwill effect.

Dear Mrs. Moore:

In accordance with our policy, we are sending United Encyclopedia, to you at the educational discount rate, to the total of $259.50. The bookcase should be along with the books sometime next week.

You were smart to order this 24-volume set while the offer was on. Do not hesitate to call on us if we can be of service to you again. Thanking you, we remain,

10. Revise the following form letter for improved order of points, you-viewpoint, positiveness, and economy of statement. It is from Minor Toy Company, Patterson, New Jersey 00863. Use a faked address block.

We are sorry to advise you that we have not made the large outdoor play blocks for a long period of time. We find that the cost of constructing these is so prohibitive that very little volume can be realized on them. It is quite possibly true that you see these in practically all nursery schools but in each instance it is generally true that one set is made up especially by hand for the nursery school. Thank you very much for your letter of March 28 and for your interest in Minor toys. You may order directly from us. A catalog and price list are enclosed.

11. Correct the following letter for acceptable use of language. Improve the negative tone and supply specific details that will also perform resale functions on dining and bedroom accessories sent from the Malcomb Furniture Company of High Point, North Carolina 27260, to Melvin P. Downing of the City Furniture Company, 113 Kress Avenue, Harlingen, Texas 75147. Sign it as the credit sales manager.

Dear Mr. Downing:
The items you ordered the 25th have been sent to you in this morning's mail. You should receive these items in time for your Saturday morning customers.
Mr. Downing, we have granted you credit, with a tentative limit of $100, at our usual terms of 2/10 n/30. The $100 limitation is placed on all new customers. After a period of six months this limitation is lifted if the customer has proven to be a good credit risk. By doing business in this manner, the customers earn their good credit ratings. One customer told us that his good credit rating was better than money in the bank. A good credit rating is also helpful when you want credit elsewhere.
Mr. Downing, we sincerely hope you will be able to obtain a good credit rating . . . and that you will like our products.

12. Analyze the good and bad elements of the following letter, considering all the points of content, tone, and method of presentation. Then rewrite it for the L. P. Hopkins Publishing Company, 2277 Forest Street, St. Louis 51462. This letter is a refusal for free material requested by Judith Ford, Lexington School, Lindsey, Pennsylvania 15767.

We regret to have to tell you, but we cannot send you *Reading for Understanding* by Preston Lake or *Be a Better Reader* by Anthony Falk and Paul Barger. With the high cost of printing and publishing you can well understand our position. We have enclosed a list of some films that can be ordered to help you teach Reading to juniors in high school. The price list accompanies the film list. Won't you let us hear from you?

13. The program chairman for the next national convention of your professional association has asked you to take an important part on the program, not as a speaker but as a chairman of a session.
Your employer encourages employees to attend and participate in the

meetings of their professional groups by paying all or part of the expenses of attending. But employees never know just how much the employer will pay until they get the answer in view of the specific situation. You have asked your employer how much expense money you may have this time but have been told that the answer can come only when your request and numerous others are considered together and compared with available funds.

Furthermore, the convention dates are December 28–30, and you have been unable to get your wife to say whether your attending the convention will conflict with her Christmas holiday plans.

You'd be glad to take the assignment if favorable answers could be had from your two bosses, both of whom are delaying. You realize that the program chairman must proceed with his plans; so you must write him a negative reply, at least for now. You still hope to attend the convention, and you will let the chairman know your decision as soon as it can be firm. If he wants to wait, that will be all right; but you advise him to get somebody else.

14. In the Department of the Interior, Washington 20008, you have been given the following letter from David Linear, 2109 Avenue Thirty-One, East, Los Angeles, California 90049, to answer:

At Cub Scout meeting the other day, my friend, Roger Barnes said you had a little book on *Living on the Moon.*
Please send a copy to me. I've enclosed 10 cents.

You can send him a booklet, *Landing on the Moon,* also done by the Department of the Interior. In sending him this booklet, minimize the negative effect of his not getting what he has asked for, emphasize efficiency in complying with his request, and favorably present your substitute. Because of so many requests the supply of the booklet *Living on the Moon* is exhausted.

15. How can you rewrite for improved you-viewpoint presentation in the beginning and in the action ending? *From:* Sinclair Manufacturing Company, 3857 Emerson Avenue, Denver, Colorado 80209. *To:* M. T. Elder, Sales Manager of Elder Company, one of your biggest agents, 2409 Paseo Road, Colorado Springs, Colorado 80902.

Dear Mr. Elder:
Our company is next month having the opening of our new warehouse in Denver the 16th and 17th. It is similar to our warehouse in Pueblo and the one which is being completed in San Francisco. It is an attractive building designed to make operations more rapid and efficient.
We would like to have you attend both days of our opening from 3:00 to 9:00 P.M. The plan is to give the customer a tour of the building, show stock, and demonstrate the handling facilities. There will also be exhibits of all types

of ferrous and nonferrous metals, as well as valves, fittings, fasteners, and gears. After speaking with someone with your experience and ability, we feel sure our customers will select the Elder Company as their best source of supply. The Sinclair company will be happy to pay your expenses if you will be kind enough to reserve the 16th and 17th of next month to see the latest developments in steel warehouse construction.

16. Rewrite the following letter to improve it in any way you can:

Dear Sir:
The Student Government committee of the University is sponsoring a book review which we think will prove to be both interesting and beneficial to all of the students in your courses. With this thought in mind we have sought to ask you to convey to your students the fact that such a review is being held and the pertinent details such as when and where the review is to take place.

Dr. A. T. Hansen of the English department will review L. M. Skidmoore's latest work, *Crisis, Where Next?* on the night of the 16th. The time is 8 P.M. and the place, University Lounge on the second floor of the Union.

We would appreciate your frequent announcement of the review to your various classes and would like to extend a personal invitation to you to attend the review. Thanking you for your time and interest, I am,
                                        Sincerely Yours,

17. Auto insurance rates depend on various facts, including type and age of car and driver, extent and kind of use made of the car, location, and so forth.

Write a form letter to go with an addressed and stamped questionnaire card to collect necessary information from a big insurance company's policyholders whose policies are about ready for renewal. The general question is whether the rates on the old policy will be appropriate on the renewal policy the company will soon be preparing. The state requires insurance companies to classify policyholders carefully and charge specified rates according to conditions. Out-of-date or incorrect information could cause the rates on one's insurance to be either too high or too low.

Filling out the reply card takes only 30 seconds. Your letter does not ask the questions but only induces the policyholder to fill out and return the card.

18. Rewrite the following letter for accuracy and better wording. *From:* Orrin Gray, Sales Manager. *To:* Fred W. Colson (a carpenter), Box 760, Acompo, California 95220. *Letterhead:* Jackson and Allen Company, Bowles Avenue, Sacramento, California 95825. The dateline is current.

Your concave and convex cutters are on the way. You will certainly receive them before the end of the month. They are being shipped by railway express —shipping charges, $2.66 plus 3 percent tax on the total purchase price of $96. So you may get the specific motor you want, please check your preference on the enclosed form and send it to us today. You are sure to be pleased with any choice you make. We guarantee all of our motors and their sheilded ball bearings are lubricoated for 5,000 hours.

Your should receive your Draftsman Sharper Table in about 10 days. Their has been a strike at the aluminum plant, and we haven't been able to get enough materials to keep our stock up. They have assured us, however, that we should start receiving our ordered aluminum in another week at the latest.

You will be glad you waited for this particular table. It is one of our best selling tables—build of sturdy aluminum and steel. The carpenters wants and need's were the factors in the design of the table.

19. Evaluate (this means giving detailed reasons) Letter A over Letter B or vice versa). Consider not only general style but also the more desirable plan.

Letter A:

Would you be interested if we could give you a considerable increase in our orders for vent caps?

After many of our salesmen reported that reluctant buyers of our end product criticize the design of the vent cap, our sales manager got our design man and me together this week to see what could be done. We agreed that the cap you supply us performs well functionally but that a modern design somewhat as suggested in the two enclosed sketches would increase our sales and probably those of your other customers (and therefore yours).

You could adapt these designs a bit for minimum retooling costs, and we believe the increased sales to us alone would soon amortize your costs, as the volume of business we have given you in the past has amortized your old molds. We sincerely believe a new design will increase sales and profits for us and for you.

We expect to retain you as a supplier for a long time, at increased volume, if we can get a vent cap that will help instead of hurting our end-product sales.

Will you strike a few examples from a pilot mold and let us see one along with your reactions to the proposal before our present stock runs out about October 1?

Letter B:

This week I was called into a meeting with our company sales manager and our design man. They discussed the design of the vent caps you regularly supply us. While it was agreed that your vent cap performs well functionally, they feel that a new, modern-design cap will enhance our end product and increase sales.

I am enclosing two sketches of vent cap designs made by our design man. Perhaps you can strike a few samples from a pilot mold, or by adapting one of the present molds. You may alter these designs to effect mold-remodeling cost savings.

We are allowing you latitude in adapting these designs so that a minimum of retooling would be necessary. As these molds, we believe, have been amortized through the volume of business we have given you in the past, we are hoping that you will see fit to absorb a retooling cost. The fact that you are given latitude in product design to most economically suit your tools, and that an increase in orders to you may be expected because of the better design, we think we are making only a fair request. It is our hope and intention to retain you as a supplier for a long time.

20. The following paragraph was written as the last in an acknowledgment of an order. Rewrite it or explain how you would revise it—as your instructor directs.

To make your future ordering easier, I'm sending along a credit application form for you to fill out. Thank you very much for your order, and you may be sure that future orders will receive our prompt attention.

21. Rewrite the following letter to improve it in all ways you can:

Dear Flexiglass Customer:

I want to express my personal regrets to you for the delay which has been incident to repairing and returning your rod to you.

As a matter of explanation to you—Swaim Industries, which manufactured Flexiglass rods in former years, went bankrupt eary this year, and thereafter, the manufacturing and sales of Flexiglass were handled by others in a rather hap-hazard manner until the middle of September. At that time, an entirely new company, Sports Universal, Inc., with no connection whatsoever with the past was organized to take over the fishing rod assets previously owned and operated by Swaim Industries and its successor. Also, this new sales company, Flexiglass Rods, Inc. was organized to distribute Flexiglass Rods through the same outlets as in the past.

We, in this new organization, have been struggling over the backlog of repair rods which we inherited and are just now getting caught up.

I do hope that you will understand our efforts to overcome the "sins" of others and we regret you were deprived the use of your rod, through no fault of ours.

Should you have any problems in the future, it will be our pleasure to help you in any way we can.

22. A few weeks ago Dr. and Mrs. Larry E. Grant of 1225 Buchannan Street, Hollywood, Florida 33024, were in your interior-decorating shop (Peacocks, 1606 Palmetto Road, Miami, Florida 33156) trying to replace some aging lampshades. They brought along a sample. You have now received samples from the lamp manufacturers and have decided that the Grants' was the Empire, and so you have ordered the two shades in that material sent directly to the Grants from the manufacturer.

The same day you sent in the order for the Maler-Weller Ez-E chair they wanted. It should arrive in about four weeks. Write the Grants for Peacocks.

23. *From:* Sales Manager, Playgate Toys, Harris Square, Poughkeepsie, New York 14303. *To:* Mrs. Marian Boles, Manager, Boles's Gift Shop,

Greenville, South Carolina 29607. Rewrite for tact and positiveness and to stimulate sales of superior Playgate toys and games for children 1–12.

Dear Mrs. Boles:

In accordance with your conversation with our salesman, Paul H. Curtis, we are mailing your Playgate toy catalog under separate cover. We did not realize hat you had a large enough store or did a big enough volume to warrant your cking our special line. Since Lionel acquired Playgate and Playschool, there been a lot of reorganizing and confusion. Please excuse our mistake. It won't n again.

nsider the following letter from the advertising manager of an company to an insurance agency that sells policies of various What about the plan? What about the tone? Rewrite to im- ay you can.

our memo of the 4th, asking whether we have any available advertising on workmen's compensation. No, we do not, y good reason. Newspaper advertising is a mass market pensation insurance is not a mass market product. thousand reading your ad in the newspaper would be ompensation insurance but you would be paying for ndred ninety-nine people who can't use what you g a special type of insurance, you would have to n the prospects for that type of insurance, such ldn't afford to pay the rates on such a trade our selling area. For instance, if your Cham- on that was sent just to your local business- e just to reach those people, then it might

ting errors and improving phras- sentation, success consciousness, ssed to Beauty Supply House, 1, and is signed by the sales Company, 1109 Lindsay the physical arrangement ents in tone and style.

en Hot-aire table-to clusive deale Hot-ai

watts. The dryer with 1000 watts sells for $290 a dozen. The Beauty-Nook dryers carry a markup of 50 percent. This means greater profits for you, the dealer. The Beauty-Nook dryers carry a greater markup for the dealer than other nationally advertised dryers.

So there will be no further delay in your order, simply take the stamped addressed card, place an X by the dryers you want and drop the card in the nearest mail box. Your dryers will be shipped COD on Fanton Truck Line Inc.

We hope you will find our service satisfactory.

26. Rewrite and type in acceptable format. Improve in any way You may assume that the kit referred to does a thorough job of ing location, improvements (paving and curbing, for example)

To: R. H. Jennings, 11 Tower Estates, Philadelphia, Pennsy
From: The real estate firm of Florida Developers, 1400 Pa
sonville, Florida 32207.

Your request for information about Florida land can b
our FLD Land Kit #8 which is enclosed. You can buy
land in the Duval County, for $35 down, $35 a mon
parcels in adjacent Union County, $20 down, $20 mo
as Florida freeways grow, as population grows.

We don't claim that you will find oil or gold. Just
shows exactly how and where to buy Florida land
Water is no longer a problem. Water lines
nected to Jacksonville.

If we can be of any further service, pleas

27. Rewrite the following letter fo
It is signed by the policy supervisor
Company, Plymouth, New Hamp
P. Henderson, District Manager
land 20903. An "assured" is the
provisions of the policy.

We are enclosing a set o
signature of the named as
named assured, attach t
one copy for your file.
Office file.

Ohio 43906, rewrite the following wordy, unplanned, and ungrammatical letter to Stanley Anderson, 11 Parkway Drive, Canton, Ohio 44319.

It was very nice of you to spend a few minutes with me last Tuesday when we discussed the opportunities available if you considered associating yourself with our good concern. Among the many things we talked about it was mutually agreed it would be best for all concerned for you to visit our main office and one of our factories to get a better picture of our operation and organization. I also mentioned that I wanted to plan a trip for four or five of your men to visit us in Youngstown making the trip over on Friday and returning to Canton on Sunday. If I recall correctly you were agreeable to make such a trip.

This contemplated trip is now definitely planned and I would like very much for you to go along. I plan to meet you and four other men at Belden Hotel in Canton at 8:00 A.M. Friday morning for breakfast, immediately after breakfast you can be off for Youngstown. All of your expenses will be paid and I am sure you will not only enjoy the trip, but you will definitely see what a wonderful organization we have. One of the other men will be using his car, so even though you may have a car we are not planning for you to use it on this trip.

When you arrive in Youngstown you will first report to our main office to meet some of the key personnel, so your attire and the clothes you will need for two evenings of entertainment is entirely to your discretion.

I have enclosed a self-addressed postcard so you can advise me by return mail, definitely, whether or not I can plan on your making this trip and if you will meet with the rest of us for breakfast at 8 A.M. Friday.

29. Rewrite the following letter for the service adjustment manager, Houston, Distribution Division for Specific Motors Corporation. The letter goes to Robert L. Le Grone, Box 754, Rusk, Texas 75785.

Dear Mr. Le Grone:

We are in receipt of your letter reporting the failure of your car air conditioning unit. Since the car and the unit are three years old I suggest you see a local reputable dealer or air condition specialists and have him repair the unit. With as old a car as you have and with as many miles as you say (40,000) you have on the car, our company is not responsible for any replacements. The guarantee on the unit is for one year. Perhaps you should investigate the new models just out and see about trading in your old car.

30. Melvin Lancaster, 88 Windsor Drive, Abbeville, Louisiana 70510, wrote Louisiana Steel Products, New Orleans, Louisiana 70125, the following inquiry:

Would you please tell me the difference between Chrome Steel and Stainless Steel and please tell me the price of these steels?

B. J. Hudson, manager of sales, in answer, wrote the following letter:

We thank you for your letter of October 17, which has been referred to this office for reply. In answer to the first part of your question Chrome Steel, as such, does not reflect any specific type of steel to us, since it could be an Alloy or a

Stainless Steel. However, for your information whenever Chromium is specified at over 10 percent this steel would then be called Stainless.

There are many Stainless Steels produced and each one reflects a different price. Therefore, if you would supply us with more information as to the amount of material needed and also the end use of this material, we would be happy to endeavor to make recommendations for you.

We thank you for your interest in our corporation and if we may be of further aid, please do not hesitate to call on us.

Rewrite the letter for Hudson, omitting unnecessary words, improving tone, correcting where necessary, and setting up in acceptable letter format.

31. As a new employee in the Council for the Blind of your state, you have the job of improving the form letters used by the Council. Here are two of them:

a) Dear Dr.

It would be appreciated if you would furnish us with appointment date(s) and time for the client(s) of this agency as indicated by the enclosed purchase order(s). It would also be appreciated if you would set the appointment(s) at least three weeks in advance in order that we can be sure that the client(s) will be notified in plenty of time. Thank you for your cooperation.

b) Dear

We understand that you failed to keep your appointment for an _____ examination which was scheduled on _____, with Dr. _____. Failure to keep an appointment for such examinations is always embarrassing for us, and it is an aggravation to the doctor as well. Please indicate on the enclosed postal card the reason your appointment was not kept, and whether or not you would keep another one if made. We cannot impress too strongly upon you the need to meet any future appointments, and cannot promise to make another one for you if this second appointment is not kept.

32. Rewrite for directness, tone, personalization, and adaptation.

Dear Mr. Prospective Supplier:

I have met with our engineers since your visit last Thursday and discussed with them more fully our requirements in a stamping press. Your model C–311–B is well suited to our needs but we feel certain accessories may not be required by us.

Would you please let me know whether we could buy these presses without the guards, fly-wheel cage, and drop chute? If this is possible, what then would be the price reduction? We have our own economical ways to provide these accessories in the presses. To be frank, we have word that we can obtain a stripped press from another manufacturer who also has an excellent tool.

Our chief accountant also asks that I check with you as to what would be our monthly payments on a 24-month basis. He has the 12- and 18-month figures. You can see he is concerned about budgeting these machine payments. I am also awaiting word from you whether the machine installment period will

be interest-free. Once operating we expect these presses to "pay their own way."

We do hope that you appreciate our viewpoints on this prospective purchase. We do want the machines, but we have our problems.

33. Make all the improvements you can in the following form letter addressed to the faculty and staff of your school. It comes from a new motel near the campus.

Good Morning:

In an effort to introduce our new dinning facilities to the xxx personell, I have inclosed a complementary card which intitles you to a $1.00 (one dollar) discount on any dinner. This card is not valid after (a date two months later). I hope this discount will encourage you to take advantage of our new policy of sensible pricing coupled with superb cuisine prepared to your taste by our continental chef. I am sure you will find dinning at The Inn Carriage Room, truely an enjoyable and ldisure evening. I invite you to inspect our 101 room "Quality" motel as well as our banquet facilities, capable of accommodating any future functions you may have. Looking foreward to meeting you in the near future, I remain,

34. Rewrite for economy and naturalness of phrasing and for positiveness, accuracy, and clarity.

Dear Mr. Unsuccessful Quoter:

Reference your letter of the 20th, may we say that we are disappointed in many ways that you were not successful bidder as per our quotation request #B–5004 (May 10). Your quote was competitive, but not the lowest received.

We would like to thank you for submitting a quotation as per our request, and to assure you of full consideration whenever in the future we prepare quotation requests for items which you manufacture.

As a possible assistance to you we would like to say that while your unit price was favorable compared to two bidders your service warranty was rather high.

We buy a fair quantity of steam equipment from time to time, and we sincerely hope that a certain portion of this business will go your way. We cannot, however, overlook high service contract costs which are an important element in overall cost.

Thank you again for your interest in our regard.

35. A big company manufacturing products competing with one you have devised is planning to put on the market one that would compete directly with yours. To help the designer of its product, the company has written you a somewhat detailed inquiry to get your suggestions. Actually the company and its designer should know about your competing product, but you are forced to believe that they do not, or they would not have had the cheek to send you the inquiry. Refuse to answer the inquiry. Consider the advisability of the straight-faced, joshing, and belittling tone you might use.

36. Assume that you are the editor of a widely distributed free-subscription magazine put out by some branch of your state or school and that you suspect that many copies are going to people who do not really want them. Write a letter to clean up your mailing list.

Unless you provide some motivation and make the action easy, many of them will simply ignore you. You may include benefits to yourself, but emphasize benefits to your readers.

Make clear that you are not interested in cutting off anybody who really wants the magazine. Also, invite them to send you the names and addresses of people who might be interested in receiving it. Check to be sure that you have the correct names and addresses of those who do want to continue on the mailing list.

37. As your teacher, assume that the chairman of the nominating committee (referred to in the letter below) asked for your suggestions on revising his letter. The letter goes to all faculty members of the college. Rewrite the letter for him.

Dear Colleague:
As you are aware, Dean X is retiring at the end of June. He has served the University as Dean of the College since 1948.
You have elected a faculty committee to serve in an advisory capacity and consult with Vice-President Y regarding the nomination of Dean X's replacement. Your committee held its first meeting with Vice-President Y on (date). It is now undertaking the task of securing nominees for this position.
You are invited to submit your suggestions to any of the members of the advisory committee whose names and campus addresses are listed below. Such suggestions should be in writing. It would be a great help to the committee if, at the time you submit names, you would also furnish any information you may have about your nominees. Additional details may be requested at a later date.
Those responsible for bringing about the appointment of a new Dean are faced with a very critical question of timing. There are only a few months available. The committee, therefore, needs to have your nomination in hand by no later than the first of next month.
All concerned thank you for your cooperation in this matter.

38. Rewrite for clarity, economy, and naturalness of phrasing.

Dear Mr. Supplier:
Subject: Purchase Order R–4610
Under separate cover we are returning 130 defective lid assemblies #243–B as received against subject purchase order on the 10th. These assemblies are returned for replacement by you as soon as possible.
The defect noted in these lid assemblies by our Quality Control department is that the threaded hub is crookedly soldered onto the lid. When the lid assembly is screwed onto shaft in final assembly operation, a flush lid fit cannot be obtained.

The lid assembly shipment of the 10th from you represents the highest reject percentage yet found—130 out of 1000—or 13 percent. Because of past mix-ups in paper work we will withhold payment on your invoice for these 1000 pieces until satisfactory replacements are received by us for the 130 defective pieces.

Our engineers again suggest that you use the lid solder jig as per the model delivered to you in May. We feel this jig can eliminate, or greatly reduce, reject percent on your lid assemblies.

Please be assured that we stand ready to work with you further on solving this hub alignment problem. We urgently need acceptable parts in the full quantities as ordered as our production requirements are running high.

39. Rewrite for positiveness, you-attitude, and success consciousness.

Dear Supplier:
Subject: *a*) Purchase Order M–4965 (appropriate date)
       b) Our Follow-ups of (appropriate dates three weeks later and one week after that)

You have failed to respond to subject follow-up forms we sent you regarding delivery information on material on subject purchase order. We are sending you this letter inquiry on delivery dates as we are in urgent need of the material on order. Please telephone or write your delivery information as requested in this letter.

We are in such urgent need of this material that we will have to shut-down our thermostat sub-assembly line next month if we do not have the material from you by then. This would disrupt our entire production schedules and be extremely costly to us.

As we plan an overall production increase of 10–15 percent these next 12 months, we are hoping that you can now prove to be a dependable supplier when our needs are not as great as anticipated later.

We will await your call or wire on this urgent matter.

40. The following postcard message was used by a large mail-order seller of superior monogrammed shirts. Many of the college-men audience who received it objected to it. Try to reason out why. Then rewrite to improve it.

Your order has been completed and shipment is being made by parcel post today.

It will expedite delivery if you will have the money on hand when the shipment is offered for delivery. Under postal regulations C.O.D. packages are held at the Post Office for only 15 days, so if the shipment is not offered for delivery promptly may we suggest that you make inquiry for it at your local Post Office.

We appreciate this fine order and hope to have the pleasure of serving you again.

41. Assume that the track coach at your school asked you to check the following letter before he sends it out. Rewrite the letter for him.

Dear faculty Member:

We are in great need of more officials for our meets in Track and Field here on our campus, therefore, we are making a survey of the entire faculty concerning their interest. We feel that we have every right to expect professors to work a little instead of just enjoying the fine exhibitions put on by the hard work of others. At present we have over 70 members who do a fine job but we need to add to this number. No previous experience is necessary, because it will be easy for us to teach anybody how to officiate at any particular area of his interest.

Attached you will find a Membership Information Sheet, which I would like to have returned if you would be willing to help us out by joining our Officials Club. During the coming year, the 25th Annual Relays will be on March 30th and on April 13, we will run the University of Kansas, who has the Worlds greatest runner in Jim Ryun. Each year we endever to bring the best possible meet here, and at the present time we are bidding for several National Meets. In order to get these meets, we need many trained officials.

Once I have received the Information Sheet, those interested will receive time skedules of all meets and a sheet to return indicating the dates they can perform duty. Information on their job assignment along with instructions will be forwarded in the near future.

Join our Club and get a first hand view of some of the greatest track in the nation.

Thank you in advance.

42. In a letter report to the dean of a junior college, a consultant wrote the following as one section. You will notice several things wrong with it. *Without changing what it says and with only minor changes within sentences,* use all of the sentences in the best rewritten version you can make.

Effective Writing (replacing EH 121). This course should be a solid college-level course in composition, not literature and not based primarily on a study of literature—certainly not on difficult selections from literature. The few students who need to and want to learn to write literary criticism can best learn it in connection with later literature courses. No one will be much concerned if your graduates cannot write literary papers, but everybody will be concerned if they cannot write effectively the kinds of things they all will have to write.

The course, therefore, should be a prerequisite to all further English courses, required for a certificate, designed to be transferred anywhere as a college course in English composition. Yet it should be concerned with topics in the students' realm of interest and orientation.

For the teacher with enough imagination to get away from the kind of uninteresting writing assignments he did as a freshman, suitable current topics from campus, town, county, state, national, international, social, commercial, and industrial affairs are endless. Much of the bad writing usually done by college freshmen can be avoided if the teacher's assignments call for writing to a well defined readership for a definite purpose. Simple news stories, editorials, letters, short reports, and explanations of processes and procedures will be more interesting to the students and more effective base for teaching composition than a psychological analysis of King Lear or an explanation of what Coleridge means by imagination.

The emphasis should be on the effective communication of what the student has to say rather than on *what* he thinks. Topics of the day, as reflected in the current press and in the student's own real or easily assumed involvements are the best bases for teaching writing. Most of your students will not easily become sufficiently involved in literary or historical topics to do their best writing. That, of course, does not rule out requirements of logical thinking, organization and coherence, and evidence in support of points made. The procedure should be preliminary instruction on how to write a given assignment, followed by careful marking of his paper and talking over his writing problems.

43. The City National Bank holds a 90-day certificate of deposit in the name of Lota M. Spell and Lota Rea Wilson (who is her married daughter). It is at 4½ percent interest and matures one month from today. The bank decided today, however, that it will start (tomorrow) paying 5 percent on all new and renewed 90-day certificates of deposit. So, within the next three months the bank must write all holders of certificates to bring in their CD's on maturity for renewal at the new rate. As the correspondence specialist for the bank, revise the following letter (addressed Lota M. and Lora Rae Wilson, 2108 Hartford Road, Gainesville, Florida) submitted by the secretary to your vice president A. J. Maloney as a fill-in form for notifying all CD holders:

Effective at the close of business (today's date) the new rate paid by City National Bank on Certificates of Deposit will be 5% for ninety day certificates. This note will effect all existing Certificates of Deposit held by the City National Bank for you; consequently, upon the next maturing date of your Certificates, the rate will be adjusted to 5%. This action will necessitate your bringing into the Bank your Certificate upon maturity and it will be reissued at the new rate. All new 90 day Certificates of Deposit will be compounded quarterly and be automatically renewed as they have been in the past. We deeply appreciate your continued good relationship with our Bank.

Very truly yours,
J. A. Maloney
Senior Vice President

PART TWO

How to win the reader's approval and motivate him to action

Neutral and good-news messages

As YOU LEARNED back in Chapter 3, messages that give the reader what he wants should do so in the opening phrases. The emphasis should be on speed, specificness, and economy. Inquiries, favorable replies, credit approvals, and adjustment approvals are typical of A-plan, direct-style letters.

Routine claims also should be direct, since they are reports welcomed by any firm as means for improving service.

Similarly, in courtesy exchanges of information about job and credit applicants—where regardless of whether the information is favorable or unfavorable to the *applicant,* it *is* what the reader wants to know—the message should begin directly with a key point.

DIRECT INQUIRIES

Any firm that stays in business welcomes *inquiries about products, services, operations,* and *personnel.* When a businessman reads an inquiry concerning the product(s) or service(s) the firm sells, the possibility of making a sale (and a consequent profit) will motivate him to reply. He may answer an inquiry about routine operations out of simple business friendship. He will also answer requests for information about people because it is an established business courtesy to give such information for business purposes (the principle of reciprocity).

In no case would the reader's attitude toward such inquiries be negative; and, if it is not one of eagerness to comply, at least it is willingness. You therefore have no problem of motivating a response; your problem is that of letting your reader know exactly what you want, so that the willing reader can give you the necessary information with as little expenditure of time and energy as possible.

Resolve this problem by beginning directly and by being specific and concise. Requests for catalogs, price lists, descriptive folders, and other information about products and services should be written with the same directness, specificness, and brevity as the following:

What choice of colors does a buyer have in the shower curtains you advertised in the November Ladies' Home Journal?

At what store(s) are they available in Mobile?

This example, you will note, gets right down to brass tacks with a direct question and the key specific phrase "choice of color" rather than the vague, stereotyped request for "more information." And the pinpointing phrase "in Mobile" further helps the replier to send exactly the information needed.

The following letter to a resort hotel is another good example of desirable directness and specificness:

Please send me descriptive material about your accommodations, recreational facilities, and rates.

My wife, 16-year-old daughter, and I are planning a two- or three-weeks' stay in the South this fall and are considering the Edgewater Gulf.

Without the second paragraph, the writer would get the most necessary information in general terms. (He would probably get much more than needed because the hotel man, not knowing just what to tell, would tell everything and thus waste his own and his reader's time.) With the second paragraph, however, the hotel man can write a reply which contains necessary general information and only the special information that would be of interest to this family group.

A specific paragraph indicating special interests, would help even more:

My wife and I are primarily interested in the golf facilities; my wife and daughter are also interested in dinner dancing; our daughter insists that she be able to ride horseback every day.

When questions require no explanation and are clear-cut, enabling the responder to supply specific data in reasonably short form (frequently by just jotting down the answers on the inquiring letter), the desirable plan of the letter is often an explanation of the purpose of the letter, followed by tabulated, numbered questions, as in the following:

SUBJECT: REQUEST FOR FURTHER INFORMATION ABOUT
            RECONDITIONED LEKTRASWEEPS

Before deciding whether to drive into Birmingham to inspect the vacuum cleaners you advertised in last Sunday's News, I need answers to the following questions:

1. Do the reconditioned Lektrasweeps come equipped with standard 1-hp. motor?

2. What kind of attachments, and how many, do you include at $49.95?

3. Does your written two-year guarantee include replacement or repairs, without charge, of any and all defective parts that might result in the unsatisfactory service of the equipment?

4. If so, will your representative make replacement or repairs in my home?

5. Is there a trial period, say for two weeks, at the end of which I could return the cleaner, if it proved unsatisfactory, and get a full refund?

I shall be grateful for this information.

But (as in most cases) if questions require detailed answers for satisfactory information, if out-of-the-ordinary questions are involved, and especially if they require explanation before the reader can get a clear picture of exactly what the writer wants to know, they are better set out in expository paragraph form, as in the following letter about a dishwasher:

SUBJECT: INQUIRY ABOUT THE $49.50 DISHWHISK

How complex—and expensive—is installation of the Dishwhisk you advertised on page 69 of the September Better Homes and Gardens?

I'm interested in a dishwasher, and I certainly am attracted
by this price. But can your unit be attached without plumbing
changes once the present unit is removed? On my sink now is a
unit with hot and cold knobs and a single mixing faucet.

Aerated suds sound economical and efficient, but will low
water pressure reduce their cleansing effectiveness? Because
low water pressure is the rule rather than the exception in
this community, this is an important consideration.

Are new soap and water used for each piece to be washed? The
use of an excessive amount of soap and water could easily
cancel the initial saving in a short time.

I shall appreciate your answers to these questions, the name
and address of a local owner of a Dishwhisk, and the name of a
local dealer.

Note that the inquiry started with a direct question. Such a beginning
is the preferable form. The request should come before explanations of
why you ask or should be interwoven with these explanations because (1)
a question commands more attention than a statement, (2) the reader sees
the reason for the explanation, and (3) such an arrangement nearly always
saves words.

Similarly, personnel inquiries should begin with the key question to be
answered and follow with necessary explanations and specific questions:

SUBJECT: REQUEST FOR INFORMATION ABOUT JAMES R. SULLIVAN

While Mr. Sullivan worked under you as a part-time instructor
in marketing, did he show an aptitude for selling? Was he
naturally friendly and able to get along with faculty and
students alike?

We are considering him for the job of head salesman in the
Georgia, North Carolina, and South Carolina territory. Since
he listed you as a former supervisor, we would welcome your
comments in the light of the following explanation.

The job will take much time and energy and will also require
that he be away from his family a great deal. Do you think he
will do his best work under these conditions? And has he
demonstrated physical stamina and willingness, suggesting that
he can stand up under the strain of much traveling for long
periods?

As head salesman he will have to supervise the work of two
junior salesmen in this territory. We are interested,
therefore, in your evaluation of his leadership ability.

Naturally we are looking for someone who will be permanent,
since our men need to know their territories and customers
quite well before they can sell enough to suit themselves or
us. Do you believe Sullivan will remain in the business world
for any length of time, or do you expect him to return to
school to continue his graduate work?

We shall appreciate your giving us this and any other
confidential information that will help us come to a decision,
and shall be glad to help you in the same way when we can.

Direct credit applications—those written when no question exists about the desirability of the account—are just as simple and concise as other direct inquiries.

Most consumers who apply for credit locally do so orally in a visit to the credit department of the business, although some do it with a telephone call. Some applicants, however, not wanting to bother with a visit to the store and realizing that certain investigation will have to be made, prefer to write a letter. This is more appropriate action when the application is directed to an out-of-town supplier.

Since requests are welcomed, a direct-style letter immediately phrasing the request and giving the necessary information is appropriate:

```
Will you please open a charge account in the name of

                  Mr. or Mrs. J. T. Holloway
                  76 Idlewild Drive
                  Dallas, Texas 75221

We have just moved here from Denver 80202, where our address
was 27 Crescent Drive.

Stores with which we have had accounts for about five years in
Denver are the White House, Foley's, J. P. Price & Co., and
the Town and Country Shop.

I am employed as a supervisor at the L. B. Price Distributing
Company, where I earn about $12,500 annually; Mrs. Holloway is
not employed.

The Merchants National Bank handles our checking account.
```

Despite having given enough information of the kind usually required as a basis for the extension or refusal of credit, the writer of the foregoing letter need not be surprised to receive an application form from the store. Most stores have standard forms which they want all charge customers to fill in and sign. In addition to blank spaces for the kind of information given in the foregoing example, they often have blanks for indicating employer or business address, whether the applicant owns or rents his home, his bank, and personal references. The information wanted and the form are so standardized and routine that an applicant may well write no more than a perfunctory sentence:

```
Will you please send me the necessary form(s) for arranging a
charge account with you?
```

Requests from business firms of national reputation, with solid capitalization and unquestioned ratings, are also perfunctory. Information about them is readily available from any number of credit sources. The acceptability of their credit is assumed; so the application for it is only by implication. Signed by an authorized agent (usually a purchasing agent), the letter might contain no more than the following:

> Please ship subject to your usual terms 6 dozen Samson 10-inch
> locking plier wrenches.

If the agent thinks the company name might not be recognized at once, he
might add:

> We are listed in Dun & Bradstreet.

If the company is not listed in any sources which can be checked readily,
he may write the following in addition to the order sentence above:

> We have done credit business with
>
>   L. B. Price Company, Dallas, Texas 75212
>   Vendo Company, Chicago, Illinois 60618
>   T. L. Painter & Co., Kansas City, Missouri 66109
>
> Our most recent certified financial statement is enclosed.

Credit inquiries from one business house to another are as routine as
those about products. Both should be direct, concise, and specific. And
because they ask for the same kind of information over and over again
(detailed under "Credit Approvals," p. 146), in most instances they should
be forms. The following form inquiry is a typical example, with a time-
saving provision for putting the answer(s) on the inquiring letter.

> Gentlemen:
>
> Will you please give us the confidential information requested
> below?
>
> In applying for credit with us, the applicant gave us your
> name as a reference.
>
> We would appreciate the courtesy. Any time we can return the
> favor, please call on us.
>
>   Very truly yours,
>
> Credit Manager
> Applicant: John Y. Bowen
> Length of time sold on credit _____
> Credit limit (if any) _____Credit terms _____
> Current amount due_____Past due_____
> Highest credit extended _____Most recent credit_____
> Paying habits _____
> Remarks _____

The letter lends itself to form treatment because the need for it comes
up frequently and no atypical, off-the-beaten-path questions are necessary.
(Most business firms have to handle inquiries about credit applicants and
job seekers with form letters because of time, money, and personnel limitations.) But whether it is a form letter or special letter, the important considerations of directness, specificness, and conciseness remain the same.

When, however, special circumstances arise which the form letter does
not cover, you're probably better off to write a special letter. Like any
direct request, it should get right down to business:

SUBJECT: CREDIT INQUIRY ABOUT MR. H. F. GREEN,
            GROCER, VINITA, OKLAHOMA

Will you please send us a confidential summary of your credit
experience with Mr. Green?

Naturally we'd like to have the usual items which reveal his
buying and paying habits.

But since we learned from one of the companies here in
McAlester that Mr. Green buys a large amount of his supplies
from you and that he has given your name as a credit reference
very recently, we'd like to have your explanation of why he
did not list your firm when he applied for credit with us.

We shall appreciate your help and shall be glad to assist you
in the same way any time we can.

When you ask your reader to give information about people, as in the
two preceding letters, both you and he face a special problem. You are
asking him to endanger himself with the libel laws. You have a duty to
help him protect himself as far as possible. Of course, if he tells the truth,
he has the one most important piece of protection, but truth alone is not
complete protection in some states. You can help by making his informative
letter what the lawyers call a privileged communication. You show him
that you have an interest to protect and you promise to keep the information confidential. As a matter of courtesy but with no legal significance, you
tell him that the inquiry was authorized (if true). In his response, then, he
shows that all those conditions exist. Otherwise, inquiries and replies about
people are the same as those about other things.

Perhaps you noticed that all of the three preceding letters expressed
appreciation and offered to return the favor. Especially when asking people to do things without any obvious benefit to themselves, courtesy demands just that. Usually the best way is in connection with your suggestion
of or request for specific reader action (generally the last paragraph). But
don't be presumptuous or jargonistic about it by using the lazy "Thank
you in advance." Instead, express it in first person, future tense—as those
writers did. And if the declarative mood (*shall* or *will*) sounds too presumptuous or imperious, change to the subjunctive (*should* or *would*).

You can increase your chances of getting an answer, or a faster answer,
if you can justifiably ask for it by a certain date. (People are inclined to
put things off—especially if the benefit is not obvious and immediate.)
Therefore you should consider justifying and end-dating:

Because Mr. Sullivan wants our decision by the end of the
month, we would especially appreciate your answer by the 25th.

The most important considerations to keep in mind about routine
(direct) inquiries, however, are to get started in a hurry, to be as specific in
your questions as you can, and to explain enough (but only enough) for
your reader to answer well and easily. The direct inquiry checklist of
suggestions will help you with most of your inquiry problems, although it
is not a prescription, a cover-all, or a cure-all.

Direct Inquiry Checklist

1. Get this letter under way quickly.
   a) A subject line may help by showing the nature of the inquiry.
   b) Start the key question in the first line of the letter.
   c) Make your question(s) specific (not just "some information" but "what colors . . .").
   d) For fast traveling in your opening, imply ideas or refer to them subordinately.
      Slow, plodding:
      > Will you please give us some information about Travis Brannon? He reports that . . . .

      Fast-moving:
      > What would be your reaction if Travis Brannon, your former assistant, walked into your office trying to sell you . . . ?
   e) When you use a subject line, don't depend on it for coherence in the letter or as the antecedent for any pronoun.

2. Cover at least the basic questions to which you want answers.
   a) Ask the minimum number of questions to get the information.
   b) Arrange questions in the most appropriate order.
   c) Provide explanations the reader needs for pointed answers.

3. Be careful about the form and wording of the questions.
   a) Ask directly for information; don't hint. "I should like to know if . . ." is wordy and slow. "Does the . . ." accomplishes the same job better and cheaper.
   b) Word your questions to get the information you want—that is, not a mere "yes" or "no" when you need explanation. Avoid leading questions (phrased to suggest a certain answer).
   c) If you want to run a series of questions, itemize (tabulate).
   d) When you need to interweave questions and explanations, vary sentence form and length to avoid a singsong effect.

4. Express gratitude cordially in first person, future tense: "I shall be grateful (or appreciate)" eliminates the awkwardness and wordiness of "It will be appreciated if . . ." and the presumptuousness of "Thank you in advance." If appropriate, offer to reciprocate.

5. At the end, confident and positive references to the reader's next action can serve as a coherent summary to the entire message, leave your reader clear as to what you want him to do, and serve as a stimulus to his doing it soon. For more likely and faster response consider justifying and asking for an answer by a certain date.

6. In inquiries about people, establish the privileged aspects.
   a) Be sure your explanation shows that you have an interest to protect.
   b) Promise confidential treatment of the information.
   c) If the inquiry is authorized, say so (for courtesy, not legal reasons).

FAVORABLE REPLIES

Any company desiring the goodwill of the public replies to all reasonable inquiries—and does so promptly. If a delay is necessary, some explanation should go forward to the inquirer indicating the reason and approximately when he can expect a complete answer, as in the following note:

> Your request for information about palletization can best be answered by Mr. J. S. McConnough, our materials-handling specialist, who will be in California for another 10 days.
>
> Shortly after he returns to the office, he will write you.

Here is another sample:

> We shall send you your copy of <u>Color Counts</u> about March 15, when we expect the revision from the printers.
>
> This new edition will show the true colors and will picture in detail all the popular patterns of Siesta ware, including the ones introduced just this year.
>
> You will enjoy it when you receive it.

The first situation appears to contain no possibilities of sales but, as in the case of any inquiry, represents a good opportunity to make a friend for the firm. The second situation obviously represents someone with an active interest in the product sold by the firm. Proper handling might well lead to a sale.

Because some incoming letters ask only for assistance, whereas others readily indicate a potential customer (and a quite different replying letter), we divide this discussion into (1) replies to inquiries without apparent sales possibilities (including reports dealing with personnel and credit applicants) and (2) replies to inquiries with sales possibilities.

Replies without sales possibilities

When someone asks you something, you say either yes or no—in an A–plan letter or a B–plan letter. For all practical purposes an undecided, noncommittal response like "Well, I'll think it over" is a refusal and needs to be handled in the inductive style (reasons before conclusion) of a B–plan letter. This discussion therefore concerns itself only with letters complying with the request. Refusals and modified refusals come later.

In letters which say yes, particular points you need to watch are the direct beginning, completeness of coverage, and (when appropriate) resale.

Direct beginning. The fundamental principle in all A–plan replies is to say yes immediately and thus gain increased goodwill, as well as save time and words. When you can do what the reader has asked you to do, begin your letter by giving the information or with a statement indicating (in line with the circumstances)

1. That you have done it (preferably),
2. That you are doing it, or
3. That you will do it.

Your compliance with the reader's request is the point of greatest interest to him—of far greater interest than any expressions of gratitude or gladness. And from the standpoint of economical writing the direct beginning cuts through and establishes many ideas by implication, thus shortening your letter copy considerably. Often the letter need contain no more than the notification of compliance, as in this example:

> We are glad to send you with this letter the last three annual reports of National Reaper, Inc., and to add your name to our mailing list to receive future copies as they are released around March 1 each year.

The direct beginning also establishes a cheerful, ungrudging tone for the letter and eliminates pompousness—at least from the all-important beginning. Observe the difference between the following slow, grudging, jargonistic original and the revision:

INDIRECT, WORDY, GRUDGING	DIRECT, COMPACT, CHEERFUL
We have your request for our HOW book.	Here is the HOW book you asked for.
It was prepared primarily for material-handling engineers, and so we were not prepared for the numerous requests we have received from schools. We are sending you one, however, and hope you will find it helpful.	It was prepared after extensive research by our own material-handling engineers with the assistance of outside consultants and plant men who specialize in material-handling methods and procedures. We're sure you'll find it useful in the classroom.
If there is any other way we can be of assistance, please do not hesitate to call on us.	Call on us again when you think we can help you.

In response to a request for a copy of a manual on letters, the following is a good example:

> Here is your complimentary copy of Better Letters, Professor Duke.
>
> I hope you'll be able to use it in developing the practical note you desire in your classes.
>
> Since the manual was compiled from company correspondence and contains actual names and other confidential material, will you please not quote directly from it? I'm sure you'll be able to use it successfully by substituting other names and figures when you want to paraphrase an example.
>
> Several Harwood graduates are doing excellent jobs with Southern Atlantic. I hope you will have other qualified graduating seniors to recommend to Mr. R. B. Jones when he comes to your campus in February.

In response to a request for material on palletization, one man wrote:

> Although there seems to be a dearth of palletization material
> in textbooks, here are two you may want to study if you haven't
> already:
>
> Harry E. Stocker, <u>Materials Handling</u>, Prentice-Hall, New
> York, 1972.
>
> Mathew W. Potts, <u>Materials Handling Equipment</u>, Pitman, New
> York, 1971.
>
> The following magazines have market research departments and
> can supply reprints of articles if you'll write them
> explaining just what information you wish:
>
> <u>Modern Material Handling</u>, 131 Claredon Street, Boston 02116.
> <u>Flow</u>, 1240 Ontario Street, Cleveland 44113.
> <u>Factory Management & Maintenance</u>, McGraw-Hill, New York
> 10001.
> <u>American Machinist</u>, 520 North Michigan Avenue, Chicago
> 60607.
> <u>Industry & Power</u>, St. Joseph, Michigan 64502.
> <u>Western Canner & Packer</u>, 121 Second Street, San Francisco
> 94101.
>
> In the attached envelope I am sending you a copy of our latest
> catalog and the last four issues of our company magazine,
> <u>Material Handling News</u>.
>
> We're glad to pass these suggestions on to you and to send
> this material along; we realize that today's students are
> tomorrow's material-handling engineers.
>
> Good luck on the thesis. Call on us again if we can help.

You will note that not one of the foregoing letters wasted any words referring to receipt of the inquiry. The direct beginning makes such references unnecessary and saves space better used for worthwhile information.

Completeness of coverage.   Obviously, you need to take up every question in an inquiring letter; when you fail to do so, extra correspondence results (or your reader marks you as careless, indifferent, or ignorant). At times, of course, you can't answer—because you don't know, or because you can't reveal the information. In either case simply tell your reader so, but don't ignore his question.

When the questions call for strictly factual answers, when the requesting letter tabulates questions and leaves space for answering on the letter, your job is easy. When the necessary answers are evaluative and expository in form, your job is sometimes not so easy.

The following personnel report is in answer to an inquiry about the subject's selling ability, personality, cultural background, character, and integrity. Note that the negative information the writer felt it necessary to establish is embedded in the letter and interpreted along with a positive characteristic of the applicant. Note, too, that the letter is *not* a "recommendation" but a *personnel report* of the writer's experience with and evaluation of the applicant.

SUBJECT: CONFIDENTIAL REPORT BY REQUEST ON TRAVIS BRANNON AS
A PROSPECTIVE BOOK SALESMAN

Mr. Brannon is a careful, accurate worker with lots of
initiative. And he makes friends readily.

I got to know Travis quite well while he made two A's in my
courses, Sales Management and Public Relations, and later
when he graded papers, had conferences with students, and did
clerical jobs as a student assistant in my office fall
semester last year. His questions in class and in conferences
showed a keen understanding of business problems and a calm,
practical approach to their solution. And his term reports in
both cases showed solid, serious, yet original business
thinking. Impressed with his scholastic performance, his
friendliness and ability to get along with people, and his
obvious wide range of interests in many things (literature,
drama, music), I asked him to be my assistant.

I particularly liked the quickness with which Travis caught on
to assigned jobs and the willingness and accuracy with which
he did a job every time it came up after I had explained it to
him only once. On many small jobs and some not so small he
went ahead and did what was needed to be done without being
told.

As he demonstrated ability, I let him do more and more. And
he accepted the added responsibility and authority with
obvious delight. As a result of such unbridled enthusiasm, I
occasionally had to change a grade or contradict what he had
told a student in conference. When that happened, he was
noticeably silent for a few days; then he apparently forgot
the incident and became his cheerfully helpful self again.

I must say, Mr. Parks, that I never had to lower a grade
Travis gave a student. And he was hardest on his friends. I
never had one single reason to suspect that any student had an
inside track with him. He was completely trustworthy with
examinations, grade records, and the like.

Perhaps the most noticeable things about Travis are his
eagerness to do his job, his efficiency in making use of all
his time, and his general alertness. These qualities, though
they sometimes made him officious in interrupting my
conferences with students and colleagues, stood him in good
stead with students and faculty alike.

I feel sure that if Travis walked into the office of a college
professor on almost any campus, the reaction toward him and
your company would be favorable.

In probably the majority of cases requesting information about an
applicant for credit, all you'll need to do is look at your customer's record
and fill in the blanks provided on the inquiring letter. But when some
atypical factor presents itself (or when the inquiring firm does not provide
a blank to make your reply quick and easy), you'll need to write a special
letter.

We do not mean to imply here that all credit reports are letters, for
most of them are not; the bulk of credit information distributed in this
country from credit-rating and credit-reporting agencies goes out in special

report forms. This is a small point, however, for in report form or letter form the useful credit summary covers essentially the same material:

—Age of account (how long on the books)

—Credit or trading limit (maximum allowed; sometimes labeled "highest credit extended")

—Buying habits (typical or average purchase, annual volume)

—Paying habits *in relation to terms* (identify the terms and show how the customer meets or does not meet them)

—Present status of the account (amount now on the books, what part is overdue, and how long overdue).

In addition to the foregoing information, you may want to incorporate explanations of the effects of local conditions on the size and timing of purchases or on paying habits. And of course, any unusual question—like the one about Mr. Green (p. 115)—requires special attention. Since it is usually the reason for the special letter, it often merits the beginning position, like this:

SUBJECT: CREDIT REPORT ON MR. H. F. GREEN, VINITA, OKLAHOMA

Mr. Green, your applicant for credit, has been on our books since August, 1967. Since our relations have always been satisfactory from our point of view, I suspect that he failed to list our name as a reference because he was a little miffed with us about a month ago because we guessed wrong on one of his vague orders.

We've been safe in allowing him credit up to $700 several times. He has a yearly account of about $4,000; his monthly purchases vary from $30 in the summer to $700 in the fall. When crop money in the fall spurs payments, Mr. Green generally takes advantage of our 2/10 EOM discount. With only a few exceptions, he has paid his net bill by the 30th. On the two occasions that we had to press him for collection, he paid up promptly.

Right now is the slack season in the farming regions; so Mr. Green has let ride his May and June accounts totaling $700.30. Of this amount, only the May bill of $382.40 is now overdue. Since, on June 16, he sent in his $366.60 check in payment of his April account, we know that Mr. Green pays his bills as soon as he gets his money. A retired farmer who still owns three farms, he is the sole owner of his modest store.

I am glad to send you, at your request, this confidential letter about Mr. Green.

Completeness of coverage does *not*, however, mean recommendation. Note that neither the preceding personnel report nor the credit report recommends the applicant—and hence such letters should *not* be misnamed "letters of recommendation."

Resale. Perhaps our suggestion to incorporate resale material in a reply to an inquiry without sales possibilities may strike you as unnecessary—even odd. But look back a moment at the contrasting examples (p.

Favorable Reply Checklist

1. Make your opening establish the fact that you are doing as asked.
    a) When you are saying yes, sending something, or giving information, do so immediately!
    b) The most effective way to show that you're glad to do something is to begin immediately to do it: not "I am very glad to tell you . . ." but "Henry Benton, about whom you inquired, has served us well as . . . ."
    c) Don't emphasize the obvious: "This is an answer to . . ."; "Concerning your inquiry . . ."; "We have received . . . ."
    d) Consider using a subject line to get you off to a fast start.

2. Specificness and correctness are essential.
    a) Answer every question—direct or implied—of the inquiry.
    b) You want to evaluate when evaluation will be helpful. But do more than editorialize with "fine," "splendid," "excellent." Back up your statements with specific evidence. In a personnel report, for instance, tell things the applicant did, work habits, personality.
    c) Scant, skimpy treatment implies that you are unwilling to extend an ordinary business courtesy or that you are dubious.

3. Tone is all-important.
    a) In a personnel report:
        (1) Remember that you are reporting, not recommending.
        (2) Beware of superlatives, for accuracy and believability.
    b) Don't do anything grudgingly or parade your generosity.

4. You often have negative material to handle.
    a) Be honest; don't ignore the shortcomings and mislead.
    b) Watch the space, word choice, and position to avoid overemphasis.
    c) When you must restrict the use of what you give, be definite—but place the negative in the middle of the letter.

5. Remember the privileged aspects when you write about a person.
    a) Label the letter confidential.
    b) Indicate that it has been requested.
    c) Incorporate these ideas in the beginning or ending statements.

6. When sending something tangible, add a few words of resale.
    a) Make them short.
    b) Make them as specific as you can.

7. End graciously and confidently.
    a) Your expression of willingness—more appropriate here than in the beginning—nullifies any possible curt impression.
    b) Don't suggest inadequacy: "I hope" or "If this is not . . . ."
    c) Omit bromides: "Please do not hesitate" or "Feel free to."

118) relating to the HOW book, and note the different impressions created. The revised makes comments on the book in such a way as to make the reader realize that he is getting something special. Furthermore, it enhances the cordiality established by the direct beginning and eliminates any impression of curtness and abruptness that might be reflected from a one-sentence letter.

Note how in the following letter the writer not only applies resale on the booklet requested but goes a step further by sending something additional and offering to do more:

> Of course you may have copies of our booklet; four of them are enclosed with this letter. They'll certainly help to show those future business leaders you spoke of something about how a direct-mail agency operates.
>
> We're also sending you a dividend: a copy of the speech Mr. Ray made at the DMAA meeting in Detroit last month. Some folks have said that it makes some pretty arresting statements about the uses and limitations of direct mail. You and your students will get something from this too, we think.
>
> Call on us again; we're always glad to do what we can.

Certainly you can't use resale in every reply. But in situations where you send information (especially in the form of booklets, brochures, or leaflets) you have every reason to enhance the desirability of what you've done and to offer to help out again (unless you specifically do not want to).

The reminder checklist on page 122 summarizes the more important points to keep in mind as you write replies complying with a reader's request which has no sales possibilities.

Replies with sales possibilities

Failure to answer inquiries and requests of the types we have been discussing will mark you as an uncooperative boor and probably lose you a good many sales in the long run, but failure to answer inquiries with direct sales possibilities is sooner or later business suicide.

When someone sends you an inquiry about your goods or services, he shows clearly that he recognizes an unsatisfied need or desire; he further implies that your product might satisfy it. Whether he asks for manufacturing data, a price list, a catalog or descriptive folder, or the name of your nearest dealer, he seems to be an *interested,* potential customer—in other words, a prospect. *If* he receives satisfactory information and treatment, he'll probably be a real customer.

Your job of giving him what he wants is certainly much easier than making a sale through the usual sales letter that has to start from scratch with a "cold" prospect (as discussed in Chapter 9), because the inquirer is already interested. He has practically invited you to send him a sales letter.

Although you will be able to write better invited sales letters after studying special sales techniques, we take them up here because they are the most significant kind of reply any business firm sends. They are more than goodwill builders; they are sales clinchers. Accordingly, they draw heavily on the principles discussed in Chapter 3.

In answering an inquiry with sales possibilities, you have no problem of securing attentive interest; your main problem is to tell enough to overcome reluctance, to tell it interestingly and convincingly, and to get the reader to take the appropriate steps that lead to a sale. Your effort, then, must be given to getting started favorably, answering all questions, subordinating unfavorable information, handling price positively, and stimulating action.

Getting started positively. When a prospective customer writes you the equivalent of "Tell me more," he certainly is going to feel that he has had cold water thrown in his face with an indifferent reply like this:

> There is an Endurtone company in your locality. Kindly
> contact them with your problem.

Such unconcern sends many readers to other sources for their needs. This, of course, is an extreme example, but it happens often enough to merit special warning.

The thing the reader most wants to know is the information he has requested—as specifically as you can give it to him. He is far more interested in such information than in any of your expressions of pleasure or gratitude. But in most cases involving a detailed inquiry, you will want to check the order of your reader's questions before framing your reply. Some of his requests for information you can answer with more positiveness than others; one of these is what you should start with, as in the following examples:

> With your Pow-R-Pac you will feel safe even when traveling
> alone at night on the country roads you spoke of.
>
> --
>
> The Rover bicycle you saw advertised in U.S. Youth is made of
> lightweight, high-grade steel of the same quality used in
> motor bikes.
>
> --
>
> Yes, Mr. Baines, the base and standard of the Roanoke lamp you
> saw in Home and Yard are of solid brass. They will blend in
> tastefully with almost any style of 18th-century furnishings.

When you can answer yes, that is the information you should choose for your opening. Such positiveness stimulates enthusiasm and increases the desire to read further.

Answering all questions. In some instances you cannot give the information your reader has asked of you. For example, the letter about the Stair-Traveler (p. 64) could not give cost details because installation varies according to the placement of the machine in a particular dwelling.

The visit of the representative (clearly referred to) would have to clear up that point. If you cannot supply an answer, do not ignore it. Such action only leads to suspicion, irritation, or disgust. Indicate that you are supplying the information in some other way or that you are in the process of finding out.

Most of the time you can give all the information the reader has requested, even though it runs to considerable length. The following reply to the request for more information about reconditioned Lektrasweeps (p. 111) is a good letter not only because of good you-viewpoint and positiveness but also because it answers every question of the inquiring letter:

The reconditioned Lektrasweep that you asked about has the following attachments: a 6-inch upholstery brush, a 6-inch lampshade brush, a 12-inch prober, and a plastic blower attachment, in addition to the standard 12-inch rug brush.

These are the same attachments as with vacuum cleaners costing $40 to $80 more. Were we to include a 1-hp. motor (necessary only for spraying attachments), the price would have to be considerably increased. Since most users want their Lektrasweeps for cleaning purposes only, we eliminate the spray attachments and thus are able to give you a good low-cost cleaner operating efficiently on a ½-hp. motor.

Next time you're in Birmingham, come in and let us demonstrate a Lektrasweep. After a thorough test of its effectiveness in picking up dust, lint, and other particles from rugs, upholstery, and walls, you'll see why we are so confident of the Lektrasweep. Although we consider all sales final (another of the economies resulting in the low price of your Lektrasweep), the Lektrasweep guarantee protects you against mechanical failures for a full two years.

If any of the parts fail because of defective workmanship, specially trained servicemen at the central plant in Cleveland will put your Lektrasweep in service again and return it to you within a week's time. As long as the machine shows evidence of proper care, as explained on the written guarantee, we absorb the charges for servicing and new parts, and return your Lektrasweep charges prepaid. The few returns to the central plant have been handled to the customers' satisfaction.

I believe we have the sweeper you'll find convenient for your cleaning. The brown crackle finish will resist nicks and scratches and will be easy to keep clean. The quiet operation of the motor is especially desirable in small living quarters. Another convenience is the 20-foot cord, which enables you to clean an entire room without having to switch from one wall plug to another.

If for some reason you'd like your Lektrasweep before you can get over to Birmingham, use the enclosed order blank and reply envelope for sending us your payment and instructions. You can be enjoying easy Lektrasweeping the day after we hear from you.

This was a particularly difficult letter to write because so many of the questions had to be answered with limitations, reservations, or an implied no, as you can see by comparing the inquiry and this answer.

To get full value out of the replies about Lektrasweeps and Roanoke lamps (next section), you need to look at each a second time. Both effectively illustrate two aspects of you-viewpoint especially important in all sales writing—including the answers to the questions of a product inquiry:

1. Psychological description.—Except in the first paragraph of the Lektrasweep letter, every time the writers give a physical fact about the product, they *tell* and *emphasize* a resultant benefit. As you look again, see how many more pieces of psychological description you can find like the italicized part of ". . . 20-foot cord, *which enables you to clean an entire room without having to switch from one wall plug to another.*"

2. *Dramatization.*—The most effective kind of sales writing gets the reader to visualize himself actually using and enjoying the benefits of the product. Where else in the two letters can you find dramatized copy like "You and Mrs. Baines will agree that the Roanoke is a handsome, efficient lamp when you place a pair in your own living room"?

For further help on answering all questions, see the second group of form enclosures, p. 132.

Subordinating unfavorable information.   It would have been very poor salesmanship if the Lektrasweep letter had started with

    The Lektrasweep is equipped with a ½-hp motor.

or with

    No, the Lectrasweep does not have a 1-hp. motor.

Likewise, if the writer of the Stair-Traveler letter had begun with

    The Stair-Traveler you are interested in will not work on a
    stair with a turn in the middle,

the lady's interest would very likely have decreased immediately and maybe vanished. But by establishing favorable information before stating this negative fact, and by stating the negative in its positive form ("as it is designed only for straight stairways"), the writer hoped to overcome the effect of the disappointing news. Explaining the necessary installation in terms of simplicity and economy (the positive corollary) further helped to cushion the effect.

Another case will more firmly implant the reasons for positive handling of unfavorable information in invited sales. The inquiry asked whether

the lamp was three-way

the shade was of parchment or paper

the shade was available in a design

the lamp was weighted to prevent tipping

the base was real brass or an alloy

a pair could be returned for full refund if they didn't fit in with the 18th-century living room.

Answers to four questions contained negative information. Here is one way of handling this inquiry to turn it into a sale despite the unfavorable circumstances:

> Yes, the base and standard of the Roanoke lamp you saw in Home and Yard are of solid brass, which will blend in tastefully with almost any style of 18th-century furnishings.
>
> For durability and ease in cleaning, the 10-inch shade is lightweight metal. Either the forest green or the royal red shade will contrast effectively with your drapes, and the quarter-inch gold bands around the top and bottom give the Roanoke lamp a distinction which most of our customers prefer to a design.
>
> The white lining of the shade and the milk-white bone china reflector enable the single 150-watt bulb to give you good reading light—10 foot-candles within a radius of 8 feet, which is more than the minimum recommended by the American Institute of Lighting. Then, too, the indirect lighting reflected from the ceiling is pleasant for conversational groups.
>
> To make the Roanoke more stable than other lamps of this size and shape, our designers put six claw feet instead of the usual four on the base and thus eliminated the necessity for weighting. Claw feet, as you know, are characteristic of much 18th-century design.
>
> You and Mrs. Baines will agree that the Roanoke is a handsome, efficient lamp when you place a pair in your own living room. Should you decide to return them within 10 days of our shipping date, we will refund your money less shipping charges.
>
> Use the enclosed order blank and envelope to tell us your choice of color. Include with the order blank your check or money order for $80 (including shipping charges). Within five days after we hear from you, you will be enjoying your Roanoke lamps, which will give you good lighting at a moderate price and will make appropriately decorative additions to your living room.

The letter wisely begins and ends with positive ideas and, as positively as circumstances permit, establishes the negative answers of "No, the Roanoke is not three-way; no, it is not weighted; no, the shade is not available in a design; no, we won't refund *all* your money if you return the lamps." It does so through the usual means available to any writer: embedded position and positive statement.

Handling price.   In most business situations no other talk is so loud as that concerned with dollars and cents. Receiving money is pleasant; parting with money is hard.

When you have a genuine bargain, a real price reduction—one which the reader will recognize as such—that information may be the best lead you can choose for your message.

Most of the time, however, you are trying to sell at an established price. And most of the time you are writing to someone who wishes the price were less! For these two simple and obvious reasons, good sales writers attempt to minimize the effect of price by one or more of several methods:

—Introducing price after most of the sales points have been presented.

—Stating price in terms of a unit ("50 cents a wrench" rather than "$6 a dozen").

—Identifying the daily, monthly, or even yearly cost based on an estimated life of the product ("10 cents a night" for a good mattress sounds much easier to pay for than "$79").

—Suggesting a series of payments rather than the total (an alumnus is more likely to contribute "$10 a month for the next year" than he is to contribute "$120 next year").

—Comparing the present price with the cost of some product or activity the reader accepts readily. ("For the price of six cigarettes a day your child can have better schools" was the punch line of an ad promoting a school-bond drive. And an Episcopal bishop drove home his point with "This means 17 cents per week from each communicant—not a large sum for the kingdom of God, when we realize that many of us spend twice that amount *every day* for tobacco." Likewise, a sales writer sells air-conditioned sleep for the price of a daily coke.)

—Associating the price with a reminder of the benefits to be gained.

The first and the last of the suggestions you can always apply; you may want to use the others as indicated by the following varying factors.

In general, the higher the income bracket of your audience, the less desirability for applying the techniques.

The higher the price of your product or service, the greater the desirability for minimizing price in one or more of these ways. The less familiar your audience is with your product or service, the greater the desirability of justifying price. Such devices are incorporated more frequently in consumer letters than in letters to dealers.

Often you will be able to omit direct price talk because a salesman will handle it in a face-to-face interview or because you need more information before determining price; sometimes you can shift the burden of price discussion to an enclosure. But when you are trying to close a sale, you must identify what it is going to cost your reader and help him justify the expenditure.

Securing action. Having convinced your reader that your product or service is worth the price, you want him to take action before he changes his mind, before he forgets about the matter, before he spends the money for something else, before any of the things that could happen do happen.

A word of caution here, however: The bromidic, high-pressure, general expressions like "Act today!" "Do it now!" "Don't delay!" are more likely to produce reactions ranging from indifference to disgust than the favorable reaction you seek.

As in all persuasive letters, your good action ending

—Makes clear the specific action you want your reader to take

—Clears up any question about how the action is to be taken

—Makes the action easy (and makes it sound as easy as possible)

—Supplies a stimulus to action, preferably immediate action

When your reader finishes your letter, he should know just exactly what you want him to do. In invited sales letters you usually want him to send in an order or take some step in furthering the order, such as to invite the visit of a salesman, make a visit to a demonstration or salesroom, or try out the product. The psychological urge is stronger if you name the explicit action rather than resort to the vague "Let us hear from you soon" or any of its equivalents. At times you will have to name two actions and ask the reader to take one or the other; if you possibly can, avoid doing so, for the simple reason that some folks faced with a choice resolve their dilemma by doing nothing.

Facilitating devices—order blanks, order cards, and postcards or envelopes already addressed and requiring no postage—remove some of the tediousness of taking action. References to them—*preferably directing the reader to use them* (see *enclosures*, pp. 31, 130)—reassure your reader that what you are asking him to do is simple, requiring little time or effort.

Moreover, through careful wording, you can further this impression. "Write us your choice" suggests more work than "Check your choice of colors on the enclosed card." "Jot down," "just check," "simply initial," are examples of wording that suggests ease and rapidity in doing something. Wording like this will help to reduce some of your reader's reluctance to take action.

The final suggestion for a good action ending—that of supplying a stimulus to action—is a matter of either threatening your reader or promising him something. Talk of limited supply, price rises after a certain date, introductory offers for a limited time, premiums, and the like is all very well *provided it is true* and *provided it is specific,* so that the reader is likely to accept your statement as one accurately depicting the conditions. Otherwise, readers of average intelligence and experience read such statements with some skepticism, for two good reasons:

1. They have seen too many instances in which such statements were not true. They have also seen "introductory" offers repeated over and over and over.

2. Especially in the United States, talk of limited supply raises questions about the desirability of the article. "If it's so good and so popular, why aren't more of them made?" Why a premium? Is the product overpriced? Is there some drawback for which the premium is sop?

Records of mail-order experiences over the years have shown that such hurry-up devices do increase returns in some instances. Scarcities, for instance, during national-emergency periods certainly make a difference in a person's decision to buy. And the desire to save money before another round of inflation hits makes many a buyer reach for his checkbook. But such devices are not universally applicable and far less so in invited sales letters than in uninvited sales.

In many circumstances you have nothing you can use as a stimulus but the desirability of your product or service. You *always* have that, however. In the final analysis your reader bases his buying decision on what the product contributes to his life; when you ask him to part with his money, *remind him again of what he will receive as a result.* (This is called a "stimulus" or a "clincher." But since many sales writers refer to the four steps of the action ending as the "clincher," we think it's simpler just to call this restatement of benefit the "stimulus.")

Such a stimulus comes appropriately as the ending idea of your letter. This placement has decided psychological value too, for it emphasizes the service attitude—rather than the greed that would be stressed if you ended with dollars and cents talk or the mechanics of ordering.

Desirably, the stimulus is short—often only a phrase, at most a short sentence, restating the theme of the letter. The Stair-Traveler letter, for example, could have ended effectively with

```
Mr. J. B. Nickle, our Memphis representative, will be glad to
call at a time convenient for you.  Fill out and mail the
enclosed postcard, and he will come to your home and explain
how simply and economically your Stair-Traveler can make your
daily living more pleasurable.
```

Another example of the built-in stimulus is this ending from a letter to a farmer about an automatic milking machine:

```
And for $77.75—less than you pay for 10 sacks of feed—Farm
Master Milker can go to work for you.  Just leave the enclosed
card for the mail carrier tomorrow morning, and our
Philadelphia representative will soon be up to give you a
demonstration of how Farm Master Milker will increase your
dairy profits.
```

For other examples, reread the endings of the Roanoke lamp letter and the letter selling the Lektrasweep.

A final reminder: Invited sales are sales letters in the truest sense; you should therefore apply all the points discussed in Chapter 3. The following checklist summarizes the most significant points to keep in mind for a good invited sales letter.

FORM ENCLOSURES AND LETTERS

Invited sales letters like those you read in the preceding section (and various other kinds of letters) do take time and therefore money—more than many firms can wisely spend unless the prospect for sizable profit is strong.

Unless a firm has practically unlimited money and trained personnel, it

Invited Sales Checklist

1. Get started in a hurry!
   a) The direct, specific, favorable answer to one of your reader's questions is the surest way of maintaining his interest.
   b) At least give a good sale point if no anwer can be affirmative.
   c) "Thank you for"—while perfectly nice—is slow.
   d) Keep out the selfish sounds like "We're glad to have . . . ."
   e) Do not begin with an answer containing negative information.
   f) You don't need to work for attention: you already have it.

2. Arrange points for natural coherence and favorable information at the beginning and end of your letter (and preferably of paragraphs). Embed touchy points.

3. Answer every question, stated or implied, or explain why.
   a) You need specific statements for conviction.
   b) Avoid denied negatives. If a product isn't something, what is it?

4. Psychological description (you-viewpoint) is good selling.
   a) Put the product to work in the life of the reader right from the start, and let reader-use sentences predominate throughout to make him visualize how he benefits.
   b) Depict reader possession and/or participation instead of mere mechanical you-beginnings.

5. Consider using an enclosure for details, economy, and pictures.
   a) Don't mention it too early.
   b) Don't emphasize that you have enclosed it; what the reader is to do with it or get from it is what counts: not "Enclosed you will find a folder," but "Read on page 2 of the enclosed folder the comments of some of the more than 8,000 owners of XXX."

6. Adaptation is easy here; your reader's letter gives you cues.
   a) Maybe use his name a time or two beyond the salutation.
   b) Work in a reference to his town, firm, or organization.
   c) Refer casually to a commonplace action or event characteristic of his job, community, area, or economic status.
   d) Fit your style to the person and his way of life.

7. Try to cushion the shock of price when you have to settle it.
   a) Use the appropriate method(s) of minimizing price.
   b) Make price payment method clear, or give a reason.

8. In a full-fledged four-point action ending (what to do, how, aids to easy action, stimulus to promptness) confidently ask the reader to take some action (preferably order).

needs to use form messages some of the time for desirable speed and economy in handling inquiries with sales possibilities.

Form enclosures and letters can decrease the cost of correspondence by cutting time needed for dictation, transcription, handling, and filing. The closer you can come to completely eliminating one or more of these steps, the more you can save. The big problem is to determine when you can save enough in costs to justify the loss in effectiveness.

Before you can decide, however, you need to know the potentials of forms.

Three classes of *form enclosures* deserve our attention:

1. Forms which are the basic reason for the mailing;
2. Forms which give supplementary information; and
3. Forms which aid the reader in responding.

Since the first group are the key things in the envelopes (checks paying for services, interest, dividends, purchases, and deserved refunds; requested pamphlets, brochures, and the like), they deserve to come to the reader's attention immediately. In some cases they may properly be the only thing necessary. In most situations, however, you should *make something of them* by saying something about them—if for no reason than goodwill. You've already seen earlier in this chapter under "Resale" the reasons and approaches for comment when transmitting requested booklets. Similarly, simple and typical covering letters (often forms themselves) beginning something like the following could hardly help making their readers feel better:

> —We're glad to send you the attached quarterly dividend check (our 200th without interruption, raised to 50¢ a share this time) and to thank you for your continued confidence in MMM.
> —The enclosed check paying for your services as consultant carries with it our thanks for the good advice you gave us.
> —The enclosed check will tell you more clearly than words that when we guarantee satisfaction with Acme products or your money back, we mean it.

Unlike the first group of form enclosures, the enclosures in the second group are *not* the basic reason for writing but are helpful to give additional details and thus avoid cluttering and lengthening the letter unduly. Most frequently useful in sales letters as brochures and detailed price lists, they also help in application letters (as résumés or data sheets) and in answering various inquiries about products (as installation, operating, and repair guides). As supplements to letters, these informative enclosures do not deserve mention until late in the letter—usually the next-to-last paragraph, *after* the letter has covered the key points and near enough to the end that the reader will finish the letter before turning to the enclosure (perhaps never to return). As with the first group, the important thing to say about these enclosures is *not* their mere existence—NOT "We have enclosed . . . ," and certainly NOT "Enclosed please find . . ." (the reader has probably already found)—but what the reader should get from them.

—As you'll see from the enclosed brochure, . . .

—The illustrations and explanations on pages 3 and 4 of the enclosed installation guide will answer, better than I can explain in this letter, your questions about wiring the two thermostats in combination.

—All the references listed on the enclosed data sheet have agreed to answer any inquiry you may want to make about. . . .

The third useful group of form enclosures (reader aids in replying) naturally deserve mention only in the ending—where you are asking for action. Order blanks and reply or return cards and envelopes (usually stamped and addressed—but NOT properly called "self-addressed," unless you insist on being jargonistic, illogical, and wordy) can often help you get an answer when the reader would not go to the trouble necessary without them. As in referring to other form enclosures, the point to stress is NOT the idea that they are enclosed but the suggestion that the reader use them. If you'll use the word *enclosed* as an adjective instead of a verb, you'll probably put the emphasis where it belongs in referring to all three classes of form enclosures, like this:

—By filling out and mailing the enclosed reply card promptly, . . .

—Sending in your order today on the enclosed form will bring you. . . .

Although most readers like the implied extra consideration of the individual letter, few business people will object to a *form letter* because it is a form but only if it seems to give them less attention than they desire. New correspondents and those writing you about important affairs are most likely to feel that way. Anybody, however, will rightly object to a sloppy form or a form message which does not contain the necessary information. And some people will object to a form which tries to masquerade as an individual letter but fails because of discrepancies in type, faulty alignment, or inept wording. But the undisguised form can successfully carry its message in many situations, especially those involving many similar inquiries to which you can reply somewhat like the following:

Here's Your Copy of
The Buying Guide
to Fine Furniture.

You will be delighted with the wealth of information condensed into this conveniently indexed booklet.

For here, in a comparatively few pages, are guideposts used by experts with a lifetime of experience in weighing true furniture values. Here are features which help such experts actually judge furniture "upside down" as well as right side up.

> And here are features illustrated and described to guide you
> in your purchases of furniture so that the pieces you select
> to furnish your home will give you utmost pleasure as the
> years roll by.
>
> We're glad you've given us this opportunity to send you this
> information, for we love fine furniture . . . take great pride
> in making it . . . and enjoy distributing information about it
> that may be helpful to you in establishing standards of value.
>
> Even though every piece of furniture bearing the Langston seal
> is handcrafted to certified standards of quality, nationwide
> popularity makes possible budget prices. For a pleasant
> surprise, see your dealer, whose name is imprinted on the back
> page of the booklet.

Even the signature of this letter is processed. When an inquiry comes in, the letter and booklet are inserted in an envelope addressed to the inquirer; addressing the envelope is the only time-consuming step. Thus a reply which could easily cost $3 or more if individually handled runs to no more than a quarter. And the firm gains extra goodwill by a prompt answer.

You can run off completely processed forms (*strict forms*) by the thousands at very low cost. The only additional expense is for addressing (of course, you have mailing expense and advertising expense in securing the inquiry, but these are the same whether your message is processed or individualized).

Thus, *completely* processed messages are the cheapest. And they can be adapted in talking points and references even to a large mailing list. But completely processed letters have limitations. Personalizing is impossible. And if you process the body and then insert individual inside addresses and salutations, you have two additional problems: greatly increased costs and likely discrepancies between the two types. Unless you sell only one product or have a different form for each product, you can't include resale talk on the goods, although you can for the firm. Completely processed messages can, however, indicate the disposition of the inquiry (or order), express gratitude, convey some evidence of service attitude, and look forward to future business relations, as in the following postcard acknowledgment:

> We are glad to give your recent order our immediate careful
> attention and to follow your shipping instructions exactly.
>
> You may be sure we appreciate this opportunity to serve you
> and shall be happy to do so when you again decide to order
> Wolf's fine confections for yourself or as a gift.

Fill-ins enable you to be more specific than you can be in a strict form. For example, the strict form above could read like this as a fill-in (the filled-in parts being in parentheses):

> (January 15, 19—)
>
> We sent a carefully packed (2-pound box of Wolf's famous Texas

Chewie Pecan Pralines) today, as you requested, by (parcel
post) addressed to (Mr. and Mrs. E. F. Blanton, 2443 Hathaway
Road, Syracuse, New York 13247).

When it arrives within the next few days we know (they) will
enjoy the rich, nutty flavor of this fine candy.

Many thanks for your order. When you want more of Wolf's fine
candies for yourself or for pleasing a friend with an
inexpensive gift distinctly different, we shall be glad to
serve you again.

But even though you do a good job of matching print and type in a fill-in like this, in almost all instances the irregular spacing calls attention to the fact that the message is a form fill-in. The first two insertions in the example above extend the line of type far beyond what any typist would do if the letter were individually typed. And see what happens when the recipient's name and address are something as short as "Mr. J. P. Ames, Opp, Iowa"! The line then would be much too short. That is one of the reasons why so many of these forms are filled in with pen and ink, with no attempt to disguise.

With proper planning, equipment, and patience, however, fill-ins can appear to be individual letters. The following is a good example, where the necessary insertions are the name of the city (at the end of a line, please note), the name of the dealer (displayed attractively with additional spacing all around), and the reader's name (again, at the end of the line and with enough space to allow for a "Miss Rives" or a "Miss Getzendannerich"). In this case you would also use full inside address and dateline.

Dear Miss Rives:

The enclosed literature describes several Phenix models we
believe will be of interest to you. Although the literature
illustrates and describes the instruments, you cannot fully
appreciate the beauty of the cabinetry or their magnificent
tone without seeing and hearing them.

Phenix instruments are designed for discriminating buyers—for
those who have genuine appreciation for refined furniture
styling and truly fine musical tone—and they are sold only
through high-grade music dealers and selected quality
department stores.

We urge you to see these instruments and have them
demonstrated to you. You will be thrilled by the perfection
of tone that Phenix has attained.

Phenix instruments are on display in Austin at

J. P. Read Music Company
855 Congress Avenue

This dealer will be delighted to have the privilege of
demonstrating Phenix instruments to you without any obligation
whatever, Miss Rives.

Plan to go by for a demonstration.

For greatest economy the preceding letter would be printed; then, when an inquiry *that this form would be a satisfactory answer for* came in, a typist would need only to fill in the blanks—a matter of two or three minutes. Addressing and stamping (or metering) the envelope would take another two or three.

But because type is hard to match and exact alignment is difficult to make, some firms use an automatic typewriter (also called "robot") for multiple correspondence like this. After the contents of the letter have been decided on, the secretary cuts a kind of stencil of the pattern to guide the automatic typewriter. She inserts paper, types the necessary dates, inside address, and salutation, then presses a button, and the machine takes over the typing job. When it comes to the necessary individualized parts, the machine stops, and the secretary types in whatever is necessary and pushes the automatic button.

The economy over straight manual typing would not be great with only one such machine; most companies, however, have a secretary running two to five at one time! When you consider that these machines produce copy at about twice the speed of the fastest typist and that one typist can easily take the place of three, you can see the economies.

This economy measure can apply to form paragraphs as well as to whole letters. The procedure is to write an excellent paragraph covering each frequently recurring point in the firm's correspondence and assign it a code number. These paragraphs are then carefully classified. Some of the classifications may be by type of letter in which the paragraphs are useful. For instance, most of the collection man's paragraphs would be useless to the man acknowledging orders, and vice versa. Usually half a dozen ending paragraphs and a dozen beginnings will cover most situations. Other paragraphs will be about the various products of the company. Each company correspondent and each typist then gets a book of the coded paragraphs, which may be typed manually or made into record rolls for use on an automatic typewriter.

When the letter writer starts to dictate, he may write a letter simply as 13, 27, 16, 42. That would mean a four-paragraph letter made up of those standard paragraphs in that order. If he finds no ready-made paragraph for what he wants to say in the second paragraph, he dictates 13, special, 16, 42, and follows with the wording for his special second paragraph. If the same point comes up frequently enough, the firm will prepare a good paragraph for it and put it into the correspondent's book.

Because the paragraphs are used over and over, they are carefully prepared and are therefore better than most correspondents would write quickly under the pressure of dictation. Obviously, the same advantage applies to an entire form letter.

And simple arithmetic shows you that even if you spend 30 to 50 hours on one letter, when you send it to a thousand people, dictation time and transcription time are only a fraction of the time individual letters would require. In a nutshell, this is the whole theory back of form letters. They have to be used to cut correspondence costs, to reduce the burdensome human aspects of the ever-increasing correspondence problems of management, and to expedite replies to people who want information as quickly as they can get it.

Certain dangers exist, however. The greatest is the tendency to use a form when it simply does not apply. When a person asks if Pepperdent has chlorophyll in it, he does not want the answer that "Pepperdent will make your smile brighter because of its new secret ingredient urium! Leading stars of stage and screen praise its refreshing cleansing effectiveness"—all of which may be true but has nothing to do with the inquiry. One good solution, if a form does not answer one specific question, is to add a postscript. If you cannot answer all questions by adding a little to an existing form, you need to write an individual letter.

Another danger is in broadcasting that the message is a form with such references as

To all our customers:

Whether you live in Maine or California. . . .

In a broadside (circular) such mass impersonality may be necessary. But in a letter the personal touch pays off. The wording of even a form letter, then, should give each reader the feeling that it applies to him. And remember that in every test ever made, the form letter that makes no pretense of being anything else (like the furniture letter on p. 133) results in more returns than the imperfectly disguised form, whether the slipup is due to poor mechanics or inept wording.

Still other dangers are in the use of form paragraphs. Unless one person prepares all the paragraphs, readers will notice stylistic differences. Unless the writer of the paragraphs is careful, he may make them too polished to sound natural in a letter. And even though the paragraphs pass on those two counts, if a poor writer has to write one special to go along with four of the good ones from the correspondence manual, his special may stand out like the proverbial sore thumb.

But form messages can help you do a correspondence job that would otherwise prove excessively burdensome.

The question of whether to use a form or not depends on the recurring nature of the problem, the degree of expediency necessitated—but most of all, on your own good judgment of whether it will do the particular job. Whether a letter is a form or an individualized letter is not the significant consideration; whether a letter does all it can do to cement goodwill and build sales is what counts.

The suggestions made about form letters in this chapter should help with any repetitive letter situation, whether it is one involving replies to inquiries, acknowledgments of orders, sales, credit, collections, or adjustments. So except for occasional incidental references pointing out the ease or wisdom of form treatment in a particular situation, the remainder of this book deals with individualized, personalized letters because

1. You can learn more about letter principles and their application that way.
2. As a result of such specific study and practice, you will write much better form letters when you need to.
3. In most circumstances calling for a letter, a personal letter will do a more effective job for you than a form.

SHORT NOTE REPLY

In an effort to expedite many day-to-day answers to inquiries (and reduce correspondence costs), many executives turn to the SNR. One leading copying-machine manufacturer in its advertising explains this way:

1. Just jot a personal note on the margin of the letter you received—no wasted time in dictation.
2. Insert the letter and a sheet of copy paper into a copying machine.
3. In just four seconds you have a Short Note Reply copy of the letter ready to mail back to the sender—plus the original for your files.

Certainly most readers will appreciate the thoughtfully fast answer. The practice seems to be gaining favor—rightly so, in our opinion. One question we raise, however: Why doesn't the sender mail the original with handwritten notes and keep the copy for his files (unless for contractual/legal reasons)?

ORDERS

Since 1963, the former huge business of buying and selling by mail has had a series of shots in the arm through repeated editions of a new book, *International Yellow Pages,* currently about 2,000 multilingual pages listing about 3,000 categories of products available in 136 countries from over half a million suppliers (full addresses given).

Buying and selling by mail never has been just through the big mail-order houses like Sears, Ward's, and Spiegel's, as many people seem to think. It has long included mail sales through large department stores like Macy's, Hudson's, and Field's; the national marketing of seasonal and regional produce like fruit, game, syrup, and candy; and farmers' orders for various supplies, machinery, and replacement parts.

Although the old standbys still account for the main volume of mail sales, today more than ever before you can sit at your desk and almost literally buy a variety of products in all the markets of the world; you can make the world your market. Unless you travel widely, not to use the mail is to build a fence of regionalism around yourself.

Furthermore, to overcome the disadvantage of buying without seeing, feeling, and trying the product, sellers by mail usually provide pictures and fuller, more reliable information than you can get from salesclerks about local goods; and they offer excellent guarantees and return privileges, and provide any necessary installation, operation, and service manuals.

Since sellers by mail usually provide well-designed order blanks and addressed envelopes with their catalogs, the only problems connected with writing an order appear when you do not have the blanks and must write a letter.

An order is probably the easiest kind of letter to write. You have no problem of getting attention or interest, and no conviction or persuasion is necessary in this A–plan letter. The reader is in business to sell goods. If you write clearly enough to let him know what you want and make satisfactory plans to pay for it, you'll get an answer. A poor order letter may, however, cause the reader some trouble and bring results different from what you really want.

As a considerate and efficient letter writer, you should write orders that will be easy for a clerk to fill and that will bring you just what you want. The basic requirements, as you can see from almost any order blank, are five (which will serve as a checklist for order letters):

1. Make them orders, not just hints. The acceptance of a definite offer to sell or an offer to buy is contractual. The usual beginning for an order is "Please send me. . . ."

2. Describe the goods completely. Although the catalog number alone usually identifies adequately except for color and size, give four or five clean-cut columns of information, preferably in this sequence:
   a) Quantity desired.
   b) Catalog number, if any.
   c) Name of product and as many details as are appropriate of model, color, size, material, grade or quality, pattern, finish, monogram initials.
   d) Unit price (sometimes not given as a separate column).
   e) Total price for the designated quantity of the item (column a times d).

   In the absence of a catalog, your information will likely go into two or three columns: quantity, name and description, and perhaps estimated total price. To supplement the inexact information, then, you may need to explain more fully by telling how the product is to be used, and in some cases by sending exact drawings.

   In ordering replacement parts for machines, be sure to give the name and model number of the machine and the name and number of the part. Frequently, you can find the number on the part itself if you have no parts list.

3. Write a separate, single-spaced paragraph for each item, with double spacing between paragraphs.

4. Make clear how you expect to pay. If you have not established credit but want goods charged, you should provide credit information with the order (see pp. 113 and 147).

   If you want neither credit nor c.o.d. shipment (which costs you more), several methods of remitting are open to you: personal check, money order (postal, express, or telegraph), certified or cashier's check, or bank draft.

Regardless of how you remit, you should refer to the remittance in the letter and tell its form, amount, and intended application.

5. Be sure the *where* of shipment is clear—and also the *when* and *how* unless you want to leave them to the seller.

The following typical order letter illustrates the five points:

Please send me the following items listed in your current spring and summer catalog:

1	60 C 6587L	Glass casting rod, Model 162, extra light action, 5 ft. 8 in.	$ 8.95
1	60 CP 6302	Pflueger Summit reel, Model 1993L ...	13.75
2	60 C 6846	Cortland "Cam-o-flage" nylon casting line, 10-lb. test, 100-yd. lengths @ $2.30	4.60
	Total	....	$27.30

The enclosed check for $29.63 covers the price, sales tax, and parcel post charges.

As I plan to go fishing a week from next Saturday (June 26), I will want the equipment by that time.

The following letter did a much more difficult job of ordering. Test it against the five requirements set up for a good order letter. Note how the writer made very clear just what he wanted without benefit of a catalog or parts list to give him the code numbers and prices of the items.

Please send me the following parts for Little Giant Shallow Well Water System P4/12818. Since I have no catalog, I am describing each part carefully.

1 Valve rubber, 1¼ inches in diameter with 5/16-inch hole. It is one of four that work under springs on the valve plate.

1 Crank pin. Apparently this is a steel pin of a highly special design. Its threaded end, 7/16 inch in diameter and 11/16 inch long, screws into the eccentric arm on the end of the drive shaft so that the rest of the pin forms the crankshaft. That is, the big end of the connecting rod fits around it. (See drawings on the attached sheet.) The crankshaft part of this pin is an eccentric ½ inch in diameter and 11/16 inch long.

1 Connecting rod, as shown on the attached sheet. Apparently it is brass or bronze. Please note the specifications as to size of hole. For other models, I know that the sizes are a little different.

I estimate that these parts will cost approximately $14. I am enclosing my check for $15 to cover all charges, including tax and parcel post. You can send me your regular refund check if the charges are less or send c.o.d. for the difference if they are more.

I'll appreciate your trying to fill the order promptly. My pump, much needed these days, is about to quit on me.

STANDARD ACKNOWLEDGMENTS

Poorly written orders cost their buyer-writers much delay in getting the desired goods, and they cost sellers lots of headaches and money (spent on letters required to get the needed information). But poor acknowledgments, for which the sellers are wholly responsible, cost them much more—in loss of goodwill and customers.

The acknowledgment letter should be an effective means of increasing goodwill and promoting business. A man who orders from you evidently has a favorable attitude toward your firm and its goods, or he wouldn't be ordering. That is a healthful climate for business. Your job is acknowledging his order is to keep it that way by giving him satisfaction.

He expects to get what he ordered, to get it promptly, and to have his business appreciated. If not, he expects a prompt and reasonable explanation. To give him less is to make a customer for somebody else.

Frequently a businessman who handles a large volume of orders, however, comes to look upon them as routine matters and to write his answers accordingly. In so doing, he forgets three things: (1) The individual customer usually sends comparatively few orders, and they are not at all routine to him; (2) a routine acknowledgment of them strikes him as indifference; and (3) indifference, according to a U.S. Department of Commerce survey, is responsible for at least 67 percent of lost customers.

Justifying reasons (strikes, impossibility of always estimating demand accurately, as well as incomplete orders from the buyer) may prevent a businessman from filling some orders promptly, or at all. But no reason justifies his not acknowledging the orders promptly, as the following fill-in form postcard reply from a large department store does.

Dear Customer:

Thank you for your letter ordering <u>a ladder</u>.

We're processing your order now, and you should receive the shipment promptly.

Though a form postcard can reflect a service attitude and thus help to retain goodwill, it cannot do all a letter can.

Least of all can a seller find any reason for not showing appreciation for orders, as in this card reply (underscored words are the fill-in—typed if you can, penned if you're swamped):

As you requested, <u>the turntable for Scrabble has been sent to Mrs. M. W. Colby</u>.

Thank you for calling on us. We try to make our service convenient. Order from us again when we can serve you.

There is scarcely any excuse, either, for the seller who does not do more than the minimum the customer ordinarily expects. A good businessman therefore usually makes even a small first order an opportunity to cement a lasting business relationship through a well-written acknowledgment letter.

The most important acknowledgment is the standard—acknowledging an order you can fill immediately. It is an easy letter to write.

Clearly the standard acknowledgment is a good-news letter. The beginning should be a direct answer to the biggest question in the reader's mind —what you are doing about his order. You tell immediately the *when* and *how* of shipment, preferably timed and worded to indicate that the goods are on the way. (And remember that you are sending goods, not an order, which is what he sent you.) The approximate arrival date is also desirable, not only as a convenience to the customer but also for the psychologically favorable effect of his visualizing himself actually receiving and using the goods.

In talking about the shipment, of course you need to identify what it includes, the charges, and (right there or later) the financial arrangements. The identification is by date and one or more of order number, exact relisting, or sometimes merely a general naming of the class of goods. When the list is long or the value great, you might best list them on an attached invoice or shipping list and refer to it in the letter. On small orders to customers who have established credit or sent the exact amount with the order, you may omit the financial arrangements because they are already clear to both parties.

If you are acknowledging the first order from a new customer, the acknowledgment will certainly include a hearty welcome and will stress resale and the forward look even more than a letter to an old customer. The welcome may be interwoven or implied in what you are doing about the order; but ordinarily it comes later, frequently combined with an expression of appreciation.

Whether new or old, the customer will probably like you better for expressing appreciation, perhaps even interwoven in the first paragraph. In most cases, however, you can demonstrate gratitude more effectively with statements of how you've handled the order, resale talk, and offers to be of service again.

The middle section of the standard acknowledgment is the place for the financial details not already completed, any resale talk of more than phrase length, and explicit evidence of service attitude. For instance in acknowledging dealers' orders, you often need to devote a paragraph to how you help the dealer to sell. You might talk about having your salesman set up window and counter displays. Perhaps you offer free mats (which the dealer can give his local newspaper for running ads with pictures of the products). You might provide free envelope stuffers (small promotional pamphlets about your products for the dealer to send to his good customers—usually at no extra cost because they are "stuffed" in the envelopes carrying monthly bills). Often you will want to talk about your radio, TV, and magazine ads that call customers' attention to your products and help the dealer sell more.

Encouragement to future ordering in a success-conscious forward look to the future (just preceded by any appropriate sales promotion material) is almost invariably the best ending for the standard acknowledgment.

Here's an example of how the parts go together for an effective personalized acknowledgment covering all points specifically:

> You should receive your eight cases of Tuff Paper towels in time for Friday afternoon shoppers; they were sent by prepaid express this morning.
>
> The $2.27 voucher attached to this letter is your change after we deducted $44.80 charges and $2.93 express from your $50 check.
>
> Thank you for your order. We're glad to serve you with this first shipment of paper products to you.
>
> You'll find that these Tuff Paper Towels have a fast turnover, Mr. Ford, because housewives like the way they soak up grease, dust off spots, and save cloth towels from many dirty jobs. And you'll like their attractive small packaging that takes up a minimum of display and shelf space. Your markup figures out at exactly 29 percent.
>
> For more information about Tuff Paper dishrags and window washers, colorful shelf paper your customers will like for their pantries, and other paper products every household needs, look in the enclosed booklet. Notice that each article carries the usual Tuff Paper margin of profit.
>
> Perhaps you'd like to take advantage of our regular terms of 2/10, n/60 on future orders. If so, we'll be glad to consider your credit application when you fill in and return the enclosed form. And when you order, if you want window and shelf displays to help you sell, just say so. Then watch Tuff Paper kitchen paper products bring Altoona women into your store for frequent repeat sales.

The trouble with this kind of acknowledgment is that it costs dollars, not cents. To be specific on all points, to adapt the message to an individual, and to make it persuasive require an average-length, individually dictated letter. But when the prospect of numerous future orders depends on the letter, the businessman would be foolish to do less. In some situations enough is involved to make him willing to spend even more to produce the most effective letter he can rather than risk an unfavorable reaction on the part of the customer to a quick brush-off or form reply.

The inability to recognize situations that deserve full treatment and the general inclination to save even a little time and money on correspondence frequently lead to trouble. Pinching pennies by dashing off personalized letters that are just a little too short to be adequate, or resorting to forms that don't do the job, is poor economy. The result is comparable to throwing out *almost* enough rope to reach a drowning man. If you are going to write a personalized letter, make it a good one. Its cost does not increase in proportion to length. A question you should always answer before cheapening your correspondence is whether you lose more in results, including goodwill, than you save on costs.

But in many cases a form card or letter serves admirably as an acknowledgment, as we illustrated in the discussion "Form Letters" (p. 133). The preceding Tuff Paper letter could be handled in a form message like this one (which, incidentally, *could* serve for acknowledging a repeat order):

You should receive the Tuff Paper products you ordered in just a few days; they are already on the way.

Thank you for your order. We are glad to serve you in this way.

You'll find that Tuff Paper products have a fast turnover; housewives like the way they can be used for many messy household cleaning jobs and then be disposed of quickly and easily.

You will like their attractive packaging that takes up a minimum of shelf and display space. And the sizable markup!

Read the enclosed booklet for more information about Tuff Paper dishrags, window washers, colorful shelf paper, and other paper products every household needs.

Use the handy order blank and business reply envelope in the back of the booklet when you want to order the additional Tuff Paper products your customers will be asking for.

(<u>Signature</u>)

If the situation is one in which specificness would add to the effectiveness of an acknowledgment, a fill-in rather than a strict form could serve. For instance, you could add a postscript of special material to the preceding letter. The letter writer will have to weigh the relative advantages and costs. Fill-ins can serve to make the essential information of the acknowledgment more specific, enhance the service attitude, and provide specific resale talk.

The use of forms in acknowledgments to customers whose orders you can fill may be summarized as follows:

1. Nothing else can quite replace the personalized letter for special, important business requiring full details, specific treatment, persuasion, adaptation, and evidence of personal attention.

2. But even very inexpensive forms (strict forms and fill-ins) may do the job adequately on numerous small orders where profits are low, where an obvious form will be excused, where not all kinds of acknowledgment content are required, and where generalities may suffice.

3. The more expensive forms are still much less expensive than personalized letters, and in the hands of a skillful user they have most of the advantages of the individually dictated letter, including the important points of *seeming* like one to each reader as he reads his copy.

Checklist for Standard Acknowledgment

1. Of greatest interest to the reader is the complete, accurate shipment.
   a) Emphasize the good news by sending the goods in the first sentence, preferably also indicating arrival.
   b) Clearly identify the order by one or more of date, number, reference to the goods by name—perhaps a complete listing.
   c) If you list, tabulate—in the letter if short; on a referred-to invoice or shipping list if long.
   d) Clear up any confusion about payment details.
   e) Consider whether method of shipment should be identified.
   f) Appreciation (and a welcome to a new customer) may come early in the letter but probably will fit better near the end—if not adequately implied.

2. Resale is part of acknowledgments to reassure the reader.
   a) Make it specific.
   b) Keep it short.
   c) Adapt it to your product and reader (consumer versus dealer).

3. Service attitude, especially important to new customers, may help with others.
   a) For a consumer: personal shopping, delivery schedules, and credit possibilities.
   b) For a dealer: salesmen, manuals, displays, and advertising aids and programs (mats, envelope stuffers, etc.)
   c) If you talk advertising programs, give the names of publications and radio or TV stations, amount of space or time, and schedules; and emphasize how the advertising promotes sales: "Your customers will be asking for . . . because of the full-page ads running. . . ."
   d) If you talk credit, invite application without promising approval.

4. Sales promotion material can indicate service attitude and build sales.
   a) Keep it appropriate—usually on seasonal or allied goods.
   b) You-attitude and specificness are necessary in sales promotion.
   c) Emphasize your service to the customer—how the suggested product might help him—not your selfish desire to sell more, as implied by "Our product . . . ," "We also make . . . ," or "We'd also like to sell you. . . ."
   d) Emphasize reader action when referring to enclosures.

5. Look forward to future orders.
   a) If sales promotion is the basis, suggest specific, easy action.
   b) If resale talk is the basis, continue in terms of reader satisfaction rather than suggest that something will go wrong.
   c) Guard against bromides and Greedy Gus wording as you close.

The man writing acknowledgments should study his situation and make the wise choice of (*a*) whether to use forms; and (*b*) if so, which kind. He can be foolish either way. Economy dictates that he choose the cheapest that will do the job, but probably the poorest economy of all is to send a form when the situation justifies a carefully prepared personal letter.

CREDIT APPROVALS

In Latin, *credo* means "I believe." Woven firmly into the meaning of the English word *credit* are the basic ideas of trust, faith, honor, and integrity. Hence, in naming what is commonly called the three *C's* of credit—the bases for evaluating credit applicants—credit men name character first, followed by capacity and capital (some credit men add a fourth *C*, conditions).

Character is honesty. It is one's good word. In business it is living up to the spirit as well as the letter of the contract. And creditwise, it is meeting obligations as one promises to do.

Capacity is the ability to produce or to earn and thus furnish the means for payment. For a business firm it is the present or potential profit from a business operation such as manufacturing or marketing; for an individual it is usually wages, salary, fees, or commissions.

Capital is the money behind the debtor. It may be cash, of course; but it is also other assets in the form of land, buildings, securities, patents, and copyrights, to mention the more common forms. It could as a last resort furnish the money for payment in the event of reversals.

Conditions (plural) has two parts. One is general business trends. The other is special or local conditions or the trends of the debtor's business as shown in his comparative financial statements.

Because all these four *C's*—especially the first two—are reflections of personal qualities of an individual, credit letters are surcharged with negative possibilities. When you question a man's honesty, earning ability, or judgment, you are treading on potentially dangerous ground. Credit letters can be one of a firm's greatest means of killing off the goodwill the sales, advertising, and even adjustment departments work to build up. With tact, patience, and a positive attitude, however, your credit letters can be goodwill builders.

One of the fundamental concepts that will help you to write successful letters about credit is this: The credit privilege is *earned;* it is not handed out indiscriminately, given away—or sold. For that reason your letters should not talk about *granting* credit; more appropriate terminology is *approval* or *extension* of credit.

On one or more of the four *C's* an individual or firm merits credit. For many people, character is the primary reason they enjoy credit. They earn little, and they have little or no capital, but they pay their bills and thus earn the right to credit. And this is the bedrock of credit extension. Firms or individuals may enjoy high earnings but will not continue to enjoy ordinary credit privileges with a record of not taking care of obligations as promised (although they will be accorded more leniency by most firms than the debtor of low earning power). Most customers in a good capital position rate high on both capacity and character. Certainly this statement is true with respect to business firms (they are usually the discounters). An occasional individual in a favorable capital position may have no earning power and may let bills accumulate, but he does not continue in such lackadaisical fashion very long; the ax inevitably falls.

Anticipating those who may be unable or unwilling to pay is one of the primary functions of the credit manager. He evaluates applicants' credit records and estimates their financial stability in the light of general business ups and downs. He does the same for customers already on the books. Periodically, he reviews accounts (and for business firms, financial statements) for danger signals. He must be on his toes to hold down losses from bad debts.

But if he approves only gilt-edged accounts, he will seriously curtail sales. His job is to contribute to the profits of his firm, not just to conserve them. Accordingly, he must be sales-minded. He needs to be well informed about the firm's goods as a means of making his letters build customer confidence and increase sales. But even more significant, he must realize that marginal risks are vital for profitable operations and that he must give a great part of his time to evaluating and encouraging borderline cases. For his firm and his customers he is part counselor, part salesman, and part detective. To play these many roles, he must keep well informed.

An efficient credit man need not want for information about his customers. He has many sources available to him.

The customer himself is a source. Most Americans are fairly well credit-educated and expect to give evidence of credit responsibility. A consumer applying for credit is usually willing to supply information about his means of livelihood, names of firms with which he has done business on credit, the name of his bank, whether he owns real estate, and his approximate annual income. Most business firms, in seeking credit, furnish financial statements and references, many of them unsolicited (and they keep right on furnishing those statements year after year). If for any reason the customer does not furnish all the information desired—or if you want to verify what the customer has stated—you have several reliable ways of finding out.

Other business firms with which the applicant has done credit business expect to furnish details of their experience when asked—but (for legal reasons) *only* when asked by somebody *with an interest to protect*. Banks supply information about both individuals and businesses. Local and national credit bureaus (such as the National Retail Credit Men's Association and the National Association of Credit Men) maintain files on concerns and individuals with whom their members have done credit business, and this information is available (on request) to any member. Credit-rating agencies (like Dun & Bradstreet) publish volumes containing credit reports on business firms; if a firm isn't listed and you are a subscriber to its service, it will furnish a special report. Your salesman can help to fill in the picture. And a trade association in many instances can give you pertinent information.

When the information you receive is favorable, you will of course approve the application and set up the account.

Certainly the extension of credit calls for a good-news A–plan message! The customer is pleased at the confirmation of his good standing and at the prospect of being served by a good business firm. And the members of the firm are happy to add another good name to the list of customers.

The one invariable essential function of such a message is that it must confirm the new credit relationship. Although some credit approvals are oral (in the case of firms of national repute and sound capital structure a credit-approving letter is not written because the credit standing of the firm is assumed), in most cases some written message notifies the customer.

Because of the sheer weight of numbers, most credit approvals are form messages, especially when no purchase (and shipment) of goods is involved. Many stores do no more than send a printed announcement card like the following:

THE J. P. BOWEN COMPANY

Is pleased to open a charge
account for you and welcome you to
our family of regular patrons

We hope you will make regular use
of your charge account

Such a notification sent promptly is certainly better than nothing. Yet it falls far short of what a good credit letter can do to strengthen the credit relationship, promote goodwill, forestall collection problems, and stimulate sales.

Establishing the basis for credit

In credit approvals you may, as an effective credit device, take advantage of the simple, obvious psychology of praise or approval. If you place a customer on the credit list because of a prompt-pay rating, you should tell him so; having been told, he is more likely to strive to maintain that rating. The same is true for some reflections of favorable capacity or capital positions.

The reference should not be lengthy; in fact, it is preferably absorbed subordinately in the extension of credit or the explanation of terms. It is a significant reminder to the customer that credit is an earned privilege for which he must exert care, thought, and effort if it is to be maintained. Too, thus established, it may serve as an effective collection appeal to the customer if the account begins to get slow.

So forceful is this device in the opinion of one experienced credit manager that his letter to credit applicants with prompt-pay records is only one sentence:

```
We have received from your references the reports of your fine
pay habits and shall be very happy to have a regular monthly
charge account with you.
```

Obviously, this letter should accomplish more than it does. But it is a good example of the significance of the credit basis.

Here are two other examples of how you can establish the basis:

```
Your excellent credit record in Joplin establishes you as a
preferred charge customer at Allen Tilby's.  The charge
identification plate enclosed will make available to you a
wealth of quality merchandise gathered from the four corners
of the world.
                              --
Because of your good credit standing, earned by your personal
honesty and the sizable amount of property you own, we have
placed your name on our list of regular credit customers.
```

Form letters can—and do—through careful wording, employ the strategy; the one-sentence letter to prompt-pay accounts is a good example. You can phrase the credit extension and the basis in broad enough fashion to cover a large number of cases.

Explanation of terms

Unless a firm wants to encourage delayed payments, the initial extension of credit should make unmistakably clear how payments are expected, with the confident assumption that the customer will comply with the terms. Even a form card or letter can easily incorporate a simple statement like one of the following:

```
On the first of each month you will receive an itemized
statement of your purchases made through the 25th day of the
preceding month; purchases made after the 25th appear on the
following month's bill.  Your payment is expected by the 10th.
                              --
Under our system of cycle billing your statement of a month's
purchases will be mailed to you on the 17th of each month;
settlement is expected within 10 days.
```

(Under cycle billing, bills are prepared and mailed at various intervals throughout the month: names beginning with *A*, on the 1st; with *B*, on the 2d; with *M*, on the 16th and 17th, etc. It is a simple matter to match names and dates in form mailings.)

In special letters the clear, specific explanation of the terms not only can prevent misunderstanding and delay but can also serve as a stimulus to prompt pay. How far to go depends on the reader's credit knowledge and class. If you think he knows and respects credit practices, you would only tell what the terms are; explaining that 2/10, n/30 means he may deduct 2 percent if he pays in 10 days or pay the whole in 30 days would insult such a reader. To a reader who is new to credit business or just barely passes your credit evaluation, however, you had better make the terms not only clear and emphatic but concrete (i.e., show him the prompt-pay benefits as savings in money, what it will buy, and the continued credit privilege):

> Under our regular credit terms of 2/10, n/30, you can save
> $1.36 on this order alone if your check is in the mail by
> July 10—which will almost pay for another enamel display
> tray. Your check for the net of $68 by July 30, however, will
> keep you in the preferred-customer class.

Such specificness is not possible, of course, except in an individually written letter or special paragraph. But the credit extension, whenever possible, should be an individual letter; it is worth the extra money in its salutary effect on the customer.

To stop with the approval, the basis, and the terms would be foolish, however; a good credit man can also help to further sales—through resale material on goods, resale on the house, or sales-promotion material on other allied goods. All should focus on repeat sales.

Stimulating sales

In credit approvals, sales-building passages should definitely be low pressure; if the service attitude does not dominate, the greedy overtones can repel the reader. But the writer of the following letter, you will note, is careful to tie in a service-to-you reference to all his sales-building passages and thus make the customer feel welcome rather than pounced upon:

> Your excellent credit record in Joplin establishes you as a
> preferred charge customer at Allen Tilby's.
>
> The charge identification plate endorsed will make available
> to you a wealth of quality merchandise gathered from the four
> corners of the world.
>
> On the first of each month you will receive an itemized
> statement of your purchases made through the 25th day of the
> preceding month; purchases made after the 25th appear on the
> following month's bill. You'll be prompt in paying your
> account on time, we know, for our terms—payment in full by
> the 10th—are the same as the terms of the stores with which
> you've been trading in Joplin.
>
> You'll find that our merchandise is just as close as your
> telephone when you haven't time for shopping. Ask for Paula
> Penn, our personal shopper, who will be glad to assist you.
> We'll have your purchases at your door by 5 o'clock if you
> order no later than noon.

When you come down to Allen Tilby's, you'll find hundreds of
sales personnel eager to help you find exactly the things you
want. For all-day shopping or just for a delightful downtown
luncheon you may enjoy the Oval Room on the eighth floor. The
spacious parking lot just across the street is available to
you when you shop at Allen Tilby's.

Since you have just moved to a new home, you may be especially
interested in the Home Furnishings Sale, which will extend
through next week. Whatever you need, come in soon and let us
serve you.

The same considerations enable you to write good credit approvals to
dealers. Two minor differences exist in circumstances (but not as far as
writing principles are concerned): One is terms (discounts, datings, and
number of days allowed); the other is the identification of the credit limit.
Few letters to consumers ever identify a limit (although one may go on
the office record); most mercantile credit arrangements include limits as
part of the explanation of terms.

To prevent—as much as possible—the limit from appearing to be a
penalty, with consequent negative reactions by the customer, a good
writer phrases it in positive language, as (underscored) in the following:

The No-Flame you ordered

    20 gallons @ $6 ....$120

was shipped to you freight prepaid this morning by the L & M
Railroad; it should arrive in Jackson by the weekend. The
amount of this shipment has been debited to your newly opened
account, which we are glad to open on the basis of your strong
personal capital.

Under our regular terms of 2/10, n/60, your No-Flame will cost
you only $117.60 if you send your check by May 2; the full $120
is due on June 21. In any one 60-day period you may purchase
as much as $250 worth of No-Flame or other Bronson products.

With the increasing demand for No-Flame you will find it a
rapid seller—and a good profit item at the usual markup of $3
a can. With your shipment you will receive attractive window
displays which our other dealers have found helpful.

Silentol, a flame-resistant, sound-decreasing plaster, is
another item your home-building customers will like. The cost
is only a fraction more than for conventional plaster. For a
trial shipment, just fill out the enclosed order blank and
drop it in the mail; we'll send your Silentol to you—along
with display material—within a few days.

Making the customer welcome

Much is said and written in credit circles about making the customer
feel appreciated. Indeed, the opening welcoming the customer to the
"growing number of satisfied customers" or to the "X, X, & Y family" is
standard with so many credit writers that it is stereotyped. The customer
is more interested in finding out the decision on his application than he

Credit Approval Checklist

1. The direct opening:
   a) When you are shipping goods, say so in the first line.
   b) Shipping the goods first also implies credit approval.
   c) Inject a cheerful, welcoming, ungrudging tone in approving credit, neither condescending nor preachy.
   d) Name the goods specifically (don't call it "order"!); state the amount (of goods and dollars, or send an invoice).
   e) In general, you'd better identify the method of shipment.
   f) Choose words that get the goods to the reader; don't stop with just getting them onto a freight car.
   g) A touch of resale (say a favorable adjective) is desirable early.
   h) But don't slow up your opening with much resale/goodwill.
   i) Use figures and symbols in order and acknowledgment letters.
   j) Take care of all legal details: item prices, freight charges, total. You may assume an invoice or tabulate here.

2. The credit agreement/relation:
   a) For restraint, explain how the customer earned this credit.
   b) Although you might identify terms incidentally in the opening, later (for people who might not understand or respect them properly) you'd explain by
      1) Attaching your interpretation of the terms to the purchase.
      2) Concretizing the discount with specific savings figures (maybe a free unit of the purchase, a month's phone bill . . .).
      3) Bringing in prompt-pay education, in a tone that implies your confidence that the reader will comply.
   c) With its negative potentialities, any credit-limit talk needs a you-viewpoint introduction and positive statement. You might want to label it temporary.
   d) But you don't want to imply "If you don't like these terms, we'll change them."

3. Your resale or sales promotion material in closing the letter:
   a) Include comments that reassure the reader of his good choice.
   b) Mention store services and selling aids concretely.
   c) Consider selling the reader some allied or seasonal goods.
   d) Regardless of how you close, let it point to future orders.
   e) Be specific, not wooden and dull, as in "We have enjoyed serving you and look forward to supplying your future needs."

4. Your appreciation is best worked in incidentally, subordinately.

5. Transitions are easier with a logical order of points.

6. Watch the tone throughout the letter.
   a) Avoid FBI implications about the credit investigation and condescending, mandatory, or selfish explanation of terms.
   b) Proportion affects your tone too; don't talk terms too much.

is in such welcomes or in any of the writer's personal (especially if selfish) expressions of happiness at adding another name to his list. If you approve the credit (implied by sending the goods immediately when the application accompanies an order), establish the basis, explain the terms positively, and then follow with resale and sales promotion material concretely implying the desire to be of service, your reader will not be in doubt over whether you're glad to have his business. By implication you adequately establish such welcomes and thank-you's.

If, despite these suggestions and illustrations, you feel the necessity for either of these expressions, place it near the end of your letter.

The checklist (p. 152) summarizes our major suggestions about credit approvals, although, as always, you should apply them with discretion. We *know* they don't apply in all cases.

SIMPLE CLAIMS AND ADJUSTMENT APPROVALS
[When things go wrong, see that you don't go with them.]

Claims offer you as a buyer the opportunity to get adjustments on unsatisfactory goods and services you have bought. If you are a seller and therefore the receiver of claims, you welcome them! They offer you an opportunity to discover and analyze defects in your goods and services as a basis for correcting them. And your adjustment letters are excellent opportunities for you to build or destroy goodwill. Whether you make the most of your opportunities in either claims or adjustments depends heavily on your attitude.

Any claim and adjustment situation necessarily involves negatives. Somebody is dissatisfied and unhappy. One of the major jobs in writing either claim or adjustment letters is to keep these emotionally based negatives from stealing the show and making the situation worse. What you have learned about goodwill, resale, and handling of negative material is especially important in adjustment letters.

Direct claims

You will probably write good claim letters if you remember these often-forgotten points (which serve as a checklist for direct claims):

1. *Progressive firms like claims, instead of disliking them, because they suggest ways of improvement. So if you think you have a just claim, go ahead.*

Many firms even advertise the request: "If you like our products, tell others; if you don't, tell us." Often they encourage claims by "double-your-money-back" guarantees and the like. For example, one manufacturer of lingerie made such an offer in full-page advertisements in national magazines. The conditions were that the products be worn, washed, and returned with an explanation of any dissatisfaction. The company hoped to get some constructive criticism whereby it could improve its products.

2. *When things go wrong, the firm surely did not intend to mistreat the customer. Almost certainly the reader of the claim letter had nothing to do with the dissatisfaction. So keep your shirt on!*

Very few manufacturers expect every item they manufacture to be perfect. They know that even after careful checking some defects may sometimes show up. Nearly always they expect to replace or repair defective merchandise which is returned. This is a more efficient system than to insist on perfection in manufacturing and consequently higher prices. The consumer who gets defective merchandise and takes the attitude that the seller tried to take advantage of him, then, is usually wrong in his attitude. In most cases, to get satisfaction, all he has to do is to make a simple claim such as the following:

> When the set of Syracuse dinner dishes I ordered from you on November 1 arrived the day before Thanksgiving, I found that one of the coffee cups was cracked and one of the dinner plates had a defective design.
>
> The excelsior around the cup was thin—evidently too thin to protect the cup from jars in transit.
>
> I am returning the two imperfect pieces by express. Will you please replace them to complete my set?

Even though a product is defective, almost certainly the fellow who reads your claim letter probably didn't make it, check it, or sell it to you. To be nasty to him is to be quite unfair and unreasonable, even foolish. Instead of putting him in a favorable mood so that he will be inclined to help you get satisfaction, you turn this possible ally against you if you write a nasty letter.

3. *When you know just what is wrong and what is required to set things right, you should make a definite claim; otherwise, explain and ask for an inspection.*

Sometimes you can be sure that the only fair adjustment is a refund of your money or a complete replacement of the product. On other occasions you can see that replacement of a part or proper adjustment of a machine will correct the trouble. You therefore ask definitely for what is necessary to make things right, as in the preceding letter.

Sometimes, however, the product just isn't right, but you don't know exactly what is wrong. Your claim then should be an explanation of how the product is failing to satisfy you and a request for the necessary action. You can make your own estimate and request that action (as in the illustration on p. 156), call in third parties to estimate (as on automobile insurance claims, like that on p. 157), or ask the firm to investigate and take the indicated action. Here are two examples:

> I think you will be interested in my experience with XXX outside white house paint used on my house this past summer.
>
> A union painter applied three coats according to directions on the can. About three months later black streaks began to appear where water runs from the eaves and valleys.

At first I thought the discoloration was from the green roof paint or the stain of the cedar shingles, but the same thing appears on the garage, which has an unpainted tin roof.

Various theories have been advanced concerning the smutty streaks. Some friends have suggested mildew, but my common sense says no. Some have suggested dirt, but it will not wash off. A chemist friend says that the sulfur in the atmosphere here may combine with the lead of the paint to make a sulfur-lead compound that is a smoky color.

So you see that I don't know what the cause is. But if your paint didn't hold its color, I'm sure that you are interested in knowing why. And I feel sure that if you find your product at fault, you will want to grant me an adjustment.

Will you please investigate and let me know your decision?

--

The Dexter fluorescent desk lamp I purchased at your store October 5 has been satisfactory in every way but one.

When in use, the lamp operates coolly and soundlessly; but as soon as the lamp is switched off, something inside produces a humming sound. Not only is the hum annoying, but I fear that it suggests a fire hazard.

I'm returning the lamp to you for repair or replacement, whichever you find necessary.

Since I've lots of reading to do, will you please rush it back to me?

4. *Sometimes a touch of humor can relieve the pressure in small claims.* Somewhat like the nasty tone (Point 2), another common error in writing claim letters is the writer's becoming deadly serious about small matters. A claim for replacement of a defective $3 item makes the writer look silly when written as if it were a matter of life and death. If the situation is really serious, of course, you would not want to treat it lightly. But to avoid the too-serious tone in small matters and make the reader an ally instead of a critic, you can often use humor effectively. You may inject only a touch or two in the letter, or the whole thing may be humorous.

Several dangers confront you if you decide to be humorous:

1. A failing attempt to be funny is worse than no attempt.
2. Humor may make you write a longer letter than necessary.
3. Humor at the reader's expense will nearly always be resented.
4. Humor which verges on the vulgar or sacrilegious may offend.

The following successful letter, which was wrapped around the returned fountain pen, avoids at least the last two dangers:

GENTLEMEN: ATTENTION THE DOCTOR OF THE PEN HOSPITAL

This faithful old "lifetime" has served me well through 10 years. But now, like an old man or an old horse, it needs rejuvenation—perhaps monkey glands.

Here's my diagnosis:

1. The threads are stripped, causing the barrel and cap to part company in my pocket. You know what that means!

2. At times gobs of ink come out.

3. Even though I like a point a little finer and more flexible than this one ever was, it seems to be getting blunter and stiffer.

I know what your lifetime guarantee is; so I'm looking forward to receiving a rejuvenated pen ready for 10 more years of service.

Usually a firm will grant an adjustment merely on the strength of a customer's explanation of what is wrong and what he considers a fair settlement. In that case you would make yourself ridiculous by misjudging the situation and writing a too-strong claim. Unless you have good reason to believe otherwise, you should therefore assume that the firm will be cooperative. Your letter should simply explain the specific facts and state your claim. Little or no persuasion is presumed to be necessary; hence you use no appeal beyond brief reference to a guarantee, reputation for fair dealing, and the like.

This kind of direct claim (A–plan) may start with the requested action, or it may start with the date and conditions of purchase. Beginning with the history of the case is a little less antagonizing and a little more persuasive. The middle part is a carefully planned, complete, and specific explanation of the facts. A test of the adequacy of the explanation is to ask whether it is all you would want to know if you had to decide on the claim. The ending, then, is a request for action. It should be as specific as the conditions will permit (Point 3, p. 154). Here are two examples:

I'm sure you will want to know that the Etherwave console model radio I purchased from you on June 5 is not giving the desired performance.

I was well pleased for the first two weeks; but now I am getting some interference, and the tuning knob seems to slip. At least turning it does not change the tuning after the machine is warmed up.

Since I know very little about a radio, I asked a friend to look it over. He thinks that the condenser plates are somewhat loose and have shaken out of tram and a small belt in the tuning mechanism has come loose.

I feel that since this radio is only a month old and is also fully guaranteed, you will agree with me that your firm should take care of the necessary adjustments to insure perfect performance again.

Only one local radio shop has the necessary equipment for tramming radio plates, and the charges are $7.50. However, this shop has no belt to fit my radio.

I see two possibilities for action. One is that I send the radio to you for repair. The other is that you send the correct belt to my local shop (XL Radio Shop, 122 East Washington) and pay the cost of installing the belt as well as the $7.50 for tramming the plates.

I shall appreciate your prompt reply, as I am especially
interested in good radio reception during the baseball season.

--

Gentlemen:

CLAIM FOR DAMAGES DONE TO MY CAR BY YOUR CLIENT
(Mr. K. C. Hall, Gary, Indiana—License CG 3035)

On June 9, about 15 or 20 miles west of Decatur, Illinois, on
Highway 48, I was driving 55–60 m.p.h., and I overtook a car
going about 35. When I was almost even with this car, passing
it, something bumped my car hard on the left rear fender and
door, shoving me hard to the right and damaging my car.

The something that hit my car (a new four-door XXXX, Illinois
license 885–009) was a late-model green XXXXXXXX driven by
your client, Mr. Hall. I estimated that he was driving at
least 70, for he whisked on by me before stopping, just as I
went on around the car I had overtaken.

Inspection revealed that his car was damaged on the back part
of the right front fender and on the right front door, mine on
the left rear fender and door.

Certainly the accident was no fault of mine, for I was driving
in an entirely normal and legal manner. Good judgment on his
part would have told him that I was going to pass the car
ahead, since I was overtaking it at an estimated difference of
20 m.p.h. Thus he should have checked his speed and waited.

He probably blew his horn, as he said he did, but I could not
hear it because a diesel train on a nearby parallel track was
blowing very loudly. He probably realized that I did not hear
when I continued to pull left to pass, but he was driving too
fast to control his car.

Since I consider him completely responsible for the accident
and damages, I hereby make claim for repairs to my car, as
listed on any one of the three enclosed estimates.

Adjustment approvals

Adjustment policies. Invariably a claim represents loss of goodwill
and of confidence in the goods or in the firm. The adjustment writer's key
job is to minimize those losses by satisfying customers as far as possible at
a reasonable cost to the company.

Some companies try to dodge the basic problem by almost literally
adopting the policy that the customer is always right (the *caveat venditor*
philosophy). They figure that the few unfair claims cost less in adjustment
losses than the liberal policy pays in goodwill.

Other firms take the opposite view (*caveat emptor*) and make all
sales final. Usually they depend on low prices rather than goodwill to
attract a type of customer to whom price is the strongest possible appeal.

The great majority take the middle ground between those two extremes: *Treat each claim on its merits, and lean a bit toward giving the
customer the benefit of the doubt for the sake of unquestioned fairness and
the resulting goodwill.*

This seems to be the most ethical and the most satisfactory policy to most people. Generally a customer will not leave a firm or product after only one disappointment if the firm applies this honest and reasonable policy with finesse. Usually a reasonable person will allow at least a second chance, unless the adjuster loses further goodwill by his attitude toward the claim or by his bungling techniques in handling it.

Carrying out the recommended policy therefore requires

1. Careful analysis and classification of each claim according to the cause of dissatisfaction and consequently what adjustment is fair.
2. Retaining a reasonable attitude even with testy claimants.
3. Skill in the use of the tools and techniques of adjustment.

Analysis and classification of adjustments. If the evidence in a claim (and from inspection when deemed necessary) shows clearly that the company or the product was at fault, you may replace the article free with a perfect one, repair it free, or take it back and refund the money.

The last is the least desirable for both buyer and seller. He bought the article for the service he thought it would render; if you take it back, he has to make other arrangements or do without that service. If you replace or repair it, you give him the service, regain his goodwill, and make him a satisfied customer who will perhaps buy from you again and pass on the good word about you and your products to other prospects. Indeed, about the only occasion when you would refund the money is when you see that a perfect specimen of the article will not do the job for him. And even then, if you have another (perhaps larger or of better quality) which you think will satisfy, you should try to give him the service he wanted and justify any higher price in terms of advantages.

If responsibility for the dissatisfaction is clearly the buyer's, you will ordinarily refuse the claim. In rare cases you may decide that a compromise or even a full-reparation adjustment will be the wise thing because of the amount of goodwill you can regain at small cost. The weakness in this decision is that it implies your acceptance of responsibility and increases your difficulty in regaining confidence in your goods and service.

Whatever your action, your major job is justifying your decision and usually (if he is at fault) educating the customer. By writing your letter as education to the buyer in the proper use and care of the product (perhaps regular oiling), you may establish the responsibility by implication, avoid irritating the claimant, and prevent future trouble.

If responsibility for the dissatisfaction is uncertain or divided between buyer and product, you will suggest a compromise or make a full adjustment. Again the educational function of the letter is usually important.

When you approve the adjustment, the discussion of favorable replies to inquiries and requests prepares you rather well to write full-reparation adjustment letters, which are in fact answers to requests (claims). They are essentially the same in organization and psychology, but with some

basic differences. In answering requests you have no legal or moral obligation to do anything against your will; in answering claims, you have a legal
and moral obligation to be fair.

Attitude of the adjuster. If a firm's adjuster looks on claims as largely
the unfair requests of dishonest people or chronic gripers, in time he may
reduce the number of claims. People will refrain from making many
claims to such a firm—if they don't stop buying there—because they do
not like to be considered either dishonest or unreasonable.

Most of them aren't, anyway. Out of 5 million customers on the list of a
big mail-order firm, only 2,712, or one twentieth of 1 percent, tried to take
advantage of the firm in five years. So the adjustment man who looks on
everybody who makes a claim as a person trying to take advantage is
wrong in fact and wrong in attitude.

Such an attitude not only drives away customers and claims, but it also
logically prevents the adjuster from making wise use of the claims he
does receive. A wise business firm keeps records of claims for statistical
analysis, to show weaknesses in its products, methods, services, and
personnel. But if the adjuster considers most claims dishonest, he could not
logically use them as a basis for making changes.

If, on the other hand, you start with the attitude that a claimant may
be misinformed but is honest and reasonable, you will be right much more
frequently, and you will do much better. You will use all claims as pointers
to improvements in the firm's goods and operations, and your adjustment
letters will show appreciation for the help the customer has given. (Even
those claims where the buyer is completely at fault point to a need for
better instructions to users.) But more important, you create a much more
pleasant situation in which people buy more freely because they know that
they can get reasonable adjustments if anything goes wrong.

In addition to this sound attitude, you need a thick skin to be an
adjuster. Many claimants will not have learned to remain calm. As a wise
adjuster, therefore, you will make it a part of your attitude to ignore personal taunts. There is the old saying, "You can't win an argument with a
customer; even when you win, you lose." So you defend yourself, your
firm, and your products insofar as you can by explanations; otherwise, you
accept the claims made. Thus you create a climate of goodwill and good
business.

A claim represents customer dissatisfaction all right, but it does not
necessarily involve really strong negatives which you cannot almost completely overcome with your fair-minded attitude and skillful use of the
adjuster's tools and techniques.

Adjustment tools and techniques. Using resale. Since the adjustment writer's main job is to regain goodwill and confidence, you will
find resale a highly useful tool. Probably nowhere else in letter writing is it
more important. Indeed, the main job of an adjustment man is essentially
the same as the purpose of resale—to recover or strengthen goodwill and

confidence in the integrity and efficiency of a firm and/or the quality of its goods. Naturally, then, resale is the main tool for doing that job.

Making positive explanations. Effective resale is impossible, however, unless you avoid the following special pitfalls which frequently trap the untrained adjustment letter writer:

1. Inadequate or inept explanation that leaves the reader thinking slipshod methods of manufacturing or marketing caused the trouble. Explain how careful you really are.
2. Dwelling on the reader's dissatisfaction or the likelihood of his being a lost customer.
3. Passing the buck by attributing the difficulty to a new clerk or an act of God.
4. Trying to hide in the bigness of your firm. About the only way you can use bigness as an acceptable explanation is to sell it in terms of reader benefits along with its weakness.
5. Stressing your openhandedness. The reader does not want to be considered a beggar, given things he doesn't deserve.
6. Suggesting future trouble. You only put undesirable ideas into the customer's head if you say, "If you have any more difficulty, let us know," or even "I don't believe you'll have any more difficulty." In fact, a big problem in adjustments is what to do about the inherent negative in them.

Handling inherent negatives. As an adjustment writer, you therefore need to be a master of the techniques for dealing with negatives. They will be one of your stumbling blocks, for every adjustment situation is full of them. You'll do well to remember the letter writer's definition of *negative* as anything unpleasant to the reader. Moreover, you should remember that a letter writer avoids negative material when he can and subordinates it when he can't. You'll find that you can usually avoid most of the goodwill killers like the following, which creep into the letters of untrained adjustment writers:

you claim	policy	damaged	delay
you say	amazed	broken	inconvenience
you state	fault	defective	regret
you (plus any accusing verb)	surprised	unable	sorry

Such wording need not appear. Prune out the negative wording (and implications). Substitute positive phrasing.

Letters approving the adjustment. When you decide to approve an adjustment, you have an easy letter to write. Since it is a good-news letter (A–plan), you answer the reader's big question in the first sentence as fast as you can.

Not only should this sentence tell him that you are approving the adjustment, but it should also be worded carefully to avoid any grudging tone and to refrain from recalling the dissatisfaction any more than necessary.

You might almost as well not approve the adjustment, insofar as goodwill is concerned, as do so in a grudging tone. And of course, reminding him of his trouble by using negative words would hurt rather than help.

The fact that you have approved the adjustment gives you a natural basis for some resale talk on the house. You should use it by interpreting the facts as evidence that you stand behind guarantees and treat the customer right, or something similar.

Somewhere in the letter, but not necessarily right after the good news and its interpretation, you should express appreciation for the claimant's calling your attention to the situation (because the information helps the firm to keep goods and services up to par). This thank you does several important things quickly: (1) It shows the reader that you are fair-minded and do not take a distrusting or bitter attitude toward claims. (2) It is basically resale in showing that you are interested in retaining (if not improving) your standards for goods and services. (3) It makes the customer feel good because his claim seems welcome and appears to get careful consideration.

Of course, if you are taking any steps to prevent recurrence of claims such as you are answering, you should explain them (to rebuild confidence) and give the customer as much credit as the facts allow. It sounds good to almost any reader to hear that "On the basis of helpful suggestions like yours, we have decided . . . ."

The biggest part of your letter will be an explanation of the situation. If the product was obviously defective or the firm was at fault in some way, for no good reason or explanation that will put either in a better light, you'd better accept the fact and frankly admit the error or defect rather than make excuses. If you explain specifically how your firm tries to see that everything goes well, most readers will accept it as due precaution and will understand that mistakes do occasionally creep in, despite reasonable care. If you have statistics to show how effective your system is in avoiding mistakes and defective goods, they may be effective in rebuilding the customer's confidence and goodwill. You want to be careful, though, not to present such data in a way that seems to tell the reader he must be odd to have trouble when nearly all your other customers don't.

Although you can't honestly or safely promise that it will never happen again, you can end pleasantly. Having covered the good news, the explanation, the thanks, and any necessary action of the reader, you can end looking forward, not backward. Apologies or other reminders of past dissatisfaction merely leave a bad taste in the reader's mouth. A light touch of resale—or even sales promotion material, if you have a related article you think would serve him well—can boost his spirit and provide you with a sincere, success-conscious look forward to future business. The customers so well treated will probably return.

The following letter illustrates most of the points:

The enclosed credit memorandum for $39.60 is an example of Strong-Arch's continuous effort to satisfy our customers in prices, merchandise, and service. We are glad to make this adjustment, requested in your letter of November 28 on the 2 dozen pairs, assorted sizes, of Cordovan Brogues we shipped you last week.

How your shoes were billed can be explained by a look at the mechanics of our Billing Department. Whenever our salesmen take an order, they enter a symbol for the particular style, size, and color of shoe. In preparing the invoice, the Billing Department automatically enters the latest price, which in this case was $21.50. At the time Mr. Green took your order, this price had been in effect only two days. He erroneously entered the old price of $19.85, which was detected and changed in billing. On future orders any discrepancies between salesmen's orders and current price lists will be referred to one individual for special handling.

We are grateful for your first order. As these shoes become popular with your customers, we know you will want to add some other Strong-Arch models and styles to your stock. All give long wear and comfort to the customer and good profit margins to the dealer.

In addition to the Cordovan Brogue, you may want to offer your customers a new style, the Strong-Arch Loafer. It is made of top-grain cowhide, with leather soles and rubber heels, and is double-stitched for longer wear. Page 4 of the enclosed leaflet shows you the Loafer as advertised in this month's Esquire.

When you order these loafers (at only $14.95 a pair), we'll include in the shipment a split sample shoe so you can show your customers the exact structure.

Although the letter below does not actually send the check in the first sentence, as is usually desirable, it does say emphatically that the adjustment has been approved. This letter is in answer to the claim letter on page 324.

You most certainly will get a refund on the XXX suit you purchased, for we support our salesmen in whatever they promise a customer.

The salesman who told you that there would be no sale on XXX suits was sincere. The XXX manufacturers have never before allowed their suits to be sold at reduced prices. We were notified one week before our summer clothing sale this year that they were permitting a reduction for the first time.

We thank you for calling our attention to this situation, and we are glad to enclose our check for $13.80.

When you again need clothing, see our salesmen in the men's department. You can rely on what they tell you, with full confidence that we will back them up.

Sometimes you will need the customer's help on a few details such as filling out blanks for recovery of damages from a transportation company and returning defective articles. Be sure to cover such points in the one letter to avoid unnecessary correspondence; be sure, also, to make the reader's action as easy as possible.

> Your Old South cream and sugar set is being mailed prepaid today so that it will arrive two or three days before the wedding.
>
> Since the Old South set is in keeping with southern traditions, it will attract favorable glances and comments as guests look over the gifts.
>
> The set is being carefully wrapped with plenty of newspaper and shipped in a corrugated box of 3/16-inch thickness. This is thicker than required by shippers, but it will be standard packing for all Old South china from now on. Your report has helped us to improve our service. Thank you.
>
> To avoid your having to pay for the second shipment and then getting a refund from the Postal Service on the first shipment, we are sending a claim form completely filled out except for your signature. Will you please sign it and use the reply envelope for mailing it back to us?
>
> The bride and groom will like the antebellum motif of the Old South set and will attach many pleasant memories to it as the years go by.

The checklist for approving adjustments (p. 164) is comprehensive enough to cover most situations, but not all points are likely to apply to any one letter.

DIRECT INQUIRY CASES

1. As John Madison, director of marketing, Furina Foods, Yorkshire Avenue, Battle Creek, Michigan 49017, write to the placement director of your school for a lead on an ambitious, quick-thinking graduate. Your company has just put out a new vitamin-fortified minute-flow cereal for babies and has plans for other quick-frozen baby foods. You need a hard-working man who is willing to travel and who is also willing to live in different places in the United States or Europe. The first six months are to be spent on the usual type of training program (visiting plants, writing reports, selling, and keeping records). The starting salary is $11,000, but raises will be frequent and rapid. You're interested in talking with students whose grades average B or above.

2. Assume the role of the recently appointed director of the new Southwestern sales division of Hunter & Davis in Dallas, Texas 74219. Your job is to push the adoption of Hunter & Davis textbooks in Arkansas, Oklahoma, and Texas. The major part of the job is getting first-rate men who have the personality and background for contact work with college professors and the perseverance that will let enthusiasm be foremost despite much travel, absence from family, and day-and-night hours. From the Placement Bureau of Indiana University, you secure the name of Robert

Checklist for Approving Adjustments

1. Make the beginning fast, informative, pleasant, and reassuring.
   a) Open with the full reparation—a specific statement of what you are doing.
   b) Avoid any grudging tone.
   c) Build up the favorable reaction with a few resale words.
   d) Too much resale on defective products before explanation may bring an "Oh yeah?"
2. Throughout the letter, avoid emphasis on the disappointing aspects by avoiding negative words.
3. Explain fully, honestly, and reassuringly any favorable facts.
   a) Include a goodwill-building sentence—either that you're glad to make the adjustment or that you welcome the report as an aid in maintaining quality and service.
   b) Whichever you choose, be sure your facts follow logically from your wording of the adjustment you've made.
   c) Judicially, impartially—and preferably impersonally—establish the reason for the mishap in the minimum number of words. Often you can effectively imply the reason in your explanation of corrective measures taken or the ordinary care taken.
   d) Whether you name or imply the source of error, give concrete evidence of normally correct, safe shipments of high-quality goods, or—if applicable—explain changes you are making to prevent recurrence of the difficulty.
   e) Be quick to admit error; don't appear to be buck-passing.
   f) Avoid suggesting frequency of error.
4. Ask for any necessary cooperation from the customer. For example:
   a) Be definite and polite in asking the customer to sign necessary blanks.
   b) Clear up what is to be done with the original article if you're replacing it.
   c) Make the customer's action as little trouble as possible ("When the expressman calls to pick up the original shipment, just have him . . .").
5. Close pleasantly with a forward look.
   a) Don't tear up your good positive efforts with a backward look apologizing or otherwise recalling the disappointing aspects.
   b) Do leave the customer with a pleasant reminder of the pleasurable use of the perfect article now in his hands, if applicable.
   c) You may end the letter with resale talk, but sales promotional material on an allied article may well suggest your additional thoughtfulness—and just may pick up an extra sale.

Hartig, a 30-year-old former Army captain winding up his degree in marketing. He seems bright and eager to please, and he apparently wants to tackle the job—even though it would mean being away from his wife and his three-year-old child a good deal of the time. He knows little about the book trade, but that is a deficiency that can be easily remedied. Back in the Dallas office, thinking it over (after a pleasant morning and a quick luncheon with Robert), you decide to write to several of the men whom Robert mentioned. The letter you are going to write is to Dr. Grant Bailey, professor of marketing, in whose office Hartig worked as a student assistant the first two terms of his senior year. You want Bailey's evaluation of Hartig as a tactful, producing book salesman. The big question in your mind is whether the man is too forceful (too bossy, too emphatic, too opinionated) for good public relations. Of course, you won't use this terminology, but you want to try to get an answer to this big question in your mind. In addition, you want to know something about his cultural background and traits and training implying effective salesmanship.

3. As vice president in charge of training for the Bank of Louisiana (with headquarters in New Orleans but with branches all over the state), you have the job of interviewing and screening several hundred applicants a year. Yesterday a personable young man came in and presented a good case for your employing him. Barry J. Blakeney, graduate of Ohio State University School of Business with a major in banking and finance, August, two years ago; 25 (two years of Army service), single; part-time work selling school supplies in a campus shop while attending the University. He said he wanted to concentrate on investment analysis after the six-month training period was completed.

When you asked (after looking over his filled-in blank) what he had done from graduation until now, he replied, "Oh, I worked for a while at the First National Bank in Springfield, Illinois, but I quit to come here." As you talked with him, it became clear that he had enjoyed New Orleans so much while in the Army that he was determined to live in this city. When you pointed out to him that after his training period there might not be an opening in the New Orleans bank, that he might have to work for a while in one of the branches upstate, he said he didn't mind, that he would sweat out a branch job for a while.

Although his training is good and his scholastic record apparently excellent (from his own statement), you can't help wondering about his experience with the First National Bank in Springfield. And you also wonder if his temperament is best for investment analysis; such work in your bank calls not only for long hours of tedious study but also for considerable tact and patience in dealing with older people (especially widows) whose funds are handled by the trust department. You routinely requested his transcript and sent two other letters to references listed from the University; now write to the officer in charge of employment at the

Springfield bank, trying to find out whether his experience suggests promise for effective work in the trust department as an investment analyst (a position which he'd not work up to for at least five years; in the meantime, he'd go through several training stages and work with senior analysts and customers).

4. As the person in charge of personnel placement with a big chain of department stores, Quarters, Los Angeles, California 90058, you interview and place in stores (after a management training program of one year) able men first as assistant managers and then as managers. This morning you talked with a volatile but nervous 24-year-old man, Ernest Gregory. As he is soon to graduate from the University of Nevada, Gregory applied for work in your training program. He seemed to be ambitious, energetic, and determined to please. While working on his business administration degree (majoring in marketing), he clerked 22 hours a week for four years at El Cortez Men's Store, 239 West Second, Reno, Nevada 89505. Besides waiting on customers, he sometimes helped decorate the windows, move merchandise, and mark goods. As an enlisted man in the Army, he did routine work. The only other work experience he had was checking stock, sweeping out, and carrying out packages in Alpine's Supermarket the summer after he was a junior in high school. As you talked with him, you noticed how much he interrupted you—was this just a nervous habit? Apparently he has plenty of determination. In some ways you felt that he was so busy thinking about his own ambition that he didn't follow what you were saying. To answer your questions about him, write Phillip Bowers, manager of El Cortez Men's Store. Also find out if Bowers thinks Gregory would irritate customers. Would he be able to direct salespeople?

5. Write the Pleasant View Home for Senior Citizens, El Charro Drive, Scottsdale, Arizona, 85251, and ask for details about making arrangements for a 78-year-old relative of yours. Find out what the monthly or yearly charges are, and ask about facilities (single, double, or ward). Ask what down payment is necessary and what the charges cover. Many homes for older people include nursing care. Ask if the Pleasant View Home will take care of bed patients or semi-bed patients. Your relative insists she will not live with you but wants to live near her hometown, and that is why you considered this home. She has been a victim of anemia and so will need a liver shot every week or 10 days, but otherwise she is in excellent health. You want her to have a comfortable place to live, but the cost of comfort is a real consideration. You have limited funds, and so does she.

6. An ad in the *Atlanta Constitution* featured the sale of land on the shores of Morgan Long Lake, located 45 minutes from Birmingham, 12 miles from Talladega, and two and a half hours from Atlanta. Write the Continental Resorts, Inc. 1104 Montgomery Highway, Birmingham, Ala-

bama 35216, for information on the cost and size of the condominium apartments. The ad said that there would be a country club, yacht club, and racquet club, but it did not say whether a homeowner or apartment owner of Continental could have membership in these clubs. If he is entitled to membership, find out if there are dues and what the dues would be. According to the ad, there will be a Continental Hotel which will have a theater, specialty shops, and gourmet restaurants as well as a health spa with sauna and whirlpool baths. Find out if there is any restriction against subletting the home or apartment.

7. Clip from the pages of any newspaper or magazine an ad featuring a product in which you are interested. Write an inquiry to the manufacturer or distributor asking for details not furnished by the ad. Price and local availability are possibilities. Servicing is another. Ask four significant questions, at least one of which requires explanation on your part. Attach the ad to your letter.

8. Because executives of your National Electric Company, Kansas City, Missouri 64114, have more to read than they have time for, and because many of them are slow readers, you, Nathaniel Black, the communications counselor, are starting a reading program to help them increase their speed and comprehension. In an educational magazine you found an ad from Miami Instrument Company, 1657 Alton Road, Miami, Florida 33132, describing two types of machines for improving speed and comprehension. The ad reads as follows:

The Technic-Mach is used at all levels of education for the individual student and the Electri-Mach is used for group training. Following the excellent results in plane and ship recognition achieved in World War II, training in hundreds of schools shows that serious use of these machines can often result in doubling of speed along with gains in comprehension from 2 to over 10 percent. Results vary widely, depending on kind and length of training, but the main fact is that almost everyone can improve his reading ability by use of these devices.

The ad does not give model numbers, shipping information, cost of either machine, or cost of operation. You have 10 overworked executives who could benefit from reading help; and probably, if the machines helped these men, you could use the machines for their assistants and secretaries. Ask the Miami Company which machine is best for your needs. How expensive and how complicated are targets (cards) to make? Specifically, can these cards be typed on any typewriter, or is special equipment necessary?

9. Assume that you are at 11 Park Lane Drive, Decatur, Illinois 62522. As a do-it-yourself type of man, you want to build a cabinet that will hold your cassette recorder and TV as well as a radio. You plan to put it along a wall of your 15- by 15-foot family room. Write Slintwood Television Company, Allston, Massachusetts 02134, manufacturers of sets designed for built-ins. Besides wanting to know price, you are also interested in size of screen. Find out if the controls go in the frame next to the picture or are mounted below. Even though you think you know how to build the set, ask the company if it is easy to install. Will the present aerial (desgined for an 18-inch Solorus) do? Does this built-in TV come in color, and if so, what is the difference in price between the black-and-white set and color?

10. To honor a retiring head of the marketing department, your business fraternity, Alpha Kappa Psi, agreed to have an oil portrait unveiled at a banquet this spring. The local photography shop on campus could copy a picture, but it does not have the facilities to do fine oil painting. It suggests sending a picture of the head of the department and getting information from the Quaint Paint Shop, Intervale Avenue, Lynn, Massachusetts 01902. Ask what an 18- by 24-inch oil painting would cost. You need to know details about lighting the frame and about different types of frames. One strand of hair is hanging loosely in the photograph, and you need to find out if this hair can be shaded out. Can the eyes be made clearer?

11. For the basement of one of your three condominium apartments (four apartments in each building), write the Bardy Company, San Diego, California 92410, to find out the sizes of the Bardy Splash-Swish, Model B-432, commercially built washing and drying machines. Ask which type of dryer Bardy recommends (gas or electric). Do the machines have to be bolted down, and do the coin meters come on the machines, or do they have to be mounted? If the meters have to be mounted, who mounts them? Do the machines have special cycles for synthetics? Assume that you are at 499 Yosemite Avenue, North, Stockton, California 95203.

12. With emphasis more on do-it-yourself type of products, you decide to see if it's practical to install automatic, coin-operated dry-cleaning machines in your fraternity house and in all the other 30 houses on campus (assuming you could get the franchise or finance it individually). First you would like to know if these dry cleaners you see advertised in *House Beauty* could be used economically in the houses (around 40 men to a fraternity and 60 women to a sorority). As a student with more ambition than money, you are looking for an opportunity to earn extra money while putting your spare time to good use. General Products Conglomerate, Commercial Laundry Equipment Sales Department, Bellaire, Ohio 43906, probably can give you the answers on cost, feasibility, power requirements, safety precautions, and financing for both an individual fraternity and a franchised agency. Some of the sororities have installed coin-operated washing machines on a franchise basis (they keep 15 percent of the money collected).

13. You have tried all the local stores for a funnel which will strain water and trash from gasoline. Some clerks don't even believe such a thing exists, but you have had one for years. What you want is about a half dozen, in about 6-inch size, as gifts for your friends with whom you go fishing. Everyone has trouble with his outboard motor because of water in the gasoline—in most cases from condensation in the tanks. Write an inquiry to the Robert Sonneman Company, 5620 47th, Long Island City, New York 11101, for descriptions, sizes, guarantees, prices, and anything else you would want to know before ordering.

14. Morris Carlisle, purchasing agent, University of Colorado, 1105 N. Nevada Avenue, Boulder, Colorado 80903, bought 20 overviewers (school net price of $260 each) from a well-known overhead projector company. The company recommended and he bought Ferma-trans, thick plastic sheets that are typed on or drawn with a fine steel point. Each sheet costs 10 cents. Several teachers complained about the Ferma-trans, saying that it took too long to print them and that no test could be typed on them, for they were too thick to go into the typewriter. Carlisle complained to the company about Ferma-trans but got no satisfactory answer.

A friend put a leaflet on his desk from Tools Unlimited, Meriden Avenue, Meriden, Connecticut 06450, concerning Transpare, a material designed for use with an overhead projector. The plastic sheet can be typed on, drawn on, and written on, the leaflet states. Carlisle wants to know the cost of the sheets and the procedure for making transparencies. Can they do such work on Transpare sheets? Many teachers prefer to put a typed test on the projector and have the students answer the questions from the projected material. He wants to be sure that these sheets will slip into any normal or regular-size typewriter. What if a Transpare is left on the machine—will it curl up and be of no use? Is it any more work to prepare typed copy or to draw maps, charts, and graphs than on ordinary paper or a stencil for mimeographing? Is there a local dealer? The leaflet says "usable on either side." If both sides can be used, considerable savings could be realized. Find out the answers to these questions and any others you deem important in a letter prepared for the signature of Carlisle.

15. Write the Heath Company, Benton Harbor, Michigan 48089, and ask for details on the new Heathkit Ignition System Analyzer you saw advertised in *Hot Rod* magazine. Ask if any special training is required to operate this analyzer and ask if it will stand rough treatment. You also want to know the name of a local owner of the Heathkit. The ad said that this easy-to-assemble kit cost $89.95 (IOW–20) or a factory-assembled model (Kit IO–20) cost $169.95. The copy stressed the point that with this analyzer a driver could find ignition defects while the engine is operating and without removing engine or ignition parts. The analyzer indicated shorted plugs, defective points, incorrect dwell time, coil and condenser problems.

16. Despite all the adverse publicity about insecticide, you would like to control the insects in your back yard, especially around the pool and patio. In the "Modern Living" section of *Time* magazine last week you read of a new product called Feller-Matic Insect Control Unit which is designed to be death on flying insects, harmless to people, pets, wildlife, and vegetation. A network of copper or plastic pipe is laid around the garden, patio, or swimming pool, with nozzles set inconspicuously at intervals. The plumbing is connected to a tank of water-base Pyraid insecticide; when the owner flicks a switch, a pump jets the lethal mist over the area. A two-minute spray is effective for about half a day and gives off a pleasant lemon odor. The device is made by Feller Chemical Company of Woodside, New York 11421. Ask what the price would be for coverage of 5,000 square feet. Ask if there is an owner of Feller-Matic nearby. Also find out installation procedure and cost of installation.

17. "How do you fix a flat tire late at night on a lonely highway in 60 seconds?" the ad in *Car and Driver* reads. The ad goes on to say that Dapper Dan is a spare tire in a can that can be kept in the glove compartment—and it's not even a tight fit. It has du Pont Freon and I.C.C. sealant in it. When the tire goes flat, just flip open the glove compartment, and slip out of the car. In 60 seconds the tire is properly inflated, with the puncture sealed. Dapper Dan is guaranteed. Money back if it does not inflate and seal a flat for at least 100 miles of continuous travel. The price is $2.98. As a consumer (on personal letterhead), write an inquiry to Bernz Company, Moundsville, West Virginia 26041. You want to know if there is any danger of Dapper Dan exploding. Also find out how long the Freon and I.C.C. sealant is effective. Can this can be used on more than one tire?

18. A friend told you about the Steamatic soil extraction system, which is superior to any other cleaning method for rugs. It is the only cleaning process ever developed that actually extracts deep-down, ground-in dirt and grime. A controlled jet of wet steam solution penetrates deep into fabric . . . soil and residue are suspended and actually extracted in one easy operation. No harmful chemicals or messy powders ever touch the carpets. From your home in Reform, Alabama 35481, write the Steamatic Company, 1109 Fern Avenue, Birmingham, Alabama 35223, for the cost of cleaning wall-to-wall carpeting in a room 15 x 30 feet. The rug is part wool and part acrylic and you need to know if that type of mixture can be cleaned. For several years there has been a stain from a soft drink. You want to know if the cleaning process will remove that stain. Also, you have a baby grand piano and you do not want the steam to damage the piano; so ask about the possibility of moving the piano or of protecting it from the steam in some way. The reason you are writing to inquire about this process is that you have phoned several times and have never reached anyone at the place of business.

19. After a summer in Europe where you stayed in youth hostels for as little as 50 cents a night, you want to find out from the Department of Interior, Parks and Recreation Division, Washington, D.C. 20006, if there are any hostels in the United States. If there are, you need to know where they are located and the cost per night. A friend told you that a system of hostels was recently started on the east coast.

20. Assuming that you coach the high school football team of your town, write Pro-Style Athletic Goods Company, Newark, New Jersey 07105, for information about nylon-covered protective equipment (shoulder pads, with neckroll protection, rib pads, hip pads, arm pads, knee pads, thigh guards, and shin guards) as advertised under the trade name Pro-Style in this year's *Sports Illustrated.* You are especially interested in the protection afforded by the mouth guards. In the past the equipment you have had has absorbed perspiration and therefore slowed the players down because of the added weight. Will the Pro-Style shock-absorbing mouth guards resist moisture readily? Because you are operating on a limited budget, you want to know the school discount. What would the price be for 50 complete sets? Will the company make the breakaway jerseys to go with the game uniforms?

21. While talking with a salesman of school supplies for the Loffitt Company, Box 102, 669 South Lawrence Street, Montgomery, Alabama 36101, you learned that the 6M Company will send a representative to any school to conduct a program to help teachers make transparencies for the overhead projector. Many teachers lack the "hands-on" training needed to effectively use the equipment and make transparencies. The salesman did not say whether this representative would come at no cost. Also, there was no mention of materials that would be needed. Write a letter to George M. Shoop, director of sales at Loffitt, and find out the cost to have an in-service program for 10 teachers two months from now. You can assume that you are writing the letter for Thomas P. Killough, principal of University Place School, 1198 Rees Avenue, Huntsville, Alabama 35805.

22. A helpful hint in yesterday's paper says "Readers who want the Veterans Administration's findings on the quality of hearing aids can get free hearing-aid advice." Write the nearest VA office for *Hearing Aid Models for Veterans.* The booklet lists all types of aids and explains which aid is best for different kinds of hearing deficiencies. Your brother needs something for his hearing; so you write the VA office in your state capital. Both he and you are veterans.

23. The ad of Concord Electronics Corporation (1935 Armcost Avenue, Los Angeles 90025) makes its Concord F-400 portable stereo-tape recorder sound good. But you have some questions. Who is the dealer nearest you? Can he provide service, additional tapes, and the like? What are the size and weight of the recorder (is it suitable for carrying with books to college classes)? How is background noise controlled (shuffling feet, crackling papers, coughing in a lecture room)? Is it always on batteries or can you use house current when available? What is the price, fully equipped?

24. Fill-mark Co. (67 Centerville Road, Warwick, R.I.) advertises an apparent bargain in do-it-yourself seat covers for various sports cars. What is the price for your car? Specifically, what is the guarantee? "Easy to install," the ad says. You wonder if this is true even for a person who has never done such work. Are any special tools needed? Is it easy to clean the covers? Can Fill-mark send swatches for color selection?

25. The Sunbeam Appliance Company, 5410 S. Wells, Chicago 78109, didn't tell enough in its COSMOPOLITAN ad about the Lady Sunbeam Hair Curler. Will hairdos hold up in your high-humidity climate? Will the preheated rollers damage color-treated hair? What are the price and guarantee? Of the 20 curlers, how many in each of the four sizes? Can you get a set with all largest curlers (diameters)? If not, what is the extra charge for them? (You prefer a smooth, natural-looking hairdo and are likely to use only large curlers.)

26. Your 12-year-old Fedders Model 10 (14,000 BTU) has been keeping your connecting dentist's offices, labs, and waiting room reasonably cool. The area is 25 x 35 feet. You know, however, that you are going to need a replacement before another season; so you are interested in an ad by K-Reyes, 1541 N. 164 Street, Miami Beach, Florida—now (October) of all this year's models of Friedrich air conditioners at a year-end closeout with $50 off. In Hollywood, Florida, you are closer to the store than people who live in South Miami. Nevertheless, before you drive over to take a look and try to close a deal, you would like to know size recommended; price; whether that price includes free delivery or installation on this deal; if not, what the charges would be; whether you can get one in mahogany or something which will match your mahogany decor. Can you assume that the machines are new, unused? What is the warranty? Can you buy on credit?

27. While already planning an extended trip next summer with your wife and two children, five and seven years old, you notice an ad in the paper by Coastal Camper Sales and Service, 3049 Phillips Highway, Terre Haute, Indiana—a closeout sale on this year's models of Swinger motor homes.

As a start to considering the purchase of one, you wonder how many people the motor home, 24 feet long, sleeps comfortably, whether it has a complete kitchen and bath, how much it weighs, whether it is safety approved by the National Motor Home Association, and whether it meets the laws of all states for traveling. If not, what are the exceptions? Write Coastal Camper.

28. The B. F. Goodrich (Akron, Ohio 44313) ad in last week's *TIME* pictures a new housing development wherein the floors, inside walls, and siding are glued on with a new B.F.G. glue. First, it was useful only for indoors, but the new glue is now suitable for outdoor use and is compatible with all kinds of painting materials, says the ad. Does that mean that you could use it in paneling the inside of your fraternity house (assume that you are an advanced architecture student working out the plans for proposed fraternity house changes)? The walls are concrete block 11 feet high plus 4 feet of plaster at the top. Will the B.F.G. adhesive bond the paneling there? Would furring strips be necessary? In your sometimes humid climate those walls are almost wet. Will the stuff stick?

If the B. F. Goodrich glue will do the job, you will need lots of it. What quantities does it come in? What's the rate of coverage? What's the price? Is there a local outlet? If so, can the fellows there answer further questions? You need to know pretty soon; the fraternity wants to start to work.

29. Assume that you are Mrs. E. C. Bartelsmeyer, Main Cross Road, Taylorville, Illinois 62568, and that you want a waste disposer for your aged but comfortable farm home. You have been in to look at disposers in nearby Springfield, Illinois, but you did not get some clear-cut answers to your questions.

One of your friends suggests that you write the Waste Queen Universal Company, Chicago, Illinois 60602, to find out if you can install a disposer when you have a septic tank. Also, find out the best kind of Waste Queen (Model 8000 or 7000) and prices.

30. No-Insect Strip works like magic, the ad in *Living* reads. Unique insecticide, Repella, seeks out and kills flies, mosquitoes, and other annoying insects wherever they are flying or hiding in an average-size room. *Just what* other annoying insects does it kill—roaches, for example? And moths? And if No-Insect is so effective in annihilating insects in the kitchen, what does it do to open pots and pans on the stove? And open milk bottles and the like? And dishes set out on which to serve meals? What is the price? And where can one get the product locally? Each strip lasts up to three months, according to the ad. A three-month accumulation of insects on a strip would hardly be a welcome sight in the kitchen, family room, or bedroom—or *any* room, for that matter. Even if this question can be answered to the consumer's satisfaction, there are still the questions of attachment to walls and surfaces and of colors to fit in with varying interior designs. As a consumer (on plain paper), write an inquiry to get answers to these questions and any other question you consider pertinent, addressed to Riley Chemical Company, Knightstown, Indiana 46148.

31. Living in Trenton (20 miles from Gainesville), you read an ad (Rhodes Furniture Company, 2305 N.W. 13 Street, Gainesville, Florida 33022) in the Gainesville paper for some $8 Manor Lane carpeting. What are the colors—anything close to emerald green? Does $8 cover necessary padding? Will Rhodes lay the carpet (work included in price)? If not, how much for padding and laying? What is estimated total cost for living room 14′ 6″ x 21′ 3″? Is the carpeting nonallergic, stain-resistant, mothproof? One of your children is allergic to certain materials.

32. A recent *Wall Street Journal* ran an ad by World Business Machines Corporation, Office Products Division, 9765 Michigan Avenue, Chicago, Illinois 60608, on a new, advanced dictating instrument, the Prospector. "Small and compact, the new WBM works behind your desk, in conference, on trips, and anywhere you think," the copy says. It gives no price. After looking in the Yellow Pages under "Dictating Machines" (as the ad suggested) and finding no WBM dealer listed, write directly to the company and ask for price, warranty, and details of construction, size, performance, and use. Ask if the machine uses tapes or belts that can be reused. You have been using a machine which records on belts, and you have found it handy to mail the belt back to your secretary when you were traveling. Ask if this machine can be used on an airplane. Also, find out when the delivery date could be, assuming no local dealer is convenient to you. As an executive, you dictate at least 20 letters a day, and many days you dictate 50 letters —while traveling, at home, or in the office.

FAVORABLE REPLY CASES (NO SALES POSSIBILITIES)

1. You have been asked by TUCA (Teaching Underprivileged Children Association) to work for $50 a month (living arrangements are provided) in the ghetto in Chicago from September 4 to June 10 of next year. You will be working mainly with high school students and will be concentrating on English and reading. The job appeals to you even though the salary is low; so you are going to accept. All acceptances must be in writing. Address your letter to Mr. Charles P. Dendy, Director of TUCA, 2446 Fillmore Avenue, Chicago, Illinois 60607.

2. As promotion director, American Advertising Association, 339 Amsterdam Avenue, New York City, New York 10023, write Professor Joseph Spann, Box 4456, University of Illinois, Urbana, Illinois 61801, and agree to send the requested direct-mail campaigns that won awards during the last five years. They may be kept two months so students can study them. You will send them express collect, to be returned express prepaid.

3. You are Dr. Grant Bailey, professor of marketing, Indiana University, Bloomington, Indiana 47712, and you are answering the confidential inquiry of Hunter & Davis, Dallas, Texas 75219, about Robert Hartig (Case 2, p. 163). When Robert worked as a student assistant, he graded papers, recorded grades, kept records, and even taught for you two days when you were ill. He kept accurate and neat records, but there was some criticism about his teaching. Several of the students told you afterward that he was too opinionated and too dictatorial. He had made up a test and given it without consulting you, much to your surprise. The students resented the test; but by doing this on his own, Robert showed initiative. Robert seemed happily married and devoted to his three-year old child. He appeared to be determined to make his marriage a success and was willing to work hard to support his little family.

4. As a young executive trainee in Louisville, Kentucky, you have frequently attended alumni meetings of your professional business fraternity, Lambda Theta Iota. It's a good group; you enjoy the programs and contacts. At a recent meeting you met the national president, and the two of you talked enthusiastically about the worthwhile activities of the fraternity for college men as well as businessmen. You knew you made a favorable impression on him, but you're surprised to receive his letter this morning, asking you to become the state supervisor for Kentucky. A quick look in your directory shows you that there are only five chapters, no one of them more than 150 miles from you. And, you reason, all the meetings are in the evening—you wouldn't have to miss many working hours; the fraternity pays traveling expenses; it means only about three trips a month (none in the summer). The more you think about it, the more the idea appeals to you. So you write Harvey Baines, 1140 Woodstock Drive, SW, Atlanta, Georgia 30331, telling him you'll accept the appointment and asking for further necessary instructions and materials.

5. As John Madison (Inquiry Case 1, p. 163), you got the name of Dudley Davidson, 606 Crawford Avenue, Milwaukee, Wisconsin 53221. He apparently is an ambitious, quick-thinking graduate. Write him and ask him to come to your office a week from Tuesday (New Products, Furina Foods). Davidson wrote you a very detailed application letter persuasively setting forth why he thinks he'd be a good choice to manage the Rome office your company plans to open in about a year.

You have an opening for a young man. And even though Davidson has been working for your competitor for three years and still is, he would have to go through an indoctrination period. Set the time and ask him to confirm the appointment. Naturally you expect to pay his expenses. Offer to make a hotel reservation for him.

6. For Mrs. Eugene Garner, manager, Pleasant View Home for Senior Citizens, Scottsdale, Arizona, 85251, answer an inquiry about your home for senior citizens (Case 5, p. 166). The new wing should be finished in two months, and it will accommodate 30 residents. Residents will pay rent 90 days in advance and thereafter pay by the month. The rates depend on the facilities taken and range from $175 for a small room with group bath to $250 a room with private bath. The rent includes room, meals, laundry, and personal help with dressing and hair. Medical attention is furnished by a contract doctor. Meals are served in the rooms of residents unable to go to the dining room. The home does not furnish nursing or hospital care. Each resident must carry his own medical and hospital insurance. Upon becoming bedridden or needing hospital care, the resident will be removed from the home and cannot return until the doctor certifies that the patient can take care of himself. Application for admission should be made directly to Mrs. Garner. Suggest that application for admission be made right away because so many senior citizens want to enter the Pleasant View Home for Senior Citizens.

7. You are Phillip Bowers, manager of El Cortez Men's Store, 239 West Second, Reno, Nevada 89505, and you are answering the confidential inquiry about Ernest Gregory (Case 4, p. 166), as fairly as you know how. In the four years Gregory worked for you, you got to like him, and you understand him. Gregory is determined to be a success (and to him, success is to make money and a place in society). He came from a poor farm family and has always wanted to better himself economically. You had to watch him or he would have taken over some of the duties of your regular employees. You felt that he was so eager to please because this clerking job after school meant bread and butter to him. Inwardly he feels insecure, and that is why he pushes himself and often interrupts a conversation to talk about his ambitions. With the help of a training program and a prospect of being a store manager, Gregory probably would feel more secure and would be a well-adjusted person. He seems to get along well with the other employees, and he was an effective salesman.

8. "Barry Blakeney!" you exclaim as you read the letter from the vice president in charge of training at the Bank of Louisiana (Case 3, p. 165). You remember him well. He came to work for you last fall when you started about a dozen August graduates in various jobs at the First National Bank in Springfield, Illinois. Blakeney had made a good impression when he came in and talked earnestly about eventually working in investment analysis; his references from Ohio State University and the character references he gave among Ohio businessmen who had known him since childhood spoke well of him. He was put to work first in the small-loans department, then in the department appraising real estate loans. He learned the details of a job rapidly and did the work assigned to him accurately. But he pestered his supervisors constantly with suggested changes and once told the head of real estate loans that he was behind the times —in front of a customer too. Shortly afterward, he came in to you and

announced that if his leaving at the end of the week would be satisfactory with the bank, he thought he would; he had made up his mind to go to New Orleans. You were a little surprised—after his initial enthusiasm—and somewhat disgruntled; training programs cost money! But you wished him well and sent him on his way. Your records show that he was on the payroll for 13 weeks. Write the letter to the Bank of Louisiana candidly and without rancor.

9. Sit in for Rodney Holder, director of HUD (Housing Urban Development), Washington, D.C. 20005, and write Melvin R. Patton, director of Operation New Cincinnati, 11174 Maple Knoll, Springfield Road, Cincinnati, Ohio, 45202. Holder agrees to speak to the ONC group from 7 to 8 P.M. the 20th of next month and to answer questions for another half hour afterward. The only prop needed is an overhead projector. He will arrive by plane 4 P.M. You will appreciate Patton's suggestions. Can he meet you on arrival? You will also need a hotel room.

10. For John E. Cooper, professor of zoology, University of Kentucky, Limestone & Euclid, Lexington, Kentucky 40506, write Claude Hinton, director of the Committee for Leaving the Environment of America Natural (CLEAN), 223 Walnut Street, Starkville, Mississippi 39759, that he will come (by plane, arriving at 9 A.M.) the 12th of next month. He will address scientists and conservationists from five Southeastern states. He will not attend the dinner party for the National Audubon Society, but will fly back on the 5 P.M. plane. His talk will be on his recent study on the environmental effects of pollution of the Tennessee-Tombigbee Waterway.

11. As Dale Wittner, prominent lawyer in Los Angeles (Equitable Building, 6253 Hollywood Boulevard, Los Angeles, California 90028), write William Vining, Student Life Committee, Sacramento State College, Sacramento, California 95819. Wittner agrees to speak at Focus, a student-sponsored event, from 2 to 3 P.M., the 11th of next month and to answer questions for another half hour afterward. To help illustrate his talk on the "Crisis in the Courts in the United States," he will need a movie projector. He will arrive by plane at 11 A.M. and will return by plane at 5:45 P.M. of the same day.

12. Today's mail brings a letter from Kerry Olson, store manager of Olson Galleries, Taos, New Mexico 87571, asking you (an artist at 4 Colt Hill in Abbott, Arkansas 71744) to send samples of your acrylic and silk-screen work. All artists will send samples at their own expense, but Olson will sell the artwork at the prices the artists put on their samples. The show will be held for one week beginning two months from this Friday. Write the letter to Olson Galleries accepting the invitation. You can send four silk-screen prints and three acrylic paintings.

13. Write an acceptance for Milton Fuller of the Fuller Direct Mail Association, 900 Sasser Drive, Mobile, Alabama 36609, to address the Marketing Club at the University of Alabama, Tuscaloosa, Alabama 35401, three months from Wednesday at 7 P.M. As an alumnus of the School of Commerce of the University, prominent in the activities of Student Government, he is glad to fly his private plane to Tuscaloosa to talk to the more than 100 members on "The Future Is Now." John Rose, president of the Club, invited Fuller to be his dinner guest before the meeting; Fuller is accepting.

14. The Michigan National Bank, East Lansing, Michigan 48823, each year awards a $1,500 scholarship to an Ingham County high school senior. The winner is a student who writes the best essay on a subject the bank selects and who scores high on achievement and personality tests. The subject this year is "Inflation in the Seventies!" The high schools in Ingham County administer the written achievement and personality tests. As professor of finance at the University of Michigan, Ann Arbor 48105, you have been asked to be one of three final judges to read about 20 essays which will have been selected from all the essays turned in. From these, you and the other two judges will pick the three best. Then in about two weeks you'll need to be in East Lansing to interview the three candidates and decide on the winner. The bank will of course pay all your expenses. It's a time-consuming job but in your opinion a most worthwhile project, and so you are accepting.

15. *Southern Living*, 1012 Young Avenue, Memphis, Tennessee 38117, a monthly publication, sent Professor Reuben Wright, professor of anthropology, at the University of Georgia (his address: 1105 Milledge Avenue, Athens, Georgia 30601) to Africa for three months in exchange for his promise to write an article. Back from Africa, Wright must answer the publication's request to send a biographical sketch with information on the books he has written and the article describing the course he has developed on African culture. Write the letter for Wright telling the publisher that the information will be along within 10 days.

16. Help Marilyn Davis, correspondence supervisor, International Electric, Long Island City, New York 11101, by answering the request of Joel Berryhill, an instructor in communications at your school. Davis will be glad to send Berryhill the film *How to Improve Your Listening* at no cost, so that he may show it to his 300 students by next week, shipping charges collect. He may keep the film one week, returning it shipping charges prepaid (a stipulation clearly stated in your offer).

17. Joel Berryhill (preceding case) also teaches a course in direct-mail selling. As Fulton Henderson, Henderson Advertising Agency, New York,

New York 10022, tell Berryhill that Henderson is (as requested) sending him *Flip* (a collection of unsolicited sales letters, collection letters, and various other material) which will be effective illustrative matter for his course.

18. For one of the major bottling companies of bottled drinks, answer the complaint of a customer who objects to your apparent practices:

emphasis on no-deposit, no-return bottles, six 10-oz., 89¢; six returnable (at 12¢) half-quarts, 71¢. You seem to try to make price comparison difficult and hide the fact that the price is 1.5¢/oz. in no-returns and 0.6¢ in returnables.

Facts: Local retailers, not you, determine what they will stock. They generally don't like the bottle-return nuisance any better than customers generally do. You still bottle your beverages in returnable 6-oz. bottles, but the demand from stores has declined greatly in recent years. You deny any intention of making price comparison difficult. The main reason for the lower price in bigger bottles is the usual price differential between sizes. Packaging and handling of many consumer products is a major cost contributing to the prices; and the cost of packing and handling a small quantity is often (as in bottles) almost the same as for a larger quantity.

19. As the banker for a well-to-do, only slightly financially informed, and busy widow (social life, many public-service activities through clubs) with three children still too young and inexperienced to manage their own business affairs, you have advised your client to get an attorney to prepare a will and a revocable living trust for her. She has asked you to put your advice in writing (said she didn't understand and wanted to think about it —and you feel sure she wants to consult with friends and perhaps an attorney).

Reasons for will: Yes, insurance and retirement benefits go to specified beneficiaries; recipients of other assets will be determined by state law, in a likely slow and costly process, unless a will names recipients and an executor to carry out the distribution.

Reasons for revocable living trust: flexible, changeable; provides professional management (even if you are absent or disabled) for you and children (to age specified) for greatest benefits from income-producing property; cuts red tape and delay in settlement of estate.

Strongly encourage seeing an attorney, and offer to work with him and/or her.

20. For *Consumer Reports,* answer the complaint of a longtime subscriber who appreciates your excellent research and reporting except for one thing: She says you seem to study products available in the East and Midwest but generally ignore brands sold in the West. The subscriber wants to know if she can do anything to help correct this situation.

Facts: You try but are frustrated by the near impossibility of complete coverage of the great variety of brands and models of products. You give no special consideration to the East—try to select products under consideration by the largest number of readers.

Usual Criteria: extent of promotion and distribution, sales volume. *Consumer Reports* has so many California subscribers, it sometimes covers products available there even though they don't meet usual criteria. CR has more shoppers (who make your store surveys) in California than anywhere else. Subscribers can best help by telling you dates and page numbers of reports not covering desired brands of products.

21. As a *Consumer Reports* correspondent, answer the letter of a subscriber who wants you to push for harsher legal fines of companies that cheat consumers; who says the minimum fines assessed three big food-products companies recently guilty are inadequate deterrents to continued or repeated chiseling; the companies lose more in staples or paper clips. He suggests 100-fold fines.

Points for explanation in answering:

—Unfavorable publicity about cheaters is probably best deterrent. Consumers cheated can do more than the law on small chiseling:

—Chide the press for not helping more with unfavorable publicity.

—Speak up against attempts of industry to stop regulatory agencies from giving the press news about cheaters.

—Fight laws and judges that gag the news sources (like the Federal Trade Commission and the Food and Drug Administration) and news media against reporting business cheaters.

—Fines alone can't stop cheats; if big enough to stop the big boys, fines would wipe out the little.

—Revision of libel laws to keep them from protecting the guilty as well as the innocent can help more than increased fines.

22. *A goodwill-building explanation.* In the editorial offices of *Consumer Reports,* you receive a postcard castigating CR for a postcard reply to a letter the subscriber had sent in—impersonal, unresponsive, not up to standards a subscrbier expects of CR, the complainant says.

Facts and attitudes to choose from for reply (by letter, this time):

—Many letters received require expert knowledge or research for reply.

—Policy is to answer as many letters as possible with facts from previous research; acknowledge others by postcard and send inquiry on to staff researcher most concerned with the subject.

—Letters received sometimes prompt new research projects leading to published results. If the problem seems of wide interest and importance, you circulate the letter for staff consideration.

—Not indifferent to letters; do take them seriously. A postcard reply is not a quick brushoff.

—Over 100 letters a day received from subscribers.

—Limited staff of experts, mainly to do research on products and publish find-ings for benefit of large numbers of subscribers. Experts answer all letters they can without taking away time unduly from main research projects. Spe-cial attention to problems of health or safety.

23. As local food inspector, John Hodge, write a directive to O'Neill's Grocery & Pawn Shop, 1801 N.E. 8 Avenue in your town, directing him to clean up and repair his small grocery store and meat market within 10 days.

Your recent inspection was prompted by a letter from the Northeast Neighborhood Citizens Association which listed 14 complaints against O'Neill's store. Basically the complaints were that much of the food on the shelves was stale as well as unsanitary. Evidence of rodents, cockroaches, and the like were everywhere. Your investigation showed that the citizens' letter was well justified. Your carbon answers the citizens' letter.

You do not need to spell out in the letter all the details that you pointed out to O'Neill during your recent inspection. You do need to make clear that he must dispose of all food unsuitable for human consumption, clean up the place, and make the necessary repairs to keep vermin and rodents out of the food. You also need to make clear that you will inspect more frequently for a while to assure compliance.

The citizens' accusations of charging 30 percent for credit, 25 cents for cashing checks, and charging taxes on food items are outside of your authority. They do, however, go into the report you must send to your state office and will most likely be passed on to the proper authorities.

REPLIES WITH SALES POSSIBILITIES

1. As manager of the Steamatic Company, 1109 Fern Avenue, Birming-ham, Alabama 35223, answer direct inquiry 18, p. 170.

Facts on case: The cost for cleaning the wall-to-wall carpeting (15 x 15 feet) would be $72.90. A 100-percent wool rug cleans better than a rug that is part acrylic and part wool. The piano will not have to be moved because you have a tool that cleans right up to each leg of the piano. The steam jets will not bother the piano, for you can hardly see the steam when it comes out. Generally stains from soft drinks can be removed unless a chlorine bleach was used on the stain. It is impossible to remove urine stains from carpeting.

Inclose a reply card setting up an appointment for the cleaning of the rug.

2. As director of sales, Feller Chemical Company, answer direct in-quiry 16, p. 170.

Facts on case: Give them the name of Howard V. Shumaker in a nearby city who owns the Feller-Matic Insect Control Unit. The cost for coverage of an area 5,000 square feet would be $295. Installation would have to be done by a reputable plumber. Cost of installation would be up to the plumber.

3. You have been asked by Marguerite Krause, owner of the Quaint Paint Shop, Intervale Avenue, Lynn, Massachusetts 01902, to answer Lewis Bills, president of Alpha Kappa Psi, about the oil portrait of the retired head of the marketing department (direct inquiry 10, p. 168). A fine oil 18 by 24 inches would cost about $450 and the frame another $100–$200, depending on the style Mr. Bills selects. For $25 a simple light can be installed, but many times a light is not needed if there is desirable lighting around the area where the picture is hung. The strand of hair can be shaded away, and the eyes can be made to look clearer. Before Marguerite Krause could start on it, however, she would need samples of the hair, of the clothing, and a specific description as to skin tones. Generally she prefers to see the person, but her artists can do almost as good a job from a photograph as from a real-life sitting.

4. *Your company:* Tools Unlimited, Meriden Avenue, Meriden, Connecticut 06450. *Your product:* Transpare, a material that can be written on with ball-point pen or other markers, or typed on, or run through a Fermo copying machine for a transparency. Transpare sheets are designed for use with any type of overviewer or overhead projector. They can be used on just one side. They always stay flexible and will not curl when left on an overhead projector. Transparencies are easy to make (just set the Fermo copying machine at about 2½, and place a sheet of Transpare on the face of the material to be copied). Transpare is available in boxes of 202 sheets (two sheets free to cover experimenting) at $15.50 per box (about 7 cents per 8½ by 11-inch sheet). *Your Potential Customer:* Morris Carlisle, purchasing agent, University of Colorado, 1105 N. Nevada Avenue, Boulder, Colorado 80903. Answer all the questions he asked (Inquiry Case 14, p. 169). Many of the teachers at the University will enjoy making their own detailed tests on Transpare, which would save mimeographing costs. Graphs, maps, charts, tables, pictures, and in fact any copy can be transmitted to Transpare. Urge Carlisle to get in touch with the local dealer, Ward Supply Company, 1109 Colorado Street, Denver 80211, phone, 456-8765.

5. As sales manager of Miami Instrument Company, 1657 Alton Road, Miami, Florida 33132, answer the inquiry from Nathaniel Black, communications counselor, National Electric Company, Kansas City, Missouri 64114. From Black's letter (Inquiry Case 8, p. 167), you believe that the Technic-Mach instrument which is used for individual help would be best. It has an extremely accurate timing device—an electronic flash unit, which gives square-wave presentation of light. It has a carefully controlled wiring system that is virtually foolproof. The reflection surface is made of two thin sheets of diffusion-gray Flexiglas designed to prevent glare from outside light sources. The resulting light closely simulates actual daylight. This allows longer practice sessions with less eye fatigue. With individual training the price, material, and length of a session can be adjusted to each executive's ability and progress. Slow readers will not be lost because the speed is too fast or the material too difficult, nor will others be bored because everything is too easy.

Specifications of the Model PT–800 Technic-Mach are as follows: rise time, 1/1000 second; shutter speeds, 1 second, 1/10 second, 1/25 second, 1/50 second, 1/100 second, and time. Standard 115 volts, alternating current, 25 to 60 cycles. Power, 20 watts. It costs no more to operate one of these machines than it costs to operate a 100-watt light bulb. *Cost:* The price includes 500 targets (5- by 5½-inch cards) and is $98. Extra blank cards (5 by 5½ inches) run $1.75 per 100 and $12.50 per 1,000. The targets are designed by reading experts. Training should be carefully planned; a definite program should be followed to its completion. The special terms or phrases used by the National Electric Company could be typed on the blank cards or targets with any ordinary typewriter for pertinent on-the-job training.

Shipment by c.o.d. or submit credit and banking reference at time of order. All prices are f.o.b. Miami; subject to change.

For group training, the Electri-Mach, Model MT–900, priced at $320 is recommended. This unit automatically changes slides at 5 seconds, 8 seconds, and 15 seconds. External timer jacks are provided for longer or shorter change intervals if desired. After each new slide is inserted, the shutter triggers automatically. The shutter may, however, be triggered between slide changes by the subject or operator. Shutter speeds are the same on this machine as on the Technic-Mach, and shipping is handled the same way.

Robert McMillan, representative in the Kansas City area, will be happy to demonstrate both machines and to work out details next month. If Black wants to try the machine right away, he should use the enclosed order form for the machine he feels will best work with his group. All purchases are final.

6. As director of sales, Slintwood Television Company, answer product inquiry 9, p. 167.

Facts on case: Price for black-and-white runs around $135. Slintwood features a 19-inch (diagonal measure) screen, which allows the housing to be less than 10 inches deep. This depth makes the right kind of space for a bookcase to be worked in around parts of the built-in. Model 800 has all controls grouped on the set, whereas model 905 provides controls on a remote unit. It is easy to install. Present aerial should do. Many people prefer joining the cable if it is available. Built-ins come in color ($400).

Many television stations use Slintwood home receivers to monitor their own broadcasts.

7. Answer product inquiry 11, p. 168. No bolting necessary for dryers or washers. Ten inches of free space at back recommended for repairman to remove back panel in order to have access to transmission and water-mixing valve. Buyer pays for installation. It is impossible to estimate installation cost from home office. Price of washer delivered, $260.50. Price of automatic gas dryer No. 236, $230.00; and for automatic electric dryer No. 208, $270.75. Electric dryer is safer and more dependable than gas dryer. Meters can be mounted in porcelain top or on side of this model, whichever is preferred. Price includes mounting of meters. Dryers and washers are 42 inches high (including a 6-inch dial panel), 26 inches deep, and 25 inches wide. The washing machines have special cycles for synthetics. Send pictures of automatic dryers and washers, and ask for an appointment for one of your representatives to go to Stockton.

8. Answer the letter in product inquiry 20, p. 171, for the Pro-Style Athletic Goods Company, Newark, N.J. 07105. Pro-Style's shock-absorbing, synthetic-covered protective equipment (shoulder pads, rib pads, hip pads, arm pads, knee pads, thigh guards, mouth guards, and skin guards) resists moisture readily. School discount for complete sets is 15 percent less than regular price, making each complete set cost $12, or $600 for 50 sets. Pro-Style's breakaway jerseys can be made to go with the game uniforms. The company has a new fabric that is coated with Synolite synthetic latex on the fabric back. The coating prevents raveling and seam slippage and helps the jersey wear longer. This new type of jersey has been tested on the Dallas Cowboys' 200-pound fullback. Eighty yards and a dozen tackles proved that the material is built to take punishment.

9. As director of sales, Bernz Company, Moundsville, West Virginia, 26041, answer product inquiry 17, p. 170.

Facts on case: Your company has no record of a can of Dapper Dan exploding. According to your chemists, the Freon and I.C.C. sealant should be effective for one year. This can should not be used on more than one tire. Send a brochure with pictures and written testimonials about the new product, Dapper Dan. Invite a direct order.

10. Answer product inquiry 12, p. 168, with the following information: Do-it-yourself dry cleaner economical in fraternity or sorority houses. Choice of two power systems—115 volt, 60-cycle, single-phase system; and 230-volt, 60-cycle, three-phase system. Installation requires only power supply and a vent to the outside. No hazards. All wiring is covered and insulated. User has no direct access to the cleaning fluid. Unit costs $600.

With 60 members in a chapter averaging $6 a month for cleaning expense, the coin-operated machine could soon be paid for. One machine holds 9½ pounds of clothing. Cleaning takes 20 minutes. Wash-and-wear clothes can be worn without any ironing as can perma-press clothes. Suggest you call on potential customer and work out payment details. Usual charge is $2 per load. Operating the machine for one load costs the owner about 50 cents.

11. You have been asked by L. P. Heath, owner of Heath Company, Benton Harbor, Michigan 48089 (Case 15, p. 169), to answer the inquiry about the Heathkit Ignition System Analyzer.

Facts on case: No special training is required to operate this analyzer. It will stand rough treatment according to the engineers at the plant. You have no name of a local owner of the Heathkit in the inquirer's area, but you can send him many names of owners in the Michigan-Wisconsin-Illinois area. The Heathkit Ignition System Analyzer has been used recently in the races at Indianapolis.

12. As director of sales, Featherglide Door Company, 819 Main Street, Morgantown, North Carolina 26855, answer the letter of a home-building contractor, Lynton Forest, 9698 Yorkshire Estates, St. Louis, Missouri 63126. Forest explains that he saw on a recent vacation in Michigan one of your new Featherglide doors that operated with one and two transmitters. He was impressed with the smooth operation but wants information on price, size of control panels and receiving panels, and guarantee.

Facts on case: Number 74 F 5609 Opener with one transmitter, $185.00; Number 74 F 679873 Opener with two transmitters, $209.90; extra transmitter with battery Number 74 F 659243, $24.95. Guarantee is for one year. When button is pressed, transmitter sends silent pulse-tone signal to receiver in garage from up to 75 feet away. Receiver relays message to power unit housed in handsome fixture. Featherglide clutch system goes into action . . . moves door without jerking or bouncing. Going down, door automatically reverses when obstacle is touched. Receiver and transmitter trimmed in vinyl woodgrain finish. Permanently lubricated ¼-horsepower motor provides smooth handling. Concealed head track. Handles doors up to 18 feet wide, 8 feet high. Counter-mounted T-rail chain drive. If power fails, door may be operated manually. Automatically reconnects when power resumes. Needs only 1½-inch clearance over high point. FCC certified. UL listed. 110–120 volt, 60 cycle AC.

Here's what the buyer gets: power unit with light, track, chain drive, transmitter with battery, receiver, separate lock for opening door electrically with key, hardware, instructions. Uses two bulbs up to 60-watt size (not included). Shipped freight (rail or truck) or express. Receiver is coded to the transmitter's signal only. Has built-in pushbutton that lets the driver operate door when car and transmitter aren't present.

13. Answer product inquiry 32, p. 174. World Business Machines Corporation has developed a 28-ounce compact, portable dictating machine, the Prospector, which sells for $425 and uses a magnetic belt. The belt is reusable, and it fits a standard envelope. If an error is made, the error is simply erased as the erasing is done for a tape recorder. Additional foot controls and headset can be hooked in. These additions cost $25. The machine dimensions are 6½ inches long, 4½ inches wide, and 1½ inches deep. It operates on a single mercury-alkaline battery providing 16 hours of dictation. Color is hickory-brown case with beige front panel and green trim, and each unit is delivered with a hickory-brown leather carrying case, one battery, four magnetic belts, four mailing inserts, one erase magnet, and one pad of index slips. The Prospector has a completely transistorized amplifier; unlimited measured review; instant, audible scanning; adjustable recording volume control; full-range playback volume control; alert and end-of-belt warning signals; dictate-listen interlock; indexing for secretarial instructions at end of letter; automatic shutoff at end of belt; built-in battery-life indicator; built-in motion window; and fine-line tuning controls. The guarantee covers parts and workmanship for one year. The Prospector can be used anywhere (on planes and trains, in the office, or at home). Because of the fine workmanship, it takes about three months to get one. Supply the name and address of the nearest local dealer.

14. Sit in for George M. Shoop (Case 21, p. 171) and answer Thomas P. Killough's inquiry.

Facts on case: A 6M representative will conduct the program or assist the audio-visual director or a teacher in conducting the program at no additional cost to the school. The program takes about one hour. However, if additional time is available, the time may be expanded. Each teacher will make five or more transparencies. The framework of the program is teacher participation. It will be necessary for the school to have the 6M Teacher In-Service Kit which contains instructor's manual, 200 sheets in color and black line transparency film, color adhesive film, tape, rub-on letters, coloring pens, 10 printed original packets, frames, and 10 creative teach booklets. The cost of the kit is $124.95 (order number 15–1078–9). Ask if your in-service representative, John Boles, can go two months from now to University Place School.

15. From Mrs. E. C. Bartelsmeyer, Main Cross Road, Taylorville, Illinois 62568, comes a letter asking about food waste disposers and the installation of them. As director of sales for the Waste Queen Universal Company, Chicago, Illinois 60602, answer her questions with the following information: If her home has a cesspool, she probably cannot install a waste disposer. If she has a septic tank and if the tank is big enough, she probably can install one. A plumber should be able to tell her whether her drain system can take the strain without choking, and a septic-tank specialist should be able to advise her on the adequacy of the septic tank.

To answer her question about the best buy in a disposer, suggest she investigate the Waste Queen 8000 (See Inquiry Case 29, p. 173 and substitute Case 6, p. 309). The Waste Queen 8000 sells for $140, and the Waste Queen 7000 sells for $112.

16. You are one of the sales consultants writing under the name of Elizabeth Baines in the office of Apasco Instruments, 7500 Birchwood Avenue, Chicago, Illinois 60625, manufacturers and distributors of hear-ing aids. You sell direct to individuals after they submit their hearing charts signed by their doctors. Your advertising stresses the idea, "Let Elizabeth Baines help you. . . ." A Sonictone costs $100 ($20 in advance and $10 a month for nine months if the purchaser wants to buy on time payment; for such a plan you require a signed statement about employment, a bank reference, and three other references; before shipping the aid, you have the purchaser sign the customary promissory note). When an inquiry comes in, you always send along with your individual-letter reply the chart and your booklet *Future Living*, which describes living with a Sonictone. It shows pictures of other users (from 8 to 80), with testimonials. There's a section on hairstyling for wearers of hearing aids. You will not sell a Sonic-tone without signed evidence from a doctor that the hearing deficiency is bad enough to be helped with one. Hence you will not refund the money paid within the first six months after purchase—and then only upon presen-tation of another signed statement by the doctor signing the original chart that he has examined the purchaser again and finds no difference in audioreception of the patient when wearing the Sonictone and when not wearing it.

In the light of this information, sympathetically and persuasively answer the following letter from Miss Janice Cobb, 12 Sunnyside Drive, Helena, Georgia 31037:

Dear Miss Baines:
I am really very unhappy. I am 23 years old and do not think a person my age could possibly need a hearing aid. Yet I find in my work as a secretary that I fail to get many things straight, to the embarrassment of my employer and me. And on dates and at parties the same sort of thing happens. I have not gone to a doctor, hoping that it was a temporary condition due to a severe cold and complications I suffered last winter. Yet I find myself subconsciously trying to lip-read. I dread the thought of having such an unsightly thing hanging on my ear and the bulge of the battery, not to mention its weight. I would appreciate full information about the Sonictone, for I feel that I must do something.

As you read the letter, you make a mental note to tell the young lady that 800,000 people in the United States wear hearing aids and that you have a style in imitation pearl, not as big as many earrings are, which is worn behind the ear. The Sonictone requires no separate batteries be-cause it has tiny self-contained power units (good for about a year like those in electric watches) and integrated circuits, called IC's. These circuits or components are built-in inseparable parts of one solid chip, and they have just recently displaced the transistor type of hearing aid. Instead of weighing three-quarters of an ounce, this aid weighs just one-half of an ounce; yet it provides both moderate amplification and high tonal quality. Sounds and speech become intelligible within a frequency response of from 500 to 4,300 cycles per second. It is attractive because it has no dangling cords, nothing to make bulges in pockets. The sound moves from the flesh-colored case behind the ear through a short plastic tube, and then into the earplug. The Sonictone has a built-in volume control, an on-off switch, and four different earplugs. An instruction booklet that accompanies the aid gives details. Try to get Miss Cobb to take the chart to her doctor and then return it to you with her authorization to send her a Sonictone. Include the necessary papers for buying on time if she cares to.

ORDER CASES

1. Assume the conditions of any of the acknowledgments (next section of the book). Write the order letter in the situation.

2. As the interior decorator of a quality department store, order four Bengali all-wool rugs from Kushman Importers, 230 Fifth Avenue, New York, New York 10001, for your department of Filenes, Pembroke Mall, Jacksonville, Florida 32210. All rugs are to be in cream and tan, 9515 design, and stock number 1674. You want three 3 x 5 feet rugs for $65 each and one 4 x 6 feet at $80. Ship motor freight collect.

3. Assume that you are writing for Mrs. Weston Pendleton, Red Eagle Lodge, Boulder Junction, Wisconsin 54512. From The Knit-Wit Shop, 1785 Benedict Avenue, Kalamazoo, Michigan 49007, order 12 2-ounce skeins of Renee Courtelle acrylic yarn in avocado green at 80 cents each. She has the needles and pattern from work on another sweater. She wants the skeins sent parcel post and charged to her account.

4. You are to represent an organization to which you belong (assume a social or professional fraternity, a religious group, or a civic organization) at its national convention in San Francisco, California 94106. Headquarters are at the Fairmont, 950 Mason, where you would prefer to stay for the two nights and three days the convention is in session. You prefer a single room at the minimum rate. Ask for such a reservation, and ask that the Fairmont confirm it.

5. For the attention of the personal shopping department of some large metropolitan department store (Marshall Fields, Chicago; Hudson's, Detroit; Macy's, New York; or Rich's, Atlanta), send an order for two items of clothing for yourself, one gift item of clothing for a friend of the opposite sex in another city, and one gift item of clothing for a five-year-old godchild. The last two are birthday gifts which you want gift-wrapped with

an appropriate card inserted. You have the current monthly shopper's catalog, so you have catalog numbers and specific prices. A flat fee of 50 cents
is charged for shipping and handling one article, 75 cents for two articles
going to the same address; the gift-wrapping cost is 30 cents per package.
You do not have a charge account at the store, so you'll send either a check
or a money order for the total price, tax if applicable, and shipping expenses.

6. Order: On the following form (a speed letter), order four Model 58
Crown Power Return Electric typewriters, beige, $225; three Model 88
Bohn Contex electric calculators, brown, $230; one Model 3897 steel typing
table $45.

```
To: Ashcroft Office Supplies
    Admiral Drive
    Charleston, South Carolina
    29401
                           From: Shade Insurance Company
                                 981 Main Street
                                 Mullins, South Carolina
                                 29574

                    Date _____ 19_____

Subject: _____
                            MESSAGE
_____
_____
_____
_____
_____
_____
_____ Signed _____

                    Date _____ 19_____
                            REPLY
_____
_____
_____
_____
_____ Signed _____
```

7. Many dealers, like City Office Supply, 315 Warwick Avenue, Warwick, Rhode Island 02888, have to write proposal letters as well as order
letters. A proposal letter tells the manufacturer what you propose to order.
This letter usually goes to a salesman. To Eastern Manufacturing Company, Allston, Massachusetts 02134, write a proposal letter about the ma-

chines you plan to sell this season: one dozen Coronable electric office typewriters, $290 each; one Selecto electric typewriter with 13-inch carriage, $400; one M. P. Schick Model 75 electric folder, $254; one Undergrain Audit 304 numerical accounting machine, $1,265. You are a customer of good standing, who usually takes advantage of the net discount. Ask for confirmation of prices and shipping dates.

8. To help Johnny Spell pass the time while he is recovering from a car accident, you order for him from the Spiller Pet Shop the following items: one 10 gallon aquarium, $10.50; one thermometer, 70 cents; one cover with incandescent lighting, $9.50; one thrifty pump, $4.25; four guppies and four goldfish, 60 cents. Johnny's address is Rural Route 5, Marks, Mississippi 38646. Spiller Pet Shop is 444 East Rankin, Jackson, Mississippi 39209. Send a check to cover supplies and shipping charges.

9. As owner-manager of the Campus Art Supply Company, 2212 Guadalupe, Austin, Texas 78712, order from Tyndale and Lenoir, Inc., 3200 Lanier, Baton Rouge, Louisiana 70814, the following art supplies:

12 boxes No. 546 Sargent oil pastels @ 60 cents a box	$ 7.20
1 dozen No. 378 acrylic sets @ 4.70	56.40
1 dozen charcoal pencil sets @ $1.50	18.00
6 sketch boxes 13" x 17" @ $6.00	36.00
	117.60

For the shipping charges, add $3.06. Enclose a check to cover supplies ($120.66).

10. To help a neighbor with a science project, you order from the Brunswick Biological Supply Company, Roanoke, Virginia 24011, the following living zoological materials:

PL 321 bullfrogs, per 3	$6.00
LI 231 amoeba proteus, class of 12	2.30
LT 243 euglena gracilis, class of 12	1.50

All living materials are sent by special delivery, parcel post. Money order is enclosed.

11. While Mrs. Steven McCamy was visiting her parents in Tulsa, Oklahoma 74106 (11 Sheridon Road), she ran out of the following cosmetics: skin freshener, night cream, and moisture cream. Write a letter for her to Mrs. Franklin Posey, 54th Circle N.W., Oklahoma City, Oklahoma 73129, ordering the following items:

1 12-ounce bottle of Truzier Skin Freshner
1 8-ounce jar of Lumar night cream
1 8-ounce jar of Truzier moisture cream

She wants these cosmetics sent c.o.d. to her home address, Route 12, Box 241, Oklahoma City, Oklahoma 73115.

12. From The Herb Shoppe, National Cathedral, Washington, D.C. 20006, order the following herbs: oregano, sesame, turmeric, rosemary, and thyme. All spices are in 1¾-ounce jars at 35 cents, except the turmeric which sells for 10 cents more. Since this is an out-of-state purchase there is no sales tax. Shipping charges add $1.49 more, however. Send a check to cover the purchase. Write from your address.

13. As a thoroughly satisfied old customer, you are going to take the form-letter suggestion of the Collin Street Bakery (Corsicana, Texas 75110) and order now (November 1) Christmas fruitcakes—one for yourself (2–lb., $4.55 including postage) and two for friends in different cities (one 3–lb., $6.50; one 5–lb., $10). As suggested, be sure to give full names and addresses (including ZIP code), to enclose the exact amount of money as a check or money order, and to indicate desired arrival date (otherwise shipment is immediate).

14. As a Florida fisherman, order the following from Herter's, Inc., large sporting goods supplier on Route 1, Waseca, Minnesota 56093. Since you've used or lost all the order blanks that came with your catalog, you'll need to set the information up in seven columns (catalog number, quantity, style or color, size, name of article, price, and shipping weight): 100 each of sizes 5/0 and 7/0 Kirby Hooks (Cat. No. 31385T, at 59¢ and 84¢, respectively, weighing 40 oz./100); 300-yd. spool of No. LC2D nylon monofilament line in natural color, 30-lb. test, $2.08, wt. 9 oz.; a No. 25–6000 Pylon Minnow Bucket, $2.75, 64 oz.; a dozen each of sizes 1 and 2, No. AH5B Ball Bearing Snap Swivels, 8 oz. dozen, prices 88¢ and 98¢, respectively; a RB6U Heavy-duty Rod Kit (with red thread), $14.08, 96 oz.; and four Plastic Shell Boxes, Style II, SPIE, $1.68, 32 oz. Since you can't figure transportation charges exactly (for the 14 lbs., 1 oz.), send your check for the goods ($23.88) and ask that shipping be express, charges collect.

15. Priester's Pecans (Fort Deposit, Alabama 36032) specializes in nationwide selling by mail of shelled pecans and pecan-filled candies and fruitcakes. As an old customer, you have Priester's brochure picturing, describing, and pricing 25 items. The price list gives the identifying numbers, the name, and the net weight of each item. But you have no order form— you used it a few months ago. For the next holiday season (Christmas, Mother's Day, or the like) or special occasion (birthday, wedding, anniversary) you want to send gifts to two friends in different cities: a Captain's Chest (No. 108, 10 Pecan Logs, net weight 20 oz., $5.25) and a

Fiddle Sticks (No. 97, 1 lb. and 10 oz., $5.35). In the same letter, you want to order (for your own cooking) some Small Pecan Pieces (No. 90, 4 lb. bag, $8) and some Mammoth Pecan Halves (No. 56, 1 lb. tin, $3.45). Prices include postage, but you have to add sales tax for items to be delivered within Alabama. Send your check. Be sure to make clear *where* and *when* to send the gifts.

16. You are the manager of Stegall's Drug Store, 639 9th Street, Huntington, West Virginia 25706. Send a rush order to Elizabeth Barden, Inc., a cosmetic company, 8654 Upland Road, New Rochelle, New York 10803), requesting two dozen Elizabeth Barden lipsticks (assorted shades), $1.40 each ($33.60); one dozen 13-ounce cans of Volvo-5 hair spray, $1.10 each ($13.20); one dozen 2-ounce jars moisturizing cream, $8.50 each ($102); one dozen 10-ounce jars of cleansing cream, $2.00 each ($24). Total runs $172.80. You want these cosmetics sent air express, charges collect. You are a long-established credit customer.

STANDARD ACKNOWLEDGMENT CASES

1. As your instructor directs, write the appropriate acknowledgment for any of the order cases detailed in the preceding section.

2. As correspondent of Manning Brothers, national hardware dealers, 100 Biscayne Boulevard South, Miami, Florida 33131, you are asked to acknowledge receipt of the following order, dated three days ago, from the Grove Hardware Company, 1106 Gunter Avenue, Tallahassee, Florida 32304:

1 doz. MRPT Premore hedge trimmer @ 35.00	$420.00
2 doz. MPRT Oxmore bow saws (36″ size) @ 1.00	24.00
2 doz. MTRP Lopping shears @ 3.20	76.80
	$520.80

A check for 10 percent of the total was enclosed. Send the garden supplies freight collect plus shipping charges, invite credit by sending a credit application blank, and tell Grove Hardware Company about an allied product. You are sending separately 400 envelope stuffers with descriptions of the electric-powered Edger Trimmers. These trimmers have an 8″ edger blade, 9″ trim blade, and five-position swivel adjustment for edging, trimming, and three trenching positions. There is a lock for all positions.

3. You are the sales manager for Sawyer Manufacturing Company, Hyattsville, Maryland 20781. Today you receive an order from a new customer, Cook Office Supply Company (R. T. Cook, manager), in Abell, Maryland:

```
4 doz. boxes Kleen-Rite legal-size stencils @ $3.40 ............... $163.20
5 doz. boxes Nu-Kote 8½ x 11½ #3–064 carbon @ $6.60 .........   396.00
1 gross ball-point pens No. 649 (assorted colors) @ 50 cents .......    72.00
                                                                    ————
                                                                   $631.20
                                                                      2.25
                                                                    ————
                                                                   $633.45
```

The goods are being sent c.o.d. as requested. What can you say in the way of specific resale about these items? What other items do you have in stock that this dealer might want to handle? An electric pencil sharpener sharpens standard-size pencils, costs only $7.00 but can sell for $13.50. It is two-tone blue plastic with 110-120 volt, AC, UL listed. Separately, you are sending a catalog describing your various sales helps such as window and counter displays, promotional leaflets, advertising mats, and self-mailing folders; and a new catalog of Sawyer products. What other points do you want to bring up? Credit application; salesman in Cook's territory?

4. Acknowledge an order for restaurant equipment from a new customer, Francis T. Cobb, owner of the Cobb Restaurant, Honey Creek Parkway, Huntingburg, Indiana 47542:

```
1 refrigerator, Model PA–808 ................................. $ 750
1 Lambert dishwasher, Model MAW ...........................   1,365
1 Thrifty ice maker, FT–75 200 Size ..........................    753
                                                              ————
                                                              2,868
              Shipping charges                                   55
                                                              ————
                                                              2,923
```

Your company, Tilden & Todd Equipment Company, 6399 Wrightwood Ave. West, Chicago, Illinois 60650, included the installation cost in the price. Equipment is to be paid for in 60 days. Include resale on all or one of the items and sales material on any appropriate item, such as the sturdy aluminum trash toters that have 7″ rubber tires, plastic grips. They hold two large square or round garbage cans. The totes sell for $7.50, while the cans sell for $8.90 each. These trash can toters move up to 300 pounds, yet their engineering and jumbo wheels make the job so easy that most women can do the moving.

5. As correspondent for Florida Hardware Company, Inc., 3200 Shamrock Road, Tampa, Florida 33610, acknowledge receipt of the following order dated four days ago from the Bordeaux Hardware Company, Metairie Mall, Metairie, Louisiana 70005: 1 doz. F–28 54–inch ironing boards @ $11.50; 1 doz. F–11 no-burn pads, $3.50 each; 2 doz. F–21 ironing caddy and drip dryer @ $2.50. A check for 10 percent of the total was enclosed, with a request for c.o.d. shipment. Motor freight charges are $8.50. You can send as requested. Enclose a credit application. Tell Henry Bordeaux about an allied product. You are sending along with the shipment 300 envelope stuffers with description of the double sweater dryer (F–18). This dryer will go over the tub, floor, or table. It has a steel frame and nylon netting. When not in use, it folds up. Cost is only $1.50.

6. *To:* The Stork Shop, Platte Shopping Center, Platte Avenue, Colorado Springs, Colorado 80909. *From:* Lipsey-Scott Supply House, 215 Dearborn, Pasadena, California 91103. *Send:*

1 doz. MHB Gro-Tub 26½ x 15½ x 8 @ $4.00	$ 48.00
1 doz. TPN nursery scales @ $4.50	54.00
2 doz. RPM electric sterilizers @ $10.50	252.00
Shipping charges	11.20
	$365.20

Terms: 2/10, n/30. *Sales promotion material:* 40-diaper, 20-quart diaper pail. Chrome-plated metal handle. 12¼ x 13½-inch diameter. Deodorant well in white lid. Sells for $2.50 retail ($1.50 wholesale).

7. Paul Powers, owner of the Pro-Slim Salon, 1198 Water Street, Bloomington, Illinois 61701, orders the following from National Athletic Company, 699 Schiller Avenue, St. Louis, Missouri 63134, enclosing a check to cover charges, less 2 percent, as well as shipping charges: two All-American jogging exercisers, No. LPN–442, at $99.95 each; three light-way exerciser bikes, No. RET–332, at $50.95 each; one Twin-post Massager, No. RMP–445, $160.70 (has two cotton belts with nonstretch leather ends). You can send the exercisers as ordered. Tell Powers about your envelope stuffers and newspaper mat service. You'll send by REA Express, as directed; the machines should be in Bloomington in about two weeks. Suggest any other appropriate merchandise for his Salon such as the dry-heat electric sauna, No. TRY–432, $270.00. It needs no plumbing. Can be plugged in anywhere. Has efficient 1350–watt heating element which generates invigorating, low-humidity heat of over 150 degrees and circulates this heat all around the person in the sauna. Leaves skin vibrant and tingling. Helps person feel relaxed and refreshed.

8. Yesterday an order came to you from the Albuquerque, New Mexico, Trunk Shop, 1109 Arvada Avenue, 87107, for the following leather goods, to be sent c.o.d.:

5 PNY–2234–F olive brown attaché cases @ $20.00	$100.00
1 doz. PHT–2233–F ebony black flight bags @ $40.00	$480.00
Plus shipping charges	10.80
	$590.80

As sales manager for M. P. Mappin Manufacturers, 1399 Washington Street, Spokane, Washington 99206, you welcome this new customer.

You'll ship the leather goods within the next three days. Separately, you'll send a catalog describing your other luggage items, and you'll want to tell him about your national advertising—quarter-page ads, September through June, in *Holiday*. This month your ad features the Two-Suiter (25 x 19 x 17) that weighs only eight pounds and sells for $45 ($22.50 wholesale).

9. Howard Bills, manager of the Erie Country Club, Erie, Pennsylvania 16509, orders the following items from United Golf Products, 1102 Dexter Avenue, Colton, New York 13625, enclosing a check adequate to cover charges as well as shipping expenses:

2 gross Jerry Wright medium-high compression golf balls @ $10.25 a dozen
3 gross Jerry Wright high compression golf balls @ $9.25 a dozen
1 dozen Jerry Wright putters (right-handed) @ $20 each
1 dozen Jerry Wright vinyl golf bags (assorted colors) @ $20.00 each

In sending the merchandise ordered, tell Bills about your special on Jerry Wright set of 8 irons (numbers 1, 3, and 4 for right-handed people only). Regular price $69.00, now on special for $60.00. Send Bills a credit application blank (terms 2/10, n/30).

10. As a correspondent in the sales office of Crew and Drew Hardware Company, 11 Orange Blossom Drive, Daytona Beach, Florida 32019, you have to acknowledge an order from Joseph Little, carpenter, 444 South Edward Street, Destin, Florida 32541:

1 MPY–332 dual-action sander @ $50.00	$50.00
1 MPY–43 lamb's wool polishing pad @ 80¢	.80
1 PTR–555 craftsman pipe cutter	22.00
Shipping charges	4.12
	$76.92

Little's check for $76.92 covers the cost of the items and mail charges; you can send the supplies today, and they should be in Destin in two days. Since he is a new customer, remind him of your fast mailing service and invite his credit.

11. Acknowledge the order for Herter's (Case 14, p. 191), acknowledging the check, saying the minnow bucket is no longer available, saying you'll have to back-order the rod kit (probably arrive in about 10 days), sending the other items, and explaining the finances. Include anything else you think you should.

12. For Priester's Pecans (Case 15, p. 191), acknowledge the order with thanks and tell the customer that her pecans are on the way, and the gifts are or will be, according to the directions given in the order. There's a fly in the goodies, though—that price list the customer used became out of date two months before the order (because of rising costs for just about everything: labor, packages, postage . . .). You're enclosing your new brochure and price list, a couple of new order blanks, and envelopes. You're also asking for a supplementary check for $3.20, the increase in the prices of the items ordered. Call attention to the fact that the old price list states the end date of its effectiveness.

13. Assume that as an authorized agent of Ashcroft (order case 6, p. 189), you can ship all the items asked for. Use the space on the reply form to indicate what is coming, how it is coming, and when it should arrive in Mullins. (You may assume the necessary signed second copy.)

14. As a correspondent in the sales office of Elizabeth Barden, Inc., a cosmetic company, 8654 Upland Road, New Rochelle, New York 10803, you have to acknowledge an order from Louis Stegall, Stegall's Drug Store, 639 9th Street, Huntington, West Virginia 25706:

2 doz. Elizabeth Barden lipsticks (assorted shades)	$1.40	each	$ 33.60
1 doz. 2–oz. jars moisturizing cream	8.50	each	102.00
1 doz. 10–oz. jars cleansing cream	2.00	each	24.00
1 doz. 13–oz. cans of Volvo-5 hair spray	1.10	each	13.20
			$172.80

You are sending these cosmetics air express, charges collect to Stegall, a long-established credit customer. Tell Stegall about Elizabeth Barden national advertisements in *Seventeen* and *Glamour* and about the spot commercials on NBC-TV by the well-known Maurine Frances. Spot TV commercials are in the late afternoon and evening, Monday through Saturday. Suggest that if Stegall would like to increase his sales by tying in his local advertising with this national campaign, you can send him mats. Also tell Stegall about an allied product such as bath oil, eye shadow, or night cream.

CREDIT APPROVAL CASES

1. James Adkinson, your salesman, has sent in an order from Howard Gilmore, owner-manager of the Gilmore Furniture Company, 1400 Laurel Avenue, Shreveport, Louisiana 71103, for four three-position rocker-recliner chairs No. T–S 250 for $150.50 each; 12 fiberglass swivel armchairs No. W–M 360 for $20 each in colors turquoise, coral, and white (four in each color); 12 captain's chairs, No. T–P 430 for $20 each. To this total of $1082.00, add freight charges of $32.40—along with a request from Gilmore for open-account terms. He refers you to his Dan & Broadstreet rating, which you, as credit manager for Spiller Furniture Manufacturing Company, Fayetteville, North Carolina 28306, discover is excellent. Adkinson also reports quite favorably that Gilmore has been in business at his present site for 25 years—his is the only furniture store in the large Shreveport Mall. His store is modern and well arranged, with a good full inventory. You're glad to extend your standard terms of 2/10, n/60. Write a letter that will tell him so and build future business.

2. As credit manager of the Southern Electric Company, 700 Park Road, Louisville, Kentucky 40216, credit a first order from Young's Appliance Store, 411 Main Street, Thunderbolt, Georgia 30581, for one dozen Teflon-coated waffle baker and grills, No. MT–606 at $19.00 each; six roaster ovens, No. YU–506 at $50.50 each; six eight-speed blenders, No. PL–504 at $30.25 each; shipping charges $25.25. The company has a well-established credit rating. Resale (on the blender): Deluxe five-cup glass container is dishwasher washable. The eight-pushbutton speeds have a special on-off switch. Stable, nonsliding base and lid are made of tough white plastic with a die-cast, chrome-plated metal top. Cord storage is in the base, which makes for no counter clutter. National ads run in *Home Beautiful* (always full-page).

3. Larry McMillen, one of your salesmen, has just written you, the credit manager of the Rosenbush Paper Products Company, Indian Trail, Racine, Wisconsin 53403, about David Bolling, formerly a general manager for a large office supply store, who has opened a business of his own in Mansfield, Ohio 44093 (80 Wolf Avenue). As general manager, he bought about $3,000 worth of your merchandise a year, and now he would like to stock the same products. According to McMillen, Bolling will place a first order of $600, but he needs 90-day terms while he is getting started. You know that Bolling has borrowed on his life insurance and home and has used all his savings. He is a good businessman and understands office supply work well; so you write him allowing him the 90-day terms he wants, with a top limit of $600.

4. As credit sales manager of Big Town Camera Company, 5400 Flamingo, Houston, Texas 77020, acknowledge the first order of M. T. Elliott, Elliott's Photo Shop, Alpine, Texas 79830, for five dozen flashcubes, No. ST–450 at $1.00 a dozen; six enlargers No. WT 659 at $40 each; one dozen lenticular screens, No. YT 432 (4 each 40 x 40, 50 x 50, 60 x 60) at prices $25, $35, $45, respectively. Elliott has built up a good camera business during the last three years, and now he wants to build even further. He has no credit established with any jobbers because he always paid cash for the few accessories he bought. His bank notifies you that Elliott has built a successful business with some savings and some borrowing and repaying of small amounts under $200. Because the good camera season is near (spring holidays, weddings, and summer vacations), you grant credit, but you carefully and specifically remind him of due dates and the advantages of the cash discount. You'll have to tell him that jobbers expect their money promptly within the terms of the sale—in your case 3/10, n/60.

Make it clear that the 3 percent discount may be taken only if his check is in the mail by the tenth day from the date of the invoice. Work in the idea that he has earned the credit. Tell him about some of your various services, sales helps, and other merchandise. Because transportation is good between Houston and Alpine, he'll have fast deliveries, which will keep him from carrying a big inventory. You are shipping his camera supplies today.

5. William P. Curtis, manager of the Curtis Shoe Store, Gainesville, Florida 32601, sends in to the Green Shoe Company, St. Louis, Missouri 63116, a first order amounting to $3,500. Curtis submits the following information to show his financial condition: annual sales, $400,320; total assets, $150,000; accounts payable, $500; accounts receivable, $6,000; no liability as bondsman or endorser. His references report him in good standing with all creditors. Write the letter to Curtis granting the credit and shipping the goods, sending a new catalog and envelope stuffers.

6. Mario M. Rogers, owner of Rogers Gift Shop, Doylestown, Pennsylvania 18901, orders from the Martin Supply Company, 299 West Liberty, Cincinnati, Ohio 45230, the following items for shipment on your usual credit terms (2/10, n/60):

6 prs. 417 Fidelity book ends @ $5.50	$ 33.00
1 doz. cork bulletin boards @ $3.00 (18″ x 24″)	36.00
1 doz. baroque-style lighted mirrors @ $10	120.00

An investigation reveals that some of Rogers's recent creditors report him as 30 to 60 days late in paying. Nevertheless, in view of his good location and thriving business, you decide to give him a try, with a tentative limit of $300 and the usual 2/10, n/30 terms. Write Rogers a cheerful (but not casual) letter, shipping the goods and granting the credit. Without preaching to him, make him realize the seriousness of the credit relationship and the happy days ahead for both of you if it is maintained. You are the credit manager.

7. As the credit manager of the Washburn Jelly Company, 3400 Vest Mill Road, Winston-Salem, North Carolina 27103, acknowledge the first order and credit application from Ezra P. Martin, owner of the Martin Fancy Food Shoppe, Emery Avenue, Greenville, South Carolina 29611, as follows:

1 case grape jelly @ $4.50	
1 case strawberry jam @ $6.50	
1 case pepper jelly @ $4.00	
_____Total	$15.00
Shipping charges	1.80
	$16.80

According to reports from the Greenville National Bank and the Grant Wholesale Grocery Company, Martin's new store is making progress and meets obligations in satisfactory fashion. Explain the details of your terms (2/10, n/30), and send him some merchandising aids along with the sweets. The usual markup is 50 percent.

8. As credit manager for the Walton Manufacturing Company, 1105 Reeder Avenue, Flushing, New York 11378, approve the request for credit of Mrs. Larry Sparks. She operates a small figure-slimming salon, 119 Main Road, Garfield, New Jersey 07070. Although her patronage is modest, more and more women have been signing up for the three-months course at $40. And the half-dozen references listed report her as paying within the terms. She has added a cosmetic bar and a wig shop to her reducing salon in the last year. Now she wants to add to reducing equipment. Send her by motor freight three W 28546N stationary bicycles at $37.88 each; four T 38765W belt machines at $40.55 each; four W 2897L vinyl-upholstered exercise boards with leg bands to hold feet at $14.25 each. Tell her you expect your money promptly within the terms of the sale—3/10, n/60. Make it clear that the 3 percent discount may be taken only if her check is in the mail by the tenth day from the date of invoice. Tell her about new Flex-a-Muscle machine that allows the customer to row, pedal, or do sit-ups on the padded slat board. The customer lifts the board for rowing exercises, yet she lies prone and pushes the end of the machine in the air for pedaling work. This versatile exerciser costs only $35.50.

9. Noble H. Pitts, who owns and manages a large furniture store in Athens, Georgia 30601, has sent a first order to the Fling Manufacturing Company, Mayhill, New York 12117. Gary Ross, your salesman who visited Pitts's store, reports that he seems to have a good turnover, an orderly store, and a good rating in Dan & Broadstreet (which you verify). There are only six furniture stores in Athens, and his is the largest and one of the oldest (in business 20 years). Grant terms of 2/10, n/30, and send a solid maple deacon's bench, eight hefty captain's chairs, and a two-drawer buffet, $290.88. Tell him of your full-page monthly ads in *House Lovely*. Encourage other orders.

10. Thomas B. McCollum, proprietor of the McCollum Shoe Store, 819 Carmen Avenue, Sarasota, Florida 33580, sends in to the Clark Shoe Company, 3709 McPherson Avenue, St. Louis, Missouri 63108, a first order amounting to $2,550. McCollum submits the following information to show his financial condition: annual sales, $325,000; total assets, $139,000; accounts payable, $400; accounts receivable, $6,000; no liability as bondsman or endorser. His references report him in good standing with all creditors. Write the letter to McCollum granting the credit and shipping the goods (on enclosed shipping list), sending a new catalog and envelope stuffers.

11. James P. McDade, owner of Hanes Office Supply Company, 2098 Van Dyke Street, Warren, Michigan 48091, orders from the Fidelity File Box, Inc., 312 North Second Street, Minneapolis, Minnesota 55401, the following items for shipment on your usual credit terms (2/10, n/60):

2 Model 418 Fidelity nonsuspension files @ $30 (15" x 18" x 52") (four
    drawers) $60
2 Model 218 Fidelity nonsuspension files @ $20 (2 drawers) (15" x 18" x
    30") 40

An investigation reveals that some of McDade's recent creditors report him as 30 to 60 days late in paying. Nevertheless, in view of his good location and thriving business, you decide to give him a try, with a tentative limit of $200. Write McDade a cheerful (but not casual) letter, shipping the goods and granting the credit. Without preaching to him, make him realize the seriousness of the credit relationship and the happy days ahead for both of you if it is maintained. You are the credit manager.

12. As the credit manager of the Quality Baking Company, 206 Maple Avenue, Elmira, New York 14902, acknowledge the first order and credit application from Harvey P. Moffit, owner of the Moffit Fancy Food Shoppe, 11 Spring Dell Road, Rutherford, New Jersey 07070, as follows:

24 2-lb. Quality White Fruitcakes @ $3 .... $ 72.00
12 5-lb. Quality Cheesecakes @ $3 .... 36.00
12 5-lb. Quality Dark Fruitcakes @ $6 .... 72.00
                                                            $180.00
Shipping charges 2.75
                                                            $182.75

According to reports from the Rutherford National Bank, the Staley Canning Company, and the Birchwood Wholesale Grocery Company, Moffit's new store is making progress and meets obligations in satisfactory fashion. Send him some merchandising aids along with the cakes (2/10, n/30). The usual markup is 50 percent.

13. As credit sales manager of Delta Automotive Parts Company, New Orleans, Louisiana 72568, acknowledge the first order of H. P. Culp, Culp Service Station, Baton Rouge, Louisiana 72599, for three dozen batteries, totaling $504. Culp has built up a good gasoline business during the last five years, and now he wants to go in for accessories. He has no credit established with any jobbers because he always paid cash for the few accessories he bought. His bank notifies you that Culp has built a successful business with some savings and some borrowing and repaying of small amounts under $300. The Baton Rouge Credit Bureau reports that he is slow in paying his personal bills. Because the good battery-selling season is near, you grant credit, but you carefully and specifically remind him of due dates and the advantages of the cash discount. You'll have to tell him that jobbers expect their money promptly within the terms of the sale—in your case 3/10, n/60. Make it clear that the 3 percent discount may be taken only if his check is in the mail by the tenth day from the date of the invoice. Work in the idea that he has earned the credit. Tell him about some of your various services, sales helps, and other merchandise. Because transportation is good between New Orleans and Baton Rouge, he'll have fast deliveries, which will keep him from carrying a big inventory. You are shipping his batteries today.

14. You are credit director, Pittman Biological Supply Company, Burlington, North Carolina 27216. *Send to:* Specks School Supply Company, 1191 Piedmont Avenue, Charleston, South Carolina 29405, the following: Four LA 500 extra-large desert terrariums at $11, two LA 362 woodland terrariums at $5, and one LA 315 aquarium and aquarium assortment at $21. *Terms:* 2/10, n/30. Shipment will go express collect. *Allied sales:* Recommended specimens for the aquariums are a set of three tadpoles, six snails, three mussels, and one turtle or newt, for $3.50 a set. Send catalog that gives valuable information on all the plants and animals available.

15. You are credit manager, Materials Center, P.O. Box 2079, Jacksonville, Florida 32203. *Send to:* The Art Supply Store, 1896 Mulberry Avenue, Pensacola, Florida 32505, one dozen Ap 42 Modern Word and Sentence Printers, $120; one dozen Ty 28 Hobby Oil Painting Sets, $126.50; and one dozen Ty 45 Hobby Watercolor Sets, $60.30. To this total of $306.07, add mailing charges and tax of $12.43. Resale on the Hobby Oil Painting Set: It comes in a 9- by 12-inch sketch box made of heavy cardboard, wood-grained, with hinged lid, metal catch, and leather handle. Features the eight colors of the Color Mixing Guide in seven full-size studio tubes of color and a large tube of white. Also 2½-ounce bottles of linseed oil and turpentine, three good-quality brushes, palette knife. *Sales:* Liquitex is a new tube color that provides the artist with a "paste" acrylic polymer paint that has the response to brush and knife handling that artists are accustomed to in oil painting. Metal tubes, 1½ by 5 inches, sell for $1. *Markup:* Generally around 40 percent. Fast deliveries.

16. As credit manager of the Eastern Electric Company, Monroe Avenue, Rochester, New York 14618, credit a first order from Rainer's Appliance Store, 35460 Woodbridge Avenue, East Haven, Connecticut 06512, for one dozen deluxe hair dryers, $30 each; one dozen toasters, $20 each; six floor washer-dryers, $70 each. Total, $1,020. Shipping charges, $22.49. The company has a well-established credit rating. *Resale:* With the Eastern floor washer, there's no need for sore hands and knees, no mops, and no pails. The Eastern puts clean water and detergent on the floor, loosens the dirt with bristles, and then vacuums up the dirty water. Floors get clean and dry enough to wax or walk on. *Sale:* Eastern Electric has had high-volume sales with the nationally advertised Sensor, a high-intensity lamp. Sensor is ideal to read by in bed, to sew by, to use as a makeup lamp. Generally retails for $19.95 (40 percent markup). National ads run in *Future* and *Live* (always full-page). One-year guarantee.

17. As credit manager for Debcraft Manufacturers, Atlanta, Georgia 31210, you approve Daniel Wade's request for credit. He operates the small Toggery Shop, 445 Prince Avenue, Athens, Georgia 31412. Send him the following men's robes on terms of 2/10, n/30:

6 navy rayon robes, sizes 38, 40, and 42, @ $15	$ 90
6 wine rayon polka-dot print robes, sizes 38, 40, and 42, @ $12.50	75
	$165

The robes are lightweight and easy to pack; have own matching snap-close case. Besides three roomy pockets, they have shawl collar and self-belt.

Two references stated that on several occasions, especially during the summer, Wade had to be reminded of his overdue account. Another reference said he had always paid on time, and still another said only once in five years had he been reminded. His store is not in a busy district of Athens. He just relocated it, and his capital investment in the business doesn't make you feel that it is a thriving business. Until you determine whether or not he is keeping his account up to date, you are limiting his credit to $250. You need to explain your credit terms and to educate him on the value of his taking advantage of the discount. You might want to tell him about your special on tan leather, soft-soled slippers by Aristo. They're usually $7.50 but are now reduced to $6.25 (sizes 6 to 14 in medium and wide widths). Send a catalog which describes these slippers on page 47 and which describes some of your other products.

18. As credit manager for the Swartz Manufacturing Company, White Hall, Georgia 30603, approve the credit request of John P. Stephens. He operates a small sporting-goods store, Stephens's Sports, 609 Edmund Avenue, St. Louis, Missouri 63110. Although his volume is modest, it is steadily increasing. And the half-dozen references listed report him as paying within the terms (but none report his discounting) on monthly invoices ranging from $2 to $500. Send him 24 No. U—300 official instructor's shirts (eight small, eight medium, and eight large) at $4; 12 No. U-400 official instructor's caps at $3.50; and six No. U-100 official instructor's jackets at $18. To this total of $246, add $2.67 shipping charges. The jackets and shirts have the blue-and-white Swiss-embroidered instructor's emblem on the left-front side, and the cap has the official emblem in the center front. The jackets are 100 percent wool, with trim set-in sleeves, snap fasteners, and heavy-knit worsted wool collar, cuffs, and bottom. The smart and distinctively styled shirt is made from top-grade heavyweight jersey with full-cut set-in sleeves.

Two references stated that on several occasions, especially during the summer, Stephens had to be reminded of his overdue account. Another reference said he had always paid on time, and still another said only once in five years had he been reminded. His store is not in a busy district of St. Louis. He just moved his store to a new location, and his capital investment in the business doesn't make you feel that it is a thriving business. Until you determine whether or not he is keeping his account up to date, you are limiting his credit to $350. You need to explain your credit terms and to educate him on the value of his taking advantage of the discount. You might want to tell him about your special on the 100 percent wool official instructor's pants. They are usually $14.95 each but now are reduced to $11.95 (sizes 32, 34, 36, 38, 40, and extra long). Send separately a booklet which describes these pants on page 7 and which describes some of your other products.

CLAIM CASES

1. Though you and your family encountered six bites with stale pecans in your 2-lb. fruitcake (Case 13, p. 191), you ate most of the cake and are not making claim on it. Indeed except for the six bad bites—bad as only a stale pecan can make them—your last fruitcake had the same delicious flavor that has kept you ordering from Collin Street Bakery for at least 10 years. You wrote your friends and asked them to tell you frankly the condition and edibility of the cakes. They all wrote back that the cakes had stale pecans. So you are asking that the cakes be replaced. (You'll need to give the names, addresses, and sizes of cakes again. You sent some 2-lb., some 3-lb., and some 5-lb.)

2. Now three weeks after returning from a trip to Florida, you receive your statement and billing invoices for gasoline purchases on your oil company credit card. All seem to check with your copies except one— where your copy shows no amount of gasoline and a charge of $3.85 but the duplicate from the company has been filled in to show 22.3 gallons and $8.85. You've never spent that much for gasoline at once, partly because your small car's tank holds only 15 gallons.

Your first inclination is to write the oil company; but, as a member of AAA, you decide AAA should know about such shenanigans. So you mail copies of both the purchase tickets (which show the name and address of the particular station on the Florida Turnpike) and send them to AAA with a letter asking AAA to look into the matter for you and get your bill corrected.

3. As vice president of the Peninsula Motor Club (the Florida branch of AAA), you are doing as asked (see preceding case) by writing R. F. Langford, chief of the Florida Turnpike Authority. Besides the facts of the particular case, you want to make the point that travelers on the turnpike

are essentially "captive" buyers of gasoline at stations that have concession contracts and therefore the turnpike authority is responsible for seeing that they get fair treatment. Should you remind him, too, that your newspaper (*The Florida Explorer*), which goes to all members, regularly carries stories about incidents like this case (including what was done about them) as warnings to members of gyps being perpetrated on the traveling public at specific locations? Should you send a copy of your letter to the governor?

4. In March you purchased by mail a portable AM-FM radio cassette from a well-known, highly respected company in Larchmont, N.Y. 10538 (Americana). It was a graduation present for your son.

In no time at all, the music began coming through garbled and would cut out intermittently. After three weeks, you returned the device for repair under the 90-day warranty. You said in your transmittal letter you would prefer a refund rather than repair. In May and in July you wrote again, both times requesting a refund. You did not receive the repaired radio cassette either.

Finally on August 31, you got a form reply stating your correspondence was received and the firm's data processing department had been asked for a report on your account. You were told to disregard any bills from the company for the time being, but it so happened you owe the firm nothing. You have no further word from the firm, no refund, and no repaired graduation present. Write the Americana and try to get a refund.

5. Using the information in the preceding case, ask for help from *Action Line,* the subscriber-problems section of your nearest metropolitan newspaper.

6. Traveling from Los Angeles to your home in the East, on September 4 you noticed undue vibrations in your car. At lunch time, you saw a good eating place and a large service station just off the highway (Interstate 10) in the south edge of Tucson, Arizona, and turned in.

The man at the service station (one of the many major oil companies, with a slogan stressing that you can depend on the man at its stations for all your car's needs) told you that you needed two new tires, all tires balanced, and new front shock absorbers. He did the work while you and your wife ate.

To your considerable surprise, the bill was $148.18—$114.58 for tires (including $5.68 federal tax and balancing of all five tires), $27.90 for shocks installed, and $5.70 state tax (4 percent). You questioned the prices on shocks and tires but paid the bill without argument.

Back home, while wondering about those prices, you found that the local Goodrich dealer would sell you the identical tires for $85 (including tax), balance all five tires for $4.50 ($25.08 cheaper for tires and work), and install the same shocks for $15.90 ($12 cheaper). Of course the federal tax on tires is the same; and of course the 4 percent state sales tax, versus the local 3 percent, is not in question.

Though you have a carbon of the bill, it does not give the name or address of the station—it's a standard form used by all the big oil company stations, giving the New York address of that company. You decide, therefore, to write the Public Relations Department of the oil company and make claim for at least $35 overcharge. Send your carbon of the itemized bill and ask its return. You happen to be a small stockholder and regular customer of that company, but your main appeal should be based on the facts in relation to the company slogan. You admit that the workman did a good job in correcting your troubles.

7. A month has passed and you have not heard further from the investigation of the Tucson service station's prices (preceding case). Write a follow-up letter to show that you aren't forgetting and you don't want the Public Relations Department to forget either. Be careful about your tone, however, to avoid implying any unsavory assumptions that you might be inclined to make to yourself. Give a face-saving way out, but assure the company of your continuing interest.

8. When Herter's partially filled your order (Case 11, p. 195), it returned a thermofax copy of your order with "out of stock" stamped across the minnow bucket item and "back ordered" by the rod kit, and sent the other items prepaid parcel post (65¢). Ten days later the back-ordered rod kit came, showing $3.15 for parcel post and 20¢ for guaranteed delivery prepaid on it—and saying you owed $3.35.

You don't want to be picayune, but you can't figure their invoice out. Show Herter's how you figure it (and ask for corrected invoice), remembering—you got no minnow bucket, and under the circumstances you don't mind the prepaid parcel post shipments (though contrary to your order); but you do mind the unauthorized 20 cents for guaranteed delivery.

You like all the things sent except the figures on changes.

9. Harry Hickel, Route 4, Brighton, Colorado 80601, bought two tires for his car from a local dealer, J. R. Bowman, The Auto Rite, two months ago. The tires were labeled "for nonhighway use" and carried no warranty. After just 1,000 miles both tires show a loss of ¼ inch of tread. Bowman will not make them good, but suggested that Hickel write the manufacturer, L. P. Goodspeed Company, Akron, Ohio 44312. Write the claim letter for Hickel asking for a refund of $68 ($34 for each tire).

10. You ordered a Spanish floor candlestick from an advertisement in a widely read women's homemaking magazine. The order was with the Waymart Candle Shop, Wayne, Pennsylvania 19087. You sent a check for

$10.80 for payment and postage. A week later you got a letter from the company stating the price of the item was $2.15 more than you had enclosed and the shop asked you to specify gold or black wrought iron. You sent the company an additional $2.15 and said again that you preferred black. Both checks cleared your bank. It is now a month since you first ordered the candlestick. Today you are going to write the shop and ask for your candlestick. Be sure and explain again that you sent two checks and that they have cleared your bank.

11. You purchased a set of early American furniture 16 months ago for $587.45 from a local furniture store. Four months ago you finished the installments on your account and asked the furniture store to repair at no cost the sofa and a chair which were coming apart and a lamp which shorted. The furniture was then just a year old, but the store said the set was not guaranteed at all in spite of the price. The manager said over the phone that he would pick up the furniture and see what he could do. When he didn't have the furniture picked up, you called again. This time he said he would have it repaired by a manufacturer, and he'd pay the bill. The firm he used verified your contention that some of the seams were not sewn correctly when the furniture was fabricated. The repair bill was $85. The furniture store now says it will split the bill with you. You can't afford to pay this. You had to scrape and save to pay for the furniture and believed that it would last a reasonable length of time, certainly more than a year. To get help, you are writing the Better Business Bureau in your community describing your problem and sending a carbon to the manager of the furniture store.

12. You drove your car through a tunnel car wash for cleaning. This type of car wash allows you to sit in your car while it is pulled through by chains. When the wash job is complete, the chains release the car.

On this day, however, for some reason, the mechanism did not release the left rear side of your car for 15 or 20 seconds. When it did release the car, your left rear tire was completely flat. The attendant at the car wash saw your tire and told you it was just one of those things. The attendant didn't offer to change the tire; so you sent for a man from a service station across the street. This service station attendant said the tire couldn't be repaired because there was a three-inch cut all the way through it. You asked the car wash attendant for the manager's name and phone number and you contacted him but were told the tire was probably cut like that when it was driven through the car wash. You told him that there was no way one could drive on a tire like that when it was flat all the way to the ground. The cost of a new tire is not the only matter upsetting you. Mainly, it's the principle of the thing and the attitude of the businessman. To help you in your plight, write a letter to Action Line of your newspaper asking for help.

13. A little over three months ago you wrote two letters a week apart arranging with Mutual Savings Institution (1005 Congress, Austin, Texas 78767) to group two of your small accounts into one two-year savings certificate (9052697) for $10,000 at a higher interest rate (6 percent). In each letter you said that you wanted earnings paid each time (quarterly) by check to you—not added to the account as had been the practice on the old accounts. Today, the end of the first quarter, instead of a check you received a form note showing your quarterly earnings of $150 *added to the account.* Write Mutual to get the check.

14. Five years ago the H. J. Heinz Co. (Pittsburgh, 15212, famous for "57 varieties") started selling its tomato catsup in squat bottles with wider mouths, while also continuing its long-neck bottle that makes catsup hard to get out and usually wastes an ounce or so. You (Mrs. J. J. Moeller, 2108 Hartford Road, Austin, Texas 78703) liked the new bottle much better despite the slightly higher price. Now you can't find any of the low-profile bottles; so you are going to write some of your thoughts to Heinz:

—The compliments you should have sent, but didn't, five years ago on consideration of the consumer in offering the better bottle.

—Why did the price have to be higher? Amortized over the years the new bottle should not cost more than the old.

—Have you discontinued the desirable bottle? If so, why? Want consumers to waste some catsup so you can sell more?

—If they are still made, where can you get the squat bottles? Why not in Austin?

Obviously your objective is to get them to resume production and distribution of the wide-mouth bottle.

15. Knowing that you are taking a course in business communication, your 19-year-old sophomore friend asks you to write this letter for him. Of course he will sign it. His father made a deal with him last week to pay off the indebtedness of his souped-up sports car and he has sent in the information for his own insurance (when he becomes the full owner the middle of next month). Of course the dealer that sold the car has been carrying the insurance.

Your friend applied to the insurance company that has insured his father's cars for years. Now he has a reply—a bill to issue the requested insurance. Wow! The charges for liability and collision insurance on his car are about double what his father recently paid on a bigger and more expensive car. How come? He says he's a better driver than his father, and he can't afford any such prices. Ask the company if it has not made some mistake in figuring the charges. To be on the safe side, give full car data again.

16. This morning when you returned to your car on the supermarket lot, it had been kissed hard, pushed several feet backward, and smashed up in front (bent bumper, hood, radiator housing, broken lights). An elderly gentleman approached and gave you a paper on which he had written his name and address and the license number and description of the car he saw hit yours (before the driver, a woman about 60, quickly backed up and then drove off hurriedly). He said he didn't want to get involved but didn't like to see hit-run drivers get away either. Though your insurance does not cover the situation, and though hit-run driving is a serious offense, you do not want to cause the driver undue trouble by reporting to the police before knowing more; and your insurance company did get and give you the driver's name and address (based on the license number). You could drive out to the small town where Mr. and Mrs. W. M. Tabor operate the Tabor Motel (your AAA book tells you), but you want to avoid the likely emotional face-to-face encounter; so you decide to write, asking about Tabor's insurance company (or other arrangement for paying the repair bill on your car—estimates for which you already have: $215, $230, $235). Keep it calm but make it persuasive. You do not need to reveal reporter's name; only by implication would you chide Mrs. Tabor for hit-run driving. You have to report to police if you don't get satisfaction.

17. Mr. Tabor (preceding case) was most cooperative (even relieved) on hearing from you. So he called you. When he confronted Mrs. Tabor about the damage to his car, he finally pumped the whole story from her: awkwardly got foot on gas instead of brake while parking, excited, left scared (not knowing how serious hit-run is). He told her, but good, to never, never leave an accident unless to go to an emergency room. And he feared you *had* reported to the police and she—a not very good driver, especially of his new car—would be in serious trouble. So he gave you his insurance company name and address (use any one you want), thanked you for your kindness, and said let him know if you didn't get satisfaction. Now you are to write the company. Send the three estimates (standard procedure) and offer to settle for any one plus the $80 you've found you'll have to pay for a rental car necessary for the week repairmen say your car has to be in the shop (painting takes time). You know that auto insurers do not ordinarily pay for rentals; so you need to make this part of the claim particularly persuasive. Send Tabor a copy.

18. Since the insurance company in response to your letter refused (Refused Adjustment Case 7, p. 290) to pay the $80, write again that you still think it is due and you are giving ten days to get your money or you'll send copies of your correspondence to the state insurance commissioner to get his advice. (Insurance companies dread this action if they have been anything but fair but have no fear when they have been fair and honest.)

19. Since the insurance commissioner agrees with the insurance company (preceding case) and since Tabor said let him know if you didn't get satisfaction (preceding case 17), let him know that you are still out $80 (besides a lot of trouble) through no fault of your own and you think he should pay it or make his insurance company pay.

20. Mrs. Paul Terry, 765 Sycamore Lane, Anderson, Indiana 46014, ordered from Marshall Miller, 500 Tremont Street, Indianapolis, Indiana 46255, a Raybeam iron with Meflon coating for $24.75. The directions said that the ironer just added water to the spray, steam, and dry iron. Mrs. Terry found that the iron worked smoothly except when she ironed her husband's shirts and her son's blue jeans. Although she had used a little spray starch on these garments, the material stuck to the iron and made tiny scorched places. Mrs. Terry cannot drive into the city to return the iron, but she wants Marshall Miller's to mail her a new one without Meflon coating. She will be glad to mail this "nonstick" iron that she has had for two weeks to Marshall Miller's. Write the letter for her.

21. Foreman's, Inc. 65 Madison Avenue, Chicago, Illinois 60675, wholesale distributor of trophies, will replace all merchandise that is defective in workmanship or material if claims are made within 10 days after purchase. The customer should state date, number of invoice, and reason for returning. Foreman's reserves the right to refuse any returned merchandise unless permission is first obtained. All returns must be prepaid by the customer. The Racket Club 1409 Edgeway, Waco, Texas 76708 (for tennis players aged 6–18), ordered one trophy from Foreman's three weeks ago, invoice No. 9876, 25-inch classic walnut trophy, No. T654, $40.50 plus $4 engraving cost for "Central Texas Tennis Meet." The handsome trophy with the gleaming metal figure of a tennis player arrived at the Racket Club yesterday, but the engraving said "West Texas Tennis Meet." As the tennis coach of the Racket Club, ask Foreman's to replace this trophy with one that has the correct engraving. Urge immediate action. You certainly do not expect to pay $4 more for correct engraving.

22. *Company:* Jo Ann's Beauty Salon, 4499 Highland Avenue, Charlotte, North Carolina 28213. *Product:* Handmade wig, made by Favorite Tress, 4876 Otis Avenue, Lansing, Michigan 48911. The $300 French-made wig, style No. 33, was delivered a month ago. You have kept it in the wig box and on the styrofoam head all the time except when you have shown it to customers. Three weeks ago, Mrs. George Alston, 11 Park Place, Monroe, North Carolina 28544, bought the wig. Today she came in with it and complained that the hair was falling out. You are mailing the wig back to Favorite Tress for replacement. Mrs. Alston has been a good customer of yours, and you want to see that she has a fair deal.

23. Your firm, Smith and Gregory, 599 Laird Avenue, Youngstown, Ohio 44505, purchased a $65 Selecto typewriter two months ago from the World Business Machines' representative, John Blake. The main selling point of this machine is that the typist can change type styles in seconds to fit the typing job. Your secretary found that the Selecto was versatile and easy to use, but, when she made duplicates of bills and letters, the copies did not come out clearly. Blake said there was nothing he could do about the typewriter, for there was nothing wrong with it. Today you and the secretary write a letter with two duplicates to World Business Machines Corporation, 987 Elmhurst, Flushing, New York 11352. Explain how unsatisfactory the machine is for making copies. Your firm has many needs for duplicate copies but prefers not to use a copy machine. Ask that WBM either make adjustments on this machine or replace it with one that will turn out distinctly clear carbon copies.

24. As Scott Hunter, 984 Lazycreek Drive, Muncie, Indiana 47304, write the United Victor Company, 574 Birch Avenue, Orange, New Jersey 07052, that the left speaker of the solid-state component system, which you ordered two weeks before does not work. You have set up this $90.95 system carefully according to directions. Your system has not been in use longer than the warranty card specified against defects. Ask for your money back or a new component system.

25. Francis Cook, salesman for Warner & Hopkins Company, 777 Commerce Street, San Antonio, Texas 78209, took a first order for five dozen pairs of Built-Rite all-leather children's shoes, style PY45876, in assorted sizes, from you, the owner of the Kiddie Korner, 997 Main Street, Round Rock, Texas 77654. When Cook sold you the shoes, he quoted and entered on the order a price of $7 a pair. When the invoice from the home office came today, you were billed for $7.95 a pair. Write a good and specific claim letter to the Warner & Hopkins Company, stating the facts in the case and asking that you be charged $7 instead of $7.95 a pair.

26. Step into the shoes of Mrs. Odessa Hudson, a secretary, 654 Lincoln Street, Peoria, Illinois 61607. Your employer is getting married, and you want to give him a nice, practical, but inexpensive, wedding present. In the gift catalog of the exclusive Hitching Post Gift Shop, Lake City Avenue, Rockford, Illinois 61108, you saw a good-looking glazed casserole dish for $9.50. The copy said: "Sparkling glazed white ceramic casserole, smart contrasting black metal cover, on a gleaming brass stand that holds candle to keep food warm. Cover lifts with brass knob. Holds two quarts; measures 8 inches high overall. Unusually attractive on colorful buffet dinner cloths." You ordered it to be sent right away. But when it came, the stand was bent and the dish broken into many pieces—the only thing left was the lid. Ask the Hitching Post Gift Shop for a new casserole dish right away so that it will get to Peoria in time for the wedding.

27. After having three new soap dispensers put on your automatic dishwasher (model No. EW–567) during the one-year guarantee period, you refuse to pay the serviceman from Western Electric, who came today to put on the fourth dispenser. It is true that the one-year guarantee has expired; you are now into the eighteenth month of using the machine. When you called the local store and talked with the manager, Tim Reasoner, he suggested you write the home office in San Diego, California 92115 (643 Camino Del Rio), requesting payment of the service call. Explain that you have always used the prescribed kind of soap and that you have been running the machine yourself. You have always been careful to set the dial in the correct position and not spin it around haphazardly.

ADJUSTMENT APPROVAL CASES

1. As manager of the Collin Street Bakery, answer the claim letter for (Case 1, p. 203) with these points: evidently your precan supplier sent you some stale nuts (about 20 claims the past week, including the 3-lb. fruitcake of one of the present addressee's friends; so far all claims are on 2- and 3-lb. cakes, which come from same mixing machine (different from 5-lb. cakes); since your shelled pecans come in 10-lb. cartons, most likely you got only one or two cartons of stale pecans, and probably all of them went into the same mix (about 50 lbs. of 2- and 3-lb. cakes). Nevertheless, you're writing the requested follow-up on the 5-lb. cake (enclosing copy). You're making good on all claims immediately by replacing all cakes (including addressee's cake). When you think you've cleared about all the claims, you'll make a claim yourself to the pecan supplier—want to keep him on his toes and keep up your quality and reputation.

2. Write the follow-up letter (referred to in the preceding case), indicating a copy goes to orderer of the 5-lb. gift cake.

3. To answer the spate of claims on your 2- and 3-lb. fruit cakes (Case 1), you've decided to use a form letter where only one cake is involved. Write the letter.

4. Read Case 6, p. 204. As Chairman of the Board (the top office in a corporation), you insist on seeing all correspondence from unhappy stockholders. You decide to start an immediate investigation of the Tucson station's prices, and you promise that the unhappy stockholder-customer will receive your report shortly. Your main purpose, of course, is to regain lost confidence and goodwill by making deserved adjustments or necessary explanations where no adjustment is warranted. Certainly you can't now promise anything except the investigation, a fair handling, any needed corrective measures, and your interest in seeing that customers are treated right.

5. As Chairman of the Board (in the preceding case), you have your report from your investigator in Tucson and are to write the promised letter to the unhappy customer-stockholder. The men who operate service stations and carry your name and products are independent businessmen leasing the stations and hence can set their own prices and procedures—within broad contract limits. You select them carefully, however, and exercise some supervision and loose control. The leases are for short terms, renewable on mutual agreement. Your main methods of control are by suggestion, persuasion, and advice—decisions to renew or discontinue leases are usually handled by regional representatives.

The Tucson representative found considerable variation in prices on tires and shocks in his marketing areas and has figured the averages. He has informed all leaseholders in the area of what the averages are and of the dangers in being too far from the averages in either direction. He found that the station where the unhappy customer went was among the highest —but not the highest. He has talked specifically with the manager, got him to agree to reduce his prices to the averages, and got him to write a check to you for $19.20 (the resultant reduction on the questioned bill). You have that check in hand. Send it, with the best adjustment letter you can write, to the unhappy customer-stockholder.

Return the carbon copy of the bill, as requested.

6. Before attempting this case, read Claims Case 10, p. 205. As the owner of the Waymart Candle Shop, Wayne, Pennsylvania 19087, write Mrs. J. T. Collins, Box 781, Corsicana, Texas 75110, and tell her that a refund of $2.15 and the Spanish black wrought-iron floor candlestick will be mailed within 10 days. The retail price of the candlestick had gone up, but since the shop's advertisement still ran the old price, you are willing to make this refund. For possible further sales, talk up a special you now have on ice-white 10-inch and 15-inch candles. These odorless and dripless candles sell for the low price of $1.50 for the 10-inch size and $2.25 for the 15-inch size.

7. As R. F. Langford, answer the letter described in Claims Case 3, p. 203. Facts: The turnpike service inspector and the involved oil company have both made investigations. An employee of three weeks at the service station had altered two gasoline invoices. He has been fired, though the other customer had not caught the "error" and had paid. The oil company is sending refund checks to both customers and asking the reporting customer to pay the bill as submitted to keep the record straight. You agree with the motor club's point of view on your responsibility to the public and appreciate the information as helpful in your constant work with service station managers to improve the service in all areas. Should you admit that this is not the first, and not the only kind, of gyps you have tracked down and squelched? Should you send copies of your letter directly to the customers? You are now fingerprinting all employees.

8. Assume that the insurance company (where you are *approval* adjuster) does have different men approving and refusing claims. Write your part of the answer to Claim Case 17, p. 208—the Tabor case.

9. As Mr. Tabor, you agree that the $80 car rental should be paid, that the insurance company is justified in refusing, and that therefore you should pay. Do pay it; and again express your kind feelings to the claimant, who has been very nice and patient.

10. As sales director for Sarah Jane's (bakers of fine white and dark fruitcakes, thousands of which are sold by mail), 4446 Pine Ridge Avenue, Evansville, Indiana 47714, answer the letter from one of your unhappy customers, Louis M. Simpson, Apartment 202, The Williamsburg East, Urbana, Illinois 61801. He reports in sharp language that over a month ago he sent his order and check for one 5-lb. Sarah Jane's White Fruitcake along with his card to be sent to his hostess of several days in Des Plaines, Illinois 60018, Mrs. Hamilton Fish, 399 Thacker Drive. In Des Plaines again last weekend, he called the Fishes and discreetly found out that the gift had never been received. "Unless you have gone out of business— in which case you'd surely return my check for $7.95—will you please trace this *or* send at once *and* write a note to Mrs. Fish confirming that I *did* order this gift very shortly after I was a guest in her home?" he ended. The facts are (*a*) you were caught short on the special raisins from Turkey and currants from California, without which Sarah Jane's White Fruitcakes would not be the distinctive culinary treats they are and (*b*) someone slipped in not notifying the buyer or the recipient of the atypical delay in shipment. You've resumed baking and shipping, filling orders in the order received; the cake in question is en route and may already have arrived. Write the necessary letters to both Simpson and Mrs. Fish. (You should send Simpson a carbon of your letter to the lady.) Certainly you'll want to try to convince both that a Sarah Jane's White Fruitcake is an appropriate gift any time and is well worth waiting for.

11. As adjustment manager for Foreman's, Inc., 65 Madison Avenue, Chicago, Illinois 60675, write Coach Harvey Kemp, Racket Club, 1409 Edgeway, Waco, Texas 76708, that you will be happy to have him send the trophy back to you right away. Tell him there is a way the expert engravers can change the wording to say what he prefers: "Central Texas

Tennis Meet" (Claim Case 21, p. 209). For the next big tennis meet, urge him to order less expensive sport "Oscars" (durable plastic bases with gleaming metal figures). These come in three sizes: 10-inch, $7, 11-inch, $7.50, and 12-inch, $8.

12. As adjustment manager for Marshall Miller's, 500 Tremont Street, Indianapolis, Indiana 46255, write Mrs. Paul Terry, 765 Sycamore Lane, Anderson, Indiana 46014 (Claim Case 20, p. 209), that you will send her a new Raybeam iron without Meflon coating when she returns the Raybeam iron she bought from you two weeks ago. Because of reports from other customers, the Raybeam people frankly admitted that Meflon coating had not been perfected. The iron worked fine on all material except material that had been starched. Mrs. Terry is a customer of long standing, and you want to keep her account on the books. The iron you are sending her has the new Scorch-Gard feature. The Scorch-Gard tells her when it's safe to do the delicate wash-and-wear garments. If she has ever scorched a delicate wash-and-wear garment because she didn't wait long enough for the soleplate to simmer down after ironing cottons or linens, she'll appreciate the value of the Scorch-Gard feature.

13. Favorite Tress, 4876 Otis Avenue, Lansing, Michigan 48911, will repair Mrs. George Alston's wig (Claim Case 22, p. 209), at no cost to her or to Jo Ann's Beauty Salon. Although the wig had had some severe brushing and too much rolling up, it is now in excellent condition and should last many more years with good care. Favorite Tress uses this opportunity to sell more wigs to Jo Ann's Beauty Salon (now has pink, green, and pale blue wigs for those who want to be exciting). The Italian and French handmade wigs are lighter to wear, but the machine-made wigs are much cheaper (retail price, $85.50 to $200). And for even less money you can supply the shop with modacrylic wigs (the synthetic hair that looks real). These wigs won't frizz up in rain, wilt in humidity, or fade in the sun. Retail price, $20 to $35. Most beauty shops take a 100 percent markup. Many wig customers have more than one. Special brushes for wigs retail for $3.00 and wig spray runs $2.50 a can retail.

14. As adjustment manager for World Business Machines Corporation, 987 Elmhurst, Flushing, New York 11352, write the firm of Smith and Gregory, 599 Laird Avenue, Youngstown, Ohio 44505, that your company has improved the typefaces on the Selecto and that you are replacing the round snap-off-and-on typing element (Claim Case 23, p. 210). The new element should be in Youngstown in a week's time. Include some resale about the machine, based on the following facts: margins and tabs are conveniently located on the keyboard control area. Stroke-storage error control stores the second of two rapidly struck characters until the first is printed out, eliminating type-bar pile-up and clash. Dual stroke control prevents printing if two keys are struck simultaneously. Sculptured keys and curved keyboard fit the typist's natural reach. The convenience of interchangeable fabric ribbon cartridges insures easy, clean, and fast ribbon changes. The five different type styles can be used in various ways. The new element prints so clearly and firmly that copies are almost as clear as originals.

15. Send Scott Hunter, 984 Lazycreek Drive, Muncie, Indiana 47304 (Claim Case 24, p. 210), a new stereo solid-state component system, and ask him to send collect via REA Express his first system to United Victor Company warehouse, 574 Birch Avenue, Orange, New Jersey 07052. Despite careful checking of all elements in the system, the delicate parts necessary to the tone quality you insist on sometimes shake out of adjustment from jars in shipping and installing. Try to tell him subtly to handle with care. Suggest to him your stereo tape recorder, the Hallman VI. Tell him that it is now available to him at a discount price because of clearance sales. Inform him of your pay-by-the-month plan, which would cost him little more than the discount price. Point out that the tape recorder is made to fit into his component system and that he can record right from his record player or built-in AM-FM stereo radio. Tell him to get in touch with United Victor as soon as possible while supplies last.

16. As adjustment manager for Franklin Sandwich-Glass, 543 McDuff Street, Los Angeles, California 90017, answer the claim letter of Mathew Gray, owner and manager of the Little Travelers, 943 Panorama Drive, Colorado Springs, Colorado 80907. Gray, an old customer of yours, complains that the last shipment of sandwich glass from Franklin seemed to be all right when he unpacked it, but when he placed it in his show window the sandwich glass cracked or popped. None of it seemed to crack in the same place, he explained. Your explanation: Probably the glass was removed from a colder room to a warmer part of the store. Sudden changes in temperature can make glass break. But, because Gray is a reliable customer, and because you want to keep his goodwill, you are sending him three vases, two pitchers, and four candy dishes (the replacements for his broken sandwich glass). In your full-reparation adjustment, explain that sudden changes in temperature can cause breakage even when the glass has been made to top-quality specifications.

17. Mrs. Owen Dodson, 876 Retirement Village, Tempe, Arizona 85281, ordered from Ventura Specialty Company, 9870 East Washington Street, Fresno, California 93728, a mother-of-pearl Victoria Carryall with the initials BTD on the front. The carryall is practical for it has a lipstick case, mirror, and cigarette case all in one. The price, as advertised in last month's *Vogue*, $14.50, includes the charges for initials and shipping. This morning she wrote you (the adjustment manager) that she got her Victoria Carryall (which she paid for by check) with the initials DBT and that she is sending it back; she wants it either fixed right or her money back. When you check her order, you see that she is correct; and the only explanation you can find is that Victoria has added new help in preparation for the Christmas rush. From now on, you will have one worker be responsible for checking the initials before the Carryalls are mailed. In two days the correct initials BTD can be put on the case, and it can be mailed to her by the first of next week. Make the adjustment approval and keep Mrs. Dodson pleased with Carryall.

18. At the manager's desk in the Colonial House, a gift shop selling artistic, unusual items (76 Charles Street, Williamsburg, Virginia 23185), answer the letter from Harding Long, 342 Whitley Drive, Norristown, Pennsylvania 19406. When Long and his wife were in Williamsburg visiting, they bought from you a handsome parchment lampshade with color photographs of Williamsburg landmarks (Williamsburg Inn, Governor's Palace, etc.) and asked that you ship it to their home address, since they had little space in their car and did not want to run the risk of soiling or crushing it. But apparently in shipment the lampshade got smashed up. Long wants another one right away. He offers to return this one (which is not necessary, but you will have to ask him to sign a statement-of-damage form you are enclosing so that you can collect from the insurance company under the blanket policy covering your shipments). To be sure that his new 15-inch shade gets to him safely, you are packing it in one of your stronger $\frac{1}{8}$-inch corrugated boxes (the original box was $\frac{1}{16}$ inch), to which you'll attach the letter you are going to write.

19. You are the adjustment manager for the Fincher Jewelry Company, 1320 Duquoines Avenue, New Orleans, Louisiana 71007. Ten days ago Milton Barger, 765 Longleaf Street, Abbeville, Louisiana 70510, ordered and charged to his account one American electric wood-case clock with an alarm and recessed, luminous hands—the Markathon, a rather distinctive model at $32. He reports the arrival of the clock "with the glass broken and the wood scratched. Please send another just like it. What do you want me to do with this damaged one?" You are having packed and sent another Markathon in a larger carton with more plastic packing around the face of the clock to protect it. Ask him to return the damaged one to you, shipping charges collect.

20. Mr. and Mrs. Samuel Murchinson, 405 Quincy Street, Olathe, Kansas 66061, have been desirable charge customers of Wimberly Company, one of the large department stores in Kansas City, Missouri 64164 (4320 Deramus Avenue). During a period of over eight years their purchases have averaged about $300 a year, and they have always been prompt in their payments. Almost a month ago Mr. Murchinson ordered an electric chime clock to be sent as a wedding present to Mr. and Mrs. Edward Weller, 98 Tierra Amarillo, Gallup, New Mexico 87301. When the Murchinsons received their monthly statement they found they had not been charged with the cost of the wedding present, $45. An investigation disclosed that through an error of a clerk, the present was sent c.o.d. because the name of Edward Weller did not appear among the charge accounts of the store. Mr. Murchinson sent a scathing letter to the company concerning the difficulty, which it is your job to handle. The company responds with the type of adjustment letter which the situation requires—an adjustment approval—and a letter to the Wellers.

FROM THE PRECEDING discussions and illustrations of various kinds of letters, you certainly realize that all letters should retain and even try to increase the reader's favorable attitude toward the writer and his firm while working primarily on something else.

Certain letters, however, have no other immediate purpose than the cementing of friendly relations between the customer and the house. Although they may not ask the reader to take any immediate action, indirectly these special goodwill letters pave the way for continued business from old customers and new business from prospects.

Because your readers know you do not *have* to write special goodwill letters, these unexpected letters are especially effective in overcoming the impression of indifference—indifference to business given and to serving new customers.

All too often the only times a customer receives word from a firm are when someone wants him to buy or to pay for something or when he demands attention by making a claim or threatening to close his account. This apparent lack of interest is borne out in practically all reliable surveys of why firms lose customers. About 7 out of 10 lost customers just drift away. Yet 8 out of 10 are reclaimable if given some attention. Only 1 percent of lost customers have real grievances that need adjusting. And a large part of the 70 percent who do drift away would undoubtedly not do so if they were reminded that the business firm appreciates their patronage and has a continuing interest in their welfare.

Where people take their trade depends not just on quality, price, and convenience; these are usually comparable in several different outlets. Most of us trade where we do partly because (1) we like the people and (2) we appreciate the extra-service considerations—the personal and friendly aspects.

In theory, goodwill letters sell only friendship. Some do no more than that—ostensibly. But we should admit to ourselves in all honesty that "pure" friendship is a commodity not bought and sold. We should also admit that a letter on a firm's letterhead, signed by a representative of the firm, is promotional, regardless of its personal nature. The cultivation of business is inherent in the circumstance itself. No writer need be reluctant to establish the virtues of his firm's services and goods and to place them at the disposal of his reader. But he should be frank from the outset. The main thing to guard against is appearing to be offering only friendship in the first part of the letter and then shifting to an obvious, immediate sales pitch.

Most special goodwill letters are low-pressure messages with potential or postponed sales possibilities. These are more accurately called business promotion letters (or just "promotional" or "promotion"). They should be differentiated both from the personal letter that is a friendly note with no sales ax to grind and from the obvious and avowed sales letter. It is impossible to draw a fine line of distinction between the two, however, or to establish definitions and classifications that conform with the varying ways different people use the terms.

Some of these "unnecessary" business letters are of such highly personal nature that to use an obvious form would be insulting, to include sales talk or resale talk on either firm or merchandise would be ludicrous, and to write very much would likely result in gushiness. Letters of deserved praise and of sympathy certainly fall into this category. Letters expressing appreciation, extending seasonal greetings, issuing invitations, accompanying favors (or services), or offering helpful information do likewise if they are strictly goodwill letters; but the majority of these are form letters including sales-building talk and thus are promotional.

Letters of deserved praise

Letters praising people are essentially congratulatory. Although they may not contain the word *congratulations,* the spirit is there. In them you are recognizing a significant event or accomplishment in the life of your reader: a job promotion, election to an office, receiving an honor, winning a contest, graduation, marriage, birth of a child, completion of a new plant or office, a project or a report successfully completed. All these and many more are instances when you can show not only customers but also friends and acquaintances that you are interested in what happens to them. Some of the better ones are just a few lines:

When I saw that you've been named plant manager of Tri-States,
I was delighted!

It's a well-earned recognition.

And it couldn't happen to a more deserving fellow!

(Any salutary effects of the foregoing passages would be lost if the writer
followed with such an idea as "Now that you're earning more, surely you'd
like to consider more insurance" or ". . . buy more clothes.")

I have just completed your article about credit control in the
recent issue of Credit World.

Heartiest congratulations on a job well done!

--

I can appreciate your deep satisfaction and pride in John's
graduation cum laude from Haverford last week.

Congratulations to him—and also to his parents.

--

Congratulations to you and your wife on the birth of your son.
And good wishes to all of you.

--

We share your pride and happiness in the completion of the new
Henderson plant.

It is a criterion of business, as well as civic,
accomplishment.

Good wishes from all of us.   (Or Sincere wishes for your
continued success.)

If these examples strike you as being more like telegrams than letters, remember that timeliness is important in letters like these, probably of equal
importance with what you actually say. The friendly thought behind the
message counts most.

A note like the following would certainly engender good feeling (and
probably stimulate the salesman to greater productivity):

Congratulations, Steve Mason, on winning the home movie
camera!

I know it took a lot of planning and hard work to exceed your
previous records and to nose out every other salesman in the
Midwest district.

You have the personality, the drive, and the intelligence to
take you places in your career with General Milling.

Incidentally, I'm glad that you have the camera while your
children are little. The film record of their growth will
become more treasured by you and your wife as the years go by.

Or this:

Your analysis of production difficulties at the Saginaw plant
was one of the clearest, most easily read reports I've ever
been privileged to study.

We're carrying out some of your recommendations immediately.

```
Several of us look forward to discussing the report with you
when you return to the home office.
```

```
In the meantime, thanks for a job well done.
```

Many people in both their business and their private lives have discovered the gratifying responses of associates, customers, and personal friends to the receipt of a newspaper or magazine clipping of interest to the reader. A simple greeting (it may be no more than "Good morning") and a line or two like "This clipping made me think of you" or "I thought you might be interested in this clipping" are enough. A folder is a common form. People who could expect to use such a mailing often would find a printed form a great saving of time; others would probably send a handwritten or typewritten note like

```
Let me add my commendation to those you've undoubtedly already
received as a result of the enclosed clipping.
```

```
It's a pleasure to know a man like you.
```

The obvious substitutions like "to be associated with" or "to serve" or "to have a friend" readily suggest themselves on the appropriate occasions.

Still another variation of a letter deservedly praising someone is one you write to a third person about a second person who in your opinion merits recognition or appreciation or both. The man who wrote the following letter to an airline official made at least two friends for himself:

```
On your Flight 127 from Chicago to San Francisco last Tuesday,
I was pleased with every phase of the service.  But I was
especially pleased with the conduct of Captain A. L. Lutz.
```

```
While at the controls he kept us well informed on flight
conditions and frequently pointed out places of interest en
route.  When he walked through the cabin, he was the soul of
hospitality and courtesy to every passenger—particularly to a
six-year-old boy who was making his first flight!
```

```
As we came in at San Francisco in bright moonlight and
crossed the Bay, Captain Lutz pointed out sights of interest;
it was a thoughtful gesture that all of us appreciated.
```

```
The smooth, pleasant ride was made memorable through the
"little extras" of Captain Lutz.
```

```
My thanks and commendations to the line and to him.
```

Any time someone renders outstanding service is an appropriate occasion to relay, via letter, your understanding and appreciation of its significance. Such a gesture not only impresses the reader with the writer's "humanness"; but it can also and often does earn him preferential treatment on subsequent occasions.

```
When I brought my two children to the glove counter of
Burger's today to purchase a Christmas gift for their mother,
I appreciated very much the patience and courtesy of the
saleswoman who assisted us.
```

```
I did not get her card, nor can I find the sales slip to give
```

you her number. She is of medium build and has black hair (my
daughter says she was wearing a beige knitted outfit).

We were in the store about 1 o'clock, and the children had not
yet had lunch; they were therefore fidgety and a little
difficult. They asked to see at least a dozen different
styles and colors, some of which even I recognized as
duplicates. They asked many pointless questions. They
argued with one another. But in helping them arrive at a
selection, the clerk remained calm and patient. And she was
certainly tactful and diplomatic when our 11-year-old spilled
a box of glove powder all over the counter and onto the floor!

No doubt she will remember us. . . . But please tell her that
we remember her too—with gratitude.

--

Last Friday your representative, Mr. John Wade, answered our
call for help when one of our motors failed at a crucial time.

We appreciated the promptness with which he came, of course.
But we appreciated even more the efficiency he displayed in
getting it running again. He was considerate of all around
him and thoughtful enough not to leave a mess for us to clean
up.

Our thanks to you and to Mr. Wade; we shall remember on other
occasions.

Obviously, under such circumstances you could also write directly to the
person whose performance you praise, as in the following instance:

If such an award were given by the U.S. Chamber Workshop,
you'd certainly get the "E" for excellence, John.

Your Thursday afternoon clinic met with more enthusiastic
reactions than I've observed in a long time.

It is a rewarding experience to work with people like you.

With a second letter to the speaker's dean (taking only two minutes' dictation time), the writer could spread goodwill all around:

Everyone at MSU working with us on the U.S. Chamber Workshop
contributed and cooperated in exemplary fashion, Dean White.

We are most grateful to all of you.

John Fohr's Thursday afternoon clinic met with such
enthusiastic response that I feel I should report the group
reaction to you. He had men like Ed Sherrer, the Memphis
division manager, eating out of his hand!

Deservedly so, in my opinion.

Congratulatory letters, including birthday and anniversary greetings, are
practically always individualized. Sympathy letters—the most personal of
any special goodwill letters—must be.

Letters of sympathy

Most of us are accustomed to lending a helping hand and extending
expressions of encouragement when friends and family suffer some ad-

versity. The same sympathetic attitude should prevail when a business friend experiences misfortune. Admittedly, letters of condolence are some of the most difficult of the special goodwill letters to write because of the melancholy circumstances (which can be reduced by avoiding specifics). But they are certainly appreciated by everyone. When a report of a retailer's illness reaches a wholesaler (or a manufacturer), he can gain goodwill with a short, human, and essentially positive note like the following:

```
Sorry, Sam—

—to hear that you're in the hospital again.

But with rest and good care you'll be back at the store sooner
than you think.

I've always enjoyed you as a friend and valued you as a
business associate; so for two reasons I hope all goes well
with you again soon.
                        --
We were distressed to learn of the automobile accident that
hospitalized you and Mrs. Sigler recently.

It's good to know, however, that you are now up and about.
We certainly hope that Mrs. Sigler's condition will improve
and that there will be no further complications.
```

As a result of accident, illness, and advancing age, most of us find ourselves having to write letters concerning the death of someone we've known. To the surviving partner of a business, for example, the following letter would be a comfort. It would help to convince him of the writer's friendly interest and concern.

```
We were genuinely distressed to learn of the death of Mr.
Guin, your partner and our good friend for many years.

Although the firm of Guin and Beatty will feel the effects of
his absence, it is too well founded and has been too well
operated over the years for any serious dislocations to
happen.

The great loss is to the community and the Guin family.  The
good judgment, vision, and integrity Mr. Guin displayed as a
business leader in your city undoubtedly were also reflected
in his private life.

In extending these words of sympathy, we should also like to
add a few of encouragement and confidence in the future; we
feel sure that would have been Mr. Guin's attitude.
```

Even though the writer of the preceding letter might not have met the widow (and/or the surviving offspring), certainly none of them would take offense at a message such as the following:

```
For many years we enjoyed a business friendship with Mr. Guin.

We respected him as a good businessman who insisted on high
standards in serving the public and was always just, fair, and
cooperative in his relations with us.  We admired the good
judgment, vision, and integrity he showed as a business leader
in your community.
```

> To you who saw these and other fine qualities in greater
> detail and frequency than we were privileged to, we offer our
> sympathy in respect and humility.
>
> May his contributions to your life in former days make the
> days to come easier to cope with.

Such a letter will necessarily have an emotional impact. But the effect can be lessened if writers will refrain from quoting Scripture or poetry. And sepulchral overtones will not be so powerful if death is accepted as the inevitability it is and the word itself used rather than euphemisms like "passed away," "passed to his reward," and "departed." Such a letter is going to be a greater comfort when it emphasizes the good characteristics and the outstanding contributions of the dead individual rather than the sorrow and anguish of the survivor. Possibly you will find writing such letters a little less difficult and will write more truly comforting messages if you accept the thought that good, worthwhile people continue to exert their influence in the hearts and minds of those who knew them.

Adversity also strikes in other forms—fires, floods, accidents and law-suits, labor unrest and work stoppage. When it does, the victim(s) will appreciate a message that says, "We're your friends; we understand the significance of this to you; we hope everything will work out successfully." If you really mean the offer and are in a position to extend it, you can add the equivalent of "Call on us if we can help." The following are examples:

> All of us were sorry to hear of the fire that destroyed your
> warehouse night before last.
>
> It's a tough break.
>
> We're sure, however, that the same determination and ingenuity
> that helped you to build your business so successfully will
> also see you through this temporary setback.

Now, if this writer had some unused storage space and wanted to offer it, he might very well close with

> We have a 30 x 40 room that we won't need for another 90 days;
> if that will help tide you over in any way, give me a ring.

But to propose to rent the space would change the complexion of the letter and destroy any goodwill built up in the opening passages.

If a supplier were writing the foregoing to an out-of-town customer, he might want to close with

> We want to do all we can to help you over this emergency. For
> a customer like you we certainly can stretch our credit terms
> and expedite deliveries if you want us to.

He might even want to add:

> We'd like in some way to demonstrate our appreciation of the
> cooperation you've always shown in our relationship.

Even in letters of condolence, a deftly phrased reference to your appreciation can be appropriate.

Letters of appreciation

You have no doubt observed that most congratulatory messages also involve an element of thanks; likewise, most thank-you letters contain some commendatory passages. It's really just a question of where you want your emphasis to go.

Letters that emphasize appreciation for strictly goodwill purposes are not nearly so numerous as those that are also promotional. When you thank a customer for patronage, for prompt payment, or for recommending you or your firm to a friend, these are business promotion letters with obvious tie-ins to service (including quality of merchandise).

Strictly goodwill thank-you letters—in response to a favor extended, for work on a project (member of a fund-raising team, for example), or for a contribution—have their origins in civic, educational, and religious surroundings rather than in business.

Many thanks for the untiring, cheerful way you worked on the recent Red Feather Drive.

Through effort like yours we exceeded our goal.

Possibly the knowledge that you have helped materially to provide clothing, food, and medical care during the coming year for underprivileged children will be slightly more gratifying with this expression of appreciation.

--

For the 32,000 youths of Athens . . .

Thanks a million!

Your generous gift to the new "Y" building is another evidence of your concern for the boys and girls of our city and county.

We want you to know how much we appreciate your cooperation in this project. As citizens and parents, we'll all be happy about our share in it for years to come.

--

Thank you   Thank you   Thank you

To you these tickets mean an evening of top-notch entertainment, but to the children of Jefferson County the price of these tickets will buy many things.

Every cent of profit from the Junior League's presentation of "Jubilee" will be spent in Jefferson County for Jefferson County children to provide

Medical care for children at the League's Children's Clinic held every Friday.

Dental care for children at the League's Dental Clinic every Thursday.

Milk for undernourished children who attend these clinics.

A nursing scholarship of $250 to a student in the School of Nursing who needs assistance.

In addition, the League furnishes clerical help to the

Crippled Children's Clinic, maintains a Clothes Closet for needy families whose children attend our clinics, and sponsors the annual Christmas caroling with the cooperation of the Boy Scouts and Girl Scouts.

League members and the children of our county thank you sincerely for your part in making all this possible.

As a matter of fact, you can't call the preceding letters pure goodwill letters, for obviously the resale phrases are designed to convince the reader of the worth of the projects and thus prepare him for the next time a request comes along.

Letters written by business firms are even more definitely promotional.

Any time is a good time to send an expression of appreciation to good customers for their patronage or for handling accounts satisfactorily. Even the rubber-stamped notation on a current bill, "One of the pleasures of being in business is serving a good customer like you," has a heartening effect. But most stores do more. Upon the first use of the account—or later in the first year—some stores send a thank-you note like the following:

We've tried to see that you enjoyed the initial use of your recently opened account and that you were entirely satisfied with the merchandise and service.

If you have any suggestions to offer that will help make the account more convenient, however, we shall welcome them. We want to serve you well and to merit your continued patronage.

Thank you for the patronage you have given us; we cordially invite you to make further use of your account.

Because of the rush of business, such letters too often go out only around holiday and special-event times. In too many such cases they don't do the effective job they might because too many other people and stores are sending greetings and goodwill letters on those special occasions. Arriving unexpectedly and without apparent reason at some other time, the following note is probably a more effective pleasant reminder of the firm's appreciation:

Believe us—

—your continued patronage and friendship are appreciated

And to hold your friendship and patronage, we certainly intend to continue giving you the sort of service and honest values you deserve.

Come see us often.

When an account has not been used for some time and then a debit appears on the ledger, many credit men wisely send a thank-you note:

Thank you for the purchase you made recently.

It's good to hear you say "Charge it" again, for we've really missed you.

To serve you so well you'll want to come in more often is our constant aim.

Letters thanking customers for paying promptly are simply a more specialized version of the ones we've been examining. They are also effective means of discouraging or reducing collection problems. Such a simple note as the following not only pleases the customer; it reinforces his determination to maintain the good habit:

> Your check this morning in prompt payment of last month's purchases made me think, "I wish all our accounts were handled so efficiently."
>
> It's a real pleasure to service an account like yours, and we thank you sincerely for your cooperation.

You can also easily tie in the expression of appreciation with a concrete reminder of the benefits the customer gains from taking care of obligations as he has promised:

> Thank you for the splendid manner in which you paid out your recent account.
>
> With your record of prompt payments, your credit at Black's is firmly established. You needn't postpone adding fresh, new things to keep your home alive and interesting. It's thrifty and wise to enjoy these things while you save for them on small payments.
>
> Come in often and make full use of the many services this large, complete home store can render you, whether it's just a window shade or a complete houseful of furniture.

Such letters may appropriately be detailed developments of the theme:

> It's sad but true . . . that 95 percent of our customers rarely hear from the credit department.
>
> But believe me, people like you who unfailingly take care of your obligations as promised are a continual source of pleasure.
>
> Month after month, year after year, your prompt payments have enhanced the desirability of your account. Continuing your fine record increases the esteem in which we hold you.
>
> We know that with the ups and downs of business, some payments may come pretty hard—all the more reason why we appreciate your record.
>
> The excellent business judgment and vision behind such a record is the surest signal of continued success. We are grateful for having been allowed to contribute in a small way, and we look forward to continued happy relations.

If you keep your eyes and ears open, you'll find many other occasions for saying thank you to your customers and clientele. When a customer recommends you or your firm to another person, you'll certainly benefit in the long run by sending a cheerful, personalized note like the following:

> It was a pleasure to have you bring Mrs. Stallings into the shop recently. We enjoyed meeting her and seeing you again.

Thank you for this expression of confidence in us. We shall
do all we can to serve her well and to continue to merit your
patronage and recommendation to your friends.

--

It was generous of you to suggest to Mr. Lee that he come to
us for quality men's wear.

He came in yesterday and seemed pleased with what we were able
to show him.

Thank you. We're looking forward to his next visit.

When a firm writes such letters of appreciation to an individual, no
reply is expected. And when an individual takes the time to pay a business
firm a compliment or to express appreciation for good service, no answer
is *required*. But you establish yourself as a courteous, polite person if you
do reply. Furthermore, appropriate resale talk helps to strengthen the
friendly feeling as well as to pave the way for future business. The following letter emphasizes gratitude for kind words but adroitly stresses
service:[1]

The personnel of our Birmingham station quite proudly sent us
your letter complimenting Delta personnel for their assistance
in transporting Otto to his new home.

It was a real pleasure to receive such an excellent
commendation, and we're happy to pass this along to all those
who assisted.

In these days of rapidly growing transportation problems, and
with the volume of traffic mounting so fast, we sometimes feel
that Delta's past record of outstanding personalized service
may not be attainable today in spite of our best efforts.

Then, at just the right time, along comes a letter like yours
to show that our station personnel are still doing a good job
of public relations. It is a genuine pleasure to hear of the
excellent way they handled the many details, and we do
appreciate your taking time to tell us.

When you receive suggestions for improved service (some of which
will be outright complaints requiring adjustment letters), an acknowledgment *is* required, particularly if you have invited the suggestion.

We certainly thank you for pointing out how we can improve our
system for providing free parking to shoppers at Wiesel's.

Starting next Monday, we shall have all customers pick up their
tokens at the cashier's booth on the ground floor. And we
shall have the parking lot entrance to the store completely
cleared for easier flow of customer traffic.

We welcome your suggestions for better service and are sure
that this change will make shopping at Wiesel's a greater
pleasure than it was before.

[1] Reprinted with the permission of the author, W. D. Huff, manager of customer
relations, Delta Air Lines, Inc., Atlanta.

Letters of seasonal greeting

A modified form of the thank-you letter is the one of seasonal greeting. By far the most common time is around Christmas and New Year, although some stores send such letters shortly before Easter, Valentine's Day, or Thanksgiving, when they do not have so much competition from other mailings. Since they must be mass mailings in most firms (to keep down costs), they are rarely personalized.

It is pertinent to point out that the Red Feather letter, the "Y" letter, and the Junior League letter (pp. 225–26) were all obvious printed forms, thus conserving the funds of the organizations for more worthy causes. Business organizations, too, despite their size and resources, must also conserve employee effort and time (as well as funds) by using some modifications of form treatment in many of the thank-you and seasonal greeting letters they mail. Ideally, these letters would be individualized from inside address through signature; as a practical matter, they often are not. The undisguised form can be successful, however:

```
Business firms, too, pause at this season to count their
blessings.

Good friends and customers like you are one of our greatest.

So we want to tell you how much we appreciate your patronage
at the same time we send heartiest wishes for

    A VERY MERRY CHRISTMAS AND A HAPPY, SUCCESSFUL NEW YEAR!
```

With the references to customers and patronage, the letter is promotional in effect. Most emphatically, you would not want sales material in a letter with such an opening theme. The following holiday greeting letter, however, is an overt attempt to cultivate business, and perhaps wisely so in the light of how a savings and loan association functions and the kind of service it provides members:

```
GREETINGS AT THE NEW YEAR!

Hearts are never as full of peace and happiness as when friends
and loved ones gather in the home at this season of good cheer
and fellowship.

Through the years your Association has played a part in
providing homes for its members through sound home-financing
plans that lead to real debt-free home ownership.  Won't you
please tell your friends about your Association and recommend
its services to them?  They will appreciate knowing of the
easy, convenient terms upon which a loan may be repaid.

Our officers and directors join in thanking you for your help
in the past year, and wish you happiness and health in 19—
and for years to come.
```

Most of the time, however, you will be on safer ground if you exclude such promotional passages and concentrate on a simple wish for the customer's well-being, along with an expression of gratitude.

Letters of welcome and invitation

One of the most popular forms of goodwill letter is that greeting newcomers to a community and offering to be of assistance, particularly during the orientation period. Almost always it is an invitation to come in and get acquainted; it also emphasizes the services of the inviting firm. One usual and unexpected example is the following from a public library:

Welcome to Evansville!

We're glad to have you as new members of our progressive city.

Your library card is ready for your use. We hope you'll be down soon to pick it up and to become acquainted with the staff and the services. For your reading pleasure and research over 100,000 volumes are available. Staff members will gladly assist you in finding what you seek. All of the leading magazines and newspapers are available in the lounge.

The children's room is also well supplied with both fiction and nonfiction books on a wide variety of topics of interest to youngsters 6 to 15.

If you enjoy musical recordings, you may want to check out some of the thousand-odd albums ranging from the most recent popular music to the classics.

We shall be glad to give you maps of the city, to supply directions—in short, to help you in any way we can to know Evansville better.

The library is open from 9 a.m. until 10 p.m. every weekday. We are glad to answer telephone inquiries during that time.

Please come in soon.

Such a letter—with no sales ax to grind—is the essence of goodwill in its spirit. It is more likely to be accepted at its face value than the usual letter from a firm with commercial/profit aspirations, such as the following:

As a new resident of our friendly city, you are cordially invited to visit the Federal Bank. We should like to get to know you. Even though you may already have selected a bank, it would be a pleasure to welcome you to Blankville personally and to explain the many services the Federal offers its customers.

The Federal has given prompt, courteous, and efficient banking services to the people of Blankville for over 75 years, and we would appreciate the opportunity of serving you.

Among the conveniences in Federal's modern banking quarters are the four drive-in teller windows that enable you to bank without alighting from your car. And in the parking garage right in our own building you may have 30 minutes of free parking while taking care of your banking business.

You may also bank around the clock at the Federal; a complete
mail deposit service and a 24-hour depository are located in
our parking garage.

Furthermore, branch banks in Freeport and in Norwood can
accommodate you when you do not wish to come downtown.

You have complete banking facilities when you bank with the
Federal.

Won't you come in for a friendly visit soon?

Most readers would probably recognize this letter for the wolf-in-sheep's-
clothing it is. It is an obvious attempt to get a new account, and the attempts to establish friendly feeling are thin and transparent. Better to discard the talk of "get to know you" and "friendly visit" and get right down
to brass tacks established with an opening like "Since you are a newcomer
to Blankville and will need a conveniently located bank with complete
facilities, may we tell you what we can offer you at the Federal?"

On the other hand, the invitation to a special event extended in the following letter would probably be read with interest; it builds goodwill because it expresses a desire to render service; no resale (except that inherent
in the action itself) or sales talk distracts:

Will you be our guest?

Beginning next Thursday, May 31, and every Thursday after that
for the rest of the summer, Brentling's will present prominent
lecturers and editors reviewing the most talked-about recent
books.

All the reviews will be held in the auditorium on the sixth
floor (air-conditioned, of course, like the rest of
Brentling's) and will begin promptly at 2 p.m.

This Thursday Miss Evelyn Kuppenheimer, popular literary
editor of the Times, will review Angeline Locke's Voodoo on
the Levee—a powerful, gripping story of the antebellum South.

We hope you will be with us to enjoy this initial literary
treat and as many of the others as you possibly can.

Someone connected with credit control can easily maintain a list of
newcomers to the community and mail a form letter (easily individualized, which does not promise credit, please note, but only invites the
application):

Welcoming you to this community gives us a great deal of
pleasure. We hope soon to count you as one of our good
friends. Our Credit Department will be glad to handle your
credit application at your request.

We invite you to use our lounging and rest rooms on the
mezzanine or the fountain luncheonette, where you can get a
deliciously prepared, well-balanced luncheon at a reasonable
price. Rollins' spacious parking lot, located only 15 feet
from the rear entrance to the store, is absolutely free to you
when you shop here, no matter if your purchase is only a spool
of thread. On Rollins' remodeled third floor you'll find home

furnishings. The advice of our interior decorators is
available to you with no obligation. And in the remodeled
downstairs section you'll find an entirely new and complete
food mart and new homeware department.

We are here to serve you. And we hope that you too will soon
feel as one of our customers recently was kind enough to say
to us, "The longer people live in this community, the more
they trade at Rollins'."

--

This is just a note to express our appreciation for the new
account you have just opened with us. We are happy to welcome
you as customers and thank you for your confidence in us.

Please call on me or any of our officers whenever we can be of
assistance to you.

The following letter to a new shareholder is typical of what many corporations do to cement goodwill (and possibly forestall some gripes when things don't go too well for the corporation):

Welcome to the Marquette family! We earnestly hope you find
your association with us a thoroughly satisfying experience.

Since lasting associations are based mainly on mutual
understanding, we try to keep our shareowners fully informed
by means of reports and other publications devoted to the state
of the business and its prospects. These are issued regularly
throughout the year.

If you should ever find this material inadequate on any point,
don't hesitate to write us for clarification. We are always
glad to hear from the owners of the business.

When you can verify credit reliability (usually an easy thing to do), you may elect to set up the account and so inform the reader:

We know that stores, too, make a difference to a person
establishing a home in a new community.

To serve you in as friendly manner as possible is one of our
aims. As an earnest assurance of our desire to show you every
possible courtesy that will make for a permanent and happy
business friendship, we have opened a convenient charge account
in your name.

The next time you are in the store, simply say "Charge it" to
the person waiting on you.

We hope to see you soon—and often.

The following special invitation letter is frankly a low-pressure sales letter. It does offer a service in making shopping easier, but the primary emphasis is on sales.

For our best customers we're having an Open House the evenings
of Wednesday, December 7, through Saturday, December 10. The
store will be open until 9 these evenings, and you are invited
to come and "just look" to your heart's content.

Refreshments will be served from 6 to 8, and our sales

personnel will simply act as hosts.   No public announcement
will be made of this event.

With an eye to Christmas giving, you may want to examine some
of the popular pocket-size transistor radios or portable TV's.
Many GE and RCA models will be available for your inspection.
The Whirlpool portable dishwasher is an especially welcome gift
for a busy wife and mother.   And of course, the 19— models in
GE refrigerators, washers and dryers, and other appliances will
be on display.   Any attendant will gladly demonstrate one of
these for you.

This Open House is intended as a departure from business
routine—one that will give us a better opportunity to get
acquainted with you and give you the opportunity of working
out your Christmas gift problems at leisure.   Won't you come
in one or more of these evenings?

Letters seeking the revival of an account are but modified versions of
invitation letters. When an account remains unused for any length of time
—say three months or six months, depending on management's choice—it
may be a signal that the customer is drifting away because of store indifference, or it may be the result of a real grievance. Letters inviting the
customer back to the store, reselling the store's merchandise and services,
stressing "How can we serve you better?" and finally asking forthrightly,
"May we continue to serve you?" can be mailed individually or in a series.
One of the finest we've ever seen is this one:

Spring fever?

Here's a SURE cure—a Beachstone suit, coat, or dress, spiced
with the right accessories.

Easy to choose, easy to buy too.   Simply use your charge
account at Wilson's.   It's as good as new and just waiting for
your "charge it" to be as useful as ever.

So come in soon!   See and try on the beautiful new spring
apparel, millinery, shoes, and other accessories we have
assembled for your Easter pleasure.

You can easily pattern any such letter after this one, which is built on sales
promotion material and an action ending suggesting a visit to the store.
Letters built around special events, such as Christmas, readily supply a
theme (although they may lose some effect by competition with many
others):

A welcome warm as Santa's smile awaits you at Bowen's!

We're all decked out with our Christmas best; so it's an easy
job to find the right gift for everyone on your Christmas
list.

Practical gifts, starry-eyed gifts . . . and all conveniently
in one store . . . Bowen's . . . where you can just say "Charge
it" for ALL your Christmas giving.

                                        Warmest holiday greetings!

Accompanying a new credit card, one letter solicited the renewal of the customer's business with:

> Ordinarily we'd send you this enclosure with our monthly statement. Since your account hasn't been used recently, we're sending it along with some back-to-school suggestions.
>
> Whether you're thinking of complete outfits for your child or a back-to-school gift for a favorite niece, nephew, or friend, you'll find complete selections of dependable quality Bowen merchandise in every department.
>
> Your charge account is just as good as ever—whether you come to the store, phone, or shop by mail.

Some writers studiously avoid asking whether anything is wrong (see p. 399). Some stores send a dozen or so mailings before asking. A favorite form is the letter written on only one half of the page (usually the left side) with the caption "Here's Our Side of the Story." At the top of the right side blank space appears another caption, "Won't You Tell Us Your Side of the Story?" Regardless of the format, most of these letters make a request much like this one:

> One of my duties as credit manager of Bowen's is to check up on our service to keep it up to par.
>
> Since your account has not been used for quite some time, the only way we can be sure we have pleased you with our merchandise and service is to hear directly from you.
>
> Just use the handy form and the convenient stamped envelope enclosed to tell us whether you want us to keep your charge account open.
>
> We will certainly do our best to please you.
>
> Will you write us . . . now?
>
> > We'll surely appreciate it!

Letters accompanying favors

Often as a goodwill reminder a businessman or firm finds some novelty or favor that can be mailed inexpensively along with a note reiterating the desire to be of service, such as the following from a women's shoe store:

> The specially treated purse-size brush accompanying this letter is for your use in keeping your handsome Everett shoes spotless wherever you wear them.
>
> Accept it with our compliments and the hope that you will be completely happy with your recent selection from Everett's collection of footwear for the discriminating woman.

In a somewhat humorous vein one company recently mailed a pocketsize calorie counter to an extensive list of customers and prospects with this short note:

"Everything's expanding—especially my waistline," grumbled a
friend recently.

Just in case you (or someone you know) may need to fight this
perennial battle of the bulge, we're sending you this handy
calorie counter that you can use at home or at a banquet or at
a lunch counter.

Accept it with our compliments—and the hope that we'll be
seeing you soon.

Small gadgets galore are used in this manner. Like tricks in sales letters,
however, they are better if related to the product or service of the firm. A
real estate agency might appropriately send a pocket- or purse-size map
of the city to which a person has just moved, along with the following:

Welcome to Jacksonville.

To help you get places faster and to know your new city
better, we're sending you a map showing the principal
thoroughfares and location of the principal landmarks and
facilities.

Note that the Coleman Agency is located in an accessible area
with adequate parking facilities nearby.

We would welcome the opportunity to help you in any way we can.

Letters offering helpful information

Large companies sponsoring radio and TV programs, as well as research
projects and publications, rapidly accumulate names and addresses of people who are interested in being kept informed. As part of the public relations or goodwill program, many of these companies periodically send
letters like the following (usually to selected lists of people supposedly
interested):

Perhaps you will be interested in a program, "Life under the
Sea," scheduled for Sunday, January 22, at 8 p.m. over NBS-TV.

"Life under the Sea" was directed by Emile Ravage, with the
assistance of the marine biologist Albert Gaudin. It is the
third in a series of such productions sponsored by the
Rawlston System.

We hope these programs will help to broaden public
understanding of science and to encourage some young people at
least to consider scientific careers.

We shall welcome your comments after you have seen the program.

--

As a teacher of advertising, perhaps you will be able to use
the accompanying brochure, "The Evolution of a Woman's Home
Journal Ad."

You are welcome to quote liberally in your classes and to
reproduce anything in it.

At least we hope you will enjoy reading it.

--

The exciting events in Detroit leading up to the introduction
of the new models last month made a story too detailed to
print completely in <u>Tempo</u>.

If you read the condensed version in the issue of two weeks
ago, you'll agree that the accompanying report-analysis we're
sending to selected educators and businessmen is a worthwhile
expansion and supplementation. If you didn't . . . well, we
think you'll want to now.

Letters anticipating resistance

In the interest of forestalling complaints and minimizing dissatisfaction,
many business executives give advance notice when something like an interruption of service, a curtailment of service, or a price increase is scheduled to take place. (The same kind of advance mailing can also pave the
way for the call of a solicitor for charitable contributions.) In almost all
instances these letters (often only postcards) must be obvious forms. They
need to stress service—improved service, if possible; at least, maintaining
superior service or quality of goods—as an antidote for the inherently
negative material the message has to establish. This message of a power
company is typical (dates and times varied according to areas and so were
stamped in):

In order to provide better service for you and our other
customers in your area, we have installed new equipment, which
we plan to place in service

April 15, 19—
between 1 and 2 p.m.

To safeguard the men who do this work, we shall have to shut
off power during this time. Service will be restored as
promptly as possible. We appreciate your cooperation in
making this improved service possible.

A notification of a price increase is really just a modified sales letter.
Admittedly, it is never an easy letter to write. But with specific details supporting the increase, it may be successful in retaining some customers who
would otherwise be lost. The following notice went to all customers of a
diaper service:

Dear Crib Customer:

In the early 1940s when we first started lending mothers a
hand with laundry for infants and babies, diapers cost 90 cents
a dozen. Now they cost $3.61.

Paper during the same period increased from six to 27 cents a
pound and soap from eight to 32 cents.

To continue giving our customers satisfactory service, we had
to increase our prices in the late 40s and again in the 50s.

In the meantime all these items have continued to increase in price and now are from one fifth to one half more than they were then.

Wages for our help, taxes, and other costs we cannot control have also risen appreciably.

And so in order to continue the same twice-a-week pickup and delivery, and the same high standards of cleanliness and sanitation that we know you as a parent want for your child, we shall have to receive payment for services as listed on the enclosed card. These prices will go into effect at the beginning of next month.

Please note that these increases average approximately three cents a day. You still are paying only 50 cents a day for service that makes life much easier for you, conserves your strength, and provides your child clothing that is sterilized to a degree impossible in most homes.

We appreciate the opportunity to serve you and shall continue to do all we can to merit your confidence and your patronage.

--

To Our Residential Customers:

As you know, prices for almost everything we use in our homes and businesses have risen sharply in recent years. The cost of living has increased dramatically in the last few years; in fact, it has gone up about 40 percent since 1948. This increase has been caused by higher prices for almost anything we can name—clothing, food, housing, medical care, transportation.

By carefully controlling our expenses and by building larger and more efficient electric service facilities, we have made electricity one of the biggest bargains in your family's budget. But, our costs, like yours, have continued to rise at a steeper and steeper rate. For example, the cost of building one mile of a typical electric distribution line in a residential neighborhood has increased some 31 percent since 1957.

Such increases in the cost of providing electric service finally have forced us to ask the Public Service Commission for a modest increase in some of our rates. On the average, this increase would add only about three cents a day to the electric bills of our residential customers.

This is the first time in our more than 50 years of service that we have asked for an overall increase in residential rates. And even with this increase, our rates will remain among the lowest in the nation. In fact, last year the average cost of residential electric service from Alabama Power was almost 20 percent below the national average.

I wish it were possible for me to talk with each one of you personally to explain the need for this increase and how little it will actually affect most of our customers. Since I'm unable to do that, I am taking this means to tell you of our request to the Commission and to promise you that we shall continue to provide you with electricity at the lowest possible cost consistent with reliable, dependable service.

We could classify and illustrate hundreds of situations in which a special goodwill letter would be appropriate and would cement a friendship for you and your firm. If you are alert to conditions, if you keep informed about what is happening to your clientele, if you honestly like people and enjoy pleasing them, however, you'll see plenty of opportunity to write such letters. You'll be surfeited with occasions! In this short treatment, therefore, we have tried to concentrate on the most common instances; it is intended as a springboard for your thinking and practice rather than an extensive catalog.

Special goodwill letters can do a big *extra* job for you, but remember that *all* your letters should build goodwill through courteous, sincere tone and the service attitude.

Crass though it may sound, one businessman realistically summarized the function of goodwill letters this way: "Especially on the executive level, hundreds of letters must be written just to keep in touch and to keep business on the personal basis that we have learned pays off."

We encourage you to

1. Write all you can of these "letters you don't have to write but should."
2. Make them specific enough to fit and be meaningful even when forms (NOT as one big company began, "If you are one of the many motorists enjoying the benefits of an XX credit card . . .").
3. In these most personal of business letters, get names, addresses, and facts right (if you write Mr. Wilkinson, he does NOT like to be addressed as Mr. Wilkerson; nor does Menning like to be called Manning).
4. Don't gush in tone or length.

GOODWILL CASES

1. With its fourth quarterly stock dividend check, Dow Chemical Co. (Midland, Michigan 48640), sends stockholders their W-2 forms. Since Dow has 91,000 stockholders, it saves $7,000 a year on postage alone (the check and W-2 form can both certainly ride for the same first-class stamp). You wish other companies in which you own stock would exercise this and other similar economies, and you want to commend Dow for doing so. You also appreciate the clear explanation (on the W-2 forms) of what part of the annual dividends is income-tax free (return of capital) and how much is taxable. You can't figure it exactly, but you would guess other savings (extra envelope and extra runs through the envelope-addressing and stuffing machines) at least equal the savings on postage.

2. Now safe and comfortable at home (1009 West Healey Street, Lisbon, Ohio 44432), you want to express to the doctors, nurses, and staff at the J. Hillis Miller Health Center's Shands Teaching Hospital and Clinics (the University of Florida Medical School in Gainesville 32601) your appreciation for the hospitality and many kindnesses—as well as your commendation for the excellent professional care and attention—given your son and you during the three weeks he was in the hospital (nine days in critical condition) after an automobile accident. John is now well on the road to complete recovery. As a retired R.N. (registered nurse) you know that it is professionally improper to single out specific names of doctors and nurses for commendation, but all those you met were deserving anyway. You want to make the point that when one is 1,000 miles from home, the friendliness of service personnel is an important part of professional care —well done in this case. And you want to suggest that your letter be submitted to the hospital newspaper (THE CENTER) and to the *Gainesville Sun* to remind the citizens of Florida (especially Gainesville) how fortunate they are.

3. As David T. Lamme, Jr., president of world-famous Lamme's Candies of P.O. Box 1885 at Austin, Texas 78767, you want to promote early Christmas orders from your former customers (for themselves and friends) by stressing the service angle.

All the customers on your list know your general reputation for quality candies since 1885 and know from experience the delectable taste of at least one of your variety of candies. So your present promotion letter in October is not intended to stress those points (though you may tuck them in as reminders) and is not intended to have any specific sales push of any particular candy. Your enclosure will be a self-sealing return-addressed and stamped envelope, the inside of which (opened flat as mailed) is a complete price list and order form with colored pictures of the main kinds and sizes of boxes, and spaces for quantity and shipping address by each item.

Your present form letter, therefore, is to stress service and grows from these jottings of points on your note pad: like orders any time; appreciate opportunity to serve you; heavy mails at Christmas, slow delivery; plan ahead; specify shipping date (otherwise immediate);—if gift, name and address of recipient; lots of experience; always improving service; orders out promptly, just as you want. Write the letter.

4. As the now happy customer-stockholder, write a cordial letter to the Chairman of the Board (see Case 5, p. 212 of Adjustment Approval letters and Case 6, p. 204 of Claims).

5. Before writing this letter, reread Case 7 of Adjustment Approvals, p. 212 and Cases 2 and 3 of Claims p. 203. You see that you need to write another letter to go along with the refund check to the customer who did not catch the "error" (really a crook's altering a sales invoice) and overpaid. Write the gypped customer a goodwill letter to go with his refund. (You may assume the same facts as in the reported case.)

6. As the now mollified lady (Case 6, p. 289), write a letter of apology to Priester's and thank the nice man who "showed himself bigger than I am" by keeping his hackles down and explaining "so calmly when I got my dander up unjustifiably." Tell him he has reminded you of the good advice your college teacher of business communications once gave: If you ever write a nasty letter, put it in a soaking drawer at least overnight, then rewrite it the next day after you've cooled off. Also refer to the enclosed order form (assumed to be there, ordering one of the several enticing new items Priester's is now offering).

7. Though goodwill letters should not be direct-hit sales letters, actually most of them are at least somewhat sales promotional. With that in mind, and with a service attitude toward its customers, the Florida branch of a New York Stock Exchange member (Walston & Co., Inc., 206 N. Hogan, Jacksonville 32202) wants to invite its regular stock-investing customers to hear a famous speaker it has scheduled: Dr. R. H. Montgomery, chief economist of the New York investment-management firm, Distributors Group, Inc.—7:20 P.M., Tuesday two weeks from now, Windsor Room of the Meyer Hotel, 315 Julia Street.

As chief account executive at Walston's Florida branch, you are to write the strict form letter of invitation to go to all regular customers, yours and those of the other account executives. Because you can seat only 250 and you expect great interest, you will admit only the first 250 who return the (assumed-to-be enclosed) reservation card.

Montgomery is an articulate and widely respected lecturer. His speech on "The Economic and Investment Outlook," including a unique slide presentation, will last about 40 minutes and leave about the same time for questions. It should give a good insight into the current battle between the bears and the bulls as a basis for predicting which side will win.

8. Assume you are the owner of any business you are familiar with and write a form message that could be sent to any credit customer a year after the account was opened. All his obligations have been paid promptly.

9. To build and maintain goodwill, *Time, Life,* and *Fortune* (all with executive offices in New York) send reprints of articles to a wide variety of people. A letter always accompanies each mailing. As the director of educational activities, write the letter to accompany *Fortune's* annual directory of the 500 largest industrial corporations. Since it analyzes the list —with special comment on newcomers, dropouts, and shift of position—it is an important analysis of industrial developments and trends. The directory goes to teachers of business writing, counselors, deans, and directors of placement bureaus in about 2,000 colleges and universities in the United States. The directory appeared as a supplement in last month's issue of *Fortune.* Besides names and titles of major officers in each company, it contains useful data concerning financial standing (capital issues, sales, and return on investment, for example) and number of employees.

10. As director of educational activities for *Time* (see preceding case), write a letter to accompany a reprint of your recent article analyzing business conditions and titled "The Soaring Years!" The mailing is to go to college teachers of marketing.

11. Assume now the role of sales manager for *Life* (see the two preceding cases), and write a letter to go along with your brochure "How an Ad Comes to *Life*." It describes step by step how an ad promoting Birdsview frozen foods was developed from its original suggested form to the finished four-color, full-page appearance in a recent issue. The mailing goes to college teachers of advertising.

12. Prepare a letter for inactive accounts for use shortly before one or more of the following special times, as your instructor directs: Valentine's Day, Easter, summer vacation time, Independence Day, Labor Day, back-to-school time, Thanksgiving, Christmas, or winter vacation time.

13. Assume that you are the owner of any business you are familiar with. Write a note expressing appreciation for business given you by your customers. It will be an obvious form letter. Adapt your message seasonally as indicated by the assumed date of your letter.

14. As head of a public library in a city of between 60,000 and 120,000 population, write the letter you would send welcoming newcomers to the community and extending your services. The letter should resell the community and the library. Assume the enclosure of a small map of the city which conveniently folds to pocket or purse size. The letter will be personalized with inside address and salutation and mailed as you receive names and addresses from the local credit bureau.

15. For your gas dealer (filling stations—though any firm could use it) prepare copy for a form letter to accompany a calorie counter. The counter is a handy pocket-sized rotating disc that enables anyone to keep accurate count of meals away from home as well as at home. Name and address of the sending firm are imprinted on the counter. The letter establishes the sending firm's identification in the signature. The sending firm orders whatever number he needs for his local list. You have the counters and letters printed in large quantities and inserted in envelopes (at about half the actual cost). The sending firm makes arrangements for addressing the envelopes. Although you want to include some resale on gas products and service, your primary emphasis is on the convenience of the calorie counter.

16. The public relations department of the *Commercial Appeal*, 500 Jefferson Street, Memphis, Tennessee 38102, invites boys to a camp for two weeks (June 10–24). Assume that you are to write the form letter addressed to principals of elementary schools in Memphis asking them for the names of desirable students. Each school is entitled to send 15 applicants to Camp Cloud Mount, Mentone, Alabama 35985. The *Commercial Appeal* pays all expenses, but the campers can take a little money to buy snacks if they want to. Qualified counselors supervise the campers in tennis, crafts, swimming, boating, horseback riding, and archery. The newspaper also furnishes transportation to and from the lovely wooded camp. Word your letter so that the reader knows that the *Commercial Appeal* wants deserving and appreciative boys.

17. Assume that you are in the credit department of a hardware store you are familiar with and prepare a letter to charge customers who have not used their accounts for three months. Build the letter around sales promotion material on seasonal goods. The obvious action sought is to get the customers back to the store. It will be a personalized letter.

18. Prepare a follow-up letter to be sent at the end of six months to those charge customers whose accounts are still unused (see preceding case).

19. Prepare a third letter for sending, one month later, to the people in the preceding case. Without suggesting poor merchandise or service, invite the customer's comments and suggestions.

20. Doster Mullins, salesman for Liberty National Insurance Company, 432 Rainbow Drive, Ventura, California 93003, sent $10 and filled out an application blank for membership in the United Credit Club. Over the signature of Harvey Mappin, president of United Credit Club, Box 786 Baltimore, Maryland 21224, welcome Mullins as a member. Enclose his United Credit Card (honored throughout Europe and the Western world), which is good for 12 months, and resell him on the convenience of being a member—as well as the protection for income tax purposes.

21. You are president of your professional fraternity. Gordon Lloyd, an outstanding man in the profession, has just driven at his own expense from a nearby city and talked to your group on a professional topic. Write a thank-you note to Lloyd that is specific enough to assure him that you and your group appreciated his generosity and realized something beneficial from his efforts. Mention a specific highlight of the speech.

22. Select some school, civic, or professional group of which you are or have been a member (or would like to be). As president, write a letter to members explaining why the dues are being raised. Explain the increase in terms of additional goals of the organization and higher production costs of the journal members get.

23. Write a letter of congratulations to someone you know who has been honored, who has accomplished something outstanding, who has been promoted, or something similar. Include enough specific comment about the event or deed to show your realization of its significance.

24. For your independent group, fraternity, or sorority, set up a form letter that can be sent to the parents of your members. The letter tells the parents how proud the organization is of their son or daughter. Perhaps the student made outstanding grades this semester, or perhaps he was elected to an honorary fraternity or taken into Phi Beta Kappa, Beta Gamma Sigma, or Theta Sigma Phi. Perhaps the student did some worthwhile charitable deed.

25. As assistant sales analyst for Fuller and Fuller, St. Louis, Missouri 63136, you write letters aimed to get customer reaction to how store personnel handle adjustments. Today's letter goes to Mrs. Hampstead Hutton, 8765 Alton Place, Cario, Illinois 62330, who returned a McGregor knit pants set, $30, size 12, and a sports jacket, $35.95, size 14. You want to find out whether she was served promptly and courteously, whether the adjustment was handled satisfactorily as well as to invite any other comments or suggestions she wishes to make. You are enclosing a stamped, addressed envelope for her convenience. The objective of the letter is, of course, to build goodwill by stressing the service attitude.

26. As the credit sales manager of your firm, manufacturers, take time out to write a short personal note to the many accounts who pay promptly within your 30-day terms, commending them for their efficiency, stressing the desirability of their account, and subtly reselling your line. Let the sample you write to Frederick Henry, 555 Tracy Avenue, Rockwell City, Iowa 50483, serve as the guide for letters you will write to others.

27. Write the letter that Frederick Henry (in preceding case) might wisely send to his retail customers expressing appreciation for prompt payment (note that there is no discount here; also this letter can refer to items from a much wider range of stock).

28. To encourage better spelling among school students, the *Chicago Tribune* sponsors a spelling contest every March. Each elementary and junior high school is invited to enter the contest. The children who enter the contest are sent books with spelling lists, and they are free to study them for several months before the contest. The winner from each elementary and junior high school is given a paperback dictionary and competes against the other winners of elementary and junior high schools. The winner of this contest goes on to a state meet. Assume that you are Cecil Bonner, associate editor of the *Chicago Tribune*, Wacker Drive, Chicago, Illinois 60609. Write the letter to the schools inviting the students to participate in the contest. There's no charge for the spelling booklets. All the judges serve on a voluntary basis; so there's no expense for the school. Children can study the words independently. Any child who wants to participate in the contest is invited to join. Only the winner from each school is given the dictionary, however.

29. You are president of Beavers Brothers, 7654 East Princeton Street, Pontiac, Michigan 48057, soap manufacturers. To tell your stockholders about the promotion your company has been giving the new nonpolluting dishwasher soap, All Clean, you are sending a form letter to them. During the rest of the year you plan to promote All Clean with a million-dollar television advertising budget. Walter Cronk, whose news program has become a household institution throughout the country, went on the air for All Clean a month ago under a long-term contract. The board of directors feels that concentrated television programs are better than expensive soap samples distributed to homes. All Clean has proved itself worthy of all-out promotion, and the sales power of Walter Cronk with American consumers is well known. In addition to having considerable impact on All Clean sales, sponsorship of these programs is certain to enhance the prestige of the company and the remainder of the product line. Write the letter designed to win stockholder approval, and plug All Clean and the company behind it.

30. For 12 years Douglas Blair, 629 Lucerne Avenue, Cleveland, Ohio 44137, has used Writex individual postal cards. In his letter to the Writex Company, 4370 Center Avenue, Pittsburg, Pennsylvania 15235, he complains that the cards are made too thick to slip easily into his typewriter. The local stationery store from whom he ordered the cards suggested that he write direct to Writex. As Alton T. Fines, vice president in administration, you investigate the stock of the cards. You find that when the last order was entered, Writex purchased it from another supplier, and this supplier used too heavy a stock for typewriter use. To welcome Blair back and to keep him as a satisfied customer, Writex will send him an adjustment order of normal-weight Writex individual postal cards.

31. You have just finished heading a campus drive collecting funds for crippled children. Write a note to one of your divisional chairmen that will serve as a guide for all the others you'll send. It should express gratitude and congratulations for the good job done in addition to reselling the cause.

32. At some point in your life you have been impressed with the attention given you by an employee of a firm. Perhaps it was a clerk who went out of the way to find something for you or who took special pains to see that you were fitted well or who made a special effort on a rush order. It might have been a reservations clerk for an airline, or a steamship company. It might have been a hostess or a stewardess on a plane. Write a letter to the business, commending the employee. Recall the instance, and be specific in telling why and how the employee gave you good service. Use the employee's name or describe the circumstances so exactly that there could be no mistaking who it was. Assume that you are writing the letter two or three days after the happy incident.

33. As treasurer of the Book-of-the-Month-Club, Inc. (345 Hudson Street, New York 10014), prepare a form letter to go to all club members outside New York State. Facts: Some states' court decisions have been requiring the Club and other sellers by mail to collect state sales taxes on mail sales to customers in those states, regardless of where the seller is. A recent U.S. Supreme Court ruling says on sales by mail (as all the Club's are) a seller is not to collect state sales taxes from customers outside the seller's state.

Most people already know about the new ruling if they read the newspapers. The new ruling makes clear that the seller is not required to refund sales taxes already collected, but it does not make clear whether a seller is to collect on sales already made but charged. The Club has decided to cancel all sales tax charges now on out-of-state customers' accounts. An enclosed statement shows the customer the resultant revision of his account.

On this form letter (as on all Club letters), put in a noticeable place the request: Please include your account number in any communication to us.

chapter 7

Disappointing messages

[*Character requires the courage to say no firmly
but pleasantly when it would be easier to say
yes or to say no unpleasantly.*]

FOR THE SAME REASON that good news is its own best harbinger, bad news is not. If you do not recall the suggestions about handling disappointing messages in Chapter 3 (pp. 56–58), turn back and quickly review them.

REFUSING THE REQUEST

If you care little or nothing about your reader's continued good feeling toward you, you can quickly and easily write a refusal like this:

```
I'm very sorry, but company practice forbids giving out
information such as you requested.
```

Even if you care a lot, you *can* write a believable turndown letter that begins with the refusal—for example:

```
I'm very glad to explain to you, Mr. Willet, why Rigate spends
```

its advertising dollars on radio time and magazine space rather
than on the distribution of samples.

But most correspondence supervisors and correspondence counselors advocate what they call the "reason-first refusal." The brevity of the first example above and the dispatch of the second are not desirable in refusals because most people are disappointed, irritated, or downright angry when
told they can't have something or can't do something. And in any of these
emotional states they will not give full attention to your explanation.

Back of most refusals is some good reason dictated by sound business
judgment. And usually it can be told. That is why we say that most refusals have an educating job to do: They usually have to acquaint the
reader with some circumstance of which he is apparently unaware. Hence
the emphasis on *explanation before refusing*.

Furthermore, one of the first lessons in good human relations any sensitive person learns is that when you take something away from someone or
deny him something, you give a reason, you give him something else to
compensate for the loss when you can, and you try to extend some gesture
of friendliness.

Simply stated, the desirable pattern for most refusals is

—A buffer beginning (establishing compatibility; defined and illustrated below)
—A review of facts (reasons)
—The refusal itself, subordinated ⎤   *or* a counterproposal which implies the
—An off-the-subject ending   ⎦   refusal

Before studying an analysis of this suggested structure, however, read the
following refusal of the request for toothpaste samples (p. 319):

Sales-minded businessmen are keenly aware of the advertising
possibilities which usually accompany such an occasion as "A"
Day at your university.

If they have found such advertising to be sufficiently
productive to warrant the cost, they are quick to take
advantage of the opportunity, and we here at Rigate are no
exception.

After experimenting with many different forms of advertising,
however, we have found that we obtain best results at the least
expense by advertising in nationally circulated magazines and
by sponsoring the Picote Theatre, which millions of Americans
enjoy every Sunday night.

The results of advertising by distributing sample tubes of
Picote did not warrant the relatively high cost of
manufacturing, handling, and mailing the samples; so we now
concentrate on magazine and radio-TV promotion. As a result,
we have been able to make a substantial saving, which we have
passed on to the users of Picote by lowering the price of the
product.

In addition to this price reduction, in January and February
Rigate will offer an economy-size tube of Picote for just one

```
additional penny with the purchase of a bottle of Rigatine.
The first time you drop by your drugstore in January, take
advantage of the savings Rigate passes on to its users.
```

The buffer beginning

When the reader starts to read your refusal, he is hoping for pleasant news. He has probably done a good job of ferreting out reasons why he thinks you should do as he has asked. The refusal presented immediately appears to ignore his feelings and his reasoning and is likely to arouse a negative reaction, causing him to close his mind to anything else you say.

If you pitch right in with a presentation of your reasons, you appear to be arguing with him—and his dander, or at least his suspicion, rises.

To prevent mental impasses and emotional deadlocks, show your reader that you are a reasonable, calm person by indicating some form of approval of him or his project. This is your buffer. Frequently you can agree completely with some statement made in his request. At the least, you can say something which will establish compatibility, even if it's nothing more than that you have given his proposal serious thought.

The turndown of the request for the correspondence manual (p. 57) could easily begin with

```
You are certainly right about the pressing need that is facing
most business firms for more effectively trained business
correspondents.
```

Or it could start this way:

```
Students attending Harwood College are fortunate to have a
faculty who try so conscientiously to correlate college
training and business practice.
```

Both beginnings acknowledge the receipt of the request, clearly imply that the request has been considered, establish compatibility, and set the stage for the review of the facts resulting in the refusal later.

Three warnings should be sounded here, however. The first is that if you appear to be granting the request, you are building your reader up to an awful letdown! The resultant reaction undoubtedly arouses more negative feelings than the abrupt, unmotivated refusal. Such beginnings as these would mislead most readers:

```
I certainly would like to see each Harwood letter-writing
student have access to a copy of the Southern Atlantic manual.
                              --
"A" Day surely would be a good opportunity to acquaint
potential customers with Picote toothpaste, Mr. Willet!
```

The second warning is against beginning so far away from the subject that the reader isn't even sure the letter is a reply to his request. The buffer beginning must clearly identify the general subject. Otherwise, incoherence and rambling are inevitable results. Even such a beginning as the following is irrelevant:

```
Your interesting letter describing "A" Day brought back to
mind many pleasant memories of my own college days.
```

The job of getting to the facts would be harder with such a start.

Despite the fact that many writers advocate beginning refusals with

```
I really wish we could. . . .
```

we do not believe it can do as good a job for you as some other opening. It is stereotyped, it sounds insincere to many readers, and it invites the belligerent response "Then why don't you?" But the greatest disadvantage (and the third warning) is that it establishes the refusal unmistakably in the opening line before showing any reason why.

Reasons rather than apologies

If you will apply the positive thinking and positive phrasing we talked about under "Positive Statement" (p. 65) and "Success Consciousness" (p. 67), you will resist the common impulse to apologize anywhere in a refusal *and especially in the beginning.* Apologies are no substitute for action or explanation. And they inevitably force you to phrase in distinctively negative terminology the very idea you should be avoiding, the fact that you *will not, cannot, are unable to, do not have,* and similar negative expressions.

You will of course run into some situations where there are no reasons (nonexistence of certain information or plain and simple unavailability) and some where the reason is so obvious that it need not be put into words. But in most cases when you have to refuse, that refusal is based on policy. And back of that policy are good reasons. Those reasons—not the policy—form the bedrock of your explanation. As much as possible you will want to search out and emphasize those reasons which reflect benefit to the reader—if not directly, then indirectly by identification with a group with which the reader might be sympathetic. This, we will admit, is one of those things more easily said than done. But the writer of the Picote-sample refusal letter did a good job of relating reader benefit to his refusal. So did the man who had to tell a 10-year-old boy that a big mail-order house could not take the time to put commemorative stamps on packages sent to the boy's mother:

```
A stamp collection can certainly be fun, Tommy!

And commemorative stamps can teach you a lot about geography
and people.

To get your mother's packages to her as quickly as she likes
to get them, however, we use canceled stamps and postage-meter
machines.  They enable us to cut down on shipping time here at
Glover's and help the men in the Postal Service to save time,
too.  They also help us to reduce our expenses.  Those are two
good reasons why your mother likes to buy from Glover's and
two good reasons why we use only these means for paying
postage.
```

I'll bet you can get all the commemorative stamps you want if
you'll just ask some of your relatives and friends to save
them for you. Try it and see.

Did you see the big write-up about stamp collection in <u>Life</u>
magazine of June 24? You'd enjoy reading it and looking at
all the pictures, I know.

The following letter from a manufacturer refusing a dealer's request for
samples also stresses reader benefits:

Congratulations on the 25 years of service you have given to
your community!

Through continued association with retailers, we know that
only those whose businesses are based on sound managerial
policies and services succeed over so long a time.

We have tried to help in these successes by cutting costs
whenever possible and passing these savings on to retailers in
the form of lower prices. This aim led us to eliminate the
high (and often unpredictable) manufacturing and shipping costs
of special samples. You and hundreds of other druggists have
benefited from these cost reductions for the past five years.

If you'll fill in and mail the enclosed card, Mr. Robert
Abbott, your Walwhite representative, will be glad to arrange
a special Walwhite exhibit for your anniversary sale. This
attractive display will attract many customers.

Such reader-benefit interpretation cannot be applied in every case. To
attempt to would result in artificial, insincere talk. The following letter
refusing a request for permission to reprint some sales letters of a mail-
order house would not be likely to offend when stripped down to its fundamentally selfish message:

You can count on a large, interested readership for the
article you are writing about the importance of sales letters
in business.

In our company, as you know, we depend upon letters exclusively
for sales. Of necessity, then, we have tested extensively to
find out the most effective procedures. Our highly paid
writers are continually revising, sending expensive test
mailings, and comparing the returns. The best letters
represent a considerable investment.

In the past we have had some of our standard letters used
without consent by rival companies; so we now copyright all
our sales forms and confine them to company use. Should we
release them for publication, we would have to incur the same
expense once again, for their effectiveness for us would be
materially decreased.

I'm sending you some bulletins and a bibliography which may
help you with your article. Will you let me know the issue of
the magazine your article appears in?

Even though the reasoning is frankly selfish, it is reasonable, and the
writing is friendly and positive.

If you establish good reasons, you have no cause to apologize.

The derived, positive refusal

Ideally, as your reader reads your explanation, he sees that it justifies you in refusing; and by the time he finishes the explanation, he has inferred the turndown. Thus prepared, he is far more likely to accept your decision without ill feeling.

But you cannot always afford to depend exclusively on implication to establish the turndown unmistakably. The refusal must be clear, but the statement of it need not be brutally negative; in fact, it need not be negative at all.

If you will look back at the sample refusals in this section, you will see that the writers established the idea of what they were not doing by a statement of what they were doing. To establish the idea of "We don't distribute samples," one writer said, "So we now concentrate on magazine and radio-TV promotion." He might have expressed his idea more definitely with "We advertise exclusively through magazines and radio-television." Instead of saying, "We cannot let you have samples of our sales letters," another phrased it, "We copyright all our sales forms and confine them to company use." When you incorporate the limiting words *only, solely, exclusively* (even phrases like *confine to* and *concentrate on*), there's no room for doubt.

Saving some of your reasons until after establishing the refusal enables you to embed the disappointing news and thus, you hope, to reduce the impact of the refusal. In any event, you certainly want to take leave of your reader on a more pleasant note than the refusal.

The pleasant, hopeful ending

In some cases when you must refuse you can do little but reassure the reader through a few additional words that you are not utterly callous —or even merely indifferent. Good wishes for the success of the project, the suggestion of other sources, possibly the suggestion of being helpful in other ways, sending something other than what the reader has requested —all these are possibilities for ending your letter with a friendly gesture.

Sometimes you cannot comply with your reader's request but can suggest an alternative action, a "counterproposal" or "compromise proposal," which will be of some help to him. In many instances it can successfully absorb the statement of the refusal and furnish you with the positive ending you seek. The following letter is an example of this technique:

```
Prudential's employees and clients will no doubt benefit
materially from the reports manual you are planning, Mr. Lee—
especially if it is the same caliber as the letters manual
your staff prepared recently.

I'm sure many college teachers would be glad to furnish you
illustrative material.  And I am no exception.  In the past 15
```

Checklist for Refusing Requests

1. Your buffer opening must pleasantly establish compatibility.
   a) One of the poorest starts is talk about how pleased or flattered you are. It's vain and selfish.
   b) Shift the emphasis to your reader.
   c) Don't appear to be on the verge of granting the request.
   d) Nor do you want to intimate the refusal at this point.
   e) Beginning too far away from the subject results in incoherence.

2. Your transition must continue the same line of thought as in your buffer.
   a) To avoid selfish-sounding turns, keep the emphasis on the reader.
   b) *Although, however, but* and *yet* signal a turn for the worse. Avoid them as sentence beginnings.
   c) Avoid also the insincere "Although I should like to . . . ."
   d) Supply the bridging sentence showing why you are explaining.

3. Give at least one good reason before implying or stating the refusal.
   a) Emphasize reasons which are for the benefit of someone other than yourself if you can.
   b) Don't hide behind "our policy." Policies merit little respect; the reasons behind them merit a lot.
   c) For believability, you need specificness.
   d) Stick to plausibilities.

4. The refusal itself should be
   a) A logical outcome of the reasons given. Ideally, the reader should deduce the refusal before he sees your definite indication of it.
   b) Presented positively—in terms of what you can do and do do.
   c) Preceded (and preferably followed) by justifying reasons.
   d) Unmistakable but implied or subordinated (maybe counter-proposal).
   e) Written without negative words like impossible, must refuse, or very sorry to tell you that we cannot.
   f) Without apologies, which just weaken your case. Concentrate, instead, on what is hopeful.

5. Continue to convince your reader of your real interest in him and his problems, without recalling the refusal.
   a) Your ending must be positive and about something within the sphere of the reader's interest.
   b) Watch for bromides and rubber stamps in the end.
   c) Be wary of the expression "If there is any other help I can give you, please let me know." It can produce some sarcastic reactions.

years of working with business and college people trying to improve the quality of their reports, I've collected much HOW NOT TO and HOW TO teaching material.

For most of this I have only my single file copy, which I use in teaching a report-writing course three times a year and which I carefully keep in my office.

Although I have no secretarial assistance, one of the students just finishing the course is an accurate, rapid typist who is familiar with the material. I'm sure she would like to do the necessary copying at her regular rate of $1.60 an hour. Since the job involves no more than 50 or 60 pages, I feel reasonably sure that securing the material this way would cost you no more than $10, probably less. Or possibly she could Xerox it for you for a little less (including cost of materials and her time).

I shall be glad to make the necessary arrangements if you would like me to. I'm sure I can have the material to you within four or five days after hearing from you.

Please note again that this writer does not resort to negative phrasing, nor does he mouth apologies. You too should resist the common tendency to resort to such expressions as "I regret, I assure you, my inability to do as you asked," "I'm sorry to have to refuse your request," or—much worse— "I hope you will understand our position," especially at the end. For these weaklings, substitute appropriate positive ideas such as those used in the examples in this section.

For writing goodwill-building refusals, keep in mind the reminder list of points on page 252.

REFUSING THE ADJUSTMENT

The letter refusing an adjustment is obviously a bad-news (B–plan) letter. Your psychology of saying no is therefore important. So unless you thoroughly understand it, read the explanation beginning on page 56 and 246.

For your buffer-paragraph beginning, you look for something in the situation which you and the reader agree on and which is pleasant to him. Appreciation for the information could serve in most cases, for he was certainly right to come to you.

The dangers to avoid in writing the buffer are

1. Stating or implying refusal before reasons ("We wish we could . . .").
2. Misleading your reader into thinking you are going to grant the adjustment ("Our policy of making fair adjustments . . .").
3. Talking irrelevantly or too far off the subject.
4. Recalling the disappointment too vividly ("We regret your dissatisfaction . . .").
5. Making the buffer too short to get in step or too long to suit an impatient claimant.

6. Making an awkward transition to the next part because the buffer is not well phrased.

Although you may introduce a sentence that serves as a transition and resale on the house, you need to get to your explanation or review of facts and reasons fairly early. And you need to give the facts and reasons fully in a clear system of organization.

Several special techniques are important if the explanation is to rebuild goodwill while refusing to do what the reader asked. You already know better than to hide behind the word *policy* or to give no reason at all. A flat-footed announcement of what the guarantee states is just as bad as unsupported talk about policy.

Since you are refusing, obviously you are not charging responsibility for the dissatisfaction to either the firm or the product. You must clear that point up with adequate explanation as a basis for refusing. Resale at this stage (before the explanation) in the area of the trouble is *not* the way, but only a head-on collision with what the reader thinks. You *have to* give the basic fact(s) on which your refusal depends. This of course, makes the reader guilty; but you don't want to accuse him directly. Preaching to him or belittling him will only make matters worse. Your best technique is to fall back on the impersonal presentation (something "was not done" instead of "you didn't"), rather than accuse. The reader will be able to see who is responsible if you explain well that your goods and your firm aren't.

In fact, if you arrange your reasons and explanations carefully, they will probably make the negative answer clear by implication without the necessity of stating it. Thus you may subordinate the negative refusal. If not this way, at least you subordinate it by burying it (that is, putting it in the middle of a paragraph where it doesn't stand out unduly).

After the refusal, which must be clearly there whether by implication or by direct statement, you may do well to add some more reasoning and explanation in support. Be sure you say enough to make your refusal convincing and justified.

Your ending then becomes an attempt to get agreement or the reader's acceptance of your refusal as justified. That is, you write with as much success consciousness as seems reasonable about the future outlook. This does *not* mean that you write and ask for an answer as to whether your action is all right. If it isn't, he'll let you know without your asking.

Often the best ending assumes that the preceding explanation and decision are satisfactory and talks about something else. Rather than looking backward, it may better look forward to the next likely relationship between writer and reader. The following letter illustrates most of the points, especially the clear reasoning that makes direct refusal unnecessary:

We certainly agree with you that your company has always ordered high-quality products to sell to your customers. We, too, try to keep our products up to a high standard.

That is why we appreciate your fairness in giving us a chance to analyze the sample of screws you sent.

Our chemical analysis shows that the screws are brittle because they are high in phosphorus and low in carbon and sulphur steel, whereas our screws are of a very different analysis. Physical analysis shows that the sample screws have been severely cold-worked without stress relief, whereas our screws are never made that way.

To check our laboratory report, which practically proved that we could not have made those screws, I have checked your former orders and found that the screws we have sent you were always blue steel finish, instead of the cadmium finish of the sample.

We should be glad to supply you again with our hard but tough screws that will give your customers the quality they have come to expect from you. Our descriptive price list is enclosed. May we look forward to your order?

For a more subtle illustration, analyze the following letter to a customer who had taken his suit to another tailor in another city and asked for payment of the tailor's bill long after the usual free-alteration period ended. (The owner-manager knew all of his student customers fairly well.)

You're right!—your Smart Marx should fit you well. When you buy a suit of that quality from us, we try as hard as you do to see that you are satisfied in every way before we turn it over to you with our blessings.

I well remember how you liked the rich sheen of the tan 100 percent wool cloth and the casual look of the patch pockets. But for comfort and becoming fit, we decided that the sleeves should be half an inch longer and the collar taken up an inch —the same directions that are on the sales slip and the alterations slip which I have, and which bear the initials of one of our tailors. When you came back in the next day and tried the coat on, I honestly thought that it clicked all the way around; and after carefully noting it from every angle, you agreed with me. I thought we had achieved our goal—your satisfaction.

But we owe you something else: the best quality at the lowest price possible. And one of the small economies that helps to keep the price of your suit lower is that it does not include costs of altering suits for men who have become heavier or lighter. In order to protect all Smart Marx buyers, we limit free alterations to two weeks after purchase, thus giving the wearer ample time to become accustomed to the feel of his new suit and take advantage of the free-alterations privilege.

After that time we're glad to make necessary alterations at regular tailors' rates to readjust Smart Marx suits to a wearer's changes in weight that sometimes come during the long life of such good suits.

Since you'll probably want to wear your suit well into the coming season, you might enjoy a pair of the Floorshine shoes we've just received. In russet calfskin, they're good for all-around wear. May we show you this style when you return to school early next month?

Refused-Adjustment Checklist

1. Make your buffer positive, related, adequate, and progressive.
   a) Reflect pleasant cooperation (try to agree on something).
   b) But begin closely enough to the situation to acknowledge.
   c) Don't imply that you're granting the request.
   d) Avoid recalling the dissatisfaction more than necessary.
   e) Watch buffer length: neither too breezy nor too long.
   f) Early resale in the trouble area bluntly contradicts.
   g) Should you show appreciation for the report?

2. Make your facts and reasons courteous, thorough, and convincing.
   a) An immediate plunge (beginning of the second paragraph) into "our guarantee" or "our policy" is abrupt.
   b) Don't accuse the reader or preach at him. Phrase your explanation impersonally—and let him derive his own guilt.
   c) Establish the explicit, adequate facts—the basis for refusal.
   d) Even intimating refusal before reasons is bad psychology.
   e) When possible, interpret reasons to show reader benefits.

3. Make the refusal logical, subordinate, and impersonal but clear.
   a) Preferably the reader sees the refusal coming.
   b) Give it little emphasis. Consider implying it.
   c) Keep it impersonal and positive—in terms of what you do.
   d) Be sure it is there, however; unclear is as bad as too strong.
   e) Follow the refusal with reasons, showing any reader benefits.
   f) Customer education or counterproposal may imply the refusal.
   g) What about the returned product (if applicable)?

4. Make your ending pleasant, positive, and success-conscious.
   a) An off-the-subject ending about store services, seasonal goods, or some topic of interest is appropriate.
   b) Don't suggest uncertainty of your ground. Watch hope/trust.
   c) Apologies are unnecessary reminders of trouble; your explanation has already made the best apology.

For the COMPROMISE ADJUSTMENT, use these for Items 3 and 4:

3. Make your counterproposal as logical, helpful relief.
   a) Be careful to make a smooth transition from the explanation (which implies refusal) to the counterproposal.
   b) Offer it ungrudgingly, without parading your generosity, but let the service element prevail.
   c) Don't belittle it ("the best we can do") or make it sound like a penalty ("a service charge will have to be made").

4. Use a modified action ending.
   a) Ask permission; you wouldn't go ahead without agreement.
   b) Tell what the customer is to do, but don't urge acceptance.
   c) For service attitude, talk prompt satisfaction.

The checklist on page 256 reviews the highlights of refusing adjustments.

COMPROMISING ON THE ADJUSTMENT

When you decide to try to compromise—usually because of divided responsibility, or uncertainty about responsibility or correction for the trouble—you may use either of two plans.

In the first you follow the refused-adjustment plan exactly down *to* the refusal. There you make your proposed compromise instead, explicitly. In effect, you are refusing the adjustment requested and are making a counterproposal—a compromise. When you ask acceptance of it, your success in getting a favorable reply will depend not only on how well you have presented facts and reasons to justify the compromise but on your success consciousness in presenting it and on your phrasing it to encourage rather than discourage acceptance.

The following letter in answer to a strong request for removal of the heater, cancellation of remaining payments, and refund of the shipping and installation charges illustrates the points. You will notice that it offers to compromise to the extent of canceling the remaining payments, but it proposes another action instead.

You are right in expecting your Warmall heater to heat a large room such as your entire store, for that was what it was designed to do.

To do so, however, it must be located so that the air currents can carry its heat to all parts of the room. Our engineer reports that the stove was installed in the proper position but that later remodeling of your store has blocked circulation of air with a half partition.

Removing your stove would be useless, for it can be all you want it to be when properly located. That would mean losing your down payment and what you have paid for shipping and installation, although we would of course cancel the remaining payments. Moreover, you must have heat, and the Warmall will do the job.

We have absolute faith in our engineer's judgment, but your satisfaction is more important. So we want to do what is fair to us both.

At your convenience we can move the stove to the position suggested by our engineer; and, if it does not heat to your satisfaction, we will not charge you a cent.

Will you suggest the most convenient time for the change that will make your store warm and comfortable? We can do the job so quickly and efficiently that your business can continue as usual.

(For a checklist following this plan of compromise adjustment letter, see p. 256.)

A second method of compromising—usually called the full-reparation beginning compromise—sometimes works better. You follow the plan of the letter *granting* an adjustment at the beginning, through the explanation. The facts, of course, will indicate divided responsibility or uncertain responsibility. Your resale talk will indicate that the repaired product (or a replacement up to par, in case the original was beyond repair) will give the service the customer wanted. Since he presumably still wants that service, you ask him to take his choice—the refunded money or the product. And of course you word it to encourage him to choose the product, because that way you have a customer satisfied with your products as well as your fair-minded practices.

Your main purpose is to restore goodwill and confidence. Your success depends on a start which offers him all he requested and thereby pleases him; your explanation, which shows the justice of a compromise; and your fair-mindedness in letting him be the judge and take his choice. The danger—not a very serious one—is that some people might try to keep both the money and the product. Here are two examples—one to a consumer and one to a dealer.

The enclosed check is cheerful proof of our "money back if not entirely satisfied" guarantee on the Corone cigarette lighter you purchased last December.

Because such a guarantee can be given only on a lighter that usually satisfies entirely, we examined yours very carefully in our service department. The shop foreman reports that the sparking ridges on the flint wheel were clogged to a smooth surface with flake particles from a soft flint. After he cleaned the wheel and installed a Corone hard flint—the type, recommended on the instructions enclosed with each new lighter —your Corone worked well.

You probably remember, Mr. Lewis, that one flick brought an instant flame before the hard flint wore out and was replaced. Now that your lighter has been returned to that condition and still has the attractive styling that caught your eye the day you bought it, you'll probably want it back.

We will be glad to absorb the normal 60 cents cleaning charge and return your lighter to you if you wish. Just send the check back in the enclosed envelope, and your lighter will be in your pocket within two days after we hear from you—ready at a flick to show your friend in Jackson that your Corone really does the job.

--

Attached to this letter is a credit memorandum for $43.75, which we cheerfully send you for the five Bear Mountain hunting jackets you returned, as an indication that you'll always be treated fairly at Bowen's.

Under the assumption that these jackets would find a ready sale at a reduced retail price despite slight imperfections (a button mis-matched, a crooked seam, or maybe a little nick in the fabric), we offered them "as is" and priced them at $8.75 instead of the regular $12.75. We felt that marking them "as is" indicated special circumstances.

Generally we follow the accepted business custom of making all
such sales final for an entire lot. But as you are a customer
of long standing and valued patronage [Better: But as we
evidently did not make the situation perfectly clear], we are
leaving the decision up to you; if you feel that you're
entitled to the adjustment, it's yours.

Many of your customers, however, would probably be glad to get
nationally advertised Bear Mountains at perhaps $21 instead of
the standard $25. And even if you sell these five at, say,
only $16, your profit will be about the same as if you sold
perfect jackets at full price. So if you'd like to reconsider
and want to offer these jackets at a saving, just initial the
face of this letter and send it to us with the credit memo.
We'll absorb the freight charges.

Even though slightly imperfect, these jackets are still ready
to stand a lot of hard wear. They are made to suit hunters'
needs, with ample pockets for shells and with comfortable
tailoring. Selling them should be easy, especially at a
discount. We'll look for your decision, but we think you can
make a good profit on them at the special price.

Application of the checklist for compromises with full-reparation beginning (p. 260) to these two letters will show that they are pretty good and
will review the principles for you.

REQUESTS FOR CREDIT INFORMATION FROM CUSTOMERS

Many applications for credit do not give all the data you must have. You
therefore write the customer, asking him to supply you with the information. The major problem is to avoid arousing the customer's suspicion or
his indignation.

To soften the effect of the delay and to quell possible suspicion, you
begin with some pleasant buffer material, stress benefits to him for complying with the request, show him that he's being treated as all other customers are, make action easy, and promise quick action. If character is not
in question, be sure to say so. And to encourage response, use resale or
sales promotion as the matrix for your explanation.

The following letter to a housewife is typical in stressing "All our customers fill out this application . . ."; it is an appropriate covering letter for
the form request discussed on page 113.

It is a pleasure to know that you want to take advantage of
the conveniences of an Allen Tilby charge account, Mrs. Lee.

So that we may assist you as quickly and as easily as possible,
will you please fill out the routine credit application which
is enclosed? All our customers fill out this form as a help
to both them and us. The information is strictly for our
confidential files.

You can be sure that we will give your request our immediate
attention. A stamped, addressed envelope is enclosed for your
convenience in returning the application.

Checklist for Compromise with Full-Reparation Beginning

1. The beginning giving the customer everything he has asked for is basic—to dissolve his wrath and get him to listen to reason.
   a) Make it immediately, specifically, and completely.
   b) Build up the wholesome effect by a friendly, adapted expression to emphasize your integrity and reliability and prevent a curt tone.
   c) Don't apologize more; Item 1(a) is an apology of the most concrete form.
   d) Carefully avoid unnecessary negative reminders.
   e) Beginning with the compromise suggestion would infuriate most readers. Since they think they're entitled to what they asked, you have to show otherwise before compromising.

2. The explanation must show that the customer is expecting too much.
   a) Don't be too slow about getting to at least some of the explanation.
   b) Interpret it with a reader viewpoint and positive statement.
   c) Do not directly accuse; show blame impersonally (perhaps by customer education on the use and care of the article).
   d) Establish the facts to show the customer that he is at least partly responsible or is overestimating his loss.

3. Show the service attitude and your fair-mindedness in your proposal.
   a) As the foundation of your proposal, stress serving your customer.
   b) Recall the original desire for the service the product can render.
   c) Continuing the reader-benefit interpretation, state your proposal.
   d) Follow your suggestion with any other plausible sales points.
   e) Don't parade your generosity in the loss you take.
   f) Suggest—don't command or preach or high-pressure the customer.

4. The modified action ending should give a choice but encourage the one you prefer.
   a) Tell what you want the customer to do: reject (return) the full reparation and accept your proposal.
   b) As in any action ending, make action easy.
   c) Do not bog down with apologies or emphasis on the full reparation.
   d) End with a short suggestion of his satisfactory use of the product.

A letter to a dealer employs the same strategy:

```
Corone fishing gear is a good line to handle.  Dealers
throughout the country report favorable reaction of fishermen.
And our advertising in Field and Stream, Sports Afield, and
True continues to create demand for Corone dealers.

We're just as eager as you are to have your Corone sales start;
so will you supply the usual financial information that all
our dealers furnish us, along with the names of other firms
from which you buy on credit?  Most of our dealers use the
enclosed form, but if you prefer to use your own, please do.
This confidential information will enable us to serve you
efficiently—now and in the future.
```

Occasionally such a request backfires, with a protest from the customer (sometimes quite vigorous!). In such cases all you can do is write again, using a pacifying buffer, and then pointing out the value of credit and the necessity for careful selection of credit customers. The letter reiterates the normalcy of the request and closes with a request for action. It is also a modification of the B–plan letter, as in this example:

```
We're glad you let us know unmistakably how you feel about
sending financial information concerning your business.  And
we're sure that as an open-minded businessman you'll want to
look at your supplier's side of the story.  Only through
complete frankness can a dealer like you and a supplier like
us work together successfully in a credit relationship.

We have some pretty definite ideas too—ideas which are the
result of selling about 2,000 successful dealers like you
several million dollars' worth of Corone fishing equipment in
the last 20 years . . . about 90 percent of it on credit.

Because of our credit arrangements, Corone dealers can do a
large amount of business on a small investment.  In effect, we
take the place of your banker, for the goods we send you on
credit are the same as cash.  And we don't ask for payment for
30 days.  Like your banker, we can make loans only when we
have evidence of ability and willingness to pay later.  The
only way we can protect all our dealers against price rises
due to losses from bad debts is to examine the financial
statements of every credit applicant and to secure statements
from his references.  If you applied for a loan at your bank,
you'd expect to show your financial statements to your banker.
We are in the same position as he—except that we have no
mortgage to protect us, and we are not so well informed as he
is about you and your local market.

The confidential information we've asked you for is strictly
for business purposes.  It helps both of us.  Since the peak
sales months are close at hand, I'm enclosing another form
and an addressed envelope with a special-delivery stamp so that
you can get this information back to us in time for us to get
your fast-selling Corone fishing gear started to you by the
first of next week.
```

(Because most requests for credit information from customers are simply modifications of direct requests and refusals, we run no checklists or cases.)

CREDIT REFUSALS

In the light of unfavorable reports from references or unfavorable financial position as shown in the applicant's statements, your job will sometimes necessitate refusing credit outright or suggesting some modification of the arrangement the customer has requested. In the case of an old customer it may be a refusal of a credit-limit revision or a suggestion of curtailed buying. All these situations are inherently disappointing; they are a reflection on the ability of the customer; they *may be* interpreted as a reflection on his honesty; and so they are fraught with negative possibilities.

As in any disappointing-news letter, you need to analyze the situation, search out any hopeful elements (especially character), line up your reasons, and write a B–plan letter.

As in any refusal, you have to have a reason. The applicant may be too slow in meeting obligations, his receivables or payables may be out of line, or he may be undercapitalized. Whatever the reason, you have to establish it, and in this function you have some educational work to do—without offense if at all possible.

You certainly do not want to close the door irrevocably on any debtor (except possibly deadbeats). A poor account at the time of writing may be a good one a year from then (and if your wise counseling has helped in the improvement, you have established yourself favorably in the eyes of the customer and are thus more likely to receive his business).

For that reason, most credit refusals follow a presentation that establishes good feeling in a short buffer, establishes the reasons in an analysis of the circumstances, identifies the deficiency, refuses in positive fashion, suggests how the customer can remedy the deficiency, and invites a later application. If possible, the letter may make a counterproposal and point out its advantages and then ask for action on that basis. The best ending is an attempt to sell for cash. After all, the reader wants your goods and possibly can't get them on credit elsewhere either.

In the following instance, involving an order for $176 worth of workmen's overalls, the dealer quickly responded with a financial statement and references in response to the request for them. Accounts receivable and payable were both too large; the trade association reports offered the explanation that strikes in the mines of the dealer's community affected all local trade. Since the references reported that the customer's payments were good enough during normal times, the credit man sought to cultivate potential business while declining the account at present:

Your large order for Stalwart overalls suggests the prospect of an early strike settlement in your area. We're glad to hear that.

When the miners go back to work, the steady revival of business in and around Canyon City will no doubt help your collections so that both your accounts receivable and accounts payable can

be reduced. In that way you can probably quickly restore your
current ratio to the healthy 2:1 we require, since we've found
over the years that such a ratio places no burden on our
customers. Such an improvement will enable us to consider
your credit application favorably. Will you please send us
subsequent statements?

You'll probably need your Stalwart overalls sooner than that
time, however; they're a popular brand because they wear well.
Workmen like the reinforced pockets and knees. They'll easily
outsell other lines you might carry.

You can stock this popular brand and thus take advantage of
present demand by paying cash and taking advantage of the
liberal discount we can give you (on this order, for instance,
the discount would amount to $3.52—more than enough to pay
interest for three months on a $100 bank loan). You might cut
your order in about half and order more frequently. With a
$100 bank loan at 8 percent and a stock turn of 12—which is a
conservative estimate, Mr. Wolens—you'd make an annual saving
of $16 after paying your interest charges. I don't need to
tell you that that's 5 pairs of dependable Stalwart overalls
absolutely free—overalls that you still sell for $5.50 a pair.

To handle the order in this profitable way, attach your check
to the memo I've enclosed and mail both of them back to me in
the enclosed envelope. We can have your Stalwart overalls to
you in about five days.

Usually you can specifically isolate the sore spot in a dealer's situation
and by impersonal, positive phrasing save the customer's pride, suggest
the remedy, and leave the way open for future negotiations. In consumer
letters involving a retail customer, however, nine times out of ten the
reason for the refusal is the customer's failure to take care of obligations.
This is a highly personal reflection, one which many retail credit men shy
away from by feigning incomplete information and inviting the customer to
come in and talk the matter over. We do not agree with the philosophy or
the dodging procedure involved in a letter like the following, but some
authors do:

We heartily thank you for the implied compliment you paid the
Bowen Company when you applied for a charge account.

According to the usual procedure in opening a new account, we
sought information which would serve as a basis for extending
credit to you. While we have gathered some very fine reports
of a personal nature, the business reports we have been able
to accumulate do not allow us to make a definite conclusion
right now.

We realize that we have only one side of the story; so if you
would care to come to the store and talk with us, we shall be
glad to have you call at your convenience. Perhaps we can
arrive at a better understanding.

In the meantime may we serve you on a cash basis? We want to
serve you to the best of our ability and to continue to merit
your goodwill.

One of the reasons for writing such a letter, according to its sponsors, is that to tell a customer that you have unfavorable reports is a violation of the confidential aspects of credit information exchanges. To this, we can only raise a polite eyebrow. A Supreme Court decision now says you have to if asked. We feel that you're doing a customer a service by pointing out what he must do in order to earn (or restore) his credit standing.

We think, however, that better procedure is the forthright credit refusal in the usual pattern of buffer, reasons, positive refusal, forward look, and counterproposal in the form of a bid for cash business.

We appreciate your request for a credit account at Aiken's as a compliment to our way of doing business.

For 50 years Aiken's has been bringing its customers quality merchandise at fair prices. This, as you realize, requires careful merchandising policies on our part. Not the least of these savings—the policy of paying cash for merchandise, thereby receiving discounts and eliminating interest charges, which we are able to pass on to Aiken customers in the form of lower prices—necessitates that we receive prompt payment from our credit customers.

As you were an applicant for a credit account, we followed our usual practice and asked for information from retail credit sources.

We realize that it is often temporarily difficult to meet all obligations promptly and that very likely in a short time you will have qualified for a charge account at Aiken's by taking care of your other obligations.

Meanwhile you will continue to receive the same courteous treatment that made you favor Aiken's in the first place. We certainly want to have you as a customer. With our will-call, budget, or layaway plans at your disposal, you may own anything in Aiken's within a short time by making convenient payments of your choice. Come in soon and let us serve you in this way.

The following letter refusing credit to a young man just out of college and with unsteady, low-income employment talks concretely and sensibly; it's a good credit-education letter. Note how the writer stresses the idea that character is not the basis for refusal.

When you wrote to us last week asking for credit, as a member of the Illinois Credit Union we automatically asked the Union for your record. You can well be proud of the report we received. The complimentary reports on your excellent character indicate a promising future.

There is absolutely no black mark against your record. The fact that you have never defaulted or delayed in paying an account means that you will be able to get credit without any trouble when your income increases.

We could extend credit to you on the basis of your personal record alone, for we know that you fully intend to meet any obligations you undertake. But if some unforeseen expense should come up, with your present income you could not pay your account. As a cooperating member of the Credit Union, we would then be compelled to submit your name as a poor credit risk. Such a report would limit your chances of obtaining credit in the future—perhaps at a time when you need it more than now. For your own benefit you'll be better off to stick to cash purchases now.

Thank you for thinking of us. We shall look forward to the time when you can comfortably and safely contract for credit purchases with us. Meanwhile you can make your dollars reach further by buying from Bowen's for cash, for we can buy in quantity, save on shipping costs, and take advantage of discounts. We pass these savings on to you in the form of lower prices. When you buy at Bowen's, your income is inflated because you get quality merchandise at low prices.

Letters limiting the credit of an old established customer are no different from refusals to new customers; they just adapt the talking points.

It is certainly good to see how well you are selling Carlton heaters. The $635 order for September delivery you gave Mr. Ray indicates a bright outlook for fall sales.

We want to work right along with you. In trying to be of service to you always, however, we often make constructive suggestions. Now, for example, the large order you placed in March, together with this current one, leads us to believe that you may be overstocking Carltons. With this shipment your account would stand about $500 beyond the limit we agreed on when you first started to deal with us five years ago. Since we believe that the proposed balance would be too great a burden upon you because it would throw your payables out of line, we suggest two alternative courses of action.

If your ordering such a stock of Carlton heaters indicates that there is an extensive home-building program going on in Fairview, your comments on local conditions and the information requested on the enclosed form may serve as a basis for extending your credit limit to the point where it will take care of your needs.

Or we will extend to July 10 the 5 percent discount on your $940 March order. By sending us your check for $893, you will not only put your account in shape for the present order; you will also mark up greater profits on the sale of your Carltons.

We're just as anxious as you are, Mr. Skinner, to send you this latest shipment. Please take one of these courses so that we may ship your new stock of Carltons in time for the fall season.

As in any good refusal, none of these letters apologize or hark back to the refusal in the end. To do so indicates that you are not confident in your decision. The checklist on page 266 incorporates the major suggestions for handling credit refusals or limitations.

Credit Refusal Checklist

1. Your opening:
   a) Your best beginning talks about something pleasant: the market; the timeliness; the reader . . . .
   b) Beware the selfish note of "We are glad to receive . . . ."
   c) To keep your reader from considering buying elsewhere, get resale (product and/or house) early in the letter: consumer pleasure in use or dealer profit possibilities.
   d) References to the order, if there was one, should be worked in incidentally while you say something of more significance.
   e) Be careful not to mislead the reader.

2. Your explanation and refusal:
   a) Stick to the theme of a strong, healthy financial condition.
   b) Do not begin your explanation with writer-interest reasons.
   c) Give some justifying reasons before the refusal.
   d) Meet the issue squarely, making clear whether character is or is not the reason. Advantages in cash buying are not reasons for refusing credit.
   e) Avoid the negative, critical, nosey, or patronizing tone; state your reasons as helpfulness to the reader. Give just enough facts to show that you know without implication of FBI investigations.
   f) Be sure you've made clear that you will not now approve credit.
   g) Hiding behind policy evades the issue (and appears selfish).
   h) Phrase your reason in terms of your experience with others.
   i) Always leave the way open for credit extension later.
   j) But you can't make promises, except to reconsider.

3. Your counterproposal:
   a) Introduce a cash, reduced-shipment, or other plan as the solution.
   b) But first show why (help to the reader).
   c) If you propose cash with a discount, figure the savings.
   d) Possibly project the savings over a year's business.
   e) Can you suggest smaller orders? Local financing?
   f) Use the conditional mood in your explanation and proposal.

4. Your ending:
   a) Leave no details uncovered in your present proposal.
   b) In regular action-ending style, drive for his acceptance.
   c) Success consciousness precludes the use of "Why not . . . ."
   d) You have to get approval before taking unasked action.
   e) Your last picture should show the reader's benefits.

5. Your tone:
   a) Throughout your letter retain an attitude of helpfulness.
   b) Sales promotion material on other goods is inappropriate.

ACKNOWLEDGMENTS OF INCOMPLETE OR INDEFINITE ORDERS

You would think that anybody could write an adequate order, but only one day's work in the order department of a big mail-order house would convince you that many people don't.

When you get an order that is incomplete (and therefore vague), you can either try to guess what the customer wants and thereby risk extra costs and customer dissatisfaction, or you can write for the needed information. Usually you write.

Your real problem is to *keep the order,* instead of causing the customer to neglect your request for the information or to write you in disgust to cancel the order. Drawbacks to your success are the inevitable delay, the extra trouble to the customer, his embarrassment at having written a poor order, and (unless you are very careful) his irritation at the way you write to him about it. The big problem, then, is to avoid or overcome the negatives inherently in the situation.

Since it is a *bad-news* letter (because of the additional trouble and delay), you will wisely use a buffer. Resale, thanks, and (if a new customer) a hearty welcome are all good buffer material and need to come early in the letter. A problem here is to avoid misleading the customer into believing that you are sending what he ordered. Otherwise, his disappointment when he learns the facts will be greater.

Very early—perhaps by starting to interweave some of it into the first part of the letter—you should stress the resale element. The more specific it is, the more emphatic it is. If you tell him he will like the product, also tell him specifically why you think so. By reassuring the customer that the product he ordered is good, resale will help to overcome the drawbacks. In this case it has a much more important role than in the standard acknowledgment. Although small bits of it may be scattered throughout the letter, at least some of it comes before the reader learns the bad news —to bolster his original desire in his moment of disappointment. It can be very short:

Fashion-conscious women everywhere are wearing Ban-lon sweaters like the one you ordered, not only for their wide color choice and style but because of their ability to be tossed around and still keep looking nice.

When you have thus prepared the reader psychologically, you should let him know the bad news by asking for the needed information. Thus you save words, weaken the bad news by putting the reader's main attention on complying with your request, and avoid any goodwill-killing accusations. More specifically, your technique at this important crux of the letter is: In one key sentence beginning with a reader-benefit reason for your request, ask for the information. For example:

So that we may be sure to send you just the sweater that will suit you best, will you please specify your color choice?

Now, if you add a touch of satisfaction-resale to motivate the requested action, do what you can to help the reader decide and answer (to overcome the extra trouble), and promise speed (to overcome as much as possible of the delay), you'll probably get the information you want, without ruffling your reader's feathers:

> Coming in four subtle shades of harvest brown, lettuce green, tile red, and sky blue, Ban-lon sweaters provide you a pleasant color to match any complexion or ensemble.
>
> Just use the handy return card, and you'll be enjoying the sweater of your choice within two days after we receive the information.

Notice that although they treat an inherently bad-news situation, nowhere in the four paragraphs of this letter is there any negative expression ("delay," "inconvenience," "incomplete," "regret," "sorry"). Most of all, the acknowledgment does not irritate by accusing with such expressions as "you neglected," "you forgot," or "you failed."

The following letter illustrates good technique for an acknowledgment when you can fill part of the order but have to get omitted information about another part. If you want to consider it as a simple acknowledgment of an incomplete order, however, you can read it without the first paragraph and the phrase "the file and" in the next-to-last paragraph.

> Soon after you get this letter you should receive the very protective locking and fire-resistant Chaw-Walker file you ordered October 2. It is to go out on our Meridian delivery tomorrow.
>
> The sturdy but light Model 94 Royal Standard typewriter you specified is our most popular one this year, perhaps because of its wide adaptability. Readily available in two type sizes and six type styles, it is suitable to all kinds of work and to various typists' tastes.
>
> To be sure of getting the size and style you like best, please check your choices on the enclosed card of illustrations and return it.
>
> Although your letter was written in Executive style elite (12 letters to the inch), you may prefer the more legible Professional style pica (10 letters to the inch) if you are buying for your reporters. It is the most widely used in newspaper work.
>
> All prices are the same—except $10 extra for the modish Script style, which you probably will not want—and your check exactly covers the file and the three typewriters you ordered in any other choice.
>
> By returning the card with your choices of type size and style right away, you can have your three new Royals Friday, ready for years of carefree typing. We'll send them out on the next delivery after we hear from you.

For requesting additional information in business-building fashion, apply the suggestions in the checklist for incomplete orders (p. 269).

Checklist for Acknowledging Incomplete Orders

1. If you are sending any goods, say so immediately and give necessary details.
   a) If not, begin with a short buffer which is basically resale.
   b) Quickly but subordinately identify the order by date, number, and/or description.
   c) Slow: "We have received . . . ," "Thank you for your . . . ."
   d) Selfish: "We're glad to have . . . ."
   e) Provide some resale on the problem article before the bad news, but don't imply that you are sending the article now.
   f) Make the resale specific, not "We're sure you'll like these shoes." Why?
   g) Use only brief phrases for resale on goods sent, or for any new-customer aspects, until you've asked for the missing information.

2. Ask for the information naturally, positively, and specifically.
   a) The natural transition to the request follows from preceding resale talk.
   b) Preface the request with a reader-benefit phrase—something like "So that you'll be sure to get just the X you want, please . . . ."
   c) To avoid puzzling, make the request fairly early—but not too quickly or abruptly.
   d) Avoid the accusation and wasted words of such phrasing as "You did not include" or "We need some additional information."
   e) Name the customer's options: color choices or different models, for example.
   f) Add explanations to help in the choice (or decision), to resell, and to show your interest in satisfying.
   g) Keep the you-viewpoint: "You may choose from . . . ," not "We have three shades."

3. Close with a drive for the specific action you want.
   a) If many words follow the first indication of what you want done, repeat specifically.
   b) Make replying easy (maybe a return card to check).
   c) Refer to the enclosure subordinately; action deserves the emphasis.
   d) Stress your promptness and his—preferably a date of arrival if he acts now.
   e) But keep it logical; post-office speed is not that of an automat.
   f) Try to work in a last short reference to reader satisfaction.

If resale on the house and/or sales promotion material would be appropriate—as the first surely would be in a new-customer situation—use Items 3 and 4 of the checklist for standard acknowledgments (p. 145) as additional Items 4 and 5 here.

DELAYS AND BACK-ORDERING

Sometimes the problem in an acknowledgment is that you can't send the goods right away. In the absence of a specified time limit, sellers-by-mail usually try to keep the order on the books if they feel they can fill it within a time that is really a service to the customer—that is, if they feel the customer would prefer to wait rather than cancel the order. After a buffer, they tell when they expect to fill the order and usually assume (without asking) that such an arrangement is acceptable. If the date is so far off that doubt arises, they may ask instead of assuming. In either case the wise businessman will acknowledge the order promptly.

Again your main problem is keeping the order. This time, though, the only drawback to overcome is delay. Your main element is resale—to convince the reader he wants the product enough to wait. It may include both resale on the house and resale on the goods. If the order is the customer's first, resale is even more important and more extensive.

The plan and technique are the same as for the acknowledgment of an incomplete order, at least through the first paragraph and some resale talk.

> Your order 5B631 of April 7 for Tropical brand playsuits in the
> new Wancrest Glachine material is another reflection of your
> astute buying. From all indications they will be the
> prevailing style this season.

The parting of the ways comes where the incomplete asks for information and the back order explains the situation. The explanation should picture the goods on their way (and imply receipt of them) in the first part of a sentence which ends with a clear indication that that does not mean now (usually by giving the shipping date).

> By making every effort to get your supply to you before
> spring, when your customers will start calling for these
> popular playsuits, we are able to promise you a shipment by
> April 27.

As always in letter writing, it is better to explain in positive terms what you can do, have done, and will do than to tell in negative terms what you can't do, haven't done, or won't do. As the writer of the preceding paragraph did, a good letter writer will avoid such unnecessary negatives as "out of stock," "cannot send," "temporarily depleted," "will be unable to," "do not have," and "can't send until."

Only a poor businessman is caught short without a justifying reason. When he is, he will be better off to admit it frankly than to give some weak or false excuse. A good businessman will have a reason. He should explain it to his customer to avoid the impression that he is inefficient. Often it is basically strong resale material if properly interpreted. For example:

The Wancrest people have assured us that although we're
insisting on the top-quality material which has made these
playsuits so attractive to store buyers, they can catch up to
our recent order and have a new shipment to us by the 21st.
Thus we can promise yours by the 27th.

More resale may follow the explanation to make the reader want the
product badly enough to wait. Because it has such an important job to do,
it is probably more important in the back-order acknowledgment than in
any other. It should be short, specific, and adapted to carry its full effect.
It may include both resale on the house and resale on the goods. Since so
much of both kinds has already appeared in the letter we're developing
here, however, more hardly seems appropriate.

The ending of the back-order acknowledgment may go either one of two
ways:

1. You may ask outright whether you may fill the order when you have said you
   can. This plan is preferable if you seriously doubt that the customer will
   approve.
2. You may phrase it so that this letter will complete the contract unless the
   reader takes the initiative and writes back a cancellation. That is, you look
   forward with success consciousness to filling the order when you have said
   you can. You assume that your plan is acceptable unless and until you learn
   otherwise. Your assumption will hold more frequently if you never suggest
   the thing you don't want your reader to do—cancel.

The following letter illustrates the handling of a back-order problem:

You will be glad to know that the women's playsuits you ordered
April 7—

　　4 dozen—style No. 16J7 women's playsuits 1 dozen each in
　　sizes 12, 14, 16, and 18, in full color assortments, @
　　$39.50 a dozen; terms 2/10, n/30

—are leading the summer sportswear sales of more than 400 of
our customers from Maine to California.

We are increasing production on this model and have booked
your playsuits for rush shipment April 27 by air express.

The unusual preseason popularity of this trimly cut playsuit
owes much to the shimmering Wancrest Glachine fabric of which
it is made. We used up our stock of this genuine combed-cotton
and acetate-rayon material, and rather than use a substitute,
we shut down production on this model. A large stock of
Glachine fabric is already en route here from Wancrest's
famous North Carolina mills; thus we are able to promise your
shipment by April 27.

For this chance to prove once again Tropical's continuing
fashion superiority, we thank you sincerely.

Much of the back-order acknowledgment technique is the same as
that used in standard and incomplete-order acknowledgments. The checklist for back-order acknowledgments points out the similarities and additional considerations (p. 272).

Back-Order Checklist

1. If you are sending any goods, say so immediately and give necessary details.
   a) If not, begin with a short buffer which is basically resale.
   b) Quickly but subordinately identify the order.
   c) Slow: "We have received . . . ," "Thank you for your . . . ."
   d) Selfish: 'We're glad to have . . . .'
   e) Provide some resale on the problem article before bad news.
   f) Make the resale specific, not "We're sure you'll like . . . ."
   g) Use only brief phrases for resale on goods sent, or for any new-customer aspects, until you've handled the key point.

2. Handle the bad news as positively as you can.
   a) Picture the goods moving toward or being used by the customer *before* indicating that you do not now have them.
   b) Avoid negatives: "out of stock," "can't send until . . . ."
   c) Adapt to the one situation rather than a universal, like "In order to give you the very best service we can . . . ."
   d) Explain the reason for being caught short (if any)—preferably resale in effect.
   e) Do make clear when you can ship.
   f) To avoid cancellation of the order, some resale is important.

3. Resale on the house helps too, especially with new customers.
   a) For consumers: personal shopping, delivery schedules, credit. . . .
   b) For dealers: salesmen, manuals, displays, advertising aids.
   c) If you talk advertising, give publications or stations, amount of space or time, and schedules; show how it promotes sales.
   d) If you talk credit, invite application rather than promise.

4. Sales promotion material shows service attitude and builds sales.
   a) Keep it appropriate—usually on allied or seasonal goods.
   b) You-attitude and specificness are necessary to effectiveness.
   c) Emphasize service to the customer, not desire to sell more.
   d) In referring to enclosures, put the emphasis on reader action.

5. Look forward to future orders.
   a) If sales promotion is the basis, suggest specific action.
   b) If resale is the basis, talk of reader satisfaction.
   c) Guard against bromides and Greedy Gus wording as you close.

6. Word the back-order action phrase to stress the action you want.
   a) Ask only if you doubt that your plan is satisfactory.
   b) Suggest acceptance; avoid the idea of cancellation.

ACKNOWLEDGMENTS DECLINING ORDERS

Only three likely reasons might make you decline an order:

1. The customer has asked for credit, and you are not willing to sell to him that way. In that case the problem is a credit problem and is discussed on pp. 259–66.

2. You don't have the goods (or a suitable substitute), and you don't expect to get them in time to serve the customer. You then simply thank him, explain the situation, tell him where he can get the goods (if you know), maybe present resale on the house and sales promotion material on any other goods which seem likely to interest him, and end appropriately.

3. You don't market your products in the way he has proposed. Most of these problems arise because of one of the following two situations: (*a*) the orderer is an unacceptable dealer; or (*b*) you sell only through regular merchandising channels and he does not propose to go through those channels.

Declining because you don't have the goods is well illustrated by the following letter from an orange grower to a former customer:

Thank you for your recent and additional order for one bushel of navel oranges.

Although this valley is known as the land "where sunshine spends the winter," a snowstorm and freeze in early January caused extensive damage to our current fruit crop. Some of the fruit looks and tastes good, but we do not trust it to keep more than a week after it has been picked.

Since one of the qualities you have a right to expect in fresh fruit is its ability to keep, and since we are unwilling to risk the chance that you might be disappointed, we are returning your check for the one bushel of oranges.

The damage to our trees is only temporary. We are looking forward to another crop of high-quality fruits next year. May we serve you again next season with some of our choice fruits?

Unacceptable dealer

A dealer may be unacceptable because (1) you sell only through exclusive dealerships and you already have a dealer in his territory or (2) because he does not meet your requirements for a dealership. For example, some manufacturers will sell only to those who propose to follow standard fair-trade practices.

The first part of the declining letter would be the same in each case and (except for the omission of resale) the same as the beginning of other bad-news acknowledgments we have discussed. In the first case your explanation would be how you operate and why you operate that way plus the simple fact of the existing dealership. In the second case it would be a simple explanation of your requirements, with justifying reasons. The ending for the one would be a purely goodwill ending of "keeping him in mind" in case you should later want him as a dealer. The other would end with an offer to reconsider if a change or additional information shows that he does meet the requirements.

Improper channels

Some buyers think that all manufacturers or producers should sell to anybody who has the money and omit the middlemen who add so much to the cost of goods. Those who howl the loudest on this point also howl loudly when a producer from afar does not make his goods available in the local stores. Both methods of merchandising have advantages and disadvantages. Which is the more desirable is a question we need not answer. We must grant, however, that a producer has the right to sell his goods the way he wants to. And whatever his plan, he has no doubt chosen it for certain reasons. At least some of them should be in terms of how he can best serve his customers.

Assuming that the firm has taken the customer-service attitude, you are in a good position to acknowledge the order of a person who does not (through ignorance or intent) choose to follow your plan. Usually he will be a consumer asking for goods from a wholesaler or producer instead of through the regular retail channel. Some of the customer-service reasons you can point out to him for selling only through local retail stores are the advantage of being able to get goods quickly from local stores; of being able to see, feel, and try them; of being able to get adjustments and service easier—indeed, all the disadvantages a seller-by-mail usually has to overcome are now in your favor.

Your bad-news letter begins in the same way as those acknowledging incomplete orders and orders you cannot fill immediately: with a buffer, including resale to help keep the customer interested in the goods (on which you *do* make a profit, of course). As before, you are careful not to mislead.

After this beginning, you explain how you merchandise your goods (not how you don't, except by implication) and why you operate this way. As far as possible, you explain the why in terms of benefit to the customer (you-viewpoint). He will not be much impressed by the benefits to you. At least a part of the reader-benefit *why* should come before the part of the explanation which conveys the bad news (by implication) that he can't buy that way, that his order is not being filled.

If your explanation is good, he will agree that this is the best way for him. If your resale talk has been good, he will still want the product, although he can't buy it from you. You tell him exactly how and where he can get it, and you give him a last touch of resale to make him place his order the way you suggest.

If you have several equally convenient outlets, you name them all to give him a choice and to be fair to all. This letter follows the directions:

```
Karsol shower curtains like the ones you saw advertised will
give you the wear you want for rental units.

So that you will be able to select personally the exact
patterns you prefer (from eight different designs offered),
we have set up a marketing plan of bringing Karsol shower
curtains to you through local dealers only.  This way you will
save handling, shipping, and c.o.d. charges.  You will be able
to get your curtains at the White House, located at 300 Main
Street in Montgomery, thus speeding your purchases and
avoiding unnecessary delays ever present when ordering by
mail.

We have recently sent a large shipment of Karsol shower
curtains to the White House, and you will be able to see for
yourself that although these waterproof curtains are of
exceptional strength and durability, they are soft and pliable.

Stop by the White House next time you are in town and select
your favorite pattern of Karsol shower curtains that will
satisfy your tenants.
```

If you are really a good businessman, you will notify the retailers, so that they can write or call the interested prospect if he doesn't come in (especially if the order is for a big-ticket item).

The reminder checklist on page 276 summarizes most of the guide points.

SELLING A SUBSTITUTE

Many times you will receive orders you can't fill exactly because you do not have the special brand, but you have a competing brand or something else that will render the service the customer obviously wanted. You know that in most cases people buy a product not for the name on it but for the service they expect from it. If you think your brand will serve (and ordinarily you do, or you wouldn't be selling it), you remember your service attitude and try to satisfy the orderer's wants. As a point of business ethics, you should not try to sell a substitute unless you sincerely believe you can truly serve by saving the customer time and trouble in getting what he wants or by giving him service at least comparable to what he can get elsewhere in terms of cost.

Once you decide that you are ethically justified in selling the substitute, you need to remember several working principles:

1. Don't call it a substitute. Although many substitutes are superior to the things they replace, the word has undesirable connotations that work against you. Burma Shave once used the connotation effectively in a roadside advertisement reading "Substitutes and imitations—give them to your wife's relations. Burma Shave."

Checklist for Diverting Orders

1. Your buffer beginning is a good place to work in resale.
   a) An exact reference to the merchandise ordered is a form of resale in that it attempts to etch the choice in the reader's mind. Other identifications (quantity, date of order, and the like) aren't so important here, since this is an outright refusal.
   b) But don't even intimate the refusal at this point.
   c) Nor do you want to imply that you are shipping the goods.
2. To avoid abruptness, continue the idea of reader benefit as you turn from the resale to your explanation.
3. Think—and write—positively in your explanation.
   a) As appropriate to your reader (a consumer or a dealer), focus on his benefits (fresh stock, less inventory, savings on shipping costs, examination of all choices before purchasing, credit and adjustment services).
   b) Establish at least one good reason for the policy before stating it (the statement of the policy is the refusal).
   c) State the policy in terms of what is done.
   d) Make it clear; otherwise, you may get a second, more insistent order.
   e) Follow the statement of the refusal with additional customer advantages.
   f) Is there any advantage in pointing out benefits other than those for the customer?
   g) When there is a price difference (and there usually is), admit it, but minimize it.
4. Your action ending should urge the reader to place the order with the appropriate outlet.
   a) Be as specific as you can (name and address if only one place and hence no playing favorites), and build up the image of service.
   b) Work in specific resale material as a safeguard against the possibility of brand switching when the reader places the order again.

2. Don't belittle the competitor's product. Not only is this questionable ethics, but it criticizes the orderer's judgment—after all, he wanted to buy that product.

3. Don't refer to the ordered product specifically by name any more than you have to—perhaps not at all. Once should be enough. You want him to forget it and think about yours. When you use its name, you remind him of it—in effect, you advertise it. Conversely, stress your product, perhaps repeating the exact name several times.

Except for the fact that the identification and resale are in general terms broad enough to encompass both the product ordered and the substitute, and show their basic similarity, your beginning of the substitute-selling acknowledgment is the same as other buffers for bad-news acknowledgments. If you phrase the beginning well, you'll have no trouble making a smooth transition to further talk about the substitute.

```
Your repeat order of September 10 for 60 regular-duty
batteries suggests that you have found your battery business
quite profitable.  We're glad to hear it, but we think we can
show you how you can do even better in the coming season.
```

You arrange to introduce at least one sales point favorable to the substitute *before* revealing that you can't send what was ordered. You need to convey the negative message fairly early, however, to keep the reader from wondering why all the talk about the substitute. Your best technique is the standard one for subordinating negative messages: Tell what you *can* do in a way that clearly implies what you can't.

```
In our continuous effort to find the best automobile
accessories and equipment at reasonable prices, we have found
that the new Acme battery excels others of its price class in
power, endurance at full load, and resistance to cracking.
Because of those desirable qualities, we decided two months
ago to stock the Acme line exclusively.  Although Powell of
Dayton still has the Motor King, we think your customers will
be ahead in service and you'll make more profits with the
Acme.
```

Once you are over that rough spot, clear sailing lies ahead. You continue your sales talk, concentrating on why you carry the substitute and what it will do for your reader, not on why you do not carry what he ordered. You give a complete, specific description of the substitute's good points in terms of consumer or dealer benefits (as the case may be).

A good test of the adequacy of your sales talk is whether it is all *you* would want to know if you were being asked to change your mind about the two products.

```
Because of its 115-ampere power and its endurance of 5.9
minutes at full load, your customers will like the fact that
the Acme keeps a hard-to-start engine spinning vigorously and
increases the chance of starting.  They'll also like the tough
new plastic case that avoids the cracking and loss of acid
sometimes experienced with hard-rubber cases.
```

Sometimes your price will be higher than that of the product ordered. If so, presumably you think your product is better. Your method of meeting the price competition, then, is to sell the advantages and then point to them as justifying the price.

> When you explain the advantages the Acme has over its
> competitors, you justify at least a $2 higher price in the
> customer's mind—and you produce a prompt purchase. The Acme
> battery will back you up, too, in the customer's long
> experience with it. It carries the usual 24-month pro rata
> replacement guarantee. And the fact that it wholesales to you
> at only $1 more means an extra $1 profit to you on each sale.

Sometimes you will have to admit (tacitly) that your product is inferior but adequate. Your technique then is to sell its adequacy and the fact that it is a good buy because of the price. If the customer had ordered a higher priced battery than you now sell, for example, you could replace the three preceding paragraphs with these:

> In our continuous effort to find the best automobile
> accessories and equipment at reasonable prices, we have found
> that the Motor King is a leading seller. Because of its low
> price, strong customer appeal, and complete range of sizes, we
> now offer only the Motor King for all cars. The fact that you
> could fit <u>any</u> car would give you a big advantage over
> competitors selling brands that come in only a few sizes.

> The $2 saving you can offer on the Motor King will have a
> strong appeal to many of your customers who are unwilling to
> pay higher prices for more than standard specifications for
> regular-duty batteries: 105 amperes, 48 plates, 5.3 minutes'
> endurance at full load. The Motor King meets these
> specifications, and it carries the standard 24-month pro rata
> replacement guarantee.

> And while your customers would be saving, we estimate that you
> would be making more profits because of increased volume that
> would almost certainly come from a complete line at favorable
> prices.

Usually, however, quality and price are about the same, and you simply sell the product on its merits and as a service or convenience because it is available.

When your selling job is done, you are ready to try to get action. You can do either of two things:

1. You can ask the orderer whether you may fill his order with the substitute, or ask him to fill out a new order specifying it; or
2. You can send the goods and give the orderer the option of returning them entirely at your expense—that is, you pay transportation both ways. Thus no question of ethics arises.

The second way will sell more goods if you word the offer carefully to avoid a sound of high pressuring. You should use it, however, only in an attempt to give the best service you can— for example when the customer indicated pressing need, and transportation costs are small, and you are reasonably sure he will accept. Indeed a recent Supreme Court decision seems to relieve the receiver of any responsibility for returning or paying for unordered goods.

If you do send the goods on option, you can greatly affect your chance of having them accepted by the wording of your offer. Note the difference between these two ways:

1. We believe you will find the Acmes satisfactory. Therefore we are filling your order with them. If you don't like them, just return them to us collect.
2. Because we are so thoroughly convinced that you will like the Acmes, we are filling your order with them on trial. When you see how they sell and satisfy your customers, we believe you will want to keep the whole shipment and order more.

The second puts the emphasis on the customer's accepting the merchandise, where it should be; the first, on his returning the goods. The second way will sell more.

Wether your acknowledgment letter selling a substitute asks approval or explains that you are sending the goods on trial, you should merely ask or suggest the action and make it convenient. A last touch of resale may help, but action should not be urged—certainly not commanded. This type of letter has the onus of suspicion on it from the outset. High pressure is out of place anywhere in it, especially in the end. Here's a good substitute letter:

Your request for another Simpson product shows that you have been well satisfied with these high-quality electrical supplies. One of the reasons we've been able to please you is the practice of introducing new and improved products first.

Our latest electric fan featuring the newest improvements is the Matthews. Because of the new-style oscillating gear, this new fan delivers 12 percent more cubic feet of air per minute than any other fan of similar size. A crackle finish looks new longer because it resists scuffs and scratches.

Since the demand is rapidly growing for the improved Matthews, we now stock it exclusively. You may still be able to buy the Seabreeze from Gardner, Perkins, and Simons in Cleveland. We believe, however, you'll prefer the Matthews.

In addition to the standard 10-inch Matthews priced at $10.83 and the large 12-inch at $14.16, with the Matthews line you can also cffer a new model, the Matthews Midget. This is an 8-inch fan priced at only $7.08. The Midget has all the new improvements found on the larger fans. Like all Matthews fans, the Midget also carries a one-year guarantee.

To order, simply fill out the enclosed card and mail it. We will ship your Matthews fans by freight collect. When you see how well the Matthews fan sells, you will fully realize that you made a sound buy.

The checklist for selling substitutes (p. 280) summarizes the points you'll want to observe in writing successful letters of this type.

Checklist for Suggesting a Substitute

1. Your opening:
   a) For acknowledgment, rely mainly on implication: maybe the date of the order and a general reference to the class of goods.
   b) Make the reference broad enough to encompass A (product ordered) and B (substitute).
   c) But don't call either by specific name, model, or number yet.
   d) Let the buffer be resale in effect, but not specifically on A.
   e) Intimating at this point that you're going to ship anything could mean only A to the reader.
   f) Establish early the kinship—the similar nature—of A and B, with emphasis on points in B's favor.
   g) Show gratitude for the customer's return to you with his business (if it applies).
   h) The routine "Thank you" or the selfish "We're glad to have" is usually not the best way.

2. Your transition:
   a) Introduction of B should follow naturally from what precedes.
   b) Before revealing that you can't send A, introduce B and at least one of its strong points.
   c) Calling B a substitute or "just as good" defeats your strategy.

3. Your statement of unavailability:
   a) Stress what you can do, not what you can't; saying that you can send only B makes adequately clear that you can't send A.
   b) Identify A by name no more than once—when you clear it out of stock.
   c) Present the bad news early enough to avoid puzzling.
   d) Make perfectly clear that you can't send A.
   e) Stress why you carry B rather than why you don't stock A.

4. Your sales message on B:
   a) Sell B on its own merits; it's a good product; no apologies needed.
   b) Seek out the sales points, and apply them specifically.
   c) Interpret these points in terms of reader benefits.

5. Overcoming price resistance (See p. 127):

6. Your action ending to keep the order and goodwill.
   a) Make responding easy, as always.
   b) Work in a last plug about satisfaction with the product.
   c) High pressure is out of place in this letter, especially in the end.
   d) If you send the substitute, make returning it a free option.
   e) But emphasize keeping, rather than returning.

COMBINATIONS

In acknowledging orders, you will often find one for several items, some of which you have and others of which you don't. To answer such an order, you have to combine the principles discussed for different types of acknowledgments. The writer of the following letter to a new customer had to combine several types because he could send one item immediately, he had to delay another shipment, he couldn't provide another item, and he had to substitute for still another:

Your two dozen 7.50 x 15 Firestone tires are already on their way to you. They should arrive by Motor-Van truck Thursday, ready for your weekend customers.

Welcoming a new customer to our long list of dealers who look to us for automobile supplies is always a pleasure. We shall always try to serve your needs as best we can, by keeping up with the market and providing you with the best goods available.

The 8.50 x 14 tires are a case in point. In another effort to assure our customers of the advertised quality of all products we handle, we returned to the manufacturer the last shipment of 8.50 x 14 Firestone tires because they had been slightly bruised in a shipping accident. Since we are assured of a new shipment in two weeks, may we fill this part of your order then?

In trying to keep our operating costs and consequently our prices at a minimum, we have discontinued handling 4.50 x 21 tires because of the small demand for them. Probably your best source for them is the Kimble Supply Company, 401 South State Street, Chicago 61382, which carries a large stock of obsolete auto parts and supplies.

When our buyer was in the market last year, he found a new automobile paint that seemed superior to other paints he knew. It is a General Motors product in all colors, with the standard General Motors guarantee. Our other customers have been so well satisfied with its quality and price (only $2.85 a quart and $9.85 a gallon) that we now stock it exclusively. As I feel sure that you, too, will be satisfied with this new product, I am filling your order with the understanding that you can return the paint at our expense unless it completely satisfies. I think you will like it.

Since I am awaiting the return of the enclosed card with your decision on the paint (sent with your 7.50 x 15 tires) and the 8.50 x 14 tires to be sent in two weeks, I am holding your check to see how much the refund is to be.

For your convenience and information, I am sending a separate parcel of our latest catalog and a supply of order blanks. We shall be glad to handle your future orders for high-quality automobile supplies.

Note how the letter would have read if the order had been for only the paint. Read only the second, fifth, and seventh paragraphs.

The checklists on preceding pages for standard (p. 145), incomplete (p. 269), back-order (p. 272), diverting (p. 276), and substituting (p. 280) acknowledgments apply to the combination cases which follow.

CASES FOR REFUSAL OF A REQUEST

1. Before you write the refusal for this case, read Case 22, p. 171 (a direct inquiry). The paper didn't tell the whole story: *Hearing Aid Models for Veterans* is available only to doctors and others trained and licensed for fitting hearing aids. The point the pamphlet stresses: The VA will pay for suitable hearing aids for veterans (under the same conditions the VA pays for other medical service). But, many veterans have bought hearing aids without professional fitting and have asked the VA to pay. Professionals generally agree that the chances of satisfaction in such cases are low. Hence the VA requirement of professional fitting or no pay. The pamphlet (prepared by a group of ear specialists) is a guide to competent hearing-aid fitters who do not have the time to keep well informed on the quality and varying characteristics of the hundreds of aids on the market. Suggest getting a doctor to check Arthur's hearing—and to write for the pamphlet if he needs it.

2. A state legislature passed a loyalty oath (loyalty to the state and the U.S.) to be required of all persons on the state payroll. When you (the state university president) sent copies of the oath on forms to be signed by all your employees just before the effective date of the legislation, just 10 days before next pay day, Dr. Norman Zeman (Professor of Philosophy and chairman of the campus chapter of ACLU—American Civil Liberties Union) wrote you a strong letter of protest for ACLU, enclosing a resolution urging you to resist and delay enforcement of the law. The new law has been challenged for its constitutionality and is now in the courts.

Base your refusal to violate the law on the following jottings on your note pad: political question, and I'm not in politics; delay impractical—signed oaths required for next payroll; agreed to *administer* university according to law and policy of board of regents; if courts reject, will discard signed oaths; Zeman's letter might better go to regents or governor.

3. As the editor of *Southwest Review*, a literary and critical magazine published by Southern Methodist University, Dallas 75221, you decline to publish an article submitted six weeks ago by Professor Arthur Anderson, Texas A & M University, College Station 77801. Return the manuscript and encourage Anderson to rework and resubmit. Among comments you and the two specialists you sent it to for advice have made: good topic ("Backwoods Humor") well fitting your magazine; interesting collection of jokes, anecdotes, and humorous regional incidents and phrasings well categorized; lacking interpretation, philosophical or critical insights (in other words lots of good research and facts that the author makes nothing of—no conslusions, principles, ideas); lively, clear style. You want to suggest about 50 percent more length, additional words all devoted to analysis and interpretation making the article one of literary criticism.

4. Answer the complaint of a local citizen who thinks your TV and radio station should list (mainly for newspapers) actual starting times of events (especially ball games) instead of lumping the main events and preliminaries and giving the starting times of the whole package. You know picture shows do the same thing in their announcements, and you have to call in to find out when the feature begins. You *are not* changing your procedures.

5. As the secretary of the English Department in X University, you receive a memo from Professor A in another department saying he will be taking a group of students (14 names listed) on a three-day field trip 10 days hence. He asks that you inform English teachers and request that they excuse the student absences, though students will be expected to make up missed work.

Your department has 59 teachers and 5,800 student enrollments in 89 courses (many of which have several sections). You aren't about to look through all the rolls to see what teachers have the listed students—or to pester all 59 teachers with a memo about the absences of the 14 students. Of course you won't tell all of this to Professor A. You do want to be helpful, but he's expecting too much. You wonder if he's unthinking, inconsiderate, or just trying to pass the buck of a lot of work to you. If he wants you to notify the professors involved, Professor X will have to tell you the English course (or courses) and section(s) each of the 14 students is taking.

Send his list back to him and explain.

6. As manager of Sunoco Travelguide Bureau, 2009 Darland, San Francisco, California 94110, you have the following problem to deal with: Thirty years ago as a goodwill gesture you started issuing marked maps and illustrated booklets to anyone who wrote in requesting such service (an expensive one). But you found through checking names of people who requested the service against your holders of Sunoco credit cards that 90 percent of the service you provide is apparently for customers of other companies. The object of such booklets is, of course, to get travelers to purchase Sunoco gas and oil. After consultation with sales and advertising personnel and many of your dealers, management decided to issue such booklets only to those people who request them through Sunoco service stations. It is really a dealer's service to his customers. In a letter designed to set the pattern for handling all such requests, tell Clyde Davis, 49 Crestmont Drive, Colorado Springs, Colorado 80904, that you honor such requests only when they come to you through one of your dealers. Many such requests will come from residents of cities where you have no outlet; so you'll have to phrase your message to include the possibility of the reader's requesting the booklets through a dealer other than in his home area. Stress the service idea.

7. As the family insurance agent, answer claim 15, p. 207. You have to educate that sophomore a little on insurance and driving. Points to explain (not in this order):

—Yes, you make money on policies carried by good drivers like the sophomore's father, who gets a 15 percent reduction from basic rates because he hasn't had an accident chargeable as his fault in 10 years.
—All insurance companies base rates on experience tables.
—Rates are 50 percent higher on his kind of car (than on his father's kind) because insurance companies (not just yours) have found that they pay out at least that much more in settling claims.
—Rates are much higher for unmarried male drivers under age 25 because experience shows that they are responsible for a comparably higher accident frequency.
—You have checked your figures carefully, and they are right for the kind of car and driver the policy covers.
—The rates are based on experience with millions of cars and drivers, and one car or driver may be an exception. But in this situation you know that his case is not. You know that he has already had one costly accident in the three months he has had his present car. Furthermore, the only claims you have paid on his father's insurance in the past three years were all three on accidents that happened when the son was driving his father's car. The father paid much higher rates when the son was listed as a driver of the car.

8. As personnel manager of Bolling and Strickland (700 Savannah Avenue, Pittsburgh, Pennsylvania 15212)—a worldwide manufacturer-supplier of paper products (napkins, facial tissue, plates, hand towels, etc.)—you have a request from Dr. Clark Mayer, president of Centerville College, Centerville, Pennsylvania 18506, asking for your help. He is preparing a series of articles for *Centerville News* dealing with large companies where outstanding Centerville graduates work and the areas in which they work. What he requests of you is a list of Centerville graduates in your employ and the duties they are currently performing for you. Although routine, such a job would be exceedingly time-consuming; it would necessitate examining the individual records of approximately 8,000 salesmen, 5,000 technicians, and 3,000 office and managerial personnel to be certain of accurate, complete information. That would require about 200 working hours, you figure, which would involve more time and money than you feel called upon to donate even to such a worthy cause. In refusing the request, offer the use of the files to Dr. Mayer or any of his office staff whom both of

you could depend upon to exercise the necessary judgment and care in handling the material. The researching would have to be done during the regular hours, 9–5:00.

9. For the signature of the advertising manager of Whitehall, Inc., 2987 987 Maryville Avenue, Charleston, South Carolina 29408, write a refusal to Mrs. Dollie Watson Hendrix, Apartment 203–B, University Court, Richmond, Virginia 23201. She has asked for a few pairs of Curity rubberized baby pants as a contribution to be auctioned off at the annual Dame's Club bazaar. The Dame's Club, she explained, is made up of young married women of students at the University of Virginia, many of whom are also mothers. The bazaar proceeds go toward financing the one big social event these young marrieds have each year. Although it represents a favorable opportunity to build goodwill with a group in which sales certainly will emanate, you have to say no; you have entirely too many requests like this. Your contributions (always money) go exclusively to orphanages and other such facilities for unfortunate and underprivileged children. You confine your advertising dollars to national magazines like *Parents'*.

10. As Wilbur Rathborne, former publisher-owner of the defunct *Morning Gazette*, Chicago, Illinois 60689, refuse the invitation addressed to you by Professor Edward M. Eddins, School of Journalism, University of Illinois, Urbana 61801, to speak to Sigma Zeta Omega (professional journalism fraternity) members at their national convention luncheon to be held in Chicago in about six months. He has suggested the topic "The Pentagon Papers on the War." Although you concede that such a talk might have some salutary effects on present and future newspaper men and women, you are saying no primarily because of the recent Supreme Court decision; what you think on the topic would be recalcitrant, repetitious, or academic and possibly misleading. Furthermore, you are reluctant to commit yourself six months in advance.

11. As John Jolly, vice president in charge of personnel, Moore-Handley Manufacturing Company, 1111 Paddington Road, Kalamazoo, Michigan 49001, write Daniel Brennan, chairman of University Day, Box 666, Michigan State, East Lansing, Michigan 48823, that you cannot send five company representatives to appear on panels planned for the event two months from now. By the time you figure lost work time and expenses for five people, the outlay would run far beyond what you consider wise for the purpose. You can't tell the chairman that in so many words, however. You can tell him that Moore-Handley spends personnel procurement funds on two college recruitment officers. From September 15 to the first of May they visit college campuses, concentrating on seniors, who usually have a good idea of what they want to do. One such officer will be at Brennan's school for about a week the first part of December; the other will be there the first week in April. Their purpose is to tell people about the company. Announcements are posted on bulletin boards at least two weeks in advance of the visits. Interviews are arranged through the university placement office. Since you need to recruit more in accounting this year than in any other area, you offer to send one man for that panel.

12. As the private secretary for Mara Stratford, famous operatic and concert singer, Allied Artists, Life Building, New York 02014, write the chairman of the Committee for Action, Box 999, Youngstown, Ohio 44502, that Miss Stratford is forced by her Allied Artist contract to limit her concerts to paying patrons only without special permission. In view of her recent objections to being overworked, she doubts that permission would or should be granted for the requested benefit performance in her own home town.

13. *From:* Meredith Miller, correspondence supervisor, Royal-Rand, 2876 Newburgh Street, Boston, Massachusetts 02176. *To:* Milford Smith, instructor in communications at your school. *Case:* Royal-Rand charges $8.50 to send the film *Accountability.* The film cost $3,700 to produce, and the company feels that it must be sent on a rental basis. Copies of the company's annual report are free if Smith would like to have them. These are good examples of business writing—a significant part of the communication process. Also you can send free brochures about your varied kinds of audio-education equipment.

14. As Morris Dykema, Dykema Advertising Agency, New York, New York 10021, write John Pearson, instructor in communications at your school, that you cannot send the first month's issue of *Review* (a collection of unsolicited sales letters, and various other examples of material) free. The charge of $75 is standard practice to help defray some of the expense of the compilation designed primarily to help sell your services, which are now being requested by many do-it-yourselfers.

15. Because being turned down by a university is at best a slap in the face to a would-be student, the admissions committee has asked you (your school's public-relations man) to draft pattern letters (to be Robotyped, as explained on p. 136) to send to the numerous applicants who don't make the grade. Facts and policies: controlling board has limited admission of new freshmen to 2,800 a year, 95 percent of whom must be applicants highest on statewide tests (assume either SAT or ACT) given high-school seniors in the state (or equivalent scores on National College Board exams); other 5 percent are admission-committee approvals after correspondence and/or interview with applicants not qualified in the 95 percent but asking for committee consideration and showing other promise of success in your high-standard curricula. Write the letter (for signature of the dean of admissions) to go to applicants not in the 95 percent (i.e., you have 2,660 applicants with higher scores).

16. See the preceding case. Write the comparable letter to go to applicants who tried the second door and didn't know the password there either.

17. *From:* Direct Advertising Association, 202 Wilson Avenue, Glendale, California 91204. *To:* You, a professor of advanced sales writing, your school. *Case:* You asked DAA for the direct-mail campaigns that won awards during the last five years. The usual fee for the current year's campaign is $75. You have no fund to take care of such a fee. You would like these campaigns for two months, and you will be glad to pay the postage on them both ways. *Refusal:* DAA gets requests like this all the time and has formed a policy that all institutions and individuals who want the campaigns must pay for them. There is no educator's special rate. Suggest that the professor can raise the money to cover the fee. How? Assess students—as part of text costs?

18. Among the 300 applicants to Goodlife Rubber Plant, Jasper Highway, Acton, Indiana 47544, for summer work is the son of a prominent lawyer, Hugh Jacob Roberts, Big Four Building, 105 South Meridian, Indianapolis, Indiana 46225. Hugh Jacob Roberts, Jr., proved to be physically weak, shy, apathetic, and insecure. Because of the prominence and influence of the elder Roberts, you feel that a form letter to turn down his son is inappropriate. Write a friendly letter explaining that you have 300 applicants for a limited number of summer jobs.

19. A recent *Riplinger Washington News Letter* contained this entry: "How to Stop Pollution on the Home Front. Write the Director, Extension Service, Department of Agriculture, Washington, D.C. 20016, for a free copy of *Pollution at Home*. It tells how to use nonpolluting soaps and other household cleaners." Requests poured in, and you no longer have any copies. As director, prepare a letter that informs the numerous requesting individuals that your supply is exhausted, and, because the U.S. Government Printing Office has so many printings already scheduled, it will be two months before any additional copies are available. Name is being put on mailing list, and copy will be sent as soon as available. No need to write again.

CASES FOR REFUSED ADJUSTMENT

1. Mrs. Courtney Champion, Box 432, Pana, Illinois 62557, bought a Regina synthetic wig from the wig department of Gafers Department Store, the Downtown Mall, Decatur, Illinois 62522. She charged this $30 wig and $4.00 for styling to her account last week. Today, she returns the wig with a letter saying she wants her money back for she is not able to style it herself and make it look like it did when she purchased it. You, as the hair stylist and manager of the wig department, have the job of refusing her request. In your letter explain that you have signs around the department clearly saying that there are no returns/refunds. Also, try to get her to buy the special spray for wigs called La Donna Wig Spray and the special metal brush for synthetic wigs. The spray sells for $4.00 and the brush for $1.50. A plastic wig block (foam head) would also help her to keep her wig in shape when she is not wearing it. The wig block also sells for just $1.50. You are writing her and asking her to come in for a styling and instructions on how to care for the wig to give her complete satisfaction.

2. For the Better Business Bureau of your community (see Claims Case 11, p. 206), write a letter explaining to the person who bought the early American furniture that he has no written agreement with the furniture store. The store contends it never made other arrangements with the claimant. His best bet now, other than legal action, is to accept the partial payment of the repair bill by the furniture store.

3. As editor of your local Action Line, write a letter to the claimant in Claims Case 12, p. 206. The manager of the car wash refuses to make the adjustment: chains are not attached to the tires. The car wash mechanism is a roller attached to a dolly, the dolly pushing the car through. The dolly pushes the lefthand front of the car, not the rear. He contends it is impossible for the car wash to damage a tire, and he invites the driver of the damaged tire to inspect the mechanism again. He offers no recompense, since he feels claimant's rear tire must have been damaged before the car entered the car wash. If the owner of the damaged tire still disagrees, he can contact Lawyers Referral Service at the local courthouse. The service fee of $15 includes first consultation with a lawyer skilled in handling this type of problem.

4. *Refused adjustment with a generous compromise offer.* As adjustment manager for L. P. Goodspeed Company, Akron, Ohio 44312 (see Claims Case 9, p. 205), turn down the request of Harry Hickel to refund the $68 for the superwide 70 Dynaglass tubeless tires. Explain that the government is trying to end a racket in which some dealers sell defective tires for high-speed highway use. Two dealers have already been fined and other fines are expected. Some defective tires, judged unsafe for normal use, are destroyed by manufacturers; but this year 185,000 of them were labeled "for farm use only" or "for nonhighway use" and sold to retailers.

Officials of the National Highway Safety Bureau said some of these rejects from the major tire manufacturers have begun to show up in some retail stores—their labels buffed off and the tires represented as being safe for high-speed driving. Some of the tires have been channeled into used car lots and put on secondhand cars to make buyers think they are equipped with a new, first-class set of tires.

A recently approved amendment to tire safety regulations, to become effective December 1, will require manufacturers to stamp rejected tires as "unsafe for highway use." Goodspeed also is required to attach a label to the tire stating that there is a $1,000 maximum fine for selling the tire for use on a passenger car.

The circumstances strongly suggest that Hickel purchased two of these defective tires that were not manufactured by Goodspeed.

However, tell him that you are writing J. R. Bowman, The Auto Rite in Brighton, Colorado, suggesting that he take in the two defective tires on two new (genuine) Dynaglass 70 tires that are guaranteed for 36 months. A company investigator for Goodspeed has been in touch with Bowman, and the defective tires have been removed from the stock at Auto Rite. To help Bowman, Goodspeed is making a good price ($50, which is at cost) on the two new tires.

5. In the role of public relations assistant for the Neenah Paper Company, Neenah, Wisconsin 54956, you handle requests for adjustments on the printed monogrammed stationery and postcards you send to thousands of retail outlets handling stationery supplies. Ordinarily when a request comes in for correction (and such requests are rare), a company policy is to print and ship the corrected copies without question and without charge. But one customer, Rose's Gift Shop, 1005 Fifth Street, Tuscaloosa, Alabama 35401, stands out in your mind because it has sent in so many requests in the last few months. Today you have another letter, asking for replacement of 100 personalized postcards which Stanley M. Washburn, 10 Freemont Drive, Northport, Alabama 35476, ordered through Rose's and which were delivered with the street name "Fairmont Drive," and for a replacement of a box of 200 sheets and 100 envelopes for Miss Sarah Wentworth, Montevallo University, Montevallo, Alabama 35215, who received her stationery with the imprint "Alabama College." Checking back, you find that the order forms filled out by someone at Rose's clearly printed in both cases what your printer faithfully followed in printing the items ordered. And so you are going to refuse to furnish the replacements gratis; they will be billed to Rose's at the usual wholesale prices. You are enclosing with your refusal 3-M copies of the original orders.

6. When the lady sent in the $3.20 supplementary check (Case 12, p. 195), she also sent you "a piece of her tongue." She didn't like your treating a good customer that way—raising your prices unannounced. Facts: You *did* send her, and other regular customers, the new brochure and price list a month before change of prices (and some changes in your listed items). For economy's sake, you sent it third-class mail (usual everywhere for such things, though third-class is not forwarded except by special arrangement

—and you now notice that her address has changed since her preceding order). By appreciation, service attitude, and careful wording of the factual explanation, try to mollify the lady and keep her as a customer.

7. As an adjuster for Mr. Tabor's insurance company (Claims Case 17, p. 208), answer the claim against Mrs. Tabor. You decline to pay the $80 for car rental—auto insurance companies don't; that coverage not listed in the policy (or competitors'); rates based on repair costs (which, God and you know, are high enough—and rising so fast you can hardly keep your rates adequate). You are sending the check for $215, along with the standard release-of-further-responsibility form to be signed and returned. Both the good and bad are in the same letter. Send a copy of the letter to Tabor.

8. In the Tabor case (Claims, Case 17, p. 208) the insurance company sent out a $215 check and release form and declined to pay the $80 rental. Cash the check and return the form unsigned with a letter to get the $80 before signing a form.

9. As an adjuster for Mr. Tabor's insurance company, explain why you won't pay the $80 for car rental (see Claims Cases 16, 17, 18, and 19, p. 208 and the two preceding cases).

10. You are the adjustment manager of the Dartmoor Company, 604 Flossmor Avenue, Evanston, Illinois 60201, a quality establishment catering to many of the wealthier residents of your community. Mrs. Donald Henderson, 11 Deerpath Drive, Dundee, Illinois 60118, a good customer who for six years has spent an average of $700 each year, writes:

Gentlemen:
    I bought a "Rathmore" pearl white coat from your store last week.
    Since then I have decided that I do not care for this coat, and so I am returning it. This was a charged purchase.
    Will you please credit my account with $120, the purchase price.

After reading her letter, you carefully examine the handsome coat (a routine procedure before returning any item to stock) and find that it has been worn. There's evidence of powder stain at the neck and lipstick stain at one pocket. To protect your patrons, your company has a policy that clothes cannot be worn and then returned. Write a tactful, polite letter to Mrs. Henderson, explaining that you cannot accept the coat for credit. She will find the coat with its special lining warm. The Scotch-guarded wool is treated to resist soil and dirt.

11. As advertising manager of *Tempo* magazine, you are to handle the request of the Rhodes Supply Company for a discount because the correction Rhodes made in the proof for a recent ad did not appear in this month's issue. You'll have to refuse the request (even though Rhodes is a regular advertiser, usually buying at least half a page, frequently full page) in the light of the following fact: Your rate card (based on 400,000 circulation) clearly emphasizes that all copy and revisions must reach you by the 18th of the month preceding publication. On the 10th you sent proof of the ad. Rhodes made a couple of minor changes and returned the proof to you on the 20th, after you had already run off 15,000 copies. However, there was a mechanical breakdown, and the press had to be stopped. This gave you the opportunity to make the corrections the Rhodes people had made in the ad. Contractually, of course, you were not obligated to do it, but as a matter of customer service you were glad to do so. Then the press resumed and turned out the other 435,000 copies with the changes as specified. In inductive order you'll review the facts and, of course, send the page proofs of the original and the corrected ads. The answer—as positively as you make it—is no. Incidentally, the first-of-the-month Audit Bureau of Circulation figure will be 450,000—but with no change in rates.

12. In the service division of the Raybeam Electric Company, 9945 Paseo Del Sierra, Los Angeles, California 90049, you have the following problem to deal with. Mrs. Fred Temple, 666 Cook Street, Big Sandy, Montana 59520, returns a Raybeam dual-control, four-slice toaster that was given to her two years ago. She stored the toaster at her mother's cottage on Echo Lake. After she discovered that it wouldn't heat up, she took it to a local repairman and he estimated the parts and labor to be $15.50. The toaster retails for $28.95. She requests that you fix the toaster free. Write the refusal in the light of the following fact: the coils are rusted and broken (a condition more probably due to heavy rust than to jars in shipments). You wonder how it could have rusted so much without having been washed or having been stored for two years in a very damp spot. The instruction booklet and the terms of the guarantee make very clear that the toaster should be wiped clean with a dry or slightly moist cloth, never washed. Your year's guarantee covers defective workmanship or material which reveals itself under normal use conditions within 12 months; likewise it exempts the company from mechanical failures due to accident, alteration, misuse, or abuse. Because of these facts you must refuse Mrs. Temple's request for free repair. The toaster will have to be rewired, at a cost of $10.25 (actual cost). You'll need her authorization before you repair it. You'll return it c.o.d. or if she prefers to save c.o.d. charges, she can send you a payment of $11.75 (including return shipping charges). You can have it to her within a week.

13. *From:* Service Department, City Electric Company, 2720 Overlook Drive, Atlanta, Georgia 30310. *To:* Lieutenant Steven McCamy, 505 Octavia Street, El Paso, Texas 79910. *Case:* Refuse to replace the twisted and bent blades for the electric food chopper Model BP-5. The blades were used to mix up frozen foods, seeds, or bones. As the booklet that accompanied the electric food chopper said, the chopper was designed to slice vegetables and fruits (after all large seeds were removed). New blades cost only $6.50 and can be sent direct to the customer. Before mailing back his damaged blades, write him and ask him if he wants the new blades.

14. In the adjustment department of Fuller and Fuller, 911 Locust, St. Louis, Missouri 63199, you acknowledge the following letter from Mrs. Hamilton Staley, 6987 St. Regis Avenue, Jackson, Mississippi 39206:

My son received as a gift from my mother the green pullover sweater I am returning in the accompanying package. He does not want to keep it. He would like to exchange it for two hunter green sport shirts, size 15–15½. If two good-quality shirts cost less than the sweater did, please send them and include a credit memo for the difference; if they cost more, notify me and I will send a check for the difference.

The rich all-wool Esquire sweater sells for $22.50. This sweater, however, had obviously been sold some time ago. The plastic bag had been torn. There was hair oil on the neck. It could not be put back in stock. You don't make exchanges after two weeks following purchase date—and then only when the goods show no sign of use, wear, etc. The sweater will give lots of service once it has been laundered or dry cleaned. This particular sweater is popular, smart looking, and warm. Your first objective is to show Mrs. Staley the justice behind your refusal, but you'll also want to convince her and her son that the sweater is still a fine gift. What about the shirts? Mention your perma-prest tapered sport shirts at $6.50. You can send his size right away. Add current sales points in your letter.

COMPROMISE ADJUSTMENT CASES

1. It was nighttime when you, Henry MacMilan, interior decorator, (MacMilan's Interiors, Sunshine Plaza, Miami, Florida 33126) came to Mrs. Ethel Weller McKenzie's home, 1215 Buchanan, Hollywood, Florida 33020, to measure for new draperies. Together you selected the *right* shade of green (No. 546) for the silk draperies ($300). While she was visiting her family in Illinois, her maid let you in to hang the new draperies. Instead of being the soft gray-green she thought she ordered, she has lime-green draperies that clash with the walls. Today you get a letter from her from the Dude Ranch, Antiago Road, Albuquerque, New Mexico 87105. She demands that you make new draperies in the appropriate color. Because you showed her the color number, and she agreed to number 546, you are going to compromise with her. You will furnish all the new material, but ask her to pay $100 for the labor.

2. As adjustment correspondent for the Whitehall Manufacturing Company, 6543 Whitehall Road, Athens, Georgia 30601, you get the following complaint from J. P. Kilgore, a dealer in Muncie, Indiana 47305 (Kilgore's General Store, 954 Liberty Street):

Three weeks ago I ordered aprons at a special price and advertised a big sale. White across the street did the same thing. I spent lots of money on advertising. But Saturday came and no aprons. White got his. I'm through with such an outfit. The aprons came today. You can do what you want with them. I've lost enough money on them and you.

Your records show that both shipments were made at the same time. When you checked, you found out that the railroad carried one past Muncie and didn't get it back until too late for the sale. The railroad won't stand the loss; yet the fault is not yours. As you look at the invoices, however, you decide that rather than pay freight both ways and handle the goods once more, you'd rather give him the gross (144) of aprons for $1.75 apiece (20 cents less than the original price). You offer to take the aprons back, explain your failure in service, and then try to sell your idea.

3. As adjustment manager of International Candy Company, 4398 Stone Street, Joliet, Illinois 60199, you have a claim from a brand-new customer, the Lindsey Candy Shop, 7654 Audubon Avenue, Evansville, Indiana 47711, that three dozen one-pound boxes of Queen Miniatures out of a case shipment received March 1 have their wrappers torn and show stains as if they had been wet. The case, which showed no outward signs of damage, was checked in and stored for a week, as the candy was ordered for a special Easter sale. On opening the case today (March 9), Mr. Lindsey says, he finds that the cardboard cartons holding the boxes by dozens are buffed within the cases by layers of excelsior on all sides but the top, where some four inches of open space had allowed the carton tops to come off and let the boxes jostle around. He is sure, therefore, that the packing was careless; and, as for the moisture stains, he can't explain those, because he has kept the case stored in a dry place. Five dozen boxes are in good condition and Easter sales are beginning to pick up. He asks you to "take care of the matter promptly," but doesn't say how.

Your decision is to rush three dozen carefully packed boxes to him by express prepaid and to authorize the return of the unsalable boxes. Extra transportation and repackaging, however, will be expensive; so you suggest that he keep the undamaged contents for bulk sale at 35 percent discount.

4. To your desk as sales manager for the Eastern Office Equipment Company, 755 Brewster, Springfield, Massachusetts 01119, comes the following letter from Alton Burr, Burr Insurance Company, 943 Main Street, Bondsville, Massachusetts 01214:

I'm returning the file cabinets you shipped me in response to my request of two weeks ago. I specified No. 3 PT 543 four-drawer steel files at $40, and you sent

No. 3 PT 763 at $60. If there were only one file involved, I'd probably pay the difference, but, as you can see from the invoice I'm returning, there are four. Please refund the $10.87 shipping charges that I paid and send me a credit memo for $240. I'm returning the four, shipping charges collect. As far as I'm concerned you can forget the whole thing.

Burr has ordered various supplies and equipment from you for at least 10 years, has always handled his credit purchases satisfactorily, and has requested few adjustments. You're sorry this happened, of course. Several months ago you sent out a correction slip for your current catalogue indicating that you no longer carry the No. 3 PT 543. Since you notified everyone to whom you had mailed a catalog, you assumed that Burr realized you'd fill his order with No. 3 PT 763 (as your correction slip indicated). Possibly it didn't reach him; maybe some of the office help threw it away. Whatever the reason, you certainly want to sell him this superior file with its improvements: heavier steel, baked-on enamel colors (instead of sprayed), satin-finish aluminum drawer pulls (instead of chrome-plated) plus automatic stops that prevent drawers from rebounding or being accidentally removed. You are convinced that they are well worth the additional cost. Before you can hope to convince Mr. Burr, however, you'll need to refund the $10.87 and assure him that you'll send him a credit memo for $240 as soon as you receive the file cabinets. You'll also want to explain why you did not follow his original instructions. But most of all you want to sell him No. 3 PT 763. You'll be willing to ship the four cabinets charges prepaid if he'll reconsider.

5. The Seabreeze Shoppe, 5427 Sanderson Avenue, Panama City, Florida 32401, writes you, Luxeer, Inc., 399 East 20th Street, New York City, New York 10025, that the large order ($525) of Luxeer perfume, toilet water, hand lotion, powder, and eye makeup requested by air express was sent by ordinary parcel post. As a result, the stock arrived after the season, and many good sales were lost. Because of limited storage space, the Seabreeze Shoppe wants to return $339 worth of the order. Since the instructions were not followed, you should pay shipping charges both ways, the letter says. You check the record and have to agree on the facts. You also note that shipping charges were $12.87 (but would have been over twice that for air express). Nevertheless, you are reluctant to charge off about $24 and handle the cosmetics all over again, when you feel sure that in a short while the shop will be ordering more. To keep this good credit customer happy, you offer to credit the account for $50 and try to get the manager to keep them on hand. Write the appropriate compromise. Remember that if the customer insists, you have no alternative but to accept the returned stock.

6. Mrs. Paul Terry, 765 Sycamore Lane, Anderson, Indiana 46014 (Claim Case 20, p. 209), ordered and paid for the Raybeam iron with Mef-

lon coating two months ago. Today she writes that the "nonstick" iron does all right on unstarched clothing but sticks on starched garments. She wants her money back because she plans to buy an iron without Meflon coating.

As adjustment manager for Marshall Miller's, 500 Tremont Street, Indianapolis, Indiana 46255, write Mrs. Terry. Before you send her money back, encourage her to use only liquid starch on the clothes. As the direction booklet indicates, liquid starch (such as Ray-Flo) will work. Call her attention to the Scorch-Gard. If she has ever scorched a delicate wash-and-wear garment because she didn't wait long enough for the soleplate to simmer down after ironing cottons or linens, she'll appreciate the value of the Scorch-Gard feature. If she is not satisfied with the ironing of starched clothes (the only ones she complained about), you will send her an iron without Meflon coating. Both irons cost $24.75. Enclose ironing directions for the Raybeam Meflon-coated iron and an envelope for her reply.

7. Although your company, Hamilton-Sydney Company, 6532 Van Slyke Avenue, Schenectady, New York 12302, is now engaged in an extensive advertising campaign stressing the dependability of its Chopaid electric chopper, you receive a letter today from one customer who hasn't found the Chopaid dependable. Mrs. Andrew Alexandra, Sherbrooke Residence Hall, 400 University Avenue, Syracuse, New York 13218, writes:

> The chopper has been carefully taken care of because my son Harry, an experienced automobile mechanic, has oiled the bearings a time or two. I wipe it off after I use it each time and am careful not to let it drop into the dishwater when I wash it off. With all this good care, it smells as if it is burning when I plug it in, and it leaks oil right into the food I'm chopping. So, gentlemen, I'm sending it back, and I want my money back to buy a Raybeam.

Quickly you see what's wrong. The instruction booklet that goes with each Chopaid says that the gears are enclosed in grease and should not be oiled by the user. Furthermore, it warns that oiling the Chopaid machine with a light oil will dissolve the heavy grease in which the gears are sealed. Evidently, Mrs. Alexandra's son used light oil. Your service department will clean the working parts and reseal the gears in grease—free of charge —if Mrs. Alexandra will try the Chopaid once more. Because your company has the guarantee "satisfaction or your money back," you send her a check in full payment, $35.95. But because you believe that a Chopaid, properly cared for, is as dependable as the high-priced mixers, you want Mrs. Alexandra to accept your offer and return the check.

8. While Terry Farmer, 11, was visiting his grandparents in Denver, Colorado, he spent time shopping for a beginning set of golf clubs and bag for, according to his father's instructions, around $50. Terry and his grandfather on Terry's next-to-last day in Denver bought from Haines & Essec, 1876 Overton (80209), a blue vinyl golf bag (vinyl pouch on pocket, all-

leather strap with snap, leather-faced handle), $25; five irons (Nos. 2, 4, 5, 6, 9) and putter $72; two woods (Nos. 1 and 3), $34. Terry had saved $60, and grandfather gladly paid the rest. Before boarding the plane for home (6189 Travis Avenue, Dallas, Texas 75238), the boy and grandfather played nine holes at the country club. When Terry got to Dallas and showed the clubs and bag to his father, his father was furious that the store would sell him a man's set that costs $131 instead of the $50 beginner's youth set he thought the boy should have. Despite Terry's saying that he liked playing with the clubs and that he would give his father $10 from his savings account in order to keep them, Mr. Farmer sent them back to Haines & Essec, demanding the boy's money back (he'll refund the grandfather's money). In his letter he made it clear that he thought a beginning golfer didn't need five irons, nor did he need such a fancy bag. Also he felt that the shafts of the woods were too long for an 11-year-old. From a mailorder catalog he could order a canvas bag, three irons, putter, and two woods for $47.95.

As correspondent in the Adjustment Department, you feel that a compromise is in order. But with Mr. Farmer in his present state of mind, you couldn't sell him anything. So you send the full refund, then concentrate on selling the same Palmer clubs and bag back to him at a bargain price of $106. Though you do not write this to Farmer, when the boy played with the set, the clubs acquired some grass stains and a few scratches; Haines & Essec would have to sell them as used merchandise anyway. In selling these well-made clubs to Mr. Farmer, some of the points you might bring out are that the set will last him all his life; even if the shaft is a bit long now, he can "choke" the cork neoprene grips for one or two seasons. The vinyl bag with leather trim will take the hard wear that an 11-year-old will give it much better than the light canvas bags the beginning sets come in. The woods with their metal soleplate that is precision-weighted for extra yardage without extra effort make driving easier for a youngster as well as a man. The select persimmon heads have improved lofts that give more angle to the face for more lift and truer shots. Of course, the clubs are highly rated by the United States Golfing Association. Convince him that he should send you a check for $106 so that you can send him the Palmer clubs that will last a lifetime. You'll also gladly pay the shipping charges.

CASES FOR CREDIT REFUSALS AND MODIFICATIONS

1. Paul Powers, owner of the Pro-Slim Salon, 119 Water Street, Bloomington, Illinois 61701, writes your company, National Athletic Company, 699 Schiller Avenue, St. Louis, Missouri 63134, for two all-American jogging exercisers, No. LPN-442, at $99.95 each; three eight-way exerciser bikes, No. RET-332, at $50.95 each; one twin-post massager, No. RMP-445, $160.70. Before filling his order you wrote and asked him to fill out a credit

application blank. After reviewing what two reliable sources said about his credit and after viewing his application, you have to decline his order. Two sources reported he paid his bills 30 to 60 days slow and his financial statement showed that he is undercapitalized. With a conventional loan he can take advantage of your discounts which will offset his interest costs. Drive for the order on a cash basis.

2. As credit sales manager of the Robinson Company, Kansas City, Missouri 64105, you have to acknowledge the order of Victor Van Law, who (according to the financial statements he sent with his application for credit and for his first order for work pants amounting to $300—he buys for $3 and sells for $6) is the sole owner of the Van Law Dry Goods Company, Eureka Springs, Arkansas 72632. You followed up the references he gave, and they spoke well of his personal integrity and indicated that he is a reasonably good payer. Two sources said he pays within the terms; three said he was 15–45 days slow; one said "slow but sure." You are reluctant to extend credit to a man in a predominantly agricultural area who, at a time when farm income is high, has allowed his current ratio (quick assets to liabilities) to fall closer to 1:1 than to the desirable 2:1. Furthermore, with the uncertainty of the government's action on farm supports, you think now is a poor time (from Van Law's point of view as well as your own) for him to be taking on new obligations without straightening out his present ones. You suspect maladjusted inventories and lackadaisical collections. As much as you'd like to fill this order, you have to refuse. It's wiser for him to cut his order in half and pay cash (he'll still get the customary 2 percent discount). Since rush orders can be handled within four days, he can keep adequate stocks on hand. Perhaps later on when he has reduced his current liabilities and strengthened his cash position, your regular credit privileges of 2/10, n/30 can be made available. After you give him the business reasons for refusing, offer a compromise solution as attractively as you can, and strive to convince him that Robinson pants are the best buy he can make.

3. As credit manager of the Hickory Furniture Company, 9876 Chatham Road, Winston-Salem, North Carolina 27105, you are not going to extend credit to the Lowman's Furniture Company, 222 Cleveland Street, Canton, Ohio 44720, on its order for two dozen ladder-back chairs ($480), three early American dining tables ($300). William Simpson, manager who formerly managed a successful store in Cincinnati, Ohio, and to whom you regularly sold on open terms, sent you an application today for credit. Although you think well of Simpson, the reports from two references show that the store owes accounts overdue from 30 to 90 days. The financial statement shows less than the desired 2:1 ratio of quick assets to liabilities and the income statements reflect disproportionately increasing expenses.

Your low prices are governed by your terms of 3/20, n/60. Even though Simpson feels that he can put the store in good standing through his hard work, the only concession you can make is to give him a 5 percent discount for cash. You suggest the possibility of reduced shipments or of additional long-term local loans. You can make prompt shipments. Work to keep the door open for the time when he is in better financial shape.

4. *Your company:* Eastern Electric, 985 Appleford Road, York, Pennsylvania 17404. *Write:* Kelly's Television Sales and Service Company, 444 Monroe Street, West Chesterfield, New Hampshire 03466. *Case:* Kelly's has been slow in paying. The last bill (invoice No. 3209), amounting to $650, became due two months ago. You made several attempts to collect it, but in answer to your last two letters your company received two remittances totaling only $150. Today you receive a check for $125 and an order for new goods amounting to $565. *Action:* The present order will have to be c.o.d. On c.o.d. shipments you require a deposit of 10 percent. You will deduct $56.50 from the present check upon his authorization to make the current order a c.o.d. shipment and credit his overdue account with the remainder.

5. Milton-Bradley Toy Company, 654 McCormick, Des Moines, Iowa, 50309, has the job of refusing to extend credit to Hugh Nelson, owner of Nelson's Gift Shop, Aaron, Kentucky 41621. The firm has sold this customer for eight years on its regular terms and has given a high credit of $2,000. The books show $2,100 now, $800 of which is due. The payments are made slowly. On the one hand, because of the amount still on the creditor's books, it will not be advisable to refuse the order outright; on the other hand, because of the long history of delayed payments, the amount now due, and the large increase in size of the order, it will not be wise to grant the full credit. Sit in for the credit manager and write Nelson to cut the order to $1,300 and pay the $800 now due.

6. The Fair Lane Women's Store, 98 Palmetto, Pasadena, Texas 77507, five years ago was extended a $2,000 line of credit with your company, Drury Manufacturing Company, 3700 Fairview Avenue, Dayton, Ohio 45414. The store exceeded that amount twice recently, and you allowed it in the light of a reasonably prompt payment record. On the second occurrence about two months ago, however, you wrote Mrs. Edna Schuster, manager, to keep within the limit or send financial information as a basis for upward revision (which information you have not received). Now she sends you an order for $2,210 which with the unpaid balance on the account would bring the debt balance to $3,000. Write her that you are processing the order but before making shipment will require a check for at least $1,000 and her most recent financial statement. Perhaps the business has outgrown the present limit.

7. Mrs. O. C. Leslie, 5 Country Club Estates, Henderson, Texas 75652, has applied for credit from Norman and Mark, Dallas, Texas 75241. The reports you've gathered indicate that Mrs. Leslie's husband earns around $30,000 a year—but apparently Mrs. Leslie spends money faster than he can earn it. From the dozen retail outlets in both Henderson and Dallas whose reports you have, she buys self-indulgently (high-quality merchandise) and pays the same way. The account consistently shows some balance past due. Two of the reports labeled her a typical "grief case." Write the letter that will keep her goodwill and encourage her to make cash purchases, but refuse the credit.

8. Robert Cochrane owns and operates a farm implement store in Moundville, Alabama 35474. For 10 years he has been an excellent customer of your Farm Machinery Company, 1559 Elm, S.W., Birmingham, Alabama 35207. He owes your company $4,500, 45 days past due, which is $400 over the credit limit established for him three years ago. Yesterday you received an order for $300 more equipment with a note at the bottom of the order:

I know my account is past due, but farmers around here are short of cash because of the corn blight. We've had some hope that the blight won't be as bad as it was last year. I think I can take care of the amount I owe in six months.

This is a request you cannot grant (your terms are 60 days). He can pay cash for the order (less 2 percent) or sign a promissory note at 8 percent for the balance past due.

9. Codpak, manufacturers of cameras and camera equipment, Zuber Road, Rochester, New York 14621, received an order for miscellaneous camera supplies amounting to $550 from Sydney Alexander, 987 Water Street, Sioux City, Iowa 51108. Paul Stern, your salesman, reports that Alexander, a former clerk in a larger camera store, has just recently opened his own shop. He has invested all of his savings. Although Stern reports that Alexander is an alert, promising, and progressive young man of excellent reputation and good standing in the community, his investment in the business is decidedly limited. You are writing Alexander and suggesting that he cut the size of his order in half and that he pay cash less 2 percent discount. You will be glad to handle all of his orders on this basis until the time when his financial situation warrants the extension of credit. To help him display the new ST–400 camera, you can send him effective displays. You'll also be glad to send a catalog and sales manual.

10. As credit manager of the California Grocery Company, 765 MacArthur Street, Oakland, California 94612, refuse credit to T. P. Sullivan, proprietor of the Health Food Store, 530 Euclid Avenue, Anaheim California 92805. Sullivan has a small store in an unadvantageous section of this tourist town, according to your salesman, Albert White. Although his references report him to be a dependable young man and his business to be taking hold in the season, still it is your experience that a business of this type has to establish itself on a year-round basis before it becomes a worthwhile credit risk. The mortality rate for small grocery stores is high. Sullivan has made occasional cash purchases from your company during the past few months. Naturally, you would like to increase this cash business and, if the account proves stable, cultivate it later on a credit basis. Write Sullivan a definite but tactful refusal, but leave the way open for credit extension later. Stress the value of the 2 percent discount and smaller, more frequent orders (you can give him one-day delivery service).

11. Today you have to refuse credit to an applicant, John Andrews, 5432 University Avenue, Bloomington, Indiana 47709. You are the credit manager of the Wilmington Equipment Company, 4400 Monarch Avenue, Baton Rouge, Louisiana 70809. Andrews, in a persuasively written application, asks for too much credit for his own good and for your own company's safety. He's planning to open a small school supplies store, and he's sure he can make a go of it, especially if he can get some extended credit right at first. He has grown up in Bloomington, worked there as a clerk in one of the stores, is a member of two civic organizations, and has a background of business training at Indiana University. His order to you is for $900 worth of supplies, for which he proposes to pay $300 down and the rest in three monthly installments.

He proposes to start with about $5,000 worth of stock—and you assume that he is making the same proposal to three or four other potential suppliers. You have to refuse because your terms are definitely 2/10, n/30 and because you adhere to the 2:1 ratio of quick assets to liabilities as a rock-bottom requirement. But you'd like to have him stock Wilmington supplies now and in the future. So you point out to him the benefits of getting more capital to start with. Offer him a 5 percent discount for cash with order, and try to build longtime goodwill and immediate cash business.

CASES FOR INCOMPLETE (OR INDEFINITE OR VAGUE) ORDERS

1. Assume that it is late summer and you have an order (from your Christmas catalog) from a former charge customer, Major Kelly Spivey, HQ USAR EUR, WM Division, APO New York, New York 09403. As the personal shopper of Hudsons, 987 Madison, Chicago, Illinois 60686, write Spivey to get the size small girl's slip he wanted: he did say he wanted No. W 230, white perma-prest, $3.50. They come in sizes 3, 4, 5, 6, or 6x. He failed to give the color of the dacron polyester blouse, No. W456, sizes 12 ($8.50). He may choose it in light gray, white, medium pink, or tawny gold. You have the two gold shirts, No. W 432, 15–15½ at $5.50 and, as soon as you get the complete information, you can mail the three gifts to Spivey's relatives in Macon, Georgia.

2. Write the copy for a postcard, vague-order acknowledgment for Carter Office Supply, 988 Old Line Highway, Cambridge, Massachusetts 01409. Leave space to ask the customers for the specific information you need to fill the order satisfactorily. This is an obvious form message.

3. In the gift department of Piedmont Products, 400 South Elm Street, Greensboro, North Carolina 27405, you are to handle an order from Mrs. James McLester, Apt. 303 Chatteaux Village, 399 Wilson Road, West Palm Beach, Florida 33406, for six china loving cups. Each was to have one name on the cup. She sent the names of Sarah, Mary, Ellen, Horace, and Frank; but Mrs. McLester failed to give you the name to mark on the sixth cup. The milk-glass cups with flower design and name sell for $2.50 each. So that you can mail them all in one express package, send a letter asking what name is to go on the sixth cup.

4. *From:* Lively Music Store, 1999 Brinkley Street, Houston, Texas 77049. *To:* John Boles, P.O. Box 89, Route 55, Big View, Texas 76543. *Facts:* When Mr. Boles was in your store he selected a colonial style, compact-size phonograph and record cabinet, for $75, to be shipped to his home address. He gave the store his personal check for the cabinet and shipping charges ($90.87). As soon as he returned home, he dropped you a note saying that he had changed his mind and wanted the full-size cabinet to put his records in at $150 that he had talked about while in the Lively Music Store. The colonial full-size cabinet sells for $160, the mediterranean, $150, and the contemporary, $145. Find out which one he wants. And clear up the money details.

5. *From:* Weinburger's Trunk Factory, 459 Benton Street, Kansas City, Missouri 64164. *To:* Mr. Edward Bounds, 543 Ellis Avenue, Abbyville, Kansas 67510. *Facts:* From your recent catalog, Mr. Bounds ordered a V-87 Harmon all-leather flight bag at $25.95 in brown. You do not have a flight bag at that price nor do you have a bag listed at that number. Your M-78 all-leather brown bag two-suiter with three outside zipper pockets (22 x 13 x 8) is priced at $35.00 ($1.75 shipping cost). You also have the M-45 brown two-suiter bag of vinyl with two outside zip pockets for $21.95. The all-leather flight bags have the approval of the National Luggage Dealers Association. You'll charge this bag to Mr. Bounds's account.

6. As correspondent for the General Electric Company, 8976 Greenwood Avenue, Nashville, Tennessee 37207, you handle the occasional mail orders of the store, which retails electrical equipment. This morning you received from Daniel Lyles, 46 Blueridge Road, Piney View, Tennessee 37452, an order for "one Proxodent electric toothbrush as advertised in the *News* Sunday, c.o.d." Your advertisement to which he doubtless referred listed closeout prices on your Proxodent cordless, self-charging toothbrush, $19.50, and your Proxodent electric toothbrush with cord, $22.50. You are not sure which type you should send him. Both models come with four extra toothbrushes. Write to ask which Lyles prefers. No c.o.d. shipments on closeouts. Remember that this is your first contact with your customer. Try to cement goodwill by your tactful letter.

7. In the sales department of Gipsom Mills, Inc., 1940 Danville, Virginia 22201, you are to handle an order which comes in the morning's mail from University Women's Shop, 9876 Lavaca Street, Austin, Texas 78754, for three dozen pant-sets No. MP–456 Jantzener knit for a total of $540 in sizes 34, 36, 38 (one dozen in each size). The order does not specify the color assortment. The pants come in solid colors of gray, green, blue, black, brown, red, or purple. The tops come in solids or in checks or stripes to match the solid pants. Ask for the color preference before making the shipment.

CASES FOR BACK ORDERS

1. You are the owner of Gateway Store, 3100 Agate Street, Eugene, Oregon 97405. Today you have an order from Mrs. Eugene Fillmore, president of the Dexter High School P. T. A., P.O. Box 547, Dexter, Oregon 97431, for one black leather scrap book 11 x 15 ($5.95) with 50 extra filler pages ($3.95) like the scrap book she bought from you last year. She wants the dates for the current year and the name of the school to be put on the cover. Because so many clubs have wanted these scrap books, you have had to back order them. You should have a new supply in two weeks, and it will take you a day or two to do the lettering on the cover. The cost of lettering has gone up from what Dexter paid last year ($2.50) to $3.75, an increase of 25 cents for each of the three words, Dexter High School, and for each date. Ask for her approval to engrave the scrap book at this higher price.

2. To your desk in the sales division of Carter Brothers, 998 Old Line Highway, Cambridge, Massachusetts 01409, manufacturers of office equipment, comes a letter from the Meredith Office Supply Company, 897 Oxford Street, Meredith, New Hampshire 03462, authorizing the shipment of six dozen heavy-gauge black steel wall safes ($16\frac{1}{2}$ x $12\frac{1}{2}$ x $9\frac{1}{2}$) at $25. Because of a recent and long-drawn-out steel strike, you have not been able to make this safe during the last month. Now that the strike has been settled (as of yesterday), you should be getting the steel and hopefully can ship the six dozen safes to Meredith in three weeks. Write the letter.

3. Prepare the copy for a regular-size postcard acknowledging an order received by Hill's Inc., 1499 Vermont Street, San Francisco, California 94116. It should be worded to apply to any of Hill's hundreds of specialty products sold by mail at $2 to $20. The purpose of the postcard message is to inform the reader that delivery will be delayed. Plan for a blank after the signature block that enables a clerk in the order department to hand-write or typewrite the specific article and quantity ordered. Although this is an obvious form ("Dear Customer" is an appropriate salutation), it can be phrased positively in readable, lively style.

4. Before solving this case, read the sales situation as described in Sales Case 20, p. 377. You are director of sales, Starwick Clock Company, 8998 Custer Avenue, Flint, Michigan 48566. The mailing your company did to holders of the United Express cards was so successful that you are now out of the Starwick grandfather clock in cherry fruitwood, mahogany, and maple nutmeg. By hiring extra workers, you hope to fill all your orders in a month. Write a form letter that can be processed with the receiver's name and address. For our situation assume the name of Mr. and Mrs. Clyde Powers, 11 Acorn Circle, Beaumont, Texas 77701, and assume that they wanted their clock in cherry fruitwood. Tell them what a fine clock this is and urge them to wait the necessary month for delivery.

5. *To:* Gypsum Service Station, Buena Vista, Colorado 81211, Paul Gypsum owner. *From:* Bernz Company, Moundsville, West Virginia 26041 (Case 9 of Invited Sales, p. 184). Back order the 24 Dapper Dan cans (designed to inflate flat tires) that Mr. Gypsum ordered from you as a result of your ad in *Automotive News*. Unit is $1.98 wholesale; retail price, $2.98. Dapper Dan inflates the tire in 60 seconds and seals the puncture. It has Du Pont Freon and I.C.C. sealant in it. Dapper Dan is a spare tire in a can that can be kept in the glove compartment—and it's not even a tight fit. Reason for back order: Du Pont (supplier of certain chemicals) has emergency government orders that must be filled before resuming production of Dapper Dan. You can promise delivery in about two weeks.

6. The Harachi Japanese Importers, 1185 Market Street, San Francisco, California 94187, receives a first order from the Sun-Way Gift Store, Deltona Plaza, Deltona, Florida 32763, for two dozen Ikebana vases in assorted colors and designs as marked on an order blank from the Harachi catalog. According to Mrs. Waverly Barbe, owner of the Sun-Way, the garden clubs in Deltona are concentrating on Japanese flower arranging (called Ikebana). To hurry up the delivery of these vases, Mrs. Barbe enclosed a check covering the purchase and shipping charges ($55.60). Write Mrs. Barbe welcoming her as a new customer but telling her that because of the great demand at this time for the Ikebana vases you will not be able to send any for three weeks. You will hold her check and mail the vases to her.

7. *To:* Miss Betsy Mund, 1102 Cook Street, Elkhart, Illinois 62634. *From:* Helm House, 987 Mesaba Avenue, Duluth, Minnesota 55806. *Product:* Easy-grip, all steel hand embosser that makes expensive looking, raised letter impressions of three-line name and address on any kind of letter paper and envelope. Easy, inexpensive way to have personalized stationery for only $5.50. You can assure her of delivery in two to three weeks. Backlog of orders.

CASES FOR DECLINING ORDERS

1. When Edward Barton graduated from junior college last spring and decided to open a variety store in his hometown (698 Main Street, Millican, Texas 77866), he wrote to you for suggestions about what paper products he should carry in stock. As sales manager of the Celluton Products Company, Dallas 75204, you drove out (30 miles) to see him. He appreciated your suggestions; but, because of limited finances and heavy expense of getting the business started, he cut your suggested order drastically.

Since it was late fall, the two of you settled on a good stock of toilet and cleansing papers and your colorful Christmas papers. When the order totaled only 18 cases, you told Barton about your policy of not accepting orders for less than 25 cases; but you agreed to accept this first order anyway, to get the new customer started handling your products. But you asked for, and got, Barton's promise of his financial statement at the end of the year.

Barton ordered 15 cases of school writing supplies and toilet and cleansing tissues in January, when you were in the hospital, and the order was filled by a clerk who saw that you had approved the previous order for only 18 cases. You wouldn't have filled it in view of the financial statement Barton sent January 4.

Now it is March, and you have an exact duplicate of the January order. Barton seems to expect to make these small orders about every two months. There is no use to let him get by with this plan, contrary to your policy, which was established as much for his benefit as for yours. Besides, he has not even tried some of your products.

In the spring and summer the need for school supplies will decrease; but the people of Millican do lots of picnicking and use lots of paper cups, napkins, and plates.

For businessmen, you have memo pads and blotters in various sizes and colors. Housewives will be doing spring cleaning. Your decorative shelf papers might help. Your tough, chemically treated special paper for washing dishes and windows is catching on everywhere that housewives have tried it.

Barton, now financially able to order more heavily, could easily make up an order of 25 cases of quick-selling paper products if he would. Then he would not need to order so frequently; he would comply with your policy; and he would enable you to keep your prices to him down where they are by keeping your per-unit costs for handling, packaging, and transportation down to the minimum.

Instead of filling his order, hold it and write him a letter. He has your complete price list, unchanged since last fall.

2. On your desk in the office of the sales manager of the National Cellog Company, 5799 Nokomis, Minneapolis, Minnesota 55440, appears an order for two cases of Instant Breakfast (one of your most popular low-calorie, high-protein cereals), to be shipped direct to Floyd Taylor, Health Food Shop, McFarland Mall, Beulah, North Dakota 58001. His check for the correct amount at your jobbers' prices is pinned to one of your current mimeographed jobbers' lists. You don't know how he got the list, and you don't propose to mention it in the letter. You cannot sell to him direct or at jobbers' prices, list or no list. Your exclusive distributor for his district is the Dwight Wholesale Grocery Company, Bismarck, North Dakota 58501. You want Taylor to handle your popular new breakfast dish; so you will return his check and ask him to place his order with Dwight. In the light of the ultimate advantages to retailers, make a presentation that emphasizes Taylor's advantages rather than your own or your jobber's.

3. Your company, Regis Candy Company, 3400 Highland Avenue, Shreveport, Louisiana 71106, receives an order for a 75-pound shipment of Regis hard candies in 1-, 2-, and 5-lb. special Christmas boxes to be shipped c.o.d. to Joseph Morrison Young, president of the A Club, 405 First National Bank, Atlanta, Georgia 30306. A check for 10 percent accompanies the order. The order comes to your desk (you are the sales manager) because the order department has been instructed not to sell to clubs, fraternities, and similar organizations. Complaints from retailers about wholesalers selling to these groups have made it necessary to have a policy of selling to dealers exclusively. Urge Young to place his order through one of the retailers in the Georgia area who stock the Regis candy.

4. Jane White, Peak's Nursing home, 643 Cheyenne Avenue, Colorado Springs, Colorado 80908, requests the new Beckite cordless toothbrush that operates on integrated circuits. Only your dealers sell this 12-ounce tooth brush, and the nearest dealer to Miss White is Harvey Cobb, 2400 Yates Street, Denver, Colorado 80211. Encourage her to write this dealer for this modern toothbrush, which comes with six extra brushes for easy replacement.

5. Mr. Clyde Tanner, 698 Randolph Street, Kingsport, Tennessee 37664, writes your company, the Alden Paper Corporation, Market Street, Akron, Ohio 44310, for six dozen disposable pillowcases to be sent c.o.d. Although your current series of institutional advertisements has brought the company quite a bit of correspondence in the form of inquiries from industrial prospects, you have had relatively few direct orders from consumers. Since you don't sell direct to consumers, you quickly check and see that it's Rutger's, Memphis, Tennessee 38122, which handles your Carall disposable pillowcases. Keep Mr. Tanner sold on the pillowcases, urge him to order directly from Rutger's, and point out to him the advantage of buying there.

CASES FOR SUBSTITUTE ACKNOWLEDGMENTS

1. As director of sales, United Toy Company, Bryan, Ohio 43506, answer the letter of one of your dealers, Clark M. Myers, 4700 Kenwood Ave., South, Chicago, Illinois 60615. He ordered one gross of Clasp cap guns at $1.45 each. You have stopped making this gun because tests showed that the sound hit a peak of 150 decibels (db). When fired indoors, the gun produced a peak of at least 155 db. Testers who fired the pistol experienced a brief sensation of deafness and some momentary roaring or ringing in the ears. To replace this cap gun, you have the improved Secret Agent allmetal gun that tests in your anechoic chamber (echo-free chamber) at only 90 decibels. At a distance of one foot it measures a peak sound of 95 db and when fired indoors, the gun produced a peak of at most 95 db. The Secret Agent gun is heavier and better built. Because of the better quality of the metal, it sells for $1.65, but this 20-cent difference will be made up in longer durability and greater customer appeal.

2. The United Toy Company, Bryan, Ohio 43506, today received a request from Roger M. Peake, buyer of toys for the chain of Gaynor's Stores, 3300 Eucalyptus Avenue, Riverside, California 92503, for one gross of Western-Trac toy tractors with swiveling front wheel. Though the swiveling front wheel can give greater maneuverability, it also confuses a youngster and can cause loss of control on a downhill slope. An improved Ranch Trac toy tractor has two front wheels for safer driving. Also, the pedals of the Ranch Trac remain stationary as the vehicle coasts instead of continuing to turn. If the child should lift his feet while riding downhill, he may be unable to get his feet back on rapidly rotating pedals. But with the improved Ranch Trac, he can find the stationary wheels. For additional safety, the Ranch Trac has a dished plastic steering wheel and the seat has a back rest. The cost for the Ranch Trac ($18) is no more.

3. You are chief clerk for Nelson-Lamb hardware wholesalers, 1780 Hudson Road, St. Paul, Minnesota 55103. You have an order from Patton Brothers, 1699 Wallace Avenue, Duluth, Minnesota 55802, for three dozen

Flame-Free fire extinguishers, auto size. The file reveals that about 13 months ago you shipped Patton Brothers four dozen Flame-Free extinguishers in the larger sizes. Four months ago you acquired the Minnesota distribution of the nationally advertised Stampire extinguishers and have sold out your entire supply of Flame-Frees in the size ordered. The Stampire is a more effective and dependable instrument than the Flame-Free. The Stampire fights all fires (flammable liquid, cloth, wood, paper, and electrical equipment). The clean, odorless carbon dioxide gas smothers fires and won't conduct electricity. It is also approved by the Underwriters' Laboratories, Inc., and the Coast Guard. The 1-quart size comes with clamps prepared for installing it on the automobile steering post without drilling holes or inserting screws. This model is $6 a dozen higher in price than the Flame-Free, but the Stampire line sells better—possibly because of its vigorous national advertising. Since the Patton Brothers firm has formerly sold the Flame-Free line and may still have some on hand and, because of the difference in price, you need to ask permission before substituting the Stampire. If the Patton buyer still prefers the Flame-Free, he can get the line from the Hardy Hardware Company in Minneapolis, the nearest distributor you know of.

4. As director of sales for the Arwin Company, Cincinnati, Ohio 45211, you are to handle an order from Mrs. Harry Post, Post Jewelry Store, 522 East Monroe Street, Springfield, Illinois 62705. Mrs. Post wants one dozen Arwin clock radios (No. 56875), "like she ordered from you last year." Your company found that the dial was too dim on the Arwin No. 56875; so you have an improved Manasonic clock radio with a dial design that is uncluttered and easy to read at night as well as in the daytime. Also, the Manasonic has a light that indicates whether the alarm is set. Ask Mrs. Post if you can send one dozen of these improved Manasonic and on regular terms (2/10, n/30). The price ($18) is the same. For added business, talk up the Sony 8RC25 clock with digital dial. Instead of a clock face, a window displays the three or four numbers that give the time (such as 2 05, or 11 37). In addition, it shows A.M. and P.M. The alarm works on a 24-hour basis, so that you can set the clock at, say, 3:15 in the afternoon, to ring at 7:30 the following morning. Mrs. Post can buy the Sony for $18 and sell it for $25.00. National full-page ads in *House Lovely* have promoted this clock during the last three months.

5. Today's mail brings a request for a Lifto Vertical Broiler from Mrs. Thurman Colburn, Box 789, Eau Claire, Wisconsin 54701, to the University Electric Appliance Company, 456 Bascom, Madison, Wisconsin 53716. Mrs. Colburn wrote that she had been trying to buy another one of these $29.95 broilers like she got three years ago. After visiting many appliance departments, she could not find any Lifto Vertical Broiler, but found only horizontal broilers that took too much counter room. She wants to know if she can buy one directly from the company, and if not, she wants the name of a dealer where she can get the broiler.

As director of sales for the University Electric Appliance Company, explain to Mrs. Colburn that the Lifto Vertical had many problems (pieces of food of uneven thickness, such as chicken, tended to slip to the bottom of the broiling rack where they browned unevenly; soft foods, such as hamburgers, oozed through the wires of the rack and came out slightly mauled; the ordinary method of heat regulation in a broiler—varying the distance between the food and heat source—cannot be used with Lifto Vertical Broiler; the drip tray had no handles and the adjacent areas got pretty hot so that it was virtually impossible to empty the tray in midst of cooking without spilling fat. Because of these problems, you have taken Lifto off the market and in its place have promoted a wall-mounted unit named Showcase. It can be folded up when dinner's done. In its folded configuration, it looks rather like a large metal attache case, 27¼ inches long, 13 inches high, and 4½ inches deep. It opens up to become a fairly respectable broiler, too. In addition to a stretch of wall at least as long as the unit, Mrs. Colburn will need a total vertical clearance of 16 inches between counter top and wall cabinets—including 1⅝ extra inches above the unit and 1⅜ inches below it to provide room for unfolding. If her counter has a shallow backsplash, she will need 14⅝ inches of unobstructed wall space above the backsplash. She also needs a wall outlet nearby. The Showcase comes with a 6-foot cord that plugs into the right-hand side of the unit. The unfolded upper leaf (actually the front cover of the folded unit) acts as a hood over the broiling surface, protecting any wall cabinets above it. The lower leaf, which contains the broiler's heating element, remains relatively cool on its underside; it shouldn't hurt a counter top close beneath it. And the back cover has a reflective surface that shields the wall from heat and spatters.

Although its proper station would seem to be the wall, the Showcase comes easily off the wall as a neat, self-contained unit that can be carried by its handle like a suitcase. With its storage compartment full of accessories—spit, rotisserie motor, detachable power cord, meat holders, skewers, and motor mount—it weighs 28 pounds.

Why would she want to move it? Well, for example, if she bought an extra wall bracket ($1.50), Mrs. Colburn could readily transfer the unit to a summer cottage. As a matter of fact, nothing has to be mounted on the wall. With an optional free-standing bracket ($5.00), she can use it on any horizontal surface, just as she would use an ordinary broiler.

The rack area of the Showcase is 155 square inches, and its effective broiling area is 105 square inches. The rack area can be put at two heights; the rotisserie, at six heights. With hood up, as when the broiler is mounted on the wall, it can handle roasts up to 10½ inches in diameter; without hood, as when the broiling unit is removed from the wall, it can take meats up to 14½ inches in diameter. Some other notable features: a separate on-off switch for the heating element, so she doesn't have to plug in and unplug the power cord to turn the heat on and off; and a tip switch that prevents the unit from running when it's folded up—a good safety device. The Showcase which sells for $79.95 has the *Good Living* stamp of approval and the guarantee of UL.

6. *Product:* A food waste disposer which is a motor-driven grinder that's installed in and under the drain opening of the kitchen sink. Impellers (small upright metal sections) or a whirling turntable slings wastes out into the notched edges of a ring that girds the grinding chamber. The high speed of impacting material gives the cutters great cutting power; they fragment the material into particles fine enough to pass through the notches in the grinding ring or through small holes in the turntable down into a drain chamber below. A steady flow of cold water—cold, to congeal greasy matter in the waste—facilitates the whole process, cleans the unit, and flushes ground-up matter through the household drains. Disposers come in two generic types: batch-feed and continuous-feed. The major difference between them is the way in which the owner turns them on. To turn on a batch-feed unit, he positions its stopper in a certain way to operate a built-in switch; since that blocks the drain opening, he can't feed the unit while it's running but rather has to feed it one batch at a time. He turns on a continuous-feed unit with an ordinary switch, which means that he can continue to drop waste down through a splash guard over the drain opening after the disposer has been started.

Problem: A plumbing supply company, Cole Company, Roebuck Road, Atlanta, Georgia 30308, orders six Coldpoint disposers of the batch-feed model 511098. In the Coldpoint, the very feature that was supposed to make batch-feed models safer than continuous-feed models posed a distinct mechanical hazard. The starter button in its throat, which is activated by pushing in and turning the stopper, could easily be activated by an arm reaching into the grinding chamber. Also, your testing laboratory found that the Coldpoint ground too slowly and left corn husk so coarse that it could clog some plumbing.

In place of the Coldpoint, you have the Waste Queen Universal 8000, which is a continuous-feed model. The Waste Queen grinds a test load of bone (750 grams, or about 26 ounces of steer rib) in a little over two minutes. The Waste Queen grinds corn husk finer than any other disposer your lab checked. It grinds them to short threadlike fibers and tiny bits and pieces, with a few longer hairlike fibers.

As director of sales for the Universal Plumbing Company, Norfolk, Virginia 23510, suggest that the Cole Company try the Waste Queen Universal 8000 which sells for $140 retail versus $119.50 for the Coldpoint.

7. The Bendix Audio-Visual Company, 638 Congress Street, Portland, Maine 04105, today received a request from Mrs. Howard Davis, 444 South Edward Street, Abbot Village, Maine 04406, for another Raybeam transistor portable radio like the one she bought from you five years ago. She enclosed a check for $20 and said she wanted the radio mailed to her. She is confined to a wheelchair and cannot shop and has no one to shop for her. Since Mrs. Davis bought the Raybeam, you have found an improved AM-FM pocket portable with a 2¼-inch speaker, yet only 2¾ x 4½ x 1½ inches deep. The new improved Canton portable is made with integrated circuits, which take much less room and power; thus even the smaller batteries last longer. Like the Raybeam, this portable has fold-down carrying strap, handsome top-grain cowhide cabinet, and an earphone attachment. Since the cost is $25, you'll keep her check and suggest that she send $5 more for the smaller portable. The lower cost of batteries alone over a five-year period will make up the difference. You could send her the old type of AM-FM portable (Harachi—made in Japan); but because you think she'll be more pleased with the Canton, you want her approval and money before you fill the order.

8. An order from Mrs. Eugene Grady, 99 Lake Estates, Barrington, Illinois 60010, for three (black, red, and blue) Stop-and-Go travel umbrellas "like she got two years ago" has to be handled by you, the personal shopper, Hampton's, Detroit, Michigan 48203. Because you had so much trouble with the Stop-and-Go umbrellas, you do not stock them any longer. Your store carries an eight-ribbed umbrella with shoulder strap and plastic handle. When closed the length measures about 12½ inches (telescopic style). These sell for the same price, $8.00. Ask Mrs. Grady if you can send her the three umbrellas and charge them to her account.

9. Mr. Anthony Hull, 325 Sunnyside Drive, Columbia, Tennessee 38401 (whose account in his and his wife's name has been on your books for eight years), ordered from M. P. Allen & Co., 705 Broadway N.E., Knoxville, Tennessee 37920, one pair of white six-button Kinglav kid gloves (he did not specify price, but these retail at $27.50) and one pair of white three-button Kinglav kid gloves (retail price $21.50), both in size 7, to be gift wrapped and mailed to his office address, 432 Columbia National Bank Building, and charged to his account. Kinglavs are the finest in French imported gloves. But because you have found that the French kid glove, Longvette, sold better than the Kinglavs, you now carry only the Longvette. Longvettes have probably sold better than Kinglavs because they are less expensive ($21.50 for six-button, $15.50 for three-button) but equally long-wearing, luxurious, and beautiful—and they wash much more satisfactorily. Ask if you may send the Longvette gloves and also a box of Longvette cold soap (six packages to a box; one package will wash two pairs of gloves) at $1.50. Make action easy for the gentleman and write him at his office address. (The letterhead on his letter read Anthony Hull and Associates, 2408 Sixth Street).

10. From his room (543), Valley View Nursing Home, Los Altos Drive, San Jose, California 95143, David Peak writes you, New Products Division,

Merriam Instruments, 754 Frederick Avenue, Plainfield, New Jersey 07060. Peak had bought a transistor hearing aid from your catalog several years ago for about $90. Somehow in his move from his home to the nursing home he misplaced the aid and so wanted another one for about the same price. He would send a money order after Merriam assured him he could buy one like he had.

Since the time Peak bought his hearing aid from you, your scientists have manufactured a superior aid called the Appolo. It is operated by integrated circuits, and so smaller and fewer batteries are needed. The Appolo, which weighs only half an ounce instead of three-fourths of an ounce, provides both moderate amplification and high tonal quality. Sounds and speech become intelligible within a frequency response of 500–4,300 cycles per second. It is attractive because it has no dangling cords, no bulging pockets; sound moves from the flesh-colored case behind the ear through a short plastic tube, and then into the earplug. Like the one he had, the Appolo has built-in volume control and an on-off switch, and comes with four different earplugs. The instruction booklet that accompanies the hearing aid gives details. The cost of the Appolo is $110, but the buyer is free of most of the worry and expense of buying and changing batteries. Generally batteries cost $1.60 for four, and one package lasts about a year, depending on the use of the hearing aid. Answer Peak's letter by suggesting that you send the improved Appolo to him at the nursing home. The money order should be made for $112.50 (mailing charges included).

11. Assume that another letter from David Peak (of the preceding case) is about an electric razor. He has a hard time shaving, for he is confined to his bed. His electric razor is almost worn out, and he would like another Vanguard razor with double rotary shaving heads. This time he enclosed a money order for $20 which he assumed would cover the cost of the shaver and mailing charges. Because Peak is confined to bed, you think a battery-operated razor which sells for $10 more would be desirable. It recharges overnight and gives up to seven days of shaving without recharging. But even better for Peak's needs might be the new cordless Vanguard 908, which operates on integrated circuits. This 14-ounce razor with self-sharpening blades gives a smooth, clean, and comfortable shave every time, even through thick whiskers. Built-in, pop-up trimmer helps keep neck and sideburns neat. Just press a button to release. It can operate in any country in the world, since it is not dependent on current. One-year guarantee. Has nylon housing but comes in attractive all-leather travel case. Suggest Vanguard 908 ($30.95 with mailing charges). He need send only $10.95 to complete payment.

CASES FOR COMBINATIONS

1. An old customer of yours, Green Thumb Nursery (Mr. Thomas C. Milan), 1877 University Avenue, Austin, Texas 78610, orders from your company, Jackson Deluxe, Inc., Harrisburg, Pennsylvania 17103, 36 Scott R9 broadcast-type lawn spreaders at $49.95 each. Because of a recent strike, you have to back-order these broadcast-type spreaders. He can expect delivery in 30 days. Remind Mr. Milan, however, that these spreaders sling the material to the sides and in front from 2 to 5 feet. This type of spreader appeals to the man who has a big job to do in a hurry. He also ordered 12 of the Rare Devil drop-type spreader at $19.95 each.

The other type of spreader for lawns, the drop-type, appeals to the meticulous gardeners. Mr. Milan ordered one dozen of the Rare Devil drop-type spreader, but you have replaced it with an improved spreader, Gardenmet. The Gardenmet puts out limestone (and other material tested) in a steady flow rather than in pulses. Also, the Gardenmet is easier to push than the Rare Devil and it has an on-off control within easy reach of the pushing handle. Ask Mr. Milan for his permission to send the improved drop-type spreader, the Gardenmet.

2. Because of the success of a recent promotional campaign, the Bennington Company, Bennington, New Hampshire 03310, manufacturers of popular cassette player-recorder, must back-order one dozen sets (at $75) for the Central Audio Company, 976 South Avenue, Gary, Indiana 46404. Three weeks from the date of this letter, the well-made play-back cassettes in full-toned stereo should arrive at Central. As sales director for the Bennington Company, offer to substitute a "personal" TV Solorola for the General American "personal" TV set he ordered (six at $60). The Solorola is available with batteries, which makes it truly portable. A view screen only 5½ inches high and 8 inches wide makes it fit easily on a bedside table or on a desk. It weighs only 10 pounds; so it is easy to carry around. The General American weighs 14 pounds and costs $70; the Solorola costs $85.00. Picture quality of the Solorola is rated high by rating agencies for detailed, crisp outlines of objects, sharp and evenly spaced horizontal scanning lines, correct geometrical shape of objects, and horizontal linearity (in a set with incorrect linearity, objects or people on one side of the screen look stretched).

Address your letter to David Bailey, owner of the Central Audio Company.

3. An old customer of yours, Hargrove Green, owner of Green Sporting Goods Store, 406 North Broadway, Baltimore, Maryland 21203, ordered from your wholesale catalog six 30-second (1/10) sweep stopwatches at $11.95 each. He did not specify if he wanted No. B, which starts, stops, and returns from stem with a 15-minute center recorder, or No. C, which has a side return button. The center dial records up to 30 minutes. As sales manager for Blakeney Fine Sports and Gym Equipment Company, 735 Chestnut Street, Springfield, Massachusetts 01107, find out which type of stopwatch he wants, and back order the dozen tetherball sets No. MTS ($10.95 a set) he ordered. The tetherball set (9-foot post of 2-inch galvanized steel tube with full-size tetherball) has become very popular in schools throughout the country. You have the manufacturer's assurance of a new shipment of No. MTS sets within 10 days and will ship them express collect to Green.

4. Acknowledge the order for Herter's (Order Case 14, p. 191), acknowledging the check, stating the minnow bucket is no longer available, saying you'll have to back-order the rod kit (it will probably arrive in about 10 days), sending the other items, and explaining the money details. Include anything else you think you should.

5. *Write from:* Singer and Skinner, shoe manufacturers, Bosley Spring Road, Nashville, Tennessee 37203. *Write to:* The Locker Room, Lennox Shopping Center, Tulsa, Oklahoma 74152. The order is signed by Harry White, owner. A check for $415.37 accompanies the order. The calculations of shipping weights and charges are correct, but the catalog number for the boots, with foam insulation and cushioned insole, is not correct and the jogging shoes (M9876) are not in stock.

12 prs. No. M9876 white jogging shoes, D width, men's sizes 9, 10, 11, 12 @ $6.00	$ 72.00
12 prs. No. S4329, boots, men's sizes 9, 10, 11, 12, D width @ $20	240.00
12 prs. No. S5429, hip boots, men's sizes 9, 10, 11, 12, D width $8	96.00
Shipping charges $7.37	7.37
	$415.37

Find out whether he wants boot No. S3492 at $18 or No. S2328 at $22 and what color (dark green or brown). Both boots are insulated. The $22 pair has silicone-treated leather uppers and is glove-leather lined. The $18 pair has silicone-treated cowhide uppers and is lined with cotton.

Because of their popularity the jogging shoes have been back-ordered. You expect a shipment next week. *Money details:* Hold Mr. White's check until you hear from him. Send him a credit application blank and financial statement form for him to fill out and return. *Sales talk on house:* Establish profitability of your shoes (50 percent markup) and talk concretely about the dealer aids you furnish: quarter-page ads in *Field and Stream,* counter displays, and envelope stuffers (which you'll furnish on request). *Allied sales:* Knee fishing boots made of multiply rubber with rubberized cotton lining, deep-cleated sole, heel, semihard toe. They come in green or slate color and sell for $3.00 (retail $6.00).

6. *To:* Mr. Lawrence Coffee, City Furniture Company, 1987 Fifteenth Street, Spartanburg, South Carolina 29301. *From:* Hickory Furniture Company, Henderson, North Carolina 27536. *Facts:* The Hitchcock chair (No. WR6789) he ordered has been discontinued. A similar chair (No. RT6798) as described in an enclosed folder could be ordered. Ask him for his action on this chair order and send him the mahogany cocktail table (No. TR567 at $120) he ordered. Tell him about your special on the one-door, 18-inch diameter, 20-inch-high column table (No. TY576). It regularly wholesales for $35, but you have a special price of $25 this month.

7. *From:* The Linen Department, Gayloafs, Michigan Avenue, Chicago, Illinois 60606. *To:* Mrs. Harry Friedman, 11 Main Cross Road, Pana, Illinois 62557. *Case:* Acknowledge the order for two St. Ann's thermo-weave blankets (one queen—90 x 90 in federal blue at $12.50; one king—108 x 90 in tawny gold at $14.50); and two dozen perma-prest percale sheets, twin-bed size at $7.00. *Action:* You can send the king-size blanket as ordered. Find out if Mrs. Friedman wants the sheets in white, or designs of tiny checks, bold stripes, or field flowers. Also tell her that you have the queen-size blanket in sky blue (not federal blue), avocado green, tawny gold, white, or strawberry pink. *Enclosures:* Besides an envelope stuffer promoting perma-prest percale fitted sheets, send a reply card for her convenience.

8. James Howard, colonel in the Army and stationed in Alaska (APO Seattle, Washington 98749) orders from Vining's (retailers), 1254 California Street, Washington, D.C. 20008, the following gifts to be sent to his brother, John, and niece, Sally Brewton, 11 Park Lane, Green Cove Springs, Florida 32043:

1 Chantilly sterling serving spoon
1 pair of gold cuff links to be initialed with an H.

To be certain that Sally Brewton will receive a serving spoon that is not a duplicate of something she already has, ask the customer to specify whether he wants to send a sugar shell, $15; table spoon, pierced or nonpierced, $25; bonbon, $11.75; chafing-dish spoon, $50, or jelly server, $15. Enclose a folder with pictures to help him choose. Ask him if he wants the traditional or the wrap-around cuff links and what price does he want to pay. Gold-filled run $8 to $15 and 14-karat run $30–$40. Ask if these are gifts for special occasions and if he'd like them gift-wrapped and sent with appropriate cards. Gift-wrapping will cost 50 cents per package, and there are shipping charges. Colonel Howard has had an account with you for several years.

9. *From:* Spencer's Detroit mail-order outlet, 3585 North Parkway, (48237). *To:* Mrs. Hugh Sullivan, P.O. Box 78, Albany, Kentucky 42602. *Case:* She orders from an old catalog an all-rayon zipper jacket (No. 987 M 4432, medium size at $9.80) for her son, and three New Tide acrylic sweaters, size 12. She mentioned no color for either item. Also, she can substitute for $12.80 a rugged perma-prest zipped-front jacket with fabric that's treated to be water repellent (65 percent dacron polyester and 35 percent cotton). Or, for $19.90 she can buy a zipped-front jacket with 100 percent dacron polyester lining. Ask her to state even chest size (36–46,

regular, and 38–46, tall). Jacket colors are: chamois gold, medium blue, medium green, tan, or federal blue. Justify the price increase with these facts: dacron polyester is treated to be water repellent; machine washable; two-button collar with storm tab; two button adjustable cuffs and elastic inserts at sides of waist. She may select the sweaters in Sahara tan, bronze olive, berry red, white, or navy. *Action:* See which of the jackets she wants. Have her select the color and the correct size for the classic pullover sweaters. Make action easy. You will charge the coat, sweaters, and mailing charge to her account.

10. Before mailing a trophy shipment to the Goodrand Rubber Plant, Ada, Minnesota 56510, you must write a letter to Gordon Lloyd, public relations. Lloyd ordered three S660 10-inch trophies at $16 each, but he failed to tell which figure he wanted on the top of each marble base. He may choose a figure bowling, running, holding a basketball, swinging a golf club, or holding a tennis racquet. A trophy figure is available for any sport or event. Also, tell him that the walnut plaques he ordered (five R875, 9 by 12 inches, at $21 each) should be mailed within two weeks. A special-metal shortage has kept your company from meeting deadlines. The practical award he ordered, P409, has been replaced in your line by P566, an improved marble perpetual calendar. The advantage of P566 is that it has a pen and pencil set as well as the calendar, but it costs only $2 more ($20.20 instead of $18.20). Under the signature of promotion director in charge of sales for Cushing's, Inc., 9764 Leland Avenue, South Bend, Indiana 46628, wholesale distributors of trophies, handle this letter, which involves a vague order, a back order, and a substitute.

11. You are one of the personal shoppers for La Fontana & Company, 6th Avenue, Denver, Colorado 80204, handling the order for Mrs. William Wilson, 1499 Acoma Street, Colorado Springs, Colorado 80901, a good mail-order customer whose address has been carried on your books for three years as Scott Field, Illinois, where her husband was a captain in the Air Force. With the necessary change-of-address information, she also included a notation that Major Wilson would be stationed in Colorado for two years and she'd be calling on you for lots of shopping help. She enclosed two cards, asking that you send two weeks from now to her nephew, Master Louis Lauria, 8703 Lynn Street, Springfield, Virginia 22150, one heavyweight athletic jacket with wool chenille letter L, advertised in this month's *La Fontana Modes,* at $10.99 plus $1.50 for initial. The size 10 jacket No. R432 is wanted in royal blue. One week later send to her niece, Laura Lauria, same address, gold sweater-knit skirt No. W3654 ($5.99) with matching pullover gold knit sweater ($5.99) No. W3256. Both are birthday gifts, she says.

Since Mrs. Wilson failed to give you the size of the girl's skirt and sweater, ask her for the girl's size (or measurements of chest and waist). These separates made of duPont orlon acrylic are amazingly light in weight yet feel like wool. They're nonallergenic; moths have no appetite for them. Machine-wash and tumble-dry. Probably because the athletic jackets wear well, and are easy to wash, you have sold almost all your stock and have none in size 10. And a month from now is the earliest the manufacturer will promise them to you. If Mrs. Wilson would like to make another choice, you'll be glad to handle it for her. If she'd prefer, you can mail Louis one of your special children's birthday-gift announcement cards, which will arrive for his birthday, telling him that he will receive a gift about a week later. It includes a blank for indicating the name of the donor. Word the message so that Mrs. Wilson will give you the necessary information and agree to the delayed birthday gift.

12. *From:* Irving Manufacturing Company, 1106 Milledge Avenue, Dayton, Ohio 45420. *To:* Moeller's Gift Shop, 987 Avery Avenue, High Point, North Carolina 27263. *Facts:* George Ayers Moeller ordered the following merchandise:

6 games Monopoly @ $3.40	20.40
6 games Meet the Space Age @ $3.40	20.40
6 Milton-Bradley jig-saw puzzles @ $2.20	13.20
	54.00

Indefinite part: Milton Bradley jig-saw puzzles are priced at 50 cents (No. 954), $1.00 (No. 987), $2.00 (No. 956). The differences are in size and complexity. Ask Moeller to check the reply card for information. *Back order:* Because of their popularity, the Meet the Space Age game will have to be back ordered. Moeller should get these games in 15 days. *Charges:* The $54 plus shipping charges will be debited to Moeller's account. *Added sales:* Tell him about the portrait-size jig-saw puzzles that are now available for $3.40 (retail $6.75). Many customers enjoy having the puzzles framed after they have assembled them.

13. You are sales manager for Shelburn Clothing Company, 987 Fair Oaks Road, Toledo, Ohio 43613. Today you have an order from Edward Essex, buyer for P. L. Harrison & Company, 29th and Buchanan, Ogden, Utah 84402, for four dozen perma-prest shorts for ladies, style No. 96543, one dozen each of sizes 10, 12, 14, and 16, at $4 each. Because of the unexpected popularity of the shorts, your stock is exhausted. You've ordered new perma-prest material, and it is due within a week; so Harry James, the production superintendent, tells you that he'll have the shorts ready to ship within 10 days. Write the letter to Essex, asking about the color choices and explaining that the shorts will have to be given a back-order listing. Word it so that Essex will accept this method of handling the order. Include some resale talk on these easy-to-wash, never-iron shorts. P. L. Harrison & Company is a good credit customer of yours. Color choices are blue, yellow, green, pink—all in pastels.

| # Persuasive messages: Requests

Special requests
   Securing interest
   Justifying the request
   Minimizing obstacles
   Positively anticipating acceptance
Persuasive claims and policy complaints
Persuasive requests for credit

SPECIAL REQUESTS

ALTHOUGH REQUESTS for information about products, services, and people constitute the bulk of businessmen's inquiries, sometimes they need special favors from people who have no built-in motivation to reply. These special requests are more difficult writing problems than direct inquiries —and for a highly understandable reason: Most people, when asked to do something even slightly out of the ordinary, can think of two reasons why they should not comply with the request for every one reason why they should.

No one ever has enough money or time to give either of them spontaneously and unquestioningly. No one is willing to reveal business information without knowing how it will be used and deciding that the purpose is good. To put the question directly in these cases is to get an immediate no. So the special request has to be a persuasive letter. Like the simple inquiry, the special request is specific and concise, but it is not direct; and because it usually requires more details in development, it is usually longer.

Favor-seeking letters are C–plan letters, as already discussed in Chapter 3. As explained there, the secret of successful persuasive copy is to (1) offer, suggest, or imply a benefit to the reader—at least talk about something of interest to him; (2) explain the worth of your proposal to justify it in your reader's eyes; (3) try to foresee and preclude objections; and (4) after giving necessary details, confidently ask the reader to do what you want.

Securing interest

If you are going to strike the appropriately persuasive theme, you need to analyze the situation to select the most pertinent and applicable *motive* that might cause the reader to do what you want.

Dollars being what they must be in American business thinking, the strongest appeal is one that holds out to the reader the prospect of sales, of saving money, or of promoting goodwill with an audience wherein sales may ultimately materialize. Such potential-dollar themes offer your reader the most concrete form of reader benefit and are responsible for this opening to an advertising manager of a manufacturing company:

    What would it be worth to Rigate to add some 8,000 potential
    customers to its prospect list?

and this opening to the circulation manager of a magazine:

    Who will be your readers ten years from now?

If you can apply such reader-benefit themes appropriately and remain within the realm of good taste (avoiding the suggestion of bribery), you undoubtedly have the strongest appeal you can make.

In many instances, however, such dollar-minded talk would arouse indignation (especially from professional people who do not advertise) or would not apply. But you need not despair of finding a talking point which will stress the reader's benefit or interest rather than your own. The letter to the correspondence supervisor (on p. 58) that begins

    How often have you received—from well-educated people—
    letters that are not worth your attention?

clearly holds out a benefit to the reader by talking in terms of making his job easier. Many times the basis for a busy businessman's filling out a time-consuming questionnaire (or one that asks for information ordinarily restricted to the firm) is his realization that as a result of the information thus gathered and made available to him, he will be more efficient at his job.

Indirect benefits may serve too. When you can show your reader how your project (and his contribution) will promote the welfare of a group of which he is a member or in which he has an interest, you can write a strong letter. On this basis you might write a letter inviting a public accountant to speak to a college accounting club or a correspondence supervisor to address a group of teachers of business writing or an alumnus of a professional fraternity to take on a responsible office in the organization.

Although many special-request letters are written with appeals to altruism,[1] in business situations you will write more successful favor-seeking

---

[1] Letters seeking funds for worthy causes are special-request letters and thus within the scope of this analysis, but we think it best not to take them up here because they are too highly specialized and because of their frequent civic, religious, and fraternal

letters if you select and emphasize reader-benefit talking points. The following letter (asking an advertising manager for free samples) stresses reader benefit throughout—so forcefully as to be almost browbeating, in fact:

> How much would it be worth to Rigate to add some 8,000 potential customers to its prospect list?
>
> You can increase the goodwill toward your company of even more people than this—and at a relatively small cost.
>
> Attracting around 300 contestants and 8,000 onlookers, "A" Day each spring at the University is a festival of fun—a program of pie-eating contests, sack races, beauty contests, and other collegiate horsing-around.
>
> Prizes for the winners of these contests are contributed by local merchants who realize the sales-building value of such donations. But if we had some prizes which we could give to each participant—winner and loser alike—they would introduce under most favorable circumstances someone's product and house.
>
> The loudspeakers would blare out, "And in addition, each participant will receive one tube of Picote tooth paste!" Some 8,000 people would hear this . . . and would laugh . . . and would remember your brand name. And 300 would actually receive your product to use and tell their friends about.
>
> The special "A" Day edition of the student paper will carry an account of all prizes given, and the program will also list all contributors.
>
> A man of your experience knows the value of such advertising.
>
> Won't you, then, write me (in time for our February planning) that you will send us 300 sample tubes of Picote? You'll be getting some low-cost, effective advertising.

If you look back at the letter beginnings quoted in this section, you will note that in addition to highlighting reader benefit (or at least reader interest), these openings are questions. You will note, too, that the questions are rhetorical (not asked to get their answers, as in inquiries, but to start the reader thinking and make him read on).

We do not mean to imply that all persuasive requests must begin with a question. In the preceding letter, for example, you could omit the first sentence (a question) and interweave the figure into the second (a statement). But the question beginning commands greater attention than a declarative statement and can be phrased more readily to lead your reader to a contemplation of your suggestion. Too, a question is never as challenging as some statements are, and it can be subtly flattering.

---

manifestations. When faced with such problems, you can be sure that the fundamental principles we present here will apply; but for more detailed techniques and "tricks of the trade," check some books like Margaret Fellows and Stella Koenig's *Tested Methods of Raising Money for Churches, Colleges, and Health and Welfare Agencies,* Harper & Bros., New York, 1959.

In phrasing such questions, however, you will be on safer ground if you eliminate the possibility of either a yes or a no answer. To make the reader contemplate the circumstance that will lead up to the request, the following opening employs the strategy:

```
What Ford philosophy of management caused the change from
                "Made in Texas by Texas Labor"
to
                "Made in Texas by Texans"?
```

We do not mean to imply that to secure interest in favor-seeking letters you must studiously avoid questions that can be answered with either yes or no. The following opening addressed to a retailing man of national standing contemplating entering the Texas market is certainly a good one:

```
Wouldn't you consider the respect and attention of some 200
key Texas retailers a valuable opportunity to test the true
business conditions in that state?
```

The mental response to such a question is positive. And as long as you can be fairly sure of getting a positive reaction, you are probably on safe ground.

The danger lies in getting an irritated answer—whether that answer is a yes or a no or any of the variants of "So what?" The student who invited the head of a large public accounting firm to speak to a college group and began with

```
Do you believe in preparing for the future?
```

apparently gave little thought to the probable snort or burst of laughter that would result from such a question. He eliminated the irritating aspects (and got closer to the subject of his letter) when he changed his opening to read:

```
What, in your opinion, are the desirable personal
characteristics of the successful public accountant?
```

True, that beginning implies no reader benefit; but it is certainly a subject of practical interest to the reader. Of possibly greater reader-benefit implications is this one:

```
What does it cost you when you have to dismiss a well-grounded
junior accountant because of his poor personal characteristics?

The actual cost of additional recruiting and training isn't
the only loss either:  The loss of prestige and possibly of
clients is a greater threat.
```

Careful study of the preceding beginnings will show two other advantages that come from question beginnings implying reader benefits: (1) They are more likely to keep the reader in the picture, and (2) they make the transition to the explanation easier.

Justifying the request

Having secured your reader's interest with a beginning which holds some promise of benefit or at least talks of something of interest, you usually need to devote the greater part of your letter to explaining what your project is and what good comes of it. Two cautions need to be inserted here, however. The first is that you should not be writing the letter unless you cannot get the necessary information or assistance by your own efforts. The second is: *Do not begin your letter with explanations or details of circumstances.* As in the simple inquiry, you certainly want to be specific. But, as they start to read, uninvolved readers aren't even faintly interested in

```
The National Association of Advertising Teachers of America,
which is made up of some 600 teachers in all sections of the
country, is planning its annual convention in New York at the
Madison Hotel on July 10, 11, and 12.
```

Of course, a member of the Association planning to attend the meeting would be. Even a nonmember would be, after having been almost or completely persuaded to give a talk to the group. Indeed, he would *have* to be so informed. Details concerning who, what, when, where, why, how (sometimes how much) always need to be clarified—but not until after the big idea of the reader's benefit or contribution has been highlighted. A speaker, for instance, needs to know the nature and size of his audience, the time and place, the facilities available to him, the amount of time allotted to him, and the topic (if you are assigning him one). He may need to know about other speakers who will precede and follow him. But such details are not appropriate lead-off points to secure interest. Furthermore, they should be incorporated subordinately as much as possible.

Nobody would read with immediate enthusiasm a beginning like this:

```
As a Master's candidate at Harwood University, I am planning a
thesis on palletization.  Professor H. D. Brunham of our
marketing department has suggested that I write to you to find
out the results of your experience.
```

Notice in the following copy how the young man seeking this information not only changed his opening to an interest-arousing question but also *subordinated* the necessary but uninteresting details of the original opening:

```
Just what are the economies of palletization?

Are they as great as my experience in the service led me to
believe?

Has palletization been adopted by an increasing number of
business firms in recent years?

Regardless of your experience in using pallets, your comments
in answering these questions could contribute materially in
making a worthwhile, authentic, down-to-earth thesis of the
one I am preparing as partial requirement for an M.S. degree
```

at Alabama. Too, the finished thesis may well be of practical interest to all users and potential users of pallets.

Perhaps you have some printed material which you can simply enclose in the stamped, addressed envelope I've included. If not, will you take a few minutes to tell me your experience with pallets, the cost of palletizing (with particular emphasis on warehousing), current uses or ideas in palletization, and/or possible sources?

Although I don't have to, I'd like to be able to quote you; but I'll handle the material with whatever degree of confidence and anonymity you specify. And no part of this correspondence will ever be used for any purposes other than research, I assure you.

Since I have to assemble material and start writing by June 1, I'd be most grateful if you'd let me hear from you before that date.

If you would like to read the finished thesis for a new idea or two that you might be able to put to work, I'll be glad to lend you my personal copy shortly after August 25.

Why—besides the interest-arousing question beginning and the skillfully subordinated facts justifying the request—did seven copies of that letter bring five detailed replies? Did you notice (fifth paragraph) how clear and specific the writer made the requested action and how easy he made it seem? Did you notice (last paragraph) how he reminded the reader of possible benefits at the end? And how (preceding paragraph) he avoided seeming to push the reader around by justifying his request for action by a necessary end date? And did you notice (sixth paragraph) how he reassured against any fears as to how the information might be used? Any one of these points (explained in the rest of this discussion) may make the difference between your getting nothing and getting what you want in a persuasive favor-seeking situation.

Minimizing obstacles

Even though your beginning may have supplied a very good reason which highlights the reader's advantage or interest, in most circumstances there is some fly in the ointment: a negative factor you have to overcome. It may be a sum of money you are asking for, which you feel reasonably certain your reader is going to consider out of line; then you break it down into several payments. It may be that you can offer no fee or a smaller fee than a program speaker is accustomed to receiving; then you cite other (perhaps intangible) rewards. It may be that you're asking for secret information. If so, assure the reader that you will do all you can to protect his interest. Regardless of the case or the circumstance, you can usually find some positive corollary to the drawback.

As added inducement, you want to make the job sound as easy as possible and as pleasurable as possible. Phrasing can do a lot here. The following letter is a good example of establishing a negative idea in positive language. The fourth paragraph implies, "See, Mr. Philipson, this really won't be much extra work"; and the fifth one implies, "Sorry, there's no pay in this deal."

> Don't you agree, Mr. Philipson, that a business leader who's on the firing line every day can lend real punch to Tau Kappa Rho activities?
>
> Of course, we give TKR's the benefits of brotherhood and a certain amount of social life, but our real reason for being is to get these promising young men realistically oriented to business life while they're still in school.
>
> So that these future business leaders will get superior guidance, will you be TKR's Midwest district supervisor? As you know, the district supervisor, through letters and visits, helps the local chapters develop and expand business-orienting programs.
>
> Frequently you'd be able to combine business and fraternity trips, I'm sure, for the Midwest district of six states and 22 chapters almost corresponds with your sales district. You'd be able to spend many pleasant evenings telling the boys how American does it! And you'd undoubtedly spot a number of promising candidates for work with your company two, three, and four years from now.
>
> Of course, you'd have an expense account for stationery and traveling. But your real pay would come from seeing these boys get a head start in their professional lives.
>
> Won't you therefore write me that I may nominate you to the General Executive Committee when it meets here in Chicago on May 21?

Finally, the mechanical aspects of complying with your request should be reduced to the minimum of detail, time, and money. That is why most questionnaires are fill-in or checkoff forms and why a return-addressed reply device requiring no postage ordinarily accompanies such requests.

Positively anticipating acceptance

After establishing the reader's benefit or contribution, making clear exactly what you want and why, and minimizing obstacles, you should confidently ask the reader to comply with the request. Hesitant, apologetic expressions belittle the request itself and have the disadvantage of suggesting excuses as reasons for his refusal. Such expressions as the following hinder rather than help:

> I realize you are a very busy man, but . . . .
> I'm sorry to trouble you for such an apparently insignificant matter; however . . . .
> I hesitate to bother you with such a request . . . .
> If you consider this a worthwhile project, ...

Eliminate such thinking (maybe by rereading the discussion on "Success Consciousness," p. 67) and forthrightly name the specific action you want the reader to take. Although you may have referred to it earlier, be sure to ask for it or at least refer to it near the end.

In your favor-seeking letters apply the summary of points on page 328.

PERSUASIVE CLAIMS AND POLICY COMPLAINTS

Sometimes you will have good reason to believe that you need to be rather persuasive to get results on your claim. Your reason may be that you know the reader to be rather reluctant to grant claims, that your case is subject to some question and you need to make as good a case as you can within the facts, or (most frequently) that you have already tried the direct claim and have been turned down.

Whatever the cause, you write a C–plan letter (similar to the special request) when you need to be persuasive, and you can appeal to any desire that might motivate the reader. Some of the main appeals (more or less in ascending order of force and objectionable tone) are to the reader's desire for (1) customer satisfaction, goodwill, and favorable publicity; (2) a continued reputation for fair dealing; and (3) legal meeting of a guarantee.

Again your letter is divided rather distinctly into three parts, but their contents are somewhat different from those of the direct claim:

1. You begin by stating and getting agreement on the principle which is the basis of your claim. (In logic, it would be called the "major premise.")

2. You explain all the facts in detail, as in any claim. (The term in logic is the "minor premise.") This part may be several paragraphs long. In it you show clearly the reader's responsibility.

3. You apply the facts or minor premise to the principle or major premise so as to draw a conclusion, as the logician would call it. The conclusion will be that the reader should act in a certain way. You request that he act as the logic has clearly shown that he should.

Here are two examples of how the system works. The first was an initial claim. It was successful, in spite of the fact that a glance may suggest that the writer had no justified claim. A closer look, however, will make clear that he did. The situation was quite different from a person's just buying something and finding a few days later that the seller has reduced the price. The key difference is the salesman's assurance to the claimant that he would not save money by waiting. The appeal is therefore to the reader's desire for customer confidence.

```
If your customers do not trust your salesmen, going to a lot
of trouble and expense in selecting and training them
doesn't do much good, does it, Mr. Barnes?  That's why I'm
writing to you.
```

On July 5 I was in your store looking at an XXXX suit priced at
$97.75. I decided to leave and wait for a late-summer sale,
as I frequently do. But your salesman assured me that there
would be no sale on XXXX suits, that the manufacturer had
never allowed its suits to be sold at reduced prices and
would not do so this year. So, since I wanted the suit, I
bought it.

Now I notice that the price has been reduced to $83.95 and
that you are selling at that price.

My plan, you see, would have saved me $13.80. Because I was
induced to buy through your salesman's assurance that I could
not get the suit cheaper by waiting, I believe you will agree
that I am entitled to a refund of $13.80.

I am sure that you want me to trust your salesmen. You can
renew my faith by standing behind what they say.

The following illustration is a persuasive claim written after a first claim
brought a proposal to compromise. It got the money, the full amount without compromise, by appealing to fair-minded analysis of the facts (and
hence the injustice of compromise in the case).

Gentlemen:

Subject: Claim No. 070–6289

If a salesman for the XXXX Casualty Company were trying to
sell me a policy and I offered to pay him half the premium he
requested, do you think he would take it? I don't. That
would be a compromise.

Compromises are for cases involving doubt about responsibility
or about the amount of damage done. In my claim no doubt
about either arises.

Analysis of the facts will show that Mr. Hall ran up behind me
so fast that he could not control his car and hit the left rear
part of the side of my car. Clearly he was responsible.

I got three estimates of the repair job to be sure of having a
fair appraisal of the damages. The lowest of the three was
$86. So there is no doubt about the damage.

I am therefore returning the Release and Settlement form you
sent and asking that you send another based on one of the
estimates I formerly sent in. That is the only fair
settlement.

I know that your job is to keep your loss ratio down as low as
possible while being fair about the obligations the company
assumes in insuring clients. The solution is to settle on the
basis of one of the estimates submitted.

I look forward to receiving that settlement.

The policy complaint may be like a direct claim or a persuasive one, but
it is more likely to be persuasive.

Whereas claims ask restitution for mistakes, damage, or unsatisfactory
products, policy complaints request correction of poor service or unsatisfactory policies and practices. The following are two typical situations:

If our customers like anything better than XXXX strawberry ice cream, it's XXXX chocolate or vanilla. That's why many people were disappointed last Sunday when we received an entire delivery of strawberry instead of the chocolate and vanilla we ordered.

If you remember last Sunday, you know it was a pretty hot day —a good day to sell ice cream. We sold 2,000 cups but turned away hundreds of tired, hungry swimmers because they insisted on chocolate or vanilla. I believe I could have sold the remaining 1,000 cups had they been those flavors.

Our customers like XXXX ice cream so well that we'd like to continue selling it. Perhaps a little more care in packing, or a little better system of labeling, will assure you of delivering the right flavors for my future orders, and thus increase both our sales.

May I depend on you?

--

Am I right in thinking that Racine Motors wants its policy on direct-sale commissions and cooperative selling campaigns to promote long-range goodwill and increased sales in this territory?

Because I think so but find the present practice is not working out that way, I think you will want to review your policies in view of my experience.

Recently one of our salesmen called on a prospect in our territory and found him already enjoying the reliability and efficiency of a 20-hp. Racine motor, which we normally stock. Further investigation revealed that he had bought the motor directly from you at a price below our selling price. Yet we have received no dealer's commission on this sale. This is one of several occasions brought to my attention in the past year which prompt me to ask you for clarification of our agreement.

Admittedly with the helpful assistance of your missionary salesmen, we have been able to sell a substantial group of the industrial users in this area on the economy and dependability of the Racine electric motor. We want to keep and expand this patronage, but it will be difficult if we are working at cross-purposes with you. It will be to our mutual good if we and you quote uniform prices and if we get our dealer's commission on any direct sales. You gain by being relieved of the marketing functions and by having a ready-made market for your motor, and we gain by getting our just profits and keeping the goodwill of our customers.

We have been contemplating an expansion of our stock to include your 60-hp. motor, which would play an important part in our sales program. Please give us a definite working policy so we will know where we stand.

PERSUASIVE REQUESTS FOR CREDIT

You can write the application for credit in direct, brief style when you are reasonably sure that you can meet the firm's credit tests. When you know you are going to have to ask for special concessions, however, a persuasive letter patterned after the special-request, C–plan letter may be in order. The presentation establishes interest by stressing potential profitable business, stresses the capacity of the management, establishes a sensible plan for meeting the obligation, and confidently asks for action. Like all the letters in this chapter, it is a modification of the AICA (attention, interest, conviction, action) of sales letters.

In the following case the young man was asking for 150 days' credit, knowing that 30 days was the usual time allowed by the Long-Shearer Company. Although the letter is unusually long, detailed, and persuasive for a credit application, it was written for an unusual situation.

Lots of auto-accessories dollars are floating around in booming Lubbock. Yet the chains sell only a standard line.

An alert independent retailer offering a complete line of parts and accessories could certainly count on the reputation of Long-Shearer accessories to give him a rapid turnover and a good chance to get his share of this increasing market.

Hence my optimism about the store I plan to open on June 24. Right on Main Street, near several garages and body shops, the 50-foot-front store is out of the high-rent district, yet accessible enough to get me my share of the walking trade. The market survey I made last week indicates that conservatively I can expect 300 people in my store every day. And the managers of all the garages and body shops within four blocks of my store have promised me they'll buy from me.

They got to know me while I worked in my father's Ford service shop during and after high school. We became better friends in the year and a half I spent in the parts department after serving in the Navy and before returning to the University of Texas to complete my B.B.A. degree. I made friends with them —and I learned a lot about the business. I also made friends of most of the young businessmen in town through membership in Rotary and serving a term as president of the Jaycees.

Although my father's death stops my chance to go into the Ford agency because there was a survivor-take-all clause in the partnership agreement, I'm willing to put every bit of the $20,000 insurance money he left me into the new store. My wife and I have no illusions of getting rich quickly and are fully prepared to plow profits back into our store so that it will get started on the right foot. You can see from the following allocation of the $20,000 that the store will be financially sound.

With $2,000 for store equipment, $3,600 for operating expenses (including six months' rent at $250 per month), and $3,600 plus a small personal fund for six months' personal expenses, about $10,000 will be left to buy an initial inventory. For the sort of stock I'll need to have an edge on my competitors, I should have an initial inventory of $20,000. I would like to finance a $10,000 Long-Shearer accessories stock by paying $5,000 now, $2,500 in 120 days, and the other $2,500 30 days after that. I plan to finance a $10,000 parts stock from the Auto-Life Company in the same manner. With Long-Shearer accessories selling as well as they do, plus living close to my budget with a wife who's able to give me plenty of help,

Special-Request Checklist

1. Your opening should be dominated by something of reader interest.
   a) The unmotivated request is likely to defeat your purpose.
   b) When you can, develop a reader-benefit theme.
   c) The question with an obvious yes or no answer stops rather than starts consideration of your proposition.
   d) Are you promising too much (like total attendance of a group) or so bluntly as to be suspect?
   e) Don't depend on obvious flattery to win the reader's help.
   f) The use of a subject line is unsound in any C-plan letter.
   g) Explanations do not arouse interest; put them in the middle.

2. For clear, natural transitions, keep the reader in your explanation.
   a) Give necessary details to prove that your project deserves his consideration and to enable him to act as you request.
   b) But subordinate these details to what the reader gets.
   c) Adapt your letter; when you can, personalize it.
   d) If it is long, consider using his name in the second half or referring specifically to his city, work, or . . . .
   e) Don't phrase the exact request until after most of the benefits.
   f) Make the reader's participation sound easy—maybe even fun!

3. The potentially negative element requires careful treatment.
   a) Elimination of the negative element is unethical and wasteful.
   b) Minimize it by positive statement, embedded position, and minimum space.
   c) Maintain a tone of confidence; avoid apologies; but, to avoid presumptuousness, also use the conditional mood in talking about what the reader is to do: *not* "you will be scheduled to speak . . ." but "you would (or could). . . ."
   d) Don't supply excuses for your reader.
   e) Give assurance that you will handle the confidential or other restricted material in whatever limited way he specifies.

4. Introduce any enclosure skillfully:
   a) Not too early, or he'll leave the letter and maybe not return.
   b) With emphasis on what he is to do with or get from it.

5. After justifying it, ask confidently for the reader's action.
   a) Good action endings indicate specifically what to do, how to do it, helps and/or suggestions for ease of action, and reason for prompt action.
   b) If there is a time limit, justify and establish it specifically but subordinately.
   c) Establish appreciation cordially in first-person future conditional. Offer to reciprocate if appropriate. Don't "thank in advance."
   d) When you include a return envelope, subordinate it.
   e) Inject a last punch line on reader benefit.

I'm confident that these estimates allow an adequate margin of
safety.

An accessories stockturn of 3 and a markup of 50 percent
should give me a gross profit on accessories of $10,000 in 120
days. Since I've budgeted my own money for operating expenses
for six months, almost all of the $10,000 should be left to
pay for the credit stock and to reorder another $10,000 of
accessories stock. Look over the enclosed order and see if
you don't agree that the accessories I've ordered will sell
quickly.

You'll notice that the enclosed list of references is a
diversified group of Lubbock businessmen, ranging from Mr.
Logan, president of the Lubbock National Bank, to Ed Duffie,
manager of the Fix-um Garage. Any one of these men, as well
as the Lubbock Retail Credit Bureau, will be glad to write to
you about me.

I shall be grateful for your help in starting my new store.
With business progressing as it is in Lubbock, and with
fast-moving Long-Shearer accessories to sell, I feel certain
that the new store will be a success.

CASES FOR SPECIAL REQUESTS

1. You've just read an interesting article in *Conservation* (an important
magazine devoted to wildlife) on recent nesting failures of the osprey. The
article by Dr. Peter Meyer said nothing about DDT as a cause of failure;
but you, a researcher for your state's department of wildlife, are doing research on DDT effects on wild fowl. You wonder if, in his research, Dr.
Meyer saw anything that might be pertinent to your study.

2. Assume that you are head of the chemistry department in your school
and that you are working closely with the architects planning a new chemistry building. Before you can decide on space and layout of the store room,
you must settle on the best methods of storing, dispensing, and holding
students responsible for chemicals and equipment used in the labs. You
have designed a questionnaire you want answered by at least a dozen
schools similar to yours. Now write a covering letter to induce those schools
to fill it out and return it.

3. For the big fuel oil, gas, and gasoline company in a farming area,
write a letter to farm equipment dealers in your trading area to induce
them to fill out and return a questionnaire on the trends and outlook in
fuel for farm tractors. You are particularly interested in the prospects for
increasing use of LP gas.

As the only major tractor fuel dealer for miles around, you want to be
prepared to give good service if more and more farmers are going to be
changing their tractors over to using gas, or buying more new tractors designed to use gas.

4. Write Dr. Milford Farnsworth of Little Rock, the country's main supplier of rats for research labs (mainly in medical schools and psychology and zoology departments).

As the man in charge of the animals used for research in a large university medical school, you are interested in designing the best possible cage for rats—one that will hold the most rats per square foot without causing the rats to develop unnatural (and undesired) behavioral patterns. Ask for his suggestions.

5. The main interchange on I-75 at Gainesville, Florida, is seven miles west of downtown on the Newberry Road, which is called University Avenue for the five miles within the city limits. Because of I-75 and the rapid residential growth between it and town, the state highway department and the city have had to make their respective parts of the route into a four-lane divided thoroughfare. Because it is the main entrance to the city, the city beautification board and the county commission recently agreed to landscape (plant with azaleas and other shrubbery) and maintain their respective parts of the divider islands on the route. For the same reasons, however, advertisers are lining both sides wherever they can with billboards that vitiate the efforts to make the route a beautiful entrance to the city, passing right by the University of Florida.

As a professor at the University and the owner of a new home in one of the best residential developments just off the route, write a letter, assuming copies are to go to the county commission and the mayor, pointing out the futility of trying to beautify when advertisers are working at cross-purposes with you, and asking your addressees to try to ban the ugly billboards.

6. As chairman, Joe Billiard, of your university's annual week-long program designed to involve students in the serious problems of the world (called ACCENT), write a letter to one of the following men to induce him to make one of the 12 major speeches scheduled for this year's program February 8–14: U.S. Secretary of Transportation, U.S. Secretary of the Interior, and Harvard Professor Rene Debos. (Insert current names for the secretaries.)

This year's ACCENT program, "Tomorrow in Perspective," will concentrate on the change or influence science has had on society. You want speakers who will speak on the legal, moral, educational, and economical aspects of their special area of interest.

7. One of the main streets of your city has a large pothole on one of the railroad crossings. Damage to tires and front ends of all cars (including those owned and maintained by the city) results. Write a letter to the street department urging the necessary repairs (for the benefit of residents, lower maintenance for the city, and favorable attitude of the voters). The letter will come to the attention of an elected official. You have called three times about this situation.

8. In an effort to upgrade student-housing garbage disposal, large mechanical containers have been placed around. One serves four wings (16 families). Since the placement of these containers, flies and mosquitoes have so infested the area that you cannot enjoy sitting out in the yard. Write a letter to the director of students telling him of the discomfort and the health hazard, and urge him to do something about the problem.

9. As a student in mechanical engineering, you took your professor's suggestion and selected a machine-design problem growing out of your experience—two summers of experience working with Bemis Bag and Paper Co., St. Louis 63155.

There you learned about the hard time Bemis had in meeting the price competition of inferior pasted bags because its superior sewn bags are more costly to manufacture. You also saw that Bemis would almost have to find methods of cost reduction, change to cheaper bags, or give up to competitors. Furthermore, you realized that the costly part is the time required for changing the feeder chains on the machines to sew bags of different widths.

As your course problem, therefore, you decided to design a feeder device to adjust quickly by dialing to handle all the different bag widths handled by the machines. You have the design worked out; but the professor and any manufacturer will insist on a prototype for testing to see if your device will really work. For $100, which you don't have—plus ten tubes (unsewn bags) of each width for testing—you can build and test the device.

You want to persuade Bemis to supply the test tubes and the $100. Since you have to run your tests within the next three weeks (course deadline) and you need at least 10 days for constructing the prototype, you need an answer in 10 days.

If your gizmo works, Bemis can have all rights to it—you'll send your full report with drawings, specifications, even the professor's comments. You do not intend to patent your device or make any contractual arrangements with anyone else.

10. As an advanced student in industrial design at the University of Illinois, you are working on an ideal design for automobile instrument panels. You are particularly concerned with the facts of human body measurements, mental response, and muscular movements—the human engineering, more than the mechanical. Therefore you were much interested in the exclusive article in this month's *Road & Track* on the XXX prototype sports car. It showed that a lot of thought had gone into the design of the instrument panel. Since your study will cover design and placement of controls as well as gauge design, however, you feel that XXX designers might well be interested in seeing your report when you've finished—necessarily in three weeks.

One thing now puzzling you is a vague reference the article made to the XXX prototype's unique gauge illumination system. You suspect that the article was vague because XXX does not want to reveal some secrets to competitors; but you're no competition, and you would like to know the colors used and any reasons for assigning particular colors to particular gauges. Naturally you'll give credit for any special information received from a particular source. Furthermore, though you now foresee no publication, you will get approval from your sources before publication, if you ever publish.

11. For a bulletin you are writing on various machinery, procedures, and techniques in the processing of forest products, you have devised a two-page questionnaire to be sent to a sizable mailing list of small mills. The bulletin, to be published by your state university extension service, is to cover your three years of research on the best methods of processing different forest products for different purposes. You are a professor of forest products in the state university—half-time teaching and half-time research through the extension division.

In return for each filled-out questionnaire, you will send the small mill a marked copy of the bulletin—plus a brief statement of recommended changes for improving its operations.

Your research is completed and written up except for a section on current practices and problems. You and the bulletin editor have therefore scheduled your bulletin to go to press in two months—two weeks to get the questionnaires back, four weeks for analysis of the data, and two weeks for writing and editing. The data from mills will be presented statistically —no names attached—and you will later get specific approval before writing up about any individual mill's problems your questionnaire asks for.

12. While trying to work out a good questionnaire (see preceding case), you decided that a questionnaire really couldn't get the information you need. So instead of sending one, you worked out a series of one-day visits to a sound sample of 25 mills on your list.

You still need to write a persuasive-request letter, however, to go to each of the sample mills to get approval of your coming and snooping, and asking a lot of questions. You'll use essentially the same letter (changing names, addresses, and dates for the visits). You will want the mill to provide a well-informed company officer to go along with you through the plant and answer questions.

Of course you'll still send a copy of the completed bulletin; but worth more, you think, will be your willingness to answer questions as well as ask them, and to make suggestions on the spot for improving operations. In effect you are offering your services as a consultant for one day free—the kind of thing for which you usually charge $100 plus costs.

13. As a graduate student in the School of Police Training and Administration, Michigan State University, you are writing a thesis on the use of photography in law enforcement. A part of your research method is a questionnaire which you will send to a large number of reputable law-enforcement agencies.

Write the covering letter you will send to induce Mr. Karl Engel, a lawyer who is secretary to the Florida Chiefs of Police Association, to fill out the three-page questionnaire. Data from returned questionnaires will be largely statistical (no specific names attached); but for any quotes you want to use, you will write to get specific permission. The questionnaire takes only ten minutes (it's largely a checkoff form), a return envelope is enclosed, and you're sure Engel has information that will be helpful and appreciated. You suspect he will be interested in your findings, an abstract of which the *Police Gazette* has already said it wants to publish. Your schedule means that you'll have to start tabulating and interpreting results in two weeks to meet both University and *Gazette* deadlines.

Engel's recent speech before a national convention of law-enforcement officers, reprinted in the current *Police Gazette,* shows his concern for the bad reputations some law-enforcement agencies have developed and his interest in improving methods of investigation and data collection for courtroom use.

14. For many years Montgomery's Index of Status Characteristics has been used to determine social classes among white people. Psychologists have found, however, that the status characteristics of black people differ a great deal from the status characteristics of whites. Before going into a thorough study of these differences, you, a graduate student, set up a questionnaire and covering letter to be sent to all black families in your area. Unlike the Montgomery Index, which asked about house type and dwelling area, your study asks about money spent for entertainment, for funerals, for musical instruments, etc., because these are the things you found help the blacks attain status. Write a persuasive covering letter that will encourage blacks to fill out the questionnaire. Indirectly this study should benefit all of them.

15. As the letter-writing consultant for a local community improvement association, write the copy for a form letter to local merchants for donations of money, clothing, candy, toys, canned goods, or other products to go in Christmas baskets to be distributed to needy families. The major emphasis is to be on money, but invite other contributions too. Except for the money (which they are to mail in), you will offer to pick up contributions at the merchant's convenience (they are to tell you time and place).

You have arranged with the local newspaper to list donors, without specifying what the donation was, in a story about the results of your drive.

16. Assume that you are in a large city where you have a position you
like. You are grateful to have had your training from the School of Business. You feel that you'll advance with your company and that the more
people you know, the better you will do. At lunch today with three New
Yorkers, you listened as they were talking about their alumni business administration luncheon group that meets once a month to exchange ideas
and to have fun. After hearing their enthusiastic reports on their meetings,
you decide to try to find out how many graduates from your School of
Business are in your city. Your university Ex-Student Association is cooperative and sends you a list of 300 names. Next you call the Park Plaza
Hotel and reserve the University Room for 7 P.M. on a date in the middle
of next month. And last you write the letter persuasively selling your idea
to the 300 alumni. You want them to send in names and addresses of other
School of Business ex-students, and you want them to make their dinner
reservations at the hotel early.

17. You are John Drinkwater, chairman of All-University Day, University of Texas, Austin 78746. One of your jobs is to line up speakers. This is
an annual event when outstanding people come to the campus and mix
with the students at a luncheon and in panel discussions. Student interest
in these discussions is keen; the business and industry exhibits are interesting and instructive. These sessions furnish good employment leads to both
students and business visitors. As a sample of the kind of letter you would
adapt to all your speakers, write to Larry Gaddis, vice president in charge
of personnel, Mallory Manufacturing Company, 954 Parkcrest, Houston,
Texas 77023, where many of your graduates go to work, inviting him to
send an appropriate representative from his company to each of the six
panels (name them). All speakers come at their own expense. You do,
however, have the speakers as guests at the All-University Day luncheon.

18. Sit in the chair of Professor T. D. Garner, a man of many activities
who right now, as director of the Illinois Business Conference, has the task
of lining up some 15 speakers for the meeting about six months from now
in Chicago at the Palmer House.

One man he'd like very much to speak before the retailers' group is
Marvin Bingham, president of Marcey-Dorch, New York 10086 (about
whom he has read in a recent *Wall Street Journal*). Garner wants especially
to have a headline speaker to attract these men and women to the current
meeting because their attendance at the conference has always been the
poorest of the groups attending (they don't want to be away from their
business over the weekend). So he has decided to test his ability to persuade big-time operators to come at their own expense and without a

speaker's fee (which most of the men he'd want to invite are accustomed to receiving) in this one letter to Bingham before writing all the other letters he will have to send.

The *Wall Street Journal* article tells of Bingham's metoric rise in retailing to the controlling ownership of Marcey-Dorch and half a dozen other stores like it, and quotes him as planning a chain of smaller stores all over the country. Adding to that with talk he has picked up at conventions, Garner figures that Bingham may likely be interested in looking over the situation in Illinois, preparatory to opening stores. Garner decides that this idea is the entering wedge for the letter which will ask Bingham to attend the meeting and to talk to the retailers' group meeting (Garner figures he can corral at least 150 for it) on the Friday of the meeting, 2 to 3 P.M., about bonus systems, promotional practices, or any other personnel management problem and how he has met it—and then for another hour to lead a group discussion. It's the sort of thing Bingham could do easily and well.

Since the professor needs to plan far ahead, when you write the letter for him (on university letterhead stationery), you'll ask Bingham if he can let you know within a month.

19. The Youth Neighborhood Corps of your city commissions you to write an effective appeal for raising money to send deserving boys to summer camp. The fund maintains four fully equipped camps in (assume a location where lots of boys from your area *do* go). They hope to have 2,000 boys this summer. The mailing consists of a letter, simple two-color folder, and a reply envelope with stamp pasted on. Write the letter copy, explaining that $25 will pay for one week for one boy, or $50 for two weeks. Your mailing list is made up of 15,000 doctors, lawyers, architects, and educators.

20. The Committee for Action asks you to help write an effective letter for support of the new Civic Center in your community. The center will be built next year if the money can be raised. Assume that the local newspapers have carried publicity stories about the center and federated clubs have been urged to have the Civic Center as their project. The land has been given by civic-minded citizens for the center, but the community must raise at least $500,000 this year so that building can get started. What you hope to do is to get the famous TV star, Bonnie Blagg, to come to the local theater and give two concerts, the proceeds of which will go to the Civic Center. She is a native of your town who has become nationally-known. According to her aunt she is to be in your city next summer on a visit. Try to sell Miss Blagg on coming to the theater and giving an hour-and-a-half show in the afternoon (2–3:30) and repeating it the next night (8–9:30), with the only reward being the good it will do. You can have the performance well advertised through the newspaper, television, and radio (all donated). Junior Welfare will take care of programs, ushering, and a reception on the Civic Center lawn (after the afternoon performance).

21. Patton's Cleaners and Dyers has various branches in all kinds of neighborhoods in a large city. The wife of Samuel P. Adams, a young executive, took some shirts to one in a good neighborhood, and Mrs. Brown (clerk) promised the shirts on Tuesday. At 8:15 A.M. on Wednesday, Adams asked for his shirts on his way to take his two boys to school; he himself had an office appointment by 9. Ticket? Didn't know he had to have one. On returning after going home for the ticket, "Not in yet." Under pressure, Mrs. Brown admitted that delivery had arrived on Tuesday afternoon but had not been taken out of boxes in the back storeroom and put on revolving finder racks by number; she declined Adams's offer of help in finding—against rules for customers to go behind partition. Promised and picked up in an hour, with an "I'm sorry about the delay." Question: "Whose order prevented you from letting me help in the emergency an hour ago?" Store rule—nobody behind that partition. "Aren't people in our neighborhood honest?" But they'll tear packages to find, instead of getting their tickets. "But I had my ticket. Even in an emergency, no relaxing of the rule?" Mrs. Brown didn't want to get fired.

At his office Adams decided to try to do Patton's an undeserved favor— get relaxation in exceptional circumstances of an ironclad rule that will lose customers. Called main office. Assistant manager explained: "Yes, it's a firm rule; we transfer girls among branches, some in bad neighborhoods; customers behind partitions mean confusion, maybe worse." "But I'm not a con; Mrs. Brown has seen me several times; my boys were with me." But rules are rules.

As Samuel P. Adams, write the manager, William P. Shade, to get a change in the unreasonable policy that will lose business for Patton's. Also bring in, as secondary, the importance of having things ready when promised.

22. As chairman of the city development board, you have designed a questionnaire to collect information about uses and needs of transportation facilities to and from San Jose, California. The questionnaire has five columns, headed as follows:

1. City or area destination
2. Number of trips during preceding 12 months
3. Means of transportation used (car, rail, air, or bus)
4. Means you would have used if convenient
5. Number of trips not made because of inadequate or inconvenient transportation

On the advice of a statistician, you have selected a stratified sample of San Jose people to receive questionnaires. Your immediate job is to write a covering letter that will induce these people to fill out and return the questionnaires.

23. As Roscoe W. Shiplett, Student Government Association, Florida State University, Tallahassee, Florida 32306, write Mrs. Evelyn Bankhead, organizer of National Organization for Women (NOW), 987 Belmont Street, Washington, D.C. 20008, and ask her to speak with no fee at AC-CENT, a student-sponsored event with limited funds at your university. Set the proper dates and time. Mrs. Bankhead was formerly active in network television at National Broadcasting Corporation. Her work in TV (NBC—"Face the Nation") is well known. In her present position she is editor of NOW's publication, *The Vocal Majority*. The purpose of AC-CENT is to broaden college students' interest and understanding. You can pay travel expenses.

IN THESE TIMES of mass production, products are usually made for sale to satisfy the needs and desires of other people—rarely for the maker's own use. Often the ultimate users are not conscious of their needs or desires until somebody else points them out. If such potential users realize their needs, marketing the product is a matter of making it available when and where wanted at an acceptable price, and filling the orders. If not, marketing also involves sales promotion—pointing out needs and desires, and how the product will satisfy them—by personal selling, advertising, and mail.

GENERAL SALES STRATEGY

Whether you sell by mail or in person, your procedures are essentially the same. You seek to gain the reader's attentive interest, convince him that your proposal is worthwhile, and confidently ask him to take action.

In some cases you already have favorable attention, as when you answer an inquiry about your product. In those cases your job is to marshal your sales points and adapt them to your reader in a message that answers his questions, convinces, and asks for action. You've already learned to do this in your study of invited sales (Chapter 5).

But in prospecting—or "cold-turkey selling," as many professionals label the procedure—you have the preliminary job of getting attention and arousing interest so that your reader will be eager to see what you have to say.

The surest way to get your reader to read is to stress some benefit to him. This benefit theme must come from what you have to sell. Obviously, then, you must know a good deal about your product, its uses, and the kind of people who might benefit from it. From analysis of your product and prospect comes the selection of the appeal to stress. And from a knowledge of marketing methods and people's buying habits comes the decision of what you want your reader to do after he finishes reading your message.

Analyzing the product

The first and foremost consideration in marketing any product is the answer to "What will it do for people?" You sell only when you satisfy a need or desire.

Although you need to know a great deal about the physical characteristics of the product (size, shape, color, length, breadth, height, composition, or operation, for example), physical description of the product is not effective selling. *The psychological description—interpretation of physical features in terms of reader benefits—is the effective part of selling.*

Aluminum cooking ware, for example, may be just metal pots and pans to you. But to a cook, aluminum utensils (in psychological description):

—Give lifetime wear.

—Maintain smooth surfaces because they do not nick, chip, crack, or peel.

—Provide even, uniform heat, thus decreasing the chances that food will burn on the top, bottom, and sides, yet be raw in the middle.

—Enable the cook to do waterless cooking or cooking at a reduced temperature and thus preserve food values that would otherwise go down the drain.

—Make dishwashing easier.

A dictation machine has buttons, wires, wheels, lights, and a motor. So what? It enables a business executive to record his ideas, it is true. But it also enables him to

—Release the high-priced dictation time of his secretary for other duties.

—Dictate when (and with a portable machine, where) he wants to—as time permits and as ideas occur to him.

—Arrange work for his office staff in his absence.

—Have a record which does not get "cold," which anyone can transcribe with greater accuracy than is often possible with an individual's shorthand notes.

—Have a record he himself can play back without an interpreter.

Insulation is not just pellets or bats of certain sizes and materials. To a true salesman, it keeps houses warmer in winter, cooler in summer. It thus reduces heating costs in cold months and cooling costs in warm months. It also deadens outside noises. Since it is fire-resistant, it reduces chances of fire and also decreases fire damage if and when fire breaks out. In view of all these reasons, insulation adds to the resale value of a house.

Even a child's tricycle (made of steel and chrome, with first-grade rubber tires) does more than provide pleasure for its youthful owner. It teaches him muscular coordination, helps to develop his visual perception and judgment, and develops his leg muscles. It also releases his parents from a certain amount of time spent in direct supervision.

You seek through such analysis to identify the promises of benefit you can make to a reader considering use of your product. Through psychological description you establish a worth he might not recognize if he saw the product *only* through his own eyes.

Psychological description is interpretation, which deserves primary emphasis. Physical description is specific detail, evidence incorporated *subordinately* to bear out the promises established in psychological-description phrases and passages.

For convincing your reader that your product is the one he should spend his money for rather than miss the benefits it will give him, you must have details concerning how, of what, by whom, and where it is made and how effectively it operates. The circumstances under which it is sold (warranties, guarantees, servicing) also affect your analysis and subsequent presentation. The physical description is necessary for conviction, but in the final sales presentation it is subservient to psychological description—the interpretation of the thing to be sold in terms of pleasure, increased efficiency, increased profit, or whatever benefit you can most specifically promise your prospect.

Finding the prospects

True prospects are people who need the service your product will give, can pay for it, and are not getting it. Determining who these people are and their addresses is the job of making a mailing list. Of course you can easily get names and addresses; but are all these people prospects?

Some people who appear to be prospects will already be enjoying the benefits of your product or one like it. In that case they aren't true prospects. But unless you know for certain (through a list of owners, which you may have for your own product but are not likely to have for a competitor's), you need to find out. And the cheapest way to find out is to solicit them.

If you are selling a product everybody needs, all you have to verify is your prospects' ability to pay. But few products are used by everybody (and when they are, direct mail is not the best way to sell them; direct mail is a specialized class medium rather than a mass medium).

In determining need, you have to start with logical analysis. For instance, you wouldn't try to sell bikinis to Eskimos or mackinaws to Cubans. You wouldn't try to sell a central heating unit to apartment dwellers. You certainly wouldn't try to sell yachts to government clerical workers. Nor would you sell many hearing aids to college students.

You would seek to sell a piece of office equipment to some business owner or manager, aluminum cooking ware to housewives and restaurant owners, insulation to homeowners.

Sex, age (and a close corollary, physical condition), family and dwelling status, vocation, geographical location, and financial situation are some of the more significant considerations in assuming that someone is a logical prospect for your product. In some cases you will need to go further than a logical analysis and make a marketing survey.

Most sales letters have to be turned out in large numbers to secure the volume necessary for profit. But even when they go out by the thousands, you send them to a *selected* mailing list. And no mailing will be any good if the list of names to whom it is sent does not represent enough real prospects. Once you determine the general classes of people who are prospects, your next step is securing specific names and addresses to provide yourself with a mailing list.

What you want is a list of people in similar circumstances; the more similarities, the better. You can make your own list, rent one, or buy one. If you have the time and the know-how, you may be able to make a better list than you can buy. The phone book or city directory is a list of people in one city, but they usually do not have enough similarities to justify putting all of them on the mailing list for your product. The yellow pages or other kinds of specialized directories give you at least one important similarity as a basis for selection. Newspaper clippings and trade reports are helpful in getting names for an initial list or adding names to an already existing one. Often the best list is the firm's present customers. Coupon returns in space advertising will build a list for you.

You can get a big list of low purity (that is, including lots of people who are not really prospects) and low accuracy (lots of wrong addresses)[1] very cheaply. The more specifications (similarities) you put on, the higher the price.

A list house will get you almost any list you order if you're willing to pay the price. There are so many suppliers of lists in all parts of the country that the Department of Commerce issues a directory of them.

Whether you buy, rent, or compile your list, however, for sales effectiveness it contains the correct names and addresses of people with common

---

[1] About 15 percent of Americans' addresses change yearly, according to professional mailing-list people.

characteristics. Only then can you adapt your talking points and your references in persuasive fashion, as discussed on pages 62–65.

Choosing the appeal

From the analysis of your product come your possible sales points. But you can't tell all of them in detail in one letter, or you'll have a cluttered, shotgun-pattern letter instead of a piercing, rifle-bullet message. After listing them, deciding who the prospects are, and getting your best mailing list, your next job is to select for emphasis *the central selling point*—the one big theme around which to build your letter. It is the answer to this question: *What one feature of the product is most likely to induce the prospect to buy?* Other supporting points you interweave, relegate to an enclosure, or leave for a subsequent mailing.

People buy for many reasons: to make or save money, to preserve health, to save time, to avoid exertion, to protect themselves or their families, to protect or build a reputation, and for many other reasons, which, if you want to, you can find listed in multitude in countless books on psychology, salesmanship, sociology, and marketing. Pride, love, beauty, acquisitiveness, self-indulgence, self-preservation, curiosity, and fear play their parts in inducing interest and stimulating the final action.

Man is both rational and emotional. He needs a rational reason to support an emotional desire for something. Arguing the relative importance of rational and emotional appeals in selling is comparable to a vigorous debate over which came first, the chicken or the egg. In writing good sales letters, if you remind your reader of a need your product will meet and supply evidence to back up your promise, if you stress what you think is the most important reason why the particular group of readers will buy, you won't need to worry about whether you are employing rational or emotional techniques. You'll be using both. And that's as it should be.

Certainly effective adaptation is necessary. Your choice of theme for your message will be affected by one or more of the significant considerations of the prospect's sex, vocation, location, age, source and amount of income, and social, professional, or educational status. One of the most obvious differences that affect your choice of theme is that between dealers and consumers. Dealers buy for the *profit* they will make on reselling. That depends on the *number* they can sell and the *markup*, less any expense and trouble necessary in backing up guarantees with replacements, repairs, and service calls. Consumers buy for the various services the product will render. But even in dealer letters you wouldn't write the same things to a large metropolitan eastern store that you would to a small rural southern store.

You can't be certain, either, of the wisdom of your choice of theme. Testing two or more different letters on a part of your list in a preliminary mailing (about which we'll say more later) may help you to arrive at a choice, but sometimes even testing does not resolve your dilemma.

For example, in selling steel desks and chairs to fraternity houses, two writers came up with two different themes. One played up comfort and subordinated the factor of appearance; the other stressed appearance to the subordination of durability and comfort:

How many hours of each day do you spend at your desk?

Three? Four? Maybe more?

From experience you know how important it is that your desk be roomy and your chair comfortable. You can be assured of the comfort and convenience you need with Carroll steel desks and chairs. Especially designed as a study unit for college men, they are also sturdy and good looking.

Since the desk is 31 inches high, you can cross your knees beneath the top. Or if you want to sit with your feet on the desk, propped back in your chair, you can do so without marring the surface or breaking the steel-welded chair.

Whether you choose the steel top at $20.75 or the linoleum top at $15.75, you don't need to worry about nicks and scratches. Either top, 28 inches wide by 42 inches long, gives you ample room for all the books and papers you have in use. Shelves at one end and a large drawer keep your other books and supplies at hand.

And you can have Carroll desks and chairs in battle gray, olive green, or mahogany.

After you've had a chance to read over the enclosed leaflet (which explains the attractive quantity discounts available to you), you'll see why Carroll study equipment was recently chosen for dormitories at Michigan, Iowa, and Princeton.

Wouldn't you be proud to show your rushees uniform desks and chairs?

Fine-looking study equipment will create an initial favorable impression. And they will realize, as you do, that following rush week comes work.

In Carroll steel desks and chairs you'll have study equipment that will stay good looking and provide years of comfortable use. The top has been chemically treated to avoid burns and scratches and to eliminate stains from liquids. Welded-steel construction assures you that your Carroll desk and chair will retain their attractive straight lines. And a choice of battle gray, olive green, or mahogany enables you to select a color which will blend in well with your present furnishings.

Either the steel top at $20.75 or the linoleum top at $15.75 will retain its attractive appearance over the years.

The ample work space of the desk—28 inches wide, 42 inches long, 31 inches high, with shelves at one end and a generous drawer—and the swivel chair of body-comfort design mean comfort for study as well as for long bull sessions.

After you've had a chance to read over the enclosed leaflet (which explains the attractive quantity discounts available to you), you'll see why Carroll study equipment was recently chosen for dormitories at Michigan, Iowa, and Princeton.

Both these letters are well-knit presentations of their selected themes. Each establishes the same information about the product. But we suspect that the first version would sell more chairs to house committees, because on most campuses comfortable study conditions are more important than appearance, and for a longer time than rushing conditions. You would have to test to be sure.

A letter addressed to the appropriate purchasing agent for the dormitories would wisely have stressed still a different possible theme—holding down maintenance and replacement costs.

You'll see further illustration of how sales appeals vary from letter to letter in the two series which appear in the final pages of this chapter.

Identifying the specific goal

You may know before you begin your prewriting analysis exactly what you want your reader to do. But you'll want to be sure that the action you request your reader to take is logical in the light of purchasing conditions, which are governed by the nature of the product, the circumstances of the customer, and authorized, organized marketing channels.

Many sales letters cannot and should not drive for completion of the sale. All they do is ask for a show of interest (and thus help to weed out all but genuine prospects). You may want your reader only to request a booklet; you may want him to come to your showroom; you may want him to give you some information about himself; you may want him to authorize the visit of a salesman; in many instances, of course, you can logically ask him to order. Regardless of what the appropriate action is, decide on it and identify it specifically before you begin to write.

All possible versions of the letter about fraternity desks and chairs should have some type of action ending, identifying payment and shipping conditions if an order by letter is appropriate or—more likely in this case —inviting the readers to come to a display room or to authorize the visit of a representative.

WRITING THE PROSPECTING SALES LETTER

After thorough study of your product and prospect, selection of theme, and decision on your specific goal, you develop that theme in a C–plan letter patterned by some adaptation of the standard sales presentation: Attention, Interest, Conviction, and Action. If you want to substitute *Desire* for *Conviction* in letters appealing largely to emotion, go ahead; it won't alter your basic procedure. If you want to call it Promise, Picture, Prove, and Push, you won't go wrong because of your labels.

But don't think of a presentation in four or five or even three parts—like a play in three acts. In a good letter, smoothly written for coherence and unity of impression, you can't separate the parts cleanly. Although we analyze the writing of a sales letter in terms of getting attentive interest, establishing belief and trust, overcoming price resistance, and confidently asking for action, the final version of it should be a presentation that is smooth because of its coherence and persuasive because of its singleness of purpose and progression of thought.

Getting attentive interest

If you believe in your product and what it can do for your reader, you'll have no big problem starting a sales letter effectively. All you need to do is hold up the promise of the big benefit your product can contribute to the reader. If it's a genuine benefit and your reader is a real prospect, he'll read.

Yet because of the clamor for attention which many advertisers talk about and write about, many advertisements and letters put on a show with the bizarre and the irrelevant in order to make the reader stop and listen. They seem to say to the reader: "We know you won't listen otherwise; so we're standing on our heads to attract your attention. Of course, standing on our heads won't tell you a thing about our product or what it can do for you, but it'll make you sit up and take notice."

To that, all we can say is: "Sure! The freak at the circus commands attention. And if sheer attention is all you want, walk down Madison Avenue or Michigan Avenue in a bikini or in shorts. You'll get attention. But is it appropriate? Is it in good taste? Will it really help to induce the reader to buy?"

Relevancy is important. Without it, your trick or gadget may be a distraction and a detriment rather than an assist to your sales effort. Tricks are legion, and they create talk, even notoriety, about you. But *unless they lead naturally, plausibly, and shortly to what your product can do for your reader, they're not worth the effort and expense.*

The American public is a highly educated public. It is quick to criticize or, worse yet, to laugh at advertising and its methods. It hasn't bought the Brooklyn Bridge for a couple of generations. It recognizes a gold brick for what it is worth. The farmer's daughter has been to town—even if it's only via TV. Smug patter about the 14-year-old mentality is beguiling—and dangerous. Even the 14-year-old mind recognizes the difference between "show-off-manship" and real salesmanship.

You'll read much and hear much about tricks, stunts, and gadgets. Good-luck pennies, four-leaf clovers, keys that open the door to everything from business success to a happy home life with your dog, rubber bands (which most of the time only stretch the reader's patience), cartoons, faked telegrams in yellow window envelopes, simulated handwritten messages, names of readers written at the top of the page in red, blue, gold ("the symbol of things precious, and your name means much to us!"), boldface numbers ("**2,400,001!** What's the 1 for? That's *your* copy!"), shorthand copy, Chinese writing, the early bird with the worm in its mouth, checkerboards, mirrors, alarm clocks—all these and many others may distract from your sales message rather than assist it unless they enable you to cut through quickly to the benefit your product can render.

Such tricks have been overused and misapplied in so many instances that one advertiser recently sent the following letter (which you'll recognize as a trick in itself):

```
I have never tried to fool you.

I have never sent you an order form that looks like an
authentic bank check, with or without signatures and
countersignatures!

And I've never sent you a bondlike certificate apparently so
valuable that it startles you briefly—before you throw it
away.

I have never used a brown envelope to make you think your tax
refund has finally arrived.

In fact, I've never even sent you a postage stamp!

We here at Bowen's think you're too intelligent to fall for
such nonsense!

We're convinced that Bowen customers are an alert and critical,
not a gullible, audience.  New gimmicks and catchphrases are
not going to influence you. . . .
```

You may dream up a trick or gadget occasionally that isn't old stuff to most of your audience and that naturally, plausibly, and quickly illustrates or introduces the benefit your product can render. If it can meet the tests of relevance, plausibility, good taste, and speed, you may want to use it. A fire-sale letter typed in red may have salutary appeal. A check form made out to the reader, immediately followed by the lead, "What would it mean to you to get a *real* check like this *every month?*" may plausibly preface sales talk about an annuity or health insurance.

The sales manager who sent a letter on cellophane with the lead, "Here's a value for you that is as clear-cut as the paper on which it is written," used a good (but very expensive) gadget to command attention.

So we do not mean to imply that all tricks, gadgets, and humorous letters are undesirable. Certainly you'll find occasional opportune times for the whimsical, the gracefully turned phrase, the chuckling at man and his idiosyncrasies, and the outright humorous. But before you use what you think is a bright, clever, or punny approach, recall the story that seasoned advertisers tell of the woman who asked her husband if he had seen a certain clever ad. "What was it about?" her husband asked. "I don't remember," the lady replied, "but it was right next to that homely X, X and Y ad."

If you can phrase an opening which is deft, novel, and catchy, use it—provided it paves the way quickly and naturally to the introduction of what your product can do for your reader. If you can't, forget about it.

The benefit-contribution-product beginning is always applicable and always good. Associate the benefit with your reader, then bring in the product as the provider of the benefit, and you have a good opening.

A business-reporting service used the following successful opening in a letter to contractors:

```
A lot of money spent
on new construction
in your area—

—is going to wind up in somebody's pocket . . . and it might
as well be yours instead of your competitor's!
```

Another reporting agency got good attention with this opening:

```
        WHAT SORT OF GOVERNMENT
     WILL DOMINATE YOUR BUSINESS
     IN THE DIFFICULT PERIOD AHEAD?
```

A laundry got the favorable attention of housewives with

```
We'll wash your shirts, iron them to please the man of the
house, and wrap them in cellophane—for four thin dimes.
```

and another varied the same theme with

```
Would you wash a shirt, iron it to please the most demanding
man, and wrap it in cellophane—for 40 cents?
```

A savings and loan association led with

```
Do your savings work hard enough for you?
```

And an insurance company seeking to sell education insurance to parents of small children paved the way with

```
A small monthly saving now will buy your youngster a gift
worth $154,000.  There's no catch to it.

The $154,000—an estate even a man of wealth could be proud to
leave his son or daughter—is the difference between the
average lifetime earnings of a college graduate and one
without this special education, according to a recent national
survey made by the Bureau of the Census.
```

Selling an automatic typewriter to office managers, the following opening (below a clipped-on photograph of a girl powdering her nose while surrounded by three of the machines referred to) pinpoints a real problem and its solution:

```
What happens when a girl "powders her nose" in the offices of
the Northeastern Mutual Life Insurance Company?

When her typewriter stops, production ceases.  And office
costs go up.
```

A variation of theme for the same product went this way:

```
"I've had five years' experience with the Mutual Life Insurance
Company, can type 140 words a minute, am willing to work each
day indefinitely, do not get tired, and demand no salary."
```

```
Would you hire this typist?  We did.  And she typed this letter
in two minutes.

Of course, it isn't human.  It's a machine—the Robo-Typist—
which types any letter you want from a record roll at 140
words a minute.
```

Note that in all these quoted openings the lead is simply a reminder of a need for which the product comes in shortly as an agent for satisfying that need. They do not command, preach, cajole, beg, or exhort. They do not challenge. They do not scream in superlatives (finest, amazing) with exclamation points! They do not begin with talk of the product itself ("Now you too can have XYZ dog biscuits!") or the company ("53 years of doing business").

Good openings positively, specifically, and vividly, but believably, say or imply, "As help in handling this specific problem, I suggest . . . ." They get attentive interest through psychological description of the product in use benefiting the reader. Thus they cause the reader to want more information, especially on how the product can fulfill the promise.

Establishing belief and trust

Having made the promise, a letter must quickly supply evidence to back it up. If the opening is successful, it has established tentative favor or agreeableness rather than serious doubt. In effect, the reader has mentally nodded his head in agreement. The next part of your sales letter—which ordinarily consumes the greatest amount of space—tells him how your product does meet his need and *gives specific information that will make him believe you.* You thus maintain and continue the agreement you establish in the start of the letter.

Explanations and descriptions of the product *in use* are how you handle this part. Word pictures of how it works and how it is made, performance tests, testimonials of users, statistics of users, facts and figures on sales, guarantees, free-trial offers, offers of demonstrations, and samples are some of your most common devices. Note how the following letter supplies evidence to support its opening claim.[2]

```
The Carriage Return Lever
On a Manual Typewriter
Is Costing You Money . . .

. . . and it's money you don't have to spend any more.

Human Efficiency, Inc., of New York City, has completed a
```

---

[2] Yes, this letter is long—as most effective sales letters are. If you're worried about length, remember that the firm which has tested more of its sales letters than any other, Time, Inc., never writes one-page sales letters any more—they always pulled less under test. Remember, too, the statement of one of the nation's most renowned consultants, Howard Dana Shaw, that in general a long letter will outpull a short one if it tells, in an interesting way, something of value to the reader. But don't confuse length with a lack of conciseness.

series of exacting tests and confirms that you can save as much as one man-hour each day for each typist you employ when you install Speedo Carriage Returns on your manual typewriters.

Watch one of your typists. Every time she returns the carriage to the next line, her left hand makes three movements. When the bell signals the end of a line, her hand moves from the keys to the lever, throws the lever, and then returns to the keys. It looks fast and easy, doesn't it? It is—an expert typist can do it in just one second.

Just one second, but one second becomes one minute when your typist types 60 lines. And that one minute multiplies to one hour every 3,600 lines. From your experience as an office manager, you know that 3,600 lines aren't very many for an efficient stenographer to type, especially the short lines required for orders and invoices.

Using a Speedo, your typist performs one step—not three—to return the carriage to the next line. When the bell signals the end of the line, she presses a foot pedal; the carriage automatically spaces correctly and returns to the left margin. One tenth of a second—not one second—has elapsed.

And because her hands do not have to leave the keyboard, accuracy increases when you install Speedos. Human Efficiency tested 150 typists using Speedos for two weeks in 20 different large plants. They showed a 16 percent reduction in errors. Naturally, the amount of time spent in erasing errors was also reduced by 16 percent.

Part of the explanation for the increase in output and decrease of errors is a reduction in fatigue. Throwing a carriage just once doesn't amount to much, but when your typist repeats the same act hundreds of times she uses up as much energy as she would scrubbing the floor of your office. The Speedo not only reduces the strain by two thirds but shifts it to the leg and foot, which can bear it far better than the arm. Tests of 45 typists employed by the Kenoya Wholesale Grocery Company of Columbus, Ohio, showed that after two weeks they increased by 9 percent the amount of copy produced daily.

Clamped to the carriage-return lever, the Speedo connects to the foot pedal by a thin wire. The adjustment is simple; you can put one on any standard typewriter in less than five minutes.

Turn to pages 1 and 2 of the enclosed folder and read the complete report of the tests. On page 3 you'll find comments of typists who've used the Speedo and the comments of their office managers. Read how the typists all agree that they had no difficulty learning to use the Speedo efficiently.

Page 4 gives you data on prices and shipping. Note that the Speedo with all its advantages—plus an unconditional 90-day guarantee—is yours for only $4.50. And by ordering a dozen for $46 you save 70 cents on each one.

Fill out the enclosed order blank and send it to us in the return envelope provided. We'll immediately ship your Speedos to you by whatever method you direct, either prepaid or c.o.d. Within 10 days at the most you'll be able to see the increased output and accuracy of your typists.

Surely you remember that sincerity is essential to the reader's belief and trust, that you-viewpoint description is vital, that psychological description in terms of the reader's use and benefits is far superior to mere physical description of the product, that specific words in positive language are necessary to effective sales techniques, and that enclosures (properly introduced) can often supplement letters effectively. If not, turn back and review the persuasion principles in Chapter 3 and the analysis of the invited sales letter in Chapter 5. All we're suggesting is that you apply the same principles.

Overcoming price resistance

You've already studied effective ways of handling dollar talk too (back in the discussion of the invited sales letter, pp. 127–28). The principles are the same in prospecting sales. Were we to repeat them here, we'd just take up space which would merely waste your time if you remember the former discussion.

Asking confidently and specifically for action

Likewise, if we discussed again what we've already told you and illustrated for you repeatedly about action endings (indicate what you want your reader to do and how to do it, make it easy and make it sound easy, and supply a stimulus to prompt action in a quick reference to the contribution the product can make to the life of the reader), we'd be using your time unnecessarily and adding to production costs. Furthermore, the summary checklist at the end of this chapter (p. 365) itemizes the points specifically. It helps you to review and your instructor to evaluate your letter.

ADAPTING TO CLASSES

All good sales letters follow the basic procedures advocated in the preceding pages. Only in their talking points and in their interpretation and references do they differ as they go to farmers instead of bankers, to lawyers instead of engineers, to consumers as opposed to dealers.

Much fluff is written and said about letters to women. Such talk is misleading. Lots of evidence points to the fact that the American woman—and the homemaker in particular—is a sharp customer, as demanding and calculating in reading the pages of catalogs and magazines as a purchasing agent for a firm is. She's no different when she reads a letter.

If you are a person of feeling and imagination and are unselfish enough to forget yourself in analyzing another person's (or group of persons') circumstances, you won't have much trouble writing successfully adapted letter copy.

As an illustration of how tone and talking points differ, study the following two letters. The first is to a homeowner, the second to a dealer. In both cases the product is a lawn mower which eliminates hand clipping.

```
                                          Lawn-mowing Time
Extra Time for
Summer Rest and Fun!

You can cut your lawn-mowing time in half with an easy-
operating Multimower because you can eliminate the hand
clipping and trimming.

The Multimower gathers all the grass it cuts too.

So with just one run over the lawn with your Multimower, your
lawn is in shape.  And it's just a light workout.  You can cut
your grass flush against fences, trees, and flower beds.  The
interlocking rotary cutters enable you to mow tall grass and
tough weeds with no more effort than it takes to cut short
grass.  And you're less tired when you get through because you
push only the minimum weight when you use this 28-pound
mower.  It's light enough for almost any member of the
household to use.

Even though the Multimower is light, you have a precision
mower of sturdy construction and strength-tested materials.
The drive shaft is mounted on free-rolling, factory-lubricated,
sealed ball bearings which keep dirt and water from rusting
these parts.  And the cutters are self-sharpening.  So your
Multimower is always ready for you to use.  All you need to do
is put in the gas.

If the weather keeps you from mowing your lawn on schedule and
grass gets a little too high, simply adjust the handle knob to
the cutting height you want, and push your Multimower easily
across your lawn, cutting a clean, even 16-inch swath.

Many of the 8,000 enthusiastic Multimower owners have been
using theirs for over two years.  Some of their statements,
along with illustrations and the details of our 90-day
structural guarantee, you can read on the two inside pages.
You'll see, too, that we pay shipping charges to your door at
the economical price of $89.95.  The time you save on the first
summer's Multimowing is probably worth more than that.

Use the handy order mailer to send us your check or money
order.  Within a week after you mail it, you'll be able to cut,
trim, and gather up the grass on your lawn in only one easy,
timesaving Multimowing.
```

The letter to a dealer stresses the same points, to show why he can expect sales to his customers; but it does so more rapidly and concisely, in order to concentrate on sales aids, price spreads, promptness and regularity of supply, and service as parts of the profit-making picture.

Certainly, of necessity, a dealer is habitually more money-conscious than the average consumer. And his reasons for buying are more complex. He may be more rational in his evaluation of a product than a consumer and probably is more critical. Still the approach is the same as in any sales letters: It seeks the answer to the ever-present question, "What will it do for me?" To a dealer the answer is always "profits," but profits depend on salability (the features of the product that cause people to buy), on service-ability, and on markup. Since salability—features attracting buyers—is usually the main point, the psychological description becomes *interpretation of those features in terms of consumer appeal*. A dealer is also interested in promptness and regularity of filling his orders, and in guarantee and service arrangement. And if you provide any advertising or other selling aids, he will be interested in seeing how they help him sell more—as in the following letter:

When you show a customer a Multimower, a lawn mower completely new in design and principle, which cuts and trims a lawn in one operation, you have a quick sale, a satisfied customer, and a $29.95 profit.

Men like the Multimower because it gives them more time to spend in enjoyable summer recreation. It cuts right up to walls, fences, trees, and flower beds and thus eliminates the need for hand trimming in spots not reached by the ordinary mower. Its easily adjustable cutting-height regulator and self-sharpening cutters that slice down the toughest kinds of grass, dandelions, and weeds will assure them of having a trim, neat lawn in half the time they've formerly spent.

Both men and women like the Multimower because it's light weight —only 28 pounds—means easy pushing. The quiet operation of the interlocking cutters has won approval of 8,000 Multimower users. They like it, too, because it is permanently lubricated and self-sharpening. With a minimum of care it's always ready for use. Just put in the gas, and it's ready to go.

No doubt many of your customers have been reading about the Multimower in the full-page, four-color monthly ads that started running in <u>Homeowners</u>, <u>Life</u>, and <u>Vacation</u> magazines in March and will continue through July. A reprint, along with testimonials and conditions of our guarantee, appears on the next page. Note the favorable guarantee and servicing arrangements.

In these days of high prices, the $89.95 retail cost of the Multimower will be popular with your customers. Our price to you is $60.

By filling out and returning the enclosed order blank along with your remittance today, you'll be sure to have Multimowers on hand when your customers begin asking for them.

The checklist on page 366 summarizes the significant points to keep in mind.

TESTS AND TESTING

You will probably recall that earlier in this chapter we referred to testing a mailing and to the returns or the pull or the pulling power of a letter. Testing means simply mailing the letter to a portion of the names on your list to see whether you can get a profitable percentage of people to take the action you want. You can see why a businessman would be wise to test a mailing before risking his money sending 10,000 letters, especially if the mailing pieces are expensive.

Suppose your mailing pieces cost 10 cents each (not unusual in a mass mailing) and you make $1 on each sale. Obviously, you have to make sales to 10 percent of the list to break even. Now suppose you have a 90 percent accuracy factor (that is, the percentage of correct addresses). Each 100 letters have to bring 10 orders from every 90 people to whom they are delivered. Further suppose the purity (how many names on the list are likely prospects instead of deadwood) is 70 percent. This means that your 100 letters have to bring 10 orders from every 63 good prospects (70 percent of 90). This requires about 16 percent pulling power from your letter (10/63). Most sales letters don't do so well. But you could change the situation into one that would be more likely to be profitable by increasing any or all of the accuracy, the purity, or the pulling power—or by decreasing costs of the mailing or increasing the profit on the sale.

Faced with the prospect of a required 16 percent, you'd probably revise plans in order to lower it. And then, to be on the safe side, you'd mail your proposed mailing to a part of your list. On very large mailings the percentage may be small—5 percent or less. If the replies from the sample meet the necessary percentage figures for profitable operations, you'll go ahead. If they don't, you'll revise or drop the whole plan without losing as much money as you would have if you hadn't tested.

Another reason for testing is to find out which of two or more messages has the greater pull or which of two times (day or week or month the mailing piece arrives) is more profitable. *But you can test only one factor at a time!*

You can test one color against another; but if you also vary size, copy, or time, your test doesn't mean a thing. You can test position of coupon *or* order blank versus order card; but if you allow any variation of other factors, your findings are not reliable. You can test one lead against another; but if the rest of the copy, the color and size of the paper, the envelope and stamp, and the time of arrival are not the same, you still have no basis for saying that one lead is better than the other.

Many test results have been published concerning format and timing. If you talk with enough people in the field or read long enough, you'll be reassured—often vehemently!—that every color you've ever seen is the best color for a mailing. You'll find one man swearing by third-class mail and another at it. You'll find out, however, what all experienced persons with judgment discover: Because people and circumstances constantly change, so do the results of testing; what a test suggests this week may not be true next week and probably will not be next year; the only way to be safe is to test in each new situation and then follow through as fast as you can.

Even so, you usually expect only 5–10 percent pulling power. But especially effective copy, carefully selected mailing lists, or unusual offers often increase these percentages. And obviously the reverse of these conditions decreases the pulling power sharply.

Because some series depend on large volume and succeed on small margins, even such apparently insignificant things as the time of arrival are important. Experience has shown that such letters should not arrive in an office at the beginning or ending of a week or month or at the homes of laborers or farmers in the middle of the week. Around Christmas time and April 15 (income tax time) are especially bad times of the year. In general the fall and winter months are better than spring and summer. Of course, seasonal appropriateness of the goods and geographical locations can easily affect this. Even temporary local conditions may.

By keeping careful records on the tests and on the whole mailing, through the years users develop a considerable quantity of experience data that may help guide them in future work.

Before you accept conclusions, however, know the circumstances back of the quoted figures. The results may be worth no more than the paper they're written on, but they may be reliable.

WRITING SALES SERIES

The sales letters we have been discussing are lone efforts to produce or promote sales. Because single sales letters frequently cannot do all the work a series can, probably *just as many* or more sales letters are sent as part of a series as are sent singly. Usually they are obviously processed (form) letters, sent out in large numbers by third-class mail. For further economy they use some simulated address block instead of an inside address and salutation (like some of the examples in this chapter). By careful phrasing, however, a skillful writer will make the one reader of each copy forget the form and feel that he is getting a well-adapted message that certainly fits him.

Whether a letter is a single sales letter or one in a series makes little difference in the techniques or preliminary planning, but in one of the three types of series the letter's organization is more complicated.

The wear-out series

Probably the most widely used of sales series is the wear-out. In it each mailing is a complete sales presentation sent to a large group by almost any firm with a relatively inexpensive product to sell (usually not over $25). The product almost has to be inexpensive, because one letter cannot hope to succeed in persuading most people to buy expensive items by mail from a complete stranger.

After the market analysis, preparation or purchase of a mailing list, and preliminary planning comes the writing of the letter. Probably you and several other executives, and perhaps a letter consultant, will spend hours preparing the letter, or several versions of it. These first few copies may cost several hundred dollars in time and consultant's fees.

Then you test your list, and perhaps several versions of the letter (as formerly explained). If one letter seems to have the best pulling power (and that is high enough to make it profitable), you run off hundreds or thousands of copies and mail them out at a carefully selected time. Now that the big investment has been divided among so many, the cost per letter is not so big (maybe 10–25 cents).

After an interval, usually of one to three weeks, you remove the names of purchasers (unless the product has frequent recurring demand) and send another letter (or sometimes the same one) to the remaining names. Sometimes the second or even the third or fourth mailing brings better results than the first, even with the same letter, because of the buildup of impact.

You continue to repeat the mailings as long as the returns pay you a suitable profit on your mailings—that is, until the effectiveness of the list is worn out.

The campaign series

What has been said about the cost of the first copy, the general preliminary planning, the testing, and the usual interval between mailings of the wear-out series also applies to the campaign series. But there the similarity stops.

Contrary to the wear-out series, the campaign series is preplanned not only for the construction of the letters and the intervals between them; you decide, before you start, how many mailings you will send and how long the whole series will run. It is also different in that it is used mostly to sell or to help sell rather expensive items.

This fact (cost of product) really determines its nature. The theory is that people buy some (usually inexpensive) items quickly, without much thought. These things can be sold by one good complete sales letter, as in the wear-out series. But before buying certain other types of items (usually more expensive but not absolutely essential), most people ponder for a month or more and talk over the situation with friends, financial advisers, and other members of the family. To send a letter which first introduced such an item and, after only two minutes of reading time, asked for the decision on an order card would be to pour money down the proverbial rathole. The reader would laugh at you. Instead of the wear-out, you would use the campaign series for such a situation. You usually do not talk price in the earlier mailings and sometimes not at all. Your action requests (at least in the first few mailings) are to get a show of interest: Write for more information, come to a showroom, authorize the visit of a salesman.

Having done your preliminary planning as explained, you are ready to plan the series. You decide approximately how long most people on the mailing list would want to think over your offer before making up their minds. Then you decide how frequently they should be reminded to keep them thinking about your product or service. On that basis you decide how many mailings you want to send for the whole series.

The essence of planning the series of letters (whether two or a dozen) is to make the whole series cover the parts of a complete sales presentation and knit them together. In any case the first letter will try hard to get attention and start working at interesting the prospect. Further letters will develop the succeeding sales steps until the last makes a strong drive for action.

The last is not the only one, however, to which a reader can easily respond. Mail salesmen know that they will not usually get any action from more than half of their prospects. But they also know that in almost any large group some people will be sold on the first contact. Consequently, they usually provide order forms with almost every mailing.

Because the campaign series varies more than other series from the one-letter presentations discussed earlier, we have illustrated with two typical campaigns (at the end of the chapter).

The continuous series

The wear-out and campaign series are different in many ways, but they are much more like each other than like the continuous series. Both the wear-out and the campaign series are usually complete sales presentations which try to bring in orders. The continuous series rarely does. Instead of being used by almost any kind of firm, the continuous series is most frequently used by department stores as a goodwill or sales promotion medium rather than a direct-mail selling system. The mailing list for the continuous series is usually the list of the firm's charge customers, instead of one specially prepared in view of a market analysis for a particular item or service being sold. The continuous series usually costs little or no postage because it rides free with the monthly statements; so the usual interval between mailings is longest in the continuous series. Still, perhaps the biggest distinction is the rigid planning of the campaign series as compared with the hit-or-miss, haphazard nature of the continuous series. It commonly includes special mailings at Easter and Christmas but also on almost any other special occasion the sales manager chooses. As such, it does not run for any set length of time or for any definite number of mailings; and it may *promote* a great *variety* of products while the campaign and wear-out series are *selling one.*

✸　✸　✸

The following direct-mail campaign directed to accounting firms, tax services, and law firms emphasizes the economy of making dry photocopies instantly with an Adeco Auto-Copier (costing about $350) instead of having papers and carbons typed. Although planned for firms in Alabama,

Georgia, and Florida, the letters could just as well be sent within one city or over the entire country. A salesman within a city could readily assemble his mailing list from the yellow pages of the phone book. The Atlanta district manager (for the three states) could assemble his list also from the yellow pages of phone books for the cities in his area (available in any large library, such as the Atlanta Public Library). Or he could buy the list. Certainly a nationwide mailing list would be more inexpensively purchased than assembled.

The mailings are planned for intervals of about three weeks. For economy they use a simulated address block instead of an inside address and salutation, are printed, and go third class. Each mailing includes a reply card which reads something like this:

```
Adeco Auto-Copier

Yes, I would like to know more about how the Adeco Auto-Copier
will help me.  Please call me and arrange an appointment.
```

The card provides blanks for indicating name of individual, position, company, and address.

The first mailing includes a 12-page, two-color booklet containing illustrations, savings estimates and comparisons, and information about the company and its organization.

```
You can save
Up to 80 percent on
Copying jobs . . .

. . . by letting your typists make black-and-white photocopies
with the Adeco Auto-Copier.

In less than 45 seconds an unskilled operator can turn out a
legally acceptable, error-proof copy of an original—one that
would take your typist at least 10 minutes to copy.  If your
office produces only 15 copies a day, the Auto-Copier can save
you about $3 each working day.  When you need to turn out
large numbers of copies, the Auto-Copier makes them for you as
fast as 75 an hour, at proportionate savings.

Your Auto-Copier takes a picture without using a camera.  So
in turning out copies of complicated tax forms, accounting
forms, government records, and deeds, it assures you of
error-proof, smudge-proof copies.  One compact photocopy unit
does it all; the Auto-Copier is a fully automatic, continuous
copier and processing unit combined.  Since prints are
processed and dried automatically, they're ready for your
instant use.

And you don't need a separate timer or printer either.  In
just two simple steps you can turn out prints made from any
original up to 11 by 17 inches whether printed on one or two
sides.

Just put the Auto-Copier on any convenient desk or table, plug
it in, and you're ready to start.  You can copy any
confidential material right in the privacy of your own office
in just a few seconds.  Read the description in the enclosed
folder of the Auto-Copier's easy, simple operation.
```

The Auto-Copier will actually enable you to have one unskilled clerk do the copying work of six expert typists. Just sign and return the enclosed card so that your Adeco representative can stop by and show you how to let the Auto-Copier cut the high cost of duplicating records.

(Signature)

Auto-Copies of tax forms are fully acceptable and approved by the Internal Revenue Service.

The second letter accompanies a four-page, two-color folder headlined "Make dry photocopies of tax returns instantly!" In the upper left corner of the letter appears the picture of a girl operating an Auto-Copier. To the right of the illustration is the headline

MAKE
 TAX RETURN COPIES
 INSTANTLY
with the Adeco Auto-Copier.

Now your typists can
Turn out tax return
Copies in just a few seconds!

Tax copying work which used to take hours you can now do in seconds with the Adeco Auto-Copier. And these copies are fully accepted and approved by the Internal Revenue Service.

You can actually reduce by one third to one half the number of statistical typists you employ. Since the average statistical typist in this area makes about $85 a week, you'll be able to save at least $20 each week for each one you now employ. Or your typists can use the time saved to get out your other important papers and reports.

You know how difficult it is to type tax copies speedily, align them accurately, and avoid carbon smudges. With the Auto-Copier you need to type and proofread only the original, then turn out error-proof, clean, legible copies at a rate as high as 75 an hour—copies your typists never have to align, erase, or proofread.

And on involved legal reports or contracts you'll find your Auto-Copier especially helpful. Whether your paper is opaque or translucent, you are assured of clear copies, and you can reproduce copies on both sides of a single sheet too.

Eliminate the expensive, time-consuming job of typing extra copies of tax returns in your office. Whether you're working on state or federal tax forms, corporation or individual, you can get the copies out three times as fast with the Auto-Copier. Just sign and return the enclosed card so that your Adeco representative can come by and show you all the ways you can use an Auto-Copier.

(Signature)

Turn to page 4 of the enclosed folder and note the three simple steps in making tax return copies.

Letter No. 3, accompanied by a one-page folder, drives for a demonstration (with the postcard altered in wording accordingly):

When you need copies . . .

. . . of tax forms, accounting records, government forms, or
letters, you can be confident that any made on the Auto-Copier
will be as clear, unsmudged, and error-proof as the original.
No more faulty copies because of poor alignment or carbons
that are too light to use. And your copies are turned out
from 3 to 10 times as fast as carbons ever can be.

The average typist, even the good typist, is hard pressed to
turn out in one hour even six perfect copies of a tax return
or many other government forms the average business has to
produce. The Auto-Copier can turn out 75 perfect copies. And
no proofreading or corrections are necessary.

Your Auto-Copier takes up no more space than a standard
typewriter. Just plug it in, and your typist is ready to
copy. Because the Auto-Copier is completely electric, you can
do all your copying work automatically from start to finish.

Try the Auto-Copier for a week. We'll be glad to bring one
around for you to see how easily it will fit many of your
copying needs. Fill in and return the enclosed card so that
your Adeco representative can demonstrate in your office its
value to you and your company.

                              (Signature)

Notice Auto-Copier's other exclusive advantages described in
the enclosure.

The fourth letter shows an attractive young woman turning out copies
on the Auto-Copier. She looks directly at the reader and addresses him:

I've typed thousands
of tax returns.

And I <u>know</u> the Adeco Auto-Copier can save you money because it
can reduce your tax copying work up to 80 percent.

For two years I have typed tax forms in the offices of
C. C. Putnam, CPA, 166 Stallings Building, Atlanta 30218.

Turning out an original copy of a complicated tax form is a
job in itself, but typing 10 or 12 clear, unsmudged carbon
copies is next to impossible.

Now just a minute! I'm not a poor typist. I can type 60
words a minute with no errors on a 10-minute test. That is
certainly as good as the average typist, and, I confidently
believe, a lot better. But I still have trouble aligning
carbons, making corrections, and typing sufficiently clear and
legible copies.

With the Auto-Copier I simply type the original and run off as
many copies as I need. I can now turn out in one day reports
that used to take at least two days. Each detail of the
original is accurately and legibly reproduced—and the only
copy I have to proofread is the form itself!

Our clients like Auto-Copied forms. And they're fully
accepted by the government.

In addition to tax form copies, I use the Auto-Copier for
letters, bank records, claims, graphs, or invoices. No more

costly retyping or hand copying! And no more messy, time-
consuming carbons!

My employer and I agree that the Auto-Copier is the answer to
our copying needs. Your Adeco representative would like to
show you how the Auto-Copier can solve your copying problems
too. Check the enclosed card today so that he can call on you
to demonstrate one in your office.

The letter carries the signature of the young woman, the title indicating
that she is secretary to Mr. Putnam.

The fifth mailing reestablishes the main talking points and stresses much
harder the advantages of having the salesman come in and demonstrate:

Can your typists turn out
75 perfect copies an hour?
With the Auto-Copier they can!

The Auto-Copier will enable you to have one unskilled clerk do
the copying work of six expert typists.

In addition, you are assured of perfect accuracy—each detail
of the original is accurately reproduced without any
possibility of error. And there's no need for tedious,
time-consuming proofreading and checking either.

In turning out copies of complicated tax forms, legal reports
and records, and accounting data on the Auto-Copier, your
typist can run off up to 20 clear, unsmudged copies in no more
than five minutes. Since she can't make errors on Auto-Copied
material, erasing time and messiness are eliminated.

You can put your Auto-Copier on any convenient desk or table,
since it measures 20 by 11 inches. You simply plug it in, and
you're ready to start using it. No special installation is
necessary. Anyone can run it.

Since Auto-Copies are processed and dried automatically,
they're ready for your instant use. You need no developing,
washing, drying, or printing space because the Auto-Copier
does everything in one simple operation.

Your Auto-Copier representative would like to talk with you
about your particular copying needs. He'll also show you how
other companies are using Auto-Copier to help cut copying
costs. Just sign and mail the enclosed card, and he will call
to arrange a demonstration in your office.

The sixth mailing is a copy of the first letter, with a reminder memo
attached.

Mailing No. 7 is the booklet sent with the first letter. Attached to the
booklet is a memo in simulated handwriting:

If you didn't get a chance to read the first copy of the
booklet I sent you recently, here's another.

It will show you how the Auto-Copier can help you cut the high
cost of duplicating records.

Of course, the reply card is also enclosed.

The eighth and final mailing is another memo, this time attached to the same folder that accompanied the second letter:

> You can make photocopies of tax forms instantly with the
> Auto-Copier. Notice in the enclosed folder the three easy
> steps necessary to turn out tax copies fully acceptable to the
> Internal Revenue Service.
>
> To find out how the Auto-Copier can lighten your tax copying
> problems, return the enclosed card.

The next campaign, directed to gift shops, seeks to get owners or managers to stock Jense stainless steel tableware. A list could be purchased easily. With time (lots of it if the mailing is to be extensive), it could be assembled from classified directories. Since the product is relatively new, the firm offers to sell on consignment. Because of this factor, for safety the list has to be checked for credit reliability, and the contractual phrasing of the order blank assumes greater significance.

The first mailing early in September is a box containing a sample spoon of Jense and a price list of the line. The envelope attached to the box contains the following letter and a reply card requesting more information:

> 100 percent markup—
> And it sells itself!
>
> Take this sample of Jense stainless steel tableware and
> compare it with any tableware—either in your shop or in some
> competitor's.
>
> It compares favorably in style, quality, and workmanship. It
> gives your customers more value at a lower price. It's
> durable and easy to keep. So more and more homemakers today
> are choosing Jense as their best.
>
> When your customers inquire about Jense, invite them to make
> the same comparisons you have made. Tell them how durable
> Jense is because it contains 35 percent nickel, the highest
> nickel content in stainless steel tableware. The homemaker of
> today does not have to be concerned when her maid or children
> carelessly handle her Jense, because it resists bending.
>
> Your customers will like the small amount of care Jense
> requires. It needs no polishing; it won't discolor or tarnish.
> Soap and water are all it needs to retain its luster. Because
> Jense requires only a minimum of care, it fits right in with
> today's living, which stresses ease and informality.
>
> The low cost of Jense is a good talking point too. Glance
> over the price list. Notice that a spoon like the one we sent
> you costs your customer only $2 and that six-piece place
> settings in any of the four graceful patterns run to only $12.
> And remember that on every place setting of Jense tableware
> you sell, you make a profit of $5.
>
> Jot down your name and address in the blanks on the enclosed
> reply card and mail it today for more information about Jense
> —the graceful, inexpensive, durable stainless steel tableware
> that your homemaker customers will buy when you put it on
> display.

The second mailing is a letter, a folder, an order blank, and a reply envelope. The four-page folder illustrates in color a table place setting in each of the four Jense patterns. These same photographs appear in current magazine advertising and are identified as such in the letter. Letter copy stresses the adaptability of Jense to conventional or modern surroundings, to informal or formal entertaining. Of course, it asks for an order. It goes immediately to any dealer who responds to the first mailing; others on the list receive it about two weeks after the first mailing.

About a month after the second mailing (the middle of October), the third mailing goes to all names on the list—whether they have bought or not. A 4- by 6-inch memo to the dealer is folded over an 8½- by 11-inch letter, which is a copy of a consumer sales letter about Jense. The memo reads:

```
Here's one way
We help you
Push your sales
Of Jense.

The enclosed letter is written just for your customers.  It
stresses the versatility, easy upkeep, low cost, and pattern
choice of Jense.

There's space at the bottom of the letter for you or someone
else in your store to sign, and room for a personalizing
postscript if you want to add one.  All you have to do is mail
the letter.

Any items you check on the enclosed order blank will be in
your shop within 24 hours after we receive it.

And we'll send you whatever number of letters you specify plus
the same number of the leaflets referred to in the letter.
```

When the dealer lifts the memo, he reads this letter, which is already prepared for his local distribution:

```
Made especially
For today's busy,
Discriminating hostess.

Whether you prefer traditional or modern surroundings, you can
set your table with Jense and have a harmonious setting with
beauty and charm.

The painstaking craftsmanship and the new techniques of hand
polishing and finishing are combined to give you a tableware
beautifully balanced for adaptability and harmony.  For
informal luncheons or buffets, Jense will complement your
arrangement and give it freshness and beauty.  And the
simplicity of Jense's design will add elegance and
distinctiveness to your formal table settings.

In preparation for your parties, you do not have to polish
your Jense.  Since it is tarnish-proof, its luster lasts for a
lifetime.  Just wash it with soap and water, and it will
always look its loveliest on your table.

You can have a six-piece Jense place setting for only $12—a
```

minimum investment for quality tableware that you will use on
any occasion in the years to come.

With Jense you can also have hollow ware in the same pattern
as your flatware. Notice in the enclosed leaflet the hollow
ware that matches each of the four distinctive Jense patterns.
And remember that all of this permanently polished stainless
steel tableware is equally at home on your table or in the
oven.

Come in soon and choose the pattern especially suited to you.

Around the middle of November the fourth letter (order blank and
reply envelope included) stresses the idea of Jense for Christmas shoppers.
The wording fits any dealer on the list, whether or not he has already
stocked Jense.

Let Christmas gifts of Jense
Increase Christmas sales for you.

When one of your customers enters your store "just looking
around" for Christmas, show her a place setting of Jense.

Tell her how durable Jense is because it contains the highest
nickel content in stainless steel tableware. Remember to
point out to her how pleased any owner of Jense is, since this
tableware needs no polishing, only soap and water, to retain
its satin luster.

Let her see the four lovely, versatile patterns of flatware
and the matching patterns in hollow ware which will please any
of her friends on Christmas morning and in the years to come.

And when you point out to her that Jense goes from the oven
right on to the table, she'll see how practical it is too.

You can get your Jense in plenty of time for the peak of the
Christmas trade by filling out and mailing the enclosed order
blank today.

In view of the Christmas buying season and end-of-the-year activities
claiming the attention of shop owners and managers through January, the
fifth mailing does not go out until shortly after the first of February. It is
a letter with folder, order blank, and reply envelope.

The newest trend
In tableware for
American women . . .

. . . who for years have wanted flatware and hollow ware in
companion pieces!

Today they can make their table arrangements blend harmoniously
when they use Jense flatware and the matching hollow ware in
the same pattern. That is why an increasing number of
American hostesses are setting their tables with Jense
stainless steel tableware in

    Fayette—elegant and distinctive
    Phoebe—contemporary simplicity with classic charm
    Flora—for contemporary or traditional surroundings
    Phellips—unadorned modern for today's casual mood

as illustrated in the folder enclosed.

You can offer your customers any of these patterns in more
than 200 different pieces. Whether they want a gravy boat, a
pickle fork, or a 36-inch tray, they can get it in their
chosen pattern of Jense. And every article sold carries a
printed guarantee issued by Jense. Any of your customers will
delight in using this heatproof hollow ware that they can put
right into the oven to keep warm before serving. And like the
flatware, it is tarnish-proof—it never requires polishing,
only soap and water.

Right now, take time to designate on the enclosed order
blank that you'd like to try Jense—on consignment, if you
prefer.

Approximately a month later (about the middle of March) the sixth
mailing stresses the appropriateness of Jense as a choice for brides—a reminder of the coming spring and summer buying for brides. It is a letter
and order blank with reply envelope. Note that the wording can go to any
dealer on the original list.

Today's American bride
Is choosing Jense tableware

Because

It is practical, beautifully designed, inexpensive—and made
to last a lifetime.

Today's brides who must be homemakers and career girls have to
budget their time as well as their money. Jense helps them do
both.

They can use their Jense stainless steel tableware twice a
day or oftener with the complete assurance that it needs no
polishing—only soap and water to retain its luster.

A display of each of the four distinctive patterns will be an
invitation to all brides to visit your store. Pieces of the
hollow ware in the matching patterns and a reminder that they
go right from the oven to the table convince women that never
before have homemakers been able to do so much with one set of
tableware. Whether buffet or formal dinner—family or special
occasion—they can use their Jense to make a beautiful,
distinctive arrangement that both their young friends and
traditional-minded mothers approve.

Any bride today can afford Jense, and she'll use and cherish
it the rest of her life. Even though this stainless steel
tableware contains more nickel than any other she could select,
she can choose her pattern in a six-piece place setting for
eight for $96, as compared to the $500 she would spend for the
same thing in sterling. And the bride's friends will be
pleased at the economical price range of her choice.

Make this spring the season to promote Jense. Use the
enclosed order blank and easy-reply envelope to tell us the
quantity you want.

                                        (Signature)

You can assure your customers that the patterns they choose
will never be out of stock—they can buy any piece in the

Prospecting Sales Checklist

1. Get started effectively and economically.
   a) Point up a specific reader benefit in the first sentence.
   b) Show a need for the service of the product before naming it; but usually use positive selling, not predicament-to-remedy push-overs.
   c) Concentrate on a well-chosen central selling point at first.
   d) Quickly get to the distinctive thing about your product. Avoid unnatural or delaying gimmicks.
   e) Don't begin with an obvious statement or foolish question.
   f) Suggest, remind, but don't preach: "You will want . . . ."
   g) Don't claim too much for your product. Be reasonable.
2. Back up your opening promise with a persuasive description.
   a) Interpret physical features in terms of the reader's benefit.
   b) You-viewpoint is not automatic from use of you ("you will find" and "you will note"); but as the subject or object of action verbs, you helps.
   c) Guard against stark product descriptions (beginnings like "Our goods . . . ," "We make . . . ," or "XYZ is made . . .").
   d) Specificness in description is necessary for conviction.
   e) Even in form letters, refer to some action or condition that applies and avoid references which brand them as forms.
   f) The history of the product or firm will bore most readers.
   g) Eliminate challenging superlatives.
   h) Guard against the trite "truly" and "really" and the indefinite "that" ("that important conference").
3. Be sure to cover all important points with proper emphasis.
   a) Develop the most appropriate central selling point adequately.
   b) Stress your central theme for singleness of impression.
   c) Give enough detail to sell your reader on reading an enclosure, when you have one, and even more when you do not.
   d) Provide adequate conviction through selected methods.
   e) Introduce any enclosure only after most of your sales points, stressing what the reader is to do with it or get from it.
4. Remember the price; it is an integral part of any sales message.
   a) Unless using a recognized-bargain appeal, minimize price.
   b) Keep price out of the ending, at least the last sentence.
   c) If you choose not to talk price now, offer to sometime and reassure the reader that it is not out of line.
5. Forthrightly ask for appropriate action.
   a) Name the specific action you want your reader to take.
   b) Be confident. Avoid "If you'd like . . . ," "Why not . . . ?"
   c) Avoid high-pressure bromides: "Why wait?" "Don't delay!"
   d) Refer *subordinately* to ordering aids (envelope, order blank . . .).
   e) End with a reminder of what the product will contribute.

Dealer Sales Checklist

1. A dealer sales letter opening has to move fast.
    a) Devote at least the beginning to the reader—how he can benefit —not yourself or even the product per se.
    b) Picture the act of selling and the product's consumer appeal.
    c) Stress a distinctive point; avoid obvious, slow, general copy.
    d) Avoid exaggeration and questionable superlatives.
2. Though you might mention profits, the first point to develop is salability. Without consumer appeal the product stays on the shelves and makes no profit regardless of price spread.
    a) To stress consumer demand, explain the product's points in terms of customers' reactions, demands, and approval—hence high-volume sales.
    b) Talk about the dealer's sales—not his use—of the product.
    c) Adaptation here means talking of sales demonstrations, wrapping up a purchase and handing it across the counter, ringing up a sale, answering customers' questions, and the like.
3. Show how the manufacturer helps to push the sale, if applicable.
    a) Refer to whatever dealer aids you have (advertising, displays, mats, cuts) with emphasis on how they build local demand.
    b) Give working ideas of size (quarter page, half page), extent (time it will run), and coverage (specific medium—magazine, newspaper, radio, and/or TV station—and type of audience).
    c) Interpret any advertising as promoting inquiries and sales.
4. Continue pointing to appeal and profitable selling in the price talk.
    a) Price is more appropriately handled late, most naturally as you ask for an order and talk payment details.
    b) Include a specific mention of price spread, percentage, or both.
    c) Terms and manner of payment have to be cleared up.
5. You will almost always have some enlosures to handle.
    a) Don't divert attention to the enclosure until your reader is near enough the end that he'll complete the letter.
    b) Make the reference to an enclosure carry a sales point too.
    c) Don't depend too heavily on an enclosure to do the selling.
6. Make the action ending brief and businesslike too.
    a) Probably better avoid commands to the seasoned buyer.
    b) Exaggerated superlatives are out of place here too.
    c) Of course, you name the specific action you want.
    d) And you make that action easy.
    e) Use a whip-back suggesting prompt handling and profitable selling.

pattern of their choice to replace or increase their Jense in
the years to come.

The seventh and final planned mailing goes out about a month after the
sixth mailing (roughly the middle of April). But it could go almost any
time. It is a carbon copy of the letter sent in the fifth mailing—with order
blank, price list, and reply envelope. Clipped to the carbon is a 4- by 5-inch
memo reading:

100 percent markup!

And it sells itself.

This carbon of a letter we sent you earlier is a reminder of
why American women buy Jense tableware:

It is the only stainless steel tableware with matching
flatware and hollow ware.

It never needs polishing.

It's equally at home on the table or in the oven.

The four distinctive patterns give a freedom of
choice for tableware adaptable to any occasion.

The price list tells you why Jense is a popular choice of
every homemaker. Use the order blank and reply envelope to
tell us the Jense you'd like to stock.

CASES FOR SALES

1. As an authorized dealer for United Protective Services, Inc., of your
city, write a letter to homeowners ($25,000 and up) pointing out their
need for a Selectograph Security System.

Residential burglaries are one of the biggest problems Americans face
today. More and more homeowners are finding their homes and families
the prime targets of lawbreakers.

Whether it's a drug addict in desperate need of a fix, a vandal out for
kicks, or a burglar looking for available cash, the homeowner has become
a leading target for criminal attack.

According to the FBI Crime Report, residential burglaries account for
56 percent of all burglaries. Residential daytime break-ins have risen over
286 percent since 1960, while residential nightime burglaries have increased over 109 percent.

More homes are unattended during the daytime than ever before because in many cases both husband and wife work, because more families
own two homes, and because we enjoy longer vacations. Another reason,
reports the FBI, is that prevention and detection are most difficult for law
enforcement agencies due to the tremendous volume of offenses and lack
of adequate police patrols. Also, law enforcement agencies are successful
in solving fewer than one out of every five cases of burglary. This low

clearance rate indicates the lack of deterrent and the slight risk of detection.

No lock—regardless of size or cost—will keep a determined criminal out. At best, it will only slow him down. With the Selectograph Security System, the homeowner has a system designed for his individual needs. If desired, the system can even notify the police.

Urge the homeowner to mail the enclosed business reply card for more information and remind him that there is no cost or obligation for the security survey and equipment demonstration.

You will not talk price. These installations can run anywhere from $600 to several thousands depending on degree of protection the homeowner wants (mere alarm, hookup with police or fire department and the like). These points have to be discussed with the prospect face to face.

2. Under the title of sales representative, send personalized letters to owners of homes of $30,000 value and over for Continental Resorts, Inc., 1104 Montgomery Highway, Birmingham, Alabama 35216, promoting the sale of land on the shores of Morgan Long Lake, right in the heart of Alabama. Land is one of the surest investments today, for it involves next-to-no risk, promises a healthy across-the-board return, and boasts a steadily increasing market value. This time two years from now, the 1,100 acres of rich woodland will be a beautifully landscaped, relaxingly secluded resort area complete with a luxurious Continental Hotel, Country Club, and Marina. Options for estate-sized home sites are available, as are individual suite ownerships in the condominium apartment complexes to be built. With either, the buyer can take advantage of membership in the country club, yacht club, and racquet club. Both home sites and condominia will overlook the lakefront, the golf course, or gently rolling forest land. Access roadways will be completed in two years.

Once the home or apartment is completed it can be rented or subleased during the times it is not in use. That means the investment will pay off in more ways than one.

The championship 36-hole golf course was designed by the internationally famous Peter James Trent. Also, there will be horseback riding, skeet and trap shooting, bowling, archery, and a full range of water sports from scuba diving to sailing to swimming. Morgan Long Lake is ideal for fishing all year round, for it is well stocked with bream and bass.

The Continental Hotel complex will include a theater, specialty shops, and gourmet restaurants. In addition, there'll be a deluxe health spa and sauna and whirlpool baths.

All the cultural and entertainment activities of Atlanta are just two-and-a-half hours from the development. Birmingham, Alabama's largest metropolitan center, is only 45 minutes away by four-lane interstate highway. Twelve miles away is the recently completed Alabama International Motor Speedway and the Talladega Municipal Jetport.

Invite your reader to fill out an attached coupon or to call Birmingham

822-6712, or Talladega 362-8654. Once you receive the coupon or phone call you'll send a full set of facts and a master plan of the entire develop-ment plus the architect's rendering for each of the proposed facilities. You also will send facts about Continental Resorts, Inc., how the corporation works, and proof of financial stability.

— Two weeks later, follow up the mailing for Continental Resorts, Inc. (preceding case), with a personal letter and drawings of the 36-hole golf course, the Continental Hotel, Country Club, and Marina. Also include a map showing the location of Morgan Long Lake in relation to Birming-ham, Atlanta, and Talladega. Ask your reader to call or fill out a return post card for additional information.

— A third mailing from Continental Resorts, Inc. (see two preceding cases), promotes the estate-sized home sites and the condominium apart-ment complexes. Sketches of the homes and apartments show that they overlook the lakefront, golf course, or the gently rolling forest land. The access roadways are also pictured. Emphasis in this mailing is on the idea that the home or apartment can be rented or subleased during the times it is not in use.

— A fourth letter sums up the main points of Continental Resorts, Inc. (of the preceding cases). Use the sales theme that ownership of land is a good investment. Land values will continue to go up as the population grows. Again make it easy for the reader to get additional information.

3. As Harvey L. Roberts, Director of Sales for Sunset House (P.O. Box 1063, Dayton, Ohio, 45401), you want to try selling by mail your decorator-designed, precision-crafted (by Springfield Instrument Company, a re-spected leader in its field) Clock Weather Stations to a specially purchased national mailing list of homeowners (homes tax-assessed at $20,000 and up), at $29.95, plus $1.85 for postage and handling, billed after a 15-day free-trial period (or $5.30 a month for six months, including postage, han-dling, and interest of $1\frac{1}{2}$ percent a month, 18 percent annual rate, on the unpaid balance). An enclosed franked and addressed order card states the 15-day, no-obligation, free-trial offer and has blanks for the number of Clock Weather Stations ordered (make wonderful gifts), the choice of payments plan, and the signature.

You will also include, with the letter, a full-size, full-color illustration (on heavy paper) for the reader to hang on his wall to see how it looks (gold faces with black hands in sculptured dark oak frame, blends with any decor). On the back will be directions for mounting, restatement of the basic offer, a reduced-size picture of the three-dial instrument (one right under the other), and a picture of the bonus for ordering this month —a round outdoor thermometer. By the three dials will be the wording:

Barometer—a fine instrument for weather forecasting; indicates atmospheric pressure changes preceding likely weather changes; adjustable to your altitude; enables you to check on the U.S. Weather Bureau just like a professional.

Clock—a truly fine U.S.-made clock with no wires (operates on size "C" flashlight batteries).

Temperature and Humidity—Accurate indoor thermometer and measure of the wetness or dryness of the air.

As usual, however, the main sales piece will be your letter—a strict form with facsimile inside address and salutation—which you now have to write.

4. Six months ago a major manufacturer of auto batteries decided to put out a really superior battery and sell it at a low-profit price, thinking that the public would recognize its quality (from description) and appreciate the quality enough to buy in high volume, though paying a little more than for ordinary competitors' batteries. Sales were slow. So a marketing consultant suggested trying to use members' confidence in the AAA to overcome buyer doubts. The manufacturer convinced the Peninsula Motor Club (Florida branch of AAA) to promote and back the battery, and get AAA-authorized service stations as sales outlets (sales to AAA members only).

As advertising manager in the offices of the PMC (1515 N.W. Shore Boulevard, Tampa, 33602), you have induced the service stations to handle the batteries in all sizes and have been running quarter-page ads in monthly issues of the much read and respected newspaper for members, *The PMC Explorer*. Above a picture, the heading reads, "Introducing the battery so good it's guaranteed by your AAA club." Underneath, the copy says new case more durable, 12 percent more lead and electrolyte inside, will crank your car twice as long and 29 percent faster than original equipment, more reserve power, more dependable; sellers will replace free if battery fails within 18 months or replace at pro-rata charges between 18 and 48 months. A table gives the price list (no-discount prices of $30.95 to $34.95) by sizes and kinds of cars they fit.

Now you have decided to try a sales letter to go to your membership list, as a means of selling even more of the now fast-selling battery.

5. Write copy for a sales letter going to dealers of photographic equipment in the Northwest (Washington, Oregon, Idaho, and Montana). You are the promotion director for Tell and Powell Company, New Rochelle, N.Y. 12203. The Tell and Powell Slide Cube represents the first real innovation in total projector design to come along in some years. It is different from other projectors both in the way it holds and stores slides and in the way it projects them. It holds slides in small plastic cubes, about 40 slides to the cube. Sixteen of those cubes—a storage capacity of 640 slides—take up about the same storage space as a standard circular tray that holds a mere 80 to 140 slides.

The projector itself works only with the cube; it doesn't accept any of the standard slide trays. The 40 slides lie in contact in the cube, one atop the other. The owner inserts the cube in a niche at the side of the projector and then slides the cube over to the starting position. The bottom slide drops onto a platter-like device that revolves horizontally, much like the turntable on a record player.

The platter makes four stops in its rounds, one stop each time the operator presses a button. At the first stop, he can see the slide in a preview window. At that point it is a simple matter to reorient the slide if it is upside down or backwards. At the second stop, the slide is projected. (Since the slide lies horizontally in the plate, it takes a mirror behind the lens to right the image for projection on a vertical screen.) The third stop is a waiting position; the slide rests there while the one behind it on the plate is projected. At the fourth stop, the slide has come full circle and drops into a well beneath the slide cube. When all the slides have made their rounds and have piled one atop the other in the well, the operator raises a platform at the bottom of the well. That pushes the stack of slides back up into the cube, ready to be stored or shown again.

One other innovation: The operator can shift the projected image up or down on the screen by simply turning a knob that moves the lens. To change the height of the image with other projectors, he has to raise or lower the front of the entire machine.

Tell and Powell has two models. One, the 871QZ, includes automatic-focus control and a zoom lens and lists at $194.50 retail, $116.00 wholesale. The other model, the 877Q, has a standard 4-inch lens and is focused manually. It lists at $119.50 retail and $71.00 wholesale.

Besides a tear sheet from one of your recent ads, you enclose an order card. You have card displays and envelope stuffers available.

6. *Mailing list:* Parents of students in Massachusetts. *Company:* Orlando Orchard, Orlando, Florida 32809, Quincy Hanover, owner. *Product:* Gift package containing 20 juicy navel oranges. The oranges will be delivered directly to the dormitory or house for $3.60. A special price of $6.60 would enable the orderer to send a package of 20 oranges the second week and another package two weeks later. A special gift card with the name of the sender would be enclosed with each package. Write the letter for Quincy Hanover. Adapt to any school in Massachusetts (Harvard, Wellesley, etc.) *Action:* Ask the parents to use the order blank at the bottom of your letter.

7. As sales representative, send personalized letters to owners of homes of $30,000 value and over for your local gas company promoting the new, convenient Harwick gas grill, Model M543: gives food "charcoal flavor" without the bother and mess; fast, even heat leaves no ashes; heavy-gauge steel, porcelain-enameled inside and out; weatherproof, dependable unit that lets the homeowner cook outdoors any time he wants to; heats quickly; cooking temperature controlled; convenient, economical; grate area mea-

sures 14 by 21 inches; nickel-plated grate can be raised to tilt position for cooking greasy foods, permitting grease to drain off into a disposable grease cup. Stay-cool handles make removal of grill possible without hot-pads. The grill can be removed from the post for seasonal inside storage. Grill revolves a full 360 degrees, so it may be faced into the wind from any direction. The even-heat cooking is due to the special "chunked" crushed refractory bricks which are heated by the burner and which form a bed of coals. Coals are self-cleaning. Lockable gas control (like a pilot light) prevents unauthorized use and removal. Has a high-speed gas burner for fast heating. Gas control provides a variety of cooking heats. Convenient match holder to light burner provided. Pine-green top stands 32 inches from the ground on a charcoal-black base or post. Permanently mounted post because the gas line must attach. The price of $75 includes installation; can pay just $1.49 a month, added to his bill for only five years. Since this is a local list, you'd ask homeowners to name a time they want you to come out (using the enclosed return reply card). Also invite them to come to the gas company to see the Harwick in operation.

8. Two weeks later, follow up the mailing on the Harwick gas grill (preceding case) with a personal letter to homeowners promoting the charcoal-black gas lamp, $66 installed. Install the lamp and the grill, $2.49 a month for five years ($65 for the grill, a reduction of $10 and $55 for the lamp). Lamp burns continually unless want to turn it off. No bulbs to replace. Soft-glowing odorless flame repels insects. Suggest that the homeowner have the gas company install the lamp by the grill. Invite the customer to the showroom of the gas company. For more details the company could send out a representative. Make replying easy. Assume an enclosed folder on the grill and lamp.

9. A third mailing from the gas company (see the two preceding cases) to homeowners promotes the $15 electric rotisserie that can be attached to the Harwick gas grill. The special exclusive Harwick design lets the chef remove food, spit, and rack together and take all to the table to put on a platter. The two-level, self-basting rotisserie cooks roasts, chickens, and game evenly. Rotisserie cooking adds a new dimension to outdoor cooking. An enclosed folder showing the grill, lamp, and rotisserie is included. Suggest that the homeowner let you, the personal sales representative, come and demonstrate the rotisserie.

10. A fourth letter to homeowners sums up the main points of the gas grill, lamp, and rotisserie (of the three preceding cases). Prices are the same. Installation can be done in time for the outdoor cooking season. Use the sales theme that the grill, lamp, and rotisserie are always ready. Cook-outs can be arranged in a few minutes when the homeowner has the Harwick gas grill, lamp, and rotisserie.

11. To those who responded to your mailing (preceding cases), you send another letter with a reply card for the responder to give you the name of a friend who might want Harwick equipment.

12. Send a dealer sales letter to gas and power companies of the Northeast over the signature of the sales manager for the Harwick Corporation, 869 Union Avenue, Patterson, New Jersey 07513. The companies pay $50 for the Harwick gas grill, $40 for the gas lamp, and $7.50 for the rotisserie. They sell for prices stated in the five preceding cases. Half-page ads will run for the next two months in *Life* and *Better Homes and Gardens.* You can send cuts and mats for local newspaper advertising, and envelope stuffers.

13. One of your direct-mail jobs is to write a two-letter campaign for the Mark Baldwin Company, 6719 Hanover Street, Madison, Illinois 60053, to promote a brown simulated-leather desk diary called the Executive Organizer, which sells for $4.95. Your mailing list is made up of executives, supervisory personnel, dealers, and distributors. The main theme of your first letter is "give a gift your friends will truly appreciate this Christmas." The theme of the second letter is "you are in good company when you use the Executive Organizer as a Christmas gift." The first mailing is in August and the second in September. Each mailing includes an order blank and a picture of the product.

Features that you will want to bring out are as follows: Page size is 6¾″ x 8¾″ with ruled lines spaced for easy handwritten entry. All entries are written on a flat surface from the first page to the last so the executive can see a "week at a glance," with plenty of room for notes, dates, and appointments. Gold-embossed tab indexing for every month of the year, plus a removable A-to-Z name, address, and telephone index helps the user organize and plan. There is a separate expense section for tax records, telephone area code numbers for every section of the country, automobile mileage distances between 192 principal cities, a guide to fine dining, basic weights and measures, buying power by sections and states, dates to remember, vital facts, and decimal equivalents. Every Executive Organizer comes in an attractive gift box and custom-made mailing carton at no extra charge. The name of each gift recipient can be embossed on the front cover for just 40 cents per unit. Mark Baldwin Company handles all the details except the pleasure of gift giving. In this two-letter campaign ask your reader to order the Executive Organizer for Christmas gifts to his business friends. These will be form letters.

14. To promote your Zip-Zip Electric Scissors you have a mailing list of fabric shops in the Middle West (Ohio, Illinois, Michigan, and Wisconsin). Where a woman who sews buys fabrics, she is also likely to buy sewing equipment or accessories. The electric scissors are made up of a small motor in a plastic housing from which a pair of short blades protrudes. The lower blade doesn't move; it's set at an angle to the housing so that the seamstress can slide it along a table's surface to guide and support the appliance. When the seamstress uses the thumb switch on the top of the housing, the upper blade makes thousands of tiny snips a minute. Those stubby blade jaws look ominous, but they're really quite safe. The blades don't close completely; the area that does the actual snipping is so small, and the blade opening at the cutting point so narrow, that it virtually is impossible to draw blood. It is electrically safe and has the stamp of *Good Living* as well as UL. The Zip-Zip will cut a double layer of heavy coat wool, stretch-knit material, as well as lightweight and sheer fabrics. It has three speeds (or settings) which are designed for the different kinds of material (slow speed for heavy material, medium for average weight material, and fast for lightweight material). Once a seamstress gets the hang of it, she will usually be able to make her electric scissors literally dash around the tight bends, corners, and notches of a dress pattern. Her job will be a lot easier when she uses these light, balanced scissors. These scissors are time savers for any home dressmaker and a particular boon for sewers with muscular or arthritic problems.

There are two styles of these eight-inch scissors: one type plugs into the wall; one has a rechargeable battery. According to tests run by *Consumer Report* the cordless scissor didn't seem to add to maneuverability. They found the model with the cord was easy to use, probably because the cord had enough reach (9½ feet). They also found that the scissors would not bite through its own cord unless deliberately forced to.

The Zip-Zip does not have a built-in lamp. After a great deal of testing by your laboratory, your company found that a built-in lamp made shadows. No serious sewer would work in the marginal light.

The blades will wear with normal use, but *Consumer Report* tests indicated no gradual dulling. They found, on the contrary, evidence of a self-sharpening effect. The blades will die at an early age if the seamstress runs the scissors needlessly while not actually cutting material or if she strikes one of the pins binding the pattern to the fabric. Even a brief encounter with a carelessly set pin may ruin the blades' edges. Should that happen, the seamstress may need replacement blades (available for $2) or a professional sharpening. The appliance should have a drop or two of light machine oil on the blade pivot occasionally to keep it in cutting condition. The two styles of scissors are as follows: (1) Zip-Zip 3 speed No. 2897 (wholesale $7, retail $14), compact and lightweight (4 oz.), quiet scissors with stainless-steel blades with 9½ foot cord. (2) Zip-Zip 3 speed No. 2965 (wholesale $9, $18 retail), compact and lightweight (5 oz.), with rechargeable battery. It provides about one hour of cordless operation per charge.

Write the form letter under the signature of director of sales for the Zip-Zip Electric Scissor Company, Military Avenue, Green Bay, Wisconsin

54303. Assume an illustration of the Zip-Zip under your letterhead and right above your letter copy.

15. By direct-mail letters your company, Resseller, East Orange, New Jersey 07601, is promoting the Resseller 23D11 photographic enlarger to members of camera clubs in the Southwest (Texas, Oklahoma, and Arkansas). You have also run full-page ads in *Photography* magazine the last three months promoting this improved enlarger. The copy reads:

The heart of the darkroom is, of course, the enlarger. In your darkroom you maintain full control over all the steps between the click of the shutter and the finished enlargement.

For $177, you can buy a Resseller with one lensboard and one 2¼ x 2¼-inch negative carrier. Use with 35-mm negatives and other formats from 16 mm to 2½ x 3½-inch. It has a heat-absorbing filter and tiltable lens stage for distortion correction.

The theme of this first mailing is—"If the heart of the darkroom is the enlarger, the heart of the enlarger is the lens. Resseller lens was ranked high by rating agencies last month."

The Resseller, like most enlargers, has a light source and its housing, condensers to focus the light into parallel rays, a negative carrier to hold the negative flat and steady under the light, an enlarging lens and a means of focusing it, a device for raising and lowering the unit to make the projected image larger or smaller, and a base to which the mounting column is attached and upon which to lay the enlarging paper during exposure.

The Resseller is an ideal choice for the enthusiast who has room for a permanent darkroom and who wants an instrument capable of a wide range of uses. It can handle negatives as large as 2½ x 3½-inch size used in many press-type or "graphic" view cameras. It is nicely finished, and its negative carriers are handy to use. The buyer can purchase it without lenses, and almost any lens can be readily fitted to it.

After you have explained the superiority of Resseller, ask the camera-club member to mail an inquiry card for more information.

16. To the people who responded to your mailing about the Resseller photographic enlarger (preceding case), write a letter and enclose an order blank and a picture folder on the Time-O-Lite timer for darkroom developing of pictures. In the darkroom time is of the essence. For best results, all the steps in developing film and making prints from negatives must be timed accurately. The developer will probably want two timers in his darkroom—one permanently attached to the enlarger to turn it off after a pre-set time interval, and another that works like an alarm clock to time other operations.

Facts about the Time-O-Lite: Made by Resseller. Relatively large, 8½ x 8½ x 4½ inches. Rated for 6 amp (750 watts). Maximum "on" time, one hour. Buzzer can be switched on to signal end of time interval. Safelight outlet; focus switch turns on equipment outlet and simultaneously turns off safelight outlet. No stop for repeated settings. Cost $32.50.

17. To promote your Retrojack (Retrojack, Inc., Hicksville, N.Y. 11561), you are sending a sales mailing to a list of automobile accessory dealers in North and South Carolina and Virginia. The Retrojack is a bumper jack powered by a 12-volt electric motor that plugs into a car's cigarette-lighter socket. It is a durable device that raises and lowers one corner of a car. The Retrojack resembles a conventional single-column bumper jack, though at 18 pounds it's considerably heavier. It has a detachable base, on which its motor is housed; a lift column with an unusual threadless roller screw on a smooth shaft that runs the height of the column and does the actual lifting; and a simple bumper hook, which attaches to the column with a flexible fabric belt. The driver adjusts the length of the belt and its position on the column so that, with the jack in position, the hook just slips under the lower edge of the bumper. Then the operator stands back, presses a switch located about four feet down the power cord (the cord is 16 feet long, plenty long to reach the cigarette-lighter socket), and watches the jack raise the car. It takes at most two minutes to lift a car and one minute to lower it. It consumes less power during a tire change than an electric dome light left on for 15 minutes. In the durability tests run by *Consumer Reports,* it ran some 350 flawless car-lift-and-lower cycles before any problems started to appear. The Retrojack must lift a car to the same precarious height as any bumper jack; so tire changing should be done only on level or near-level terrain, blocking the wheel diagonally opposite the jack to minimize the danger of slippage. It doesn't work, however, on cars with an inaccessible lower bumper edge. (Most of those cars provide special holes in the bumper face in which to insert a jack designed specifically to fit.) But if the car normally uses a bumper jack, and if the lower edges of the bumper are within reach, the Retrojack will probably work. The Retrojack costs $19.95 dealer price, $29.95 retail.

18. At Spell and Maxwell Company, 824 Royal Ridge Road, Northlake, Illinois 60062, where you are sales manager, you have worked up the following product description for Spell and Maxwell new Dial 15 camera:

Appearance of product: 3- x 4-inch camera with an electric eye around the lens comes with a flash mount to use with rotating cubes. A specially designed, snap-on strap can be used with the camera when it is in or when it is not in a deluxe case.

What product does: The electric eye gives correctly exposed pictures every time, or with the manual override the user can set the lens himself for special effects. Up front is a superb f/2.8, sharp, wide-angle lens that industry test reports say can compete with the most expensive made. It has shutter speeds to 1/250 second, takes film as fast as ASA 1000. It will take twice as many quality pictures on one roll of film. It will take 20 pictures in less than a minute. It will take close-ups only 2.6 feet away. The Dial 15 not only gives crisp color or striking black-and-white prints—it also makes color slides.

MAILING LIST: Parents (who earn over $15,000 yearly) of high-school graduating seniors. You can use the list by state, region—or even nationally.

Offer and Cost: Let the reader use and enjoy the Dial 15 for two weeks free. If he decides to keep it then it will be $8.88 per month or $99.95 complete. He needs to send no money and no deposit is required.

Action: Ask the graduate's parents to sign an enclosed reservation form and return it to Spell and Maxwell Company. The form includes credit details.

19. Your company, Whittier and Winston, Inc., 4100 Brighton, Rochester, New York 14619, manufactures Luxaides, dinner napkins 17 inches square made of triple-ply, fine-quality cellulose. Market research shows that some commercial restaurateurs pay more for rented table linens than the cost of these napkins (one case of 2,000 napkins sells for $25). When they use their own linens, pilferage losses and replacements due to fraying and cigaret burns amount to a significant cost. Operators who are using paper service are dissatisfied with the small size and poor quality of the napkins, but operators of fine establishments are interested in a luxury type of paper napkin for cocktail lounge or luncheon service. With economy and quality appeals, write a letter to hotel managers in the Middle West. For our sample you can write to John Boles, Hunters' Lodge, Boulder Junction, Wisconsin 54512. See whether you can convince him that this snowy-white napkin is far superior to ordinary paper napkins. It is intended for use instead of linen in the finest inns, hotels, and clubs, where patrons expect the best.

With these large paper napkins that won't slide off laps, the hotel or lodge avoids laborious ironing, sorting, counting, bundling, and handling. Also Luxaides have no holes, no frayed edges, no rust spots, or stains. Besides calling Boles's attention to the enclosed napkin, suggest that he order by filling out the reply card.

20. Under the title of sales representative, send personalized letters to cardholders of United Express. As a United Express cardholder your reader is invited to order and "live with" a magnificent Starwick grandfather clock. Each clock is individually crafted and designed. Each clock is sanded four times during its manufacture—the last two times completely by hand. In addition, each cabinet is hand-glazed, which means that the coat of glaze is carefully hand-wiped by an expert who knows exactly how to bring out the beauty of the grain in each individual piece of wood. In Starwick, there are three different finishes: cherry fruitwood, mahogany, and maple nutmeg. The face of the Signature Series is finished in brass, with elegant hands and numerals showing on a satin-aluminum background. Behind the glass cabinet door there is a 25½-inch pendulum gently moving, and three weights; the right one drives the Eastminster chime that sounds every quarter hour; the middle one drives the movement itself; the left one drives the Big Ben gong that sounds the hours in resonant, deep-voiced tones.

United Express cardholders may order a Starwick Signature Series grandfather clock for 30 days, free inspection. Simply sign and mail the enclosed reservation card. If, for any reason whatsoever, the cardholder decides that this timepiece is not for him, he is entitled to return it to United Express and owe nothing. If he decides to keep it, he will be billed on his regular United Express monthly statement. In this way the reader can "live with" a Starwick Signature Series grandfather clock for 30 days free and own one on easy terms. Enclose a reservation card and ask the cardholder to sign it. Also assume that a folder with pictures and descriptions of the clock is enclosed. Price is covered in an explanatory order form. A business-reply envelope is also part of the mailing.

21. *Mailing list:* Executives in the Northeast. *Company:* Dorsey Electronic Corporation, 1698 Trenton Street, Troy, Michigan 48084.

Product: Dorsey *Siel* Electronic Calculator: 3½ x 5½ inches, 26 ounces; adaptor (for recharging) 2 x 3 inches, 12 ounces; $345 plus sales tax, shipping and handling. Can be paid for on World Express Card (lump sum or monthly payments). Guarantee for one full year against any and all defects, with free repair for one year from the date of purchase, except in cases of misuse.

Advantages: Can use it on battery anywhere (in the office, on planes, at home). Use it for 3 hours on battery, after it's charged for 3 hours on regular current. Completely silent operation. Can plug it in and use it at office. It calculates in just milliseconds. It'll cut through sales projections, annual budgets in a fraction of time. It even charges while the executive works. Students can use it for homework and at school. Homemakers can use it to check monthly bills, balance checkbooks, etc.

How it Works: Answers can be read at first glance. It's illuminated in bright green numerals displayed against a black background to make reading easy. It adds, divides, multiplies, and subtracts. Decimal point automatically moves to the right position. Large, clearly marked, finger-contoured numeral keys are separated from the function keys for faster use and fewer errors. Minus sign indicator lights up when answer is negative. Clearing key clears the previous answer instantly from the display panel so additional calculations can be made quickly. Error lamp prevents inaccuracies. In multiplication or division, if the answer is greater than 16 digits you cannot carry this undisplayed answer in further calculations. Alarm lamp alerts you when the unit is not charging when it is plugged in.

Sales Pitch: Your time is your most valuable commodity. Show the reader how he can spend time thinking instead of pushing a pencil with the Dorsey *Siel* Calculator.

Enclosures: Descriptive folder and reply card.

22. With a mailing list of 50,000 owners of homes valued at from $40,000 to $60,000 in the Northeast, your company, Nesbitt Swift Door, 900 Nokomis Avenue, Akron, Ohio 44321, sends a letter and pamphlet on the integrated-circuit door opener for garage doors. Previously you have handled automatic door openers that operated by radio control. Some customers complained that they were highly temperamental. Now your company has perfected a garage door opener that is operated by small integrated circuits, or IC's. The garage door is automatically opened, and the light goes on automatically when the driver pushes a small panel (2 by 4 inches). The receiving panel in the garage and the pushbutton transmitter are the size of a 3- by 6-inch box. Although these operate the same way as the radio control, the units are smaller and cost more ($180 instead of $160), but they last longer. These have a five-year guarantee instead of two. They have been tested on 60,000 single and double garage doors in six major areas of the United States (East, Southeast, West, Midwest, North, and Northwest). The company will repair or replace without charge any defective Nesbitt Swift door opener within five years of date of purchase. If the homeowner has several cars, there is no problem of mounting a control set in each car. Only his garage can be opened from his car. Safety is a big selling point for this item. The family or just one member of the family can feel secure in driving up to a dark house, pushing the IC panel, and having the garage light come on and the door open. Before he leaves his car, the driver can close the door from the car panel, or he can close the door from the garage reset panel.

23. Using the information in the preceding case, write a dealer sales letter from the company to firms handling garage doors in the Northeast or influencing the decisions of home builders: lumber companies, hardware outlets—even architects and building contractors. Full-page ads are now running in *House Lovely.*

24. As director of the Convention Bureau of San Francisco, California 94114, write a letter to induce as many members as possible of the California Council of Teachers of Mathematics to attend the convention to be held at the San Francisco Hilton, 333 O'Farrell, June 29 and 30.

You are enclosing a beautifully printed and colorful pamphlet describing the accommodations, recreational facilities, and interesting activities in the San Francisco area. You have worked closely with the convention committee and can promise that the program is well planned to include something helpful and interesting to any teacher of mathematics as well as to leave opportunity for enjoyment of some of the recreational facilities. Since the meetings are on Friday and Saturday, you want to interest as many members as possible in staying over until Sunday afternoon. As a special aid, you have arranged for each convention registrant to pick up at the registration desk a courtesy parking ticket, allowing free parking at any metered space.

25. Choose from the pages of a newspaper or magazine any product selling at from $5 to $20 that could reasonably be sold by direct mail in one letter. Either copy the ad (with name of publication, date, and page reference), or cut it out and attach it neatly to a description of the mailing list you assume for your letter. (Remember to indicate distinctions of geography, vocation, sex, age, social or educational status if they apply, and any other pertinent factors.) Submit these with your letter, properly adapted to the circumstances.

26. A chemist, working under a research grant provided by the Whitman Equipment Company, Wilmington, Delaware 19809, perfected a formula for protecting tools from rot, rust, heat, and cold. Tool-Keep stops splitting of wooden handles, waterproofs joints, penetrates wooden surfaces, sets up a weather-resistant, glovelike coating, leaving no sticky surfaces, making tools grip easier, safeguards metals. As a test 5,000 tools were tested two years ago in Wilmington. During the two years the tools were exposed to rain, snow, sun, and sleet, but they didn't rust, nor did the handles deteriorate in any way. In a short time this product pays for itself. A 1-gallon metal drum, $19.50 retail, is enough to paint 600 tools. Also available in a 4-ounce plastic bottle with application top (20 tools, $1) and 16-ounce bottle ($2.95). You're going to send a one-page letter to all contractors in the New York-New Jersey-Pennsylvania area. Your mailing will be a four-page folder: the letter on the first page; two-color illustrations, copy, and endorsements on the rest. (For class purposes just write the letter and assume the rest.) On the fourth and final page will be an order blank. To cut down on the expense of mailing, use a faked inside address imitative of the three-line inside address. Even your signature as sales manager can be processed.

27. Try a mailing promoting Tool-Keep to hardware dealers in the New York-New Jersey-Pennsylvania area (see preceding case). A 4-ounce plastic bottle with applicator top wholesales for 50 cents, 16-ounce bottle, $1.75. To make ordering easier, you've enclosed an order blank along with pictures of the product. You can afford to send card displays and envelope stuffers to help promote Tool-Keep. You are running full-page ads in the monthly *Hardware Review*.

28. *Mailing list:* Parents of college students within your telephone and telegraph company's district (for example Illinois Bell, South Central Bell).

Company: Choose a telephone and telegraph or just a telephone company in the area where you live.

Product: Bell System toll credit card. It is convenient for students in placing calls to have this card. The card serves to some degree for identification purposes.

Action: Suggest that parent call the telephone company business office authorizing the card be sent to the college son or daughter. The card will have to have the phone number of the parents.

29. With the theme "Which is more important to your child . . . the size of his home or the size of his mind?" write a sales letter to parents of grade-school children promoting Tempo-Living series of *Science Series.* An enormous printing materially reduces your cost so that under the usual direct-from-the-publisher plan you can pass on these savings to the customer. The 15 volumes "televise" information with 20,467 magnificent photographs, charts, maps, and drawings. *Science Series* is the largest and most complete reference set in the field of science published in America for children, containing 25,000 pages and over 30 million words. With the book-of-the-month payment plan the set is easy to pay for. The set sells for $99 (only $6.60 for each volume). Assume a one-page descriptive leaflet and reply card. Ask your reader to fill in and mail the card you enclose so that he will receive, without cost or obligation, a copy of the beautiful new booklet which contains an exciting preview of the latest edition of *Science Series.*

30. Write copy for a sales letter going to fathers of 12-year-old boys in your community. You are the manager of the Raycraft Drug Company.

Through the courtesy of a friend who runs the leading family shoe store and maintains a list by birth dates of all children who have made purchases at his store, you have assembled your own list—by dates, name of son, name of father, and address. The letters will be individually typed, using both the father's and the son's name. Your secretary will type out the two or three (rarely more than six) letters coming up each day and mail them about 10 days before the birth date. You want to stress the desirability of having the young man start good, easy shaving habits with the Realclean Speedshaver, a shaving means which will help to keep the skin smooth and clear (no nicks and cuts) and—because electroshaving is so much simpler than other ways—promote good grooming (sometimes a matter of despair to parents of teen-agers).

The Realclean (which is pictured and described on an envelope stuffer that you'll enclose with every letter) is a rotary-blade shaver that never has to be oiled; the twin blades never have to be sharpened. The rotary blades stroke off whiskers whichever way they grow. Simplest cleaning imaginable: Simply push the button, and the head flips back for emptying whisker dust. All this whisker dust is collected in the head; does not spray around the room. The young man would not have to use the bathroom for shaving; he could shave in his bedroom. A built-in, pop-up trimmer helps keep neck and sideburns neat. Ninety-day guarantee. Cost, $22.95, including handsome traveling case. AC-DC. Ask the reader to come in for an inspection and demonstration. Suggest the appropriateness of the gift also at Christmastime. Since you would likely be on a first-name basis with many of the men on the list but not with others, after using the exact name in the inside address, in the salutation use phrase form of address like "Dear Parent of a boy who'll soon be a man."

31. As supervisor of sales promotion for Health-Action Corporation, 2399 Sleigh Avenue West, Tampa, Florida 33610, you write a letter to 5,000 YMCA's in cities over 50,000 promoting the Health-Acizor, an electrically operated machine which produces peak waves to exercise external muscles. The peak waves trim down bulges by creating a pleasant impulse that exercises the muscles. Depending upon size of unit and number of accessories desired, the machine costs either $210 (six pads, three knobs, exercises three sets of muscles at the same time) or $340 (eight pads, four knobs, exercises four sets of muscles). The Health-Acizors are guaranteed for the first two years, with free adjustments during this same period.

One third of the company's customers are men; so you figure that the "Y" is a good market. Men want to stay fit and trim and live longer too. The Health-Acizor weighs about 7 pounds, resembles a portable radio, and comes with an assortment of body belts, round rubber pads 4 inches in diameter, straps, and wires. To take a treatment, a person just puts the body belt or pad where he wants to reduce, straps it down, turns on the machine, and relaxes for 30 minutes while the machine does the work. In 30 minutes a day for a month a man can lose as much as $4\frac{1}{2}$ inches from his waistline.

Many beauty parlors have Health-Acizors and charge an average of $15 for 30 treatments. The YMCA might like to operate on this basis and let the machine pay for itself.

It has the seal of safety from Underwriters Laboratories. In the past two years the company has sold over 900,000 machines in the United States. Since you are writing a form letter, a simulated inside address would be an economical way of starting. The enclosed folder pictures men using the machine, and the enclosed reply card suggests that the receiver fill it out so that you can let your representative in the area come to see him.

32. The Panaphonic Corporation, 9765 Thunderbird Road, Dallas, Texas 75238, has been running advertisements in *Time, Business Week,* and *Harper's* plugging its dictating machine, the Sonic Time-Master. "Does Paperwork Stand in Your Way?" the ads read; "Wife-Saver—thanks to the Sonic Time-Master . . ."; "Reasons Why Sonic's Time-Master Makes Your Work Easier!"

The Panaphonic Corporation officials decide to try prospecting sales letters in addition to magazine advertising. As sales manager, prepare a personalized mailing intended for insurance companies. You may address your sample to Thomas Moore, President, Provident Life Insurance Company, 1187 Lamar Avenue, Milwaukee, Wisconsin 53204.

Assume the enclosure of the four-page folder, and try to pave the way for a salesman to introduce the free-trial plan. With the sales pitch of cutting costs and avoiding last-minute rushes, write the letter. Enclose a card so that Moore can get more information, a booklet. The machine sells for $425 plus federal and state taxes. It is an electronically controlled stenographer, made of durable, lightweight steel. Maintenance on the machine is done by factory-trained personnel. The warranty covers parts and labor for one year. This 28-ounce compact, portable dictating machine uses a magnetic belt. The belt is reusable, and it fits a standard envelope. If an error is made, it is simply erased, as the erasing is done for a tape recorder. Additional foot controls and headset can be hooked in. These additions cost $25. The machine dimensions are 6½ inches long, 4½ inches wide, and 1½ inches deep. It operates on a single mercury-alkaline battery providing 16 hours of dictation. Color is sandstone-beige case with blue front panel and black trim, and each unit is delivered with black-leather carrying case, one battery, four magnetic belts, four mailing inserts, one erase-magnet, and one pad of index slips. The Sonic Time-Master has completely transistorized amplifier; unlimited measured review; instant, audible scanning; adjustable recording volume control; full-range playback volume control; alert and end-of-belt warning signals; dictate-listen interlock; indexing for secretarial instructions at end of letter; automatic shutoff at end of belt; built-in battery-life indicator; belt-in-motion window; and fine-line tuning controls. It can be used anywhere (on planes or trains, in the office or home).

33. The Panaphonic Corporation (see preceding case) two weeks later sends a second letter to Thomas Moore, stressing how much freedom may be had when the Sonic Time-Master dictating machine is used. Mention how simple the machine is to operate. The dictator just inserts the magnetic belt into the machine with one hand, presses the mike, and thinks out loud. It is so easy to erase an error. Suggest the free-trial plan. Card is enclosed.

34. Two weeks later (see preceding two cases) your letter centers around convenience. With a Sonic Time-Master, Moore can spend more time with his family. The Sonic Time-Master is so compact, so light (28 ounces), that he can conveniently carry it home on the days he never seems to finish dictating. He can dictate when out of town and mail the recording to his secretary. Ask him to return the card authorizing the salesman in his area to call.

35. Three weeks go by (see preceding three cases) before you write that there's no need to worry about being misunderstood when you use Sonic Time-Master magnetic belts, since each message is recorded and heard with FM clarity by the transcriber. Any corrections the dictator makes are clearly indicated, so that his secretary can turn out an even flow of correctly done work. Of course, your letter will want to bring in other points, but the theme can center around the clarity of the recording. Same card is enclosed.

36. Your final letter two months later (review the preceding four cases) summarizes the main sales points of simplicity, freedom, and economy. Tell Moore that your sales representative will phone for an appointment to demonstrate the Sonic Time-Master.

37. *Mailing list:* Send personalized letter to parents of college graduates.
Company: Graduate Locaters, P.O. Box 810, Chicago, Illinois 60623. Graduate Locaters serves as a clearing house of address information for the graduates of colleges and universities who don't want to lose track of their friends.

Here is how G. L. works: 1. To apply for registration, the postage-paid enclosure must be filled out and returned to G. L. 2. Upon acceptance of the application, G. L. will mail a Locater Kit to the graduate. (Naturally, a note will be enclosed indicating who sent the gift.) The Locater Kit includes a form the graduate fills out and returns to G. L. computer center, plus additional *Information Cards* which are used to keep the computer advised of any subsequent relocation. 3. The kit also contains a number of request information cards which are used to obtain information from the G. L. computer center about the location of classmates as the graduate moves or travels from place to place.

The use of high-speed computers allows G. L. to offer this service for only $5.00 per graduate—a small sum when compared to the value of the most precious commodity in the troubled world—a lasting friendship.

Appeals: A graduate of the University of X moves to a large midwestern city and suddenly finds himself alone in a strange place. A list from G. L. computer center will tell the graduate right away whom he knows in the city, so that he can get in touch with them on the day of his arrival.

Framework: Address the letter to Mr. and Mrs. Wallace Strudwick, parents of Stacey Strudwick, 89 Country Club Lane, Warsaw, Indiana 46580. Open your letter with some reference to Stacey's recent graduation from Indiana University. Sign the letter as John Hawthorne, Vice President.

38. One of your direct-mail jobs is to write a campaign for the Florists Telegraph Delivery Association, 800 Bakewell, Toledo, Ohio 43605, to promote flowers as a profitable tool for building goodwill, creating new sales contacts, and strengthening employee and public relations. FTDA's primary function is to serve as a nonprofit national clearinghouse through which retail members can send and receive out-of-town orders through fellow florists. But member shops have come to depend on the Association for a host of other vital services, including advertising, merchandising, promotional assistance, public relations, and long-range sales planning. On behalf of the 15,500 retailers who control it (and whose floral orders by wire finance its operations) the Boston-headquartered FTDA spends $2 million a year on advertising. And it supplies members with scores of sales promotion aids ranging from electric signs to envelope stuffers.

As a sample use of direct mail, write a letter for FTDA shops in St. Louis, Missouri 63132, directed to business executives and mailed in mid-October to support Christmas flower giving or in the spring for Easter sales.

A special letterhead plays up names, addresses, and phone numbers of the participating shops, together with a dominant display of the Association's name and initials. In this, your first letter copy, point up FTDA members as the top-ranking florists in the city and emphasize their efficient, guaranteed service. But place heaviest emphasis on use of flowers for such purposes as office decorations, employee relations, and customer contact—especially at the Christmas season. Don't forget that such business gifts are tax-deductible. Emphasize this easy way of Christmas shopping.

39. Instead of showing names and addresses of participating shops, the second FTDA mailing (see preceding case) is processed on the Association's regular headquarters stationery with no identifying tie-in to local members. It goes out about November 1 and asks prospects to mail a special order form back to Boston specifying the name of any FTDA florist in their trading areas. In return, prospects receive five roses with the compliments of that shop, sent either to their business or their home.

40. As part of your FTDA campaign (see preceding case), the third mailing is a follow-up from the florist who sent the five red roses. Write this for the Flower House, 1109 Chambers Avenue, St. Louis, Missouri 63143, to M. P. Dutton, 399 Dover Place. This is on the original FTDA letterhead prominently identifying the Flower House and other FTDA shops in the area. It reiterates reasons why flowers are a logical solution to business gift problems. Flowers are distinctive, create a lasting impression, are always in perfect taste (a bid for a larger slice of the millions that business firms spend on liquor, food, delicacies, and other gifts).

41. A fourth mailing of the FTDA campaign stresses ease of ordering, availability of assortments in every price bracket, and reliability of FTDA service. The hard-sell phase of the campaign reaches its climax with a clean-up letter timed for delivery December 15, reminding executive shoppers that even the last minute is time enough to cover late additions to their gift lists with flowers by wire.

42. The fifth mailing of the FTDA campaign (see preceding case) reminds your executive that he can keep flowers on his sales force all year round, to build lasting cordial relations; to express appreciation, congratulations, sympathy, or respect; and to create lasting sales impressions.

43. *Mailing List:* Owners of homes in the $30,000 and up range in Michigan and Wisconsin.

Company: Therma-Steam Ltd., 116 Park Avenue, New York, N.Y. 10017.

Product: Therma-Steam (steam bath for tub or shower). Therma-Steam Ltd., the world's largest manufacturer of residential and commercial steam-bathing equipment, is the originator of true steam bathing in the privacy of the bathroom.

Guarantee: Should any Therma-Steam unit be found defective in parts or material within one year from installation, it will be repaired or replaced by Therma-Steam at no extra cost except shipping charges, providing the equipment has not been tampered with and the warranty card is returned to the manufacturer within ten days after installation. Therma-Steam guarantees unconditionally that there will be no steam damage to tile within bathing area, to bathroom walls or wall coverings.

How Therma-Steam Works: The Therma-Steam unit is connected to a water line (preferably hot). Then a copper line is attached from the unit to the special antiscald steam outlet head which is installed just above the rim of the tub or 12 inches above the shower floor. An electric circuit is connected to the Therma-Steam unit and the minute timer control. A glass pane or panel is added to the existing tub or shower doors (or new hinged or sliding doors are installed) completely enclosing the full bathing area. Therma-Steam baths are fully automatic and completely safe. The Therma-Steam bath is as simple to operate as a shower. Set the timer for the minutes desired for a steam bath (average steam bath is 10–20 minutes). Step in and close the door. Steam appears in about 2 to 3 minutes. The timer will automatically shut off the steam at precisely the time it was set for.

Equipment for Therma Steam: Minute timer is placed outside the bathing area (automatically controls duration of steam baths). Antiscald steam outlet head is specially designed and provides fast and even heat throughout the entire area. Laboratory tests and hundreds of field tests prove that the Therma-Steam antiscald steam head introduces steam into showers and tubs safely without any adverse effect on tile, or mastic, or sheet rock. Therma-Steam compact steam generator hides away in the closet, attic, or in the vanity. It takes up no usable bathroom space. Hinged or sliding glass doors must enclose full opening (no other special construction necessary). Shower door is watertight, but not airtight. During the steam bath, air enters continuously around the edges of the door and seams of the frame and circulates with the steam. After the steam bath, a regular shower can be enjoyed. This will cause the steam to condense and disappear down the drain.

Optional Accessories: Thermostat permits the bather to set steam bath temperature exactly to his liking and maintains it until shut off. Remote temperature. Sensor in bathing area. Eliminates need for timer switch. *Vaporproof switch:* Installed in bathing area, eliminates need to leave bath to shut off thermostat. *Deluxe steam outlet head* features special "reservoir" to permit the bather to add medication or fragrance of his choice to his steam bath.

Action: Ask your reader to return the business reply card that appears on the back of the six-page folder you have sent along with this letter. (Obviously, price will not be a part of this letter because of installation differences.)

| # Persuasive messages: Collections

THE ONLY SURE WAY to prevent collection problems is to sell strictly for cash. Even with the most careful selection of credit customers, the credit manager (who is usually in charge of collections too) will make an occasional mistake and will allow credit sales to somebody who will not pay promptly.

Unfortunately, however, strict cash selling is also an almost sure way to keep sales and profits unnecessarily low. For that reason the old battle among the salesman who wanted to sell to everybody, the credit man who would approve sales only to gilt-edged credit risks, and the collection man who insisted on prompt pay regardless of consequences has ended in compromise.

Today the thinking salesman accepts the fact that you make no profit if you can't collect; so he does not even try to sell without a reasonably good chance of collection, and he helps the credit man find out about the chances. The credit man accepts the fact that every sale he turns down for credit reasons is a lost chance for more profit; so he approves sales to some marginal credit risks. And the collection man remembers that he not only must collect the money but must retain the goodwill of customers, or he will drive them away as fast as the sales department can bring them in.

Indeed, modern credit theory stresses selling to marginal risks as a means of increasing sales and profits. If a businessman follows this theory, as most do these days, his collection problems will be numerous—but expected.

DEFECTS OF OLD-STYLE COLLECTION LETTERS

In the early days of credit sales, things were different. Only the best risks could get credit. When one of them did not pay promptly, the businessman was surprised, disappointed in his trusted customer, and irked because his bookkeeping routine was broken. The letters he wrote to collect the money revealed all these emotions. Combined with stock letter-writing phrases, these emotions led to letters characterized by curt, exasperated, injured, accusing, or self-righteous tone, jargon, strong-arm methods, and ineffective appeals to sympathy, fear of getting one's nose smashed, and fear of legal suit.

Indeed, such letters are still sent by businessmen who learned all they know about letter writing years ago only by reading and imitating the poor letters of others. With some exceptions, collection correspondence is still a notorious blind spot in business.

Besides the old faults, all too frequently collectors send obvious form letters to collect long-overdue accounts where a form hardly has a chance, or write many short letters when a good one, only a paragraph or two longer, would do the job. They then defend themselves by claiming that they don't have time or money to spend on individualized letters or long letters, or by saying (without testing to find out) that debtors won't read long letters. Tests have shown that the longer letters nearly always pull better than the shorter ones, and individual-sounding letters always pull better than obvious forms in collecting accounts that are very long overdue. The apparent reason is that in the longer letters you can present enough evidence and reasoning to be persuasive.

The approach of "several poor letters" delays collections and leaves the business to be financed through borrowing instead of through current collections. Thus it loses one of the main values of promptness.

The loss, however, is a small consideration in comparison with the main shortcoming of poor collection correspondence—its disposition to drive away customers that the sales department has brought in only at great expense for advertising and sales promotion. Here are two recent examples:

```
We are trying to avoid getting impatient over your delay in
settling your account amounting to $124.60.  The amount is
```

considerably past due, and your failure to answer our letters
(all of which we believe have been polite) has been very
annoying as well as discourteous. If you cannot pay the
account in full, we should be pleased to be favored with your
remittance for part of the amount with approximate date for
payment of balance.

Trusting that you will give the above your prompt attention,
and with kindest regards, ...

--

You have classified yourself by failure to answer our letter
Re: Olympia Clinic Acct., $8. It is therefore our intention
to seek other means of collection of this account as we do not
intend to let you beat it if at all possible to prevent. We
beg to advise that fees for medical services are held by court
to be a necessity. So remember, the time to settle a debt is
before it gets into court.

It will be to your benefit to communicate with this office at
once.

Notice that the only reason given for payment in either of those letters
is the implied threat to sue (for $8?) in the second. Such letters increase
the difficulty of collecting because they make the reader hate to pay
someone he so thoroughly dislikes, and they incense him so that he never
wants to do business with the writer again. The results of poor collection
correspondence, then, are one or more of these unnecessary losses:

1. A series of costly collection letters, when one good one would do the job.
2. Delayed collection of money needed for operating expenses.
3. Additional purchases which may be added to the account before it is closed
   (and thus will increase the loss if the account is uncollectible).
4. Loss of sales. Customers with overdue accounts commonly trade elsewhere
   rather than face the embarrassment of buying where they owe money.
5. Permanent loss of many customers.
6. The unfavorable attitudes passed on by these customers to others.

These are high prices for any firm to pay for keeping a poor collection man
—higher than necessary to employ a good one.

ATTITUDES AND OBJECTIVES OF MODERN COLLECTION WRITERS

Modern collection theory and methods are designed to prevent these
undesirable consequences. The trained collection man takes the attitude
that the debtor should pay because he promised to do so by a certain date
and the time has come. So a collector need never apologize about asking
for his money; he has every right to ask for money due him.

In asking, however, he realizes that people pay because of benefits to
themselves rather than sympathy for the collector or any other reason.
He therefore not only associates the obligation with the goods through
resale talk; but in persuading the debtor, he points out the benefits of
paying now.

The modern collection man is not surprised by a delinquency. He knows that most people who do not pay promptly are still honest and that they will pay soon. He knows that some are in temporary financial difficulty and need only a little more time. So he avoids the curt tone. He is not hurt or disappointed as if he were being let down by a trusted friend. So he avoids the injured, pouting tone. He is not the bookkeeper irked by a broken routine. So he avoids the tone of exasperation and self-righteousness. He knows that some delinquents are withholding payment because of dissatisfaction with the goods or charges and that the problem is really one of adjustment rather than collection. He knows that some will have to be persuaded to pay. And he knows that a few—but only a few—are basically dishonest and will have to be forced to pay or marked off as losses. But he realizes that threats of physical violence are illegal and threats of suit destroy goodwill. Most important of all, the modern collector (unlike his predecessors) recognizes the true nature of his job.

The trained writer of collection letters today expects his letters to do *two* jobs:

1. They must collect the money, promptly if possible.
2. They must also retain the goodwill of the customer if at all possible.

By adding the second job, the collector retains the customer, prevents the unfavorable publicity inevitably carried by a disgruntled former customer, and makes his letter more likely to succeed in its first job—that of collecting. In many cases the second job is more important than the first. Certainly to collect $4.50 by means that lose the goodwill of a customer who has been buying hundreds of dollars' worth of goods a year is bad business.

If the collector has to sacrifice anything, he will yield promptness the most willingly, despite the inherent losses (previously listed).

For effectiveness in both collection and goodwill, the modern collector cooperates with the sales department. As in acknowledgments of orders, he may even inject some sales promotion material into *early* collection letters to a good risk, when he feels that it might be of interest to the customer. It not only promotes future sales, but it shows the debtor that the firm still trusts him and is willing for him to buy more on credit. Thus it is a subtle appeal to pride which helps to save the reader's face and his goodwill. If used at the end of the letter, it relieves the sting and solves one of the correspondent's touchiest problems—how to provide a pleasant ending for a letter in which some element is displeasing to the customer.

Even when resale is not the basic collection appeal (as discussed later), the collection man introduces into his letters a few phrases of resale talk to keep the customer convinced that he made a wise decision in buying *those goods* from *that firm*—and to make the obligation to pay concrete by attaching it to the goods. The following letter includes both resale and sales promotion talk:

You probably remember your first feeling of pleasure when you saw the dark, gleaming wood and the beautifully proportioned design of the Heppelwaite bedroom suite you bought here a few months ago. The suite was one of the finest we have ever had in our store, and we were well pleased—as we thought you were —when you selected it for your home.

At the time, we were glad to arrange convenient credit terms so that you could have your furniture while paying for it. Now if you will look over your bills, you will notice that those for October, November, and December have not been marked paid. The sooner you take care of them, the more you can enjoy your furniture because each time you use it or even see it you will subconsciously remember that you are up to date on your payments.

When you come to the store to make your payments, be sure to see the home furnishings department as well as the time-payment desk. An entire new line of curtains, slipcovers, bedspreads, and scatter rugs is there for your inspection. You'll find a great variety of colors and fabrics made up in the latest styles. From the wide selection you can choose a beautiful new setting for your Heppelwaite suite.

This letter pretty well exemplifies the attitudes and objectives of modern collection writers: Ask for the money without apology because it is due, persuade by showing the reader benefits to himself, use calm understanding and patience, collect but retain goodwill, and cooperate with the sales department.

CHARACTERISTICS OF THE COLLECTION SERIES

In trying to collect and retain goodwill, the efficient collector classifies delinquent accounts and prescribes the best treatment for each. The method is like a process of repeated siftings or screenings. The procedure is a series of mailings, each of which eliminates some names from the delinquent list and aids in reclassifying and prescribing for those remaining.

To do its two jobs best, the collection series should have the following characteristics:

1. *Promptness.* Credit and collection men know that the sooner they start trying to collect after an account becomes due, the better the chance. The U.S. Department of Commerce has found that a dollar in current accounts is worth only 90 cents after two months, 67 cents after six months, 45 cents after a year, 23 cents at two years, 15 cents at three years, and 1 cent at five years.

2. *Regularity.* Systematic handling of collections increases office efficiency and has a desirable effect on debtors. They see quickly that they are not going to slip through the holes in a haphazard procedure.

3. *Increasing forcefulness.* Since the collector wants to retain the goodwill of the customer as well as collect the money, he starts with as weak a letter as he thinks will work. Like the doctor who uses stronger and stronger medicine or resorts to surgery only as the need develops, he applies more and more forceful methods and resorts to the court only after weaker methods fail.

4. *Adaptation.* Not all credit and collection men classify their customers into the clean-cut categories of good, medium, and poor risks suggested by some books; but all competent ones vary their procedures according to the quality of the risk (as well as according to the general bases of adaptation already discussed). Usually the poorer the risk, the more frequent the mailings and the more forceful the messages. Whereas three months might pass before anything stronger than a few statements go to a good risk, much less time might run a poor one through the whole sifting process and bring him to court.

5. *Flexibility.* The collection procedure has to be flexible to take care of unusual circumstances. The collector would look silly to continue sending letters every 15 days to a man who had answered an early one with the message that an automobile accident had thrown him financially two months behind but that he would pay the bill by a certain date. After all, you can't get blood out of a turnip.

STANDARD COLLECTION PROCEDURES

The exact plan of a collection series varies according to circumstances. Also, various collection theorists and practitioners use different terms to mean essentially the same things. Most well-planned series, however, are screening processes somewhat like that shown in Table 10–1.

TABLE 10–1

Stage	*Assumption*	*Nature*	*Gist*
Notification	Will pay promptly	Usual statement	Amount due, due date, terms
Reminder	Will pay; overlooked	Statement, perhaps with rubber stamp, penned note, or sticker; or form letter or brief reference in other letter	Same as above, perhaps with indication that this is not first notice
Inquiry	Something unusual; needs special consideration	One letter	Asks for payment or explanation and offers consideration and helpfulness
Appeal	Needs to be persuaded	Letters	Selected appropriate and increasingly forceful appeals, well developed
Urgency	May be scared into paying	Letter, sometimes from high executive or special collector	Grave tone of something getting out of hand; still a chance to come through clean
Ultimatum	Must be squeezed	Letter	Pay by set date or we'll report to credit bureau or sue; reviews case to retain goodwill by showing reasonableness

Of course, you would send only one mailing at the notification, inquiry, or ultimatum stage. The nature of the letters makes repetition of them illogical. The number and frequency of mailings in the other stages vary from firm to firm, and even within firms according to the class of customer and other circumstances, such as the type of business (retail or mercantile) and type of sale (open account, installment). In general, the better the credit risk, the greater the number of mailings and the longer the intervals. Usually, however, you use two to four reminders, two or three appeals, and one urgency letter at 10- to 30-day intervals (which usually become shorter near the end).

The assumption, nature, and gist clearly call for modified A–plan messages in the first two collection stages (where no persuasion seems necessary) and for C–plan letters in the last three. The inquiry stage is middle ground, where one might well use either. B–plan letters would be appropriate in collections only if the debtor had asked for an unapproved concession, such as an unearned discount.

Notification (usually a form telling amount, date due, and terms)

On or about the due date, you have no reason to assume anything except prompt payment if the customer knows how much is due, what for, the due date, and the terms. Most people will pay in response to form notices —the first sifting—which give these facts. A personal letter at this stage would insult most people by implying distrust and concern over the account. Instead of a costly letter, then, the notification is almost always a statement (bill) sent on or about the due date. The forms have the advantage of avoiding insults and saving lots of money on the large mailings while reducing the mailing list for the later, more expensive stages.

Reminder (usually forms giving basic information and adding a push)

If the notice brings no response, the collector gives the customer the benefit of the doubt, assumes that he intends to pay but forgot, and sends him one or more reminders (the number and frequency depending on the circumstances). The collector knows that most of the remaining delinquents will respond at this stage, and further reduce his list. He therefore concerns himself with avoiding offense while giving the necessary information (amount, what for, due date, and terms).

Reminders are usually forms, in order to save both money and the customer's face, but they may be of four types:

1. Exact copy of the original notice, or copy plus a penned note or rubber stamp such as "Second Notice" or "Please Remit," or copy with the addition of a colorful gummed sticker carrying a slogan. Effective examples are "Don't delay further; this is long overdue," "Your prompt remittance is requested," "*Now* is the time to take care of this," "Prompt payment insures good credit," "Prompt

payments are appreciated," "Don't delay—pay today," "Remember you agreed to pay in 30 days," and "Have you overlooked this?"

Less effective wordings, with the apparent reasons for ineffectiveness in parentheses, are:

> We trusted you in good faith; we hope we were not mistaken (undesirable implications and tone, stressing *We*).
>
> We are counting on you; don't fail us (selfish view).
>
> If there is any reason for nonpayment, write us frankly (suggests finding something wrong; lacks success consciousness).
>
> If this checks up clear, clear it up with a check (same criticism as preceding; the word play is questionable).

2. Brief gadget letter (form):

[Picture of Reddy Kilowatt, beside which is]

```
I'm wondering why—

My note to you last week didn't bring payment of my wages.

Did you by chance forget to send it in?  If you have sent my
pay within the last day or two, thanks a lot.

                          Your faithful servant
                          REDDY KILOWATT
                    --
Doe$ thi$ little note from u$ remind you of anything?

I$n't there $omething that you have meant to attend to—
$omething that ha$ nearly e$caped your attention?

If you will take ju$t a moment right now—while the enclo$ed
po$tage-free envelope i$ before you—we'll $urely appreciate
it.
Amt.      $9.08
                          $incerely your$
                          Robert W. Widdicombe

                    --
We enclose a small piece of string, just long enough to tie
around your finger to remind you that you should send your
check today for $48.50 in payment of . . . .

                    --
The little alarm clock pictured in this letterhead, like any
alarm clock, reminds you that it's time to do something you
planned to do.  This is a friendly reminder that you intended
to send your check today for $28.65. . . .
```

3. Incidental reminder (underscored in the following example) in a personalized letter mainly about something else:

```
With fall just around the corner and school starting within a
month, no doubt you have been planning to order some more
fast-selling Queen candies to have plenty on your shelves
before the fall rush begins.

By this time you have surely realized the advantage of handling
Queen products in your new store.  You will want to take
advantage of our special back-to-school offer too.  It includes
many delicious assorted candies popular with children.
```

When you mail your payment of $126 due July 30, covering our
last shipment under our invoice No. 134, dated June 30, won't
you include your next order, so we can assure you an early
delivery of factory-fresh candies? Notice the variety in our
complete line, as shown in the latest catalog, a copy of which
I'm enclosing for your convenience in making your selections.

More of the helpful window and counter displays like those
sent with your first shipment are available on request. If
in any other way we can help you to sell Queen candies, let us
know. We are always glad to be of service.

If we let XXXXX represent collection talk and————represent resale
or sales promotion talk, the reminder letter may look like either of the
following (usually the first, as in the preceding letter):

<table>
<tr><td align="center">THIS</td><td align="center">or</td><td align="center">THIS</td></tr>
</table>

THIS   or   THIS

_____   XXXXXXXXXXX
_____   _____
XXXXXXXXXXX   _____
_____   _____
_____

Some collection men prefer the second version. They feel that most
people behind in their accounts expect a collection letter and spot it as
such. Better then, they reason, to send it under no such masquerades as
the first. In the following letters, after the direct request for payment
the sales material reassures the customer that the firm feels no concern
over the status of the account. The first one is a form letter:

Will you please take a moment to fill out your check for
$69.50, the amount due for your August purchases?

And then bring it by the shop so that we can show you all the
latest fashions assembled from the choice showings in New
York, Dallas, and Los Angeles.

Whether you need a basic outfit or only accessories to complete
one, we'll look forward to serving you.

--

Now that the end-of-the-year rush has let up, won't you please
give your personal attention for a few minutes, Mr. Bowers, to
your $95 account for Columbia supplies sent you on December 3?

Personal attention is appropriate here, for you are concerned
—more so than are any of your assistants—with the
maintenance of your valuable credit reputation among stationery
supply houses. You will want to continue this good record, of
course, by taking care of your first purchase from us, sent to
you with our invoice BB103. Please sit down now and send us
your check for $95 covering these supplies.

The $42 worth of supplies ordered on January 26 and shipped
with our invoice CB345 brought your account total to $137.
Doubtless these Valentine and Washington's Birthday sets
enlivened your early February sales. With Easter almost here,
the new color books and cutouts shown in the enclosed folder
will soon be in demand. May we send you what you need?

Up through the reminder stage in the collection procedure the assumption is that little or no persuasion is necessary. Thus forms or incidental reminders can do the job more cheaply and avoid the sting that personalized, full-length collection messages would carry. You may have noticed that even the incidental reminder in the Queen candies letter is in dependent-clause structure to avoid too much sting.

4. Individual-sounding letter solely about collection. For greater force in the last reminder, or to poor risks, or about large amounts, the collector may, however, decide to write a letter that talks collection all the way and seems to be individualized. Since most of his delinquents have so much in common, he may still make it a relatively inexpensive fill-in form if he watches the tone and content carefully, typing each copy (perhaps made of form paragraphs) or matching fill-ins neatly.

The following letter for a mercantile concern, for example, adapts easily to a large number of customers. With only one fill-in (for the underscored part, conveniently placed at the end of a paragraph) besides the inside address and salutation, it will serve for a large mailing list. It has a touch of pride appeal along with the reminder to reduce the sting of the apparently individualized message.

```
As a successful businessman, you know what a good credit
reputation means.  You have one.

That's why we immediately extended you 30-day credit on your
recent order.  We know that the reports of your good credit
reputation were correct.  And we likewise know that you'll
send us payment as soon as this letter recalls the fact that
you owe $85 due November 15 for. . . .
```

Beyond the reminder stage, however, the *obvious* form letters sometimes used can hardly do the job. In the inquiry stage and beyond, the very nature of the collector's working assumptions seems to call for individualized messages.

For the later stages of the collection procedure the collection man fortunately has ample information on the credit application form and in the credit records to adapt an individually dictated letter. And his earlier mailings have so reduced the list of delinquents that he can afford to give some personal attention to each letter late in the collection procedure.

Inquiry (giving the debtor a chance to pay or explain; offering help)

When the collector has sent enough reminders to convince himself that oversight is not the cause of delay, he has to start working on another assumption. With a new customer or a poor risk he may assume that persuasion or force is necessary and skip a stage or two in the usual procedure.

With an old customer who has paid regularly, however, he will reason that unusual circumstances must be the cause of delay. He still has con-

fidence in the customer, based on past favorable experience. He still wants
to retain goodwill. And he is always willing to be considerate of a person
temporarily in a financial tight spot.

His plan, then, is to write *one* letter in a spirit of friendly understanding and helpfulness, asking for the money *or* an explanation. Because he
prefers the money, he stresses it instead of the explanation of what's wrong
or how he can help. But he is careful not to offend this formerly good
customer who is apparently in a temporary jam. And he will not suggest
that something is wrong with the goods or the billing (for reasons explained later). His only persuasion is in his frankness, his offer of help, and
his considerate attitude. Most people react favorably to requests presented
in such a spirit. The three letters below illustrate the technique for the inquiry stage:

> Because distance makes it impossible for me to come to you for
> a friendly chat, I ask you to accept this letter as the next
> best thing.
>
> You now owe us $250, due since May 31, for the shipment of
> assorted electric fans listed on invoice X-221. Formerly you
> always paid our invoices promptly. We conclude that some
> special reason causes the delay this time. As your business
> friends, can we do anything to help you over the rough spot?
>
> Of course we want our money, but we also want to keep your
> friendship. What is wrong? What can we do to help?
>
> Will you please send your payment today or let me have a full
> and frank explanation? Perhaps between us we can work out a
> plan so that you can bring your account up to date without
> crowding yourself too much and we can continue to supply your
> immediate needs.
>
> If you will use the handy return envelope I'm enclosing, your
> reply will come direct to my desk unopened.
>
> --
>
> Even though we do not send you a series of strong collection
> letters about the account you owe us, we do expect you to pay
> it as soon as you can.
>
> In view of the very satisfactory way you have paid your bills
> for the five years we have been supplying you, I feel that
> something unexpected has happened to you. Can we help you
> over the hump?
>
> May we ask that you do one of the following three things?
>
> 1. If you possibly can, send us a check today for the full
>   amount of $237.60 for the . . . .
>
> 2. Send us a partial payment today and propose a schedule
>   you can follow to cover the rest.
>
> 3. If you honestly feel that you can't spare enough to make
>   a significant partial payment, please explain what the
>   trouble is, what I can do to help, and your proposed
>   schedule for taking care of the account.

```
I shall have to be able to report some response soon, or my
boss is going to think I'm not doing my job.  May I ask you
to help by doing 1, 2, or 3?
                           --
I wish I could sit down and talk with you for a few minutes
about the circumstances that leave January and February charges
to you on the books.

But because of the distance, I can only study our past
experience with you, and various kinds of credit information.
Your past record of prompt payment leaves me unconcerned about
ultimate collection, but it also leaves me wondering what's
wrong now.

Please either make immediate payment of the $157.47 balance
due or drop me a note today telling just how you intend to
handle the account.  You'll find me cooperative in accepting
any reasonable proposal for your taking care of it—or better,
the $157.47.
```

You may have noticed that these letters avoid *two common collection-letter errors* that have their first chance to come up in the inquiry stage.

The *first* is that in writing inquiry-stage letters, collectors sometimes ask *questions about the customer's possible dissatisfaction with the goods or charges or both*. The apparent purpose of the questions is to secure some kind of answer—to keep the debtor thinking about his obligation and renew his acceptance of it.

But aren't such questions psychologically unsound? If the debtor had found anything wrong with the goods or the billing, would he not himself have suggested an adjustment? Isn't the collector practically suggesting that if the debtor will claim that something is wrong, he can gracefully postpone payment and perhaps even get an unjustified adjustment? Certainly he is working in the opposite direction from both resale talk and success consciousness.

The *second* common error is *backtracking*—that is, going back to the assumption of an earlier stage in the collection procedure (see Table 10–1, p. 393). Apparently in an effort to save the delinquent's face, a timid collector sometimes grabs back at "oversight" (the assumption of the reminder stage) after he has started a letter in the inquiry stage. If he believes that oversight is the reason for the delay, he should not advance to the inquiry stage.

The same kind of nerveless collector sometimes shows the same tendencies in two other places in the collection procedure. After his inquiry-stage offer of special consideration has been ignored, he sometimes incongruously repeats it in letters of the next stage. Not many businessmen will send an ultimatum and then back down on it—the worst kind of backtracking. Those who do merely spoil customers and lose their respect, just as many mothers do with their children by issuing ultimatums and not carrying them out.

The summing up on all three kinds of backtracking is simply this: Don't do it. Hold onto one working assumption until it seems unsound. Then throw it overboard, grab the next one, and don't be diving into the water to retrieve the discard. If you've threatened to sue or report the delinquent unless you get your money by a certain day and the money doesn't come, sue or report. Conversely, don't talk about suing or reporting until you are seriously considering it.

Appeals (basically reader benefits, made increasingly forceful)

If the delinquent does not respond to a friendly inquiry, apparently he is taking the wrong attitude toward his indebtedness. The collector's new assumption is that the debtor must be persuaded to pay. He will not backtrack from that.

Basic considerations. At the appeal stage the collection letter writer does his main work. In doing it, he keeps in mind four important points.

1. *For persuasiveness, write individualized messages.* The earlier brief notices, reminders, and inquiries will have collected most of the accounts (the easy ones) as inexpensively as possible in terms of time and goodwill. The remaining few will be harder to collect. Usually they will require individualized (or at least individual-sounding) letters rather than forms, because they have to be persuasive. By using the information in the credit records, the collector can write individualized messages that are specific and therefore persuasive to a degreee impossible in a form.

2. *Develop only one or two points.* Scattering shots like a shotgun over several undeveloped appeals weakens the message too much to reach the remaining hard-to-collect-from delinquents. Something like a rifle bullet, with all the powder behind one fully developed central theme, will be more forceful. This usually means longer letters because they must be specific and say enough to make the point emphatic, but they pay off in results.

3. *Retain goodwill as far as possible.* Because they are individualized, pointed, full-length collection messages, appeal-stage letters will necessarily carry some sting. Like doctors and patients, however, collectors and debtors have to accept the fact that the needle carrying strong medicine for advanced stages of a disease often has a sting. Still, the wise collector, like the humane doctor, will minimize the sting as much as possible without weakening the medicine.

You want to be firm without being harsh. Skillfully stimulate the customer's desire to pay and you'll both be happy.

4. *Select a reader-benefit appeal.* Successful collection, like successful selling or any other kind of persuasion, involves showing the debtor that he will get something he wants or avoid something he doesn't want—in other words, the you-attitude.

Appeals to sympathy (variously called the "poor me" appeal or the appeal to cooperation) do not meet the requirement. They are fundamentally selfish:

```
You have often heard of a business house needing money
to finance its operations, haven't you? How is a concern
going to carry on without a source of income to meet its
constantly growing bills?

That, Mrs. Rose, is our problem today; hence we are asking you
again to send us a remittance to cover the balance of your
past-due account. Won't you please accommodate us by balancing
your account tomorrow?
```

Though a cleverly and humorously overdrawn picture of the writer's family in need might bring the money, it is more likely to bring a wisecrack answer. For instance, one man built his letter around a picture of his wife and 11 children, with the note below: "This is why I *must* have my money." The answer was the picture of a beautiful blonde with the note "This is why I *can't* pay."

Basically, people want

1. To have self-respect and the approval of others (they have to live with both themselves and others).
2. To avoid loss of what they have and add to those things (money, property, and the credit privilege, for example).

So a collector can be persuasive by showing debtors how they benefit in self-respect or in economic self-interest.

The true collector is therefore really a salesman. Like a salesman, he makes a careful analysis of the customer, selects the appeal most likely to succeed with the particular individual in the specific situation, and sells him on the idea of paying by showing him the benefits he gets. The resale, pride, and fair-play appeals show the reader how to retain a clear conscience and keep his self-respect.

The resale appeal. Touches of resale belong in every collection letter to keep the debtor satisfied and to show him what he got for his promise to pay, but resale may be the theme of a whole appeal letter. Essentially it goes back and almost repeats the points a good salesman would make in selling the product. By the time the collector-salesman is through reselling, the debtor will see that he got good value. Whether you call it his integrity, his respect for his word when he made the contact, his sense of fair play, or his pride, it can prompt him to pay for his basic desire to act so that he will have a clear conscience and be able to live with himself.

Although inept phrasing may make any appeal ineffective or kill goodwill, the danger is not great in the resale appeal. Really effective use of it, however, requires skillful salesmanship. The collector must be imaginative enough to paint a vivid, interesting picture of the product in use; and he must be willing to make it complete, detailed, and long enough to be persuasive. The following letter illustrates the type:

Now that Asbex and Asbar have had time to prove their profit-making ability to you, can you say that we were right? We said that they would be a good selling team for you.

When you followed up your original Asbex order of April 15 with the April 27 order for 10 gallons each of Asbex and Asbar, you showed that you thought the fire-retarding twins would move quickly together. With your good reputation for prompt payment as our guide, we were glad to have such a desirable outlet as your store for this pair of fast sellers. Although your payment of $39 for the first shipment, invoice BT-41198, is now 10 days overdue, you can keep your record intact by sending us a check in the next mail. If you make the check for $156, you can also pay for the second shipment, invoice BT-41390, on its net date.

From all reports on the way business is in Ardmore, you'll be sending us repeat orders before long. We'll be looking forward to serving you now that you have learned that Asbex and Asbar fill a recurring need of your customers. With readers of <u>Life</u>, <u>Good Housekeeping</u>, and <u>House Beautiful</u>, and more and more satisfied users spreading the good news, you can expect ever-increasing turnover with the twins in your stock.

The following letter from a building and loan collector who made the loan originally and knew the family quite well is even more personal in its resale appeal. The reference to passing pleasures in the second paragraph is a subtle way of telling Barnes, without preaching to him, that the collector knows where the money went—into expensive parties designed to keep up with the Joneses.

When you and Mrs. Barnes moved into your new home two years ago, I was very proud that I had something to do with it, for if anything contributes to the pleasure of life it is a good place to live—and especially if that place belongs to the occupant. I feel that much more than mere sentiment is behind the words "There's no place like home."

Indeed, so much of comfort, security, and pride comes with home ownership that anyone should forgo passing pleasures that eat up his income, take the savings, and invest in a home—just as you decided to do.

The importance to you of keeping up your payments on your loan deserves your serious attention. Perhaps by now you are used to your home, and you take it as a matter of course. But take a walk around the lawn. Note the landscaping; note the beautiful architectural lines of the building. Then go inside and think for a minute how comfortable you, Mary, Jim, and Jane are there. Think where you would be without it. And suppose you were going to build today. Instead of the $18,000 you paid, you would now have to pay about $20,000 because of increased prices in general. Really, you cannot afford to stop enjoying those comforts.

So will you please come in and take care of your March, April, and May payments as soon as possible?

Pride appeal. Often resale talk joins a subtle appeal to pride, or the appeal to pride may be more or less independent of resale on the goods.

In either case the writer uses all his knowledge of practical psychology to know when to encourage pride by sincere compliments, when to needle it, and when to challenge it. If he bumbles, he may get a surprising answer, as did the collector who asked what the neighbors would think if he came into town and repossessed the debtor's new car. The answer was that the neighbors all agreed it would be a low-down, dirty trick. The collector had erred in challenging when he should have been encouraging pride.

One collector succeeded by quoting from a highly favorable credit report on the debtor, asking if he recognized the description, and encouraging him to retain his reputation by taking the required prompt action. Others have given percentages of customers who pay at different stages in the collection procedure and said that of course the debtor does not want to be in the minority groups at the end of the list. The essence of success with the pride appeal is to *encourage the debtor toward actions he can be proud of* and to avoid the use of accusations and implications of shame as far as possible.

The following examples show the methods. Note that the first (an early letter) ends with sales promotion, and the last (to a university student) incorporates a reference that is almost a left hook.

Your choice of the navy-blue suit and the light tan suit with matching shoes, purse, and gloves, for a total of $182.95, shows the care and pride with which you select your clothes.

We feel sure that you want to show the same pride in maintaining your preferred credit rating. Drop your check for $182.95 in the mail today, and your account, due on November 10, will be paid in full.

The next time you are in town, come by and look over our completely new line of Mary Margaret furs. Whether you want to make additions to your wardrobe or merely to see the latest fashions, you will be welcome.

--

When you applied for credit privileges with us, we of course checked your rating.

"Good" and "fair," some firms reported, and (according to three) "excellent." You may well be proud of such a rating.

Let us help you keep your pride in your rating by writing "Paid" after the 30-day overdue balance of $33.88 that now shows on our books for . . . .

--

Twenty-seven other Lansing residents bought Monora television sets the same week you got yours.

That was just a little over three months ago. Yet 23 of them have already been in to take care of their payments as agreed. We made a note of their prompt payments on their records. And they walked out of the store pleased with themselves, their sets, and us.

When you stop to think about it, the good credit rating you establish by promptly paying as agreed is more than a matter

of personal pride. It adds to the value and desirability of
your account with any store in Lansing. It's a personal
recommendation too, for employers often check the credit
record of an applicant for a job.

Take the two minutes now to send us your check. Or bring your
payment to the store tomorrow.

Fair-play appeal. By using slightly different wording, you can turn the
basic appeal to self-respect into an appeal to fair play. The wording may
recall the debtor's sense of respect for a contract, his feeling of duty to do
what he has promised, or his conscience that makes him do the right thing.
It develops the feeling that the debtor should carry out his part of the bargain, since the creditor has been fair in carrying out his. Integrity or
honesty may be as good a name for the appeal. Some people call it a
request for cooperation.

Whatever the name, a well-developed, positive presentation (without
accusations), showing the reader that he should pay to be fair, is an effective appeal. It goes back to the fundamental idea that the debtor promised
to pay by a certain time for certain goods or services. Since he has received the benefits, the fair thing is that he should pay for them. Almost
everybody wants to feel that he is fair in his dealings with others. Here are
two examples of the appeal:

On August 20 we filled your order for a . . . on credit because
of our faith in you to pay according to terms. It has no
doubt given you the service you expected by . . . .

We were glad to extend open-account terms to you, and since
this has run far beyond the usual 30 days, isn't it true that
we've been fairly decent about waiting this long for our
money?

I cannot believe that you want us to suffer a loss because of
our good faith in filling your order without cash in advance.

So I'm enclosing an addressed envelope that needs no postage,
and I'm appealing to you to use it—this moment—to send the
$27.60 due us and to make our contract a two-sided one, the
way it is supposed to be.

--

How would you feel next payday if you received no paycheck?
I'm sure you would feel that you had been giving good service
and that your employer should pay for it.

When we ask you for the $44.95 for the coat you bought on
November 18, we are only asking for what is due us.

At the time we placed your name on our credit list, we made
clear that accounts are due on the 10th of the month following
purchase. Perhaps more important, you accepted the terms in
accepting that becoming coat.

In fairness to us and to yourself, won't you please come in
today and give us our paycheck according to our agreement?

Appeals to economic self-interest. Even the man who has no sense
of obligation to pay for value received (as developed in the resale ap-

peal), or of pride, or of fair play in treating decent people fairly will likely pay if it is clearly to his own economic self-interest to do so. You may therefore write forceful collection appeals to a debtor's desire to retain his valuable credit privilege.

Slight shifts of emphasis in the wording, as in the illustrations below, may stress the convenience of credit in future buying or the economics of credit:

> The increasing size of your three orders for Mada irons and lamps since June 15 indicates that your business must be good.
>
> With your business growing as indicated, you'll be needing a greater variety of stock. That's just good merchandising. It's also good business to pay for your stock within the 60-day terms.
>
> Please send your check for $260, which is now almost four weeks past due. New Mada stocks are coming in now, and you'll want to be in a position to offer your customers the latest in electrical supplies.
>
> --
>
> Why is a prompt-pay rating like money in the bank?
>
> Both are able to command goods and services immediately when you want them.
>
> On the basis of your ability to pay and your reputation for meeting payments promptly, we extended credit immediately when you asked for it. Now we ask that you send your check for $98.76 to cover your August shipment of jewelry, sold to you on credit just as if you had drawn on your bank account for it.
>
> Then look through the enclosed booklet. Notice the color pictures of things you'd like to have in stock for Toledo's Christmas shoppers. The heavy hollow silver plate described on page 3 is a line for moderate budgets. It's durable as well as handsome, since it's triple-plated silver on copper.
>
> Should you care to order on our regular terms, enclose a check covering your balance of $98.76 and order the new stock; use your credit as if it were another check drawn on money in the bank.
>
> --
>
> Customers are quick to buy Presto-Lite flashlights at $3.45, aren't they?
>
> That price gives you a substantial 50 percent markup on each one you sell and helps you meet competition for sales of reliable, durable flashlights.
>
> One of the reasons you enjoy this favorable pricing is that we extend credit only to those outlets with good credit ratings and thus keep down collection costs. When our credit customers pay within the agreed-on 30 days, we can take all cash discounts available from our suppliers and pass these savings on to our customers and their customers in the form of lower prices. If they take 90 days, however, the $2 you pay us for a Presto-Lite would probably increase to $2.15 or $2.20 and would wind up costing your customers around $3.75. That affects both of us, doesn't it?

So that all of us may profit from the real economies of prompt payments, please write out your check for $51 covering the 24 Presto-Lite flashlights you received almost 50 days ago, and mail it to us in the enclosed envelope.

Though the following letter speaks of fair play, it is an appeal not to fair play, as explained before, but to the debtor's economic self-interest in enjoying the benefits of the credit privilege:

Are you playing fair—

—playing fair with yourself, I mean?

You want to continue to get merchandise promptly by merely mailing an order to your supplier. Rightfully you can expect the best of service along with good-quality products when you arrange a businesslike transaction. You will agree that you would not be fair to yourself if your actions caused you to lose this privilege.

The Reliable Paint and Varnish Company has continued to honor this privilege because in the past you have always settled your account satisfactorily. At present, however, you owe us $125, now three months overdue, on invoice 362773 covering a shipment of 35 gallons of white Reliable house paint.

To treat yourself fairly and to preserve your good, businesslike reputation, you will want to get your account balanced promptly. Please use the enclosed envelope to send your check today and put your account in good condition again.

Urgency

When the regular collector is getting nowhere with appeals like those in the preceding letters, he may continue with stronger letters, or he may turn the job over to a higher executive for the final few mailings. Sometimes he writes the letters himself and sends them out over the signature (and with the approval) of the treasurer, the president, the company lawyer, the credit bureau, or a collection agency.

The psychology is to give the reader the feeling that things are getting pretty serious when the moguls have to take over. Although urgency-stage letters are not actually the end of the collection procedure, they should seem close. They therefore answer the question of the lady in the *New Yorker* cartoon who flashed an early-stage collection letter at the collection desk and asked how many more she would receive before she had to pay.

Actually the letter sent over the signature of the higher executive is usually a forceful development of one of the appeals already discussed. It may go a bit further on the economic interests of the debtor and talk about the cost of facing suit (since the debtor would have to pay the bill and court costs), but usually not. Even now the firm is still interested in goodwill. It knows that a chance of retaining the customer remains. If he is lost as a credit customer, it desires to have him as a cash customer and to have him speak of the firm as favorably as possible. So the executive more frequently plays the role of the good fellow who gives a man a last chance. But he still does not turn the screws all the way by setting an end date. The following letter, signed by the company treasurer, illustrates:

> When you began your business, a good reputation in Ardmore
> made it possible for you to get loans, and your hard work and
> prompt payments—good reputation again—got you credit on your
> purchases.
>
> This reputation is more important to you now than ever before,
> for with the unsettled world conditions causing wide
> fluctuations in the securities market, credit agencies are
> becoming more and more strict in their policies—and
> businessmen are learning to be more insistent on their terms.
>
> We have not received your check for the $156 for your invoices
> 69507, covering our shipment of 10 gallons of Asbex on April
> 10, and 76305, covering the shipment on April 20 of 10 gallons
> of Asbex and 20 gallons of Asbar. Some arrangement for this
> settlement is necessary right away. We are willing to accept
> your 90-day note at 8 percent for this amount so that you can
> protect your credit rating without lowering your cash balance.
>
> We would of course prefer to have your check; but for the
> benefit of your business, your customers, and your creditors,
> please settle your account some way with us today.

Ultimatum

If he gets no response to the serious mood, the strong appeal, and the bigheartedness of the executive's offer of still another chance, the collector will give the screw its last turn. He now assumes that he will have to squeeze the money out of the debtor. He has decided that as long as he gives this debtor any slack, he will move around in it. The collector therefore says calmly and reluctantly but firmly that on a definite date, usually 5–10 days later, he will turn the account over to a collection agency or to a lawyer—unless he receives payment before that time.

Though the language of the ultimatum is firm, it should not be harsh. To minimize resentment, the collector commonly reviews the whole case at this point to show that he cannot well do otherwise, that he has been fair and considerate all along (but he does not become self-righteous about it), that he dislikes to take the necessary action, but that it is justified. Carefully worded, this letter may collect and still retain goodwill because of the fair-play appeal in the whole review. Usually it will at least collect, as these two letters did:

> When we sent you your first credit shipment of $95 worth of
> Christmas supplies under invoice CA-872 on December 4, we took
> the step all stationery wholesalers take when approving
> similar credit requests: We verified your good credit
> reputation with the National Stationery Manufacturers Guild, of
> which we are a member.

The Guild's certification meant that you invariably pay your
bills. When we received a second order on January 26, we were
happy to serve you again by shipping $42 worth of Valentine
cutouts and art supplies, under invoice CB-345. Since then we
have tried to be both reasonable and considerate in inducing
you to pay by our usual collection procedures. Now we shall
be compelled by the terms of our membership agreement to
submit your name to the Guild as "nonpay" unless we receive
your check for $137 by April 15.

You are no doubt aware of the effects of being labeled by the
Guild as nonpay. Credit requests to new supply houses would
be refused; old sources would be reluctant to continue
supplying you on a credit basis. We want to help you maintain
your preferred status so that you can continue to stock your
shelves on credit.

With the sincerity of a friend, I urge you to weigh carefully
the effects of a bad report and the advantages of a favorable
one on your hard-earned and well-thought-of credit rating.
I urge you to avoid the necessity of our submitting an
unfavorable report. And beyond that, of course, would be a
suit in which you would pay not only the bill but the court
costs.

All the advantages of an unmarred credit standing among
suppliers are yours now. Mail us your check for $137 by the
15th and retain those advantages.

--

Let's talk once more about your 95-day-overdue account
amounting to $68 for the butcher supplies you bought on July
15.

That buying was done a long time ago, Mr. Forrest, and the
sale was made on the basis that you would pay within 30 days.
By your acceptance of the goods, you made a contract to pay
according to the terms.

Although this contract is legal and binding, we usually use
the Wholesale Credit Men's Association, rather than the courts,
as our final collection agency. You probably know what a
stamp of "bad pay" on its record can do to you. Every supply
house is a member. It's almost impossible for any firm to
get credit on supplies with a bad record in the Association
files, and it's difficult for a retailer to operate without
credit.

Think it over and see if it's not worth $68 plus the small
amount of time necessary to write out a check. Your account
should have been reported as an overdue one before now, but I
like to give a man a warning and a last chance.

Let us hear from you, with a check enclosed for $68, not later
than the 28th.

If an ultimatum like the two above does not bring the money by the
date set, the only remaining letter to write is a courtesy letter, not a
collection letter, telling the customer of the action taken. Then the case is
out of the hands of the writer of collection letters and in the hands of a
lawyer. In any event the collection series ends with the ultimatum.

BEGINNINGS AND ENDINGS

For most writers the beginnings and endings of letters, including collection letters, are the most troublesome spots. Beginnings are more difficult than endings because the background or point of contact varies more than the desired action, and therefore the beginning cannot be well standardized.

This much, however, we can say: You have to capture the reader's attention and interest and hold it through the letter. Identification of the account (the amount due, what for, and when due) should be clear in every case, *but these facts do not make good beginnings for persuasive letters;* the reader has already shown his lack of interest in them.

Neither are references to former attempts to collect good as beginnings. Such references may sound like whining or may suggest that the debtor can again ignore the request with impunity. Since collection letters are basically sales letters—selling the debtor on the benefits of paying—the collector will do well to reapply the principle of reader-benefit beginnings.

Just as the salesman drives for an order at the end of his sales talk, so does the good collection writer strive to bring in a check or an explanation that will name a payment date. So the standard action ending—telling what to do, making clear how to do it, making action easy, and providing a stimulus to prompt action—is always proper except in the early stages of the series, where it is too forceful. There, resale or sales promotion talk rather than the request for payment usually ends the letter to imply faith, appeal to pride, perhaps promote sales, and remove the sting.

Although the collector always writes with success consciousness because he expects his letter to bring results, in none except the one serving notice that the account has been placed in the hands of an attorney does he fail to leave the way open for more severe action, as in the following forceful requests:

> Please sit down NOW—while your resolution is still strong—
> and send us your check for the balance of $225 due on your
> Christmas purchases. Your name will then remain in the
> preferred-customer file.
>
> --
>
> Won't you come by our office on Saturday night and close this
> account in such a way that we can write a completely
> satisfactory comment about you on our records?
>
> --
>
> We're enclosing an addressed envelope that we expect to see
> back in our office—with a check enclosed for $100—before the
> 15th.

Whenever feasible, the collection writer will find it advisable to make response easy for the debtor. An already addressed and stamped envelope does this and also provides a strong stimulus to prompt action. The Direct Mail Advertising Association reported that 798 collection letters sent without reply envelopes brought remittances from 42.85 percent and requests for time extensions from 6.78 percent for a total of 49.63 percent answering. A similar mailing of 798 letters which included reply envelopes brought remittances from 45.12 percent and requests for extensions from 16.8 percent for a total of 61.92 percent responding. Even the casual "Don't bother to write a letter; just slip your check into the enclosed envelope . . ." will show the debtor the friendly attitude you have toward him and will frequently produce the check.

Because collection letter circumstances vary so much, there are few universal truths about them suitable for a checklist such as we have provided for some other kinds of letters. But the suggestions on p. 414 will be helpful as a partial checklist for collection letters.

HUMOR IN COLLECTIONS

Generally, past-due accounts are not laughing matters, either for the debtor or for the collector. But small amounts early in the collection procedure are not deadly serious matters either. In the early stages, where little or no persuasion is presumed to be necessary or even desirable, the main job of the letter is to gain attention and remind the debtor. Under these circumstances a humorous letter may be just the thing. Its sprightliness will supply the attention and memory value needed. The light mood will take the sting out of the letter and make the collector seem like a friendly human being instead of an ogre.

A widely known and highly successful collection letter, the famous "Elmer" letter by Miles Kimball, pictures both kinds of collection man. The writer, a friendly human, warns the debtor against the ogre Elmer, treasurer of the company, who sometimes gets out of hand and writes letters that destroy a reader's will to live. The whole thing is a detailed and ridiculous account of the kind of ogre Elmer is and the disastrous effects of his letters, plus a brief warning to pay now before Elmer writes.

Shorter humorous letters are more usual. One merely asks for the name of the best lawyer in the debtor's town, in case the collector has to sue. One collector simply mailed small, live turtles to slow payers. *Time* has long used two humorous letters for people who don't pay for their subscriptions. One, on the back of the front picture cover of the current issue of *Time*, begins "I'm sorry—sorry I can't send you any more than the cover of this week's *Time*." It then goes into a brief resale appeal. The other begins with the assertion of how much is due, pokes fun at the usual collection letter that breaks into tears in the first paragraph and yells for the law in the second, shows how large numbers of small accounts add up, and ends with the pun that "procrastination is the thief of *Time*." Still another journal begins a subscription collection with

"CHECKING, JUST CHECKING,"

said the telephone lineman when the lady jumped out of the
bathtub to answer. I'm just checking to find out whether you
want to continue to receive. . . .

The rest of the letter is the usual resale appeal with a standard action
ending.

Another device is that called the one-sided or half-and-half letter. The
writer presents what is essentially an inquiry-stage collection letter as a
narrow column on the left half of the page and asks the reader to use the
right half to attach his check or explain.

Though such letters (usually inexpensive forms) may be effective in
collecting small amounts early in the series, they are too flippant for large
amounts or late-stage collections. The exception is that they might serve
just before an ultimatum to jolt the debtor out of his rut. But we must not
forget that

1. The credit obligation is a serious responsibility, and we can't expect the
debtor to take it seriously if we are undignified about it.

2. Written joshing is more likely to offend than oral banter.

3. Gadgeteering and humor in letters of all kinds are likely to be overrated
because we probably hear more of the occasional successes than of the numerous
failures.

COLLECTING UNEARNED DISCOUNTS

A special problem which does not fit into the regular collection procedure is that of collecting unearned discounts (that is, discounts taken
when sending payment of a bill *after* the end of the discount period).
The fact that the amount is usually small—always small in comparison with
the volume of business the collector risks in trying to collect—complicates
the problem. Moreover, some large purchasers know the collector would
think twice before losing their $200 or $20,000 orders to collect an improper
$4 or $400 discount.

Fortunately the collector usually has some advantages on his side too:

1. When the occasion arises, he is almost certainly dealing with experienced
businessmen who will understand a businessman's reasoned analysis.

2. The sizable purchaser has almost certainly investigated various sources of
supply and might be as reluctant to change suppliers as the collector would be
to lose him as a customer.

3. If the collector cannot get his money in early and has to pay interest on
money borrowed for financing, the debtor will understand that the ultimate end
to his action will be a revised system in which he has no possibility of discount
at all.

4. The fair-play appeal can include playing fair with all the collector's other

customers. That is, he cannot well allow one to take the unearned discount while requiring others to pay according to terms.

Armed thus, the collector is ready for the taker of unearned discounts. First, he can certainly start by assuming a little misunderstanding of the terms. If any doubt remains about whether the terms were clear, he may assume responsibility, make the terms clear, and overlook the improper deduction *the first time.*

When no doubt exists, the collector can certainly assume (reasonably enough) that the unjustified deduction comes from failure to check the dates—an unintentional chiseling—and that the additional money will be forthcoming after a little reminder. One writer used an analogy for the reminder by telling the story of the boy who presented nine apples as his mother's offering for the harvest festival. When the vicar said he would call to thank the mother, the boy asked him please to thank her for 10 apples.

If neither misunderstanding of the terms nor failure to check dates is the reason, the collector has a real letter-writing job. Although well armed —with justice, legal advantages, and some psychology on their side—some collectors fear to go ahead. The almost inevitable result is chaos in the collection department, or at least in the discount system. Word gets around.

The bold do better. Their appeals are Item 3 above (the economic justification of discounting practices) and Item 4 (the broadened fair-play appeal). Often a good letter combines both, as in the following illustrations:

> From your letter of May 25 we understand why you feel entitled to the 2 percent discount from our invoice X-10 of April 30. If some of our creditors allowed us discounts after the end of the discount period, we too might expect others to do the same.
>
> The discount you get from us when you pay within a definite, specified period is simply our passing on to you the saving our creditors allow us for using the money we collect promptly and paying our bills within 10 days after making purchases. It's certainly true that your discount of $4.57 is small; but large or small, we would have allowed it if we had had your payment in time to use in making a similar saving in paying our own bills. If our creditors gave us a longer time, we'd gladly give you a longer time.
>
> Since they don't, the only solution besides following the terms is stopping all discounts, taking the loss on all our sales, or being unfair to our many other customers by making exceptions and showing favoritism. I don't think you want us to do any of those things, do you, Mr. Griggs?
>
> When you mail us your check for the full invoice amount of $228.57, we know that you will do so with the spirit of good business practice and fairness.
>
> Thank you again for your order. You will find that our merchandise and attractive prices will always assure you of a more-than-average profit.

--

The fact that we are returning your check for $2,450 does not mean that we don't appreciate your business. Rather, we want you to use your money for 10 more days and, from your experience, to answer a question on which we want your opinion.

Before I ask the question, however, I want to stress the fact that we consider your company an ideal outlet for our products in your area. Apparently you also consider our products a good line to sell.

But evidently we are not in such complete agreement on the matter of cash discount as established in our terms of 2/10, n/30. The question is: Is your money worth 36 percent a year to you? Under our terms we pay you 2 percent for the use of your money for 20 days (the time between the discount date and the net due date) or 36 percent a year. We do this because it is a trade practice, but there is no justification for it unless we have the money during those 20 days. We have no right, of course, to use your money even part of that time without paying for the use of it; so we are returning your check and asking that you pay the net of $2,500 on the due date, 10 days hence.

We believe you will welcome this frank presentation so that you can give discounts your fair-minded consideration. May we have your decision?

The letter above did both of its jobs of collecting the money and re-taining the customer. Certainly it was not written by the distrusting merchant who told a new employee that if somebody wanted to pay a bill and somebody else yelled "Fire!" to take the money first and then put out the fire.

The problem of unearned discounts becomes particularly difficult after you have allowed one exception, explained the terms carefully, refused to allow a second exception, and received a reply including statements like these:

. . . I thought that an organization such as yours would be above such hair-splitting tactics . . . and I resent your hiding behind a mere technicality to collect an additional $3.69 . . . oversight. . . . If you wish . . . a new check will be mailed, but . . . it will be your last from us.

Here's how one collection writer handled this hot potato—successfully:

I appreciate your letter of December 5 because it gives me an opportunity to explain our request that you mail us a check for $184.50 in place of the returned one for $180.81.

Our sincere desire to be entirely fair to you and all our other customers prompted the request. For years we have allowed a discount of 2 percent to all who pay their bills within 10 days of the invoice date. Such prompt payment enables us to make a similar saving by paying our own bills promptly. Thus we pass on to you and our other customers the savings prompt payments allow us to make.

But if our customers wait longer than the 10 days to pay us, we make no saving to pass on. Of course, an allowance of

Collection Letter Checklist

1. Follow a reasonable philosophy and adapted procedure.
   a) Associate the specific goods with the obligation to pay for them, and show that you expect payment because it is due.
   b) Always identify how much is due and how long overdue.
   c) Except in the first two stages and the ultimatum these identifications (in b, and perhaps the point in a) are not good beginnings.
   d) Stick to your sequence of assumptions for different collection stages; backtracking shows weakness and loses reader respect.
   e) Try to get the money and keep the customer's goodwill.

2. Fit the tone carefully to the circumstances.
   a) Avoid seeming to tell the reader how to run his business.
   b) Nasty, curt, injured, pouting, exasperated, or harsh tone doesn't help; it turns the reader against you instead.
   c) Scolding or holier-than-thou attitude brings resentment too.
   d) To avoid credit platitudes, relate credit principles and regulations to the particular case.
   e) Show confidence that the debtor will pay, by
      1) Avoiding references to past correspondence (except in late-stage reviews).
      2) Stressing positive benefits of payment.
   f) Be sure any humor avoids irritation or distraction.
   g) Avoid (1) accusations, (2) apologies and—except in the reminder and inquiry stages—(3) excuses invented for the reader, including any fault he may think he finds in the goods or billing.
   h) To increase the force, use more collection talk and less sales promotion (good only in early letters to good credit customers).
   i) To decrease stringency and apparent concern, reverse (h); watch proportions.

3. For persuasiveness (after the first two collection stages):
   a) You have to stress what the reader gains by doing as you ask.
   b) Remember the effectiveness of a developed central theme.
   c) Select an appeal appropriate to the circumstance and reader.
   d) Remember that any kind of antagonizing works against you.
   e) Individualize your message for stronger effect, even in forms.

4. Guard against the legal dangers. (See Appendix B, pp. 681–86.)
   a) Reporting the delinquent to anybody except those requesting information because of an interest to protect is dangerous.
   b) Don't threaten physical violence, blackmail, or extortion.
   c) Be careful about your facts, and show no malice.
   d) Be sure that only the debtor will read.

5. Adapt your drive for action to the stage of the collection.
   a) A full-fledged action ending is too strong and stinging early.
   b) But later, anything short of it is too weak.

$3.69 is a small matter; but if we allowed it in one case, we would have to allow similar discounts to all our customers or be unfair to some.

The principle involved is a serious one, since any exception would have to become the rule if we are to be fair to all.

I feel sure that you want us to treat all customers alike, just as you do in your own business. Certainly I do not think you would like it if you found that we were more lenient with somebody else than with you. Our request for the additional $3.69 is necessary if we are to treat all alike.

Thank you again for writing me and giving me this chance to explain. May we have your check—in fairness to all?

COLLECTION CASES

1. When the Hawley Department Store, 987 Plaza Center, Ontario, California 91762, approved credit terms for Meredith Gray a year ago, it had a report from the credit bureau which said:

Mr. Gray conducts a successful laundry route in this area. Always pays promptly. His weekly income is about $130 net. Good character and well liked. Credit good to $400.

You can't understand why he'd mar a good credit standing like this by allowing a bill for a suit ($100) to be unpaid for three months. You will not insist that it all be paid at once. He can work out a time-payment plan to suit his circumstances. If he is absolutely unable to pay, you want him to come in and explain. You have sent him two other notices and have phoned him twice. According to your records he is still living at 5503 West Maitland, Ontario 91762.

2. A hematologist, Dr. Whaley McMillan, Barclay Medical Building, 422 Jefferson Boulevard, South Bend, Indiana 46622, has had as patients Nelson Janes and his wife, Route 2, Knightstown, Indiana 46148. Dr. McMillan has sent several bills to Janes for services given during the preceding six months, but as yet no payment or explanation has been forthcoming. Janes manages a hardware store in Knightstown. There is no apparent reason why payment should be withheld. Write a letter for Dr. McMillan which you think will collect the $222 due.

3. Two young women, wives of students, operate a small but successful shop, the Ginny Lee, 1109 Lincoln Street, Urbana, Illinois 61801. Three months ago they sent a reorder for four Watersword glass compotes ($40), which you sent on the usual terms of 2/10, n/30. The two statements sent at 30-day intervals have brought no reply or check. Write a collection letter for the credit manager of Watersword Imports, 500 Lenox Hill, New York City, New York 10021.

4. As credit manager for the Lipsey-Scott Company, Roanoke Parkway, Kansas City, Missouri 64109, you granted credit to Mrs. Marlin E. Williams, The Bridal Shop, 239 North Lamar Avenue, Jackson, Mississippi 39211, on terms 2/10, n/30 for four bride's dresses ($375). On the eighth day you sent her the usual form calling attention to the discount date, but when you received no reply, you took it for granted that she would pay during the net period. On the 28th day you sent her another form note telling her the amount was due by the 30th. But again no reply. So when the account was 45 days old (15 days overdue), you sent another memorandum note. Still no luck. Today write a collection letter to be sent when the account is 30 days overdue. Keep in mind the dresses she bought, her use of the credit account, and sales promotion talk for the coming bridal season.

5. The letter you wrote to Mrs. Marlin E. Williams (of the preceding case) when the account was 30 days overdue went unanswered. Fifteen days later you wrote what you thought was a persuasive letter, still confident in its assumption. The idea behind this letter was:

We know you don't like this delay any more than we do, and we are sure that you will want to send us your check for $375 for the bridal dresses sent you on account, now 45 days overdue. Your record clearly tells us you realize the value of paying promptly.

Now Mrs. William's account is 60 days overdue. Write her and tell her she should pay her obligation to keep the reputation she now enjoys.

6. Still no luck in getting a check from Mrs. Marlin E. Williams (of the two preceding cases). When the account was 75 days past the due date, you wrote:

Please check your books this morning and note especially the 75-day overdue bill for four bride's dresses, $375. As a good businesswoman, you probably don't hesitate when your customers fail to come through. And you, too, realize the importance of keeping your slate clean.

Unfortunately Mrs. Williams ignored this letter too. So now, when the account is 90 days overdue, you are to write the final letter. As a member of the National Wholesale Credit Association, you must report her if she does not pay within 10 days; she must send a check by then for her own good. Point out what she gains by paying, so that what she loses by not paying is clearly established.

7. Before repossessing a $400 phonograph and record set from Mrs. Annie Bell Mayfield, 11 Hargrove Street, Franklin, Tennessee, you write an appealing letter trying to get her to work out a payment plan with you. She is a waitress at the downtown hotel and earns about $400 a month. She's divorced and has one son aged 13. Three months ago she bought the set and paid $200 down with the understanding that she would pay the balance in six months. When you phoned her, and when you talked with her in person, she said she would pay, but she has not paid a cent. She now has one week to make arrangements before repossession by your company, Maxwell Supply and Service, 1899 Meade Avenue, Nashville, Tennessee 37217.

8. A week after the date of your invoice (Weinberg and Stein Importers, 330 Market Street, San Francisco 94132) to Mrs. Jonathan Pemberton, Jr., owner and manager of the Pemberton Gift Shop, 1109 Marcello Road, Albuquerque, New Mexico 87107, for 12 Marjorie Gregory pitchers at $6 each (express charges collect), you sent a cheerful note about the 2 percent discount. She ignored it, as well as the customary notice that you sent on schedule at the end of the net period (30 days). Instead of the customary short printed reminder note that would normally go out 30 days after the due date, you alter the collection procedure and send her a personal letter, talking about the value of a prompt-pay rating. Although this theme automatically hints that the customer *should* pay the account, you decrease the stringency of the request for payment with a sales suggestion: Isn't it about time for another shipment of quality gift items? Has she looked over the leaflet telling about Marjorie Gregory wine glasses? In case it has been misplaced, here's another. In this letter you are careful not to say or intimate that she can buy no more until the present amount is paid; you very likely would honor another credit request within the next 30 days. She has bought sporadically from you the past five years—and paid in similar fashion (never later than 60 days, however). Notice, however, the big difference in tone when you write, "If you pay, we'll send you more . . ." as contrasted with "When you send your check, include an order for . . . ." Write the letter to be sent out 30 days after payment is due.

9. Your polite letter to Mrs. Jonathan Pemberton, Jr. (preceding case) went unanswered. In 30 more days you sent another letter the theme of which was

The favorable prices on Weinberg and Stein fine imports are partly due to the fact that no collection costs are figured in; if everyone took 60 days to pay instead of 30, the cost of all items would have to be increased a few cents.

Surely, you reasoned, an owner of a small business would respond to such persuasion. But she didn't. You know Mrs. Pemberton can pay; you know she has a thriving shop that can furnish you with a sizable business for many years if your goods give satisfaction and your sales and collection divisions please her. You write her a strong letter, 80 days after the due date, pointing out the value of the credit privilege and the necessity of a sure-pay rating. The theme automatically implies that the account is in jeopardy and that Mrs. Pemberton *should* pay—and soon. You'll want to send the letter on its own merits, with no reference to any letter sent earlier or any that will follow if this one doesn't succeed. This letter talks credit and collection straight through; it contains no sales promotion material on any other goods, although it may contain resale talk on the Marjorie Gregory pitchers.

10. Still you have no answer from Mrs. Jonathan Pemberton, Jr. (of the two preceding cases). When the account was 105 days overdue, you wrote a letter to her that went like this:

For five years we have been privileged to serve the Pemberton Gift Shop by providing fine imported gift items. For five years you have met your obligations. We still believe that our original reports as to your credit integrity were correct. But you must make payment of the $72 for the Marjorie Gregory pitchers sent you over three months ago if we are to continue to regard you in that light. If you can't send the check, perhaps we can arrange a 90-day 8-percent note for part payment.

Mrs. Pemberton still didn't answer. Now it's 15 days later (the account is 120 days overdue), and you write the final letter in which you tell her she must pay or face the consequences of having her name reported to the National Manufacturers Credit Association. This letter makes a special effort to be friendly but final. Give her 10 days in which to reply.

11. As correspondent in the credit department of the Clothes Horse Dress Shop, Gateshead Shopping Center, Detroit, Michigan 48207, you are asked to write a personal collection letter to a well-to-do customer, Mrs. Pembroke Deveroux, 11 Woodland Estate, Eau Claire, Michigan 49111. Her account, amounting to $532.95, is 90 days past due. Mrs. Deveroux has ignored the routine notification, one printed reminder, and one personal note. Be courteous but definite in this second personal letter.

12. *Creditor:* The Radio Shack, 1145 Shawnee Boulevard, Oklahoma City, Oklahoma 73118. *Debtor:* George Batson, Apartment 22, Campus Inn, Norman, Oklahoma 73069. *Case:* George Batson, a university student, bought a dual-powered cassette, $77.95, on the easy payment plan. He paid $30 down, and the $47.95 outstanding was to be paid $11.99 a month for four months. He paid two monthly installments, and the third is 30 days past due. (You sent a reminder when the payment was 15 days past due). As credit manager for the Radio Shack, write the letter suitable for the situation.

13. George Batson (preceding case) ignored your letter and failed to send his payment of $11.99 for the third month for the dual-powered cassette. It is now five months from the date of purchase, and Batson has ignored all your messages. You checked with university officials, and they verified that he was living at Campus Inn and was attending classes. Before turning his name over to the University and his hometown credit bureau for failure to pay, write him an appealing letter that will get him back on a payment plan.

14. *Creditor:* Scott-Lamb, 400 Union Street, Lafayette, Indiana 47905. *Debtor:* Jack Blue, Box 4, Route 2, Star Grove, Indiana 47922, a dealer in farm equipment. *Case:* Jack Blue owes your company (a wholesale dealer of farm supplies) $3,190, which is 60 days past due. Blue is reliable but sometimes slow in payment when his own collections are slow. In response to a recent letter from you, he wrote that he would pay when his farm customers shelled and sold their corn. This will be in about a month. Write and ask him to sign a promissory note. Since he is a man who intends to pay his debts, he may think this is a reflection on his honesty. Explain that you have some exceptionally heavy bills to meet in payment for incoming stock. You can discount his note and use the proceeds for this purpose. Make the explanation and the request tactfully.

15. You are the credit manager of Moore-Macon, Inc., manufacturers of garden tools, 4324 King Street, Gary, Indiana 46420. Just eight days after the date of your invoice to L. P. Johnson, owner of Johnson Hardware Company, 444 Morgan Street, Belleville, Illinois 62221, for pruners, hose carts, and shears ($262), you sent a cheerful note about the discount. He ignored this as well as the customary notice you sent on schedule at the end of the net period (60 days). Instead of the customary short, printed reminder note that would normally go out 30 days after the due date, you alter the collection procedure and send him a personal letter talking about the value of a prompt-pay rating. Although this theme automatically hints that the customer should pay the account, you decrease the stringency of the request for payment with a sales suggestion: Isn't it about time for another shipment of pruners? Has he looked over the leaflet telling about the new garden hoses? In case it has become misplaced, here's another. In this letter you are careful not to say or intimate that he can buy no more until the present amount is paid; you very likely would honor another credit request within the next 30 days. Notice, however, the big difference in tone when you write, "If you pay, we'll send you more . . ." as contrasted with "When you send your check, include an order for . . . ." Write the letter to be sent out 30 days after the payment of $262 is due.

16. Your polite letter (preceding case) went unanswered. In 30 more days you sent L. P. Johnson another letter, but he didn't respond to it either. You know Johnson can pay; you know he has a good, thriving store that can furnish you with sizable business for many years if your goods give satisfaction and your sales and collection divisions please him. You decide to write him a forceful letter, 80 days after the due date, pointing out the value of the credit privilege and the necessity of a sure-pay rating. The theme automatically implies that the account is in jeopardy and that Johnson *should* pay—and soon. You'll want to send the letter on its own merits, with no references to any letter sent earlier or any that will follow if this one doesn't succeed. This letter talks credit and collection straight through; it contains no sales promotion material on any other goods, although it may well contain resale talk on the pruners or grass shears.

17. Still you have no answer from L. P. Johnson (of the two preceding cases). When the account was 105 days overdue, you wrote a letter to him that went like this:

We know our reports as to your credit integrity were correct when we received them. So we also know that you want to mail us your check for $262 for the carts, shears, and pruners we sold you 105 days ago when you can. If you can't send the check, however, perhaps we can arrange a 90-day, 8-percent note for part payment.

Johnson still didn't answer. Now it is 15 days later (the account is 120 days overdue), and you face the final letter in which you tell him that he *must* pay or face the consequences of having his name reported to the National Dealers Credit Association. By positively telling what he keeps for himself by paying, you establish adequately by implication what he loses otherwise. This letter makes a special effort to be friendly but final. Give him 10 days in which to reply.

18. Sixty days ago you acknowledged an initial order from the Music House, 11 Middlessex Highway, Charleston, South Carolina 29407, and shipped:

1 dozen Arch-Tip guitars @ $20	$240
1 dozen classic autoharps @ $20	$240
Shipping charges	5.27
	$485.27

You debited the total under your regular terms 2/10, n/30 to P. M. Shoop, owner of the shop. As credit manager of Richmond Manufacturing Company, Chicago, Illinois 60640, you sent a reminder of the discount. On this 60th day (30 days overdue) you write a friendly note, reminding him of the due date and containing resale on one of the items and sales promotional material on Japanese banjos (mahogany resonator with long-lasting aluminum shell for rich, vibrant sound; plastic head; 20-nickel-plated brackets; protective celluloid-bound edges; rosewood fingerboard). It would cost Shoop $20 for one banjo, but he can sell it for $40.

19. On the 55th day (overdue) you wrote another short, friendly note to P. M. Shoop (of the preceding case):

With the interest among teen-agers for their kind of music, you'll be asked more and more for guitars. In order to help increase your sales, we've designed some festive displays with pictures of the popular guitar players.

If Shoop would like some, ask him to send his check for $485.27 for the guitars and a request for the displays.

20. The good letter you wrote P. M. Shoop (preceding case) went unanswered. So did the one you wrote when the account was 90 days overdue, the long "let's talk it over" letter. Ten more days have elapsed; so you're forced to turn to outside help if the check or some satisfactory arrangement isn't forthcoming. The National Dealers Credit Bureau may not get your money for you, but the report you'll have to send within 10 days won't help Shoop's credit standing. For his sake and yours, you would prefer that he pay now and not have this report affect his business—as it inevitably will. If he pays up within 10 days, he can still get goods on credit, open new accounts, and buy what he needs when he needs it.

21. As collection manager of the Pride Finance Company, your city, you must write Henry Hendrix, 1976 Pine Avenue, a foreman in a local factory, who has borrowed $100 from you to be repaid $5 a week for 20 weeks. He has missed two payments, and a third is two days overdue. Write him a letter telling him you are going to get a judgment in court; then you'll serve a notice of garnishment on his employer, who must deduct the amount from Hendrix's wages and pay to you. How will this affect his relations with his employer and his credit reputation with local retailers?

22. As manager of the credit department of the Jordan Manufacturing Company, St. Louis, Missouri 63120, write a collection letter to Mrs. Betty Turner, owner of the Pair Tree, 1230 Commonwealth Drive, Sarasota, Florida 33580. Sixty days ago you sent her five dozen pairs Italian sandals ($10 a pair) and three dozen American Girl loafers ($8 a pair). This is your first order from her but the third attempt to collect.

23. To get the money and yet retain the goodwill of William Curtis, manager of Curtis's Appliance Store, 1101 Maple Street, Warren, Ohio 44483, write a middle-stage collection letter that shows him why it is to his advantage to pay. Sixty days ago you sent him six portable dishwashers, three Model 500 ($130) and two Model 400 ($100), which sell for $170 and $140, respectively. Curtis has been buying from your company, Mainwhisk, 1198 Continental Street, Pittsburgh, Pennsylvania 15211, irregularly (and paying the same way) for three years. Write the letter over the signature of the credit manager.

24. You are with the Brook Watch Company, 564 Albert Avenue, Providence, Rhode Island 02907. A dealer (Paul Mayer, 1409 Arlington Drive, Beaumont, Texas 77705) owes $545.50, now over a month past due. Mayer is a good customer and can be relied upon to pay his debts, although he is sometimes slow. Write him a letter based on the idea that your prices have not been advanced even though there has been a 10 percent increase in the price of gold. Maintaining the old price has been possible only because of careful management and attention to all details.

25. On the eighth day after you (as credit manager of United Products, 3000 Green Bay Road, Racine, Wisconsin 53402) sent a shipment of toys to Henry Miller, owner of the Toy House, 1230 West Grant, Milwaukee, Wisconsin 53207 (12 single-holster guns at $3.50, 12 two-gun holster guns at $6, and 24 games at $3), you sent him a cordial note about the end of the discount date, mentioning that the discount saving would buy another game or puzzle. He didn't answer the note. On the 30th day, you sent a formal printed notice, but it received no reply. So on the 45th day, when normally a second formal notice is used, you sent Miller a short personal note, with more resale and sales promotion than collection talk. Still silence. Now that the collection file reminder shows Miller marked for special attention on the 60th day ($186, 30 days overdue), you are writing another friendly note talking up as its central theme the value of a prompt-pay rating as particularly adapted to this dealer. This is clearly an early letter; there is no intimation that the account is in jeopardy, least of all with backward- or forward-looking references to other correspondence.

26. On the 75th day after Henry Miller (of the preceding case) bought guns and games from you (when the account was 45 days overdue), you wrote him another letter trying to show him that his slow-paying habits really cost him money in the long run. Apparently he didn't care, though; he didn't answer. So with the $186 account 60 days overdue, you write him a slightly firmer letter, stressing the value of a good credit rating—the reputation for always paying bills—especially to the individual proprietor with modest capital. It's the check for the entire amount that you want, not partial payment—and surely not just a bunch of excuses.

27. Henry Miller (of the two preceding cases) paid no attention to your letter written when the account was 90 days old (60 days overdue). Fifteen days after that, you wrote another letter that went like this:

Let's talk again about the $186 worth of guns and games we sold you 105 days ago. If you're experiencing a temporary slump in sales, we can take your 90- or 120-day 8-percent note and thus help you protect your good credit rating. Better yet, use the enclosed envelope to send the check—today!

It still didn't work. So 15 days later, when the account is 120 days old (90 days overdue), you face the inevitable. You must tell him that he must pay or face the consequences of having his name reported to the National Dealers Credit Bureau. By positively telling him what he keeps for himself by paying, you establish adequately by implication what he loses by failing to pay. He is no novice, it's true; nevertheless you'll want to devote a major portion of the letter to telling him how the National Credit Bureau works.

This letter makes a special effort to be friendly but final. It should not threaten; instead, it is an earnest and sympathetic plea that Miller forestall the bad results his inaction will inevitably bring about. Tell him he has 10 days more in which to reply.

28. As instructed by your teacher, assume that the letter for any one of the sales cases has been successful, that several of the buyers have not paid, and that the seller wants a series of four collection letters to bring in the money. According to your instructor's directions, write all four or any one of the stages specified.

29. Anthony Hull, owner of the Hull Nursery Company, 1109 Gurley Road, Richmond, Virginia 23222, sold Mrs. Kenmore Kendall, 11 Hunters-dell Lane, Richmond 23235, $550.98 worth of dogwood trees (pink and white), camellia bushes, roses, and azalea bushes two months ago. She said she would pay two weeks after she purchased, but she has not paid anything, nor has she acknowledged your two statements. Today, we find out from the purchaser of her Huntersdell Lane home that she has moved to 506 Rushwood Avenue, Roanoke, Virginia 24012. She is the widow of a medical doctor. The credit bureau reported that she lives on annuities of about $700 a month and that she is a free spender, often behind in payments on her many charge accounts. Although your letter is an early-stage letter, be sure you make it clear that she owes for the plantings she contracted for, and also point out the value of having a clear credit rating in Roanoke.

30. You are the credit manager of Right-Tow Auto Supplies, 3303 Noyes Avenue, Charleston, West Virginia 25311, a firm selling auto supplies to dealers, service station owners, etc. You sold supplies worth $417 to Hal McCall, 332 Main Street, Friars Hill, West Virginia 24939, five months ago. Terms were 30 days net. He has disregarded your statements and printed reminders. His credit rating is good. Write him a personal letter.

31. *Creditor:* Scan's Department Store, 2953 California Street N.W., Washington, D.C. 20008. *Debtor:* Captain John McClosky, 89 Mason Place, Tampa, Florida 33612. *Case:* Captain McClosky bought a mahogany five-drawer chest ($150) and four cherry domino end tables ($200) and one bedroom lounge chair ($110) on a budget account. He paid $100 down and signed a budget contract calling for $32 a month for 12 months for the balance. Last month and this month you didn't get his check for the $32; the two payments are now 40 and 10 days past due. Write him a letter calling his attention to the regulations of installment buying and pointing out the importance of maintaining a good credit rating, especially as a military officer. As credit sales manager at Scan's, you'd be in a rather ludicrous position to refer to the repossession clause in the installment contract— with the furniture in Tampa.

32. *Creditor:* Young and Foresman, 220 Dearborn, Chicago, Illinois 60601. *Debtor:* The Health Spa, Barrington Mall, Barrington, Illinois 60010. *Case:* Your company publishes city directories. Bills for advertisements, which are the major source of revenue, are payable upon publication of the directory. The Health Spa is now two months late in its payment of $325 for the quarter-page ad you published on contract. Write a letter based on the idea that large sums of money have to be invested before any returns come in (for materials, editorial work, labor, etc.). To pay for these costs, you have to borrow—and the terms of the loan are based on the assumption that your advertisers will pay promptly. Rates would have to go up if they didn't.

33. Because of too much overbuilding, your area is in a building recession. Hugh Barlow, 666 Cook Street, a reputable local building contractor, owes your company, Holman and Bridgers Building Supplies, $532.98, now a month past due. When you talked with Barlow two weeks ago, he promised to pay you the next day. You phoned him the day the check was to arrive, but he said he had just forgotten to mail the check. He has been a good customer of yours for five years. You are on friendly terms. Write an appropriate note.

34. *Creditor:* Mullins Paper Company, Neenah, Wisconsin 54956. *Debtor:* Good Samaritan Hospital, 1188 Acheson Street, Anchorage, Alaska 99504. Three months ago the hospital purchased from you the following:

1 gross hospital gowns	$144
2 gross paper shoe covers	36.60
4 gross paper pillowcases	144
(Terms 2/10, n/30)	324.60

You sent a discount reminder and a routine notification on the due date; now you are going to write this new customer a mild early-stage letter that is designed to get the money but—of equal significance—retain goodwill and build sales. This first order was obviously a trial. And you are eager to build volume.

35. For cards and gift paper products the Colburn Shop, 400 Alcott, Denver, Colorado 80228, owes your paper manufacturer (Hillmark, 9991 Hobersham, Savannah, Georgia 31406) $351.95, now six months overdue. Write a fourth and final letter, making it clear that you are going to report the unpaid account to the credit-reporting division of your trade association in five days unless you receive payment. Spell out what this will mean to the debtor. But remember that you still want the firm's business.

36. *Creditor:* Kushman Importers, 230 Fifth Street, New York, N.Y. 10001. *Debtor:* Filenes, Pembroke Mall, Jacksonville, Florida 32210. *Case:* Filenes owe you $300 for rugs (design 9515 and stock number 1674) bought three months ago. Despite the several collection notices and letters you have sent them, they have not paid the bill. Today they order more rugs in the same design and stock number ($150 worth). They want these rugs sent by motor freight. Write the appropriate letter in which you diplomatically point out that you cannot add to their already overdue account, that the $300 must be paid before the next order can be filled.

37. You are with Tyndale and Lenoir, Inc., 3200 Lanier, Baton Rouge, Louisiana 70814. Leigh Bain, owner of the Campus Art Supply Company, 2212 Guadalupe, Austin, Texas 78712, who is a fair risk, owes $117.60 for supplies plus $3.06 shipping charges:

12 boxes No. 546 Sargent oil pastels @ 60¢ a box	7.20
1 dozen No. 378 acrylic sets @ 4.70	56.40
1 dozen charcoal pencil sets @ $1.50 . . . . . . , ...	18.00
6 sketch boxes 13″ x 17″ @ $6.00	36.00
	117.60
Shipping charges	3.06
	$120.66

Assume that it is late July. He has not responded to three statements you have sent him for the account, which is 60 days past due. Write a letter built around the theme that it will soon be time to place an order for school season. He should clear his account for heavier buying.

38. Assume that you are the collection manager of the Manning Brothers, national harware dealers, 100 Biscayne Boulevard South, Miami, Florida 33131. One of your small customers, M. J. Grove, Grove Hardware Company, 1106 Gunter Avenue, Tallahassee, Florida 32304, three months ago ordered:

1 doz. MRPT Premore hedge trimmer @ 35.00	$420.00
2 doz. MPRT Oxmore bow saws (36″ size) @ 1.00	24.00
2 doz. MTRP lopping shears @ $3.20	76.80
	$520.80

The terms were 2/10, n/60. Although you have sent the usual notification and two letters during the last five weeks, the account remains unpaid. Write the appropriate letter to get the money.

39. Ten days after the date of your invoice to Samuel Healy, owner-manager of the Healy Condominium Corporation, Deltona, Florida 32763, for the Westgate appliances your salesman, Charles Dodson, sold him—total plus freight, $3,300—you sent him a suggestion about taking the discount. The customary notification on the due date followed. Now it's 30 days after the due date, and you write a friendly letter showing him the advantages of a prompt-pay rating and telling him about your newest

wash-and-dry appliance for clothes (retail for $490). This machine thoroughly washes and dries clothes in one operation yet takes the space of one machine. There are eight fully automatic wash-and-dry cycles. Top-mounted lint screen, safety start button, lighted console, porcelain finish, and UL listed. Suggest that he order several washer-dryer combinations and send his check at the same time. You are the credit manager of Cutler Supplies, 7100 Dixie Highway, Miami, Florida 33160.

40. Even though you and your salesman, Charles Dodson, feel that Samuel Healy (of preceding case) can pay, he still hasn't answered your letters. Since he has been the pioneer in building condominiums in Deltona and apparently has been successful with his venture, you felt that you had to be patient and wait 30 more days before sending him a second letter. So when the account was 60 days old, your letter was basically this:

Perhaps there is a valid reason why your account for $3,300 for Westgate appliances sent 90 days ago is not paid. If so, please tell me by return mail when you can pay. Like any firm that values your account, we value your goodwill. A delay in prompt payment—as long as it is explained—doesn't injure your credit rating.

Healy didn't answer this letter either; so now that it's 80 days after the due date, you write him a forceful letter pointing out the value of his credit rating that he worked hard to earn—what it does for him—why he needs it. You omit sales promotion material on any other goods, but you should have a short resale talk on the appliances ordered.

41. In the last five years William A. Jenkins has purchased over $2,000 worth of merchandise from your store, City Electric Supply, 5400 Flamingo, Houston, Texas 77020. Jenkins has a good credit rating. Six months ago he bought a 60-pound automatic icemaker for home use for $325, paying a substantial amount and saying he'd take care of the small balance later. You agreed to this arrangement. Three months later the manufacturer of the ice machine reduced the price on the model by $50 in an attempt to get more homeowners to want ice machines. Shortly after, Jenkins wrote you, the manager of the City Electric Supply, pointing out that since the reduction was more than the balance of his account ($30), he thought some adjustment should be granted.

In your reply you told him that the price reduction was that of the manufacturer, that City Electric Supply still had to pay the original cost of the ice machine Jenkins had bought. You further explained that the manufacturer made no adjustment to dealers on models already sold, and so there was no price adjustment which would be passed on to customers. Jenkins didn't reply. You have sent him first-of-the-month reminders on two occasions since, but he still hasn't responded. Write him (Deer Ranch, Baytown Road, Texas 77018), requesting payment of his account.

PART THREE

The job-finding process

UNLESS YOU ARE an extremely fortunate person, sometime in your life you will write letters to help you get work: summer jobs; jobs launching a career when you graduate from some institution of learning; a change of jobs for more money, for a better location, for work that has greater appeal to you—and even jobs for retirement or widowhood days.

And even if you never write such a letter, the assurance and confidence from realizing what you could do if you had to are good equipment for successful living. Too, from a practical standpoint the experience of job analyzing is desirable preparation for interviewing—an inevitable part of the procedure in job seeking.

As in sales, when you seek work, you are simply marketing a product: your service. You market that product to some prospect: business firms or other organizations which can use your services. In some cases those firms make their needs known—through advertisements, word of mouth, placement agencies, or recruiting personnel. In these circumstances the application is invited. In other cases firms do not make their needs known; so it's a case of prospecting. You'll find, then, that job-getting letters will be directly comparable to either the invited sales letter or the prospecting sales letter. Both must convince someone of your ability to do something; the big difference between the two is in the approach.

If you are content to accept what life doles out to you, you will probably never write anything but an invited application letter. But we assume that you would not be reading this chapter if you were not trying to improve yourself. For that reason and others listed below, we believe we can help you more by beginning this analysis with the prospecting letter.

The prospecting application is the logical first choice for learning to write applications, because you will write better applications of any type as a result of thorough analysis and writing of this kind. Moreover, in real-life applications the prospecting letter has these advantages over the invited:

—You have a greater choice of jobs and locations, including jobs not advertised.

—You don't have as much competition as for an advertised job, sometimes no competition, as when you create a job for yourself where none existed before.

—Often it is the only way for you to get the exact kind of work you want.

—You can pave the way for a better job a few years later after having gained some experience.

Of course you need to know what kind of work you want to do before you ask someone to let you do it. You may now know exactly what you want to do—that's fine! You may know exactly the organization where you will seek employment and be thoroughly familiar with its products, operations, and policies. But if you don't know for sure, the following few pages will help you in arriving at those important decisions.

And even if you think you know, you will profit from reading—and maybe revising your present plans. Life holds many changes, occupational as well as personal. Many a job plum turns out to be a lemon. One's goals at 30 often contrast sharply with those one had at 20. Sometimes changes come through economic necessity, because of health reasons, because of changes in personal situations (one's marital and family status), because of shifts in demand for a product or service (the prosperous livery-stable owner in 1900 was no longer prosperous by 1910 and was no longer in business by 1920). For you, probably the most significant reason will be your ambition to get ahead: to earn the right to assume more responsibility in work that is challenging and interesting and thus merit respect and prestige in the eyes of other people, with consequent increased financial returns.

The starting point in your thinking and planning, in any case, is yourself.

ANALYZING YOURSELF

If you are going to sell your services, you will do so on the basis of *what you can do* and *the kind of person you are*. That is your marketable product and it deserves careful analysis, as launching any product does. The education you have, the experience you've had (which is not so important in many instances as college students assume it to be), and your personal attitudes and attributes are your qualifications which enable you to do something for someone.

Of the three, attitudes and attributes may be the most important: If you don't like a particular kind of work, you probably won't be successful in it. Of all the surveys of why people lose jobs, none has ever cited less than 80 percent attributable to personal maladjustments rather than professional deficiency.

No one but you can decide whether you will like a particular kind of job or not. Your like or dislike will be the result of such general considerations as whether you like to lead or to follow, whether you are an extrovert or an introvert, whether you prefer to work with products and things or with people, whether you are content to be confined indoors all your working hours or must get out and move around, whether you are responsible enough to schedule your own time or must keep regular hours guided by punching a time clock, whether you want to work primarily for money or whether for prestige (social and professional respect and greater security can partially compensate for less money). Certain kinds of work call for much traveling, entertaining after work hours, frequent contact with strangers, staying "dressed up" and "on call" physically and mentally; other kinds are just the opposite.

For most readers of this book, education is already a matter of record or soon will be. In some college or university you are laying a foundation of courses pointing to job performance in some selected field. While graduation is a certification of meeting certain time and proficiency standards, the individual courses and projects have taught you to do something and have shown you how to reason with judgment so that you can develop on the job. Unless you intend to forfeit much of the value of your training (which for most people who go through college represents an investment of $10,000 to $30,000), you will want to find work in the field of your major preparation.

Experience, likewise, is already partially a matter of record; you've held certain jobs or you haven't. Most employers look with greater favor on the person who has already demonstrated some workmanlike habits and exhibited enough drive to work and earn than they do on the person who has held no jobs. But if you've never earned a dime, don't think your position is bleak or unique. Many employers prefer a less experienced person with vision, judgment, and a sense of responsibility to some experienced plodder with none. And as you know, many employers prefer to give their employees their own brand of experience in training programs.

Regardless of your status, when in an application you show that you understand and meet the requirements for the job, you have an effective substitute for experience. Furthermore, if you will discard the kind of thinking that brands your education as "theoretical" or "academic," you will begin to realize that it is as down to earth as it can be. And that is true whether you have stressed cost accounting or a study of man and his environment.

But since you may still need to come to a vocational decision, because your learning may be applied equally well in many different lines of business or industry and because you probably don't know as much about job possibilities as you could (most folks don't), you'll do well to do some research.

To get some idea you may want to read a description of job requisites and rewards concerning the kind of work you are considering. Publications like *Occupational Briefs* and other job-outlook pamphlets published by Science Research Associates (259 East Erie Street, Chicago, Illinois 60611), and the publication *Occupational Outlook Handbook,* put out by the Bureau of Labor Statistics assisted by the Veterans' Administration, will help you. If you check in *Readers' Guide, Applied Science & Technology Index* and *Business Periodicals Index,* or *Public Affairs Information Service* under the subject heading of the vocation you have chosen or are contemplating, you may find leads to more recent publications.

You may want to consult some guidance agency for tests and counseling. Most institutions of higher learning have facilities for testing aptitudes and vocational interests, as well as intelligence. So do U.S. Employment Service offices and Veterans' Administration offices. And in practically any major city you can find a private agency which, for a fee, will help you in this way. Reading and talking with other people can help you, but only you can make the choice.

Having chosen the particular kind of work you want to do, you will be wise to make an organized search for those who can use your services.

SURVEYING WORK OPPORTUNITIES

If you are dead sure that you have chosen the right kind of work and the right organization, that the firm of your choice will hire you, and that both of you will be happy ever after in the arrangement, this discussion is not for you.

Most job seekers, however, are better off to keep abreast of current developments as signs of potential trends in lines of employment and specific companies.

The publications of Science Research Associates (already referred to) give you business and employment trends that help you decide whether you are going to have much or little competition in a given line of work (as well as what is expected of you and approximately how far you can expect to go). The annual Market Data and Directory number of *Industrial Marketing* and Standard and Poor's Industry Surveys analyze major industries, with comments on their current position in the economy (the latter also identifies outstanding firms in each field). The *Dictionary of Occupational Titles* (U.S. Employment Service) and the *Occupational Outlook Handbook* help you to keep informed on vocational needs. The special reports on individual fields which *Fortune* and *The Wall Street Journal* run from time to time are helpful also. And study of trade journals devoted to the field(s) in which you are interested can help you decide on a given kind of work.

Once you make that decision you seek names of specific organizations which could use your services. You can find names of companies in *Career, The Annual Guide to Business Opportunities* (published by Career Publications, Incorporated, Cincinnati and New York), *The College Placement Annual,* Standard and Poor's *Manuals,* and Moody's *Manuals.* Trade directories are useful. If you are concerned with staying in a given location, the city directory—or even the classified section of the phone book—will be helpful. Even if there is no city directory, the local chamber of commerce can help you.

If willing to spend a little time, you can assemble a good list of prospects from reading business newspapers and magazines. When significant changes occur within a company—for example, a new plant, an addition to an already existing structure, a new product launched, a new research program instituted, a new or different advertising or distribution plan announced—some newspaper or magazine reports that information. Widely known and readily available sources of such information are *The Wall Street Journal* and the business section of an outstanding newspaper in the region of your interest. *U.S. News & World Report* and *Business Week* (in their blue and yellow pages) give you outstanding developments; *Marketing Communications* summarizes what is happening in marketing. From such reading you can assemble a list of companies, the nature of each business, the location, and sometimes the names of key personnel.

Many large companies distribute pamphlets dealing with employment opportunities with the company and qualifications for them; all you have to do is write for one.

If it is a corporation you're interested in, frequently you can get a copy of its annual report from a business library in your locality. If not, you can get one by writing for it. The report will also often identify key personnel, one of whom may be the man you should direct your letter to.

Certainly other people can also help you. Teachers in the field of your interest and business people doing the same thing you want to do can make many good suggestions about qualifications, working conditions, opportunities, and business firms. Before taking their time, however, you should do some investigating on your own.

ANALYZING COMPANIES

The more you can find out about an organization, the better you can write specifically about how your preparation fits its needs. And remember, that's what you have to do in a successful application—show that you can render service which fits somebody's need. For that matter, even if you are fortunate enough to have interviews arranged for you, you'll want to find out all you can about the company: its history, operations, policies, financial structure, and position in the industry—even its main competitors.

Probably the best source of such information—and the easiest for you to obtain—is the annual report. And most annual reports contain much more than financial information; their intended readership includes stockholders, employees, customers, sources of supply—almost anyone, in fact. So they summarize the year's overall activities in terms of products, employment, sales, stockholders, management conditions affecting the industry and the company (including governmental activities), and a wide range of other topics. Careful reading of the last five years' annual reports makes you well informed on the company.

Standard and Poor's *Manuals* and Moody's *Manuals* summarize the history, operations (including products or services, number of employees, and number of plants), and financial structure.

If you can't find the needed information in sources like these, you may be lucky enough to find it in some magazine. *Fortune,* for example, has published many extensive résumés about specific companies. *Time* does regularly. Indexes—*Readers' Guide, Applied Science and Technology, Business Periodicals, Public Affairs Information Service*—may show you where you can find such an article.

From whatever source you can find, learn as much as you can about what the company does, how it markets its products or services, the trends at work for and against it, its financial position, its employment record, what kind of employees it needs and what it requires of them—plus anything else you can.

FITTING YOUR QUALIFICATIONS TO JOB REQUISITES

Actually what you are doing when you analyze yourself in terms of a job is running two columns of answers: What do they want? What do I have?

The answers to both the questions lie in three categories: personal attitudes and attributes, education, and experience—but not necessarily in that order of presentation! In fact, as explained in greater detail in the section "Compiling the Data Sheet" (pp. 440–52), you will usually put yourself in a more favorable light if you follow an order emphasizing your most favorable qualification in the light of job requirements. This rarely means little personal details like age, weight, and height. But desirable attitudes and personal traits and habits are basic equipment in *any* employee (and for writing a good application). Without them, no amount of education and/or experience will enable you to hold a job, even if you are lucky enough to get it.

The right work attitude

Someone puts you on a payroll because you give evidence of being able and willing to perform some useful service for him. That means work. The simplest, easiest, and most effective way to think, talk, and write about work is in terms of doing something for someone. The only way you'll convince someone that you can do something for him—better than someone else can—is first to realize that you're going to have to be able and willing to produce; that hard work is honorable; that recognition in the form of more pay, more benefits, and flexible hours comes only after demonstrated ability; that you have to be as concerned with *giving* as you are with *getting*, and that you have to give more than you get, especially at first; that you know you can learn more than you already know, and are willing to in order to grow on the job; and that glibness does not cover incompetence or poor work habits—not for very long, at any rate.

The only way you can earn the right to stay on a payroll is to give an honest day's work and to give it ungrudgingly. That means punctuality, reliability, honesty, willingness, cheerfulness, and cooperativeness.

Without a desirable outlook toward work and the conditions under which it must be carried on, competence can be a secondary consideration. Before you can ever demonstrate competence, you have to gain the approval of other people. You can be good, but if you don't get along well with people, your superior abilities won't be recognized. Even if recognized, they won't be rewarded.

You can be very good, but if you indicate that you think you are, you're going to be marked down as vain and pompous. One of the most frequent criticisms of college graduates is that they have overinflated ideas of their worth. Of course, if you don't respect your own abilities, someone else is not likely to either. The key is to recognize that you can do something because you've prepared yourself to do it, that you have the right mental attitude for doing it under normal business conditions, that you believe you can do it, and that you want to.

Confidence in yourself is essential, but so are humility and modesty. You can achieve a successful blend if you imply both in a specific interpretation of how your education, experience, and disposition equip you to perform job duties.

Specific adaptation of personal qualities

The work-for-you attitude in an adaptation implying confidence is basic in any application. Other attitudes or personal qualities need to be evaluated in the light of the particular circumstance. Affability, for instance, is highly desirable for work in which a person deals primarily with people (saleswork, for example); it is not so significant in the makeup of an actuarial statistician or a corporation accountant. Accuracy is more to the point for them, as it is for architects and mechanical engineers. Punctuality, while desirable in all things and people, is more necessary for a public accountant than for a personnel worker; for him, patience is more to be desired. While a salesman needs to be cheerful, a sales analyst must be endowed with perseverance (although each needs a measure of both). A young woman asking to be a medical secretary would stress accuracy in technique but, equally, poise and naturalness in putting people at ease; were she applying as a technician, accuracy would be the primary consideration, probably to the exclusion of the other two. Certainly in any position involving responsibility, the candidate for the job would want to select details from his experience which would bear out the necessary personal virtues of honesty as well as accuracy.

While all virtues are desirable—and truth, honor, trustworthiness, and cheerfulness are expected in most employees—a virtue in one circumstance may be an undesirable characteristic in another. Talkativeness, for example, is desirable for an interviewer seeking consumer reaction; the same talkativeness would be most undesirable in a credit investigator (who also does a considerable amount of interviewing). Both would need to inspire confidence.

Indeed, finding the right degree of confidence and aggressiveness to sit well with the reader and the job (and reflecting it in style and content) is one of the hardest things about writing good applications. Most employers want neither a conceited, cocksure, overbold and uninhibited, pushy extrovert nor the opposite extreme. They do not want new employees to take over their own jobs in a few weeks, but they know that the meek do not inherit the leadership needed for future managers either.

In any application analysis, estimate what you think are the two or three most important personal characteristics, and plan to incorporate evidence which will imply your possession of them. The others are then likely to be assumed. You can't successfully establish all the desirable ones. Besides, you have to show that your education and experience are adequate in selling yourself to a potential employer.

Enhancing your college preparation

With the desirable work-for-you attitude, you'll think in terms of job performance. If your reading has not given you a good idea of the duties you would be expected to perform on a particular job, you'll profitably spend some time talking with someone who has done the work and can tell you. You cannot hope to anticipate everything you might be called upon to do on a given job (nor would you want to talk about everything in your application); but if you anticipate some of the major job requirements and write about your studies in a way that shows you meet these requirements, you'll have enough material for conviction.

Although recruiting ads often stipulate a level of academic attainment, the academic units of credit and the diploma are not what enable you to perform a useful service. *What you learned in earning them does.* To satisfy the arbitrary requirement when you apply to some firms, you'll need to establish your graduation (or the completion of as much work as you have done). But the *primary emphasis in your presentation needs to go on those phases of your education which most directly and specifically equip you for the work under consideration.* In planning your application (but not in writing it), you'll need to list, as specifically as you can, job duties you can be reasonably sure you'll be called upon to perform and, in a parallel column, the background that gives evidence of your ability to do them.

An applicant for work in a public accounting firm knows that he is going to be expected to analyze financial data, prepare working papers, assemble financial statements, and present a report with interpretive comments. The direct evidence of his having learned to do these things is his experience in having done those same things in advanced accounting courses and/or work experience. He must also communicate intelligibly and easily his findings to his clients; and as evidence of his ability to do so, he cites training in report writing (and letter writing) as well as in speech. If he assumes that pleasant relations with clients are a desirable point to stress, he may cite study of psychology and sociology. In helping his clients to evaluate the significance of what the accountant discovers, he may draw on his knowledge of law and statistics.

A secretarial applicant writes about her dictation performance as evidence of her ability to record her employer's ideas; as evidence of her ability to reproduce them rapidly in attractive letters, memos, or reports, she writes in terms of transcription performance. She enhances her value when she talks in terms of relieving a busy employer of much of his routine correspondence as a result of her study of business writing. Since she can be reasonably sure of having to handle callers both face to face and on the telephone, she cites her courses in speech and in office procedures.

If you are interested in selling as a career, your specific work in salesmanship (both oral and written), market analysis and research, advertising principles and practice, and report writing needs emphasis (along with any other specifically desirable preparation that you know about).

Likewise, the management major stresses study of principles, industrial management, and personnel selection and placement. And if he is particularly interested in industrial relations, he will focus on work in industrial management, motion and time study, and labor economics, law, and legislation.

In all instances, applicants need to be selective, concentrating on that study which most nearly reflects the most advanced stage of preparation. For example, the successful completion of an auditing course implies a background of beginning and intermediate principles of accounting. Similarly, a person who cites evidence of training in market analysis and research will certainly have studied marketing principles. The careful selection of the most applicable courses precludes the necessity for listing qualifying courses and thus enables you to place desirable emphasis on the most significant.

Making the most of experience

Any job you've ever held that required you to perform some task, be responsible for the successful completion of a project, oversee and account for the activities of other people, or handle money is an activity you can cite with pride to a prospective employer. You may not have been paid for it; that doesn't matter a lot. The college man who directs his campus unit of the United Fund drive gets a workout in organization, delegation of authority, persuasion, systemization, persistence, punctuality, responsibility, honesty, and accuracy that is good work experience. It is experience which is more valuable than that of the student who mans a cash register at the local supermarket four hours a day—and nothing else. Especially if both men are aiming at managerial work or some kind of contact work, the man who has earned no pay but has had more experience working with people and assuming authority and responsibility is in a more desirable position.

You may not have held the job for any length of time—maybe for only a summer or over the holidays or briefly part time while in school. But didn't you learn something that increased your ability to render service?

You may have held a job that does not appear to be related to the work you hope to do. The checker at the supermarket, for example, has punched his way through college because that is the only way he could prepare for a career in marketing. But hasn't he demonstrated vision and stickability? Hasn't he learned and demonstrated accuracy, the ability to work under pressure, the willingness to be cheerful and polite to customers? And if he has kept his eyes open, he has had a good workout in interpreting consumer demand.

Even the person of limited experience can interpret that experience in an adaptation to job requirements, giving the most significant experience the emphasis of position. The most directly related phase of experience is the one most nearly preparing you to do something. For example, if the supermarket checker had also been a fraternity house treasurer (involving handling and accounting for money), in an application for accounting work he would want to emphasize the treasurer's duties over the checker's job; were he seeking to do selling, the checker's job would be more significant.

If you are fortunate enough to have a wide range of experience, your problem is simply one of picking and choosing and presenting in an order of descending applicability to the job sought. Chronology (a time sequence) rarely should be your governing choice at graduation or even for a few years after. As an experienced employee changing companies, you may wisely elect to present job experience in chronological order (or the reverse), emphasizing progress to the present state of preparation; such order-of-time presentation suggests a well-defined goal and success in attaining it.

Whatever experience you elect to present, you want to show as directly and specifically as possible that as a result of this experience you come equipped to do the job or at least to learn how quickly. The surest way to present this information about yourself in the most favorable light is to *describe job duties* related to the job you're seeking. You will strengthen your application if you interpret the experience to show what it taught you about important principles, techniques, and attitudes applicable to the hoped-for job. Evaluating work experience is the same process as evaluating education; it's the matching-up as far as possible the answers to "What do I have?" with the requirements under "What do they want?"

You will rarely, if ever, meet all job requirements; and you will always have some points that are stronger than others. Outright lack of a specific point of preparation or below-average standard are negative points to be handled in the same manner that any writer handles them: embedded position and positive language.

Determining a favorable order of presentation

After you have listed the necessary and desirable equipment of the person who will be hired and your own specific preparation as defined by personal qualities, education, and experience, you will then need to decide on an order of presentation that is most favorable to you.

Most jobs are secured in the first place because of the employee's competence, not his personal charm or good looks. While undesirable personal attributes and attitudes can keep you from getting the job of your choice (sometimes from getting *a* job!) and may result in your losing the job even if you fool someone and are selected, good personality will not ordinarily get you the job unless you first show ability to do the work. Competence stems from good education or worthwhile experience, or a combination of the two.

If your strongest point is thorough preparation, that is what you want to start with; if it is experience, begin that way. And within each of these categories, arrange your qualifications so that the best comes first (as any good salesman does).

Without telling your reader what they are, as if he didn't know, be sure to give evidence that you meet all important job requirements. And write your evidence not in the order it occurs to you or even in an order of what you estimate is of greatest significance in the evaluation but in an order that stresses your strong points.

For this comprehensive presentation, a data sheet (often called résumé or personal record sheet) is the preferred form.

COMPILING THE DATA SHEET

The purpose of a data sheet is to help sell you to a prospective employer. It can accompany either a prospecting or an invited application letter— and often serves to start off an interview under favorable conditions. It tells your complete story—the little details as well as the big points—thus enabling your letter to be shorter and to concentrate on showing how the high spots of your preparation enable you to do good work.

As one authority said, a data sheet gives your life's history in two minutes, indicates your organizing and language ability, and leaves your letter free to sell.

Whether you call it a data sheet, a qualification sheet, or a résumé, or a personal profile, it is a tabulation of your qualifications, giving pertinent, specific details concerning your education, experience, and personal data and—except in atypical circumstances—supplying the names of references who can verify what you say about yourself.

We know that company employment forms conventionally ask for personal details first. This practice comes partially from custom and partially from the wish of some prospective employers to have a clear-cut picture of the applicant from the start: such information as physical specifications, age, and marital status. Important as this information is, it is not what gets you a job.[1]

When you are preparing your own data sheet, you want to sell yourself. Remember that the company isn't trying to sell you, but you are! You will sell yourself more by emphasizing initially your best point of preparation— either education or experience details, followed by the other. In most cases you have a stronger presentation by establishing these significant points before you take up the necessary personal details. Notice that the four data sheets which follow (pp. 441–49) desirably emphasize each candidate's strongest selling point first.

Since the data sheet must carry a wealth of detail and condense the material into a small amount of space, it follows good outlining principles and form. You need to use the space-saving devices of tabulation and noun phrases (rather than sentences and conventional paragraphs). To facilitate rapid reading, you should use headings, differentiate in type for the various classes of information, and observe uniform indentions for rows and columns of information. Parallel construction in phrasing requires special care. (If you stick to noun phrases, you'll eliminate your problems in this respect.)

---

[1] See *Marketing Insights: Dart* 1968–69 (12–9–68), pp. 12–13, for an emphatic confirmation of this point.

JOHN DAYTON HALE'S QUALIFICATIONS FOR

ACCOUNTING WORK WITH PHILCO RADIO CORPORATION

(Address: 4030 Sixth Street, Port Arthur, Texas 51205)

Professional Education

Three uninterrupted years' study summer and winter (1969–72) in the University of Texas majoring in accounting; BBA degree, August, 1972, with better than a "B" average.
Courses pointing to a thorough understanding of corporation accounting and financial analysis:

–Accounting–

Cost: Job-order and process cost methods.
Federal Income Tax: Reporting taxes for corporations, partnerships, and individuals.
Procedures: Various systems of accounting with emphasis on special items of the balance sheet––accounts receivable and investments.

Auditing: Elementary and advanced; public auditing and internal auditing with emphasis on internal control
Fiduciary: All business units in voluntary or involuntary bankruptcy; also accounting for estates.
Governmental: Accounting for all types of governmental units.

–Related Courses–

Corporation Finance: Financial policies; types of corporate securities––when to issue stocks or bonds.
Money and Banking: The theory of money and how the Federal Reserve System runs.

Business Law: Contracts, sales, negotiable instruments, corporations, partnerships, and property.
Economics: Basic understanding of the various theories.

Written Communications:
Report writing and
letter writing.

Work Experience Requiring Accuracy

1972--   Accountant for D. H. Hicks, General Contractor, Austin Texas; planning and supervision of accounting system, afternoons and evenings while in school.
1970–71:   Records clerk, Texas Fire Insurance Commission, Austin, Texas; part-time.
1969–70:   Clerk, Police Department, Austin, Texas; part-time in Corporation Court and Identification Bureau.

Impersonal style, without opinions and comments, is usually best for this concise, basically factual presentation.

The best form is that one which enables you to make a favorable presentation of your qualifications, attractively displayed and concisely stated. Study thoughtfully the four examples beginning above. Note

JOHN DAYTON HALE'S QUALIFICATIONS FOR ACCOUNTING WORK, PAGE 2

1968–69: Superintendent, Bureau of Identification, Police Department, Port Arthur, Texas
(fingerprint expert, detective, photographer, interrogator).
1967–68: Clerk, Identification Bureau, Police Department, Port Arthur, Texas.
1966–67: Airman, U.S. Air Force.

Personal Details

Birth date and place:
Born in Texas in 1948
Family status:
Married, one son.
Physical condition:
5 feet, 10 inches; 165 pounds; no
defects. No absence from work
or school due to illness in last
four years.
Glasses for close work.

Organization memberships:
Beta Alpha Psi (accounting, pro-
fessional and honorary)
Kappa Alpha (social)
Masonic Lodge
University Baptist Church
Hobbies:
Fishing (artificial lure)
Swimming (water safety and
swimming instructor)

References (by Permission)

Dr. C. Aubrey Smith
Professor of Accounting
The University of Texas
Austin, Texas 78710

Mr. Frank Graydon
Professor of Accounting
The University of Texas
Austin, Texas 78710

Mr. Joyce Campbell
City Manager
Port Arthur, Texas 77640

Chief R. D. Thorp
Police Department
Austin, Texas 78710

Mrs. Corinne Lundgren
Office Manager
Texas Fire Insurance Commission
Austin, Texas 78710

Mr. D. H. Hicks
1313 Speedway
Austin, Texas 78710

the variation in the use of rows and columns of information, in the type and placement of information, in the classification of the information, and in the points the writers stressed. One is as good as the others; they all did the job for the people who used them.

Your data sheet should be typed. When you type each presentation,

MARIAN CRANE'S QUALIFICATIONS FOR

EFFICIENT PUBLIC RELATIONS WORK

WITH SOUTHEASTERN HIGHWAY TRANSPORT, INC.

Address until
June 1, 1972
Box 1773
University, Alabama 35402

┌─────────────┐
│ Conservative │
│ picture in busi- │
│ ness dress. │
│ Front view. │
│   │
│ (Detachable) │
└─────────────┘

Address after
June 2, 1972
Box 47
Evergreen, Alabama 35411

Thorough University Training

Three and one-half years of work in the School of Commerce, University of Alabama, with only
five hours of advanced electives left (for completion by correspondence) after June 2, 1972,
for a B. S. degree.

"B" average in the following courses related to public-relations work with Southeastern Highway
Transport:

Transportation	Business Statistics
Traffic Management	Business Correspondence
Employee Supervision	Business Report Writing
Personnel Management	

Experience Working with People

Active participation in these campus organizations:

Beta Beta Alpha--organization for
women Business Administration majors.
Newman Club--organization for the promotion of religious social activities of
Catholic students.

Wica--independent women's social
organization.
Campus League of Women Voters--
meetings used for the discussion of
current events, trends, interests.

Three and one-half years of life in a cooperative house--an organization of 16 University
girls who cooperate to do all the planning, managing, and work of this living unit.

Coordinator of this organization
during senior year. Managerial responsibility.
Member of the advisory committee, with
special duties of talking to any member
of this co-op who caused any friction
within the house.

Active member of the Interco-op
Council, the board representing all
co-op houses on the campus. Working on problems of all the houses as a
whole and planning a definite expansion program.

you can desirably fill in the name of the organization addressed and make
other minor changes for better adaptation.

As a practical matter, however, you may have to run off multiple copies.
If so, printed data sheets are better than mimeographed ones. Remember,
too, that although about half the potential employers say they do not object

MARIAN CRANE'S QUALIFICATIONS--page 2

General office work with Ford Motor
Company of Evergreen, Alabama.
Typing, dictation, bookkeeping.
Summers, 1969, 1970, 1971.

Secretary to Representative Stark in
the Legislature during the last
session. Spring, 1971

Office assistant at Radio
House, University of
Alabama. General office
work of typing, dictation,
mimeographing. Part time
while in school.

Personal Details

Nativity: Born in 1952 in Alabama
Family status: Unmarried.
Physical characteristics: 5 feet,
4 inches; 120 pounds; blond hair;
hazel eyes.

Health: Good. Perfect hearing and
eyesight.
Religious affiliation: Catholic.
Hobbies: Participation in sports;
listening to classical music;
designing and sewing wardrobe.

Persons Who Will Testify

Dr. M. W. Whitman
Professor of Transportation
University of Alabama
University, Alabama 35401

Dr. John Robert Blocton
Professor of Business Statistics
University of Alabama
University, Alabama 35401

Mr. Layden D. Osmus
Director of Radio House
University of Alabama
University, Alabama 35401

Mr. D. R. Lanning
Professor of Marketing
University of Alabama
University, Alabama 35401

Mr. L. A. Jarosek, Manager
Ford Motor Company
1813 N. Main Street
Evergreen, Alabama 35411

to mimeographed data sheets, half of them do. These statistics do not imply that any potential employer prefers processed data sheets. Some will tolerate them, but an equal number will not. Unfortunately, you have no way of guessing which class the reader of your application will fall into. So if you can spare the time (or the money), send typed ones—and never a carbon.

Qualifications of Harry E. Adams

for Representing Bedford, Mace, and Company in the Field

Until June 1, 1972

Box 3652
University, Alabama 35402

```
┌─────────────────┐
│ Conservative    │
│ picture in a    │
│ business suit.  │
│ Front view.     │
│                 │
│ (Detachable)    │
└─────────────────┘
```

After June 1, 1972

Rainbow Drive
Gadsden, Alabama 35901

Education and Teaching Experience

Master of Science degree, June, 1972, University of Alabama, with major concentration
on economics and labor.

Courses of value in representing a publisher to the college trade (in addition
to specialization):

Public Speaking	Business Correspondence	Business Research
Psychology	Business Report Writing	Advertising
Marketing	English Composition	Business Law

One year (1971–72) of teaching Economic Principles, University of Alabama. Responsibility
for planning and delivering lectures and for all testing and grading.

Personal Factors

6 feet tall, 170 pounds,
  brown hair and eyes,
  dark skin, conservative
  dress.
Born January 24, 1947,
  Gadsden, Alabama.
Honorable discharge from
  U.S. Navy after 24
  months of service

Delta Chi social fraternity.
  Baptist Church.
Single (free to travel).
Active participation in tennis,
  golf, swimming. Frequent
  bridge and dancing. Wide
  reading of fiction and business
  publications.

University of Alabama References

Dr. Ralph M. Hill
Professor of Economics
University, Alabama 35402

Dr. R. E. Lampkin
Professor of Management
Chairman, Commerce
  Graduate Division
University, Alabama 35402

Mr. D. H. Brennan
Professor of Marketing
University, Alabama 35402

Dr. Paul W. Paulings
Professor of Economics
University, Alabama 35402

You may choose to omit references if you are prospecting or if you are
answering a "blind" (anonymous) advertisement and fear the effects of
an inquiry at the firm where you are working. Or you may not want to ask
references to take time to answer inquiries until you know for sure that
you are interested in the job. In either case you would need to indicate
willingness to supply the names of references upon request or after an

Training
and
Experience
REPORT
on

CHARLES E. COMPTON

To: Busy Executives, Personnel Managers, and other Company Leaders

— A one minute check list to save you time —

Do you need a career minded young man who—

IN MARKETING

1. Can adapt   ☐
2. Can help develop marketing mixes
    for nontechnical products   ☐
3. Knows basic consumer behavior   ☐
4. Can help identify new markets   ☐
5. Can structure surveys — interpret findings   ☐
6. Can write reports — present results   ☐
7. Has ideas — some good — some bad   ☐

IN ACCOUNTING AND FINANCE

1. Can analyze financial reports and data   ☐
2. Can make cost and price analyses   ☐
3. Can evaluate operating results   ☐
4. Knows something about stubborn
    overhead cost growth   ☐

IN BUSINESS

1. Can communicate with people at all levels   ☐
2. Can think in detailed or broad terms   ☐
3. Seeks continued challenge and growth   ☐
4. Works without close supervision   ☐
5. Accepts responsibility   ☐
6. Will work hard — Will study hard — to learn
    the business he serves   ☐

CHARLES E. COMPTON'S QUALIFICATIONS
for
MARKETING LINE or STAFF WORK

334 Bruce Street Apartment E
Warner Robins, Georgia 31093
Home Phone: 912- 923-7442
Office Phone: 912- 926-2151

Age: 27   Height: 6' 2''
Health: Good   Weight: 195
Married 1967, no children
Wife (Roberta) Pharmacist

Current Status: Captain, USAF   Will separate in July 1972
     Central Procurement Officer   Available upon separation

OBJECTIVE

To work in a marketing line or staff job. To handle projects and assignments concerned with the various aspects of marketing and offering cross training into other major functional areas. To gain additional business knowledge, experience, and judgment necessary for advancement.

THOROUGH COLLEGE TRAINING

**M.B.A. Degree
top third**

Master of Business Administration degree, 1968, University of Alabama, with major in General Management. Ranked in top third of class. Completed advanced courses in management, finance, accounting, statistics, marketing, business law, and economics. Earned Graduate Research Assistantship. Secretary of Commerce Graduate Association. Passed all seven fields on written comprehensive M.B.A. Field Exam. M.B.A. paper on Product Management. Other research papers on Brand Imagery, Corporate Organizational Structure, and Product Deletion.

**B.S. Degree
top 10%**

Bachelor of Science in Commerce and Business Administration, 1967, University of Alabama. Graduated in top ten percent in class of 175. Marketing major with emphasis in Sales Management and Professional Selling. Earned A's in Marketing Research, Report Writing, International Marketing, Marketing Analysis and Control, Marketing Seminar, and Industrial Marketing and Wholesaling. Earned B's in Promotion, Salesmanship, and Retailing. No C's. Elected liberal arts courses in mathematics, speech, and behavioral sciences with B average. On Dean's List junior and senior years with QPA of 2.8 on 3.0 system each year.

**College
Activities**

Alpha Kappa Psi, Professional Business Fraternity, Vice President junior and senior years. Theta Chi Fraternity, social, elected officer two years. Active member in Marketing Club. Member of academic honor society. Active in intramural sports. Earned seventy-five percent of college and living expenses.

BUSINESS EXPERIENCE REQUIRING ACCURACY AND JUDGMENT

Four full years of responsible Procurement work for the Air Force whiie stationed at Warner Robins Air Materiel Area (WRAMA), Robins Air Force Base, Georgia. Two concurrent years teaching college business courses at night.

AIR FORCE BUSINESS EXPERIENCE

March 1970 to present

Principal Negotiator

Contract Price Analyst and Negotiator — Work as a Price Analyst and Principal Negotiator on fixed price and cost type contracts in excess of $100,000. Negotiate with major defense contractors. Analyze all cost and profit elements to develop formal Government price objectives. Responsible for total negotiation and price justification. As negotiation team leader, maintain close contact work with engineers, auditors, production personnel, contracting officers, and top management.

Price Analyst

Experienced in analyzing proposals, and evaluating audit reports and technical reports. Evaluations include analysis of labor hours and rates, overhead cost and base, material costs, and profit factors. Analytical tools include variable and fixed cost analyses, weighted averages, learning curve applications, and regression analysis.

Central Staff

Negotiated twenty-four contracts across-the-table or by telephone with twenty contractors obligating about $15,000,000 during the past year. Currently work in a central staff office with fourteen analysts supporting 530 Directorate of Procurement and Production employees.

1968—1970 Buyer

Government Buyer — Experienced in Government procurement system, methods, and regulations. Wrote solicitations, evaluated proposals, made awards, and wrote final contracts up to $100,000 in value.

TEACHING AND SELF EMPLOYMENT

College Teaching

Taught seventeen quarter courses at night in Georgia colleges since April 1970 in four business fields. Course Titles: Accounting — Business Finance — Business Organization and Principles — Basic Marketing — and Wholesaling, Retailing, and Logistics Management. Held complete responsibility for developing course content and presentation.

Small Business — Advised two local retailers on product lines, product display, and accounting controls.

1968—1971

Real Estate — Worked with Georgia realtor in conducting feasibility analysis for a city trade area shopping center.

Amway Cleaning Products — Sold to institutions. Developed a small distributorship of home retail salesmen.

OTHER WORK — INTERESTS — MEMBERSHIPS

Other Work

Graduate Research Assistant, University of Alabama (1967—1968).
Timber Management of personal property (1967—1972).
General Reserve in paper mill during summer (1963—1965).
Cattle Farm work and management (1962—1963).
Retail Clerk in shoe store — Tupperware Salesman (1960—1961).

Interests

Conversation with business leaders — Travel and meeting people — Income tax accounting — Remaining current on business conditions — Stock market activities — Real estate investments — Church — Physical fitness — Hunting — Golf.

Memberships

Church of Christ — American Marketing Association.

REFERENCES

References

References gladly furnished upon request.

Résumé (or Data Sheet) Checklist

1. Give your data sheet a heading, and establish address(es) and phone number(s) quickly (including ZIP and area codes).
   a) Identify your name, the type of work desired, and (preferably) the company to which addressed.
   b) Be sure you apply for work, not a job title.
   c) Write concisely; avoid "data sheet of" and "position as."
   d) Incorporate your address(es) and phone(s) in the minimum of space.
   e) Some employers want a small photograph (but cannot legally require it).

2. Emphasis, ease of reading, and space saving are the main factors affecting the physical arrangement.
   a) Balance the material across the page in tabulated form.
   b) If you have to carry over an item, indent the second line.
   c) Centered heads carry emphasis and help balance the page.
   d) Capitalize the main words in centered heads and underline the heads. Unnecessary to underline one in solid caps.
   e) Remember to identify and number pages after the first.
   f) Difference in type and placement affects emphasis and shows that you are aware of organization principles.

3. Lead with whatever best prepares you for the particular job.

4. Education details should point up specific preparation.
   a) Establish the status of your education early in the section: degree, field, school, date.
   b) Highlight those courses which distinctively qualify you for the job. Listing everything takes away emphasis from the significant ones and suggests inability to discriminate.
   c) Give courses titles or descriptions which show their real content.
   d) You may give specific details of what you did in courses.
   e) Give grade averages in a form which any reader will interpret accurately: letter, or standing in quartiles, or percentages.
   f) Expressions like "theoretical education" deprecate your work.
   g) Arrange courses in order of significance or applicability.

5. Experience: Remember that all is good; some is just better than other.
   a) Give complete data about the experience you list—job title, duties, the firm or organization, the place, and the specific dates.
   b) If experience is part time, identify it as such.
   c) You do want the chronology of your life to be accounted for.

Résumé (or Data Sheet) Checklist

(continued)

6. The personal-details section should present a clear, true picture.
   a) It ordinarily includes physical indications (age, height, weight, general condition of health, marital status). (Though it prevents employers from asking, no law prohibits you from volunteering information about race and religion.)
   b) Tabulate, but try combining ideas to reduce overlisting, saving space and words:

Born in Birmingham, Alabama, 1951	Married, no children
5′11″, 185 lbs.	Member of (list appropriate organizations)
Good health, glasses for close work	Like fishing and reading
	Draft Status 1–S

7. References ordinarily conclude data-sheet presentation (unless there is some reason for a "blind" situation).
   a) Give the names, titles, and addresses of references for all important jobs and fields of study listed.
   b) Always give proper titles of respect: Mr., Professor, Dr., Honorable—whatever is appropriate.
   c) Unless character references are requested, omit them.
   d) Unless obvious, make clear why each reference is listed.

8. Remember these points about style:
   a) Data sheets are usually impersonal presentations; avoid first- and second-person pronouns.
   b) Noun phrases are the best choice of grammatical pattern.
   c) A data sheet is ordinarily a tabulation; avoid paragraphs and complete sentences.
   d) Items in any list should be in parallel form. See Para. in Appendix D.
   e) Keep opinions off a data sheet; just give the specific facts.

interview; the evaluation by those who have supervised you in classrooms and on jobs is of real use to the people who consider employing you.

In most cases—and always for college students seeking a career—the names of references to whom the potential employer can write are a necessary part of data sheet information. Logically, they conclude the presentation.

With careful planning and only minor changes, if any, you will be able to use the same data sheet information over and over as you mail out applications for the same kind of job. Often a simple substitution of company name in the heading is all you'll need. When the kind of work you're applying for changes, however, reevaluate your qualifications in the light of the circumstances. The data sheets shown on page 441–49 would have stressed different aspects of education had the applicants been applying for work in their majors.

The fourth résumé—a fold-out—was commercially printed on heavy paper. With the photograph, the art work, and the extra postage, the cost was far higher than many students just graduating from college can afford. It is a good example of what you might want to do after a few years of experience, however.

After studying the four examples, review the checklisted items (pp. 450–51) as a basis for preparing your own data sheet.

WRITING THE PROSPECTING APPLICATION

WITH A WELL-PREPARED data sheet you will have done a good job of lining up your qualifications, of realizing what you can (and can't) do, and of deciding on those phases which most nearly equip you for efficient performance. You are then in much better shape to write a covering sales letter (C–plan, as you know).

At times you may want to send a prospecting letter without a data sheet. That's your decision. We don't think it's the better decision if for no other reason than that most of the personnel men we've ever talked with or listened to or whose articles we've read prefer to receive the data sheet summary. Even if you elect not to use one, you'll write a better letter for having prepared one. Having prepared it, you're throwing good money away if you don't let it work for you.

You're also being very foolish if you fail to capitalize on your investment of time and effort (and maybe even cash) by slavishly following the points and aping the style of another person's application letter. The good "model"

453

application letter doesn't exist—and never will for applicants of average intelligence and above. They realize that the application letter must be an accurate reflection of the writer's personality as well as aptitudes. And so they will write their own.

Securing favorable attention

As in sales letters, the infallible way to secure interest in your application letter is to stress your central selling point in writing about doing something for the reader. Your central selling point may be an ability based on education, experience, or personal qualities or a combination of them. The young man who compiled the third of the data sheets you studied (see p. 445) successfully combined all three:

> With my college background of undergraduate and graduate work, my teaching experience, and a temperament which helps me to adapt easily to college people and circumstances, I believe I could do a good job as a field representative for your firm.
>
> And after talking recently about the nature of the work with R. D. Schott, southern representative for Leath, I know I'd have the added factor in my favor of being very enthusiastic about it.
>
> While I certainly don't know all the reasons why college teachers choose certain textbooks, I have taught enough while completing a master's degree at Alabama to realize that format and price are only minor factors affecting a teacher's decision.
>
> Possibly the most significant realization from my year as a graduate student and instructor is that there is no true "academic" personality—that a successful representative has to be prepared to meet and talk freely and convincingly with a wide range of personalities.
>
> Teaching classes in Economic Problems and Policies, discussing my thesis with committee members both collectively and individually, and talking with staff members about teaching problems (in staff meetings and in bull sessions) have helped me to think on my feet, to have self-assurance when speaking to groups and to individuals, and to adapt myself to varying situations. I've learned to feel at home with all types of college teachers.
>
> The fact that I have studied business at Alabama rather than liberal arts at an Ivy League school may actually make me a better representative, Mr. Dayton—especially if I'm assigned to the South, where I already know the territory. I could serve happily as your representative in any district, however; I've traveled over most of the U.S. (and to Europe and the Far East while in the Navy) and can adapt readily to the fine people and country one finds everywhere.
>
> I believe you'd find me quick to learn; the men I've listed as references on the enclosed data sheet will probably tell you so if you'll write them.

After you've had a chance to verify some of the things I've
said about myself in this letter and on the data sheet, will
you write me frankly about the possibilities of my working for
you?

Possibly I could talk with one of your regional representatives
in this area as a preliminary step. And I can plan to go to
New York sometime this summer to talk with you further about
my successfully representing your firm.

(You may be interested to know that the 22 copies of this letter brought
22 replies within a couple of weeks. Half a dozen of the firms wanted to
interview the applicant right away, another half dozen, within a month
afterward. The writer had four job offers.)

To get started rapidly and pertinently, one applicant began her letter to
the American Red Cross this way:

I can be the versatile type of club director the American Red
Cross seeks.

As a result of five years' specialized training in dietetics
and institutional management and 10 years' practical experience
in meeting and serving people as a volunteer worker in service
clubs from New York to Trinidad, from France through Germany,
I know the kind of program which will best meet the needs and
interests of service men and their families everywhere.

A young man just graduating from college got favorable attention with
this:

Because I have had an unusual five-year educational opportunity
combining the study of engineering and management, I feel sure
of my ability to do efficient work in your industrial
engineering department and to steadily increase in usefulness
if you employ me.

I could conduct a time study with a technical knowledge of the
machines concerned or work on the problems of piece wage rates
without losing sight of the highly explosive personnel
situation involved.

A 19-year-old girl with two years of college summarized her outstanding
qualifications in the following well-chosen lead:

As a secretary in your export division I could take your
dictation at a rapid 120 words per minute and transcribe it
accurately in attractive letters and memos at 40 words per
minute—whether it is in English or Spanish.

There's nothing tricky about these openings. They just talk work.

You may be able to capitalize on a trick in some situations—provided
that it shows knowledge of job requirements. The young advertising candidate who mailed a walnut to agencies with the lead "They say advertising is a hard nut to crack" got results from the message he had enclosed in
the walnut. The young man who, in seeking radio work, wrote his message
in the form of a radio script marked "Approved for Broadcast" and stamped
with a facsimile of the usual log certification indicated above-average

knowledge of working conditions. The secretary who started her letter with a line of shorthand characters indicated qualifications from the start. The statistical worker who drew at the top of his letter a line graph showing the Federal Reserve Board Index of Industrial Production and in the opening lines of his letter commented on the significance of its recent movements certainly had a head start on other candidates for the job. If you can think of one which is pertinent, in good taste, and not stereotyped (such as the balance sheet from an accounting candidate), it may help you. But it is by no means a must.

You do need to concentrate on rapidly and naturally establishing your qualifications with the attitude that you want to put them to work for the reader in some specific job. Having held out such a promise, you need to back it up.

Supplying evidence of performance ability

Your evidence in an application is simply an interpretation of the highlights of your data sheet. For persuasiveness, you phrase it in terms of "doing something for you." If you didn't notice how each of the paragraphs two through seven in the letter beginning on p. 454 gives evidence in support of the opening promise, go back and read the letter again.

The applicant to the Red Cross whose opening you read in a preceding passage continued her letter this way:

```
With the full realization that the Red Cross necessarily
operates on an economical basis, I can use my thorough college
training in institutional organization as a sound basis for
financial management, cost control, personnel management,
employee training, and job specification, all of which I know
are vital in a well-run Red Cross club.

When it comes to food service, I feel at home in the planning,
selection, buying, preparation, and serving of party food for
a group of 500 or 1,000 or behind the snack bar of a canteen
or in planning the well-balanced meals for the hardworking Red
Cross girls who live in the barracks.  During my year as
assistant dietician at Ward Memorial Hospital in Nashville, I
successfully supervised the preparation and serving of from
3,000 to 20,000 meals a day.

Having been an Army wife and lived in many places under
varying circumstances, I have learned to use my own initiative
in developing the facilities at hand.  I've learned to be
adaptable, patient, resourceful, and—through grim necessity
as a widow—cheerful!  I believe in puctuality but am not a
clock watcher.  And I know from experience that I can direct
people without incurring resentment.

I've always enjoyed and participated in the many sports and
social activities that are listed on the enclosed data sheet.
As a Red Cross director I could help others to share their
pleasures too.
```

The industrial-management applicant followed up his opening like this:

The program I followed at Northwestern University required
five years of study because I felt that qualification for work
in industrial management should include basic engineering
information. The scope of such courses as Business
Organization and Cost Accounting were therefore enhanced and
expanded by related work in Machine Design and Properties of
Engineering Materials.

Three years in the Corps of Engineers of the U.S. Army form
the main basis of my experience. A large part of this time I
spent as a section officer in a large engineer depot. The
knowledge, skills, and experience I gained concerning layout,
storage, freight handling, and heavy packaging relate very
closely to the problems of factory management in the production
of heavy machinery. While working with the problems of
shipping bulldozer blades, I was gaining experience that will
aid me in understanding the special techniques required in
handling cotton pickers and tractors.

I've learned how to get my ideas across in business-writing
courses here at Northwestern as well as through being a
reporter for the <u>Daily Northwestern</u>. As a member of the
student governing board and the senior council, I've had good
lessons in cooperation and patience. And despite a pretty
rugged schedule of classes and extracurricular activities,
I've kept myself in good physical condition by participating
on my fraternity's intramural basketball and football teams.

The enclosed data sheet and inquiries to the men I've listed
will probably give you all the information you want about me
before seeing me, but I shall be glad to furnish any further
particulars you may wish.

And the secretarial applicant to the exporting firm continued (after her
opening) in the following vein, drawing exclusively on her schooling:

In secretarial courses during my two years of study at Temple
College, I've consistently demonstrated my ability to handle
material at these speeds. And as a matter of practice in my
course in conversational Spanish I take down what my teacher
and my classmates say. I have no difficulty transcribing
these notes later.

I learned a good deal about your markets and your clientele
while doing research for a report I submitted this semester in
marketing, "Some Recent Developments in Latin-American
Markets." In the process I became familiar with such
publications as <u>The American Importer</u>, <u>Exporting</u>, and <u>The
Foreign Commerce Yearbook</u>.

I'm neat and conservative in appearance. Early in my life
mother impressed upon me the desirability of a low-pitched
voice and distinct enunciation; probably for that reason my
college speech teacher has been especially interested in
helping me to achieve poise and dignity before a group of
people. On the telephone or in person I could greet your
clients pleasantly and put them at ease.

After I start working, I hope to further my knowledge of the people and language of Latin America by using my vacation time for trips to Mexico, Central America, and South America.

Overcoming deficiencies is a function of the letter, not the data sheet. In almost any application situation you'll have one or more. In many cases the wiser course of action is simply not to talk about it! In other cases, if you feel that it is such an important consideration as to merit identification and possibly discussion, embed it in your letter, and endow it with as much positiveness as possible.

The young man wanting to be a publisher's representative had two strikes against him and knew it: the fact that he had gone through a commerce school plus the fact that he was a product of a state university in the South rather than an Ivy League school. Turn back and note how in the fifth paragraph of his letter he met the issue head on and capitalized on it.

The industrial-management applicant had no experience. But did he apologize for it? Not at all! He held out his service experience confidently and showed its relation to the job sought. "Three years in the . . . U.S. Army form the basis of my experience," he wrote—instead of the weak-kneed statement, "The only experience I've had was in the Army," or even worse, "I've had no experience. But I did serve with the Corps of Engineers in the Army."

Probably one of the finest examples we've ever seen of turning an apparent handicap into a virtue is that of a young woman who at first didn't know where to turn when confronted with the necessity for getting a job. After thoughtful analysis of what she had done in college and how it could be used in business, she sent the following letter to a large Chicago mail-order firm. The third paragraph is the epitome of positive thinking.

Isn't one of the significant qualifications of a correspondent in your company the ability to interpret a letter situation in terms of the reader?

Because I believe that I could express an understanding of a situation clearly and imaginatively to your customers (a degree in English from the University of Illinois, an $\underline{A}$ in Business Communication, and the editorship of my sorority paper suggest that I can), will you allow me to become a trial employee in your correspondence division?

Learning your particular business policies and procedures in writing letters would come quickly, I believe; I am used to following assignments exactly, and I have no previous working experience to unlearn.

I have a good background in writing. I can type 60 words a minute. And the varied extracurricular activities listed on the enclosed data sheet are my best evidence for telling you that I've successfully passed a four-year test of getting along with people.

Will you call me at 876-2401 and name a time when I may come in and talk with you?

It worked! And the same kind of positive approach to any handicap you may have—physical or otherwise—is probably your best way to treat it.

Talking the special language of your reader's business also convinces your reader of your performance ability and helps to overcome any deficiency. In all the examples you've been reading in this analysis, you've probably noticed that each incorporated specific and special references to conditions or products or activities peculiar to the given job. Such references certainly further the impression that you are aware of job requirements and conditions. The would-be publisher's representative referred to books, teachers, college circumstances, and adoptions (the end and aim of that particular job). The industrial management applicant referred easily and sensibly to two products of the company, tractors and cotton pickers. The applicant to the Red Cross referred to service clubs, canteens, and the hardworking Red Cross girls who live in the barracks.

From your research you can readily establish such references. If significant enough information, they may be good choices of talking points for your beginning, as in the following three instances:

```
With the recent improvements on the foot-control hydraulic-
power lift on Farmall tractors and the construction of a new
implement plant at Poplar Bluff, Missouri, the International
Harvester Company of Memphis will no doubt be selling more
farm machinery than ever before.  As a salesman of Farmall
tractors and equipment, I am sure I could help to continue
your record of improving sales.
                          --
The marked increase in General Motors sales for the first two
quarters undoubtedly reflects the favorable public reception
of the new passenger car models and the new Frigidaire
appliances.

These increased sales plus the increased production as
announced in your annual report also mean more work for your
accounting staff.  I can take care of a man-sized share of this
extra work, I believe—and with a minimum of training.
                          --
The regular Saturday night reports your retail dealers submit
show consumer trends which I want to help you translate into
continued Whirlpool leadership—as an analyst in your sales
department.
```

Each of these candidates continued to talk the terminology peculiar to the job. For example, the sales applicant referred knowingly to farmers and farming activities and to the selling activities of making calls, demonstrating, closing, and—probably most important in selling farm machinery—servicing. Such informed references are highly persuasive in any application letter because they establish in a desirable way the impression that the writer is well aware of the work conditions and requirements.

You want to show such knowledge, of course. But if you state it in independent clauses (flat facts which the reader probably already knows) you'll sound wooden and dull.

The undesirability of emphasizing analysis instead of qualifications will be clearer to you through comparing the following original letter and the revision. The original is almost painful in its flat, obvious statements. It also uses so much space stating requirements of the job that it fails to establish qualities of the applicant. The revision eliminates the flatness and preachiness through implication or incidental reference.

Although the revision is a little longer, it accomplishes a good deal more: It establishes qualifications in a good lead; it talks the special language of the reader; it establishes more qualifications. It also has a much better work-for-you interpretation. But the major improvement of the revision over the original is that it eliminates the preachy, flat statements (particularly at the beginnings of paragraphs) that made a smart girl sound dull.

ORIGINAL

It takes a secretary who is versatile, accurate, reliable and dependable for a firm like the Brown Insurance Company. I realize the importance of your having such a secretary, and I believe I have the necessary qualifications.

Having graduated from the University of Alabama with commercial studies as my major, I am familiar with such machines as the adding machine, mimeograph, and comptometer. Since my graduation I have been employed as a secretary with the Reynolds Metal Company. This has given me an opportunity to combine my knowledge with experience.

Insurance takes a lot of time and patience. A large amount of bookkeeping is required because every penny has to be accounted for. My one year of accounting at the University will enable me to keep your books neatly and correctly; and if it is necessary for me to work overtime, I am in good physical health to do so.

REVISED

My year's work as a secretary, four years' thorough college training in commercial studies, and lifetime residence in Tuscumbia should enable me to serve you well as a secretary and further the friendly relations between you and your clients.

Whether you want to send a memo to a salesman, a note to a client, or a letter to the home office, I could have it on your desk for signing within a short time. While earning my degree at Alabama, I developed a dictation rate of 100 words per minute and a transcription rate of 45, which I demonstrated daily during my year's work as secretary with the Reynolds Metal Company.

To help with the varied kinds of record keeping in a large insurance agency, I can use the knowledge and skills from a year's course in accounting and my study of filing systems, office practices, and office machines—all applied during my year of work. You can trust me to compute premiums accurately, send notices on schedule, and devise and turn out special forms when necessary.

ORIGINAL	REVISED
Since the Brown Insurance Company has many customers in different parts of the country, a large amount of business letters and transactions are carried on. As your secretary, I could take dictation at 100 words a minute and transcribe your letters accurately and neatly at 45 words a minute.	I realize that in an insurance agency everyone from the janitor to the bookkeeper affects the feeling of the public and that all must exercise friendliness and tact in any contact with a client. I anticipate the unexpected, and I meet it calmly; so I am prepared to handle a number of duties and to adjust to the demands of a busy, varied work schedule (including overtime work when it's necessary). I would expect to maintain cordial relations with all your customers quite naturally and easily because most of them are the neighbors and friends I've lived around all my life.
Even though accuracy and speed are important, personality is an important characteristic too. Because of the many kinds of people who are connected with this type of business, it is important to have a secretary who not only can file, take dictation, and type, but who can be a receptionist as well. Since I have lived in Tuscumbia all my life, I will know most of your clients as individuals and can serve them in a friendly manner.	
I have enclosed a data sheet for your convenience.	Mr. Bills and the other references I've listed on the enclosed data sheet will be glad to confirm my statements that I can work efficiently and cheerfully for you as a secretary who is able and willing to do more than turn out letters. After you've heard from them, please call me at 374–4726 and name a time that I may come in and talk with you.
Will you please call me at 374–4726 and tell me when I can talk to you?	

Asking for appropriate action

Whatever action you want your reader to take, identify it as specifically as possible, and ask confidently that he do it. Ordinarily it is to invite you in for an interview. As a self-respecting human being who has something to offer, you do not need to beg or grovel; but you do need to remember— and to show your realization of the fact—that the reader is under no obligation to see you, that when he gives you time he is doing you a favor, that the time and place of the interview are to be at his convenience, and that you should be grateful for his seeing you.

The action ending of the sales letter needs to be slightly modified in the application letter, however. You cannot with good grace exert as much pressure. For this reason most employment counselors and employers do not advocate using any reply device (an employer is happy to pay the postage to send a message to a potentially good employee, and writing and mailing a letter are routine actions for which he is well set up). But your application action ending still suggests a specific action, tries to minimize the burdensome aspects of that action through careful phrasing, establishes gratitude, and supplies a stimulus to action with a reminder of the contribution the applicant can make to the firm.

You've already seen several action endings in this chapter. But to drive home the point, let's look at the action endings of the four letters with which we started this analysis.

The Red Cross applicant definitely planned a trip to Washington for job-hunting purposes; so she concluded her letter logically and naturally with

> When I'm in Washington during the first two weeks in August, I should be grateful for the opportunity to come to your office and discuss further how I may serve in filling your present need for Red Cross club directors. Will you name a convenient time in a letter to me at my Birmingham address?

The industrial-management applicant phrased his ending in this simple fashion:

> Please suggest a time when you can conveniently allow me to discuss my qualifications for work in your industrial engineering department.

And the secretarial applicant confidently asked her exporter-reader:

> Won't you please call me at 615–5946 and tell me a time when I may come to your office and show you how well my preparation will fit into your firm?

The publisher's-representative applicant was in a slightly atypical situation. He couldn't afford to ask directly for an interview in New York because he had neither the money nor the time right then. (As it turned out, he flew to New York at the expense of the firms on two occasions within two weeks after sending the letters, but that was the result of further correspondence—and it's certainly not anything to count on!) So he wrote:

> After you've had a chance to verify some of the things I've said about myself in this letter and on the data sheet, will you write me frankly about the possibilities of my working for you?

> Possibly I could talk with one of your regional representatives in this area as a preliminary step. And I can plan to come to New York sometime this summer to talk with you further about my successfully representing your firm.

Such letters as suggested in the preceding pages and in the checklist for applications won't work miracles. They won't make a poor applicant a good one. They won't ordinarily secure a job; usually they can only open the door for an interview and further negotiations. To make yours do all it can, you may want to review the list of suggestions on pp. 468–69.

WRITING THE INVITED APPLICATION

Often a firm makes its personnel or employment needs known by running an ad, by listing them with an agency (commercial, where they'll charge you a fee, or governmental like the U.S. Employment Service offices and state-government equivalents, or college placement bureaus), or simply by word of mouth.

As you probably know, most large companies have recruiting personnel who regularly visit campuses scouting for talented young men and women. In many of these cases you don't need to generate interest. You have it! Furthermore, the ad or announcement usually gives you the analysis of job requirements or as a bare minimum identifies a job category and principal duties. If you learn of the job through an agency, someone there will tell you the principal requirements. Even when you hear of the job through a third person, he will usually tell you what you'll be expected to do. So matching up your qualifications with the job requirements is easier in the invited situation than in the prospecting, because your source will usually identify requirements in some order indicating their relative importance to the employer.

If you are equally strong on all points of preparation, you have no problem; you simply take up the points in the order listed. But such a happy condition you'll rarely find. Most often your best talking point is not the most significant requirement, and usually you'll be deficient in some way. The solution is to employ the same strategy you did in writing the invited sales letter: Tie in your strongest point of preparation with something the reader has indicated he wants done; take up those points wherein you are weakest in the middle position of the letter, and attempt to correlate them with some positive point.

Your analysis of job requirements and compilation of a data sheet are exactly the same procedures as in a prospecting situation. Adaptation is simply easier. And once past the opening, supplying evidence and asking for appropriate action are the same. Since the beginnings in the prospecting and the invited applications do differ somewhat, we need to consider why and to make some suggestions that will help you write good ones.

Whether you learn of the job through an ad, through an agency, or via a third person, your beginning is pretty much the same. The first requirement is that it talk work and qualifications; the second, that it identify the job; the third, that it refer to the source of the information (subordinately unless it is significant). The reason for naming this third function is simply that the reference to the ad, or the bureau, or the person who told you about the job is an automatic attention getter which favorably reinforces the reader's willingness or even eagerness to read your letter. One good sentence can accomplish all three functions and point the trend of the letter.

The opening of the following letter puts emphasis on work, clearly identifies the specific kind of work sought, and desirably subordinates the reference to the source. Note that after the opening the letter reads much the same as a prospecting application (indeed, if you omit the lead in the faked address block and the first two lines, it could be a prospecting letter).

Note also the adaptation of talking points—the stress on experience rather than on formal training.

```
I'm "sold
on insurance"
```

and I believe I can be the aggressive salesman for whom you advertised in Thursday's <u>Express</u>.

Five years of experience in dealing with people very similar to your prospects—in addition to technical training in insurance and salesmanship—would aid me in selling your low-premium accident policy.

As a pipeliner in Louisiana in 1967 I made friends with the kind of men to whom I'd be selling your policies. I had a chance to study people, their hopes and fears and desires for protection and security, while doing casework for the Welfare Society in San Antonio in the summer of 1968. And while working as a soda jerk both in high school and in college I learned how to <u>work for</u> and <u>with</u> the public.

The most significant thing I learned was to keep right on smiling even though dog-tired at the end of my 6–12 p.m. shift after having been to school most of the day. And I certainly learned the meaning of perseverance when I had to go home after midnight and get on the books for the next day's assignments.

The same perseverance that earned me <u>B</u>'s in Insurance and Income Protection, Liability Insurance, and Personal Salesmanship will help me find leads, follow them up, persuade, and close a sale. I know an insurance man makes money for himself and his company only when he sticks to a schedule of calls. But I'm equally aware of the value of patience and the necessity for repeat calls.

Because I'm friendly and apparently easygoing, your prospects would like to see me coming. I was elected a Favorite at Schreiner Institute, and at the University of Texas I was tapped for Silver Spurs, a service-honorary organization. Making these many friends has resulted in my knowing people from all sections of the state.

My build and obvious good health inspire confidence. And since I'm 24 and single, I am free to travel anywhere at any time, as well as to work nights.

Dr. Fitzgerald and the other men I've listed on the enclosed information sheet can help you evaluate me professionally and personally if you'll write or call them.

I should be grateful for your telling me a convenient time and place when I may talk with you further about my qualifications for being the hardworking salesman you want.

Frequently your source—especially an ad—gives you an effective entering cue and provides you with useful reference phrases throughout the letter. From the key phrases you can almost reconstruct the ad the young man answered in the following letter:

Because of my college training in accounting and my work

experience, I believe I can be the quick-to-learn junior
accountant for whom you advertised in the May Journal of
Accountancy.

Having successfully completed down-to-earth studies in tax
accounting and auditing while earning my degree in accounting
at Alabama, I should be able to catch on to your treatment of
these problems quickly.

And while working as assistant ledger clerk for the Grantland
Davis firm in Atlanta one semester, I developed a great respect
for accuracy as well as an appreciation of the necessity for
the conscientious, painstaking labor so essential in public
accounting. There, too, I also saw clearly the necessity for
absorbing confidential information without divulging it in any
manner to others.

My natural aptitude for synthesis and analysis, strengthened
by special study of the analysis of financial statements and
reinforced with a broad background of economics, law, and
statistics, should enable me to handle the recurring tasks of
compiling comparative statements of earnings and net worth.
And my training in writing reports will help me to tell the
story to my seniors as well as to clients.

Realizing that the public accountant must gain the confidence
of his clients through long periods of accurate, trustworthy
service, I welcome the offer of a long-range advancement
program mentioned in your ad. I'm not afraid of hard work.
And I enjoy the good health essential in the long, irregular
working hours of rush business seasons.

Will you study the diversified list of courses and the
description of my internship listed on the attached data sheet?
Note also, please, the wide range of activities I took part in
while maintaining an A̲ average. Then will you write the
references I've listed as a basis for letting me talk with you
further about my qualifications for beginning a career of
immediate usefulness to you?

I can start to work any time after graduation on June 4.

A variation of source doesn't affect your procedure—except that you
emphasize a source that would be influential in your getting the job; otherwise, subordinate the source. If you learn of the work through an agency
or a third person, the procedure is still the same. Here are some openings
bearing out our statement:

Since I have the qualifications necessary for successful
selling that you listed in your recent letter to the dean of
students here at the University of Illinois, I believe I could
serve you well as a salesman.

--

When I talked with Mr. Hugh Lomer this morning, he assured me
that I am qualified by experience and professional training for
the duties of a field auditor with your firm.

--

During the four years I worked as a branch-house auditor for
the L. B. Price Mercantile Company to put myself through
school, I became thoroughly familiar with every phase of
accounting work necessary for a branch office of a large

```
installment concern and with the reports required by the home
office.
I'd certainly like the chance to prove that my education and
personal characteristics parallel the description of the
desirable management trainee that you gave to Dr. Morley, head
of our placement bureau, when you visited the campus last week.
```

Two warnings need sounding, however. The first is to guard carefully against the stupid question, the one with the obvious answer. It is usually the result of asking a question which is made perfectly clear from the ad or the situation. When a young lady began her application to a legal firm with—

```
Are you looking for a college-trained secretary who can do the
work in your law office efficiently and accurately and who is
eager to learn law work?  If so, I think I can meet your
exacting requirements for a legal secretary.
```

—she was earnestly trying to highlight the employer's needs. But the reader had made perfectly clear in his ad the answer to her question! And an efficient candidate only looked silly in the eyes of this reader.

You don't need to worry about setting out requirements; they are already clearly established. Even this opening is questionable because the answer is so obvious:

```
Wouldn't that junior accountant you advertised for in the
Tribune be more valuable to your firm if she had a sound
understanding of accounting theory and principles and basic
training in industrial accounting?
```

The reader would probably snort, "More? She wouldn't be valuable if she didn't!"

The second warning is against showing signs of selfish glee over having discovered a job possibility of your choice. When you read or hear about the job, you may rightly think, "That's just what I want!"—but don't write this or any variation of it. Resist the impulse and start writing in terms of doing something for the reader: what you can give instead of what you hope to get.

Perhaps a third warning should be sounded against assuming that you don't have much of a selling job to do because the reader is on the asking end. Nothing could be further from the truth. The competition you're up against for an advertised job is keen even in the heyday of prosperity. And because many others will apply, you'll have to write a superior letter to be chosen as one of the final few for interviewing.

In fact, the reader may find such a heap of letters on his desk that yours may not even get read. For that reason you may want to do one of several things so that your letter will command attention and thus be selected for reading. Most of these have to do with the physical impression or the mechanics of sending.

A favorite device is sending the letter by special delivery. Few personnel men ever object. If you are in the same town, you can deliver the letter yourself, with the request that it be turned over to the appropriate reader.

If you insert the letter in an envelope large enough to accommodate an 8½- by 11-inch page without folding and put a piece of cardboard under it to keep it smooth, the contrast between your letter and all the others that have been folded will call attention to yours.

Cutting out the ad and pasting it neatly at the top of the page may single out your letter for attention. Beginning your message with a faked address block which quotes from the ad is another device. Hanging indention may help to make a rushed reader reach for your letter instead of another. Even appropriate color may cause the employer to read yours rather than another in the stack.

When competition is keen, you'll need to take the time and exert the effort to be sure that your letter is one of the earliest arrivals. This may mean getting up early to get the first edition of the newspaper and having your material in such shape that you can have a complete, well-written letter and data sheet in the hands of the employer hours or even days before less alert candidates get theirs there. Even though you may not get the immediate response you want, your letter (if it is good) becomes better in the eyes of the employer as poorer ones come in through the mail.

But none of these devices will make much difference if your letter is not written from the viewpoint of contributing to the firm through effective, efficient work.

As you already realize, the items we suggested to you in the prospecting application checklist (p. 468) apply equally when you write an invited application. Study them again, and review the additional items at the end of that checklist which are peculiar to the invited application.

CONTINUING THE CAMPAIGN

Regardless of the results from your application, you have some follow-up work to do.

If you get an invitation to an interview, you know how to handle it. Accept promptly, pleasantly, and directly (if that's your decision) as suggested in Chapter 5. Just remember to continue your job campaign by indicating continuing interest in serving. If you decide to turn down the invitation, Chapter 7 has shown you how; but remember, also, the adage about never burning your bridges behind you.

If within a reasonable time you do not hear from the person or firm you've applied to, you'd probably better send a follow-up letter indicating continuing interest.

Follow-up letters

A good salesman doesn't make one call and drop the matter if he doesn't close the sale. Neither does a sales-minded job applicant.

Prospecting Application Checklist

1. The prospecting application must generate interest from the start.
    a) Establish early your central selling point of education or experience or both, in terms of doing something. You may also cite your research on the company or the field, or tell a human-interest story; but they postpone the real message.
    b) Avoid the preaching or didactic, flat statement.
    c) Avoid implying that your up-to-date techniques are better, or telling the reader how to run his business.
    d) Make clear early that you are seeking work of a specialized nature, not just any job.
    e) Be realistic; talk work and doing, not "forming an association with."—Avoid *position, application, vacancy,* and *opportunity.*
    f) You need verve and vigor, not stereotypes like "Please consider my application . . . ," "I should like to apply for . . . ."
    g) Don't let your biography drown out what you can do now.
    h) By the second paragraph, start talking your qualifications.
    i) Mere graduation (rather than the preparation back of it) is a poor lead anywhere, especially at first.
    j) Eliminate selfish-sounding statements or overtones of them.
    k) Don't give the reader an opportunity to shut you off with a negative response.

2. Interpretation and tone are important from the start.
    a) Maintain a consistent, acceptable tone, neither apologizing for what you don't have nor bragging about what you do.
    b) For conviction, back up your assertions of ability with specific points of education or experience as evidence.
    c) Generalizing and editorializing are out of place: "invaluable," "more than qualified," even "excellent."
    d) Avoid needlessly deprecating your good qualifications.
    e) Project your education or experience right to the job.
    f) Use enough "I's" for naturalness, but avoid monotony.
    g) Show the research and thought which have gone into the project. Address the letter to the appropriate individual if at all possible; talk about company operations and trends in the industry; even a deft, tactful reference to a competitor can be a point in your favor.

3. Your education and experience are your conviction elements.
    a) Talk about your experience, schooling, or personal characteristics in terms of accomplishing something. For example, you may register for, take, attend, study, receive credit for, pass, learn, or master a course.
    b) The emphasis should go on a phase of work connected with the job you're applying for.

Prospecting Application Checklist
(continued)

c) Refer to education as work preparation (in lowercase letters) rather than exact course titles (in capitals and lowercase).

d) You need highlights rather than details in the letter.

e) But even highlights need to be specific for conviction.

f) Your data sheet supplies thorough, detailed coverage in most cases. Refer to it incidentally in a sentence establishing some other significant idea after stating your case and just before asking the reader to take action.

4. Reflect your personality in both content and style.

a) Refer to the more significant personal characteristics affecting job performance, preferably with concrete evidence that you have them.

b) Incorporate phrases which reveal your attitude toward work and your understanding of working conditions.

5. Ask for appropriate action in the close.

a) Name the action you want; make it specific and plausible.

b) Don't beg and don't command; just ask. And avoid the aloof, condescending implications of "You may call me at . . . ." Usually you ask for an appointment to talk about the job.

c) Eliminate references to application, interview, position. Use action references to work and the necessary steps in job getting.

d) Clearly imply or state that you will be grateful. But "Thank you for . . ." in present tense sounds presumptuous.

e) Show success consciousness without presumptuousness.

f) A little sales whip-back at the end will help strengthen the impression of what you can contribute.

FOR WRITING INVITED APPLICATIONS

6. When writing an application in response to an ad or the suggestion of an agency or friend:

a) Primary emphasis should be on putting your preparation to work for the reader. But since your reference to the source is an automatic way of securing attention, you should identify it early and emphasize it if it carries an implied recommendation.

b) Avoid stating what the reader would infer ("I read your ad").

c) Don't ask questions or phrase assumptions which are clear pushovers: "If you are seeking X, Y, and Z, then I'm your man." "Are you looking for an employee with X, Y, and Z? I have X, Y, and Z."

d) Postpone salary talk until the interview if you can. If the phrase "State salary required" is included in the description, your reply of "your going rate" or "your usual wage scale" is acceptable to any firm you'd want to work for.

In order to have a reason for sending a follow-up letter within two or three weeks after the original application, some applicants intentionally omit some pertinent but relatively insignificant piece of information in the original. Even if you receive the usual noncommittal letter saying that the firm is glad to have your application and is filing it in case any opening occurs, you need not hesitate to send another letter two, three, or six months after the first one. It should not be another complete application (yours will still be on file); it is just a reminder that you are still interested.

> I noticed in rereading my copy of the application I sent you three weeks ago that I did not list Mr. Frank Regan, manager, Bell's Supermarket, Anniston, Alabama.
>
> Since I have worked under Mr. Regan's direct supervision for three summers, he is a particularly good man to tell you about my work habits and personality. I hope you will write to him.

Such a subterfuge we cannot commend, if for no other reason than that so many other approaches are available to you. One acceptable one is this:

> I know that many organizations throw away applications over six months old.
>
> Because that much time has elapsed since I sent you mine (dated April 15), I want to assure you that I'm still interested in working for you, in having you keep my record in your active file, and in hearing from you when you need a man with my qualifications.

Only a lackadaisical applicant would end his letter there, however. With just a few more words he could bring information about himself up to date and perhaps stimulate more interest in his application. He could add something like this:

> Since graduation I have been doing statistical correlations at the Bureau of Business Research here at the University. I've picked up a few techniques I didn't learn in class, and I've certainly increased my speed on the adding machine and calculator.
>
> I still want that job as sales analyst with your firm, however.

The foregoing two paragraphs could be a follow-up letter in themselves.

Election to an office or an honorary society, an extensive trip that has opened your eyes to bigger and better possibilities of the job, a research paper that has taught you something significant to the job, and certainly another job offer are all avenues of approach for reselling yourself and indicating continuing interest.

Thank-you letters

Following an interview, whether the results seem favorable or unfavorable, your note of appreciation is not only a business courtesy; it helps to single you out from other applicants and to show your reader that you have a good sense of human relations.

Even when you and the interviewer have agreed that the job is not for you, you can profitably invest about two minutes writing something like this:

> I surely appreciate the time you spent with me last Friday discussing employment opportunities at Monitor and Wager.
>
> The suggestions you made will help me find my right place in the business world now.
>
> After I get that experience you suggested, I may be knocking at your door again.

When you are interested in the job discussed and feel that there's a good chance for you, you're plain foolish not to write a letter expressing appreciation and showing that you learned something from the interview.

> Your description of the community relations program of Livania has opened new vistas to me, Mr. Lee.
>
> The functions of the public relations department in your company as you described them made me much more aware of the significance and appeal of this work.
>
> As soon as I returned to the campus, I read Mr. Fields's book that you suggested and the pamphlets describing U.S. Steel's program.
>
> Many thanks for your suggestions and for the time you took with me.
>
> I shall be looking forward to hearing the decision about my application as soon as you can make it.

Job-acceptance letters

When an employer offers you a job and you decide it's the one for you, tell him so enthusiastically and happily in a direct A–plan letter that keeps you in a favorable light.

> I certainly do want to work with Franklin & Franklin—
>
> —and I didn't need a week to think it over, Mr. Bell, although I appreciate your giving me that much time to come to a decision.
>
> I've filled out the forms you gave me and enclosed them with this letter.
>
> Anything else?
>
> Unless you tell me differently, I'll take off two weeks after graduation. But I'll call you on Friday, June 11, to get report-to-work instructions for Monday, June 14.

Job-refusal letters

Sometime in your life you'll have to tell someone that you don't want what he has to offer. And you may feel that it's routine, that it doesn't mean anything one way or the other to a busy man who interviews many applicants and has many possibilities available to him. Remember, though, that a human being with all his pride and ego is going to read the letter. And make yourself think, "I don't want that job *now*," for you may want to reopen negotiations at some future point.

To wind up negotiations pleasantly and leave the way open for you, write a B–plan letter with a pleasant buffer of some favorable comment about the company or the work, some plausible and inoffensive reason, the statement of the refusal as positively as you can phrase it (possibly with the statement of where you are going to work), and an ending expressing good feeling and appreciation or both. The following letter is a good example:

> Meeting you and talking with you about working for Bowen's was one of the more interesting job contacts I have had.
>
> The opportunity to learn the business from the ground up and to grow with an expanding company is a challenging one, one for which I am grateful.
>
> As I told you, however, I am primarily interested in product research. Since I feel that my abilities will best be utilized in that way, I am going to work for [a company] that has offered me such employment.
>
> I shall certainly continue to watch your company's progress with interest, and I shall look forward to reading or hearing about the results of your prepackaging program.

Letters of resignation

Resignation letters, like job-refusal letters, are modified B–plan letters. When you have worked for a firm, you have benefited in some way (in addition to the regular pay you have drawn). Regardless of how you may feel at the time, remember that you can say something complimentary about how things are run, about what you have learned as a result of your experience, or about the people with whom you have associated. By all means, say it! Then announce your plan to leave, giving consideration to the necessity for ample time in which to find a replacement. In some cases no more than two weeks is enough advance notification; sometimes it should be long enough for you to help train the person who will take your place.

Remember, however, that you want to stay in the good graces of the individuals who have assisted you in your career. You will be wise to give ample notification, to give credit where credit is due. The suggestion to "Be kind, courteous, and considerate to the people you pass on the way up the ladder of success; you will likely meet them on your way back down" is good advice to keep in mind when you leave a job.

In many circumstances your resignation can be oral. And in many circumstances it may be better that way. But when you need to write a letter, consider adaptations of the following:

I've certainly learned a great deal about the clothing market from my work as sales analyst at Foley's the past 18 months.

I shall always be grateful to you and the other personnel who have helped me to do the job and to prepare for a more challenging one.

You will perhaps recall that when I had my interviews with you before starting to work, I stressed my interest in working toward a job as a sales coordinator.

Since I now have such an opportunity at Sakowitz, Inc., I am submitting my resignation. Apparently it will be some time before such an opening is available for me in this organization.

I should like to terminate employment in two weeks. But I can make arrangements to work a little longer if this will help to train the person who takes my place.

My thanks and good wishes.

Often when another offer comes your way, you'll feel free to discuss the opportunity with your current employer before making a final decision. Such a conference has many advantages for both employee and employer. Often a counteroffer results, to the mutual satisfaction of both, and the job change doesn't take place. If, despite a counteroffer, you still decide to make the change, you can resign in good grace with a letter somewhat like this:

Your recent offer is one I appreciate very much, and it made me give serious thought to continuing at Bowen's.

Let me say again how much I have appreciated the cooperation, the friendliness, and helpfulness of everyone with whom I've been associated here.

After considerably more evaluation, however, I believe I can make a greater contribution and be a more successful business manager by accepting the position offered me by Lowen's.

I hope that I can leave with your approval by [specific date]; I feel sure that all my current projects will be completed by that time.

You'll hear from me from time to time—if for no other reason than that I'll be interested in how the new credit union works out.

But I'll always want to know how things are going for Bowen's and the many friends I've made here.

When appropriate, a possible talking point is the suggestion of a successor to you; often this is a big help. A constructive suggestion, phrased positively, implies your continuing interest in the organization.

Letters of resignation written by college students who resign after having agreed to work for someone but before actually reporting for work are something we take up with reluctance. Many personnel men regard them as a breach of contract. Certainly a practice of sliding out from under such agreements will soon give you a black eye employmentwise.

We would urge you to give serious thought before definitely accepting a job offer. Don't make the mistake of grabbing the first job offered you, only to have something infinitely more to your liking come along later. We'd further urge you never to let yourself get caught in the position of being committed to two employers at the same time. If you have agreed to go to work for a firm and then you have a later offer which you want to accept, do not accept it until you are released from the first contract. To the second potential employer, reply in some vein like this:

I certainly would like to accept your offer to come with your firm. As attractive as your proposal is, however, I must delay accepting it until I can secure a release from the Jenkins firm in Blankville. After my interview with you, I accepted this position, which at the time appeared to be the most promising available.

Can you allow me enough time to write the Jenkins personnel manager, explaining my reasons and requesting a release? (I can give him the names of two friends who might be suitable replacements.)

This shouldn't take longer than a week to settle. I appreciate your offer, regardless of how things work out.

If necessary, phone the second potential employer, explain frankly, and get his consent to wait. But for your own protection, get his consent before writing a letter like the following:

As you know, I am now planning to report to work as an executive trainee shortly after the first of June.

Before I made this agreement with you, I had talked with a representative of the Larkin organization in Sometown concerning possibilities of my working there as an analyst in the quality control division, which is the kind of work I have specifically trained for and know I want to do.

I believe I'd be a better adjusted and qualified employee in the Larkin job. That is the main reason I ask that you release me from my commitment with you. The fact that Sometown is a considerably larger city and that the starting salary is somewhat larger are only secondary considerations.

No doubt you have other people you can call on to take my place, but you may be interested to know that Don M. Jones and Peter Lawson are interested in the Jenkins program. You can get portfolios on both of them through the placement bureau here at school.

Since the Larkin people have agreed to postpone a decision until I have heard from you, I should appreciate a quick reply.

You can rest assured that I shall keep my word with you and that if your answer is no, I shall report to work as promised and do all I can to be an efficient, cooperative, and cheerful employee.

Only a Simon Legree would say no to the foregoing letter. If the man releases you, you'd then write the appropriate acceptance letter to the second firm; but you should, as a matter of business courtesy, write a short thank-you letter to the first man.

TWO USEFUL MODIFICATIONS OF APPLICATIONS

The following two letter possibilities for helping you get the job of your choice are not printed here with the implication that they will take the place of the complete sales presentation we have suggested to you. Because they may help you sometimes, we simply remind you of them.

The job-anticipating letter

Most personnel men are willing to give advice. And most of them are pleased with a show of interest in their companies and evidence of long-range planning on the part of a student. Several of our students have had successful results from letters like the following, sent in the junior year of college:

A course in the operation of business machines under Mrs. Lora Osmus in the Statistics Department at Alabama gave me skill in their operation and showed me the tremendous possibilities of Burrows equipment for business use.

After comparing Burrows and ABL equipment that was on exhibit on Commerce Day and talking with the Burrows representative in charge of your display, I am coming to you directly and frankly for some help.

Since I have completed practically all of the courses required for the B.S. in commerce, I am free to elect practically all courses I shall study next year before June graduation. On the attached sheet I've listed the courses I've completed and those I'm contemplating. Will you please rank the ones you consider most beneficial for a prospective Burrows representative?

Naturally, I will regard your suggestions as off-the-cuff assistance that implies no commitment. I'm just trying to equip myself as well as I can to meet the competition for the first available job with your company after I graduate.

I shall be most grateful for your comments.

The telescoped application inquiry

We realize that good applications take time. They're worth the time, however.

But we also know that sometime, somewhere, you may need to send some inquiries in a hurry and simply cannot write a complete one. You may be able to make profitable use of the services of your college placement bureau in a letter, as one young man did. He was too busy writing a thesis and sitting for graduate examinations to prepare a thorough application. He sent the following request and a reply card to six firms:

With completion of an M.S. degree in accounting at the
University of Alabama and two years of retail merchandise
accounting experience, I believe I could make you a good
accountant with a minimum of training—and be able to advance
more rapidly than the majority of accountants you could hire.

I am not just an accountant: A well-rounded background of
finance, transportation, economics, and other related subjects
will enable me, in time, to do managerial work as well.

May I have the Placement Bureau here at the University send
you a transcript of my college record together with a detailed
record of my experience, faculty rating statements, and names
and addresses of former employers?

I shall be happy to furnish any additional information you may
want and to be available for an interview at your convenience
later if you will check and return the enclosed card.

He received replies from all six firms, it's true. But only one resulted in an interview.

This may be a stopgap measure sometime. But this young man's experience simply reconfirms the fact that an applicant must tell a complete story if he expects to get a show of effective interest.

Although letters exchanging information about applicants are a part of the employment routine, applicants themselves do not write them. For that reason, and because you studied them in Chapter 5, we see no point in taking them up here. They are A–plan letters, characterized by directness and conciseness.

Likewise, we do not think you need to study or write the kinds of letters an interviewer or employer writes to an applicant who is accepted for a position (clearly an A–plan good-news letter) or to an applicant who is not accepted (a B–plan disappointing-news letter). With but simple changes of talking points and references, they follow the principles of their basic plan.

Letter cases for part three

Prospecting applications

1. Assume that you are in your last term of school and graduation is around the corner. Your greatest interest is in finding work which you like, for which you have been preparing for about four years, and in which you could support yourself now and a family later as you win promotions.

The want ads of newspapers and trade magazines list no job of your choice. No placement bureau provides anything to your liking. So you decide to do as any good salesman does: survey the product (yourself); then appraise the market (companies which in the scope of their operations could use a person who can do what you are prepared to do); then advertise (send the companies a data sheet with a covering application letter); and then follow up with another letter if you don't hear from them. Such a procedure sometimes creates a job where none existed before; sometimes it establishes a basis for negotiations for the "big job" two, three, or five years after graduation. And very frequently it puts you on the list for the good job which is not filled through advertising or from the company staff.

To analyze the high points of your preparation, you will need to study the lineup of courses that under your curriculum you expect to complete by the time you graduate. *This means you'll have to study your college catalog.* It also means that you will have to make a temporary decision about the kind of work you want to do. If you haven't the faintest idea of what you'd like to do, follow the suggestions in Chapter 11.

Use the courses you have had and make plausible assumptions (don't go daydreaming and woolgathering; stick to probabilities) about the courses you will have completed on graduation.

Distinguish between those courses which actually qualify you to do the type of work you are seeking and those which give you background education. If you've had experience directly related to the job you want as a career, that's fine; but any work you've done means qualifications (military experience—active duty—is in almost the same category as on-the-job experience). With these training and work sections mapped out, complete a tentative data sheet with personal details and some appropriate references.

Then study the market, as suggested under "Analyzing Companies" (p.

433). In actual practice you would compile a list of companies and send them an application. For this assignment, after some preliminary digging around, select one company and plan a letter–data-sheet combination addressed to that company. Adapt it as specifically as possible to the one company. You may or may not be able to find out the name of the specific individual to address it to. If not, address it to the personnel department or to the head of the particular department in which you are interested.

You will benefit from this exercise in application letter writing only if you approach it earnestly and seriously. It should be a job utilizing your college training. It should be a job geared to what you could reasonably assume will be your level of performance at the time of graduation. Few just-out-of-college folks can expect to be sales managers, chief buyers, senior accountants, copy chiefs, and the like; you'll have to begin at a subordinate level and work up; you'll want to show in your letter that you realize this fact. On the other hand, don't waste your time and your instructor's applying for something that you could readily do if you had never gone to college.

Preferably, you would confine your presentation to a one-page letter and a one-page data sheet. But don't be afraid to go to two pages for either. As in sales letters, some highly successful ones run to two and sometimes even three pages.

In actual practice you would send the letter and data sheet together. As a work control measure in a classroom situation, however, your teacher may allow you to submit the data sheet (which you should in actual practice prepare *before* writing the letter) and a few days later, the letter.

In a job campaign like this, you would do well to get a reply to each of your letters. If half these replies asked you to send more information, you'd be lucky. If a fourth of your replies asked you to come for an interview, you'd be hitting a jackpot. If even one offered you a job without an interview, you could consider your letter phenomenal!

2. Write a job-seeking letter for work next summer. It should not only enable you to earn some money to apply on your college expenses; it should also be work which will be good preparation for the career you plan when you finish your degree and/or leave college. Too, consider the prestige value of the company name on data sheets you will prepare later in your life.

This may well be the company to which you would send an application upon graduation; if so, shape your letter presentation accordingly.

3. Look over your local situation for part-time job possibilities, perhaps on your college campus or in the college community (close enough for you to arrange a schedule of classes that would permit you to work five afternoons a week). Since you plan to attend school straight through, you could talk in terms of two years of work. Word the application so the reader will understand that between the end of summer school and fall registration you will either have to work full time or go to your home. Prepare a data sheet and letter that summarize and interpret your background up to the time of writing (of course, you would include subjects you are now studying).

4. You've decided that you want to earn some money, see some new places, and have some fun this coming summer. So you're going to address an application for summer employment to an inn at a resort (possibly one of the national parks). You'll have to indicate a willingness to do house-keeping duties (including kitchen and dining room duties), although if you have enough maturity and the right kind of experience you may be able to get some kind of clerical or even more specialized assignment. Since college students chosen for such jobs are really hosts (and hostesses) to the guests, stress poise, dignity, and cheerfulness, as well as any talents for entertaining.

5. Modify the preceding problem to this extent: You want to be a coun-selor at a summer camp for children at least five years younger than you. Choose a camp with which you are familiar, or find out about one from a friend. Address the letter and data sheet to the camp director (by name if you can get it). Note here the importance of understanding and getting along with youngsters, the ability to direct activities, and the emphasis on athletic abilities. Apply to a camp which is not in your hometown or your college town; it should be a residence camp, not a day camp.

6. With plausible assumptions and appropriate modifications, write a job-anticipating letter to the company of your choice. Assume that you have one more year of college studies before graduating.

Invited applications

1. A good starting point in job getting is the want-ad columns of news-papers and magazines (especially trade magazines). Study the ones of your choice and find an ad that describes a job you would like to have, requiring qualifications you could reasonably assume at the time of your graduation (or some other assumed time as affected by your intentions). It should be a job utilizing your college training. And it should indicate clearly that letter—not telephone—answers are wanted. Clip the ad neatly to your letter; or if you find the ad of your choice in a library copy, make an exact copy, with exact reference: name of publication, date of the issue, and page on which you found the ad. You may instead choose one of the ads listed later in this problem.

Draw on imagination, experience, and whatever information you can find out to bring the situation as close to reality as you can. Read the ad thoughtfully for what it says, and search mentally for those qualifications which it only implies. Then evaluate your own training and experience in the light of the specific job. You can readily distinguish between courses that actually qualify you to do the job you're considering and those which are only background. You can certainly classify your work experience in an order of applicability to the given job. Further, analyze significant personal factors. And finally, decide upon references. In actual practice you would want to send a data sheet. For this problem assignment you may assume a data sheet much like the one used with the prospecting application and refer to it in your letter.

Submit the letter trying to get the one job for which you are best suited, either from an ad you've found or one of the following (assume the city):

a) Sales Trainee. College graduate, preferably in business administration. No traveling. Well acquainted in city. If you have limited opportunity to increase your income in your present position and are interested in training for sales career with national firm, you can earn from $8,000 to $25,000 annually. Adequate starting salary. Write full details to Box B–65, c/o *News*.

b) Credit and adjustment manager of national dress manufacturer needs assistant. Handle routine correspondence, supervise clerical help. Bright future for right man or woman. College training, business experience, mature judgment necessary. Salary $5,500 to $7,000, depending on qualifications. Box P–65, c/o *Press*.

c) Accountant—expanding national concern. Traveling. Good opportunity for person with ambition, personality, hard-work habits. State age, training, experience in confidential letter to M–89, c/o *News*.

d) Advertising worker for Peers-Loebuck store. Prefer experienced worker; copy, selling, layouts, with general advertising and marketing background; might consider promising beginner. Write Box 897, City. Send samples of work.

e) Secretary wanted for law firm. Write Box C–89, c/o *News*, stating training, and experience.

f) Office secretary, experienced in bookkeeping, typing, and meeting public. Must do accurate and neat work. Correspondence by dictation two hours daily. Regular salary $90 a week. Good background and personality important. Give details. Box E–98, c/o *News*.

g) Immediate opening—internal auditor. For young college graduate with major in accounting to train as internal auditor with growing national manufacturer in Ohio. Excellent opportunity for person with executive potential, ambition, attractive personality. Experience helpful but not essential. Established concern. Up-to-date employee benefits. Write giving full details of qualifications and salary requirement. All replies will be kept confidential. Write A–98, c/o *News*.

h) Insurance manager—Banker Life Insurance Company. Must be able to hire and train sales personnel. Prefer college graduate with knowledge of insurance and business. Salary override commission and renewal bonuses. Apply J. P. Morrison, Room 908, Comer Building.

i) Stenographer—general office experience. Must be familiar with office machines. Be able to start in 30 days. Good training, salary—5½-day week. Give experience, telephone, and other essential details. Write Box D–90, c/o *News*.

j) Production manager for small midtown publisher and producer of distinguished and unusual illustrated books. Good experience. Confidence guaranteed. Box 989, *Marketing Communications.*

k) Distributor wanted for Tender Vender Warmers for popcorn, Box 578, Miami, Florida 30148. To handle exclusive franchise throughout state. Distributor receives help in setting up office and in training sales force.

l) Office manager. Knowledge of all types of office machines; knowledge of accounting desirable. Must have initiative, ambition, adaptability, eagerness to learn. State full details, salary expected in letter. Large firm with sales-service outlets in key cities of the United States, Europe, Canada, Mexico. Local Box 15.

m) National concern desires insurance or credit reporter. No selling or collecting. College education preferred. Be capable of earning above $7,000 annually. Write Manager, Box 3366A, South Highlands Station 35401 (nearest metropolitan center).

2. The director of your college placement bureau (use his name) has just told you about the training program of a large corporation. The personnel director indicated in a letter to your placement officer that the company seeks young college graduates between 21 and 25 (this is not ironclad, however) to train for managerial positions throughout the organization. The training program lasts for a year. During that time trainees work in every division under close supervision and attend a series of classes. Assume a specific company, and prepare a letter and data sheet. (If you have already written a data sheet for the prospecting application, you should use that form with only slight modifications; for this assignment, then, you may just assume the modified form. If you have not already prepared your data sheet, do so for this assignment.) As in any application, indicate your particular field of interest, but reflect a receptive attitude toward the various phases of the training program, showing your realization of its benefits regardless of the specific work you'll eventually perform.

3. Your college adviser is head of the department in which you are pursuing your major studies. This morning he tells you that a firm you hold in high regard is seeking a person with substantially your qualifications for a particular job you want. Fill in with the necessary specific details and write the letter you would send, assuming that your basic data sheet presentation will accompany it.

4. The same college adviser (preceding case) also suggested several other companies as good prospects but stated specifically that he did not know whether there are openings in these companies at present. "They hire a lot of people," he added, "and if there's no opening now, you can be pretty sure there will be one before long." Using his name early in your lead, write the letter (assume the data sheet).

5. This morning, quite unexpectedly, you had an interview with the representative of a firm you'd like to work for. After half an hour of talk which appeared to be mutually satisfactory and during which time you found out a lot about the company, the representative handed you one of the company employment forms for applying, shook your hand, and ushered you out of the room, saying, "Fill this out and return it to me with a letter of application." With the form filled in neatly and completely, draft the earnest but enthusiastic letter of application this man invited. Be careful to talk work rather than employee benefits. Assume specific names for the representative and the company. He said he would write you after receiving your letter.

Follow-ups

1. Not having heard from the application letter you sent in any of the preceding situations, write a fairly short letter reemphasizing your desire to work for the firm. You may want to send it as soon as three weeks after the initial letter; you may prefer to wait longer. Clearly refer to the original application by date and type of work discussed. Include any additional data you think will help sell you. This letter, however, should not be a rehash of what you have already written. It should identify the action you want the reader to take.

2. Assuming that it is almost a year after you sent your original letter, write a follow-up letter that reassures the firm of your desire to work there. In the meantime a good deal has happened to you (or should have!). Account for the way you have spent the time in such a manner as to show that it is preparation for the job you seek.

3. Assume that you have had an interview as a result of your letter and data sheet. You know the company representative interviewed several other candidates for the job. In a thank-you letter, confirm your interest in employment by the company and add other details to show that you picked up something from the interview. The representative promised to get in touch with you in a week or 10 days.

4. As a result of your determined efforts and good showing, you've been offered the job of your choice. The letter so informing you requests you to fill in an employment form and return it and names a starting date that fits in with your plans. Write the acceptance.

5. Although you were offered a job in response to your application, you have decided that you do not want to accept it because it is not in the field of your primary interest and for other plausible reasons—not salary. Write the tactful letter that expresses appreciation for the time spent with you and the interest shown in you and that leaves the way open for you to resume negotiations later if you care to. Comment favorably on some aspect of the company.

6. You have just been informed that you were not chosen for the job you have worked so hard to get—and still want. Remember, however, that you were considered; that someone spent a good deal of time with you; and that, employmentwise, nothing is ever final. Write the letter expressing appreciation for the courtesies extended you, revealing how you have profited from the contact, and showing your determination to reach your intended goal. Above all, the letter should reflect a friendly feeling toward the company and the representative addressed.

7. In response to your application you receive an invitation to come in for an interview at a time and place convenient for you. Write the acceptance confirming the circumstances.

8. Assume that in response to your prospecting application you receive an invitation to come in for an interview at a time which would be convenient if you had the money for traveling to the distant point. Write the letter which reaffirms your interest. Admit your lack of funds and ask if it is possible to see a representative of the firm at a place which is more accessible to you.

Writing reports

HISTORY, GENERAL FUNCTION, AND PRESENT NEED OF REPORTS

IN HIS EARLY HISTORY man did not need reports. Every man operated his own complete business or directed a small group of people under his command. As on-the-spot manager he had all the facts he needed for making decisions. For example, when a shipowner captained his own small ship, he saw all the operations and consequently needed no reports. His personal observation provided all the information he needed and thus served the one general function of most reports—*to help the receiver make a decision by providing needed facts and ideas.*

Later, as society became more complex, some men gained power over large groups as their tribal chieftains, masters, or employers—and found reports essential. When one of these bosses sent an underling to scout an enemy tribe or do some work, the boss wanted a report indicating difficulties encountered or to be encountered and the underling's suggestions on such things as materials, personnel, necessary time, and plans for overcoming the difficulties. For example, when a successful shipowner built a second ship and put a hired captain on it to develop trade along a different route, the owner needed reports if he was to make wise decisions about future operations. Thus the ship's log came into being as one early form of written report.

SPECIFIC WAYS REPORTS SERVE

The impossibility of the manager's being in two places at the same time made reports necessary. Overcoming the problem of *distance,* then, is the first specific function reports may serve in achieving their general purpose of helping the receiver make decisions by providing needed facts and ideas.

When businesses and other organizations grew to where the manager could not find time to oversee all operations (sometimes even under the same roof) and some of the processes became so technical that the manager did not have the knowledge to evaluate all of them, reports became more and more widely used to solve two more specific problems: *time* and *technology.*

With the increasing complexity of society, *records* became more important too; and as their fourth specific function, written reports provided permanent records. Thus they became important in preparing tax returns, in preventing later repetition of the same work, and (through extra copies) in informing interested secondary readers.

As executives became responsible for more and more varied activities, the wiser ones also began to realize that they could not do all the desirable thinking about new products, processes, and procedures. They therefore invited employees with initiative to submit ideas in reports. Hence reports began to serve management in a fifth way as vehicles for *creative ideas.*

As managers became responsible for numerous employees, some of whom they rarely saw, they often found that the best indicators they had of how well a man was doing his job were the reports he wrote. Thus reports began to serve in a sixth way—as a basis for *evaluating the employees* who wrote them.

If you bring these trends up to the present world of large and complex organizations—

—Where top management may be thousands of miles from some operations

—Where management cannot possibly find time to oversee all the activities even in one large building

—Where some of the processes are so technical that no man can be competent to decide wisely about all of them

—Where numerous records must be kept and many people informed

—Where competition pushes a manager to use all the creative brainpower of all employees in developing new ideas, and

—Where personnel managers may never see employees they have to evaluate

—you see that reports have become essential tools of modern management.

QUESTIONS REPORTS ANSWER

In making their decisions, managers often depend on reports to answer one or more of three broad questions:

1. Should we take a certain proposed action?

A board of directors trying to decide on a proposed new product or plant will want a report showing whether expected returns will cover estimated costs and leave a profit. Often the answer is not in terms of dollars, however; it may be in terms of any kind of benefits—higher quality or quantity, or less time, material, or effort. Particularly in reports for public institutions, the benefits are likely to be in terms of better service, safety, goodwill, law enforcement, ecology, health, or education.

2. Is it feasible?

In thinking about any proposed action, the decision maker may first ask *why* it should be done (question 1); but unless it obviously *can* be done, the feasibility question will be a quick second. Can you imagine approval of proposals like constructing a bridge across Michigan's Mackinac Straits, or allocating billions to try to establish any kind of operations on the moon, without reports pointing to their feasibility?

3. Which is the best (or better) way?

Of course, the question of the best way presupposes favorable answers to the two preceding—through previous knowledge, previous reports, or previous treatment in the same report. This question also covers those numerous reports which start only with a problem, rather than a proposal. In that case the report writer has to originate as well as evaluate proposed solutions. Often the answer is a choice between the present way and a proposed new one. But it may be between or among products: Smith or Royal typewriters for our offices? Chevrolet, Ford, or Plymouth for our fleet? Repair the old or buy a new . . . ?

Any board of directors, president, governor, manager, superintendent, or department head in any organization—public or private—wants satisfactory answers to all three questions before approving substantial expenditures, changes in operations, or new regulations. Many times those questions lead to the assignment of reports. For this reason management today expects all employees (except possibly day laborers) to be able to write reports.

If you need more evidence that learning to write better reports will be a worthwhile activity for you, turn back to pages 7–8 and read "Why Study Report Writing?"

NATURE AND CLASSIFICATION OF REPORTS

Just as a building, a piece of furniture, or anything else should be designed according to its functions, so should reports. In the foregoing discussion of the functions of reports, you have seen several implications of their nature. Yet the word *report* is such a broad concept that it cannot be well defined in a few sentences. All known attempts at definition are either incomplete, too general to be useful, or not quite true. For example, if you say that reports interpret facts, you are obviously talking only about *analytical* reports and omitting the numerous *informational* reports which do not interpret the facts they present. The best way to get a clear idea of the meaning of the word *report* is to consider the usual characteristics of reports, along with the special characteristics of different types.

Usually, but not always—

1. A report is a management tool designed to help an executive in making decisions. Thus it is *functional* writing for the *benefit of the reader.* The reader, not the writer, is the important person involved. Since he wants useful information which he does not already have, a report is quite different from a term theme turned in to a professor.

The *research* report is the most likely exception. Since it is a report of pure research pushing back the frontiers of knowledge, it may not point to any immediate use by specific readers.

2. A report is an assigned job. Besides the research report, the *justification* (or *initiative*) report may be an exception, but even it may be written in response to a standing invitation to submit ideas (as in a suggestion box). Otherwise, *periodic* reports (at regular intervals, such as weekly, monthly, or quarterly) are assigned as part of an employee's regular duties, and *special* reports are assigned as occasions arise requiring them.

Usually the assigner will make clear whether he wants an *informational* report just giving the facts or whether he wants an *analytical* report (sometimes called *recommendation* or *improvement* reports) giving the facts plus interpretation into conclusions and/or recommendations. If he doesn't, the report writer should find out from him. Otherwise, the writer may be embarrassed to be called in and told to finish his job—to analyze the facts and show conclusions and recommendations. Or perhaps more embarrassing, if the writer has gone too far and seemed to infringe upon the executive's prerogative of deciding what to do, he may be told to keep his opinions and recommendations to himself and leave the decision making to the boss.

3. A report goes up the chain of command. A few reports go between people of equal rank, as between two department heads, and some (directives) go downward from executives (but most reports executives write

are to still higher authorities—boards of directors, legislatures, or the people who elected them).

4. A report is written for one reader or a small, unified group of readers for whom one is the spokesman who arranges to have the report written. A report writer can therefore adapt his talking points and language well. Usually there is one immediate reader, who may send the report on up the chain of command to just a few higher executives. The corporation annual report, aiming primarily at stockholders and employees, still aims at an unusually large readership for a report.

5. A report gets more than normal attention to organization. Of course, all good writing is organized; but because reports are usually expositions of complex facts and ideas for practical purposes and for busy readers, report writers work harder at organization than most other writers.

6. A report makes more than normal use of the techniques and devices for communicating clearly, quickly, and easily: commonly understood words; short, direct sentences and paragraphs; headings, topic sentences, and brief summaries; itemizations; graphic presentations; and specific, concrete, humanized writing.

7. A report is expected to be accurate, reliable, and objective. No executive wants to base decisions on a report writer's errors, assumptions, preconceptions, wishful thinking, or any kind of illogicality. Although no person can be strictly objective—because his selection of facts to include and his evaluation of them are based on his whole background and the kind of person he is—the report writer strives to be as objective as possible. And where the reader might otherwise question the validity, the report writer explains his sources and methods of collecting data to show the soundness of his facts.

8. A report follows the special form best suited to its particular functions. Thus we speak of such special forms as *letter, memo, credit, justification,* and *complete* (or *long* or *formal*) reports. If the word *complete* suggests that the other forms are incomplete, it is justified in doing so. The others actually leave out or combine some parts which do not need full, separate development under the circumstances. If the word *formal* suggests that the shorter reports are informal, that is usually true—although any report may be formal in situations where the relationship between writer and reader(s) is formal. Usually those situations involve the *public* reports of government and military services rather than the *private* reports of business and industry. And usually they are sizable studies that require long rather than short reports.

The *progress* report is the most flexible of all. Like other reports, in terms of subject matter, it may concern any project; in timing, it may be *periodic* or *special;* in terms of function, it may be informational or analytical; its form, length, and degree of formality may be whatever is appropriate to the situation.

For the report writer, however, much more important than knowing the classifications of reports (except possibly the distinction between *informational* and *analytical*) is close attention to the characteristics reports should have: *They should be full of useful information that is accurate, reliable, and objective; presented in functional rather than literary style; adapted to the reader; carefully organized; and clearly, quickly, and easily readable.*

PREPARING a complete analytical report is a five-step process: planning the attack on the problem, collecting the facts, organizing the facts, interpreting the facts (this step is omitted in preparing an informational report), and writing the report in appropriate form and style. Since any or all of these five steps may be necessary in varying degrees in the preparation of a particular report in any form, we present the five steps before explaining and illustrating different forms.

PLANNING THE ATTACK

Planning the attack is a job to be done at the desk—the headwork before the legwork. It involves six procedures, in the following sequence:

1. Get a clear view of what the central problem is. If you can't see the target you're shooting at, you're not likely to hit it.

This procedure requires reflective thinking. It may also require a conference with the man who needs the report. As a check, you can try writing a concise and interesting title that clearly indicates the content and scope. If you can also write in one sentence a precise statement of the purpose, clearly indicating what you intend to cover and what you don't, you have the necessary view of the problem.

2. Consider conditions that influence the report—the use to be made of it, its importance, and the attitude, degree of interest, knowledge, and temperament of the reader, for example.

In considering use, don't overlook the fact that reports commonly go in the files for future reference after they have served their immediate purpose and that therefore they need to be clear to other readers ten years later. Also, the immediate superior who asked for the report may have to send it on up the chain of command for approval before anything can happen. So it needs to be intelligible to possible readers other than the immediate one.

The reader's temperament and knowledge of the subject have considerable influence on how much background and detailed explanation you need to give, and whether you can use technical terms. His attitude, as well as your reputation as an authority, will influence how persuasive you need to be (whether you use the convincing inductive plan or the faster, more interesting, but possibly less convincing deductive plan). His known biases and special interests may influence what you should stress and whether you must use impersonal style. Your relationship to the primary reader will indicate how formal or informal the style should be.

Limitations on time, money, or availability of data may affect how thorough you can be and whether you can use costly plates and charts.

3. Divide the central problem (the *text* of your report) into its elements, the main divisions in an outline of the topic. The idea of dividing to conquer applies in report writing as well as in military strategy.

Whatever you do at this stage toward outlining will probably be only tentative and skeletal. You'll probably change it later, after you have the facts. At this point you merely need a starting guide to what kinds of facts to collect. So don't worry too much about form and accuracy; specific instruction on the finished outline comes later (pp. 506–10, at which you might well glance now, to avoid some false steps).

Of course, not all problems divide alike, any more than all jigsaw puzzles do; but the dividing process is a job of finding the natural divisions of the whole. For that purpose you should temporarily ignore the introduction and begin your tentative outline with section II.

If the problem is one of deciding between two or more things, the *criteria* are usually the best major division headings. For example, if you are trying to decide which of several jobs to take, on what bases do you decide? Maybe

II. Kind of work

III. Location

IV. Beginning pay

 V. Chances for advancement

VI. Working conditions

Some topics to consider in many problems are history, disadvantages of present system, advantages of proposed system, costs and means of financing, personnel required, effects on goodwill, method of installation, materials required, time involved, safety, increases or decreases in quality, market, competition, convenience, and availability of land.

4. Raise specific questions about each element. The questions further divide the problem, lead to subheads in your outline, and point more directly toward collecting data for answers. If cost is one of the elements, for example, you want to ask what the costs are for operating one way and what they would be under a revised system. You would then want to question further about how to find the costs in each instance. And you might do well to break the questions down further into first costs, operating costs, and depreciation; costs for personnel, for upkeep and for power; and the like. Specific questions on goodwill might include those about customers, stockholders, workers, and the general public.

5. Take stock of what you already know. You may pose a hypothesis, but don't let it close your mind to other possible solutions. Don't assume that you know the answer until all the facts are in. You certainly don't want to start out to prove a preconceived notion.

Get a clear concept of the assumptions you are willing to make, and separate those which are to be held without further checking from those which are to be checked.

Jot down answers known for the questions raised and the tentative answers to be checked. Clearly indicate gaps in information that are to be filled by data to be collected, and jot down what you think tentatively are the best sources and methods for getting the missing data—experts, books and articles, and maybe the man for whom you're writing. Or perhaps you need to plan a survey—kind and size of sample, kind of survey, and the like.

6. Make a working schedule. Assign time blocks estimated to be necessary for each of the remaining steps in producing the report: collecting remaining data, organizing, interpreting, and writing the final report. If you plan a survey, remember that the mail requires time and that people don't always respond to questionnaires immediately. For any except the most routine kind of reports, be sure to allow some time for revising early drafts to put the final report in clear, interesting, and inconspicuous style and form.

The first item on the working schedule is the next step in report preparation—collecting the facts.

COLLECTING THE FACTS

For collecting complete and reliable facts, you may use any or all of the four basic methods of securing information: library research, observation, experimentation, and surveys. The first provides secondary (secondhand) data, and the others provide primary (firsthand or new) facts. In most cases you should use at least two of the methods in such a way as to get at the essential facts and assure their reliability.

Library research

Study of published books, articles, theses, brochures, and speeches is most universally useful and is usually the best first step. When you face any problem of consequence, somebody else has probably faced the same or a closely related problem and written something worthwhile about it. And when pertinent data are already written, getting the facts by reading them in the other fellow's collection is nearly always the easiest and quickest way—easier and quicker than the laborious process the original writer went through to get the information. Besides being the quick and easy way to collect facts, it may also give a bird's-eye view of the whole problem, acquaint you with terminology and methods you may not have thought of, refer to other good sources, show formerly overlooked natural divisions and aspects of the problem, and in general help you to revise your tentative plan of attack.

Fortunately, libraries are pretty well standardized. They nearly always have at least three broad categories of materials—reference books, books in the stacks, and periodicals. Some main ones of the great variety of *regular reference books are:*

Encyclopedias (*Americana, Columbia, Encyclopaedia of the Social Sciences, Encyclopedia of Science and Technology,* and the *Britannica*)

Collections of generally useful, up-to-date statistical and other information, surprising in variety and amount (*The World Almanac* and *Facts on File*)

Census reports (U.S. government censuses of agriculture, business, government housing, manufacturing, population, minerals, and other breakdowns)

Yearbooks of various countries, trades, and professions (commerce, shipping, agriculture, engineering, and others)

Atlases (especially those by Rand McNally, *National Geographic,* and Hammond)

Dictionaries (*American College Dictionary, Standard College Dictionary, Webster's Collegiate Dictionary, Webster's New International Dictionary* [unabridged], and the *Oxford English Dictionary*)

Directories (such as Kelly's for merchants, manufacturers, and shippers; Thomas' for American manufacturers; Ayer's for newspapers and magazines)

Who's who in various fields (including the *Directory of American Scholars,*

American Men of Science, World Who's Who in Commerce and Industry,
and Poor's *Register of Corporations, Directors and Executives*)

Statistical source books (*Statistical Yearbook, Statistical Abstract of the United
States, Survey of Current Business, County and City Data Book*)

These are just a few main examples of the numerous reference books
usually placed conveniently on tables or in open shelves in a library.
Constance Winchell's *Guide to Reference Books,* Eighth Edition (with
supplements by Eugene P. Sheehy) tells about them and many more.

The standard key to *books in the stacks* is the card catalog, arranged
alphabetically by author, subject, and title. But because libraries available
to most writers will not have all the books published on their subjects;
because it takes months for books to be published, bought by libraries, and
cataloged for distribution; and because not all topics are written up in
full-book treatment, the report writer often finds that his best up-to-date
printed sources are periodicals.

Fortunately, most periodicals are covered in one or more of the numerous periodical indexes, both general and specific, for almost any field. Table
14–1 (p. 498) describes the main current indexes; but if you do not find one
for your specific field, look around and/or ask the reference librarian. And
if the abbreviations or the system of indexing is not immediately clear to
you, the preface always explains.

Whatever library key you use, you need to develop resourcefulness.
Often when you look under one topic (say "Business Letter Writing" or
"Report Writing"), you will find little or nothing. Don't give up. You
have to match wits with the indexer and try to think of other possible
wordings he might have used for the topic. He might have put "Business
Letter Writing" under "Business English" or "Commercial Correspondence" and "Report Writing" under "Technical Writing" or something
else.

When your resourcefulness brings you to a book or article that seems
to be useful, scan it to see what portion (if any) of it is grist for your
mill. A look at the table of contents may tell you whether it will be helpful.

If it seems pertinent, check its reliability. Consider both the textual
evidence and the reputation of the publisher and of the author for (1)
any possible slant or prejudice, (2) the question of whether the author
is a recognized authority in the field, (3) the question of whether the
material is up to date. Reading a review in a related journal can help in
judging the worth of a book. A sound report writer will not be duped
by the usual undue worship of the printed word; he knows that the
mere fact that something is in print does not make it true.

If the material meets the tests for reliability, take notes—*a separate
card or sheet of paper for each important note.* If you put more than one
note to the card, you will have trouble in arranging the cards later because
they will not all fit at the same place in your report. To save time later in
arranging notes, put a notation at the head of each note card (that is, one

TABLE **14–1** Main Current Indexes

Title	Coverage	Publication facts (most frequent issue and cumulation)
Accountants' Index	International; technical books and magazines	Annually
Applied Science and Technology Index	Scientific, engineering and technical American and Canadian magazines	Monthly except August; annually
Biological and Agricultural Index	International; books and magazines	Monthly; annually
Business Periodicals Index	Business, industrial, and trade magazines	Monthly; annually
Chemical Abstracts	International; all phases of chemistry	Biweekly; semiannually
Education Index	Professional literature	Monthly except July and August; three-year
Engineering Index	Domestic and foreign literature on engineering	Monthly; annually
Index Medicus	International; medicine and related fields	Monthly; annually
New York Times Index	The news in the paper	Semimonthly; annually
Public Affairs Information Service (PAIS)	Periodicals and government documents and pamphlets of general, technical, and economic interest	Weekly except only two in August and three in December; annually
Readers' Guide to Periodical Literature	General American magazines	Semimonthly; annually and/or biennially
Social Science and Humanities Index	Emphasis on history, international relations, political science, and economics	March, June, September, December; annually
Wall Street Journal Index	Corporate and general business news	Monthly; annually

that indicates where the information fits in your plan). It may well be the divisional symbol from your outline, say section III(C).

When in doubt, take fuller rather than scantier notes than you think you need; it's easier to omit later than to come back for more.

Some notes you may want to take in verbatim quotations, but usually not. Direct quotation should be used rarely, and then only to gain the impact of the author's authority, to be fair by stating exactly before criticizing, or to take advantage of his conciseness, exactness, or aptness of phrasing. If you do quote, be sure to quote exactly and not change the original meaning by lifting a small part from a context in which it meant something different.

In most cases you can save words and express the idea better for your purposes if you paraphrase. When you paraphrase, however, be sure not to change the original meaning.

In some cases you may see that you can save time later by writing your notes as a review of the article or book—that is, from your own point of view, giving the essential content of the article along with your comment on it—because that seems to be the form it will take in the final report. In other cases you will condense, digest, or abstract the article.

Whether you quote, paraphrase, review, or abstract the article or book, you need to list in your bibliography all printed sources used directly in the preparation of the report; so you need to take the necessary information while you have the book or magazine in hand. Although bibliography form is not standardized, the usual information is author's name (surname first, for alphabetizing), title of book or article and magazine, publisher and place of publication for books, edition if not the first for books, volume and inclusive page numbers for magazine articles, and the date. For use in citations in the text, you always need to record the specific pages used for each note.

Observation

The second method of collecting data—observation—is used here to include not only its usual meanings but also investigation of company records on finances, production, sales, and the like. As such, it is the main method used by accountants and engineers for their inspection and progress reports.

The job of collecting data by observation usually involves no particular problem of getting at the facts. The important part is more likely to be knowing what facts to consider. This requires keeping in mind what the purpose is, so as to notice everything relevant and to relate each pertinent fact to the whole situation.

A skilled policeman's investigation of a murder scene or of an automobile accident scene exemplifies the technique. Camera, measuring tape, and note pad are standard equipment for outside observation, just as the accountant's special paper, sharp pencil, and calculator are for inside inspection of the records. Still, the most important pieces of equipment are sharp eyes to see the situation, judgment to evaluate it, and (most important) imagination to see the relevance of a particular observed fact to the whole problem.

Observation has the advantage of being convincing, just as the testimony of an eyewitness convinces a jury more than circumstantial evidence; but it has the disadvantage of not getting at motives. That is, it may answer *what* but not find out *why*. And unless the observer is careful, he may put too much stress on a few isolated cases or facts.

Experimentation

For the most part, experimentation is useful in the physical sciences rather than in business and the social sciences, and in industrial rather than commercial operations. And of course, the methods used vary almost infinitely according to the particular experiment to be done. They are best taught by a specialist in the particular physical science, in the laboratory with equipment, rather than through a small section in a textbook mainly about something else. Regardless of his field, however, the experimenter is as zealous as the report writer about the reliability of his results. The basic requirements for reliability in experimentation are three:

1. Accurate equipment. If the laboratory balance is inaccurate, or if the tachometer or thermometer misrepresents the facts, the results of an experiment using them will be unreliable.

2. Skilled techniques. If the technician doesn't know how to set his microscope, he won't be able to see an amoeba; and if he can't pipette both accurately and fast, he will be no good at Kahn tests. But skilled techniques also include proper selection of specimens for study.

3. Sufficient controls or repetition of results. If the experimenter takes two specimens just alike, treats them exactly alike except in one way (perhaps inoculates one, keeping the other for a control), and gets different results (say one gets a disease and the other does not), he makes a strong start toward convincing us. If he repeats the experiment and exactly the same thing happens every time (100 percent), he need not make many repetitions to be thoroughly convincing. For every drop from 100 percent, however, the scientist has to multiply his tests many times to produce similar faith in them.

Testing one variable at a time is basic. If soil, seed, and temperature all change in two runs, different results cannot be attributed to any one of them.

Experts in certain phases of business can use experimentation that closely parallels laboratory methods if they are careful about their equipment, techniques, and controls. For example, marketing specialists can test the comparative effects of different advertising campaigns and media, sales promotion devices, prices, and packaging. Their problems of equipment and technique are psychological instead of mechanical and manual, and their controls are difficult to set up to make sure that only one element is changed; but experts can and do manage all three to assure reasonable reliability. (See pp. 352–54 on testing sales campaigns.)

Surveys

Often the quality to be tested is not subject to exact laboratory examination—the sales appeal of a new car, for example. The only place to get an answer to that is from the people. In fact, the survey for fact and opinion vies with library research as a method of collecting data for business and social science reports. It is particularly useful in discovering *why* people do certain things and in *forecasting* what will happen (frequently an important job of reports).

Regardless of which of the three kinds of surveys you use—mail questionnaire, personal interview, or telephone interview—certain basic problems, principles, and techniques are involved.

The first problem is determining *what people you will survey.* In some cases you may decide that the opinions of a few experts will be worth more than the answers of thousands of the general public, as they will be if the problem is technical or professional (say medical or legal). If the whole group involved (called the "universe" by statisticians) is small, you may decide to ask all of them. But in most cases you take a sample.

For sound results you then have to decide on *how large a sample* is necessary. This will depend on the degree of accuracy required and on the variety of possible answers. For instance, if plus or minus 10 percent is close enough, your sample can be much smaller than if you have to be accurate within a range of 1 percent. And if you have to forecast election returns only in terms of Democratic, Republican, and other votes, your sample can be much smaller than if you have to forecast the purchases of the 50 or more makes and body styles of cars. As an even simpler illustration, it is certainly easier to predict the fall of a coin (only two choices) than of a pair of dice with 11 possibilities.

Although a full treatment of sampling theory would require a complete book, statisticians have provided us with some *simple devices for determining adequate sample size.* The simplest is the split-sample test. You break your sample arbitrarily (that is, to avoid any known differences) into two or more parts. You then compare the results from the various parts. If the results from the partial samples are acceptably close together, the results from the total sample will be acceptably reliable.

Two more precise checks on sample reliability require only a little mathematics.

1. If your survey results are in percentages, you apply the formula

$$N = \frac{pq}{E^2}$$

Suppose you have decided that error (E) of plus or minus 5 percent will be close enough for your purposes. When you have enough returns to estimate the apparent division of answers (say 70 percent yes and 30 percent no), you can find N (the number of returns required) by

$$N = \frac{0.7 \times 0.3}{0.05 \times 0.05} = \frac{0.21}{0.0025} = 84$$

2. If your survey results are in terms of the average (arithmetic mean), the formula is

$$\sqrt{N} = \frac{\sigma}{\sigma x}$$

If you don't know how to figure the standard deviation

$$\left(\sigma = \sqrt{\frac{\Sigma x^2}{N}} \right)$$

and the standard error of the mean (σx), any elementary statistics book will explain. But for quick, easy calculations accurate enough for most purposes, use

   a) $\sigma = \frac{1}{6}R$ (range of difference between the highest and lowest figures in the sample)

   b) $\sigma x =$ allowable error in your result

Thus if you want to find the number of scores necessary on a test to establish an arithmetic mean with allowable error of no more than one point where the highest score is 76 and the lowest is 34, your figures are

$$\sqrt{N} = \frac{42 \div 6}{1} = \frac{7}{1}$$
$$N = 49$$

Even your adequate *sample must be stratified* (sometimes called "representative"), or your results can go wild. That is, each segment of the universe must be represented in the sample by the same percentage as in the universe. According to sampling theory, this will be the result if you take a large enough *random* sample (one in which each item in the universe has an equal chance of getting into the sample). In practice, however, you often have trouble making sure you really have a random sample. Unsuspected selective factors may work to produce a nonrepresentative sample.

To avoid such a possibility, you can use stratified sampling *if you have data showing the proportions of different segments in your universe.* Fortunately, you usually do. Just as a college registrar's office knows the number of students in different classes, majors, age groups, grade-point groups, and the like, the statistical source books provide breakdowns of people in nearly every imaginable way. Whatever group you may want to sample, you probably can find the proportions of the different segments making up the universe. If 50 percent of your universe are farmers and 70 percent telephone subscribers, half your sample must be farmers and 70 percent telephone subscribers.

Adequate size and stratification together make a sound sample.

A sound sample can still produce unsound results, however, unless your techniques of getting answers from it are also sound. If you start out by surveying a minimum sound sample but get answers from only half of it, the sample of actual answers is unsound because it is too small. If you survey more than enough and get a large enough sample of answers but 100 percent of one stratification group answers and only half of another group answers, your returns are not stratified and hence are not reliable. You may therefore have to toss out excess returns from some groups to keep returns from all groups in proportion to the original stratification. Of course, the best solution is to get 100 percent returns from all groups—an ideal rarely accomplished.

How can you *induce people to answer survey questions?* Sometimes the respondent is already so much interested, because his benefit is obvious, that you need not point it out to him. You can therefore begin directly with the request for help, as in the direct inquiry letters discussed on pages 110 ff. At other times you have a selling job to do, as in the persuasive requests discussed on pages 317 ff. Whether you are using a mail questionnaire, a personal interview, or a telephone interview makes little difference in the approach. But to misjudge the situation and make a direct inquiry when you need a persuasive request may result in decreased returns and hence an unreliable sample.

Fundamentally, your persuasive method is the same as in persuading people to do anything, as in sales and collection letters: *Show them a benefit to themselves.* It may be a gift or reward, direct payment of a fee, or less obvious and less material benefits such as appeals to pride and prestige (but not obvious flattery), appeals to their desire for better service or more efficiency in their kind of work, or the possibility of their getting answers to some questions or solutions to problems they encounter in their own work.

The last two are frequently the best (because they avoid suggesting a bribe or being too mercenary, as the first two might), and they are more immediate and tangible than the others. For instance, a personnel man who has to read lots of poor application letters is likely to answer a textbook writer's or a teacher's questions about what he desires in application letters —because of the possibility that he may as a result get more good applications and thereby make his work easier. A frequent method of inducing answers is the offer of a copy or digest of the survey results.

A big point to remember in making persuasive requests is to show a benefit *before* making the request. Then if you explain who is making the survey and why; make answering as easy, quick, and impersonal as possible; assure respondents that you will honor restrictions they put on use of the information; and tell pointedly just what you want them to do, enough people will usually do it to make your results reliable. Skilled approaches, both oral and written, often bring percentages of answers that surprise the untrained who have tried their hands and failed. Chapter 8 explains in detail how to induce reluctant people to respond as you wish.

The approach you use will be a major factor in determining your success in getting returns, but *the questions you ask and how you ask them will affect both the percentage of returns and the worth of the answers.* For that reason, writers of questionnaires and people planning interviews need to keep in mind the following main principles used by professionals:

1. Ask as few questions as you can to get the necessary information. Don't ask other people for information you should have dug up for yourself, possibly in the library. And don't ask a question when you can figure the answer from the answers to others. To avoid unnecessary questions—which reduce returns—write down all you can think of, group them, and then knock out the duplicates. (There is one kind of permissible duplication: double-check questions which get at the same information from different approaches as a check on the validity of answers.)

2. Ask only what you might reasonably expect to be answered. Requests for percentages and averages are either too much work or over the heads of many people. Questions requiring long memory may frustrate and bring erroneous results. And most people don't even know *why* they do many things.

3. Make your questions as easy to answer as possible (perhaps by providing for places to check); but provide for all likely answers (at least the "no opinion" answer and perhaps the blank to be filled as the respondent wants to because he doesn't really like any of your suggested answers).

4. Make your questions perfectly clear. To do so, you may sometimes have to explain a bit of necessary background. If you ask "Why do you use X peanut butter?" you may get "It is cheapest," "A friend recommended it," and "I like its smooth texture and easy spreading" from three respondents. If you really want to know how the customer first learned of X, you should phrase the question in such a way as to get answers parallel to the second. If you are interested in the qualities that users like (as in the third answer), you should ask that specific question. Questions about *how* cause as many different interpretations as those asking *why* and require the same kind of careful wording. Also, double-barreled questions (Did you see X, and did you like it?) will confuse the reader if he wants to answer one part one way and the other part another way.

5. Carefully avoid leading questions—questions which suggest a certain answer, such as one to agree with the questioner's obvious view.

6. Insofar as possible, phrase questions to avoid the "prestige" answer—the respondent's answering according to what he feels he ought to think in order to make the best impression.

7. Avoid unnecessary personal prying. When your question is necessary to your basic purpose, make it as inoffensive as possible (for instance, by asking which named *income group* the respondent falls in, if that will serve your purpose, rather than his exact income).

8. Arrange questions in an order to encourage response—not too hard or personal ones at first, related ones together in a natural sequence to stimulate interest and aid memory.

9. Insofar as possible, ask for answers that will be easy to tabulate and evaluate statistically; but when they are important, don't sacrifice shades of meaning or intensity of feeling in the answer for easy handling.

Often the most helpful answers a survey brings are those to open-end questions; but if you ask many of them, you will reduce your returns. Such questions require time and thought to answer as well as to analyze.

After you have decided on the questions you want answered, your next problem is deciding *which type of survey* (mail questionnaire, personal interview, or telephone interview) will best serve your purposes. No one type is always best. The main *bases for your decision* are as follows:

1. The kind and amount of information requested. People are more willing to *tell* you personal information—and more of it—than they are to put personal facts in writing or to do very much writing. The comparative anonymity of the interviewer and reluctance to talk long over the telephone with strangers are against the telephone method, but generally people consider talk cheaper and less dangerous than written statements. On the other hand, factual information (especially statistics, percentages, and averages) which may not be known at the moment may be dug up and written, because the respondent can take a little time with a mail questionnaire.

2. Costs. Within one telephone exchange, if your group is not large, the telephone is the cheapest method; but if it involves long-distance charges, they become prohibitive unless the group is small. The mail questionnaire has the advantage of wide geographical coverage at no additional cost; and the bigger the group, the greater the advantage, because copies of a good set of questions can be duplicated at little extra cost. The personal interview is almost always the most costly (mainly in interviewer's time) unless the group is small and close together. You need to consider cost per return, however; and since the mail questionnaire usually brings in the lowest percentage, its advantages may not be so great as at first thought unless a good covering letter and set of questions mailed at an opportune time induce a high percentage of answers.

3. Speed in getting results. If you have to have the answers today, you can get some of them by telephone (and by personal interview if your sample is not too large and the people are close together); but you can't get them by mail. Mail answers will flood you in about four days and dribble in for a week or more after that, unless you make clear that you need the information by a certain time (a point which needs careful justifying to avoid the bad manners of rushing a person to do you a favor).

4. Validity of results—all three kinds of survey having advantages and disadvantages. In personal and telephone interviews people may give you offhand answers to get rid of you because the time of the call is inconvenient, and they may answer according to what they think is your view. In mail questionnaires they can choose the most convenient time and are more likely to answer thoughtfully or not at all. But those who choose not to answer may be a special group (say the less educated who don't like to write) and may thereby unstratify your carefully stratified sample. On the other hand, certain segments of the population have fewer telephones

than others and thereby skew a telephone sample. And certain kinds of doors (maybe apartment dwellers') are hard to get into for personal interviews. But everybody has a mailing address where a mail questionnaire will reach him. On the other hand, the personal interviewer may pick up supplementary information (such as the general look of economic conditions around the home and incidental remarks of the talker) that will provide a check on answers given—an impossibility by telephone and mail. Either the personal or the telephone interview can better clear up any confusion about questions and thereby get appropriate answers. But in view of costs and time, the mail questionnaire is less likely to be limited to a too-small group or one that is geographically or economically limited.

5. Qualifications of the staff. Some people who can talk well and thus get information may not be able to write a good questionnaire and covering letter; and, of course, the opposite may be true. Even some good talkers have poor telephone voices that discourage that method. And others have disfigurations that discourage personal interviews.

If you select an adequate and stratified sample, induce the people to answer by showing a benefit, ask good questions, and use the most suitable type of survey, surveys can get for you a great variety of valuable information for your reports.

ORGANIZING THE FINDINGS

However you collect the necessary facts for your report, you have to organize them for presentation and, if you're writing an analytical report, for your interpretation. You can't well evaluate a bridge hand until you have grouped the cards into the four suits and arranged the cards in order within the suits—mentally if not physically.

Your problem of organizing is probably easier than you suspect, however, because most of the job will have been done for you by conventional practice or by someone who set up a standard plan of reports where you work. If you have no standard plans to follow, Chapter 16 gives help in organizing the widely varied kinds of short reports. Almost any long analytical report uses something approaching conventional practice (explained in the next chapter) for the overall organization.

Your only problem—and the only one we are talking about here, therefore—is the organization of the *text* of complete analytical reports. The introduction is usually the first major division of your final outline, and the conclusions and recommendations (together or separately) are usually the last one or two.

Because the text—all the report between the introduction and the conclusions—is the essence of the report, *you do not have a section heading for it.* (If you did, it would be the same as the title of the whole report.) The divisions of the text, then, usually constitute sections II, III, IV, and so on—where you present all your facts, explanations, and reasons leading to your conclusions and recommendations.

Basically, organization is the process of putting related things into groups according to common characteristics *and your purpose* (playing poker instead of bridge, for example), and then putting the groups into a desirable sequence. In the process you may find that you have insufficient evidence for some points in your tentative outline and therefore have to get more, that some of your information seems contradictory and has to be reconciled, that some data are really irrelevant or too detailed and need to be discarded, or that you need to revise your tentative outline because the information classified according to your first plan is not logically or psychologically arranged for good presentation. For instance you will want to make sure that things the reader needs to compare are close together.

Certainly you need to check your tentative outline before going further. You may now be able to see enough interpretations of your data to make a sentence outline, as you couldn't earlier, because sentences require you to *say something about* the topics. If you can, it will be easier to follow, it will force more careful thinking, and it will give your reader the essence of your report (not just the list of topics discussed but the key statements about those topics). Because of its helpfulness in writing up the report, you may want to make a full-sentence outline (like a lawyer's brief or a précis) and later change it to one of the less cumbersome forms (later discussed) for final presentation.

Whether you use full sentences or noun-phrase topics, close adherence to the following principles is necessary for a good outline:

1. Stick to the one basis of classification implied in your title and purpose as you break down any topic (such as your text) into its parts. On the basis of credit hours earned, college students can be classified as freshmen, sophomores, juniors, seniors, and graduates. You can't logically classify them as juniors, Protestants, and Democrats. Such a procedure shifts bases in helter-skelter fashion from credit hours earned to religion to politics. Thus you have overlapping of topics, whereas the divisions of an outline should be mutually exclusive.

If your title is "Reasons for (or Why) . . . ," the major divisions of your text can't logically be anything but the list of reasons. If the title is something like "Factors Influencing . . ." or "Ways to . . . ," each major division will have to be one of those factors or ways. The title "Market Factors Indicating Why a Rexwall Drugstore in Savannah Would Sell More Than One in Charleston" commits you to show for each subject—Charleston and Savannah—market factor evidence supporting your thesis. (This does not forbid giving the introduction, conclusions, and recommendations similar major-division status.)

In outlines of comparison leading to a choice, use the criteria (bases on which the choice depends) rather than the subjects (the things between or among which you must choose) as the major divisions. Your criteria are the things on which your choice will stand or fall, and hence they deserve the emphasis. In evaluating a Ford and a Chevrolet, for example, you should use both names frequently in your organization scheme, but neither would be a major heading as such. Your major headings would be the tests you decide to apply: costs (initial and operating—and possibly trade-in value), performance, comfort, and appearance. Under each head you would be obligated to analyze each subject.

2. Follow one good system to show the relationship of all the parts. The most widely used is roman capitals (I, II, III, etc.) for the major topics (which are logical divisions of your title), subdivided as capital letters (A, B, C, etc.), subdivided as arabic numbers (1, 2, 3, etc.), subdivided as lowercase letters (*a, b, c,* etc.). Various modifications of a decimal system, somewhat like the following, however, are coming into more and more use —especially in the sciences:

1.0		I.
1.1		A.
1.2		B.
1.3		C.
2.0		II.
2.1	instead of	A.
2.11		1.
2.12		2.
2.2		B.
3.0 (etc.)		III. (etc.)

3. Cover all categories—that is, all the divisions at any level must add up to the whole indicated by your title. All the roman-numeral divisions together must add up to everything covered by the title, and all the capital letters under section II must total the II data. If you classify students according to political affiliation, you would most certainly have Republicans as well as Democrats, in addition to others. If you classify according to religion, you would have to include non-Protestants along with Protestants (or word the title to show the limited coverage).

4. Use no single subdivisions. If you start to divide section I by putting a subhead A, you must logically have at least a subhead B; you can't divide anything without having at least two parts.

5. Use parallel grammatical structure for parallel things. All the roman-numeral divisions are parallel things; all the capital-letter divisions under one of them are parallel, but not necessarily parallel with those under another roman-numeral division. They may all be complete sentences, all nouns or noun phrases (probably the best), or all adjectives. In discussing the five sections of the usual application data sheet, for example, you would not list "Heading and Basic Facts," "Education," "Experience," "Personal," and "References." All except "Personal" are nouns, but it is an adjective. "Personal Details" would be all right.

6. Consider the psychological effects (reading ease) of the number of parts in any classification. Three to seven is the optimum range. Of course, the nature of the topic may dictate how many you have. For instance, according to credit hours earned, the classes in a university are just five—from freshmen to graduates—no more and no less. In breaking down some topics, however, you have some choice in the number, depending on how broadly you name the parts. Having too few suggests that there was no need for the breakdown or that you have not completed it; having too many puts a strain on the reader's mind to remember them. In some cases you may be wise to shift to a slightly different basis of classification that will lead to a more suitable number of divisions, and in other cases you can group some of the less important classes together (perhaps as "Others" or "Miscellaneous").

7. Organize for approximate balance. That is, try not to let some of your divisions cover huge blocks of your subject and others almost nothing. You probably need to reorganize on a different basis if you have five major divisions (roman numerals) and any one is more than half of the whole report. Of course, the nature of your subject may force you to some imbalance. If you are writing about American politics, for example, the Democratic and Republican parties will each be bigger parts than all the rest, which you might group under "Others" or "Miscellaneous" for approximate balance. Inevitably some parts in the outline will require longer treatment than others, but approximate balance is desirable.

8. Put the parts of each breakdown into the sequence most appropriate for your purposes and the situation. The overall sequence or plan of a report is usually one of the following:

a) Direct (sometimes called "deductive"), giving the big, broad point first and then following with supporting details. This plan arouses more interest than some other plans because it gets to the important things quickly, saves the busy reader time if he wants only the big idea, and provides a bird's-eye view so that he can read the rest more intelligently. It is therefore desirable if the reader is likely to be sympathetic with the decision or if the writer is such an authority that his unsupported word would be readily accepted, at least tentatively. But it is psychologically unsound where it risks the danger that the reader will raise objections at first and continue to fight the writer all the way through.

b) Inductive (sometimes called "scientific"), giving a succession of facts and ideas leading up to the big conclusions and recommendations at the end. The inductive plan is slow and sometimes puzzling until the conclusion tells where all the detailed facts lead to; but it is necessary in some cases for its strong logical conviction, especially when the reader is known to be opposed to the conclusions and recommendations that are coming.

c) Narrative (usually chronological accounts of activities). If no good reason argues against it—but usually one does—the narrative style of report is both the easiest to write and the easiest to read. The main objections are that it doesn't allow you to stress important things (it may have to begin with minor details, and the biggest things may be buried in the middle), and it doesn't allow you to bring together related things that have to be seen together for clear significance. The somewhat similar spatial arrangement (from top to bottom, front to back, left to right, or by geographical area) is usually the obvious choice if it is appropriate for the material at all.

d) Weighted (that is, according to importance). The weighted plan's basic advantage is that it enables you to control emphasis by putting the most important points in the emphatic positions, first and last.

For certain kinds of material and conditions, arrangement according to difficulty or from cause to effect (or the reverse) may be the wise choice.

Whatever the plan of organization, you will need to use meaningful headings and subheads, topic sentences or paragraphs, standard transitional words and sentences, and summarizing sentences to indicate organization, to show the coherence of parts in the organization, and to tell the skimming reader the essence of the sections. The summarizing sentences, however, grow naturally out of your interpretation of the facts.

INTERPRETING THE FACTS

If the report is just informational, you are ready to write it when you have organized the facts; but if it is to be analytical, you have to study the facts and interpret them into conclusions and/or recommendations for the boss, as required. Since the reader wants a sound rather than a prejudiced basis for his decisions, your *first consideration* in making the interpretation is objectivity.

Nowhere else in report writing is objectivity more important—or harder to achieve. Since you are a human being, your thinking is influenced by your whole background and personality; but you must strive to be as objective and logical as possible, and to avoid the temptation to stretch the truth a bit for dramatic effect. The following two basic kinds of unobjective attitudes require attention if your report is to be unbiased:

1. *Preconception.* If a writer thinks he knows the outcome and closes his mind to other possibilities before he collects and evaluates the facts, he may be influenced by that preconception to overlook or undervalue some facts and overstress others.

2. *Wishful Thinking.* If he has a strong desire that the investigation turn out a certain way (because of a money interest or any other kind), he finds it hard not to manipulate facts (like the referee who has bet on the game) to make them lead to the desired result.

In addition to these dangerous attitudes to shun if you are to be unprejudiced, you must avoid (as your *second consideration*) the pitfalls to logical thinking (called "fallacies"). Although some of them—like circular argument and shifting the meaning of terms—are not likely to trap an honest report writer, avoiding the following requires constant alertness:

1. Using sources (both books and people) which may be unreliable because

of basic prejudice, because they are uninformed, or because they are out of date. Although these things would have been checked in your collecting data, they might be examined again in the interpreting process.

2. Making hasty generalizations—that is, drawing conclusions on the basis of too little evidence (maybe too small a sample, too short a trial, too little experience, or just too few facts). The temptation to make hasty generalizations will weaken if you remember that sometimes no logical conclusion can be drawn. Certainly you need to remember that lack of evidence to establish one hypothesis does not prove its opposite.

3. Using false analogies. Although true analogies (comparisons of things that are similar in many ways) are effective devices for explaining, by comparing unknown things to others the reader knows, even at their best they are weak as logical proof. And false analogies (applying principles valid in one case to another case where they don't belong) are tools of shysters and traps to the careless thinker. Essentially the same error results from a false analogy and from a person's putting a thing in the wrong class (say a persuasive request situation misclassified as a direct inquiry) and applying the principles of the wrong class to it.

4. Stating faulty cause-and-effect relationships, such as

   a) Assigning something to one cause when it is the result of several. Comparisons which attribute the differences to one cause need careful controls to be valid. Otherwise, some unseen (or intentionally ignored) cause may deserve much of the credit for the difference.

   b) Attributing something to an incapable cause (for instance, one that came later).

   c) Calling something a cause when it is merely a concurrent effect—a symptom.

5. Begging the question—just assuming, rather than giving evidence to support, a point that is necessary to the conclusions drawn.

6. Using emotional suasion (usually characterized by strong and numerous adjectives and adverbs, or any kind of emotionally supercharged language like that of a defense attorney pleading with a jury) to influence the reader, instead of depending on logical conviction through marshaling of fact.

7. Failing to distinguish, and make clear to the reader, what is fact, what is opinion, and what is merely assumption.

Your *third consideration* in making your interpretation is discovering the really significant things to point out to the reader. If you avoid basic prejudice prompted by preconception or wishful thinking, avoid the pitfalls of various fallacies, and know what to look for, you should be able to interpret the facts and draw sound conclusions.

When you do, you should be sure they grow out of the facts, state them pointedly, and itemize them if they run to more than three or four. You can then turn them into practical recommendations that are general or concrete and specific, according to instructions when the report was assigned. Itemization will usually help to make the recommendations desirably pointed too.

Some bosses want answers to all of what to do, who is to do it, when, and where; others feel that the report writer with so specific a solution to the problem infringes upon their prerogatives of making decisions. But all expect you to show the significance of your facts to the problem. In addition to an organization and presentation of facts that lead to the conclusions, the reader will expect you to point out lesser interpretations along the way.

Causes, symptoms, effects, and cures are always important. So (in terms of graphic statistical data) are high points, low points, averages, trends, and abrupt changes (especially if you can explain their causes). Without going into disturbingly technical statistics, you can probably interest your reader in such measures of central tendencies as the mean (call it average), median (midpoint), and mode (most frequent item). Sometimes you might well use indicators of dispersion, such as standard deviation, range, and the -*iles* (percentiles, deciles, quartiles).

Your reader will be interested in comparisons that give significance to otherwise nearly meaningless isolated facts. For instance, the figure $7,123,191 given as profit for the year has little meaning alone. If you say it's 7 percent above last year's profit, you add a revealing comparison; and if you add that it's the highest ever, you add another. If your volume of production is 2 million units, that means less than if you add that you're now fourth in the industry as compared with 10th two years earlier.

Breaking down big figures into little ones also helps to make them meaningful. For instance, you may express the capital investment in terms of so much per employee, per share of stock, per stockholder, or per unit of production. The national debt becomes more meaningful if given per citizen; the annual budget makes more sense as a per day or per citizen cost; library circulation means more in terms of number of books per student. Often a simple ratio helps, such as "Two fifths (40 percent) of the national budget is for defense."

Whatever the analysis reveals, you need to state it precisely. Guard carefully against stating assumptions and opinions as facts. And select gradations in wording to indicate the degree of solidity of your conclusions. The facts and analyses will sometimes (but rarely) prove a point conclusively. They are more likely to lead to the conclusion that . . . , or indicate, or suggest, or hint, or point to the possibility, or lead one to wonder—and so on down the scale. Usually you can do better than stick your neck out by claiming to prove things you don't or draw your neck in too far with the timorous last three of these expressions.

But phrasing the ideas well is a problem for the fifth and last step in preparing a report—writing it.

WRITING APPROPRIATE REPORT STYLE

Your final writing of the report will not be difficult if you have done well the preceding four steps of preparation. But if your methods of collecting, organizing, and interpreting data have been faulty, you're trapped. Our suggestions for a good report style will help only if you have something worthwhile to write and a pretty good idea of the sequence of points.

You will notice that our suggestions relate more to the *effectiveness* than to the *correctness* of your writing, for two reasons: (1) Correct spelling, grammar, punctuation, and sentence structure do not assure effectiveness. We assume that you have pretty well learned these aspects of writing before studying report writing. And if you haven't, a more basic study of composition—or review of Appendix D (p. 692) or some other good handbook—may be advisable. (2) Effective writing presupposes reasonable correctness but also requires that you help your reader to get your message clearly, quickly, and easily. How to do this is our next concern.

Basics of report style

Because almost everything we said about letter style in Chapter 2 applies equally to report style—and the few exceptions are obvious—we recommend that you read that chapter carefully before going on to the special points about report style.

The discussion in Appendix A probably applies even more to report writing than to letter writing. We therefore recommend that you study that material thoroughly before proceeding to the following points especially significant in report style.

As you have already seen in Item 6, page 491, report writers use various techniques and devices for communicating clearly, quickly, and easily: commonly understood words, short sentences so direct that they require little punctuation, short paragraphs so direct that they require few transitional words, itemizations, graphics, and headings.

Even though you have read those other parts of the book, several points of basic style and some of the special techniques deserve a bit fuller treatment for report writers.

Adaptation requires that you consider not only your primary reader but likely secondary readers. Even though some readers may know the background of the problem and the technical terms of the field, others may not. The good report writer must therefore provide the explanations necessary for the least informed of important readers. This includes restricting your vocabulary to words readers will understand readily. If you feel that you must use specialized terms, you had better explain them. Usually a parenthetical explanation right after the first use of a technical term is the best way. But if your report includes many such terms, it should provide a glossary in the introduction or in an appendix—to keep it from being "all Greek" to nontechnical readers.

Coherence becomes a greater problem as the length and variety of points in a paper increase. Hence as a report writer you need to observe carefully the use of transitional words, previewing topic sentences and paragraphs, and summarizing sentences and paragraphs in the illustrations

in the next two chapters. **Coh** in Appendix D and items S3–8 in the checklist for complete analytical reports should also prove helpful.

Here is how one writer helped keep his readers on the track with good
topic statements, summary paragraphs, and transitional ideas. For economy of space, we have quoted only some of the transitional parts from
various places in the report.

II. NASHVILLE'S LARGER MARKET AREA

Since women often will travel long distances to buy clothes,
the secondary area surrounding the metropolitan area is
important in determining the location of a Four Cousins retail
store. [After this topic lead-in, several paragraphs
identifying principal communities and number of people in them
for both Nashville and Knoxville followed.]

Even though 370,000 more possible customers live within the
market area of Nashville, most of the sales will come from the
people within the immediate metropolitan area. [Summarizes II
and makes transition to III.]

III. BETTER POPULATION FACTORS IN NASHVILLE

The total population and its rate of growth, number of
women, number of employed women, and percentage of nonwhites
show more clearly the potential buyers of women's clothing.
[This topic statement preceded A, B, C, and D headings of
subsections giving the facts about and the interpretation of
the topics as announced.]

Even though Knoxville has a larger population, a smaller
percentage of nonwhites, and about the same growth rates,
Nashville has more women and a significantly larger number of
employed women. Thus it furnishes the kind of customer Four
Cousins sells to. [Indicates what A, B, C, and D add up to.]

Potential customers are buyers, however, only when they have
sufficient buying power. [Clearly foreshadows a topic coming
up and why.]

IV. MORE BUYING POWER IN NASHVILLE

Effective buying income (total and per capita), income
groups, home ownership, and automobile ownership give estimates
of ability to buy. [The information as promised then follows
in four sections.]

[This summary statement comes at the end of the section.]
The Nashville shopper has more dollars to spend, even though
home- and auto-ownership figures imply more favorable financial
positions in Knoxville families. Higher expenditures for
homes and cars in Knoxville explain, in part, why Nashville
merchants sell more.

V. GREATER RETAIL SALES AND LESS COMPETITION IN NASHVILLE

[The writer continues the use of these coherence devices
throughout the report.]

Parallelism is a special pitfall to the unwary report writer because reports so frequently involve series, outlines, and lists. Each is in effect the
partition of a whole, the sum of the parts equaling the whole. Hence the
law of logic and mathematics—that you sum up, or add, only like things—
applies. Thus the breakdown of anything must name all the parts in similar

(parallel) grammatical form—usually all nouns or noun phrases, adjectives, or complete sentences.

Timing of the verbs (tense) in reports also often trips a careless report writer. One simple rule answers most questions of tense: *Use the present tense wherever you can do so logically.* It applies to things that existed in the past, still exist, and apparently will continue to exist for a while. Otherwise, use the tense indicated by the logic of the situation. Thus in writing about your research activity, you say that you *did* certain things (past tense in terms of the time of writing). But in reporting your findings (which presumably are still true), you say "70 percent answer favorably, and 30 percent are opposed."

Ten common faults listed in American University Professor William Dow Boutwell's study of government reports (and printed in the *Congressional Record,* Vol. 88, Part IX, p. A1468) occur frequently in other reports too:

1. Sentences are too long. Voted unanimously as one of the worst faults in nearly all writings analyzed. Average sentence length in poor government writing varies from 65 to 80 words per sentence. In exceptionally good government writing (Report to the Nation by Office of Facts and Figures and President's speeches) average length is from 15 to 18 words per sentence.

2. Too much hedging; too many modifications and conditional clauses and phrases. The master writer will say, "A third of a nation ill-clothed, ill-housed, ill-fed." The amateur will write: "On the whole it may be said that on the basis of available evidence the majority of our population is probably not receiving the proper type of nutriment. . . ." Psychologists say that "conditional clauses cause suspension of judgment as to the outcome of the sentence, and therefore increase reading difficulty."

3. Weak, ineffective verbs. *Point out, indicate,* or *reveal* are the weak reeds upon which many a government sentence leans. Writers overuse parts of the verb *to be.* Hundred-word sentences with *was* or *is* as the principal verb are not uncommon.

4. Too many sentences begin the same way, especially with *The.*

5. An attempt to be impersonal, which forces use of passive and indirect phrases. Example: "To determine whether retail sales have been out of line with expectations based on the past relationship of retail volume to income, estimates of retail sales in the first half of each year . . . have been charted against income payments for the same periods, and a line of estimate fitted to the resulting scatter." The good writer would say: "Our statisticians have charted estimates of retail sales, etc., etc."

6. Overabundance of abstract nouns. Such nouns as *condition, data, situation, development, problem, factor, position, basis, case* dominate the writing of too many government documents. How bright and real writing becomes when picture-bearing nouns take the place of vague ones may be seen from this sentence: "During the lean years when salaries and wages were low and irregular, the people who drifted into the credit-union offices came around because they had dropped behind in their personal and family finances and had to get a loan."

7. Too many prepositioned phrases. In a study of reading difficulty, investigators (Drs. Leary and Gray of Chicago University) found that prepositional phrases ("of the data," "under the circumstances," etc.) add to reading difficulty. Yet, samples of government writing show that many officials use at least one prepositional phrase to every four words. Samples from good writing contain only one prepositional phrase to every 11 words.

8. Overabundance of expletives. "It is" and "there are" and their variants ruin the opening of many good paragraphs.

9. Use of governmentish or federalese. "Shop words" serve a proper purpose for "shop" audiences. But many government writers make the mistake of talking to the public in technical, office terms . . . .

10. Tendency to make ideas the heroes of sentences. People think in terms of people and things for the most part. The government official writes in terms of ideas and phenomena only. Hence, when a writer means "Employers refuse to hire older workers in defense industries," he writes instead: "Refusal of employment of older workers continues." In other words, the writer has substituted "refusal," an idea or phenomenon, for "employers"—living people.[1]

Documentation

Since a report is usually the basis for an executive decision which may be costly if it is wrong, the executive reader rightfully expects the report writer to answer two important questions: What are the facts? How do you know?

The second question means that the report writer must convince the reader that the information is trustworthy. Usually you do that by explaining your sources and methods as a basis for the reader's judgment of the report's soundness. The only exceptions are in the reports of unquestionable authorities (whose word would be taken at face value) and in cases where the methods and sources are already known or are clearly implied in the presentation of the facts.

In short reports you can best explain the sources and methods in incidental phrases along with the presentation of data, as in the following:

```
Four suppliers of long standing report him as prompt pay
and . . . .
Standard quantitative analysis reveals 17 percent
carbon . . . .
Analysis of the balance sheet reveals . . . .
```

Notice how the illustrative reports in Chapter 16 (the short ones) interweave the references to methodology of research and to published sources —right within the text of the report.

In the complete analytical report the introduction explains methods and

---

[1] An AP Newsfeature, "Gobbledygook: Language of Government," by Richard E. Myer, September 5, 1971, stresses many of the same points.

mentions printed sources (which are explained more specifically in the bibliography and in footnotes and/or other citations in the text).

At least, any report writer except the recognized authority precludes what one reader expressed as "the distrust I have of those people who write as if they had a private line to God."

Since you usually use some published materials in collecting data for reports, citing those sources is an important part of assuring your reader about the soundness of the facts.

Unfortunately, *bibliography* forms are not standardized. For the past 50 years the trend in documentation forms has been toward simplicity and efficiency, especially in business, industry, and the sciences. This does not mean less documentation, but more efficient forms. Some people in the humanities, on the other hand, have tended to hold on to the older forms, especially their punctuation. Others have adopted the library practice of capitalizing only the first word and proper nouns (specific names of people, products, and places) in titles. So unless you are sure that both you and your reader(s) understand and prefer other generally accepted forms used in your field (in the main professional journals, for example), we recommend that you use the following content and form.

Readers generally expect a bibliographical entry to give the author's name, the title (of both an article and the journal), and (for books) the edition (if not the first), the publisher and place of publication, and the volume (if more than one); the volume number (if on the magazine) and all page numbers for magazine articles; and the date of publication for anything (noting n.d. when you can't find it). Preferably the pieces of information are in that order. Some people omit the publisher of a book or put it in parentheses with the place and a colon preceding. The same people (usually in the humanities) use roman numerals for magazine volume numbers and follow immediately with the date in parentheses. In some specialized fields even the date or title may come first.

Usually the several entries in a bibliography appear in alphabetical order by author's name, which is inverted for the purpose. In some specialized fields, however, you will find other arrangements; and in extensive bibliographies (unusual in reports) you often find books and articles alphabetized separately, with headings for each group.

Unless you choose to follow the well-established form of your special field, we suggest that you be up to date and enter books as

```
Wilkinson, C. W., J. H. Menning, and C. R. Anderson (eds.),
   Writing for Business, Third Edition, Richard D. Irwin, Inc.,
   Homewood, Illinois, 1960.
```

In the humanities, however, most authors would enter this book as

```
. . ., Third Edition (Homewood, Illinois: Richard D. Irwin,
   Inc.), 1960.
```

Even in this simple entry, you have three somewhat unusual items:

1. Three men worked on the book, but the name of only the first needs to be inverted for alphabetizing.
2. Since the men were editors rather than writers of the book, you see the "(eds.)" right after their names.
3. Because the book is not the first edition, the entry tells which it is. Some writers would add, at the end, 369 pp., $7.95—two pieces of information usual in reviews of new books but not in bibliographies.

The recommended form for magazine articles is

```
Gallagher, William J., "Technical Writing:  In Defense of
    Obscurity," Management Review, 55:34-36, May, 1971.
```

Or (often in the humanities):

```
Arnold, C. K., "How to Summarize a Report," Supervisory
    Management, VII (July, 1971), 15-17.
```

If you want to be more helpful to the reader, you may annotate your bibliography with brief notes indicating the content and your evaluation of the book or article:

```
Darlington, Terry, "Do a Report on It," Business, 94:74, 93,
    May, 1969.
    Good treatment of report functions and short, simple, direct
    approach for report writing.  Especially good on five-point
    plan for organizing.
```

You need to note two points here:

1. Titles of parts like magazine articles and book chapters are enclosed in quotes; but titles of whole publications are underscored (italics in printed copy), with the first word and all others except articles (*a, an, the*), prepositions, and conjunctions capitalized.
2. Listings of magazines do not include the publisher and place but do include the volume number (if available) and all page numbers, hyphenated for inclusive pages and separated by commas for jumps in paging.

If no author's or editor's name appears on a book or article, the entry usually appears in the alphabetical list by first word of the title (not counting *a, an,* and *the*). Sometimes, however, a writer chooses to alphabetize by publisher instead—pamphlets, booklets, reports, and the like put out by corporations and governmental agencies. Thus you will see entries like

```
"Are Your Memos on Target?" Supervisory Management, 9:39-40,
    August, 1969.
Texaco, Inc., Annual Report of 1971.
U.S. Department of Agriculture Bulletin 1620, Characteristics
    of New Varieties of Peaches, U.S. Government Printing
    Office, 1969.
```

(Note that when a comma and a stronger mark—question mark or exclamation point—need to come at the same place, you simply omit the comma.)

At those points in the report text where you make use of printed sources, you also tell the reader about them by specific references or citations. One way of doing so is *footnoting,* which is decreasing in use because footnotes heckle readers. A better method for most situations, now coming into wider and wider use, is to interweave the minimum essentials of a citation subordinately right into the text, like this:

```
Wilkinson says ("The History and Present Need of Reports,"
   The ABWA Bulletin, 19:14, April, 1969) that reports . . . .
```

For other illustrations, see pages 2, 515, and 671.

Still, footnote citations (indicated by raised numbers in the text and matching numbers before the notes) may be necessary in some cases to keep long, interwoven citations from making the reading difficult. Remember, however, that a footnote at the bottom of the page is usually more of an interruption than a parenthetical citation.

The first footnote or interwoven citation, plus whatever bibliographical information may be given in the text, is a complete reproduction of the bibliographical entry with two minor changes: The author's name is in the normal order (given name or initials first), and the page reference is the specific page or pages used for that particular part of the report. Accordingly, first footnote references to a book and a magazine would be as follows:

```
J. H. Menning and C. W. Wilkinson, Communicating through
   Letters and Reports, Fifth Edition, Richard D. Irwin, Inc.,
   Homewood, Illinois, 1972, p. 469.
H. R. Jolliffe, "Semantics and Its Implications for Teachers
   of Business Communication," Journal of Business
   Communication, 1:17, March, 1964.
```

Later references to the same work can be shortened forms with the specific page number(s) and just enough information for the reader to identify the source. Usually the author's surname, the title, and the page(s) will do, whether interwoven in the text, put in footnotes, or divided between the two. Thus later references could be as shown below:

```
Menning and Wilkinson (Communicating . . ., p. 29) discuss
   letters in three broad categories: . . . .
Jolliffe ("Semantics and Its Implications," p. 18) makes the
   point that . . . .
```

The short-form citations of sources, enclosed in parentheses here, could be footnotes if the writer prefers.

The old practice of using Latin abbreviations (such as *op. cit., ibid.,* and *loc. cit.,* to mention only a few), which have long confused many people, is disappearing along with footnotes. Except in scholarly writing for other scholars, the trend is toward using English words and a few standard abbreviations like *p.* for *page* and *pp.* for *pages*—preceding page numbers which do not follow volume numbers.

Letters and interviews used as sources of information do not belong in a bibliography but nevertheless are cited by footnoting or by interweaving the information about the giver and the receiver of the information, the form, the date, and any other pertinent facts.

The newest and probably the best citation system—coming into wider use, especially in science and industry, probably because of its efficiency —involves these steps:

1. Numbering the listings in the bibliography after they are arranged in the usual way (alphabetically).
2. Using these numbers and the specific page numbers, usually separated by colons and enclosed in parentheses, at the points in the report requiring documentation—usually just before the periods at the ends of sentences.
3. Explaining the system at its first use, by footnote or something like "(4:39, meaning p. 39 of Item 4 in the Bibliography)."

Although these are the main points about documentation forms, several large books and many smaller ones, plus numerous pamphlets, deal extensively with this subject. As further illustration of bibliography forms, and as sources of more detailed information about them, footnotes, and other details of form, we list the major publications:

A Manual of Style (Twelfth Edition), University of Chicago Press, Chicago, 1969.

The MLA Style Sheet (Second Edition), Modern Language Association of America, Washington, D.C., 1970.

U.S. Government Printing Office Style Manual (Revised Edition), U.S. Government Printing Office, Washington, D.C., 1967.

Turabian, Kate L., *A Manual for Writers of Term Papers, Theses, and Dissertations* (Third Edition), University of Chicago Press, Chicago, 1967.

Turner, Rufus P., *Technical Writer's & Editor's Stylebook*, Bobbs-Merrill Company, Inc., New York, 1964.

Objectivity in presentation

Clearly the report reader expects the writer to demonstrate that he has been as objective as is humanly possible in collecting the data, in organizing and interpreting them, and finally in writing them.

That does not mean, however, that you must follow an old rule and use impersonal style (which is sometimes erroneously called "objective" style). You can be just as objective when saying "I think such and such is true" as when saying "Such and such seems to be true" or even "Such and such is true." The second and third versions mean only that the writer thinks something is true. The only sound objection to the first version is that it wastes two words, not that it is natural style.

The only real justification for recommending impersonal style in reports, as many books do, is that methods and results are usually the important things, and therefore they, rather than the person who did the research, deserve emphasis as subjects and objects of active verbs.

But since things happen because people make them happen, the most natural and the clearest, easiest, most interesting way to tell about them is to tell who does what. A report about research done by its writer therefore naturally includes *I*'s; and if the writer keeps his reader(s) in mind, it also naturally includes *you*'s. To omit them is unnatural and usually dull, because the writer goes out of his way to avoid the natural subjects of active verbs or uses too many inactive ones and leaves out the most basic element of an interesting, humanized style—*people doing things*.

Because they are professionally trained, constantly practicing, and usually writing about people doing things (although in the third person, which is considered a part of impersonal style), newspaper men often write well. An equally trained and practiced report writer (a rarity) *can* by great care write interestingly in impersonal style. But most report writers find it unnatural and difficult. Unless they exercise great care, it usually leads them into awkward, wordy, and weak passive-voice constructions; it gives away the third leg (Frequent Personal References) to Rudolf Flesch's three-legged stool of easy readability, so that the stool falls; and it *does not* gain objectivity.

Strangely, the strongest promoters of impersonal style are people who pride themselves on being scientific. They usually also insist that writing should avoid any kind of exaggeration about the true state of things. But they then argue that impersonal style gives the reader more confidence in their statements. When one of them draws a conclusion, therefore, he wants to say "It was concluded that . . . ," as if some omniscient oracle had drawn the conclusion, when all he means is "I conclude that . . . ."

Actually, more destructive to objectivity than the use of a natural style is the use of too many or too strong adjectives and adverbs, or any kind of feverish, high-pressure, hot-under-the-collar writing. Such a heightened style—using emotional connotations, fancy figures of speech, and other techniques of oratory—has its place where the author feels deeply and wishes his reader to feel deeply about the subject; but it is often distrusted, and is inappropriate in reports anyway, because both writer and reader are expected to think hard rather than emotionalize.

Simply put, then, our advice on natural versus impersonal style is this: Find out whether your primary reader thinks reports have to be in impersonal style. If so, give it to him as best you can while

1. Avoiding "It is" and "There are."
2. Putting most of your verbs in the active voice.
3. Picturing people (other than yourself or the reader, of course) taking the action of as many as possible of your verbs.

But any time your primary reader will let you, write naturally but calmly and reasonably. Where the natural way to express an idea involves an *I* or a *you*, use it. Don't let anybody talk you into referring to yourself as "the writer."

Except for the fact that letter style allows more use of emotional suasion than report style does, the discussion of style in Chapter 2 applies to reports as well as letters.

In addition, report writers also make more extensive use than letter writers of these other techniques of presenting ideas clearly, quickly, and easily for the reader: using headings and subheads, presenting quantitative data skillfully, and using graphic aids to effective communication.

Headings and subheads

Because they are usually longer than letters, and because the reader may want to recheck certain parts, reports use headings and subheads, in addition to topic and summarizing sentences, to show the reader the organization, where he has been, and where he is going. For the same reasons and purposes we have used headings in this book. If you have not thought about them already, for illustration flip back through some parts of the book with which you are well acquainted and see if they don't serve these purposes.

Skill in using heads and subheads can be a valuable technique in your writing, not only of reports but of anything else that is very long—maybe even long letters.

The only reasonable test of how far to go in putting in subheads is this: Will they help the reader? If so, put them in; if not, leave them out.

Despite the fact that headings and subheads are great helps to readers, no single system of setting them up is in universal use. More important than what system you use is that you use some system consistently and that the reader understand it. Most readers understand and agree on the following principles:

1. A good heading should indicate clearly the content below it, should have reader interest, and should be as brief as possible without sacrificing either of the other two requirements. Trying to keep titles too short, however, frequently leads to sacrifice of exactness. Usually a short heading is too broad (includes more than the discussion below it covers), or it tells nothing about the topic. Note the difference, in examples from annual reports, between "Profits" and "Profits Up 8 Percent from Last Year," and between "Position in the Industry" and "Position in Industry Changes from Eighth to Fourth." In other reports where some readers might only skim, you can help them a lot by making your headings tell the big point about the topic instead of just naming the topic to be discussed. You've already seen some good examples of helpful *informative* headings (as opposed to merely *topical* ones) in the quoted illustration on page 514. The headlines in any newspaper provide others.

2. The form and position of the head must make its relative importance clear at a glance. That is, headings for all divisions of equal rank (say the roman-numeral heads in an outline) must be in the same form and position on the page, but different from their superiors (of which they are

parts) and from their inferiors (their subdivisions). Putting heads of different levels in the same form and position is confusing; it misrepresents the outline.

3. Centered heads are superior to sideheads in the same form (compare second- and third-degree heads in the following illustration); heads in capitals are superior to those in caps and lowercase; and heads above the text are superior to those starting on the same line with the text (compare third- and fourth-degree heads in the illustration).

4. Heads should not be depended on as antecedents for pronouns or as transitions. The one word *This* referring to an immediately preceding head is the most frequent offender. Transitions between paragraphs and between bigger subdivisions should be perfectly clear if the headings are removed.

5. In capital-and-lowercase heads capitalize the first word and all others except articles (*a, an* and *the*), conjunctions (for example, *and, but, for,* and *because*), and prepositions (such as *to, in, of, on,* and *with*).

The following five-level illustration further explains the principles. If you need a further breakdown for your report, you can type the first heading in spaced C A P I T A L S and move each level of heading up one notch. Note that *above* second- and third-degree heads the spacing is more than the double spacing of the discussion.

FIRST-DEGREE HEADINGS

The title of your whole report, book, or article is the first-degree heading. Since you have only one title, no subhead should be written in the same form. As illustrated here, the title uses the most superior form and position.

Second-Degree Headings

If you use solid capitals centered on the page for the first-degree heading (title), a good choice for the second-degree headings (usually roman numbered in the outline) is caps and lowercase. Preferably, they and any other uncapitalized head should be underscored to make them stand out. If you do not need the five-level breakdown illustrated here, you could start with this form.

Third-degree headings

To distinguish the third-degree headings from their superiors, you may put them at the left margin above the text, underscore them to make them stand out, and write them in initial-cap form (as here) or in cap and lowercase (which would require capitalizing the D in Degree and the H in Heading).

Fourth-degree headings.—For a fourth level, you may place headings at the paragraph indention on the same line with the text and write them as caps and lowercase or as straight lowercase except for capitalizing the first word. These headings definitely need to be underscored and separated from the first sentence, preferably by a period and dash, as here. Some people drop the dash. This form of head saves space.

The fifth-degree headings can be integral parts of the first sentence of the first paragraph about a topic. Underscoring (italic type when printed), will make them stand out sufficiently without further distinctions in form.

Presentation of quantitative data

Most reports make considerable use of quantitative data. Consequently, as a report writer you need to know how to present figures for clear, quick, and easy comprehension. Your reader will usually want the figures on measurable topics you discuss; and unless he has made clear that he wants only the facts, he probably will want your interpretations showing what the figures mean (conclusions) and what you think should be done about them (recommendations). Even if he has the ability to make the interpretations himself, he likely will want you to make them—for possible ideas he might not see and for economy of his time.

The following brief suggestions are designed to help you present quantitative data the way most report readers want them.

1. Make sure your figures are reliable by checking your sources and derivations of them. And when you present an average, make clear whether it is the mean, the median, or the mode.

2. Write isolated quantities in one of the standard ways explained under **Fig** in Appendix D.

3. Insofar as possible, avoid cluttering your paragraphs with great masses of figures. Tables are better if you have many figures. Ordinarily, however, extensive tables are not necessary to the reader's understanding of the text but are in a report to show that you really have the facts. In that case put tables in the appendix and refer to them specifically in the introduction or text; then follow points 4–7 below for presenting necessary figures in the text.

4. Put necessary statistical information as close as possible to the place in the text where it is most pertinent. The reader will likely refuse to flip pages back and forth to find a table, or at least will resent having to do so.

5. Present the key figures as simply as possible. Usually some ratio, rank, or difference is more important than the raw data. Instead of a gross of $2,501,460.70 and expenses of $2,124,101.40, the simple figures $2½ and

$2\frac{1}{8}$ million tell the story easier. The ratio 1:7 or about 15 percent for the net certainly reads easier than $377,359.30 and is probably the more important figure. Moreover, except in bookkeeping and highly technical research, such rounded and simplified figures are precise enough for most purposes. Engineers regularly use slide rules that are not accurate even to the first decimal place. Indeed, rounded figures in most cases are as accurate as the unrounded ones on which they are based. The means of arriving at most large figures are not accurate enough to make the last few digits anything but a bogus precision and a hindrance to readability.

Another way of increasing readability is to break big figures down into so much per . . . (whatever is an appropriate divider). If the divider is the number of persons involved (employees, students, or citizens, for example), you also gain interest by humanizing the presentation.

6. Small tables (usually called spot tables), perhaps using key figures based on extensive data in an appendix, are not only easy to read but can be put close to the relevant discussion. Use them freely.

7. Help your reader by pointing out highs, lows, averages, trends, ranges, and exceptions or extremes. They are not always readily apparent, especially to the many readers who are not accustomed to analyzing statistical data; but they are usually important, especially if you can also explain their causes and/or effects.

Graphic aids as supplements to words

Since reports so frequently treat quantitative data, designs, organizational plans, and the like, you often almost have to use charts, graphs, pictograms, drawings, and maps as well as tables to present your information well. But in most cases—even for engineers and architects, who have to study drafting—these devices only assist, not replace, words. And since interpretation of graphics is not one of the three *R*'s learned by everybody, most graphics help to explain and/or support the text only if the text helps them by telling the reader how to look at them and what they mean. Skillful communication therefore often involves care in interplaying words and graphic aids.

The best procedure begins by introducing the topic; then subordinately referring the reader to the graphic aid at the point where it will be helpful, using the best type of graphic for the purpose; and then further commenting on (interpreting) the graphic device. Note these points:

1. A reader should not run onto a graphic device until he has been introduced to it; in most cases he would be confused.

2. The existence of the graphic aid, or where it is, is *not* the important thing and does *not* deserve the emphasis in your sentence referring to it. So refer to it *subordinately* and use the main clause of your sentence to tell the reader the significant point: "Twice as many men as women like X, as shown in Table 2."

3. Insofar as possible, place graphic aids close to the comments on the same point, preferably right before the reader's eyes. Unless the device is staring the reader in the face when you mention it, tell him precisely where it is.

4. Carefully label each graphic device (unless obvious) as a whole and by parts, and provide a key if necessary. Variations in color, shading, and kind of line (solid versus broken, for example) are common means for distinguishing the different kinds of data in lines, columns, bars, and the like.

5. Interpret your graphics unless doing so would insult the reader because the meaning is so obvious.

Complete discussion of the uses, advantages, disadvantages, and techniques of preparing different kinds of graphic devices is beyond the scope of this book. And extensive illustrations—which are costly to reproduce and are not very helpful except when accompanied by the relevant text— would quickly run up the size and cost. As an economical, minimum introduction to graphics, however, you should look carefully at the following illustrations of three commonly used types, with just enough text to show how the graphics should be interwoven.[1]

The federal government's share of civilian public employment has less than doubled since 1900, while the shares of state and local governments have increased nearly 9 and 2½ times, respectively, as shown in Table 14–2.

TABLE 14–2   Government employment as a percentage of total employment, United States, 1900–1965*

	1900	1910	1920	1930	1940	1950	1960	1965
Federal								
Military	0.5	0.4	0.8	0.5	1.1	2.8	3.6	4.9
Nonmilitary	1.1	1.2	1.7	1.4	2.2	3.5	3.3	1.9
State	0.3	0.3	0.5	0.7	1.1	1.8	2.3	2.6
Local	3.1	3.4	4.0	5.4	5.9	5.4	6.7	7.6
Total	5.0	5.3	7.0	8.0	10.3	13.5	15.9	17.0

* Figures through 1940 are adapted from S. Fabricant, *Trend of Government Activity Since 1900* (New York: National Bureau of Economic Research, 1952). The 1965 data are from U.S. Department of Labor, *Employment and Earnings,* June, 1965. All school employees are classified as local through 1940. For later years they are distributed between local and state governments in proper proportion. The federal figure for 1940 excludes emergency relief workers.

The commonly heard statements about the burgeoning growth in federal employment are therefore misleading. As the table shows, the great growth in our military establishment (almost a 10-fold increase) is the big factor. It and the big increases in state employment are the main causes all government's share of total employment has increased 2.4 times since 1900. As you see graphically in Figure 1 federal nonmilitary employment is the slowest growing of the four categories of public employment; and it has been shrinking since 1950.

National defense is much the biggest item in the federal budget, as shown

[1] The comments are ours, but the graphics are reprinted, by permission of the author and publisher, from Lloyd G. Reynolds, *Economics: A General Introduction,* rev. ed., Richard D. Irwin, Inc., Homewood, Ill. 1966, pp. 459 and 461, respectively.

FIGURE 1 Government employment as a percentage of total employment, United States 1900–1965

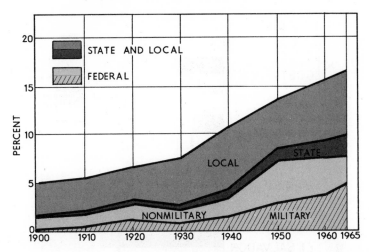

by Figure 2, almost three out of five federal expense dollars (58.2%) going there.

If we include the foreign aid and atomic energy programs as part of the defense effort, national defense absorbs about three quarters of the cost of federal services. Everything else has to come out of the remaining quarter.

FIGURE 2 Cost distribution by level of government and type of service, United States, 1963–64 (percent)

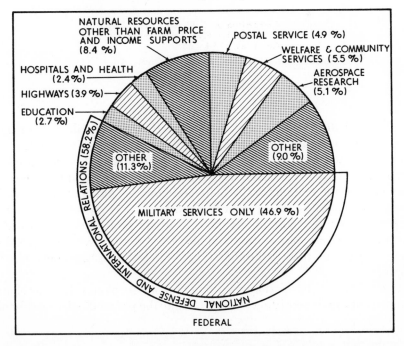

As a further illustration of the kinds, uses of, and techniques used in charts, see those illustrated in Figures 3, 4, and 5.

FIGURE 3

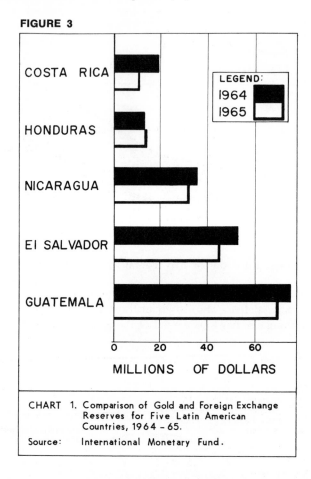

CHART 1. Comparison of Gold and Foreign Exchange Reserves for Five Latin American Countries, 1964 – 65.

Source: International Monetary Fund.

In your reading of other books, newspapers, and especially news-magazines like *U. S. News & World Report, Newsweek,* and *Time,* notice the numerous good (and some bad) illustrations. Look not only at the graphics themselves, but notice what kinds of information call for graphic presentation, whether the graphics really help, and how the authors interrelate the graphics and words so that each aids the other.

If you will make those observations, you will probably see how useful graphics can be in your writing and also learn most of what you need to know about using them skillfully. Still we think these suggestions may be helpful:

1. Use line graphs (perhaps marking the tops of columns in a bar chart) to represent trends according to time. Usually the perpendicular axis should

FIGURE 4

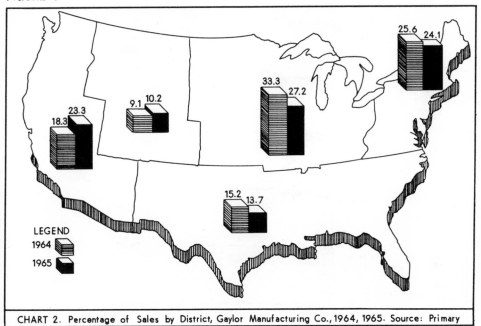

CHART 2. Percentage of Sales by District, Gaylor Manufacturing Co., 1964, 1965. Source: Primary

represent volume of the subject treated and the base (or horizontal axis) should represent time. Two or more different kinds of lines can show relative quantities as well as the absolute quantities of several subjects at any given time.

Unless you are using several lines or bars (but not so many as to confuse!) and are interested only in their comparative values rather than their individual changes, be sure to start at 0 as the base. If, for example, you use 40 as the base of the quantity scale and the first year presented has a volume of 50 and the second 60, the second year appears to have doubled the first (20 above the base 40 and thus twice as high on the scale as the preceding year, which was only 10 above the base). But actually it has increased only 20 percent (the 10 points from 50 to 60, a one-fifth or 20 percent increase)—as it would and should look on base 0.

Providing grid lines will help avoid optical illusions and give the reader a quick and precise idea of just where a line is at any given time in the graph.

Remember also to use faired (curved) lines for continuously changing data and straight lines to connect plotted points of data that change by steps, such as enrollments in a university by semesters.

2. Use segmented bars or pie charts moving clockwise from 12:00 to represent the proportions in the breakdown of a whole. Usually the color

FIGURE 5

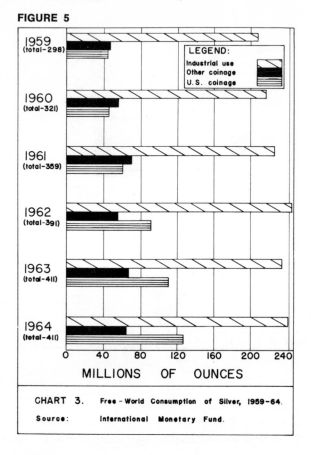

CHART 3.   Free-World Consumption of Silver, 1959-64.

Source: International Monetary Fund.

or shading of sections distinguishes the parts (which should not be confusingly numerous). They should be labeled with both the raw figures for precision and the ratio or percentage of the whole for easy comparison (the ratio is usually the more important point).

3. Use maps for geographical distribution of almost anything; organization charts of rectangles arranged and connected to show lines of authority and communication; flow charts showing movement and stages in processing; blueprints giving precise sizes and relationships; and photographs picturing accurate size, texture, and color. All are useful graphic devices in their places if you keep them simple enough for easy reading and concentrated on the point under discussion.

4. Use symbolic pictograms (like little men representing workers or bags of money representing profits) to add interest, especially for nontechnical readers, when you have the time and money and are preparing a report in enough copies to justify the cost. But keep all the little characters the same size (although each may represent any quantity) and vary

the *number* of them to represent different total quantities. Otherwise, you mislead because the volume in the pictogram involves a third dimension (depth perspective) not shown in the pictogram. Of two cylinders representing oil production, for example, one actually twice as big as the other looks only slightly bigger because of the unseen third dimension. Even in the best usage, pictograms are not precise unless you write in the exact quantities. Pictograms should be drawn to avoid prejudicial side messages too—such as the unfavorable and irrelevant suggestion that all welfare cases are diseased, decrepit, or dumb in the drawings of a pictogram designed to represent the changing *number* of welfare cases.

❋   ❋   ❋

Beyond that, the writing of a report depends on the particular form to be used, and the form you choose should be the one best adapted to the situation, as explained along with the illustrations in Chapters 15 and 16. (The cases for reports of different kinds are at the ends of those two chapters.)

chapter 15	# Analysis and illustration of complete analytical reports

[The ladder of success must be set on something solid.]

A bird's-eye view of layout
Checklist for complete analytical reports

IN PETTY DETAILS the makeup of long analytical reports varies only a little less than the organizations sponsoring the reports. Hence we cannot tell you the details of any report form that will be acceptable universally or specifically to the particular organization for which you may write.

Yet in the larger aspects of report parts and their interrelations, agreement far exceeds disagreement. In this chapter we propose to explain and illustrate report makeup with emphasis on the generally acceptable major points. Since you will also want some guidance on details, however, we will suggest *a* good way to handle them; but we ask you to remember that what we present on details of form is *not the only way.*

Even more important, we do *not* present *the illustrations as perfect reports, and certainly* not *as wording to be followed slavishly or copied parrotlike. At best, they show acceptable content, form, and general style for their particular situations as starters to your thinking—not as solutions to all your problems on these points for your situation.*

A BIRD'S-EYE VIEW OF LAYOUT

Most complete analytical reports include three broad categories of several parts each. The parts marked with asterisks in the following list normally do not appear as separate parts except in long, formal reports, but the others are almost universal.

Preliminaries
- Cover
- Title fly*
- Title page
- Letter of authorization*
- Letter of acceptance*
- Letter of transmittal
- Table of contents
- Tables of illustrations*
- Synopsis

Body
- Introduction
- Text
- Conclusions
- Recommendations

Supplements
- Appendix(es)
- Bibliography
- Index*

The following specifics will help in layout and pagination:

1. Generally each of the listed parts except text, conclusions, and recommendations begins a new page; otherwise, only the filling of one page calls for a new one. The table of illustrations goes on the same page with the contents if space allows without crowding. Each appendix begins on a new page.

2. Preliminary pages are counted beginning with the title fly, if used (and after title page get lowercase roman numerals); other pages take arabic numerals. The first page number of any part beginning a new page is centered at the bottom of the page; others appear (preferably) at least three spaces above the end of the first line. No page numbers need adornments such as parentheses, hyphens, periods, and underscores.

3. If the report is to be bound, the "bite" requires an extra wide space, so that no writing will be hidden and margins will appear equal.

Optional and minor parts

Now, before we present the parts that require full discussion and illustration, let's clear out the no-problem parts and the optional parts marked with asterisks in the preceding list.

The *cover*, much like the cover of a book, is there to hold the report together and protect it. But unless it has an open or cellophane-covered cutout, it hides the identifying title page. It then needs to carry at least the title (perhaps in shortened form) and the author's name, but it may carry the rest of the title-page information too.

As the name suggests, the *title fly* is a full page carrying only the title. Whatever its use in printed books, it is only excess paper in typewritten reports. If used, it counts as the first of the preliminary pages (lowercase roman numerals), although the page number does not need to appear on it.

Although written by the man who has the problem to be solved and pays for the report rather than the one who prepares it, the *letter of authorization* should be included when the assignment was made by letter. This is most likely to be when the assignment is a big one, especially if it is a public-affairs problem or the report writer is an outsider working on a fee basis. By showing any reader what the assigned job was, the letter enables him to judge the adequacy of the report. To make sure of getting what he wants, the writer of the authorization needs to state the problem precisely and make clear the purpose, scope, and limits on time, money, and the like. He may help further and save himself money by asking specific questions and, if he knows how, suggesting sources, methods, or approaches that might be useful.

The letter of acceptance—rarely included—is the answer to the authorization. Together they constitute the working agreement.

Tables of illustrations help only if some of the tables and graphics might be useful to a reader independently of the discussion around them. If used, in table-of-contents form they list separately the tables, charts, and figures in sequence by their identifying numbers and titles, and give the pages on which they appear.

An *index* would serve little purpose in most reports both because they are not long enough to need one and because they are not used the way a reference book is. Ordinarily the table of contents adequately serves the purpose of an index, helping a reader to find a certain point without reading the whole report. If, however, you find that you must prepare an index, take some good advice from people who have tried indexing: (1) Hire a professional indexer to do the job or (2) study at least one of the several helpful books on the subject before you start. Indexes done by nonprofessionals are mostly rather poor, including those in most textbooks—too scant and too full of errors.

Title page

The title page is usually the first of the preliminary pages (counted as lowercase roman numbers down to the introduction), but the page number does not need to appear on it. Four other blocks of information do: the title itself, the name and title of the reader, the name and title of the writer, and the place and date. In many instances the name of the organization with which both writer and reader are connected is desirable information also. When needed, a brief abstract, a list of people or departments to receive copies, and project or serial-number identifications may appear also.

Like any other heading, the title should indicate precisely (not too much and not too little), concisely (without wasted words such as "A Report on . . ." or "A Survey of . . ."), and interestingly the content of the report. If you can't do this in about 20 words or less, you might consider writing a short title and supplementing it with a secondary clarifying title (usually in parentheses a couple of lines lower); but you should not use a subtitle to dodge reasonable efforts at making one title do the job well. The main problem is to delimit the topic adequately but concisely.

In looking at the accompanying illustration of the title page (p. 536), note how the writer blocked her information into four parts, how she used balanced layout, and how specific she made her title. A report is information about a specific problem of an individual or a definite group, and the title should indicate that specificness (often to the extent of naming the man or group as well as the problem). You can't answer such a general question as "Should Spot Radio Advertising Be Continued?" Remember, however, that the title on the illustrative report is a final title, written after the reporter had made her analysis. Thus she knew what the decision was and chose to tell the reader directly. To have phrased it that way before her research would have been a preconception that could have prevented her from facing facts fairly.

Letter of transmittal

Unless the report is an extensive and formal one, including such things as a copyright notice, title fly, letter of authorization, and letter of acceptance, page ii (counted, but not necessarily numbered) is a letter of transmittal. (In a formal public affairs report with large numbers of indefinite readers, a typical preface replaces the personalized letter of transmittal.)

Written after the report is completed, in regular letter form (Chapter 1) and a style appropriate to the circumstances, the letter of transmittal must do at least two things: transmit the report and refer to the authorization. In informal situations one sentence can do both: "Here's the report on fish poisoning you asked me to write when we were talking on May 10." Usually it needs to be a little more formal than that, but it needs no bromidic "As per your request, . . ." and rarely such formality as "In accordance with . . . ." Certainly it needs to subordinate the reference to the authorization to avoid a flat and insulting sound—seeming to tell the reader that he asked for the report as if he were too dumb or forgetful to remember. In the rare cases where there is no authorization, instead of the reference to it the writer tells enough background to arouse interest in the report.

Despite the importance of conciseness and the possibility of doing in

WHY THE P. L. LYON COMPANY SHOULD DISCONTINUE SPOT RADIO

ADVERTISING AND CONCENTRATE ON NEWSPAPER ADVERTISING

Prepared for

Mr. P. L. Lyon

President

by

Mary Lowery

Advertising Manager

Paynes, Illinois

March 10, 197--

the first sentence all it *has* to do, a letter of transmittal will say more, if for no reason than to avoid a curt tone. Some additional things it might talk about (but not all in any one letter) are

—A highlight particularly significant in affecting the findings, or a reference to special sections likely to be particularly interesting to the reader.

—A summary of conclusions and recommendations if the reader is likely to be sympathetic, unless a synopsis two or three pages later says the same thing. Even then, the letter can give the general decision but not supporting data.

—Side issues or facts irrelevant to the report but interesting or valuable to the reader.

—Limitations of information and time and money if they are true provided they are not a part of the introduction, where they naturally belong—and provided that they do not sound like lazy excuses.

—Acknowledgments of unusual help given by others not cited later as sources.

The letter may appropriately end with some expression indicating the writer's attitude toward the significance of the report and/or his own appreciation for having been allowed to work on it. If you are in the business of making such studies, you surely appreciate business. If you're within the company, you certainly should appreciate the opportunity to demonstrate your ability and to learn more about the company.

The writer of the accompanying transmittal letter wisely elected to incorporate her summary or synopsis in the letter, thus saving time for her reader. Had the synopsis been longer, she would have handled it separately, immediately after the Contents.

Otherwise the content of the letter is quite typical. You will notice that it transmits the report and refers to the authorization in the first sentence and expresses appreciation in the last. Other possible contents of a letter of transmittal were unnecessary, especially in view of the synopsis.

But the layouts of the third and fourth paragraphs of the letter, although good, are individualistic rather than typical. The whole middle of the letter, giving the supporting data, could be more normally written like this:

Although the radio theoretically reaches more prospective customers at only twice the cost per family (19.9 cents per 1,000 versus 10.04 cents per 1,000), it actually reaches fewer than the newspaper and costs 27 times as much per prospect reached (82 cents per 1,000 versus 3 cents per 1,000).

A part of the reason is that whereas nearly all of the 11,354 copies of the local newspaper go to the store's trading area, many of the 21,368 radios in PQR's more extensive coverage are outside that area. Even within the area, only one out of five families listens to radio commercials, whereas at least one member of a family nearly always reads the newspaper.

Moreover, people don't remember commercials as long as they do ads in newspapers, probably because the newspaper is available for reference later.

The total effect has been that Lyon sales of individual items spot-advertised as well as total sales showed little difference (1 percent) during the time you advertised by radio. The single item that showed any appreciable increase was maternity wear—a new department without competition in the town.

Thus newspaper advertising seems not only to meet the criteria of coverage, cost, and retention value better than radio advertising but it is the only other available major form.

Letterhead

December 10, 197-

Mr. P. L. Lyon
The Lyon Company
Paynes, Illinois 61611

Dear Mr. Lyon:

Here is the report you requested two weeks ago concerning your advertising
program.

The cost figures gathered from Station WPQR and the Paynes <u>News</u> <u>Messenger</u>,
and analysis of your store sales figures, support the recommendation that
you discontinue the spot radio advertising which you started last April
and concentrate your advertising dollars on newspaper space.

Here are some of the significant reasons:

> --though the radio provides more extensive coverage, the newspaper
> circulation more nearly corresponds to the store's trading area
> and avoids wasted coverage
>
> --radio ads cost only twice as much per family theoretically reached
> (19.9¢ per 1,000 vs. 10.04¢ per 1,000) but--because only one out of
> five families listens to commercials, inattentively at that--27 times
> as much per person actually reached (82¢ per 1,000 vs. 3¢ per 1,000)
>
> --even so, people don't remember commercials as long as they do ads in
> newspapers (probably because the newspaper is available for reference
> later).

Thus the newspaper better meets the tests of coverage, cost, and retention
value.

BUT THE MOST CONVINCING REASON IS THAT

> --Lyon sales of individual items spot-advertised as well as total sales
> showed little difference (1%) during the time you advertised by radio.
> The single item that showed any appreciable increase was maternity wear
> --a new department, without competition in the town.

The newspaper thus wins the nomination by default as the only major medium
that seems likely to serve Lyon's well.

I've enjoyed making the study. Please call on me if I can help further.

Sincerely yours

Mary Lowery
Advertising Manager

We do not mean that you should copy our rewritten version instead of
the original; we mean that you should not copy anybody's word patterns,
especially if they are unusual. You should look at illustrations for ideas
and principles of communication—then express your thoughts in your
own way.

Contents

The next part, usually page iii (with the number centered at the bottom, as always on a page with extra space at the top because of a part heading), is what is commonly called the table of contents or simply contents. It sets out the headings of the report and their beginning page numbers. Thus it quickly shows the organization and serves as a handy guide for the reader, especially the busy reader who may want to check only some parts. In the absence of an index, it needs to be detailed—the more detailed, the better.

To list in the table of contents the table itself and those pages that come before it looks a little odd; the reader would already have seen them. Yet conventional practice does condone listing of preceding letters. Remember, however, that the preliminary parts down to the introduction are *not* parts of the outline and do not get outline symbols, such as *I* and *A*, but only their names and page numbers (small roman numerals). If a separate synopsis comes after the table of contents, you list it flush left without an outline symbol, usually as the first thing on the list.

Then comes the real outline of the report—the headings and subheads. In most reports you may well give all of them, reproduced in exactly the same wording as elsewhere but not necessarily in the same type. Preferably you should put the outline symbols before them—capital roman numerals for the major divisions (including the introduction, conclusions, and recommendations) and capital letters for their subdivisions, according to the system of outlining suggested earlier. (Remember that roman numerals, like arabics, line up on the right.) If any heading runs over to a second line, indent it. After each heading is a leader line of *spaced* periods leading to the page number, as in the accompanying illustration.

Supplementary parts such as appendixes and the bibliography continue the arabic page numbers of the body copy, but they do not carry roman numerals to the left in the table of contents because they are not logical parts of the discussion being outlined.

The contents may be single- or double-spaced, or single-spaced within parts and double-spaced between, whichever makes the best appearance on the page.

Synopsis

Written after the report proper has been completed, the synopsis is a condensed version of the whole report (introduction, presentation of facts and the interpretations of them, and conclusions and recommendations). It is the report in a nutshell. Usually it should be somewhere between a 10:1 and 20:1 reduction. In most cases the introduction should be reduced even more, and the conclusions and recommendations less because they deserve the main emphasis.

Since the synopsis stresses results, it should not be used in a report which

Contents

needs to be strongly convincing because of the reader's likely resistance; the condensed presentation of findings may not be adequate to do the necessary convincing before the reader sees the unwelcome conclusions.

But in a report which may properly follow the deductive plan because the results are probably welcome to the reader, the synopsis serves several important purposes:

1. It saves time for the busy reader who may find there all he wants.
2. Even for the reader who goes on through the whole report, the synopsis gives him a bird's-eye view which enables him to read the rest more easily and more intelligently because he can see how each fact or explanation fits into the final results he already knows.
3. Often the synopsis also serves as the basis for a condensed oral presentation to a group of important "readers" such as a board of directors.
4. Sometimes it is reproduced and distributed to a number of readers who do not get the whole report.

Particularly for the first and last uses, many executives insist that reports coming to their desks have *one*-page synopses. You should therefore try to keep synopses down to one page, even if you have to single-space within paragraphs.

The letter of transmittal you read earlier is also an example of synopsizing. In that report the author used no separate synopsis but wove it into the letter. For a more typical example, read the more detailed synopsis below of a different report long enough to make desirable a separate synopsis

Synopsis

Savannah people are likely to buy more at a Rexwall Drug Store than Charleston residents are, according to this market evaluation prepared for the Chairman of the Board, Rexwall, Inc., by Factseekers, Inc.

Though metropolitan Charleston merchants serve 11,000 more customers from the shopping area, Savannah retailers can expect some trade from almost twice as many out-of-town buyers (340,000 versus 184,000). Savannah's 1,000 more family units more than compensate for the fact that the Charleston family averages 3.62 people while the smaller Savannah family averages 3.4.

Savannah individuals average $85 more buying income, but the larger Charleston families average $35 more per family for a total of half a million more annual buying income. With less first-mortgage money to do it, 2,800 more people in Savannah have built homes in the past four years; but 17,000 more Charlestonians own automobiles.

The higher income of the individual Savannah buyer and the larger number of customers from around Savannah explain why $2.5 million more passed through the hands of Savannah retailers last year. Individually, Savannah residents spent $75 more; the small Savannah family, however, spent only $55 more.

Though five years ago Charleston druggists outsold those in Savannah by an average of $3,000, last year the 61 Savannah drugstore managers and owners collected about $5 million— $170,000 more than 62 Charleston druggists—for an average of $4,000 more per drugstore in Savannah.

Overall business factors also point to Savannah as the choice. Savannah's estimated business volume of $989 million is almost twice that of Charleston. Since a significant part of this difference is attributable to the 10 million more tons of

cargo handled by the Savannah docks, Savannah consumers and
retailers will feel the pinch of recessions and strikes more
than Charlestonians. The extra $36 million added by
Charleston manufacturing, however, is almost as uncertain in
the stability of that city as the effects of shipping are on
the economy of Savannah. Charlestonians benefit from $35
million more of the relatively stable wholesale business; but
$32 million more agricultural income from farms averaging
$4,000 more in value helps to bolster the Savannah economy.

Certainly Savannah's business activity has been consistently
better than Charleston's in the past four years. Though the
trend continues up in both cities, construction has averaged
$12 million more annually in Savannah. Bankers in Savannah
have consistently received about 10 percent more deposits than
their Charleston counterparts have—for $150 million more in
commercial accounts and $12 million more in savings. In both
cities postmasters have collected about 8 percent more each
successive year, but Savannah citizens have steadily paid for
$200,000 more postage than Charlestonians have.

(the better practice in all but comparatively short reports). It specifically
and concisely synopsizes a report of six major divisions (besides the introduction and the conclusions and recommendations) running to 27 pages.
Desirably, it focuses on a quick presentation of results (the decisions) in
the first paragraph, while also making clear the purpose, the readers, and
the writers. Then it summarizes, in a paragraph for each, the six data-filled
sections in the same order and proportionate space given the topics in the
full report. For readers not used to market-research data, headings like the
following for those six paragraphs might have helped:

Population and Buying Units
Buying Income
Retail Sales
Drugstore Sales
Overall Business Factors and Stability
Business Activity

Since the synopsis is derived exclusively from the report itself—which is
adequately illustrated and documented—you need neither graphics nor
citations. But you do need to give the main supporting facts. Otherwise the
synopsis becomes a nutshell with no meat. This is one reason we use the
term *synopsis* rather than *abstract*. Abstracts are of two kinds—topical,
giving only the points discussed; and informative, giving the findings about
each topic, with emphasis on conclusions and any recommendations made.
A synopsis is like an informative abstract, emphasizing results.

Introduction

The introduction to a complete analytical report serves primarily to answer the second of a report reader's two inevitable questions: How do you

know? Rarely does it answer any part of the first question: What are the facts? If that question needs to be answered briefly and early, the synopsis does the job.

But since the introduction does begin the body of the report—which also includes the findings of fact and their interpretation, the conclusions, and the recommendations if the reader wants them—the title of the whole report appears at the top of the page, which is numbered arabic 1 (centered at the bottom instead of at the upper right, as always on a page with extra space at the top because of a part heading there).

The first real problem in writing an introduction (often done after the other parts) is selecting a heading for it that gives a preview of its contents more precisely and more interestingly than the stock term *Introduction.* The following illustration, you notice, does better; but you don't need to use its wording. The heading of the introduction, the first major division of your outline, should be the same grammatical and type form as all the other major-division headings.

In explaining how he knows the forthcoming facts to be reliable, the report writer states his *purpose* and his *methods* and *scope,* so that the reader can judge whether the research would produce information that is sound and adequate for the purpose. Unless the reader sees that the research is basically sound, he naturally discredits the whole report. The introduction, then, is an important part of the conviction in the report and therefore deserves careful attention from both writer and reader.

The section headed *Purpose* may take several paragraphs for full explanation, especially if it starts with a little history of the problem; or it may be short. Long or short, it should contain some *one* sentence which is a pointed, concise statement of the problem you set out to solve.

Methods and *scope* come under separate headings or (because they are often nearly inseparable) under a combined heading. Your reader does want to know, however, what you intended to cover and how thorough your research was (scope) and how you got and analyzed your information (methods).

How thoroughly you need to explain your methods depends on two major points: (1) how new and questionable your methods and findings are and (2) your reputation as a researcher. On both bases nobody questions the audit report of a reputable auditing firm like Ernst & Ernst that says no more on methods than the following: ". . . in accordance with generally accepted auditing standards, and accordingly included such tests of the accounting records and such other auditing procedures as we considered necessary in the circumstances." Most report writers, however, cannot depend so completely on either their reputations or such well-established procedures to convince their readers.

A frequent question is how much methodology to put in the introduction and how much (if any) to relegate to an appendix or to interweave along with the presentation of findings. No simple answer fits all cases and relieves you of thinking. A general answer is that you explain your methods at the best place(s) to show your reader their soundness. He will want at least a general idea from the introduction. If he would likely forget specific details of research procedure, special materials and apparatus, or technique before he got to the resultant findings, you had better omit the specifics from the introduction and interweave them with the presentation of findings. (A specific question with its answers from a questionnaire is a good example.) Certain details of methodology may sometimes go in an appendix, but only if (1) they would interrupt or unduly slow up the fast movement of the report proper and (2) most readers of the particular report would not want or need them. (Detailed explanations of unusual statistical procedures, such as in the Kinsey reports, are good examples.)

Besides the standard parts (purpose, method, and scope), an introduction may take up one or more (rarely all) of several other possible topics. For readers who may not know the *background* to the problem, it may include a little history. If the background can be kept short, it usually starts the introduction and leads into the statement of purpose; otherwise, to avoid delaying the statement of purpose, the writer starts with it and uses the flashback method to follow quickly with the clarifying background to the problem. He may relegate any very long background story to the appendix and refer the reader to it. In the accompanying illustration (p. 545) the writer applied the flashback method and put background under the somewhat unusual heading, *Assumptions and background conditions.*

In a study involving a choice or evaluation, the introduction may well explain the *criteria* or *standards* used, as a part of method and scope or as a separate part.

Unless the letter of transmittal has already done so, the introduction should also forewarn the reader of any unavoidable *limitations* of data that make the report less than might be expected. The explanation may be a part of method and scope if it is not so extensive as to need its own heading. But in no case should it be used as excuse making for the writer's own shortcomings.

Sometimes a report uses technical words or certain terms applied in a sense unfamiliar to some likely readers. If so, you may explain them in the introduction or, preferably, in brief parenthetical statements immediately following the first use of each special term. If the list is extensive, the *glossary* may be an appendix.

The important point is for the introduction to answer the big question— How do you know?—*before* the reader asks it.

Then you are ready to present the assuredly reliable facts.

Before asking the reader to go on this mental journey, however, consider whether you can help by giving him a final reminder of his route: a concise statement of *plan.* Such a statement should not be long or detailed in its itemization of *all* your headings. Usually one effective sentence can

WHY THE P. L. LYON COMPANY SHOULD DISCONTINUE SPOT RADIO ADVERTISING

AND CONCENTRATE ON NEWSPAPER ADVERTISING

The WHY and HOW of This Report

Purpose.--After the Lyon Company of Paynes, Illinois, started
using spot radio advertising in its program, the question arose, "Is
this advertising practical enough to warrant its continued use?" This
study answers that as its major question.

By preliminary agreement, however, the study also considers the
broader question of what kind of advertising Lyon might best use. The
occasional use of envelope stuffers is not in question, however,
largely because of their small cost (about $100 a year).

Assumptions and background conditions.--Neither does the study
include the question of whether to advertise at all. The management
team assumes that for a store like Lyon, with increasing competition,
some major form of advertising is essential. I therefore assume that,
in the absence of a local TV station, the choice is really between
newspaper and radio advertising--or both if justifiable. (Professional
advertising people do not consider direct mail a good medium for more
than occasional use by retail clothing stores except in unusual
circumstances not prevailing here.)

We cannot really establish the effectiveness of our newspaper
advertising without "before-after" figures from a long-range experiment
such as we now have on the radio advertising. But to discontinue the
newspaper ads long enough for a sound test could be costly in lost sales

1

chart the way through to the end, like this: "As bases for determining the
more favorable market conditions, the report examines—in this order—
population characteristics, buying power, retail sales and drugstore sales
and the attendant competition, stability of the economy, and the current
business outlook." If you compare this statement of plan to the separate

synopsis presented earlier (p. 541), you will see that they both reflect the careful organization of the same report.

Text

Even the lazy writer who gets by with *introduction* as the heading for that part cannot get by with *text* as a heading covering the biggest part of the report, where the writer presents his findings and analyses of them. The stock term, fitting all reports and therefore useful in talking about them, fits no one report well.

But more important, the text section of the report is fundamentally the report; so if you try to phrase a suitable title for the section, it will be the same as the title of the whole report. Then the basic elements of your report —the factors or criteria which serve as the basis for the final decision— become third-degree headings with seemingly too little significance.

That is the first of the two major problems confronting the writer in presenting the text of his report: (1) showing the reader the organization carefully worked out as the third step in report preparation and (2) phrasing well the findings of the second step (collection of data) and the interpretations made in the fourth step. Satisfactory solutions to both are necessary if you are to give your reader the reliable information he wants.

Your main methods for showing the overall organization, the relations between parts, and the relation of each part to the whole are headings and subheads, topic sentences, and summary and anticipating statements. (You will find ample illustrations of all in the accompanying report.)

The headings and subheadings grow directly out of your attack on the problem, where you broke it down into its elements (capital roman) and further subdivided it by raising questions about each. Now that you are presenting the facts that provide the answers, you need only phrase these elements and questions into headings and subheads. Remember that good headings are indicative, interesting, concise, and (in some cases preferably) informative to the extent of telling the most important findings about the respective parts. (Notice the heads in the report.)

Just as a well-phrased heading may tell the main point about the section over which it stands, a topic sentence can give the essence of a paragraph and clearly foreshadow what the paragraph says. The topic sentence puts the big point across fast, arouses the reader's interest in seeing the supporting details that follow, and makes reading easier because of the preview. Although the resulting deductive paragraph plan is not the only one possible, it is the most useful for most kinds of writing, including report writing.

Reversing the plan produces a paragraph which presents a series of facts and arguments leading to a summarizing sentence at the end.

Both plans may apply to larger sections as well as to paragraphs. In fact, both a paragraph's topic sentence and the first part of a larger section may

2

if they are now being effective. I therefore have assumed, finally--
the way a doctor assumes about his prescription--that the major form
of advertising which scores the higher on the usual criteria pointing
to advertising effectiveness is the wise choice. The existing
conditions do provide an adequate basis for that kind of analysis.

The significant parts of history can be brief. While depending
almost wholly on newspaper advertising since opening its doors twenty
years ago, the Lyon Company has had steady and generally satisfactory
growth. Increasing competition in recent years has changed the story
only slightly. Nevertheless, more or less as an experiment, from May
through October of this year we decided to try spot radio ads broadcast
Monday, Tuesday, and Thursday at 12:35 P.M. over station WPQR AM/FM.
This time is in the Class A bracket ($4.25 for each spot if as many
as 104 a year), which includes the times of day when the listening
audience is the largest. As usual, advertising continued in the
Paynes News Messenger and through stuffers sent with the monthly statements.

Scope and Methods.--Those assumptions and conditions have led me
largely to a comparison of our newspaper and radio advertising. Using
the first criterion (coverage), I compared trading-area coverages of
the radio and the newspaper, based on an area map of the radio coverage
(prepared for WPQR by a radio-engineering firm) and subscription lists
from the newspaper. To identify the area from which the Lyon Company
draws most of its business, I tabulated the residence of each charge
customer. Figures on the number of families and of radio families in
each of the principal towns came from the latest Census of Population.

reflect, summarize, or provide a transition from a preceding part, as well as
give the essence and preview of what is to follow. And endings of both
paragraphs and larger parts commonly summarize them, show the significance of the just-completed part to the whole problem at hand, and foreshadow what is to follow in the next section (as does the ending of the

3

Newspaper subscription lists established number of homes reached by
newspapers.

To apply the second criterion (costs), I had to reduce the total
coverage figures to prospects actually reached for equal amounts of
time (a procedure detailed in the report) before dividing into the
known advertising rates to get the comparable costs.

To find out how many people the newspaper and the radio station
actually reached, I used statistics compiled for each of them by such
recognized agencies ás the Audit Bureau of Circulation and the A. C.
Nielsen Company. Information on the listening habits of Paynes people
came from a survey conducted three months ago by Robert S. Conlan and
Associates, Inc.

Since the comparison involves oral and visual media, I relied
on established principles and two professional advertising authories
for the comparison of retention values.

Daily sales tickets of the Lyon store showed the number of sales
of each item, which I cross-compared against WPQR records showing
the type of merchandise spot-advertised and when.

Total Lyon sales figures for last year (from the accounting department) were adjusted to find out what sales should have been this year
in the light of national sales trends as reported by the National
Industrial Conference Board publications. Comparison of these adjusted
sales figures with actual sales showed the overall effect of the
radio advertising introduced this year.

Limitations.--Comparing number of words in a spot ad to the number
of words in lines of newspaper advertising is admittedly open to question;

illustrated introduction on p. 549). Although the summaries may imply the
advisability of a certain action, they should not go further and steal the
thunder of the recommendation section by actually saying that the action
should be taken.

4

nevertheless, it is one means of evaluation. Furthermore, the number

of people listening to the radio at any one time and their concentration

or inattention are impossible to verify. And the great number of

factors affecting sales--weather, factory strikes, for example--make

it impossible to attribute fluctuations to any one cause with absolute

certainty that you are right. On the other hand, if radio spot advertising

has any effect on the sales of the Lyon Company, we can reasonably assume

that it would show up in some of the items specifically advertised or

in the total sales over the test period.

Basic plan.--To help answer the fundamental questions, this report

examines (in this order) both radio and newspaper coverage, cost, and

retention value before analyzing the sales records of radio-advertising

items.

Greater Coverage by Radio but More Selectivity through Newspaper

Both cover trading area; some waste in radio.--As you can readily

see from the three maps on the following pages [good things in the

report, omitted here for reasons of economy], both the daily newspaper,

the Paynes News Messenger, and radio station WPQR AM/FM completely

cover the Lyon trading area. This area includes all of Landu County

and also the neighboring parts of three adjoining counties.

The newspaper's coverage by carrier and mail delivery closely

resembles the company's trading area. Mail delivery, however, is one

day later than the date of publication.

On the other hand, the radio covers the entire trading area as

well as a much larger secondary area from which the company draws no trade.

Little more need be said about how to put the findings of fact and the
interpretation into words. You have already learned (Chapter 14) to use
commonly understood words, short and direct sentences and paragraphs,
itemizations, summarizing and transitional phrases and sentences, headings

5

Both the radio and the newspaper cover the trading area, but much of the radio advertising is wasted because it goes to people who do not trade in Paynes.

<u>Radio covers more families</u>.--A much better idea of the coverage comes from comparing the number of families in the trading area reached by radio and those reached by newspaper. According to the latest Census of Population figures and newspaper circulation records, the number of radio families in the principal cities and towns in the retail trading area (21,368) just about doubles the numbers of newspaper subscriptions, as shown in the following table [omitted]. Radio families are almost 100% of the total families of the area (22,204) and newspaper subscriptions about half that. Therefore most families in these principal cities and towns could be exposed to radio advertising.

Although the radio ads cover some unnecessary area, they still make it possible to reach a greater proportion of the people the company wants to reach than is possible through newspaper advertising.

Higher Cost of Radio Advertising

<u>Radio costs 4:1 for same content</u>.--To compare the costs of newspaper advertising with those of radio advertising, I experimented with different ads and found that on an average people read two column inches of advertising in 20 seconds, the length of the average Lyon spot ad. On the assumption that a 20-second spot and a two-column-inch ad are comparable in content, I determined the relative costs of $4.25 (WPQR rate chart) and $1.14 (57¢/column inch).

Those figures alone do not tell the complete story, however; successful spot radio advertising depends on frequent broadcast (1:373,

and subheads, and graphic aids to words. You know, too, that you need to support your statements of questionable fact with explanations, additional specific and concrete details as evidence, citations of sources, and any meaningful statistics.

But remember that graphic presentations are not complete in them-

6

meaning p. 373 of Item 1 in the Bibliography).

On the basis of content alone, radio spot advertising is clearly more expensive than newspaper advertising. The frequent repetition necessary for success only makes it more so. Possibly, however, a higher priced ad may reach so many families that its cost per family may be lower than a less expensive one.

Radio costs 2:1 for each family theoretically reached.--To find the cost for each family theoretically reached by radio, I divided the number of homes with radios (21,368) into the cost of one spot ad ($4.25) to arrive at a cost of 19.9¢/1,000 families. The same procedure applied to a newspaper ad shows a cost of 10.04¢/1,000 subscribers ($1.14÷11,354). Since a very large part of these subscriptions go to families (only a very few to business firms) we can safely say that to reach a family by radio costs almost twice as much as by newspaper advertising.

Radio costs 27:1 for each person actually reached.--But not all radios are turned on, and even if turned on, some will not be tuned to WPQR.

Advertisers figure that one third of the radio families will not be at home and another one third will not have their radios turned on. Of the 21,368 radios in the Paynes area, then, only 7,123 are likely to be tuned to WPQR under the most optimistic circumstances.

Paynes families listen to other stations more frequently than they listen to WPQR, however. On an average, 43% of the sets, 3,063, will be tuned to the local station (3:5). And when a Paynes radio is on,

selves, that they only help words to present facts. They cannot interpret. The reader will consider your job only half done if you present him with a mass of undigested data and make him do the interpreting. But if you put graphics and comments about them close together so that the reader can see both at once, each supplements the other.

7

1.7 people are listening. Accordingly, we can reasonably assume that
5,207 people are actually exposed to the commercial and thus arrive
at the cost of 81.6¢/1,000 people actually reached ($4.25÷5,207).

The News Messenger, with a circulation of 11,354 in the Lyon trading
area, has a secondary readership of 3.5 persons per copy (2:2). Since
the estimated number of persons exposed to a newspaper ad is 39,739
(11,354 x 3.5) and the cost of the ad is $1.14, we can for all practical
purposes assume a cost of 2.87¢/1,000. Radio, then, is about 27
times as expensive in terms of people actually reached. [A summary
table appeared here.]

Greater Retention Value of Newspaper Ads

The most significant point to establish in considering relative
retention value of advertising media, I believe, is that advertising
in a small town like Paynes to a large extent is merely keeping the
store name and the merchandise before the public. People here do not
respond to advertising as quickly as they do in large cities; they
wait until they had planned to go downtown to shop before they come
to the store.

Mr. B. T. Mills (president of Kirby and Clark, Inc., prominent
New York advertising agency), at a recent conference which I attended,
pointed out the postponed-buying habits of people in towns of less
than 40,000 population and added that for this reason spot radio advertising is impractical for stores located in towns the size of Paynes.
He went on to point out that a newspaper usually remains around the
home for some time and shoppers can refer back to an ad to get details
they might have forgotten, whereas a radio ad once heard can never be

References to the carefully chosen, most suitable graphics should be
subordinated to the interpretation of the facts shown. The mere fact that
the graph is there, or even the facts shown in the table or graph, are less
important than the significance of those facts to the whole problem or the
particular point being made at the time. So the emphasis should be on the

interpretation. (Note the references to charts throughout the text of the accompanying report.)

Here's a flat example which is short only because it forces the reader to dig in Figures 1 and 2 for the information:

> The greatest majority of the students interviewed showed their preference for buying at home in place of buying in the larger cities of Birmingham or Tuscaloosa. The overall percentage for the entire body of male students represented by the sample was 78 percent. The freshmen showed an even greater tendency for home buying by their percentage of 84.
>
> Figure 1, below, gives a picture of the place of purchase of the entire group without regard to the nature of the group. Figure 2 divides the group according to the students' rank.

This rewrite is more informative, emphatic, and readable:

> When University of Alabama men are ready for a new suit, they go home 78 percent of the time. Although 4 out of 100 will buy in Tuscaloosa and 7 in Birmingham, as shown in Figure 1, these 11 atypical cases do not warrant extensive advertising.
>
> The Alabama man, although never weaned in the majority of cases from hometown buying, does slowly shift his clothes-buying sources from home to Birmingham to Tuscaloosa. The gain of only 13 out of every 100 purchasers over a four-year span, however (Figure 2), only confirms the suspicion that Bold Look advertising dollars in Tuscaloosa would be wasted.

Although basically an interpretation may point out trends, high and low points, and significant differences brought out by comparisons and analyses of facts and figures presented, you need not waste words by talking about "a comparison" or "an analysis of" or "a study of"; if you state the significances, you imply the comparison, the analysis, or the study. And the comparisons become more significant if you put them in terms of percentages or ratios instead of, or in addition to, giving the raw figures.

To avoid monotony of both sentence pattern and length, especially in a series of similar comparisons, consider different types of sentence beginnings. Nearly always you can do better than use the expletives "It is . . ." and "There are . . . ," which waste words, delay the idea, and lead you to weak and awkward passive constructions.

And unless the logic of the situation clearly dictates otherwise, you'll do best to use the present tense for both presenting and interpreting the facts. When a reader reads it, your report analyzes, presents, takes up, examines, establishes, and finally concludes (all present tense). Of course, you'll have to use some past and future tenses; but in general, use them for matters of historical record and things not yet done. You have to assume that your most recent information is still applicable; hence, even though last year's sales figures are a historical record of what people bought, you are justified in saying, "People buy . . . ," meaning that they did buy, they are buying, and they will buy.

With the facts and analyses well organized, clearly presented, and

8

heard or referred to again.

We know, too, that almost everyone remembers things he sees longer than those he hears. And the continually confirmed fact that only about one out of five people listen to commercials attentively (4:504), clearly implies the greater retention value of newspaper advertising, and its application to the small-town customers of the P. L. Lyon Company is obvious.

We do not need to operate solely on implications, however; company sales confirm the tentative conclusions.

<u>Negligible Effect of Radio Ads on Sales</u>

<u>No significant change in sales of selected items</u>.--Sales of seven selected items for the week before and also for the week after they were advertised on WPQR were quite irregular, as Chart I shows. [At this point appeared a graph with seven different-colored lines representing sales of maternity dresses, pajamas, brassieres, hose, sweaters, girdles, and coats for two successive weeks.] The usual peak of sales on Saturday and a low on Monday is the normal pattern for the store, in no way attributable to radio advertising.

Any upward trend of sales during the second week could reasonably be attributed to the radio advertising, but sales of only one item rose significantly--maternity dresses. [Original graph omitted here.] Since this department was added to the store the week the advertising and sales were observed, the assumption that radio spot ads had anything to do with the sales is hardly justified--especially in view of the fact that this is the only maternity department in the city.

sharply summarized at the ends of sections, you have led the reader to your statement of conclusions and (if he wants them) recommendations.

Conclusions and recommendations

When you put your conclusions and recommendations into words, they should not be surprising—and they won't be if you have done an adequate job of the preceding part. There you should have presented all the evidence and analysis necessary to support your conclusions. So no new facts or analyses should appear in the conclusions or recommendations.

Whether you separate conclusions and recommendations into two headings makes little difference. Some people prefer separation because, they say, the conclusions are strictly objective, logical results of what has been said, whereas the recommendations are the individual writer's personal suggestions of what to do about the problem. Whichever point of view and plan you use, the important thing is to be as objective as possible in stating both conclusions and recommendations.

As evidence of that objectivity in your conclusions, and as a means of saving the reader the trouble of looking back into the text, you may well lift basic figures or statements from the earlier presentation and interweave them into the conclusion sentences. The writer of the synopsis illustrated on page 541 knew that the reader of his report could not possibly retain the 200 or more facts and figures given as evidence in 27 pages of analysis. In recalling to his reader the significant evidence affecting the decision in his conclusion, shown below, that writer wisely attached a specific figure to every fact. Note, too, the specific wording of his ending section—as well as the selectivity and brevity.

VII.   THE PREFERRED CITY: SAVANNAH

Although a Charleston druggist enjoys the advantages of

    --a population with a half million dollars more buying
       income annually and families with \$34 more to spend

    --11,000 additional potential customers

a Savannah drugstore would likely sell more because of these
advantages:

    --\$170,000 additional drugstore sales and \$4,000 greater
       sales per drugstore

    --\$2.5 million more retail sales and \$162 more per person
       spent in retail stores

    --1,000 more families and per capita income \$87 higher

    --four-year trend increases of 8 to 10% in construction
       (12 million more), bank deposits (\$150 million more),
       and postal receipts (\$200,000 more)

Both conclusions and recommendations need to be as pointed and positive as the facts and the writer's judgment will allow. (Usually itemization will help you to make them so and help the reader to see them as such.) If you toss the problem back to the reader with indefinite conclusions or alternative suggestions, he may feel that the salary or fee he has paid you for doing the report has been wasted. Still, he retains the right of final decision;

9

[The next three pages of the report present and interpret six
more small two-color line graphs--like the first for maternity dresses--
showing sales for a week before and a week after spot advertising of the
six other items.]

Records of sales before and after spot radio advertising of selected
items do not show that spot advertising brings significant increases
in sales of those items.

No appreciable increase in total sales.--Since advertising may
increase the number of people coming into a store without showing increased
sales of any particular item, however, total sales of the store provide
a check.

But to compare last year's monthly sales to this year's would not
take into consideration the fluctuations due to changes in general
business activity. I therefore used National Industrial Conference
Board percentages of increase and decrease of this year's sales to last
year's sales (Table 2) to see what we should expect this year without
radio advertising. [The statistical table of the original report is
omitted here.]

The difference shown in Chart 9 between what the sales actually
were and what could be expected could possibly be due to the radio
advertising. [Chart 9 is omitted here. It showed little difference.]
But the variations between actual sales and expected sales January

so even when he asks for your recommendations, he expects you to present
them as definite suggestions but certainly not as commands. The example
just cited—phrased specifically in terms of the objective of the report, to
select the city which will likely be the more profitable scene of operations
—avoids indecision on the one hand and its equally undesirable opposite,
imperative command.

10

through April, when radio advertising was not used in either year, suggest that the variations from May to October cannot be definitely attributed to spot advertising alone.

Even if we assume that the difference between what sales were and what could have been expected was a result of the radio advertising, the extra profits which <u>may</u> be attributable to it do not pay for it.

From May through October--the period observed during which the store used spot ads--sales were $750 more (1%) than could have been expected (Table 2). At the average net-profit margin of nearly 10%, this means radio ads increased the store's profits by about $12.50 a month. Such an amount is not only negligible when compared to the total monthly profits--it does not even pay for one week's advertising (3 x $4.25). Clearly, spot advertising has not paid its own way at the P. L. Lyon Company.

<u>Summary of Reasons for Discontinuing Spot Advertising and Relying on the Newspaper</u>

I recommend that the Lyon Company discontinue spot radio advertising and concentrate on newspaper advertising because

--spot radio ads have had apparently little effect on the sales of the store, either on selected items spot-advertised or on total sales

--on any basis it costs more than newspaper advertising, not only because of actual cost but also because of waste coverage

--Paynes customers, like all small-town customers, are not likely to respond to spots, preferring to depend on their newspaper for reminder when they decide to shop . . .leisurely

--the newspaper advertising not only scores higher than any other major medium available on the criteria of coverage, cost, and retention value but wins the choice by default.

Bibliography

Most reports have a bibliography. The writer of the spot radio advertising study did not compile one because her report was short and included few published references; she adequately identified these few as she referred to them.

In view of the circumstances under which she submitted her report, she was justified in omitting a formal bibliography since she supplied documentation as she went along. But this is the exception rather than the rule for any but very short reports.

For that reason (and to illustrate the economy of using numbers only for citing sources as described on p. 520) she took her sources and compiled the illustrated bibliography.

Most of the time when you use printed sources, the reader expects you to tell him what they are, not only to avoid the accusation of plagiarism but also to indicate reliability and perhaps provide him with places to get fuller information. Your footnotes and other citations in the text give the specific references. But at the end you list—in alphabetical order of authors' surnames, or titles if the sources are unsigned—books and magazines you have used for basic background information or for specific facts, ideas, or direct quotations.

The following bibliography (telescoped here for space economy) went with a 20-page report. (Usually the best spacing is single within items and double between them.) The items are numbered for concise, specific citations in the text.

PUBLICATIONS CONSULTED

1. "Airlines Will Sacrifice Power to Obtain Lower Jet Noise Level," _Aviation Week_, 66:34, February 25, 1972.

2. "Boeing Sets Suppressor Flight Test," _Aviation Week_, 65:41, April 1, 1971.

3. "Portable Jet Engine Muffler Design," _Aviation Week_, 64:74–75, April 8, 1970.

4. Richards, E. G., _Technical Aspects of Sound_, Elsevier Publishing Co., New York, 1971.

5. Richards, E. G., "Research on Aerodynamic Noise from Jets and Related Problems," _Royal Aeronautical Society Journal_, 57:318–42, May, 1971.

6. "Silencing Jet Fleet Will Be Costly," _Aviation Week_, 64:47–48, May 27, 1970.

Appendix

Although the report reproduced here in telescoped form needed no appendix, many reports do. The key is this: Use an appendix for material which the reader does not _need_ to see to understand the text but which some readers may _want_ to see to be sure your textual statements are valid. Frequent uses are for survey questionnaires too extensive for presentation in the introduction and not essential to the reader's understanding; for extensive formulas and statistical calculations; for extensive history, too long for the introduction; and for large maps, diagrams, or tables of figures that may be the basic data of the whole report but do not belong at any partic-

11

Bibliography

1. Lazarsfeld, Paul F., and Patricia L. Kendall, Radio Listening in
   America, Prentice-Hall, New York, 1968.

2. Readership of the Paynes News Messenger, Audit Bureau of Circulation,
   1970.

3. Study of Listening Habits--Paynes, Illinois. Robert S. Conlan and
   Associates, Inc., Detroit, 1971.

4. Wolfe, Charles H., Modern Radio Advertising, Funk and Wagnalls,
   New York, 1968.

ular place in the text. Often the best arrangement is to put a big table in the appendix and use appropriate figures from it as spot tables at key places in the text.

❊ ❊ ❊

For the feel of report continuity, go back and read straight through the illustrative report interspersed in this chapter and beginning on p. 536. Selected partly for its shortness (to save pages and reading time), it nevertheless illustrates adequate handling of the standard parts of a complete analytical report. (We feel that the preceding discussion and a little ingenuity will enable you to prepare other possible parts if you need to write them—cover, title fly, letters of authorization and acceptance, table of illustrations, appendix, and index.)

Because the report illustrated here is somewhat short, however, it does not need to make full use of topic and summary statements needed at the beginnings and endings of sections in longer reports. For illustration of how to use them, we refer you to Items 4–7 on page 564.

❊ ❊ ❊

Although the following checklist is primarily for complete analytical reports, many of the items apply to all reports. For greatest usefulness the sections appear in order of preparation of your material, not the order of presentation in the final report. Remember, however, that this is only a checklist. If you need fuller explanation of a point, find it in the appropriate chapter. (The index may help.)

Checklist for Complete Analytical Reports

Organization/Outlining (O)

1. Your title should make clear the nature and purpose of your analysis. Thus it will show the basis of classification as you phrase the major divisions of your subject, and prevent overlapping. (See Item 1, p. 507.) It may or may not reveal the outcome or reflect basic method. It should establish the boundaries of your treatment.

2. In comparisons, carefully distinguish between subjects of your study and criteria (tests) which you apply to the two or more subjects from which you ultimately make a choice.

3. Carefully distinguish also between a criterion (one of the tests you apply) and a method. A research procedure or a statistical procedure—which does need identification and probably explanation in the introductory passages—is the way you have gone about evaluating, not the basis of evaluation.

4. An outline in which the contents suggested by the title and by some other heading (usually II) are essentially the same thing shows no recognition of effective organization. All the basic elements of the problem are parts of the text. They are where you present all your facts and analyses.

   According to strict logic, these elements would be the only appropriate major divisions (in roman numerals in the suggested outline form). Neither the introduction nor the conclusions and recommendations (like the synopsis and bibliography) would get major-division status. They are not logically factors, or elements, or criteria, of the topic named in the title.

   Customary practice, however, does give major-division status (roman numerals in the outline) to the introduction and to the conclusions and recommendations (separately or together). They deserve emphasis, although they are not logical parts in the same breakdown of the title that gives you the text elements.

5. Customary practice also skips a heading for the whole text and gives each major element of it a separate roman number—for projer emphasis and better balance. So don't bury the elements or criteria in third- or fourth-order heads.

6. A heading must be phrased to cover any and all of the items listed under it. "Greater Number of Men in Milwaukee" does not cover the subhead "Greater Density of Population in Buffalo"; but "More Favorable Population Characteristics in Milwaukee" could cover that as well as other points like age, color, and vocations.

Checklist for Complete Analytical Reports

O—(continued)

7. Consider the function of (how you are interpreting or applying) your piece of information in maintaining a logical sequence without shifting viewpoint as you move from second- to third- to fourth-order heads. The relation of the part to the whole should always be clear and defensible.

8. Headings of the same class should be in the same grammatical form. Noun phrases are probably best. Complete sentences are perfectly acceptable, although often bulky.

9. When you have only one division under a heading, you have either omitted something or merely restated the governing head. True division gives at least two parts.

10. Make the heading tell something of the findings as well as establish boundaries. One-word headings only name the topic and are usually too general and all-inclusive (promising more than you cover). You cannot exclude properly with a heading like "Grocery Stores." Give the reader a tentative idea of findings with a heading like "The Increasing Importance of Grocery Stores in the Distribution of Cosmetics." Under a second-degree heading of "Current Business Factors Favor Milwaukee," present third-order headings such as "Milwaukee's Larger Postal Receipts," "Larger Volume of Bank Clearings in Buffalo but Greater Percentage Increase in Milwaukee," and "Milwaukee's Greater Volume of Construction."

11. Headings are like road markers: They keep pointing the way, providing reassurance and relief. Too many heads become a distraction, maybe even an irritation; too few make the going harder.

12. In phrasing headings, work for variety of wording, but retain parallelism of grammatical form. Use synonyms to prevent monotony of expression.

13. The wording of any one heading must be the same, regardless of how many times it appears—or when, or where.

14. Use placement on the page, spacing, and differentiation of type of headings (with or without conventional outline numbers) to show the relative importance and relation of parts. (See pp. 522–24.)

Checklist for Complete Analytical Reports

(continued)

Graphics (Gr)

1. Place the graph, table, or any other illustrative device as close as possible to the point discussed (in typed reports, maybe even on the back of the preceding page).

    a) Most charts and tables you can present in small enough size to splice right into your text. Part of a page of graph paper will serve well for most charts.

    b) The laziest way is to dump all illustrations in the appendix. If the reader really needs to see them, put them in the text.

2. For economical references to illustrations in the text, number all graphics and tables separately and give them complete and accurate titles, keys if needed, and any necessary explanation.

3. Adequately label all parts of a table or chart.

4. Indicate the source of your information when you use someone else's material. Write "Source:" and follow up with the same information you would use in a footnote.

5. Give the dates that apply to your material. Many current publications list information several years old. You can always list the true date in parentheses immediately after the title.

6. Put a few lines of discussion of the specific point before the chart or table and preferably a few lines after.

7. Call attention to the figure before it appears. When it is necessarily on a different page, tell the reader where it is.

8. Charts have more interest value than tables and with accurate labels can be just as exact.

9. When you have a number of items to present, consider giving them in several small charts or spot tables closely associated with the related text rather than in a collective table.

10. In line graphs for time series, run dates along the bottom line; run quantities or percentages along the side. And be sure your starting point for quantities or percentages is zero (unless your point is the relative values).

11. Select the best kind of graphic device for your purpose. Bars (simple or segmented) read as easily as pies and often more accurately —and pictographs may add interest but can distort information.

12. When chronology is not significant, arrange multiple bits of graphed information in order of importance.

13. Number charts consecutively throughout your study; number tables consecutively in their own order.

14. Use the appropriate graphic whenever one will help.

15. Avoid wasting time and space on useless graphics.

Checklist for Complete Analytical Reports

(continued)

Introduction (I)

1. Focus attention on the continuing existence of the report by talking about it in the present tense.

2. Put initial emphasis, then, on the nature and purpose of the study rather than on historical (past-tense) details of authorization, method, or history.

3. Not every report needs a history section. If yours does, it may be dealt with subordinately in conjunction with "Purpose" or may be a short flashback after "Purpose." If it is extensive, consider shifting it to a preliminary section after the introduction or relegating it to the appendix.

4. Definitions of terms aren't always necessary either. When they are, consider parenthetical or footnote explanations.

5. You do need some explanation of procedure or method. Show in the required detail how you've gone about solving the problem.

6. Such petty details as "Graphs have been included" are better omitted, however. Statistical exhibits are as expected in most reports as sentences are in building paragraphs.

7. References to limited amounts of time or money in the introduction may sound like excuses for poor performance. Such references —if true—may be better incorporated in the transmittal letter.

8. You usually do have limitations of coverage, however, which are sometimes necessary to show your reader why you are not covering some phase of the subject.

9. Have a clear indication of the order in which the various points confront the reader as he goes through the report. Peferably end your introduction with this statement.

10. Work for combinations of these various possible contents of the introduction to prevent overorganizing and overwriting. Nature and Purpose go together naturally (and may include necessary identification of who wants the report as well as who submits it); Method, Scope, and Limitations can be combined; Scope, Limitations, and Plan might well be the label for one compact section.

11. In reports that contain a synopsis (which precedes the report itself), findings, conclusions, and recommendations are unnecessary in the introduction—even undesirable. When you have no synopsis, you may reveal major findings either at the beginning or at the ending of your introduction.

12. Repeat the exact title of the report at the top of page 1 where you begin your introduction. But in the text, paraphrase it.

Checklist for Complete Analytical Reports

(continued)

Style (S)

1. Tables and charts cannot analyze. Your words do that. Put the highlights (and low points or trends) into words and establish their significance in the light of your objective. It's the message of the chart that counts, not the chart itself.

2. Refer incidentally (subordinately) to tables or charts within the sentence or at the end, not at the beginning. Don't make the figure the subject of the sentence. "Increased steel production, as shown in Chart 2, aids business in general and appliance makers in particular" puts the emphasis where you want it. Parenthetical reference (Chart 2) does the same thing.

3. Headings are only assists; the text must read coherently without them. Use no pronoun referring to a heading.

4. A clear topic identification in your text as you begin a new point is vital.

5. As you move to a detailed analysis of a point involving two or more divisions, tell your reader what those divisions are and name them in the order he will meet them. This is what report writers call a "topic statement."

6. When you've finished a detailed analysis involving two or more parts, establish the significance of the overall point in a summary statement (a short sentence or paragraph).

7. Show the relation of parts to one another and to the whole in forward-looking (and sometimes backward-looking) transitional statements. They are most useful immediately after a summary statement concluding the subject of discussion under a second-order heading. But they may coherently appear in connection with topic statements at the beginning.

8. Your topic statements should emphasize what subjects you are taking up and the order in which you take them up; they may explain why, but only incidentally; they may even establish findings or results, but this is more the function of the textual material and summary statements.

9. To enliven your style and increase readability:
   a) Choose simple, short words.
   b) Make people (not things, intangibles, or percentages) the subjects and/or objects of most of your sentences.
   c) Use mostly action verbs.
   d) Use active voice (and thus eliminate "It is" and "There are" beginnings).

Checklist for Complete Analytical Reports

S—(continued)

e) Refer to quantities in simplified form (rounded off, fraction form, simplified percentages, reduced forms within the quick comprehension of any reader).

10. Immediate and specific evidence is the essence of good analysis. A line doesn't sell "well"; it accounts for 19 percent of total sales. "Many people" can be interpreted differently by each reader; "324" or "9 out of 10" can be interpreted in only one way.

11. In the analysis, lead the reader up to seeing the advisability of an action, but leave your recommendation(s) for the ending pages.

12. Write in present tense when you are interpreting a recognizable tendency which is likely to be continuing.

13. Treat each subject or alternative you are examining under each point (test or criterion) you take up. The surest indication of a prejudiced writer is giving information about one subject and failing to give the same kind of information for another.

14. Emotional writing, persuasive passages, and ignoring of fact are marks of an amateur or biased writer.

15. Assumptions are necessary in any kind of analysis, but they should be plausible, and clearly established as assumptions.

16. Let the objectivity of your presentation be apparent from the careful, specific identification of your method, from the quality of your analysis, and from your interpretations and style. Talk about "unbiased," "impersonal," "objective" qualities brings questions to your reader's mind. If your report is all these good things, your reader will recognize it as such; if it isn't, such disclaimers only make the situation worse.

17. Remember that many factors must be evaluated relatively as well as absolutely. The relative status (percent, ratio, or rank—a qualitative factor) is often as important as the total (or quantitative)— and may be more important.

18. A natural style (using first- and second-person pronouns—I, me, my, our, we, us; you, your—when you need them) is clearer, easier for both writer and reader, and more interesting; yet some readers (and teachers) require an impersonal style avoiding these pronouns because they think (unjustly) that personal reference loses objectivity. If you must write impersonal style (which allows third-person references), you can still have highly readable copy; but you'll need to guard against dangling modifiers, an overuse of passive voice, expletive sentence beginnings ("it" and "there"), circumlocutions and other wordiness—and especially "the writer."

Checklist for Complete Analytical Reports

(continued)

Documentation (Doc)

When you use someone else's material, you are obligated to give credit to that source. The usual means are citations in the text, footnotes, source indications under graphs and tables, and a bibliography.

1. A bibliography is an alphabetical listing of all publications you have used in substantiating what you have said in the report. For the specific form, see pages 516–20 ff.

2. With a bibliography at the end, save your reader's time and confusion when you can: If you can quickly identify your reference in the text, do so. If you cite the author in the text, give no more than the publication and page reference in a citation. If you'll number your bibliographical entries, you can use parenthetical citations like (7:215) right in the text; but explain, the first time, that you mean page 215 in Item 7 of your bibliography.

3. If the reference is long and involved, relegate it to a footnote.

4. As long as you continue to draw from the same source, you need no further documentation. If you shift sources, however, you do need a new citation. When you cite a fact or figure from a table or chart, you do not need a source reference because you have the source indicated under the table or chart.

5. Source indications under graphs and/or tables are just the same as other citations of sources.

6. If you use footnotes, number them. Put a raised number at the end of your borrowed material; put the corresponding number at the bottom of the page and give the minimum required information. Separate footnotes from text by a line, and space so that the last line of footnote material falls at your normal margin point.

7. Number footnotes anew on each page; it is easier for you and your reader.

8. Interviews, speeches, letters, and questionnaires need not be in a bibliography. But credit should be given at the time of quoting or paraphrasing in the text (the person, his title if any, the date, place, and circumstances). A questionnaire is explained in the "Method" section; thereafter it need not be referred to as a source.

9. Quotations of more than two lines should be set out with additional white space all the way around (top, bottom, both sides). Further to distinguish them, they should be single-spaced. In this position, they need no quotation marks.

10. Since the synopsis and the terminal (conclusions and recommendations) are derived from the report, these derivations commonly contain no documentation.

Checklist for Complete Analytical Reports

(continued)

Terminal (T)

1. By definition, the terminal section is a derived section—a quick recap of the most important points you have covered. Any introduction of new material is therefore an indication of haphazard planning.

2. The emphasis here should be on selectivity rather than comprehensiveness of coverage. The reasons affecting your recommendation(s), arranged in order of importance, determine the order of presentation.

3. The more specific you can make this section, the better. Attach specific supporting figures or facts to your statements, so that your reader will not be forced back to preceding pages.

4. You'll almost always have to admit that you have not built a case which is completely beyond question; you'll often do well to admit that an alternative you have not chosen does have some points in its favor. Beware of overstating your case with too strong a word like "prove."

5. You might as well be wrong as inconclusive. If you vaguely toss the problem back to the reader with alternative courses of action of equal desirability, you're simply not doing the job assigned you. Remember, however, that the summary, "This report does not prove a thing," is a definite answer in the face of extensive analysis—and sometimes may be the very best conclusion.

6. The terminal must be a result of the analysis. Step by step you have arrived at tentative or implied conclusions in summary statements along the way. If you have analyzed and built the structure of your report well, you have kept your reader nodding his head in agreement and thus prepared him for the inevitable end result. The surprise ending is slipshod—and may be infuriating.

7. As a report writer, you are rarely in the driver's seat. Someone else will make the decision. You may be expected to suggest or advise but not to command. Phrasing like the two illustrative samples presented earlier in this chapter will help you to avoid appearing peremptory or dictatorial.

8. Try itemizing your conclusions and recommendations for preciseness and conciseness, but avoid overlisting. Combine points so closely related that they should be seen together.

Checklist for Complete Analytical Reports

(continued)

Synopsis (Sy)

The synopsis (or epitome or précis) should not be attempted until the entire report has been written. It is a highly condensed summary of your entire report, not a preface or foreword and most certainly not merely a rewrite of the contents table in sentence form. That would be a shell with no kernel. A good synopsis contains the most important parts of the report's kernel.

1. Preferably the first sentence of the synopsis contains a significant answer to the problem. If your report ended with a recommendation, work that recommendation in as the lead; if your report merely summarized, let your lead contain the condensed significant findings.

2. Include enough of the background for coherence; but detailed explanations of method, scope, history, and plan are unnecessary here.

3. Having effectively telescoped your terminal and then your introductory functions, follow the same order of points you have in the report itself.

4. Preferably maintain the same proportional amount of space given to points.

5. Work in as many specific, significant statistics and other facts as you can.

6. Rely on your good order of points and short transitional words and phrases for smoothness and coherence. You do not have enough space here to employ the topic statements, summary statements, and transitional sentences desirable in the longer report.

7. The synopsis should stand alone (so that copies of it could be run off and circulated to many readers for coherent reading without the complete report).

8. Use of present tense is probably even more desirable in the synopsis than elsewhere.

9. The synopsis concerns itself primarily with findings, not analysis (although there is more likely to be analysis in the synopsis than in the terminal section).

10. The primary difference between the synopsis and the terminal is that the terminal is highly selective; the synopsis covers the entire report.

Checklist for Complete Analytical Reports

(continued)

Transmittal Letter (TL)

1. The letter of transmittal should immediately and unmistakably establish the fact that the report is in the reader's hands.
2. Refer to the paraphrased topic and the time of the job assignment.
3. But tie these in naturally and conversationally. If you let the contractual aspect predominate ("Submitted herewith in accordance with your written request of April 5 . . ."), you inject an element of restraint right when you want your reader to feel most cordial toward your report.
4. If you have a synopsis a few pages later, you certainly do not want to dwell on findings, although you might reveal the final decision.
5. The introduction discusses methods and sources; rarely will you want to mention them here.
6. The emphasis of your letter should be given to showing your realization of the report's significance.
7. By implication or outright statement, express appreciation (usually your most natural way to end the letter).
8. The weak-kneed "I hope it will be useful" is unnecessarily disparaging. If you are so dubious about your report, rework it.

Authorization Letter (Au)

As the author of the report, you will of course never write your own letter of authorization. When you do have to write one, however, keep the following points in mind:

1. Since this is akin to an order letter (it just orders services instead of tangible goods), begin directly with a request for information.
   a) Make it as specific as possible.
   b) Establish the report idea early—in the opening sentence or possibly in a subject line.
2. To preclude rambling, incomplete reports, indicate
   a) The nature of the problem.
   b) The direction of the solution.
   c) How the results are to be used.
3. Suggestions for starting points and sources of material are helpful, and they frequently save the authorizer money.
4. Be explicit in identifying
   a) When you want the completed study.
   b) How much money you are prepared to spend.

Checklist for Complete Analytical Reports

Au—(continued)

5. Eliminate brusque and unfriendly overtones by exhibiting cordiality and gratitude.

Mechanics (M)

1. For the body of the report, margins on the sides should be at least 1 inch and usually no more than 1½ inches. The bottom margin is generally 1½ inches, top margin slightly less. If you will place your page number on the sixth or seventh line and then double-space, your top margin will be in good relationship to the others.

2. As long as you can insert two or three lines of your exposition, you need not start a new page (from the introduction through recommendations) when you go from one section to another. Don't isolate a caption from the beginning of the material it headlines.

3. If you use a binder, allow additional margins so that when the "bite" of the binder is taken off, your pages will still have proper margins.

4. Preliminary pages before the contents page need not be numbered; they are figured, however, in arriving at what the number of your synopsis page or pages should be. Figure it by counting every single page after the cover (lowercase roman numerals).

5. The page number for page 1 (as well as numbers for all similar first pages of report parts) appears six spaces up from the bottom of the page, centered. All other arabic page numerals generally go at the top right, marking the right-hand margin. No mark of punctuation (dashes, periods, parentheses) is desirable with page numbers.

6. For typed work:
   a) Headings in capital letters are superior to those in capitals and lowercase letters, and those in capitals and lowercase superior to initial-cap heads.
   b) Centered headings are superior to side headings above the copy, and side headings are superior to headings on the line with copy.

7. Any heading not in solid capitals should be underscored to make it stand out.

8. You need at least a triple space above centered heads, a double space below.

9. Centered captions of more than one line look better double-spaced. Center the second line too.

Checklist for Complete Analytical Reports

M—(concluded)

10. For any heading, spread the lines out; have fewer and longer lines.

11. Be consistent in whatever system you adopt for headings.

12. On the title page, display in three or four blocks:

    a) The complete report title (about 2 inches from the top).

    b) The person or persons receiving the report, plus title if appropriate, and name and address of the company if different from the writer's (slightly above the center of the page).

    c) The writer, his job title, name of company, address, and date of the report (spaced so that the last line is at least 1½ inches from the bottom of the page).

13. Center every line on the title page unless you have special ability to design some other good-looking layout.

14. The simple label Contents is adequate for the page(s) identifying your heads and page numbers.

15. By placement and type in the contents, show that the synopsis is a prefatory part. Without outline symbol, begin it at the left margin and give it its appropriate lowercase roman page number.

16. Likewise, show by placement and type that the bibliography, appendix, and index (if you have one) are appended parts by running them (without outline symbols) at the left margin. But they are numbered in arabic page numerals, since they follow the pages so numbered.

17. Use spaced-dot leader lines (. . . . not . . . .) to guide your reader's eye across the page to page-number indications. Remember to line the dots up vertically in successive lines.

18. Only the page where the section begins is listed on the contents table, not inclusive page numbers.

19. Every item listed on the contents page must have a page number indicated and must be readily seen on that page.

20. Align all numbers to the right. If you'll put periods after outline symbols (I. A. 1.) and keep the periods lined up, you'll have no trouble.

21. For letters, observe the same conventions of placement and form as for any letter. They do not have to follow the same layout as the report (indeed, they should not).

22. Even though your report is double-spaced, if you want or need to single-space letters, parts of the contents table, or the synopsis, go ahead. You should, however, double-space between headings of different levels on the contents page.

CASES FOR COMPLETE ANALYTICAL REPORTS

(Whether you are going to use Cases 1 and 4 or not, you should read them for points that should apply to nearly any major report-writing project. By reading them, you will probably get some further insights into the nature of reports. You may also get some additional tips that you will find helpful in preparing whatever major report you may be called upon to write.)

1. Subject to approval by your instructor, choose a topic for your long report. Preferably it should be a real problem actually faced by a company, organization, or individual; if not, it should be a problem likely to be faced by someone somewhere. It should be written for one reader or a very limited group of specific readers. A term-theme topic or something like a textbook chapter will not do because it is not a report. If you can't quickly give the name or title of somebody other than a teacher who might ask for such a report, your topic is unsuitable. It should be an analytical report: the relevant facts plus interpretation and evaluation of the advantages and disadvantages (the pros and cons) of at least two alternatives and the eventual selection of one in your final conclusions and recommendations. In other words, it must be a problem which you help someone to solve.

It should be a topic for which you can get information in the library *and* (not *or*) through either interviews, questionnaires, or your own observation or experimentation.

You should settle on a topic early in the term and should not change topics after midterm for any reason. The kind of problem we're talking about usually takes 10 to 20 pages for the text alone and requires most of the school term.

As your instructor directs, be prepared to submit on one typed page

a) A tentative title (not *now* worded to show a preconception of the outcome, but clear, concise and catching).

b) A one-sentence statement of the purpose of the report.

c) An indication of who the readers are and your relationship (actual or assumed) to them.

d) Sources and/or methods of collecting data, including the titles of five items from your tentative bibliography.

e) Major divisions (with subdivisions, if you like) of the coverage or body of the report.

Be prepared at any time to give your instructor a progress report in memo form, indicating what you have accomplished, what difficulties you've encountered, what remains to be done, and your plans for finishing.

At the time directed by your instructor, submit the report with appropriate cover, title page, letters of authorization and transmittal, contents listing, synopsis, body (including introduction, facts, and interpretations, conclusions, and recommendations), bibliography, and appendix if necessary.

As further clarification and suggestion, here are some of the better topics chosen by students in one class:

—Comparative evaluation of swimming pool (or goldfish pool) disinfectants under specific conditions.

—Comparative evaluation of materials and procedures to reduce black-shank damage to tobacco plants (specific conditions).

2. (Parts of this assignment probably should not be taken by a large class in a small community because too many students would be getting in too many businessmen's hair. This danger can be reduced, however, if students work in teams, at least on the data-collecting part of report writing. Also, consider the listed topics, which are *not* report titles, just suggestions to start thinking about what could be an endless list of the same kind of thing.)

For your choice of the following topics, assume that you can and will arrange amicably for access to, observation of, or experimentation with the obviously necessary facts (usually available only in a small local firm). Then write the kind of report (form, tone, and length) which the facts and the situation seem to require (or your instructor assigns). Assume that the appropriate person in the firm has asked you to do the report, and assume an appropriate position for yourself. In most cases you will likely be an employee; but in some, you might reasonably assume that you are a consultant on a fee basis. Each situation is to involve thorough study of existing conditions and application of well-established, up-to-date principles leading to recommendations for betterment of the situation.

—The letter writing done by a small local firm (only students who have studied letter writing should attempt this assignment).

—The public relations of a local firm (limited parts, if necessary).

—The accounting procedures of a local firm (limited aspects, if necessary).

—The advertising program and budget (not copy) of a small local firm.

—The advertising copy (not program and budget) used by a local firm.

—The physical layout (floor plan) of a local store (same problem a housewife works on when she moves the furniture around).

—The hiring and firing and promoting criteria (or just one criterion) and procedures.

—The financing arrangements of . . . .

—The stock control procedures . . . .

—The fringe benefits (or just one) or salary scales of . . . .

—The materials-handling procedures of . . . .

—Pilferage control in . . . .

—A motion-time study of some local processing or manufacturing operation.

—Any other problem of this type which you think of and can get facts on, and which your instructor approves.

—Proposed equipment and procedures for fire prevention and fighting in a certain forest.

—Should a given wood products company devote some of its lands to producing hardwoods?

—Solution to the problem of poor growth and fruiting/flowering of certain plants on a large lot.

—Critical analysis (with suggestions) of the company publications of a comparatively small local firm.

—Possible computer applications in a local library (or company).

—Suggestions for improving appeal and income at a small fee-charging, publicly operated park and lake.

—Would a proposed campground (private, specific location) be a successful business venture?

—Analysis of a local company's employee relations problems, with suggestions for improvement.

—Would a specific large wood products company be wise to set up a sawmill and/or paper mill in a certain locality where it has some landholdings?

—To have or not to have coffee breaks for a given company's employees.

—What the people of a 10,000–100,000 community think of their public schools, with emphasis on suggested improvements.

3. Write the long report authorized in memo problem 31, page 640. Supplement the published data with data acquired through letters and/or interviews, as agreed upon by you and your instructor.

4. One of the requests coming to your desk as director of Factseekers, Inc., New York 10032, is from the president of (name of firm supplied by your instructor). The company is a chain of retail (type of store supplied by your instructor) stores with outlets in most major cities. The chain is now contemplating opening a store in either one of two cities (names of two cities supplied by your instructor).

You are asked to make a report evaluating the two as potential locations for the new store.

The letter to you as director, signed by the company president, reads:

Will you please submit in report form your analysis of retail sales possibilities for (specific goods) in (specific cases)?

Before deciding where our next branch will be, we would like the opinion of a firm of your caliber.

Naturally we want to know the story on population, buying power, retail sales—with special emphasis on (specific goods)—competition, and current business. But please include other data which will be helpful to us in making our choice.

Please do not attempt to cover taxes, wage scales, real estate costs, or availability of sites.

Since we plan to have the store in operation within a year's time, will you please confirm that you can submit the report no later than (specific date as assigned), subject to the same rates as on previous studies?

From secondary library sources you can get all the necessary comparative data: *Statistical Abstract of the United States; County and City Data Book; Market Guide of Editor and Publisher;* Rand McNally's *Commercial Atlas and Marketing Guide; Sales Management Survey of Buying Power; Printers' Ink's* special studies like *Sales Planning Guide* and *Major American Markets;* and *Consumer Markets,* published by the Standard Rate and Data Service. The foregoing are some of your more useful sources. But they are not intended to be an exhaustive list. You will of course want to consult the censuses of population, business, and manufacturers for (respectively) breakdowns of populations, influence of wholesaling and retailing on the local economy, and the value added to the economy by manufacturing. In all cases you will want the latest reliable data; recency of information is important.

Your entire analysis should be focused on the answer to the question: Which of the two towns is a better market for selling more of the specific merchandise this store sells? Population is, of course, a factor—size as well as distribution and character. The retail market area always needs examining. Income figures are significant (a person with $4 is in a better position to buy than one with only $2). Retail sales indicate whether people are willing to spend their money (total retail sales, per capita retail sales, and retail sales figures in the particular line you're investigating—if you can find them). Sources of business strength are appropriate considerations (a manufacturing town suffers more than a distribution center during a recession; a community depending primarily upon farming for its sustenance weathers economic storms more readily than one heavily dependent upon shipbuilding, for instance). And the current business picture (as measured by construction, postal figures, employment, and bank deposits) is always examined for its diagnostic value.

The list of topics above is merely to help you start thinking about what to include; it is not intended to be inclusive, orderly, or arbitrary. For instance, no study of this kind would ever omit competitive factors.

This is assigned: Exclude any discussion of banking facilities, communications facilities (newspapers, radio stations, advertising agencies), and transportation facilities. These are adequate in both cities and so would not affect the decision. But when you set out these limitations in the introductory section of the report, indicate in a footnote the sources where the reader can quickly and easily find the information if he wants to check it or tell him frankly that such data are not available if that is the case. Furthermore, the people would have done enough reading themselves to know where the cities are—and the pertinent geographical and climate features.

Although, as an intelligent approach to the analysis, you will want to do some background reading about the cities (in a good encyclopedia, possibly in a chamber of commerce release), *you will not use these sources as documentation (evidence) in your report.*

Once you've made the final decision of what factors to include and— just as important—the order in which to lay them out, the analysis becomes a matter of simply comparing the two cities simultaneously to show which city is the better market—more people with more money to spend, and the apparent willingness to spend it, especially for this kind of merchandise.

Do not attempt to turn out a chamber of commerce root-for-the-home team piece of propaganda. Impersonally, impartially present the facts about the two cities and make your decision on the total evidence.

An analytical report is not just a compilation of tables and labels. Your report must depend on the quotation of facts from other sources; these are incorporated primarily in the wealth of statistical display (graphics primarily, for readability). Without these, your report has no base and, in the reader's mind, no authenticity. But the most significant part of the report is your own expository (analytical) comment which explains the significance of the data you have gathered.

Of course, your report will be graded on physical appearance and mechanical correctness (freedom from errors in spelling, punctuation, and grammar). It will be graded most heavily, however, on

1. Organization (the order of points for logic and emphasis).
2. Readability (stylistic factors).
3. Complete, authentic evidence and its reliability and documentation.

5. Find a recent article giving facts about some significant new findings in your field. Assume that you did the research by assignment while employed by a firm which might well put the new findings to use. Write the research and findings in a report to your boss not only telling about research procedures and results but suggesting applications in the company's operations.

(If your course involves the writing of magazine articles for specialized journals—technical journalism—your instructor may want to make this modification of the assignment: Rewrite the original article with the original and the rewrite in parallel columns on the page; cross-match changes by notations in the two, like footnote numbers in the text and matching ones on the footnotes; and justify, by explanation, every change. The instructor may or may not want you to apply the Robert C. Gunning Fog Index and/or the Rudolf Flesch Readability Formula to both versions as a part of the justification for your changes.)

6. Assume that you are a scout for any major-league baseball team and that your team faces any other team in an important game (or series). On the basis of a thorough analysis of the opposing team's and its individual players' past records, recommend specific tactics. You may assume that you scouted the opposing team many times and recorded individual and team records in detail. Since you didn't really, get your data wherever you can —next-day newspaper accounts, special baseball books, or the most recent *World Almanac* (which has a surprising amount of detail on baseball). Obviously, your report will be addressed to the manager. Would your players also read all of it or even the parts that most affect how they should play their positions? This report would not be attempted by anyone who doesn't know baseball well. And of course, it would be restricted information until after the game. (Incidentally, the idea for this assignment came from post-series newspaper accounts of just such a report prepared by the series winner and given credit by the manager for his team's winning. He admitted, however, that the players had a little to do with the win.)

7. Inspect the equipment and/or furniture in a laboratory on your campus where at least some of it needs to be replaced. Write a report which evaluates the equipment and/or furniture and specifically justifies and recommends any replacements and/or additions. To whom should you address the report? What role are you playing—i.e., who do you assume you *are* to be writing the report? What other sources of information will you use to supplement inspection? Should you recommend specific brands, models, and prices of things to be bought? If so, you will need to get acquainted with catalogs and brochures on such things—or with the famous Sweet's File, the architect's bible, available in any architect's office or architectural library.

(As a modification of the situation, write the report proposing and justifying just what equipment and/or furniture to buy for a new laboratory, a whole building, or some other new structure your school is now constructing.)

8. A few years ago you, as a research man in the Research and Development Department of your state government, compiled the following table as the start on a project. When you explained to your boss, however, he squashed the idea and has kept you busy on other things since. Then yesterday, as if he had originated the idea, he asked you to make just the study you proposed earlier. You didn't remind him, but you know you have a

Measure of personal income (millions of dollars—not adjusted for seasonal variations)

State	1957-59 Average	February, 1963	January, 1964	February, 1964	Percent Change	First Two Months 1963	First Two Months 1964	Percent Change
Alabama	$ 366.8	$ 439.6	$ 471.0	$ 468.6	+ 6.6%	$ 888.1	$ 939.6	+ 5.8%
Alaska	44.9	53.9	53.5	54.8	+ 1.7	105.8	108.3	+ 2.4
Arizona	184.4	269.1	299.0	289.8	+ 7.7	545.2	588.8	+ 8.0
Arkansas	182.3	229.6	249.0	246.8	+ 7.5	460.8	495.8	+ 7.6
California	3,160.6	4,165.8	4,425.2	4,430.5	+ 6.4	8,350.4	8,855.7	+ 6.1
Colorado	296.8	378.1	402.3	398.9	+ 5.5	754.6	801.2	+ 6.2
Connecticut	551.9	686.6	722.6	728.1	+ 6.0	1,379.7	1,450.7	+ 5.1
Delaware	103.8	124.1	137.0	133.5	+ 7.6	250.3	270.5	+ 8.1
District of Columbia	117.9	217.4	222.0	228.6	+ 5.2	436.7	450.6	+ 3.2
Florida	711.9	1,001.9	1,113.5	1,114.8	+11.3	2,015.2	2,228.3	+10.6
Georgia	477.4	605.5	659.6	660.3	+ 9.1	1,212.4	1,319.9	+ 8.9
Hawaii	98.5	136.9	141.0	142.7	+ 4.2	272.8	283.7	+ 4.0
Idaho	93.7	111.3	122.8	118.3	+ 6.3	228.7	241.1	+ 5.4
Illinois	2,048.2	2,458.0	2,597.4	2,569.1	+ 4.5	4,935.2	5,166.5	+ 4.7
Indiana	779.9	950.0	1,009.5	1,003.4	+ 5.6	1,904.8	2,012.9	+ 5.7
Iowa	438.0	529.6	581.4	553.0	+ 4.4	1,080.7	1,134.4	+ 5.0
Kansas	344.1	410.6	442.7	429.6	+ 4.6	844.1	872.3	+ 3.3
Kentucky	364.3	429.8	527.3	458.6	+ 6.7	907.5	985.9	+ 8.6
Louisiana	416.1	477.2	534.1	517.5	+ 8.4	960.1	1,051.6	+ 9.5
Maine	137.8	167.8	173.3	172.8	+ 3.0	336.1	346.1	+ 3.0
Maryland	559.9	725.5	759.1	764.4	+ 5.4	1,442.0	1,523.5	+ 5.7
Massachusetts	983.2	1,182.2	1,212.1	1,232.9	+ 4.3	2,370.5	2,445.0	+ 3.1
Michigan	1,414.7	1,696.1	1,835.3	1,801.8	+ 6.2	3,405.1	3,637.1	+ 6.8
Minnesota	537.9	653.1	697.9	681.8	+ 4.4	1,318.2	1,379.7	+ 4.7

Mississippi	191.3	238.5	258.0	256.5	+ 7.5	485.8	514.5	+ 5.9
Missouri	728.8	864.8	921.9	914.6	+ 5.8	1,747.6	1,836.5	+ 5.1
Montana	109.6	131.2	139.2	135.4	+ 3.2	268.9	274.6	+ 2.1
Nebraska	226.7	286.1	313.6	290.3	+ 1.5	597.1	603.9	+ 1.1
Nevada	58.1	94.4	104.4	104.5	+10.7	186.2	208.9	+12.2
New Hampshire	93.6	114.6	116.3	117.4	+ 2.4	231.0	233.7	+ 1.2
New Jersey	1,225.2	1,529.6	1,570.9	1,610.5	+ 5.3	3,059.7	3,181.4	+ 4.0
New Mexico	129.1	151.4	165.4	159.4	+ 5.3	307.7	324.8	+ 5.6
New York	3,568.0	4,314.0	4,473.8	4,493.9	+ 4.2	8,629.1	8,967.7	+ 3.9
North Carolina	527.6	652.2	711.3	709.8	+ 8.8	1,313.3	1,421.1	+ 8.2
North Dakota	82.6	115.5	142.8	117.7	+ 1.9	252.6	260.5	+ 3.1
Ohio	1,760.5	2,041.1	2,151.0	2,166.2	+ 6.1	4,095.2	4,317.2	+ 5.4
Oklahoma	326.5	400.6	426.3	424.9	+ 6.1	813.3	851.2	+ 4.7
Oregon	300.0	363.8	392.5	401.6	+10.4	703.2	794.1	+ 8.8
Pennsylvania	1,996.2	2,299.1	2,367.5	2,429.5	+ 5.7	4,598.9	4,797.0	+ 4.3
Rhode Island	146.2	174.5	179.0	180.4	+ 3.4	349.5	359.4	+ 2.8
South Carolina	247.0	312.3	336.8	340.7	+ 9.1	630.1	677.5	+ 7.5
South Dakota	90.1	115.5	127.0	120.4	+ 4.2	244.8	247.4	+ 1.1
Tennessee	422.9	517.6	562.7	549.0	+ 6.1	1,044.4	1,111.7	+ 6.4
Texas	1,440.4	1,697.2	1,839.2	1,798.8	+ 6.0	3,465.1	3,638.0	+ 5.0
Utah	127.8	169.0	175.7	172.1	+ 1.8	340.0	347.8	+ 2.3
Vermont	54.8	65.8	67.9	68.3	+ 3.8	131.9	136.2	+ 3.3
Virginia	557.5	702.0	751.3	755.5	+ 7.6	1,411.3	1,506.8	+ 6.8
Washington	505.0	623.0	649.7	654.2	+ 5.0	1,246.2	1,303.9	+ 4.6
West Virginia	253.2	273.5	286.4	292.5	+ 6.9	547.5	578.9	+ 5.7
Wisconsin	652.2	792.2	838.4	837.5	+ 5.7	1,595.8	1,675.9	+ 5.0
Wyoming	57.2	65.8	68.5	66.6	+ 1.2	131.4	135.1	+ 2.8
Nation	$30,353.1	$37,205.0	$39,526.1	$39,368.8	+ 5.8%	$74,859.6	$78,894.9	+ 5.4%

running start—that you will simply have to add new columns of up-to-date figures—and perhaps drop out old ones—for a broader base.

Of course, you'll have to get other kinds of information too, for the basic idea is to provide information needed by your state legislators and other government officials, and for business firms and individuals in the state and considering moving in. The publicity and advertising men in your department will no doubt welcome your report.

The nature of your work, and particularly of this report, will make it largely informational. You can draw some conclusions based on your thorough analysis, although the variety of users of the report may prevent you from making specific recommendations. In other words, the report is more like a research report than the usual analytical report.

Add other columns of information on population, percent of income spent on education and higher education, and comparative quality of the school systems—figures for all of which are available—to make this a long report addressed to the top men in education.

9. Assume that in planning to reorganize its undergraduate curriculum, the marketing department, where you are assistant to the head, has sent a questionnaire to all 152 members of the AACSB (American Association of Collegiate Schools of Business) and 395 other colleges and universities. Of these, 256 (52.4 percent) have replied, although many of them have few or no marketing courses.

The head of the department (your boss) has dumped the whole lot of questionnaires on your desk with instructions to tabulate them, study them, and write a report for him and the rest of the marketing faculty to consider before revising and rewriting for the dean, the college curriculum comittee, and ultimately the whole faculty of the college of business. Fortunately for you, the questionnaire asked that credit hours always be figured as semester hours.

You have found that 81.9 percent of the AACSB schools replied. Six replies came from graduate schools of business, so you have not tabulated them. Seventeen other replies were unusable for various reasons. Of the remaining 233 replies, which you have tabulated, 70 are AACSB schools, and 140 offer degrees in marketing.

You now have each question with the tabulations under it (the following tables). Now the real headwork begins. You have yet to organize the findings for best interpretation and presentation, to figure out the best tables and graphics to use in the presentation, to interpret the findings, and to write your results in the best form and style you can muster. Don't just sit there; do something.

For each of the courses listed in the following table, put *M* in the column indicating your opinion about its importance to marketing *M*ajors and *B* in the column indicating its importance to *B*usiness students not majoring in marketing. (Usable replies: 228.)

Course title	Required		Desirable		Less desirable		Not necessary		No answer	
	M	B	M	B	M	B	M	B	M	B
Principles of Marketing	226	199	1	21	0	0	1	3	0	5
Retailing	130	12	65	64	8	42	9	48	16	62
Retail Sales Promotion	19	1	57	9	62	38	45	93	45	87
Advertising	168	34	44	83	8	31	2	26	6	54
Advanced Advertising	18	2	62	5	70	30	40	113	38	78
Salesmanship	105	39	50	57	37	28	18	51	18	53
Wholesaling	46	1	83	21	49	44	21	85	29	77
Industrial Marketing	35	4	105	21	42	43	16	88	30	72
Marketing Management ...	139	23	54	59	8	36	6	51	21	59
Retail Store Management ...	26	0	73	14	52	43	38	98	39	73
Sales Management	104	13	72	45	10	45	5	54	27	71
Marketing Research	170	12	41	64	9	43	1	44	7	65
Advanced Marketing Theory	56	2	77	18	49	29	16	104	30	75
Purchasing	33	8	79	33	61	38	22	79	33	70
Marketing Case Problems ..	110	15	72	32	18	37	6	75	31	69
Product Development	12	1	66	13	67	30	41	107	42	77
Agricultural Marketing	6	1	33	3	75	25	69	121	45	78
Cooperative Marketing	5	0	24	5	64	17	90	129	45	77
Distribution Cost Analysis ..	40	7	95	35	39	39	18	76	36	71
Supervised Fieldwork	20	1	63	12	42	17	56	119	47	79
Independent Research	29	3	77	29	40	20	37	100	45	76
Marketing of Specific Products	1	0	15	0	36	6	111	127	65	95

Please indicate the number of semester hours you think should be required of marketing majors. (Usable replies: 231.)

	None	1–3	4–6	7–9	10 or over
Accounting	1	7	133	62	28
Business Statistics	7	135	81	5	3
Business Mathematics	82	115	31	3	0
Finance	21	116	78	12	4
Business Law	13	77	130	10	1
Business History	171	55	5	0	0
Introduction to Business ..	137	87	7	0	0
Business Cycles	116	112	3	0	0
Real Estate	206	25	1	0	0
Business Education	226	2	1	2	0
Insurance	153	66	12	0	0
Business Research	108	112	9	2	0
Management	35	139	45	10	2
Personnel	95	118	17	0	1
Policy and Administration ..	112	107	10	2	0
Production	118	104	8	1	0
Human Relations	140	75	16	0	0
Foreign Trade	166	60	2	1	2
Transportation	127	94	6	2	2
Business Writing	80	131	20	0	0
Secretarial Training	205	22	4	0	0

Please indicate the number of semester hours you think should be required of marketing majors in these nonbusiness areas (Usable replies: 224.)

	None	1–3	4–6	7–9	10 or over
Language Arts (any)		1	0	1	7
English	14	4	114	40	52
Modern language	157	8	37	5	17
Classical language	221	1	2	0	0
Speech	45	136	40	3	0
Humanities (any)		4	21	5	7
Philosophy	99	85	20	5	14
Religion	173	15	26	5	5
Literature	106	34	77	4	3
Architecture	221	3	0	0	0
Art	172	40*	5	0	0
Music	188	27*	2	0	0
Social Sciences (any)		3	12	2	17
Anthropology	193	26	5	0	0
Economics	10	3	102	48	61
Geography	146	64	13	1	0
History	88	30	94	6	6
Political Science	104	73	44	2	1
Psychology	55	102	54	7	6
Sociology	99	95	25	4	1
Laboratory Science (any)		6	59	40	10
Biology	190	18	12	4	0
Chemistry	200	13	8	3	0
Geology	218	3	3	0	0
Physics	205	9	9	1	0
Mathematics	54	51	84	21	13
Journalism	203	18	3	0	0

* Seven said either art or music.

chapter 16	# Writing short reports

THE BEST FORM for a report depends on the situation—mainly who its reader is, its purpose, and its length. This chapter explains and illustrates various kinds of short reports written in the most important forms.

Like all reports, short ones can be classified on various bases. Their most common names, however, point to two bases: form and content. To avoid making up new names for them, in this chapter we list and discuss them by their common names, although this system does not provide a strictly logical classification.

Because the reports apparently named by content have become pretty well associated with certain forms, however, the seeming violation of logic in classification is more apparent than real. The primary basis of classification here is therefore form (with the exceptions explained where they apply). Yet the primary emphasis is not on learning the forms themselves but on the uses of different forms and the information, organization, interpretation, and style in the reports.

The illustrations are not *presented as perfect reports, and certainly are* not *to be followed slavishly or copied parrotlike. At best, they show acceptable content, form, and general style for their particular situations as starters to your thinking on these points for your situation.*

Although we recognize that strictly informational, periodic reports are the most numerous kind, we do not devote our main attention to them because they are mostly printed forms to be filled in with figures and perhaps a little other writing. They are thus real report-writing jobs only to the people who devise the original forms. We therefore treat the commonly used forms which do raise real report-writing problems.

Letter reports

Many short reports, usually one to four pages, are written in regular business letter form. Usually they go between organizations rather than between departments of the same organization, where memorandums are more likely.

Since the letter report is likely to be longer than the usual letter, however, and since it *is* a report, it may take on the following special features of reports, while otherwise using the form explained in Chapter 1:

1. More than usually careful organization.
2. Objectivity (absence of emotional suasion, viewing both sides of the situation, enough interweaving or implying of methods and sources to assure soundness).
3. Use of appropriate subject lines, subheads, and itemizations where helpful.
4. Use of graphic devices where helpful and economically feasible.

Depending on whether the message will likely meet with reader approval, disappointment, or resistance, the letter report should follow the A–, B–, or (rarely) C–plan, as explained on pp. 55–59 and illustrated thoroughly in Chapters 5, 7, and 8, respectively. More specifically, any of the organizational plans discussed on p. 509 may apply to a letter report.

Although a letter report, like any other, needs to convince the reader that its facts are reliable, it rarely needs a separate section or even a separate paragraph explaining authorization, purpose, and methods and sources used in collecting data. Most likely the writer got the assignment because the boss knew he had the information in his head or at his fingertips. In other words, he was already recognized as an expert on the subject. If not, he may have been told just how to study the problem. Or for the simple problems appropriate to letter reports, the methods and sources are frequently so obvious as to need no explanation.

If any explanations are necessary, usually the best way to give them is in incidental phrases interwoven right along with the information: ". . . seems to be the best solution to our problem of . . ."; "Inspection of . . . reveals . . ."; "Legal precedent in cases like . . . is clearly . . ."; "Microscopic examination shows . . ."; or ". . . , according to such authorities as . . . ."

Indeed, letter reports are like other reports except for the form which gives them their name, the limits of length and hence of topics for which they are suitable, and their almost necessarily natural style. A letter in impersonal style would be almost a joke. Although we do not think any kind of report should necessarily be in impersonal style, even those people who do will almost certainly approve a natural style in letter reports.

Two common types of letter reports are those about job and credit applicants (personnel and credit reports), already discussed on pp. 119 and 120–21, respectively. You should study both the explanations and the illustrations. You notice that both the illustrations use subject lines effectively. Note, too, that both begin immediately with important information because they face no problem of reader disappointment or resistance.

Personnel and credit reports, however, do have the legal problem of avoiding libel suit by referring to the request for information, trying to be fair to both parties, and asking confidential use of the information. Notice how the two illustrations handle that problem.

These two kinds of reports should be informational, in that they should rely on facts and subordinate or entirely eliminate unsupported opinions —and certainly recommendations. But letter reports may be either informational or analytical. In some cases they are more nearly directives than reports, but directives are more likely to be in memo form.

A report that is quite similar to the preceding except in being analytical (first paragraph) instead of informational is the following:

Dear Mr. Linton: Subject: Charles R. Sheppard

The best suggestion I can give in answer to your request for advice is that you ask Sheppard for an explanation of his unofficial withdrawal from school here and act accordingly.

He enrolled at XXXX University for his second year last fall. For reasons which we do not know, he apparently attended no classes after the Christmas holidays. Consequently his semester grades for all five courses he was taking were F's, as shown on the transcript you have.

Since he was registered under PL 346, I have found from the local Veterans' Administration office that he did check out there by letter on January 4. He apparently thought that this was an official withdrawal from school.

If Sheppard could give a reasonable explanation of his actions during January, he would be welcome back here. His grades for the first year's work average a strong C.

If you prefer that we handle the situation, however, we will change his F's to N's and send you a new transcript on Sheppard's satisfactory explanation of his unofficial withdrawal here.

Because the following message is somewhat bad news and the reader may be reluctant to take the suggested action, the report uses the more convincing inductive rather than the faster-moving deductive plan. You will note, too, that it uses no subject line. To do so would defeat the psychological purpose of the inductive plan. As you always should when you have a step-by-step procedure or a series of pointed, emphatic principles, qualities, conclusions, or recommendations to convey, this report uses itemization effectively at the end.

Dear Mr. Rogers:

In our audit of your company's books on January 16, we discovered that for years the total net profit has been added to surplus.

This procedure is usually correct. For the past three years you have had a bond agreement, however, which specifies that a sinking-fund reserve of 3 percent of the par value of the bonds must be set up annually out of surplus. That agreement

is legally binding. Moreover, state law requires you to set
up the reserve in this situation. The remaining profit, of
course, can be added to surplus.

Laws of this type protect investors and brokers who desire a
true picture of the financial condition of companies.

The laws also give you protection. The setting up of a
separate reserve prevents the unlawful declaration of
dividends by the directors. In other words, the proper
presentation of surplus figures is an aid to better
management.

We therefore recommend that you

1. Take immediate steps to set up the reserve.

2. Transfer to it now, from surplus, 3 percent of the par
   value of the bonds for each of the past three years.

3. Regularly each year for the duration of the bond
   agreement transfer the required amount from surplus to
   the reserve.

Both the shortness and the nature of the material made divisional
headings useless in the preceding illustrations of letter reports. Conversely, both length and content make headings almost mandatory for
effective presentation in letter reports of two pages or more, as in the
following. It is a reply to a school superintendent's request that his recent
graduates tell him about college expenses for passing on to high-school
seniors. (You'll notice that the way of life pictured is not common on
college campuses today, but that does not keep the report from showing
the helpfulness of carefully classifying information under suitable headings.)

Dear Mr. Loudenslager:

I certainly was glad to receive your letter of January 20. It
is nice to know that John is not finding school as hard as he
thought it was going to be.

Here is the information you requested. These costs are based
on one semester here for the male student. Although I have
not kept detailed records, my figures are more realistic than
the somewhat outdated ones in the catalog you have.

Being neither plush nor poor, I have spent according to the
Typical column, but I have classmates whose expenses more
nearly match both the Liberal and the Conservative figures.

Estimated Expenses Table

	Conservative	Typical	Liberal
Course fee	$000	$000	$000
Room and board	000	000	000
Books and supplies	00	00	00
Physical education	00	00	00
R.O.T.C.	00	00	00
Clothing	00	00	00
Laundry and dry cleaning	00	00	00
Transportation	00	00	000
Incidentals	00	00	000

FIXED EXPENSES

Course fee.—Although the regular course fee is $000, certain courses and curricula like music, law, medicine, and veterinary medicine do require extra fees. Insofar as I know, these extra fees have not changed from the catalog you have.

Physical Education.—All students are required to take two years' credit in gym. The $10 fee is for the first semester only.

R.O.T.C.—All able-bodied male students are required to take two years' credit in military science. The fee will be refunded when the equipment is returned after completion of the course.

VARIABLE EXPENSES

Living Expense

College residence halls.—Adequate dormitories are available on the campus. Meals are served in the dining rooms seven days a week. Room and board is $000 a semester. The resident is required to supply linen, toweling, and pillow.

Fraternities.—Room and board in a fraternity may vary from a low of $000 to a high of $000. The average is about $000.

Cooperatives.—If a student desires, he may join a co-op, in which a group may defray part of the cost of living by all helping with the work. Room and board in a co-op usually runs to about $000 a semester.

Individual rooms.—Rooms in approved homes cost about $00-$00 a semester, two men to a room. Food in local restaurants costs about $000-$000. Only graduate students and married students are allowed to have apartments.

Apartments.—Rents for apartments will run from $00 for the most modest to $000 depending upon whether the student shares it or occupies it alone. Also, utilities must be paid.

Working for meals.—Male students who want to do so can nearly always find jobs working for their meals in dormitory dining rooms or in local restaurants.

Clothing.—Some students who attend college are forced to buy entirely new wardrobes. Others may get along quite well for some time with what they have. So clothing expense is highly variable, as my figures in the table show. For most students, college clothing costs should be only a little more than for high school clothing.

Laundry and dry cleaning.—Facilities are available for the student to do his own laundry in the dormitories. Several laundromats are also convenient to the area. Dry-cleaning prices are the same as at home. Again, an individual can spend as much or as little as he chooses.

Transportation

At school.—The majority of the activities are located on the campus within walking distance. Bus fare to town is 30 cents a round trip. Taxis are also available. The student who expects to have his own car will find that a jalopy is not the thing here and that keeping a respectable car can hardly cost less than $450 a semester. Depreciation alone could cost that much without anything for insurance, upkeep, and gasoline.

<u>To and from school</u>.—Most students will find it inconvenient as well as expensive to go home more than twice a semester. The round-trip bus fare, the cheapest way, is $16.80.

<u>Incidentals</u>

<u>Necessities</u>.—Students need a small amount of money to spend while out with a group for coffee, cokes, shows, and the like. Also, there is the ever-present emergency of haircuts, shoestrings, razor blades, toothpaste, etc. Normally one may expect to spend $000 a semester on such things.

<u>Dating</u>.—Taking a girl out for an evening can cost a lot of money, or it can be done fairly inexpensively. Some of the larger dances can cost up to $30 for the evening. The item is highly flexible.

If anyone in this year's high-school senior class has any specific questions about this school, I'll try to answer as best I can. One thing you can safely tell all who are thinking about coming here: They had better learn to write correctly and to handle simple math, or they will be in trouble.

Except for item 1 (on form), the checklist for memos on page 594 applies equally to memo and letter reports.

Memorandums

Just as letter reports are more likely for communicating between organizations, memorandums are more appropriate within the same organization. Along with a stock of letterheads, among the supplies of almost any well-run office is a pad of printed memo forms (usually half sheets 5½ by 8½ inches turned either way). The printed headings used in the illustrations of memorandums in this section show the main variations (see pp. 589 and 593). Item 1 of the checklist for memos (p. 594) gives further details of form.

Except for the differences in form and use, memorandums follow the instructions already given for letter reports. They are, however, inclined (1) to be ephemeral and hence less formal (often being handwritten without carbon), (2) to make even greater use of itemization (almost characteristically), and (3) to become directives going down the chain of command.

One of the most common and effective techniques is itemization. Numbering each paragraph almost forces the writer into careful organization, precise statement, and conciseness.

Two simple memos showing slightly different forms follow:

UNIVERSITY OF FLORIDA

DATE *Jan. 20*

MEMO TO: *Andrea*

FROM: *CWM*

SUBJECT: <u>*Work for today*</u>

Since I have an appointment downtown
during your working hours, please
1) record the grades of the attached
   papers in my grade book.
2) check the revised class lists
   against my rolls and return
   the lists to the Registrar with
   proper notations.
3) get the <u>Congressional Record</u>, vol. 88,
   Part 9, from the Library and
   copy Congressman Hill's comments
   on p. A-1486, and
4) make a table showing percentages,
   by class and major, of students
   on the E#255 lecture lists (both
   lists in one table).

January 12, 196–

TO: All Occupants of Business Administration Building, Journalism Building, University College Building, Forestry Building

FROM: R. F. Noonan, Building and Utilities Department

SUBJECT: <u>Interruption of Electrical Service</u>

The electricity will be off in your buildings on Tuesday, January 13, from 8 a.m. to 4 p.m.

Temporary electric service will be provided for lights in main departmental offices and for all telephones.

All electricity will be off for approximately one-half hour from 8 to 8:30 a.m. and 4 to 4:30 p.m. for the connection and removal of the temporary service.

Notice these details in the two memos: One is on an ephemeral topic to one reader; so efficiency pointed to a quick, handwritten memo. Like many, the other went to a number of people. It was a ditto form. Since some of its readers would not have known who the writer was, he gave his official title. The other writer would have wasted time even to write out his full name. The subject lines in both are carefully phrased to indicate the content concisely and are underscored to make them stand out. Since itemization seemed helpful in one but would have served no purpose in the other, the writers used it accordingly. Neither needs a signature at the end: The name appears above, and no reader will fear to act on the memo without the kind of authentic signature a banker requires on your check.

The U.S. military services make extensive use of memos, with their own slight modifications, as indicated in the following illustration:

HEADQUARTERS
SECOND UNITED STATES ARMY
Fort George G. Meade, Maryland

AIAAG-CP Byron, Kenneth Hugh   31 July 19—

SUBJECT: Promotion as a Reserve Commissioned Officer of the Army under the Reserve Officer Personnel Act of 1954

THRU: Commanding General   A—7 May XX
          XXI US ARMY Corps (Reserve)

                                    B—None

TO: Captain Kenneth Hugh Byron, 02 203 034,
        MPC, USAR
        1812 West Grace Street
        Richmond, Virginia 20020

   1. The Secretary of the Army has directed that you be informed that by direction of the President you are promoted as a Reserve commissioned officer of the Army effective on the date shown after A above to the grade in the branch and component shown in address above.

   2. Promotion service for promotion to the next higher grade

will be computed from the effective date of this promotion, unless there is a date shown after B above, in which case it will be computed from that date.

3. No acceptance or oath of office is required. Unless you expressly decline this promotion within 60 days, your assumption of office will be effective as shown after A above.

4. A commission evidencing your promotion is enclosed which will be returned in case you decline the promotion.

5. Authority: AR 135-155, paragraph 15.

FOR THE COMMANDER:

1 Incl	G. W. WILLIAMS
DD Form 1A (Commission)	Captain, AGC
Copies Furnished:	Asst Adj Gen
TAG	
CG, XXI USA Corps	
MRU	
File	

Probably the biggest user of memos is the biggest business in the world—the United States government. It has its own form and its own directions for using the form, as illustrated and applied in the accompanying memo directive (reprinted form *Secretarial Handbook*, Tennessee Valley Authority, rev. ed., 1960, pp. II–10*a*, II–10*c*).

TVA 64 (OS.4.59)
United States Government
MEMORANDUM   TENNESSEE VALLEY AUTHORITY

TO   : Maybelle Campbell,
              Reproduction and Stenographic Unit, 421 Wall
              Avenue, Knoxville (2)

FROM   : Carl Angle, Office Methods Staff, 619 LB,
              Chattanooga

DATE   : June 15, 1960

SUBJECT: STYLE FOR INTEROFFICE MEMORANDUMS

Attention: Yetta Konigsberg

This is an illustration of the office memorandum. Its use is described in the enclosed copy of the Secretarial Handbook. A style sheet for the half-size memorandum is also enclosed.

The items in the heading begin two spaces from the preceding colons, and the body of the memorandum uses the left margin established by the placement of the heading. The right margin should be at least one inch but not more than one and one-half inches.

If two lines are necessary in the "To" or "From" line, the second line is indented two spaces and the break is made between units of the address. But the line should be extended into the margin if that will avoid two lines.

Titles of courtesy, <u>Mr.</u>, <u>Mrs.</u>, and <u>Miss</u>, are omitted before the names in the heading, but professional titles such as <u>Dr.</u> are used. Job titles are not used when the organization unit provides a satisfactory address. The "To" and "From" lines should be parallel in content. No punctuation is used at the ends of the lines in the heading.

The text begins on the fourth line below the subject. (If additional space is needed on the half-size memorandum, begin on the second line below the subject.) When an attention line is used, it is typed on the fourth line below the subject, with no end punctuation, and the text begins two lines below the attention line.

Block style is used for memorandums; that is, paragraphs are not indented. Single spacing is used within the paragraphs, double spacing between them. If headings are used in a memorandum (as for a progress report), side headings and paragraph headings begin at the left margin. If numbered paragraphs or items appear in the memorandum:

1. The first line begins at the left margin. (Note that in indented style, as for formal reports, the first line—the number—is indented five spaces.)

2. Additional lines are aligned with the first word in the paragraph, as shown in this sample.

2

Maybelle Campbell
June 15, 1960

STYLE FOR INTEROFFICE MEMORANDUMS

This page illustrates the setup for the second and succeeding pages of a memorandum. Each page after the first is numbered with an Arabic numeral on the fourth line from the top of the page, flush with the left margin. The addressee's name is typed two lines below the page number, and the date immediately below the name. The subject is typed two lines below the date, and the text begins on the fourth line below the subject.

No complimentary close is used. No signature line is used since the signer's name appears on the "From" line and his initials or signature in the blank space below the text is sufficient. But if the signer requires a line, it is typed on the fourth line below the text, with the name under the line.

The attachments are identified in the memorandum; therefore, they are not listed in the attachment notation, but the word <u>Attachments</u> is followed by <u>2</u> to show how many pieces of material are attached.

Carbon copies of this memo are to go to Billie Burt and Lucy Somerville. Their names appear in alphabetic order. The address must be given for each person listed.

The word <u>Attachments</u> in parentheses after the name and address indicates that attachments (the same as those sent with the original memorandum) are being sent to Mrs. Burt with her copy of the memo. Two copies of the memo without the attachments are being sent to Miss Somerville, as indicated by the number in parentheses following the name. If an extra copy is being sent to the addressee, (<u>2</u>) is typed at the end of the "To" line.

1

2 JF:DG
3 Attachments: 2
3 CC: Billie Burt, 115 AB, Wilson Dam (Attachments)
        Lucy Somerville, 1108 Market, Chattanooga (2)

We have given you the Army and TVA reports merely to show some widely used variant forms of memos, not to suggest that you adopt them or their rather stiff, heavily passive styles. Almost any large organization is likely to establish its own simpler form and style.

The following memo on a company's printed form (essentially the form used by the United States government) shows a more usual layout, typical A-plan, and a typical problem:

OFFICE MEMORANDUM—Acme Insurance Company

Date   : 2/10/72
To   : Mr. J. G. DeWolfe, General Manager
From   : R. R. Fortune, Safety & Health
Subject: HOW TO REDUCE ABSENTEEISM CAUSED BY RESPIRATORY
          DISEASES

1. <u>Conclusion</u>.—Our recent high rate of absenteeism seems to be a result of too low humidity. Absentees reported colds or other respiratory diseases as the cause in 73 percent of the cases.

2. <u>Humidity in relation to respiratory diseases</u>.—According to the U.S. Public Health Service, the higher the humidity in buildings the lower the rate of respiratory diseases. You can see this relationship in Figure 1 on the attached pages. The explanation is that a high humidity prevents excessive cooling from evaporation of skin moisture.

3. <u>Desirable humidity-temperature relationships</u>.—Although our 70 degrees is considered the best temperature, it isn't warm enough for most people unless the humidity is about 40. Ours is 20. As Figure 2 of the USPHS study shows, a

Checklist for Memos

1. Form:
   a) Use a neatly arranged heading, including at least the company name (usually in capitals); some wording like Memo, Memorandum, or Interoffice Communication; and a dateline.
   b) Begin To, From, and Subject at the left; preferably, double-space between them; and use colons right after each or align all the colons with the one after Subject. In either case, align the beginnings of what you fill in after the colons.
   c) Use courtesy titles (Mr., Mrs., Miss) with the names of others (but not yours) if you would in talking with them; and use official titles for everybody unless all readers would know them.
   d) For emphasis, underscore or capitalize subject lines.
   e) End-of-line periods are unnecessary, even undesirable.
   f) Single-space within paragraphs and double-space between.
   g) Use itemizations, headings, tables, and charts where helpful.
   h) For pages after the first, put at least the addressee's name, the date, and the page number on the first line and triple-space below it.
   i) Use no salutation, complimentary close, or typed name of writer at the end; sign only nonroutine memos requiring authentication.
   j) When used, file and other references (including other people to receive carbons) may go under a flush-right date or to the right of the To-From-Subject block. (Carbon-copy lists more commonly appear at the end instead.)

2. Organization and coverage:
   a) Bring in your main point (whether it is a request, conclusion, recommendation, or something else) in the first sentence unless your reader might resist; and if he might, lead up to it with whatever facts, reasons, or explanations are necessary to convince him—especially any reader benefits you can point out.
   b) Be sure to make clear that your information is valid and pertinent by showing what the problem is and how you got your information to solve it; but see 3(b).
   c) Effective dates (for directives)—and when necessary, other time limits, places, and people concerned—are important points.
   d) Consider whether you should mention alternatives to your recommendation.
   e) Should you explain more specifically how to carry out your proposal?
   f) Be sure you have covered all points your reader will need or want covered—especially all steps in your logic.
   g) Check your sequence for coherence, logic, and psychological effect (A–, B–, or C–plan).

Checklist for Memos

(continued)

3. Style:
   a) Make the subject line indicate the content accurately and specifically.
   b) Emphasize the important and avoid undue emphasis on the unimportant. What you found out and the likely effect are more important than how you found out or from whom; so for 2(b), usually you should just imply or interweave in incidental phrases the necessary but unknown parts of purpose and method of the report. Usually the reader will already know the purpose; and if not, it and your method of getting information are usually implied in stating the facts you got. "Sixty-two percent of your employees favor a company snack bar" indicates both the problem and the survey method.
   c) Be sure your terminology, sentence length and structure, and paragraph length and structure make for quick, clear, easy reading. Short words, sentences, and paragraphs usually help; itemizations and tabulations may help further.
   d) Display really significant data, conclusions, and recommendations by such means as increasing white space, decreasing line length, itemizing, and tabulating.
   e) For coherence (and often for conciseness), precede displayed items with an appropriate introductory statement.
   f) Don't develop a fever (with numerous strong adjectives and adverbs, for example).

4. Tone:
   a) Soften commands for acceptable tone; sharp imperatives rankle even in directives. "You will . . ." is too commanding for most situations. Three directives from which you can usually select an appropriate one are (in descending order of sharpness): "Please . . . ," "Will you . . . ," and "I ask that you . . . ." "If you will . . ." is usually too weak.
   b) Phrase recommendations for acceptable tone (depending on the reader-writer relationship and the firmness of your conviction): "You must . . . ," "I recommend . . . ," "I suggest . . ."; "The only way . . . ," "The best solution is . . . ," and "Probably the wise decision is . . . ."
   c) Accusations are always objectionable.
   d) Positive is better than negative phrasing.
   e) Item 2(a) is an important factor in tone.
   f) Consider whether to write impersonally or (usually better) naturally ("Employees will receive their checks . . ." or "You will receive your checks . . .").

humidity above 50 makes most people feel clammy and below
30 causes them to feel a dryness in their noses and throats.

4. <u>Recommended corrective steps</u>.—To reduce absenteeism,
improve the health of our personnel, and enhance employee
relations, I suggest the following:

<u>a</u>) Raise the humidity to 40 by having a tinner make a pan
with the necessary evaporation surface for each radiator
(to be concealed from view by the radiator covers).

<u>b</u>) Assign the janitors the job of keeping water in the pans.

<u>c</u>) Purchase one temperature-humidity guide for each office.
Besides providing a constant check on room conditions,
these meters will remind the employees that you have
done something about their comfort and health.

Prices range from $2 to $200. The cheapest ones are
likely to be inaccurate; but the Wechsler at $4.50
carries the recommendation of <u>Consumer Reports</u>. It
looks like a small clock with two red hands pointing to
temperature and humidity scales. Hardware, department,
mail-order, and specialty stores carry it in varied
colors to fit the decor of any office.

Justification reports

Another kind of short report often using memo form has its own special
name. Of course, any analytical report could be called a justification report
because it draws conclusions (and makes recommendations if wanted)
and presents facts to justify them. But as used in report writing, the justification report is a special kind.

Almost invariably it is an initiating report in which the writer makes
an original proposal, rather than a requested study, although it may well
be the requested full write-up of a suggestion that has been dropped in a
suggestion box.

It is deductive (A–plan) presentation that gives the recommendation
immediately, followed by concise statements of the most important considerations and conclusions, before giving detailed explanations and supporting facts. Thus it *quickly* gives the busy reader all he needs to know
if he trusts the writer. Probably this point is the main reason for the increasing popularity of the justification report among executives. But if the
reader wants to read the whole explanation, the plan is still good. He
can follow the details better by having already read the conclusions and
recommendations—that is, what the details lead to.

You will provide good organization and coverage if you set up the
five standard headings and do the following in this order:

1. State the purpose in one sentence. The first part, in phrase or dependent-
clause structure, should mention a benefit. The second part should be the
recommendation in an independent clause.

2. State the cost and saving in no more than two sentences. Don't delay the fast
movement by explaining.

3. In a third part called "Procedure" or "Method of Installation," cover concisely such things as necessary space, men, training, special materials, time, restrictions (rules, regulations), and interruptions of work. Usually one to three sentences will do.

4. Itemize the conclusions, state them pointedly, and keep them to the minimum number that will cover all aspects. One of them has to be on cost and saving. One commonly overlooked is the goodwill of all people concerned. They are not always all benefits; some may point the other way.

5. In a discussion section (sometimes called "Discussion of Conclusions" or "Explanation of Advantages"), give all the details supporting the statements already made. Usually they should be itemized to match the itemized conclusions. Interweave into your explanations enough of your methods to answer the reader's question: "How do you know?" This applies particularly to your method of figuring cost and saving.

The following typical example illustrates both plan and technique:

HOW MECHANICAL PENCILS WOULD SAVE MONEY FOR MORGAN COMPANY

Purpose.—To save the Morgan Company more than $100 in pencil expense each year, I recommend that we purchase mechanical pencils instead of wooden ones for use by employees.

Cost and Saving.—A year's supply of mechanical pencils and refills would cost about $150 as compared with more than $250 for wooden pencils—a yearly saving of something over $100.

Procedure.—A dependable automatic pencil manufacturer—Ray & Company, Rome, Georgia—would supply the yearly need of about 750 pencils with the Morgan name on them at the quantity-discounted price of 10 cents each. The stockroom clerk could distribute them as he does the wooden pencils, and maintain records for control.

Conclusions.—The Morgan Company would enjoy four advantages by using mechanical pencils instead of the present wooden ones:

   1. We would save at least $100 a year.

   2. The stockroom clerk would have fewer pencils to store and issue—750 as compared with over 13,000.

   3. Employees would be more careful about misplacing them.

   4. Mechanical pencils stay sharp and thus provide uniform, neat writing without loss of time and patience at the pencil sharpener.

Discussion of Conclusions.—

   1. During the past three years pencils have cost us about 70 cents a year per employee, as shown by the following calculations:

	19—	19—	19—	Average
Pencil costs	$271	$227	$295	$264
Employees	450	298	395	381
Cost per employee	60¢	76¢	75¢	70¢

Converting to mechanical pencils would require, for each employee, an estimated two pencils (at 10 cents each) and 20

cents worth of lead and eraser refills, for a total annual
cost of 40 cents per employee.

Cost comparison shows a saving of $114.30 with mechanical
pencils:

```
Cost of wooden pencils, 381 employees, @ 70¢ ........ $266.70
Cost of mechanical pencils, 381 employees, @ 40¢ ....  152.40
                                                       ───────
   Saving ........................................... $114.30
```

2. In the past three years, the clerk in the stockroom has had
   to allot space for about 1,104 dozen, or 13,248, pencils.
   Also he has had to take the time (considerable in the
   aggregate) to distribute each one. With only 762 pencils
   to store and issue, he could use the relieved space and
   time for other things.

3. Since mechanical pencils are more valuable and more
   conspicuous (especially with the Morgan name on them) than
   wooden ones, I believe employees would be more careful
   about carrying them home and not bringing them back. Also,
   if employees had to sign a receipt—which is more feasible
   with the fewer mechanical pencils—misplacements would
   occur less frequently. Those misplaced might be worth at
   least a part of their cost as advertising.

4. The mechanical pencil needs no sharpening and writes with
   the same neat uniformity throughout its use, instead of
   becoming blunt and less neat progressively. Moreover,
   mechanical pencils would avoid the interruptions to thinking
   and work when employees take their wooden ones to the
   pencil sharpener (which often annoys by breaking the lead
   or needing to be emptied).

You might well notice several specifics about the preceding report. The
writer who *initiated* this idea—usual for this kind of report—moves fast
in presenting the basic idea and facts. If the boss trusts the reporter, he
may approve after reading less than the first half; but if he wants details,
he simply reads further. The clear, concise, and prominent (by underlining) but easily typed heads serve as guideposts to the reader. And the
matched pair of itemizations helps the reader relate pointed conclusions
with supporting facts and explanations. The inevitable repetition of cost
and saving is justified by deserved emphasis—you make such proposals
because benefits outweigh costs (neither of which always has to be in
dollars and cents). Perhaps most important of all, notice how the writer
concisely but subordinately interwove only what he deemed necessary of
methodology to answer the reader's question: "How do you know?" But
he wasted no words telling how he knew former pencil costs. The answer
is obvious.

Although the form of justification reports is commonly memo, it may be
letter or some other such as that illustrated. A title page like that of the
complete analytical report may precede the form illustrated. If so, the title
would be on both pages. In letter or memo form the title would serve as the
subject line. Of course, the five division heads may be centered heads or
sideheads above the text if you prefer. If you use memo form, Item 1 of the

checklist for memos (p. 594) will apply. In any form you can use items 1–5 on page 596 as the subheads under Item 2 of that checklist and have a good checklist for justification reports.

Progress reports

As the name suggests, the progress report is an interim report of how you are getting along on a project—usually a construction job. It may be a single, special report or one in a series of required periodic reports. (In the series the last one is called the *completion* report.) As a periodic report, a progress report is usually strictly informational. A special progress report is likely to be analytical, because of the special problem that caused it to be written.

The general purpose of a progress report is to keep the top men informed so that they can act wisely. If the report is for the owner, he may want to consider whether to continue as planned, change the plan or methods, or drop the project. If it is for a contractor, he may need to consider such questions as when to order certain materials, whether to increase the men and equipment assigned to the job, and whether to bid on another job.

Basic contents of a progress report are the answers to three questions:

1. Whether the project is on schedule.
2. If the project is not on schedule, why not?
3. What will be done next and what the plans and prospects are for completion on schedule.

Although neither those nor the following are necessarily the subdivision headings, a progress report may cover any or all of the purpose and nature of the project (usually the reader already knows), what has been done, present status, what is now being done, plans and outlook for the future, and unexpected developments. The last may be of major importance if the report is designed to get a decision on a problem that has arisen. In series, each progress report summarizes former work reported but stresses developments since the preceding report. Progress reports on research projects may or may not include tentative findings and conclusions —depending on the writer's confidence in them and the immediate need for them.

No single plan is always best for a progress report. What is best depends upon the whole situation, especially the content, deserved relative emphasis of parts, and the attitudes and wishes of the reader.

One thing can be said: Preferably all the reports in a series should follow the same plan. It may be topical by divisions of the subject (supervision, equipment, materials, and labor; or steps, phases, or divisions of the job); or it may be chronological (by days, weeks, or months; or past, present, and future). One simple plan calls for

1. The transitional elements of background and summary of already reported work.
2. The body giving the details of recent progress.
3. The prophetic or future prospects.

A more specific but somewhat flexible plan is

1. Quick introduction (purpose and nature of the project, unless known; summary of work to date; status, including any significant results).
2. More detailed résumé of earlier progress reported, if any.
3. New progress (work done, methods and men, obstacles and what you've done about them) in relation to schedule.
4. Realistic forecast (plans in relation to schedule, and recommendations or requests, if any).

More important than *what* plan, in most cases, is that you have *a* plan—a unifying thread to hang your beads on.

Like the plan, the form of progress reports may vary with the circumstances. Short ones usually are in memo or letter form, longer ones in some adaptation of complete report form.

Since the form, plan, and content of progress reports vary so much and we cannot well illustrate all the possibilities, we think we can help most by illustrating some common weaknesses in progress reports: (1) having nothing to say but trying to pretend that you do, (2) using pompous jargon to cover up, and (3) being nonspecific. The following illustration properly lampoons the main weaknesses.

STANDARD PROGRESS REPORT FOR THOSE WITH NO PROGRESS TO REPORT

During the report period which ends (fill in appropriate date) considerable progress has been made in the preliminary work directed toward the establishment of the initial activities. (Meaning: We are getting ready to start, but we haven't done anything yet.) The background information has been surveyed and the functional structure of the component parts of the cognizant organization has been clarified. (We looked at the assignment and decided that George should do it.)

Considerable difficulty has been encountered in the selection of optimum materials and experimental methods, but this problem is being attacked vigorously and we expect that the development phase will proceed at a satisfactory rate. (George is looking through the handbook.) In order to prevent unnecessary duplication of previous efforts in the same field, it was necessary to establish a survey team which has conducted a rather extensive tour through various facilities in the immediate vicinity of manufacture. (George and Harry had a nice time in New York last week.)

The Steering Committee held its regular meeting and considered rather important policy matters pertaining to the over-all organizational levels of the line and staff responsibilities that devolve on the personnel associated with the specific assignments resulting from the broad functional specifications. (Untranslatable—sorry.) It is believed that the rate of progress will continue to accelerate as necessary personnel are recruited to fill vacant billets. (We'll get some work done as soon as we find someone who knows something.)[1]

The following progress reporters did much better, as a writer usually does when he has something to say to somebody for some purpose. Especially if all goes well, as in the first, the report is easy to write. (All these writers used memo form; we'll begin with the subject line.)

SUBJECT: Monthly Progress Report No. 2 on Orangeville
            Expressway

Present status

1. Work on the 10.8-mile section of expressway running south
   to Brownsville is on schedule. The final surface is 80
   percent complete. We have had no delays during the past
   month and have regained the two days formerly lost and
   reported.

2. The 18.4-mile section of expressway running north to Malden
   remains approximately two weeks behind schedule. The right
   of way has been cleared all the way to Malden, and the
   roadbed is completed along the first 8.6 miles north of
   Orangeville.

3. The overpass for U.S. 1 was completed on December 14, 18
   days ahead of schedule.

Expected progress

1. During January the southern link to Brownsville should be
   completed except for the drainage preparation and the
   approaches. Work on them will most likely have to be fitted
   in between rains normally expected at this time of year in
   this area, especially in the valley of Hogtown Creek.
   Present progress and normal weather expectations suggest
   that this link will be ready for traffic just before the
   completion deadline of March 3.

2. During this month the roadbed will be extended along the
   north section to Malden. The first layer of tar will also
   be completed along a strip about 5 miles long, beginning at
   Orangeville and extending north. Additional men are being
   hired to insure completion of this section before the
   deadline of June 24.

Sometimes progress reporters must explain their difficulties to defend themselves and to justify requests, as in the following:

SUBJECT: Special Report on Interlocking Plant Installation

Because of a shortage of track cable, I would like to have
your permission to advance cutover day to at least January 18.

---

[1] So widely reprinted in the literature of report writing as to be in the public domain —like many jokes.

The installation is now about 88 percent complete, as shown by
the broken line on the following graph [omitted here]
comparing the predicted work schedule and the actual schedule.

If the track cable ordered December 1 arrives within the next
few days as promised two weeks ago, and if we have good
weather, the future work schedule should appear as the dotted
projection line. This points to 100 percent completion on
January 18.

Since progress reports often deal with technical work, you need not
be surprised if you fail to understand some things in some of them. If you
have trouble with the following, for example, remember that it was not
written for you but by one technical man to another, who understood
perfectly. This report also illustrates a not unusual organization around
topics rather than time, while the time sequence and relation to schedule
are still clear.

SUBJECT: <u>Progress on Prototype Power Supply for Collins</u>
           <u>(Job 280)</u>

At the end of three weeks on the two-month schedule for
developing a prototype power supply for Collins Radio, the
project is two days ahead of the preliminary time estimate.
The circuit has been designed and tested for dependability.
It is now undergoing final inspection.

1. <u>Results of circuit dependability test</u>.—The test circuit
   operated within the desired limits of $\pm$ 2 percent of the
   desired voltages and currents. Measured by a thermocouple
   in the 3' x 3' x 3" base mounting plate of aluminum, the
   temperature readings (with attendant voltages) ran as
   follows:

<u>Hour</u>	<u>Transmit</u> <u>Voltage</u> <u>@ 200 Ma.</u>	<u>Receive</u> <u>Voltage</u> <u>@ 110 Ma.</u>	<u>Bias</u> <u>Voltage</u> <u>@ 65 Ma.</u>	<u>Temperature</u> <u>(Degrees</u> <u>Centigrade)</u>

[No use to waste space in this book on the recorded
results.]

2. <u>Printed circuit board</u>.—The basic sketch work for the
   printed board is finished. The component placement and
   hookup connections were frozen yesterday. Now the enlarged
   negative is being drawn. It should be ready for the
   developer on January 13, five days ahead of the final
   acceptance date.

3. <u>Chassis design</u>.—The chassis drawings went to Alsfab on
   January 9. The prototype chassis, with finishes of black
   anodize on the base and gray enamel on the cover, will be
   ready on January 14. The dimensions are 6" x 4" x 3" or 2
   inches smaller than the maximum allowed by Collins.

4. <u>Remaining work</u>.—The printing board has to be etched and
   built. It will be tested in the small chassis, and the
   complete unit has to be tested for all conditions, including
   vibration, moisture, and temperature. Unless now unseen
   troubles develop, the present rate of progress should
   continue, and the prototype should be ready for shipment by
   February 7.

Credit reports

The credit report illustrated as a letter report (p. 121) is typical of those written by individual references about a credit applicant. But various trade associations, credit bureaus, and special credit-reporting agencies have to write so many credit reports that each develops special forms for convenience and the economy of standardization.

Because the purpose of a credit report is always the same and known to the reader, and because the methods and scope are always the same, the credit report omits the introduction. Because the credit report is an informational rather than analytical report, it also omits conclusions and recommendations. And because it is a short-form report, it omits other parts of a complete report—all except the text and perhaps a synopsis. But because the credit report must protect the writer against libel suit, it includes the necessary legal defenses (in addition to assumed truth in the facts presented) by specifying confidential use for the purpose mentioned when it was requested. Because credit decisions are always made on the basis of the four C's of credit—Capital, Character, Capacity, Conditions (see p. 146)—the report invariably covers these topics (but not under these headings). The information includes anything which might have a significant bearing on the credit worth of the subject (individual or firm) and omits anything else.

Different organizations still set their reports up in various forms. One of the oldest and biggest credit-reporting agencies uses the following pattern, which covers just about everything others do in different form:

1. A subject line identifying name and address of subject, kind of business, and symbolic rating of capitalization and dependability (A–1, F–2, G–5, for example).
2. A summary usually covering such things as background, net worth, payment practice, and conditions and trends.
3. Several reports from firms which have sold to the subject of the report. These —usually in tabulated columns—establish the highest credit extended (HC), amount currently owed, amount past due, the terms, manner of payment (discount, prompt, or slow), and length of the credit relationship.
4. A financial statement (signed if possible, sometimes followed by notes on facts that influence financial solidity).
5. A description of operating conditions (including type and price ranges of stock, kind of customers, cash versus credit sales, advertising and other promotion, location, competition, kind and size of building, neighbors and other factors influencing fire hazard, insurance, and fire record).
6. A history describing origin, kind of organization, shifts in organization or ownership, any changes of location, and growth of the business, with emphasis on the facts about the owners and managers (education, experience, and any significant personal details such as age, marital status, and health).

The old report on the opposite page is just one of the many kinds, but it illustrates most of the points. When you notice how the note in fine print at the bottom provides legal protection against libel suit, you will understand that Dun & Bradstreet had to get permission from Simpson to release this report for educational purposes—and why D&B sent an old report.

Annual reports[2]

In accounting to their publics for their management of funds entusted to them, corporations and governmental units summarize each year's activities in their annual reports.

In the middle of the 19th century, when annual reporting really started, stockholders were the only public considered. Since they were usually wealthy and educated—or advised by investment specialists—early annual reports were little more than financial statements in the formal accounting terms of the day. And the usual attitude of management was to tell as few people as possible as little as possible.

Today all that is changed. Stockholders have increased greatly (now estimated at about a tenth of the U.S. population, many of whom are not acquainted with accounting terminology). Labor forces have increased their power and have become intensely interested in corporate affairs. The changed thinking of the times considers corporations essentially public institutions affecting the public welfare. Management has seen that its publics include stockholders, workers, customers, government officials, and the general public. It has realized that many of these people are not educated in accounting and that many of them are interested in more than the strictly financial affairs (wages, fringe benefits to workers, products, research and development of new products, and overall policies—for example, company ecological policy).

Annual-report writers today, therefore, try to write so that everyone can understand, and they try to cover topics of interest to all publics. And with the realization that people are inclined to distrust and take a dim view of things they don't know about, management has shifted to the attitude of telling as many people as possible as much as possible (limited only by security regulations and information that might hurt the competitive position of the company).

---

[2] Although most annual reports are not short, they are largely factual reporting (informational) rather than the analytical studies of problems with conclusions and recommendations discussed in the preceding chapter. They are periodic reports and are something of a special type and form. Certainly they are the most voluminous of reports (many companies distributing more than a million copies annually), and the writings about them are probably the most numerous (we could easily give you a 10-page bibliography). Yet we do not think they deserve extensive treatment here in view of the purposes of this book. Still, you deserve some introduction to them, and it belongs in this chapter more appropriately than elsewhere.

Dun & Bradstreet Report

SIC	NAME & ADDRESS		STARTED	RATING

	CD 26 FEB 2 19-- N			
52 51	SIMPSON HARDWARE CO HARDWARE & PAINTS		1948	E 2
	SIMPSON, WILLIAM J., OWNER			Formerly E 2½

495 N MAIN ST.		TRADE	DISC-PPT
SPRINGFIELD OHIO		SALES	$89,446
		WORTH	$27,908
		EMPLS	I + I P.T.

SUMMARY   AN ESTABLISHED BUSINESS CONDUCTING A STEADY AND PROFITABLE VOLUME. FINANCIAL CONDITION IS WELL BALANCED.

TRADE

HC	OWE	P DUE	TERMS	Jan 19 19--	SOLD
1551	356		2-10-30	Disc	1948 to date
900	600		2-10	Disc	yrs
400			2-10-30	Disc	1950 to 11-1-6-
1600	300		30	Ppt	Active acct
733	112			Ppt	yrs

FINANCE

Statement Dec 31 19--			
Cash on hand & bank	$ 4,604	Accts Pay	$ 3,064
Accts Rec	1,315	Accruals	621
Mdse	19,158		
	--------		--------
Total Current	25,077	Total Current	3,685
Fixt & Equip	4,008		
Auto	2,113		
Ppd & Def	395	NET WORTH	27,908
	--------		--------
Total Assets	31,593	Total	31,593

Net Sales January 1, 19-- to December 31, 19--, $89,446; gross profit $19,551; monthly rent $175; lease expires 19--. Fire insurance on fixtures $4,000; on merchandise $20,000.
Signed Jan 30, 19-- SIMPSON HARDWARE CO. by W.J. Simpson, Owner

-----0-----

When Simpson took over the business in 1948, sales were about $45,000 a year. By working long hours and advertising in the Suburban News he built up volume a little every year. Also there has been an increase in residential building on his side of town. Profits have increased as sales have expanded. Cash withdrawals from the business have been conservative. Merchandise turns satisfactorily and Simpson has been able to improve his financial condition a little each year. Carries good balances at his bank and has not borrowed since 195-.

OPERATION   Retails shelf hardware and tools (65%), S & W Paints (20%) and housewares, cutlery, garden implements, glass, lawn mowers, seeds and sporting equipment (15%). About 90% of sales is for cash; 30 day credit is extended to contractors and householders. Two clerks, one part-time, are employed. LOCATION: Rents a store 25 x 60 in a residential shopping area on the outskirts of town. Premises are well maintained.

HISTORY   Style was registered by Simpson July 17, 1948. Used for buying and advertising. Owner purchased this established business July 1, 1948 from Ralph T. Meyers. Capital was $18,000 of which $10,000 was a loan since repaid.

William J. Simpson, born 190-, is married, a native of Ohio. After graduating from Miami University in 1930, taught school until 1936. 1937-1945 employed by the Wilson Wholesale Hardware Co., Columbus, Ohio, latterly in the accounting department. 1946-48 was a salesman for Davis & Crocker, wholesale builders supplies, Springfield.
2-2 (201 49)

Indeed, today the annual report is a major medium in the public relations programs of most corporations, a means by which they hope to tell their story to all their publics to justify their existence and their way of doing things. They know that any business firm exists, in the long run, only with the approval and patronage of a public whose goodwill it has. Most corporations therefore make their reports available to anybody who asks, and some go to considerable expense to make their reports appealing and to buy newspaper advertising space or radio and television time to tell their stories to everybody.

Some have gone so far in telling their stories that the reports seem more like propaganda or advertising brochures than objective reports—and have sometimes thereby lost faith and face. But the usual annual report today is highly informative about the organization it represents. The facts presented are quite reliable. If you read annual reports knowing that they are likely slanted (by not telling everything rather than by misrepresentation), you will be adequately cautious—and well informed.

Usually today's annual reports contain a letter from the highest official as well as financial statements and the auditor's statement of opinion (sometimes called the "certificate"). Often the letter from the president or chairman of the board is only a short introduction to a review of outstanding influences, developments, and trends affecting company operations. Frequently it is both an introduction and a synopsis. And in many cases it is the entire report, running to 10, 12, or more pages.

Either way, most annual-report writers adapt all the devices already mentioned here—readable style, liberal use of meaningful headings, graphic illustrations—to make reading easy and interesting and the reports effective public relations agents for the organizations they represent.

Annual reports deserve the study of any student of accounting. While they are not the accounting reports commonly presented by the accountant to his clients or his superiors, they are excellent studies in reporting and interpreting financial information.

You can find a tremendous volume of material about them in the library. And as we mentioned in the chapters on application letters, you can get examples by writing to almost any corporation. The annual report of a company is a source of information which anybody should read before applying for a job with that firm.

Short analytical reports

As you have seen, some of the short reports in forms already discussed have been informational, and others have been analytical. Yet the name "short analytical report" often has a special meaning in report-writing circles—a meaning indicating a certain form rather than any very definite limits of length. In that sense—the sense used in this section only—a short analytical report is like a complete analytical report which the writer has cut down by (1) omitting certain parts, (2) combining parts where possible, and (3) writing less in the remaining parts simply because their topics require no more. Even so, it is still likely to be longer (maybe up to ten pages) than what is generally called a short report (usually five pages or less).

Since the parts of a short analytical report all have parallels in the complete analytical reports discussed in the preceding chapter, we see no need to explain and illustrate them extensively here. For your study of short analytical reports, therefore, we ask you to keep in mind the following points as you reconsider the preceding chapter.

1. The short analytical report usually omits the cover, the letter of authorization, and the letter of acceptance.
2. It often also combines the letter of transmittal and synopsis, omits the table of contents and depends on headings throughout the report, omits the bibliography and provides the full references as footnotes or interwoven citations, and interweaves the essential parts of possible appendix material right into the text.
3. It may, but rarely does, also put the title-page information at the top of the first page and move right into the next part on that page; combine the essentials of authorization, transmittal, and synopsis as a summary right after the title-page information; and omit the introduction as a separate part and interweave its essentials into the text. It could thus have only three sections—the title-page information, the summary, and the text. This is about as far as it can go. Any report would have these elements, although they might be arranged differently and presented in different forms.

The following report (slightly revised for our purposes) is a good short analytical report. We know additional improvements we could make—and you may see some too—but notice particularly:

1. The exactness of the title, including the general answers to both questions (appropriate in the final title but not in a tentative one, where they would show preconceptions).
2. The telescoping (omitting certain standard parts of longer reports like those discussed in the preceding chapter and combining them with others). In this case you see the letter and synopsis combined, no table of contents but a well-displayed system of heads and subheads, and no bibliography because published sources are interwoven in the text.
3. The use of tables and charts where they help to highlight important quantities (the original contained others, omitted here because we do not think they were worth their space and costs in this book).
4. The smooth continuity and coherence of the whole report, helped by numerous beginning topic sentences and paragraphs and ending summary-transition sentences and paragraphs.

HOW A CORRESPONDENCE-IMPROVEMENT PROGRAM

WOULD SAVE MONEY AND BUILD GOODWILL

FOR BURNS, INC.

By Patricia Jean Barksdale

Assistant, Research Department

November 28, 1971

Letterhead

RESEARCH DEPARTMENT   November 28, 1971

Mr. C. D. James, President
Burns, Inc.
2619 Powell Street
San Francisco, California 81001

Dear Mr. James:

Here is the report you requested on October 20 evaluating the possibilities
for improvement and, if needed, the best methods Burns could employ to
improve the quality of its correspondence.

The report shows that Burns could both save money and improve goodwill by
instituting a correspondence-improvement program.

To achieve the quality that should be maintained in our correspondence,
Burns should employ an instructor to conduct classes, issue a correspondence
manual, and hire a permanent supervisor to maintain quality correspondence.

In the month given me to prepare this report, I have learned some interesting
and useful facts which I believe will help you in establishing a
correspondence-improvement program. Please call on me if I can be of
further help.

                        Sincerely yours,

                        (Miss) Patricia Jean Barksdale
                        Assistant

HOW A CORRESPONDENCE-IMPROVEMENT PROGRAM

WILL SAVE MONEY AND BUILD GOODWILL

FOR BURNS, INC.

I. Introduction

This report, authorized on October 20, 1971, by Mr. C. D. James, president of Burns, Inc., and submitted by Patricia Jean Barksdale, assistant in the research department, was assigned for two purposes: (1) to determine whether Burns really needs to improve its correspondence and (2) to propose and explain any needed action.

Information presented in the report comes from a survey of the quality of correspondence Burns presently puts out, current letter-improvement publications, questionnaires, personal interviews with representatives of local companies which have conducted letter-improvement programs, and an interview with a professional consultant in business letters.

The significant savings in both money and goodwill which would result from instituting a letter-improvement program are evident from the following analysis of the costs of correspondence, the present correspondence conditions at Burns, the success of correspondence-improvement programs, and the costs of methods and plans successfully used by other companies.

2

II. The High Costs of Correspondence

The average cost of business letters is at least $3 each (according
to the article "Cutting Correspondence Expense," by Henry Howard, in
the May issue of U.S. Business, p. 29).

On the basis of this figure, Burns's yearly correspondence expense
is:

          Average number of letters per business year 212,500
          Average cost per letter $3.00
          Yearly correspondence expense $637,500

This minimum cost, comprising a large part of the firm's total
expenditures, consists not merely of supplies expense but more significantly of the valuable time of dictators and typists. The high total
expenditures for correspondence seem to offer a vast area for possible
savings.

In addition to the possible dollar savings on correspondence, Burns
also needs to consider the intangible yet highly significant goodwill
value of its correspondence. The impression the company's letters make
on the public can either win or lose business. As Mr. Howard says
(p. 31), "To get your money's worth, you must be sure that every letter
helps to improve public relations."

III. Unfavorable Correspondence Conditions Existing in Burns, Inc.

A survey of current Burns correspondence reveals that it is not
creating the best public image. The survey consisted of analyzing 200
letters selected at random from the average 4,250 letters prepared in
one week by the 40 typists and 85 dictators.

Many of the company's letters contain outmoded forms, errors in
spelling and grammar, poor sentence structure, poor style, and other

3

undesirable features shown in Chart 1.

Chart 1

Form, Spelling, and Style in Burns Letters, November, 1971

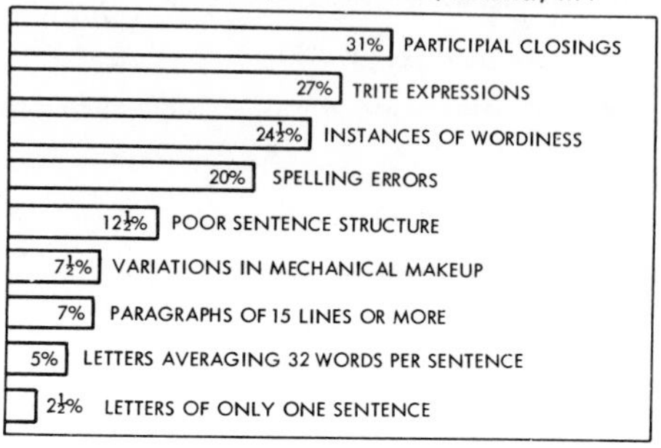

31%	PARTICIPIAL CLOSINGS
27%	TRITE EXPRESSIONS
24½%	INSTANCES OF WORDINESS
20%	SPELLING ERRORS
12½%	POOR SENTENCE STRUCTURE
7½%	VARIATIONS IN MECHANICAL MAKEUP
7%	PARAGRAPHS OF 15 LINES OR MORE
5%	LETTERS AVERAGING 32 WORDS PER SENTENCE
2½%	LETTERS OF ONLY ONE SENTENCE

A. <u>Layout, Spelling, and Style Improvement Needed</u>.--Since Burns
letters are often the only contact readers have with the organization,
the impression created by the letters is important. The quality of
the typewritten letter creates a picture of the quality of the firm.

Quality correspondence requires accuracy and attractiveness.
Spelling errors and poor sentence construction reflect unfavorably on
both the company and the company's dictators and typists.

1. <u>Variations in Mechanical Makeup</u>.--Almost one in 12 (7 1/2
percent) of the letters contains variations in mechanical makeup.
These variations often result from inconsistency on the part of various
typists when the dictator does not specify the form of letter he
desires. Such variations are not necessarily errors, since all forms
that are consistent are correct; but the outmoded or ultramodern form
does characterize the writer and his company. Since the modern trend

4

is toward simplicity, Burns could save much time and money by adopting
a simple form that would suggest that Burns is neither out of date nor
frivolously ultramodern.

2. Spelling Errors.--One out of every five letters typed by Burns
typists contains one or more misspelled words. To most people a
misspelled word is a mark of discredit on the firm on whose letterhead
it appears. The typists are responsible for not correctly spelling
the words dictated. That 20 percent of the letters sent out each week
contain spelling errors certainly indicates the need for study by the
typists.

3. Trite Expressions.--About one fourth (27 percent) of the letters
sent out by Burns contain trite expressions. These outdated phrases
dull reader interest and make the letters sound pompous and unnatural.
Use of these expressions is usually due to lack of thinking on the
part of the dictators. Triteness, like spelling errors, is not good
for public relations.

4. Poor Sentence Structure.--One eighth (12 1/2 percent) of Burns
letters contain improper sentence structure. Poorly constructed
sentences are often unclear and may convey a meaning different from
that intended. More significant than lack of clarity, however, is
the fact that poor sentence structure draws attention to the dictator's
style rather than to the more important message. Therefore poor sentence
structure decreases readability and in turn decreases the quality of
Burns, Inc., in the eyes of its readers.

5. Participial Closings.--The survey reveals that the largest
percentage of improper phrasings is participial closings--31 percent of

5

the letters end with outmoded expressions such as "Until such time, I remain, etc." This means that one out of every three letters dictated indicates to customers a lack of up-to-dateness at Burns, Inc.

6. <u>Too Long or Too Short Paragraphs and Sentences, and Instances of Wordiness</u>.--Two out of every five letters contain sentences and paragraphs of considerable length. Five percent of these letters average more than 32 words per sentence. Although an average of 16-20 words is good for readability, sentences of 32 words or more are not improper if necessary for the good presentation of the idea and if easily readable because of direct phrasing that requires no complicating punctuation.

However, 24 percent of the letters contain instances of wordiness. This indicates that the lengthy sentences are probably due to deadwood phrases rather than to good idea presentation. Wordiness indicates lack of careful thought of the dictator.

Also, 7 percent of the letters contain paragraphs of 15 lines or more. These long paragraphs are uninviting and hard to read. If the dictator dictates paragraphing, he should break up his thoughts; but if he leaves it to the typist, she must learn how to assume the responsibility.

Although short and direct sentences aid clarity, letters that are too short give the reader an unfavorable impression. No one likes to be treated in an abrupt, brush-off manner; but 2 1/2 percent of our letters contain only one sentence and therefore probably sound discourteous.

Burns correspondence leaves a lot of room for improvement. Poor style weakens the impact of the message and also indicates outmodedness

6

or inability of the employees. Much more significant than style, however, is the actual message conveyed to the reader.

B. <u>Offensive Expressions and Duplication Costly</u>.--Approximately two out of five letters leaving Burns offices are probably doing as much harm as good. Yet Burns need not feel that it is exceptional in this way. Professor C. R. Anderson reports that 40 percent of 1,000 carbons he read in a firm where he was consulting represent letters that never should have been sent ("Correspondence Inefficiencies," <u>Journal of Business Communication</u>, 4:13-18, October, 1971). Still, the fact that other firms send out bad letters does not mean that Burns should.

1. <u>Letters Containing Offensive Expressions</u>.--Of the letters that Burns sends to readers, 18 percent contain offensive expressions (Chart 2).

Chart 2

Percentage of Letters Containing Offensive Expressions, Unanswered Questions,
and Unnecessary Duplication
November, 1971

This means that Burns is spending over $100,000 a year to drive business away (0.18 x 212,500 x $3). Accusing the reader ("You failed... or neglected..."), implying distrust or stupidity ("You say...," "If so,...," "Obviously..."). and the like certainly destroy rather than build goodwill. No company can afford this loss of goodwill and waste of money. Burns dictators definitely need instruction in this area.

7

   2. Unnecessary Duplication.--About one in six (16 1/2 percent)
of Burns letters leave questions unanswered. Not only are customers
annoyed by having to write again--unless they decide to drop the
subject and go elsewhere with their business--but Burns dictators
waste time in preparing letters to answer questions they should have
answered in the first letter.

   If they have to write again for each letter leaving unanswered
questions, a waste of another $100,000 a year results (212,500 x 0.165
x $3). This problem generally occurs because a dictator reads the
incoming mail carelessly and dictates before planning carefully to
answer what the inquirer asked.

   Unnecessary duplication comes also from 8 percent of the letters
being essentially the same messages dictated to three or more individuals.
Such duplications obviously cost Burns some money. Well-trained dictators and--in many cases--use of a good form letter could save at least
part of it.

   Spelling errors, poor sentence and paragraph construction and
length, offensive expressions, unnecessary duplication, and other faults
evidence the unsatisfactory quality of Burns correspondence. Unfavorable
correspondence conditions are increasing expenses by thousands of
dollars yearly and are also causing a loss of goodwill and business.
Only 24 percent, less than one in four, of the letters Burns now sends
out are of top quality--clear, correct, complete, and considerate of
the reader's feelings.

   Correspondence improvement offers Burns a vast area for savings
both in money and in goodwill. The results obtained by companies

8

using letter-improvement programs show the success Burns might expect
from a program of its own.

IV. The Success of Correspondence-Improvement Programs

The results of companies using letter-improvement programs include
improvements in letter quality, in attitudes of correspondents, and
in customer relations.

The following excerpt from "Letter Training Program Pays Off,"
an unsigned feature on page 377 of the January issue of Printers' Week,
comments on the improvement received from correspondence instruction:
"Bring in an instructor who has had experience in writing letters as
well as in teaching. Have him conduct regular classes for several
weeks. Require each member of the firm connected with letter writing--
from the president to the typist--to attend. Then watch your letters
improve!"

The same source lists the names of 57 companies which have carried
out letter-improvement programs. The 55 replies to questionnaires sent
to these companies indicate favorable results from their programs.

A. Considerable Improvement in Letter Quality.--The first and
most important question asked was "What do you believe was the effect
of your program on the quality of the company's letters?" Almost three
fourths (39 of the 55) say they have received considerable satisfaction
with significant improvement in quality. Twenty-seven percent see no
noticeable difference, and 2 percent note slight improvement.

B. Favorable Attitude of Correspondents.--More than three fourths
of the firms--42 of the 55--report correspondents' favorable attitudes
toward their programs. Only 4 percent report unfavorable reactions.

9

One typical comment is: "On the whole, both correspondents and typists appreciate the constructive criticism of the instructor. Nearly all are enthusiastic when they realize how important their letters are in building goodwill for the company."

Both improvement in letter quality and correspondents' approval indicate that the programs improve the companies' public relations.

C. Improved Customer Relations.--To the inquiry "What do you believe was the effect of the program on your company's customer relations?" more than two-thirds report considerable improvement. Sixty-nine percent report considerable improvement, whereas 20 percent consider the improvement slight and 11 percent notice no apparent change.

A favorable comment states that "Since completion of our training program, we have received fewer complaints than ever before, and many customers have written letters of appreciation."

Improvement in letter quality, correspondents' favorable attitudes, and better customer relations show that other companies' correspondence-improvement programs are successful. The type of program which works best, however, is more difficult to determine.

V. The Costs and Methods Used by Other Companies with Successful Programs

Most companies which have successful correspondence-improvement programs use a correspondence manual, a permanent supervisor, and (to start) a special instructor.

A. Correspondence Manuals Are Effective.--A correspondence manual for reference is an important part of a letter-improvement program. The usual manual contains both instructions and examples of approved styles for company letters to serve as a guide for dictators and transcribers.

10

Of the 55 companies questioned, only a little more than half (51 percent) said yes when asked "Do you have a correspondence manual?" Those companies which use a manual, however, readily realize its importance and benefits. Of those that report using one, 86 percent answered yes to "Do you believe it has helped to improve letter writing?" Almost 9 out of 10 believe their manuals help, whereas less than 1 out of 10 gives either a doubtful or a negative answer to the question.

Evidently the others (49 percent) do not realize the benefits that users receive from manuals. They serve both as guides to new employees and as reminders and handy references to established employees. In most cases a manual seems to be most beneficial to follow up and answer questions that arise after completion of the course of instruction.

In discussing the benefits of the correspondence manual, one respondent commented, typically, that "The correspondence manual issued at the close of our training period served to crystallize the information presented by the instructor. It is always available for quick reference."

Before a correspondence manual can be justified in a letter-improvement program, however, its benefits must be weighed against its cost.

B. Cost of a Manual Is about $300.--In replies to the question concerning the cost of correspondence manuals, $300 to $500 is the most frequent answer (43 percent). One fourth of the firms (25 percent) paid $400 and over for their manuals, 2 percent less than $200, and only 1 percent spent $200 to $300.

The advantages of the savings in time and money which result from the use of a correspondence manual seem to justify the cost in the thinking of most firms. Evidently, then, a good correspondence-

11

improvement program will provide a manual.

The most successful programs, however, do not depend on a manual alone but also provide a correspondence supervisor.

C. <u>Correspondence Supervisors Maintain Effectiveness</u>.--The correspondence supervisor serves as an adviser to the employees concerning problems and as an inspector to make sure the letters maintain standards of quality. Without the supervisor, dictators and transcribers lapse into their old habits, according to companies which have tried to operate without a supervisor.

The survey reveals that 58 percent of the companies make use of a correspondence supervisor or someone else who assumes his duties under another title. But 42 percent do not have a correspondence supervisor.

A greater percentage (58 percent) of firms make use of a supervisor than make use of a manual (51 percent). And unanimously all 32 companies which have a supervisor agree that he is effective in maintaining letter quality.

The following comment from one firm further illustrates the need for a correspondence supervisor:

> The letter-improvement classes we held five years ago made correspondents conscious of their responsibilities for several months. But since we had no supervisor to encourage consistent effort to make letters effective, correspondents became lax again. Our new program provides for a supervisor who will spot-check outgoing mail and hold regular classes for discussion of letter problems.

Evidently a supervisor helps to keep the letter quality up to par. The most effective letter-improvement program should make use of both a supervisor and a manual.

12

Still an additional element appears in the most successful programs.

D. <u>All Sources Recommend Instruction to Start</u>.--All articles read, many comments made by interviewees and respondents to the questionnaire, and the advice of a professional letter-writing consultant point to the wisdom of an instructional program as a necessary start to a letter-improvement program.

Dr. R. R. Brawner of Del Monte, the interviewed professional consultant, says that in his varied experience few companies have been successful in greatly improving their correspondence without a definite program of instruction to start. Much of the job, he says, is getting employees to recognize the importance of good letters to their companies and themselves. Although inspiration and exhortation alone will not do much good, some motivating along with good instruction on how to improve usually does produce good results.

Dr. Brawner's statements are in line with specific comments heard or read elsewhere, and he offers a program based on 10 years of successful experience.

Dictators and transcribers would attend 10-week courses in separate groups. Five groups with 17 dictators each and two groups with 20 typists each would include all of the 85 Burns dictators and 40 transcribers while keeping the classes down to effective working groups. Dr. Brawner proposes to analyze letters dictated by each correspondent and to give individual suggestions on the paper (when necessary, in person). Under his professional direction, employees are practically assured of learning the much-needed fundamentals of good letter writing. His fee for each class is $500 or $3,500 for the whole instructional program.

13

By employing Dr. Brawner to conduct the proposed classes, Burns
would be taking a step that everyone with successful experience in
attempts at correspondence improvement seems to agree is essential.

VI. The Recommended Program

The high cost of correspondence and the deficiencies in the quality
of letters at Burns, Inc., definitely indicate that the company should
institute an improvement program as soon as possible.

Published articles, the experiences of firms that have worked at
improving their correspondence, and the advice of a professional consultant
all suggest that the best plan is a three-pronged attack:

1. Employ a professional teacher to motivate and instruct
   employees as the first step.

2. Provice a correspondence manual for ready reference.

3. Appoint a permanent correspondence supervisor to keep up the
   motivation, help with special problems, and spot-check out-
   going mail to catch and correct any developing laxness.

As the solution to the problem of poor letters at Burns, Inc.,
I therefore recommend that the company take these three steps in order
as soon as practicable. Specifically, I recommend Dr. R. R. Brawner
of Del Monte as the professional consultant and teacher to start the
program.

With the recommended program in operation, at a cost of about
$4,000 ($3,500 + $300 + overhead), Burns should expect to save at
least 50 times that much a year by writing fewer but better letters
and by avoiding duplication. But the biggest improvement would be
the better company image Burns correspondence would put in the minds
of its readers.

Because the short analytical reports discussed in this chapter are simply cut-down versions of the complete analytical reports discussed in the preceding chapter, you need no checklist for these. You can easily use the applicable parts of the checklist for complete analytical reports (pp. 560–71).

SHORT-REPORT CASES—LETTERS, MEMOS, ETC.

1. The Administrative Management Society conducted a survey of its members to determine their policies on office grooming. Of the 372 members responding, 52 percent said miniskirts were permitted in their companies, 48 percent said they weren't. Here are some other results:

	Yes	*No*
Colored, textured, or fishnet hose	66%	34%
Boots	25	75
Beards	26	74
Moustaches	73	27
Sideburns	46	54
Long hair (a la Beatles)	5	95
Turtleneck shirts (versus coats and ties)	23	77

As the office manager of Steck & Co., Austin, Texas 78703, in charge of 272 office employees, write a memo to the executive committee proposing revised policy on office grooming. Some of the employees—especially some young ones—are apparently not only trying to be very much up with new styles but also seem to be pushing the limits of acceptability. As a result, you have noticed many distractions from work and lots of catty remarks and resentments between the faddists and those who dress conservatively. You have these note-pad jottings of points you want to make:

—No Victorian, prudish, or puritanical interest in limiting employee freedoms when actions and dress do not interfere with work and reputation of Steck.

—In view of competition for employees, accept what others do by as much as 55–45 percent.

—As printer of school and office manuals, booklets, and forms, suggest grooming slightly on conservative side, in keeping with line of work and desired public image.

2. As a statistician in the U.S. Department of Agriculture, you have the request from your boss (the Secretary of Agriculture) for a memo on how the American farmer is doing in our fast-changing economy. (He will of course report to the appropriate congressional committee and hence to the press and the public.)

By way of preparation, you've made the following jottings from the great mass of data your department collects continuously:

—Food prices rising 7 percent annually now (meat 12 percent).

—$89.5 billion last year spent for food (up 44 percent in a decade); $28.9 billion to farmers (specific examples: 50 cents per dollar spent for milk, 14 cents for bread, 22 cents for oranges, 27 cents for onions, 33 cents for potatoes, 9 cents for corn flakes, 17 cents for frozen peas, 25 cents for margarine).

—Five percent of total living costs (not just food) goes to farmers for food (versus 10 percent two decades ago).

—Number of farms dropped from 7 to 3 million since 1935; trend line points to 1.5 million in a decade.

—Farm income dropped again to $4,526 average last year; farmer's costs up about 3 percent a year recently—twice the percentage price increases paid for his products.

—One farm worker produces food for 42 people now, versus 23 a decade ago.

—$60.6 billion of food bill goes to costs after basic food ingredients leave the farm.

—According to National City Bank of N.Y., food retailers' after-tax profits average 1.1 percent of sales (bakeries 3.2).

—Percentage price increases during the past decade among the main sharers in the $60.6 billion going to the people who store, transport, process, package, advertise, and sell food are labor 53, transporter 15, corporation after-tax profits 71, depreciation 57, business taxes 83, advertising 67, rent 55, interest 150, repairs and bad debts 71, other 22.

3. Assume that you are a research assistant in the office of a state representative. Your boss is a graduate and strong supporter of the U. of X and is from the county where the U. of X is. He has been much concerned in recent years about the small state appropriations for the University (the major university of the state) while larger and larger appropriations have been going to a lot of smaller state schools, including several new junior colleges and colleges with little or no graduate work. Anybody in higher education work knows that advanced graduate and research programs (best administered by major institutions) are much more costly than undergraduate work.

Preparing for a major speech in support of higher appropriations for the U. of X, your boss has asked you to see what statistics you can provide to support his position.

You have found that state support for higher education in the 50 states over the past eight years averaged a 233 percent increase. Many major institutions, however, have not received increases in keeping with the overall gains in appropriations for higher education in their states. The 15 institutions with the greatest gaps are listed in the following table:

| | Percentage of increase | | |
Institution	Institutional Gains	State Gains	Eight-year gap (lag)
Florida State University	144	278	134
North Carolina State University	128½	275	146½
Ohio State University	114	284	170
Rutgers University	182	288½	106½
Texas A & M University	180	259½	79½
University of Arkansas	112½	229	116
University of Connecticut	286	370	84
University of Hawaii	320	432	112
University of Massachusetts	239	417	178
University of Michigan	79½	157½	78
University of North Carolina	191	275	84
University of Tennessee	221	329½	108½
University of X	82½	278	195½
Virginia Polytechnic Institute	138	261	123
Washington State University	107½	189	81½

Give the supervisor a memo of your findings from this approach.

4. As office manager, write a memo on the memo form of the Treatolite Corporation (a St. Louis chemical research and patent-leasing firm working on petroleum processing) to go to each of your seven department heads, concerning the selection of a copying machine for reproducing letters, magazine articles, drawings, and other documents. You have looked into five already, but all of them had limitations that did not make them adaptable to all-around application in Treatolite offices and laboratories. Just recently, however, Eastman Kodak has introduced a new machine that looks hopeful.

You have literature on it and can see only one objection: Pages to be reproduced have to be laid flat in the machine. Magazine pages would therefore have to be torn out. Since your departments are all in one building, all your men have been able to get along pretty well with one copy of the numerous technical magazines which you subscribe to; and you would not want to mutilate them before binding them in volumes for your permanent library. You could, however, order duplicate copies wherever necessary—probably without excessive expense. Certainly you could, by using the machine, more economically and quickly reproduce the various papers that the departments have been asking your central stenographic pool to type up—to say nothing of the fact that many of the magazine articles have charts, graphs, tables, drawings, and pictures that your girls can't reproduce.

You have therefore arranged with the local Eastman man to give a demonstration in your office two weeks from today. You invite the department heads to attend if they want to. Whether they come or not, you want each to send you about five pages of material he wants reproduced (and can wait for until the demonstration date). You want to encourage them to select material that is somewhat typical but will truly test the machine's versatility. They'll have to mark the material as to source (so you can return it and the copies desired to the right department) and (as always) to indicate the number of copies desired. You want them to be thinking about possible ways to overcome the one known weakness of the machine so that, when they get their copied material, they can give you their suggestions on that problem, their comment on the quality of work the machine does, and their vote to buy it or not.

5. Assume that you are working for a company whose annual report is attached to your report.

Assume that the chairman of the annual reports committee (a vice president) has asked you for your evaluation of the report because (a) he has learned that you studied report writing and, (b) not having worked on the report, you can give an independent judgment.

Specifically, he wants you to point out *good* and *bad* things about the report *presentation*. The idea is how to improve future reports by keeping the good and eliminating the bad.

He does not expect you to check on the reliability of the information—in fact, he tells you to assume that the information is correct. Neither does he expect you to be a publications cost analyst, though you may suggest obvious possible savings that would not hurt the quality of presentation and though you may suggest worthwhile changes that might cost a little more.

He reminds you that each stockholder and each employee gets a copy. Additional copies must go to stock-market officials. Most companies also distribute copies, for public-relations reasons, to major newspapers, news magazines, and anybody else who asks for them. Among those people are great varieties in knowledge of the company, interests, and reading ability. The company wants to get as much as possible of its story to as many as possible of those readers. Your primary concern, then, is how to write the report so that it *will* be read and *can* be read and understood as clearly, quickly, and easily as possible by those readers.

For purposes of illustration and reference, (a) mark passages in the annual report and attach it or (b) clip the desired passages and paste or staple them to your pages or (c) simply make specific references so that the reader can find them quickly in his own copy.

You are to present your analysis in a memo to the vice president.

6. As deputy attorney general, send copies of a memo to your department's more than 1,000 lawyers. (You will attach the memo up front on a package of the time-report forms and a copy of the ten pages of instructions on how to keep the records which are devised for quick feeding into a computer. Ask them to turn in detailed daily reports of their working day.

You realize that the lawyers are likely to resent and resist the order; so you plan your memo carefully, explain that the purpose is to get relief from the heavy work load (not to increase their work or to catch loafers), and tell them that only reasonable accuracy is expected. You need the data to convince Congress that you need a bigger appropriation to employ more lawyers.

7. For the benefit of the editors of *Forbes* (a biweekly business magazine started in 1917), present and interpret the following research data you (in the Statistical Department) have collected:

Circulation (according to the Audit Bureau of Circulation) 101,900 in 1949 (versus 247,500 for *Fortune* and 192,400 for *Business Week*); 107,800 in 1952; 208,000 in 1957; 340,300 in 1962; 400,000 in 1965; 432,700 at June 30, 1965 (versus 439,400 and 504,800 for *Fortune* and *Business Week*—425,700 versus *Fortune's* 388,200 in U.S.); 450,000-plus in 1967. *Business Week* (a newsweekly) started in 1929 and *Fortune* (a story-in-depth monthly) started in 1930.

Recent analysis of subscription lists by W. R. Simmons & Associates Research, Inc., shows 19 percent of subscribers own securities worth $20,000 or more (versus 15 percent and 8 percent for F and BW); 42 percent are in professional or managerial positions in corporations with 1,000-plus employees (versus 33 percent and 37 percent); 36 percent (versus 25 and 27) in big corporations at salaries of $15,000-plus; 61 percent (versus 56 and 46) are college males; 19 percent (versus 17 and 13) scored "superior" on verbal intelligence.

8. As Professor C. E. Mounts, write a memo to the following colleagues in the English Department at the University of Florida (Gainesville, 32601): Professors Lalia Boone, W. A. Clark, J. A. Jones, G. S. Miles, T. Pyles, C. A. Robertson, R. E. Vowles, A. L. Williams.

Professor Robertson (head of the department) has asked you to take charge of drop-add (where students make changes in their schedules) in the English Conference Room, Wednesday—Friday, Sept. 16–18. You will operate 8–12 and 1–5 each day, with one person on duty each half day except for two the first session (the busiest time).

Make the schedule and the duty assignments (not including yourself and Robertson). Colleagues may trade assignments if they inform you; but if anyone can't serve at all, you want to know promptly.

9. For the librarian in charge of your school's reserve reading room, write a memo to all professors, explaining your procedures, rules, and regulations.

—Ask them to submit book lists (on the attached form, of which more copies are available on request) at least two weeks before students are to use the books. You will make books ready in the order of receipt of requests.

—Ask them not to make assignment in the reserve books until you send notice that the books are ready.

—Books not already in the Library may be ordered through the order department (but getting them usually takes longer than two weeks).

—Personal books may be brought in (when listed for the reserve), but the library will not be responsible for loss or damage. If not in hard covers, such books should be put in pam binders (available at bookstores).

10. An exercise in concise, descriptive exposition—

1. Look carefully at everything about a Sprite bottle (including the product name).
2. Assume that you had the job (for Coca-Cola Company) of preparing a bottle design for the product.
3. Assume that you have designed the bottle and written all the proposal report (including criteria, pitfalls, false starts) and have led up to and presented a full-size color picture of the bottle.
4. Now write concise, justifying reasons for each feature of the bottle. (Use a subhead for each feature.)

11. As manager of the ladies' ready-to-wear department in Adelstein's (big department store in Lexington, Kentucky, Zip), you've been concerned about the approximately 20 percent returns. When you mentioned it, General Manager E. M. Scarborough suggested that you study the situation and give him a report suggesting what, if anything, you suggest doing. Your study reveals 11 reasons for returns, with essentially the same percentages for goods delivered over the counter, by trucks, or by mail:

Reason	*Percentage of returns*
Wrong size asked for	38%
Customer change of mind	19
Sent on approval	11
Wrong color	4
Wrong size marked	1
Customer mistake in order	3
Imperfect goods	3
Wrong size sold	3
Miscellaneous	10
None given	7
Unclaimed (will call)	1
	100%

Presently any clerk has the choice of handling a return problem (and filling out a form for your office) or turning it over to the adjustment department.

12. For a variety of reasons—including state and local tax rates, competition for and pay scales of almost all classes of employees, water and power rates, transportation (both local and long-distance), real estate and construction costs, proximity to both raw materials and major markets for finished goods—the board of directors of the Acme Corporation, where you have been the traffic manager for the 15-year life of the corporation, is considering a move of the home office from Chicago to Louisville.

Because the move will involve a considerable shuffling of personnel (some will not want to move, some will not be asked to move, some from the branches all over the country will be moved up to "home," some new men will have to be employed), President Henry Harrison wants to make the major presentation on the personnel shake-up at the next board meeting. He therefore talked to you about personnel moving costs two weeks ago and asked for some guidelines so he could figure the costs when he knows who and how many families will have to be moved.

You reminded him that policy on that topic has grown "like topsy" along with the corporation and that you are having increasing problems because of ill-defined policy that leaves more or less negotiable the question of what you will pay to move old or new employees. Thereupon, President Harrison said now is a good time to firm up the policies—that with increasing growth you will have to have well-set, nonnegotiable policies. So the report due next week takes on that new hue.

You've already done your homework to supplement your experience—fortunately finding already in print two studies that you would otherwise have wanted to do: 1) *Corporate Nomads* by Atlas Van Lines, Inc., a national survey by mail questionnaire sent to corporate traffic managers; 2) an article "Help Your Family Make a Better Move" in *Changing Times* last month by a housewife and staff journalist, Katherine Slaughter, who had surveyed the wives of a hundred corporate nomads and others who had moved.

The two sources provide some relevant statistics, often essentially the same:

40 million Americans a year change addresses; 22 million of them shifting job assignments in their companies or to different companies. Of those 22 million, 90 percent are in the age group 25–45; 68 percent have moved at least once in three years, 18 percent every year, 23 percent once in two years, and many of them 5–7 times in 10–20 years before arriving at the home office.

Source 1 says additionally that 70 percent of corporations pay all moving expenses, 93 percent all *direct* costs; 87 percent place no weight limit on household goods; 95 percent of the paid-for moves cost $510–$8,850 averaging $2,767. Increasing numbers of corporations are paying indirect and "fringe" costs: 53 percent help sell old home and/or find and finance new; half will move a second car (only 43 percent two yrs. ago) and some now pay for boats, trailers, and the like (none two yrs. ago).

Source 2 adds that ¼ of corporations (twice as many as two years ago) now moving employees pay maid service (in connection with the move) at the old and new home; 67 percent pay one house-hunting trip for wives (16 percent two trips); "The moving industry and employing corporations abysmally under-estimate the role of the housewife in moving. The nitty-gritty part of moving belongs to the woman, and her attitude is crucial to the rest of the family's ac-ceptance and adjustment to the move."

Keeping in mind the proposed move of Acme, the increasing competi-tion for personnel, the trend toward paying more and more parts of total personnel moving costs, and the position of *la femme*, give President Harrison the memo he wants for his presentation to the board. (Your instructor may or may not want you to attach a copy of the best personnel-moving-cost policy statement you can write.)

13. To determine faculty opinion on the possible need for an OMBUDS-MAN (a grievance committee) at a certain university, the professional relations and standards committee sent questionnaires to the 1,900 faculty members and received 764 answers: 251 professors, 176 associate profes-sors, 258 assistant professors, and 66 instructors.

Three hundred eighty-four admitted having some problems where an *ombudsman* might help (48 in student relations, 120 in teaching arrange-ments, 131 in nonacademic personnel (hiring, firing, etc.), 80 in student enrollments, 103 in graduate school rules, 149 in research budgets, 133 in travel arrangements, and 116 in other areas. Three hundred fifty-two said they needed no help.

Five hundred eighty-seven admitted there was someone on campus to whom they usually went to discuss problems (168 to departmental col-league, 408 to department chairman, 46 to a colleague not in his depart-ment, 172 to his dean, 75 to a member of the administration, 5 to the AAUP president, and 30 to other persons; 120 answered that they went to no one.

One hundred ninety-five answered favorably when asked if an OMBUDSMAN would help more quickly in solving their problems: 494 answered unfavorably.

Of the 764 questionnaires received in answer, 99 members had been on the faculty 0–1 years, 182 members had been on the faculty 1–3 years, 100 3–5 years, and 371 for more than 5 years.

When the data were summarized by colleges, the trend was about the same as for the total university figures.

As secretary for the committee, write up the results in a memo to the other six committee members as a basis for further discussion and possible recommendations to the university senate.

14. As chairman of the high honors committee in your school, you want to call the attention of faculty members to eight students whose grade point averages (according to the registrar's records) make them likely candidates for high honors. School regulations (p. 97 of the current catalog) say graduating seniors may graduate with high honors if:

—They have an average of 3.5 or better (4.0 is highest) or

—They are recommended by at least three faculty members, and then

—They take and pass the special oral exam given (by invitation only) by your committee.

The eight students look like good prospects, but you cannot invite them to the exam without the required faculty recommendations. You will send the memo to all the departments, asking them to ask teachers to send in recommendations if they feel that the students are worthy.

15. As a technical writing specialist in the central office of your state's highway department, you are to rewrite the following. Under a big bond arrangement, the department is building lots of new highways. The chief inspector is having so much trouble that he wrote the copy. But the highway commissioner says it won't do—that you have to rewrite it. The memo goes to all inspectors.

Inspection

The inspector at one time or another is likely to be faced with the situation wherein the materials or work being produced by the contractor are not acceptable as set forth by specification requirements and the men in charge of the contractor's operations are openly antagonistic to any corrective action that should be taken to the point wherein they not only refuse to make adjustments, but continue to produce the unacceptable material or work. The inspector might even be told by the foreman that they don't have to comply with the inspector's warning concerning specification limits and claim that they "cannot be shut down." The procedures and timing may vary somewhat depending on the particular operation but there is no option but a requirement that the inspector's instructions be "carried out" or the work be "shut down." Inspection work can be a complex nature requiring a high degree of intelligence for technical matters and human relations to insure acceptable work with a minimum of interruptions and warnings. It will be attempted (in the attached procedures sheet) to set forth the recommended procedure for the inspector to follow in a situation wherein he considers the work must be suspended due to an infraction of the contract or when warning letters should be written.

It may be pointed out that it is by far the majority of contracts wherein the inspection work is carried out to its satisfactory conclusion without any particular problems and on an agreeable basis among all personnel concerned. In other words, most contractors recognize their responsibilities in the work and most inspectors carry out their duties in a fair and intelligent manner.

Obtaining good inspectors has long been a troublesome problem to the department. Inspection work is sometimes exceedingly difficult especially when the material or work starts falling outside of the specifications and the contractor's men are resisting corrective measures to avoid the additional expense. In practice it has been found that at least three types of personalities, although they may be actually desirable for other phases of our work, must be screened out of the inspection work.

1. The "agreeable type," which in avoiding arguments, possible bad feelings, unpleasant tasks of informing others, etc., will accept work or material that is completely unacceptable to the specifications.

2. The "domineering type," peculiar to their make-up, that will take the powers as authorized them through their position, and dictate, harass, or badger the contractor's personnel in an unnecessary and needless manner like a "small town cop operating the proverbial traffic speed trap." The use of these powers to domineer or for revenge due to personal differences cannot be tolerated.

3. There are inspectors, mostly through no fault of their own, that have personalities that clash with others, sometimes to the extent that they cannot tell the foreman the time of day without causing a heated argument. In some cases, even though the inspectors were far above average in intelligence and ability to conduct tests, these good qualifications were lost because of this personality barrier. If this irritating attitude (sometimes being referred to as "superior," "biased," "resentful," "overbearing," etc., cannot be effectively overcome, then this individual should be assigned to a different job—or taken off inspection work entirely.

16. Memo to all residents of university (or college) residence halls from the director of food services. During the preceding summer the food service department started a serve-yourself salad buffet. Students seemed to like it. Today you receive notice that such serving is contrary to department of health regulations. The inspector says you must stop and return to the normal salad service from the cafeteria line. But students may return for second servings, as before. To take effect beginning of next month.

17. The Electronic Manufacturing Co., Inc., is located in Kansas City, Missouri, and has affiliated plants in Akron, Ohio, and Cleveland, Ohio. The home office is located in downtown Cleveland. Sales of the electronic ovens (produced in Kansas City) have grown until the plant has become inadequate. There is no available land near the present plant, and its foundation will not carry additional stories. The company is considering building at one of three locations: a new location in Kansas City; Industrial Park, Cleveland; or Euclid, Ohio.

A new plant 450 by 250 feet, with a second floor 60 by 250 feet for offices; with adequate sources for power, air, and water; and including a building site, would cost about $950,000 in Euclid, 15 percent more in Kansas City, and 20 percent more in Industrial Park. The Chamber of

Commerce of Euclid offered to donate a site of 20 acres, served by a highway and two railroads, with all utilities brought to the site. The site, its present worth being about $80,000, lies just outside the city limits and would therefore enjoy a low tax rate—3 percent lower than in Missouri. Property tax for the Kansas City site was $5,300 last year. This tax would be four percent higher in Industrial Park.

The expenses of moving the equipment and inventories to Euclid or Industrial Park would amount to approximately $90,000. The expense of moving to a new site in Kansas City would be about $25,000. Should it move out of Kansas City, the company would have to pay the moving expenses of 15 executives, which are estimated at approximately $3,500 for each man who could be moved to either Industrial Park or Euclid.

During the past year, executives of the company spent $9,000 in traveling between the Cleveland office and the Kansas City plant. In addition, $2,500 was spent in telephone calls. Moreover, the company paid $20,000 in Missouri state income taxes for the year. No state income taxes are levied in Ohio.

Total yearly wages in Kansas City have averaged about $435,000. There will be no appreciable differences in the number of workers required in the new plant. Prevailing wage rates in Euclid would increase total expenditures per year for wages by 2 percent. Higher prevailing rates in Cleveland would increase yearly wage expenditure by 3 percent.

On the basis of these data, where should the plant move? Why? Write to T. Lee Hall, president of the company, giving him your recommendation and including comparative costs on initial expenses and operation for the first year. Submit the report in letter or memo form as your instructor directs.

18. As director of the placement bureau in the college of commerce and business administration at your university, you have been asked by the dean of students to submit a short report (for distribution to high schools in your state and to incoming freshmen) on employment of C&BA graduates using the bureau's services. Your dean tells you that the students would be interested in what fields (industry, banks, government, etc.) the graduates have entered during the past two years and in the average salary for those obtaining employment through the bureau. The dean wants to inform the students of the bureau's service to the students in arranging interviews.

Since the bureau asks graduates using the bureau to report on job placement, you have the available statistics. By knowing who the potential readers are, you are ready to prepare a report which highlights in an interesting style the two major areas of interest.

College of Commerce and Business Administration
June, August, January (most recent year)

Total number of graduates—664
Total number reporting—431
C&BA average salary (B.S.)—$704.00 monthly
Number students interviewing—485
Number individual interviews—3367

Status of Employment	Totals	Percent
Industry	104	24.1
Government	7	1.6
CPA firms	22	5.1
Banks	9	2
Family	10	2.3
Self-employed	1	.3
State institutions	8	1.8
Military	107	24.8
Staying in school	86	20
Unemployed or undecided	77	18
Total number reporting	431	100

Starting Salaries	Totals
Number reporting	144
Low	$ 394
High	$1,200
Average	$ 704

May (most recent year)

Total number graduates—314
Total number reporting—207
C&BA average monthly salary—$724
Number students interviewing—244
Number individual interviews—1284

Status of Employment	Totals	Percent
Industry	46	22.3
Government	6	2.9
CPA firms	13	6.3
Banks	3	1.4
Family	5	2.4
Self-employed	3	1.4
State institutions	0	
Military	42	20.3
Staying in school	48	23.2
Unemployed or undecided	41	19.8
Total number reporting	207	100

Starting Salaries	Totals
Number reporting	61
Low	$ 500
High	$ 950
Average	$ 724.42

19. In an attempt to improve the efficiency of registration at your school, the registrar has decided to pick the brains of as many students as he can. To that end he induced the student paper to run a brief article of explanation, including a sincere and forceful invitation to students to submit memos (form given as in your text) by hand or by U.S. or campus mail this week. The explanation made clear that the registrar does not want any waggish, unrealistic, or far-out revolutionizing of the system. A committee of seven experienced teachers and registration office employees will consider the problems and all sensible suggestions before revising the present system. Mainly what the registrar *does* want are specific troubles you had at the last registration together with remediable causes (if you know) and suggested cures (if you think you see any reasonable ones).

Write the memo based on your experience if you had as many as three specific troubles; if not, talk to a friend or friends until you have at least three different problems, and use the experiences as your own. Keep your shirt on; write a report, not a diatribe.

20. As a product designer for the Ohio Match Company, write a memo to H. N. Sparks, general manager, recommending changes in design, structure, and materials of Ohio's books of paper matches. As the main source of information, get any book of paper matches and inspect it carefully (maybe tear it to pieces), assume that Ohio made it, and think hard.

You might consider the following divisions (unless you're sure you can do better): purpose of the memo, description of the product, uses and conditions of use, and recommendations for improvement.

In the description and the discussion of uses, emphasize those points that are the bases of your proposed changes; and show clearly the interrelationships of description, uses, and recommendations. Use freehand drawings at appropriate places if they will help. Ignore the whole question of advertising. Some books have the strike plate on the front. Is that best? Some are not very rigid because of the narrow, single staple in the center. Some tear apart as a user tries to pull out one match, the stem of which is equally tough all the way down. When you put your mind to it, you can find fault with anything; perfection is a rarely achieved quality. But correcting faults without running into worse ones is hard. That's where a designer earns his money. (This report could be written as a justification report.)

21. Assume that you have graduated and acquired a job, appropriate to your training, in a big office where

a) The company has a library-lounge and buys books, magazines, and other reading material related to its work.

b) The company invites memo suggestions of any kind from all employees.

Write a memo or justification report to the person in charge of buying for the library, suggesting a subscription to a magazine in your field. Basing your comments on at least five recent issues, consider such points as the following about the magazine (and show how they make it appropriate reading for the company's employees):

—Purpose, goal, intended readers

—Types of writers and contributors

—Types of articles

—Special sections and departments

—Gist of a recent article or two

—Illustrations

—Advertising

22. Assume that you have written this first draft of a covering memo about the results of a survey study you have made. You see that the memo is not good. Rewrite it as a letter.

TO: Fellow Business Teachers

FROM: (Your name with the title "Executive Secretary,
                 United Business Education Association")

SUBJECT: Some Recent Developments in Business Education

Several months ago you were one of the 150 business teachers who were selected to participate in an experiment. This experiment was to use an "open-end" survey form to secure current information relative to recent developments in business education. We wanted to determine what changes, if any, had occurred in certain business courses during the past two decades.

It was recognized that this survey form could not be tabulated statistically and that it would be time-consuming to answer. However, it was believed that it would be more indicative of potential trends and actual change than a long check sheet. The fact that you were joined by over 60 percent of your colleagues in completing this questionnaire speaks well for the high degree of professional interest in business education.

The attached summary is a brief condensation of hundreds of pages of written material. We have tried to select the highlights and to emphasize trends. As would be imagined in certain areas, there are no really significant trends. In others there seem to be conflicting statements, or countertrends. We believe that this material will be of interest to you as it expresses the reactions of numerous junior high, high school, and college teachers throughout the United States. If you have any questions regarding the attached, I would be happy to have you contact me. Again, I want to say a very sincere thanks for your cooperation.

23. For a purpose and situation which your instructor assigns (or leaves to your imagination or clarification):

a) Introduce (i.e., lead into) the information in the following table.

b) Present the information, with a good heading, in the best graphic form you can devise for the purpose.

c) Interpret the facts fully.

U.S. family income (before taxes)

Income	1950 Average: $3,319	1960 Average: $5,417		1970 Average: $9,867
$0–$3,000	42%	23%	Under $5,000	19.3%
$3,001–$5,000	28	21	$5,000–$6,999	11.8
$5,001–$7,000	20	25	$7,000–$9,999	19.9
$7,001–$10,000	6	18	$10,000–$14,999	26.8
$10,000 and up	4	13	$15,000+	22.3

24. Get the week's closing market quotations on a blue-chip stock for at least the last 20 weeks. (A class may share the work and the information, or each student may have to find his own best way to get the information, or each student may be assigned or allowed to choose a separate stock.) Using the data, make up two different straight-line trend charts with different unit scales, and write one or both of the following one-page reports (letter or memo form):

a) Recommending that the reader (a businessman who likes to play the market) buy 100 shares.

b) Recommending that the reader not buy now.

Include the appropriate chart and a market theory within the report(s).

25. The buildings superintendent of your school has prepared the copy for a training and procedures manual for all employees doing janitorial work under his direction. (The maintenance men, doing repair and replacement work, will get a different manual.) Realizing that he is not a good writer, he employs you to organize and edit the copy for his approval before it goes to the final typist. He gives you the copy with the following headings, all in the same form, on successive sections. (From reading the copy, you've jotted down the parenthetical indications of the content under the various headings.)

You see immediately that the sequence of topics will have to be settled first because it will affect the copy editing—especially in the transitions and the avoidance of needless repetition. So your first job is to organize the sections into major divisions and their appropriate subdivisions, improve the wording of headings where you can, and put the sections in the best sequence. In other words, make a classification outline or detailed table of contents. You are allowed to combine two or more topics under one double heading if you need to, or you can phrase broader headings to cover two or more closely related ones from this list. By indention and/or outline symbols, clearly indicate the level of each heading.

Background (history and size of job; number and general assignments of personnel)

The Foreman (duties, qualities)

Leave Benefits (sickness, vacation)

Overtime (Saturday, special events; paid as hours off)

Work Schedule (foreman assigns; adapt to "open" time in offices and classrooms)

Accessory Items (mops, brushes, brooms, rags; cleaning, storing, replacing)

Showers (daily cleaning, airing)

Halls and Stairways (daily cleaning procedures and timing; weekly mopping)

Banisters (daily dusting, weekly washing)

Floors (daily cleaning each of 10 kinds)

Scrubbing and Waxing (floors; occasional)

Brick Tile (daily cleaning; occasional scrubbing and waxing)

Cement Floors (cleaning)

Soap Dispensers (cleaning, filling)

Door Hardware (quarterly cleaning)

Blackboards (daily dusting, fortnightly washing)

Chalk Trays (daily cleaning, stocking)

Erasers (cleaning)

Light Fixtures (occasional cleaning; replacing incandescent bulbs only)

Walls (cleaning as needed)

Baseboards (cleaning as needed)

Furniture (cleaning as needed)

Floor-Machine Brushes (cleaning, storing, replacing)

Buckets and Wringers (cleaning, oiling)

Supplies—Janitor Closets (stocking, cleaning, keeping orderly, locking)

Work Items and Procedures (daily cleaning entrances, rest rooms)

Glass Doors and Partitions (cleaning as needed)

Reminders—Day Crew (mainly cautions, emergencies)

Night Operations (mainly scrubbing and waxing)

Equipment and Supplies—Window Washers

Janitor/Maid Daily Duties (list)

Janitor/Maid—Not Daily Duties (list, done as directed by foreman)

Janitor/Maid—Do Not Do the Following (limitations on responsibilities)

Night Supervisor (duties)

Stripping, Scrubbing, and Waxing (procedure; done when and where night supervisor directs)

Reminders—Night Crew (details related to preceding head, plus safety precautions)

Personal Habits and Appearance (reflect favorably; some reasons for dismissal)

On-the-Job Conduct and Relationships (get along with faculty, students, fellow workers)

Reporting Maintenance Problems (emergency, general; where, how to report)

Special Events—Window Washing (same 15-man crew for setups at homecoming, commencement, registration, etc.)

Window-Washing Procedure (foreman designates when, where)

Useful Hints on Care of Janitorial Equipment (cleaning, keeping in good order; reporting needed repair)

26. For some time you, as the superintendent of the Stanhope Packing Company (Astoria, Washington), have been concerned about the condition of uniforms worn by the employees who sort and strip such foods as crab, shrimp, salmon, and tuna for canning by your company. Some of the uniforms are so soiled and stained that they'd cause trouble if an AAA inspector spotted them on an inspection visit. Others are too worn and/or ill-fitting to be considered appropriate for work. Although you have been supplying a clean white uniform daily to these employees (having them laundered and always ready for use), you decide that the system is not working the way you'd like it to. After talking with several of the supervisors and the people who do the actual food preparation, you decide to allow each employee to draw as many as five uniforms for his/her use until they wear out, but after that to require the employees to furnish their own. They will also be responsible for the care (including laundering) of them. You will grant each employee a cash allowance of $6 a week (which is not subject to taxes) to help absorb this expense. In your memo for distribution to all employees, make clear that they must wear a clean white uniform in good condition each day.

27. For some years the company for which you are plant manager has operated a company cafeteria serving breakfast from 6 to 8, lunch from 11:30 to 1:30, and supper from 4:30 to 6. In addition, a snack bar has operated from 6 A.M. to 12 midnight. But because of increased costs and difficulty in securing help and a steady decrease in number of employees eating supper in the cafeteria, you are faced with the necessity of curtailing service. As an alternative to increasing the prices employees pay at present, you and the cafeteria manager have decided to eliminate all meal service in the cafeteria, to convert the snack bar exclusively to vended foods and drinks, and to expand the selection of food in the snack bar. Address the memo to all employees.

28. To inform all employees of the local plant (where you are controller) of changes in distribution of paychecks, prepare a memo for general distribution. Under the revised plan employees will no longer go to the payroll windows in the plant administration building but will receive their paychecks in their respective departments starting at 10 and stopping at 12 on Fridays. Pay is figured, as before, on a Thursday-to-Wednesday week. Checks not picked up on Friday morning will be available at the payroll office Monday through Thursday 4–5. The change is because of the increasing numbers of employees and the long lines and waits at the payroll window.

29. You are the credit union officer of the Bowen Corporation employee credit union, which has about $500,000 representing shares bought by employees, for lending to fellow workers. It has just recently been activated.

Prepare a memo for distribution to all employees, announcing the institution of the plan and availability of the money, provided that the loan application is approved. Employees have to pay a $5 fee for membership. Invite additional investment; you expect to pay a 6 percent return. Employees pay 1 percent a month interest, figured on the exact number of days the money is used. For the time being, the three-man committee that reviews all loan applications has decided on a $500 limit for any loan.

30. Preparatory to registration for the next session of your college, write a memo for the dean (or the director, or the head) to be distributed to all staff members connected with enrolling students. Remind them to check prerequisites for each course carefully; far too many students have had to add and drop courses after classes were under way because registration or enrollment personnel put students in classes for which they were not prepared. Emphasize that the normal load for a student with a *C* average is 15 or 16 hours (or credits); that students with a *B* average may carry 18, and those with an *A* average as high as 21—but only upon written permission from the dean's (or director's, or head's) office. No student may under any circumstances carry 22 hours. Nor may any student on campus carry less than 12. Any person attempting to register for less than 12 hours should have written permission from the appropriate office indicating either that he is a nondegree (special) student or that he needs only a certain number less than 12 hours to complete his degree requirements. Only a student who has received a grade of *F* in a course may reenroll for the second time; having received a minimum passing grade or an *X* or Incomplete or Deferred, he may not begin again from the beginning. Registration officials should be careful to see that students are admitted only at the times designated for them; if they are late, they have to register the last afternoon of the last day of registration; they should not be allowed to usurp the time of students who do report on time.

31. In the role of the industrial relations director for National Rolling Mill, Inc., write a memo authorizing one of your assistants to submit a report evaluating various SUB plans now in operation in the steel, auto, aluminum, rubber, and glass industries. SUB stands for supplemental unemployment benefits. You'd like to have as thorough a study of the various plans as is possible to obtain through avaliable sources (magazine articles, annual reports, monographs, books) to aid your thinking and planning for an eventuality in your own company that is rapidly assuming the form of a reality. Indicate a time by which you want the report.

32. For the president of your institution, prepare a directive to go to all faculty and staff members reminding them of the fact that most of the buildings on your campus are equipped with automatic sprinkler protection with an alarm bell as part of the system. In all cases the alarm bells are located on the outside walls of the buildings, on the ground floor. When water begins to flow through the sprinkler system, the alarm bell rings. All persons in buildings so equipped should be aware of the fact that there is such protection and of the location of the bell. The reason for this memo is that on the 18th of last month a broken waterline of the sprinkler system in the administration building caused approximately $10,000 damage. Several people heard the ringing of the waterflow alarm bell but did not notify the police or fire department because they were unaware of what was happening. As an attachment to this memo, you are listing all the buildings so equipped and the location of the bells. You want each employee to know the status of the building(s) where he works—and teachers to announce to their classes in buildings were applicable.

33. As plant manager for Specific Motors, Inc., Pontiac, Michigan, prepare a directive in memo form for distribution to all employees: Parking control system being inaugurated; stickers corresponding to parking places are $2 at the employment office any time between 8:30 and 5:30 during the next week; after that, violators' cars towed away, released for $5.

34. As city manager in a sizable city with an excellent three-year-old city hall, you want to write a justification report to the five city commissioners, recommending two daily 20-minute breaks for employees and an arrangement for an employee snack bar in available space in the hall.

Although breaks have never been approved, your talks with the nine department heads and every 10th name on alphabetical lists of employees reveal that about 67 percent of the employees take one or more anyway (15–40 minutes); conscientious workers resent the liberties taken by others, and the others feel guilty; and department heads have quit trying to prevent the unapproved breaks.

The city attorney says your proposals are legal, within the power of the commissioners to authorize.

Your proposed breaks are in line with allowed "coffee-break" time of at least half the business and industrial firms of the city and with the nationwide practices of three fourths of such firms (as reported in a recent study by the National Office Management Association, *Coffee Breaks in U.S. Business and Industry,* Philadelphia, 1971, p. 11).

35. Leon Farris needs to repaint the interior of his men's apparel shop. He had originally planned to use the same colors he had had for the past 10 years, medium-green walls and ceiling, light-stained mahogany-colored shelves and counters. But after talking with a paint salesman, he realized that it might be advisable to consider other colors. So he asked you, one of his college part-time clerks, to look into the possibilities for decoration of the store.

The floor is covered in a light-colored rust (with green flecks) indoor-outdoor carpeting. It is in good condition, and so Farris does not want to change it. The fluorescent fixtures will also stay the same.

You talked with Lester Gould, owner of City Hardware, Inc., who reported a 16 percent increase in sales after redecorating in light colors. And the manager of the Belken Department Store reported a sales increase of 12 percent after repainting in pastels.

F. B. Phillips, lighting engineer whom you consulted, told you that dark colors absorb both natural and artificial light. Pastel colors make it possible to obtain 50 percent more light for each watt consumed, without any extra lighting cost.

Grant Uzell, a color expert whom you interviewed, recommended a light yellow for the walls and, since the ceiling is high, suggested a darker shade of yellow to make it seem lower and to harmonize with the walls. He suggested that the shelves and counters stay the same. Redecorating in these light colors will cost Farris no more than redecorating in darker colors.

Report your findings and recommendations in a direct-style memo.

CASES FOR SHORT ANALYTICAL REPORTS

1. As Mr. Buford T. Singer, P.O. Box 2715, University, Alabama 35486, you have received this letter:

Would you please send me your analysis and recommendations on the following common stocks: Canadian Breweries, Inc., Merrill Island Mining Corporation, and McLean Industries. (Substitute any three as directed by your instructor.)

I am considering the addition of shares in any or all of these corporations to my stock portfolio. I've heard that you have recently finished some research into the evaluation of stocks as an investment and would like for you to apply the criteria you have developed to these issues.

Naturally, I'll be interested in learning something about the nature of the industry in which each of these companies operates; the size of each company and its scope of operations; net assets per common share of stock in each company and the dividend histories; and any operating details which might affect future price increases.

Please *do not limit* your discussion to my suggestions, Mr. Singer. But do keep in mind that I like to move into and out of the market and that I am looking mainly for an increase in market price over the next 12 months rather than a long-range income from my investment.

Call it intuition (I've been pretty lucky on this basis before!)—but I feel I simply must have your report in my hands no later than a month from today (when I shall have a certificate of deposit of $10,000 maturing). I understand that your normal charge for this type of analysis is $25 per hour and hope that your fee will run no more than $100.

Mrs. J. H. Swindley, 41 Drury Lane Apartments, Old Selma Road, Tuscaloosa, Alabama 35401, obviously wants information and recommendations. What information is really significant? Submit the report with cover, covering transmittal letter, and the report itself. (This could readily be a letter report of several pages.)

2. Two weeks ago your boss, James Bowran, asked you to prepare a report on what kind of typewriters he should buy for use in his eight Illinois Auto Supply Stores. He will buy 10 of the same kind because by so doing, he will get a 10 percent discount.

The only other time he had called you to his office since you started working for him two months ago was to ask you what you meant by the words *synchronize* and *simultaneously* in a letter you wrote and to tell you that he likes his language straight. At that time he told you that Rudolf Flesch's book, *The Art of Readable Writing,* is the best book written in the last 25 years (and you suspect that it is the only one he has read in that time).

Although you, like the other employees, are a bit ill at ease when talking with Mr. Bowran, you admire his directness. Moreover, you know that he has you working as assistant manager in the main office in Chicago to size you up as prospective manager of the largest branch at Peoria. You suspect that your report is to determine his decision about you and the typewriters.

A hundred interviews with secretaries selected at random in Chicago offices enabled you to reduce the field to four makes of machines on the basis of secretarial preference. Since Mr. Bowran told you that he wanted to give attention to his girls' desires, even at some cost (perhaps for the same reason he has taken some of the girls to dinner and the theater), you sent them a questionnaire. Twelve of the 20 experienced secretaries working for Illinois Auto showed a preference for Regal typewriters among the four makes, as the interviews with Chicago secretaries had suggested they would.

There were other reasons for your decision to recommend 12-inch Regals, each with its special feature—a bronze platen which can be inserted in 30 seconds for cutting stencils better and making large numbers of clear carbons. The list price is $532 plus $14 for the extra platens. All the new machines have such features as automatic margin sets, choice of elite or pica type, and 12- or 16-inch platens. Each also has some special features. Besides secretaries' preferences, you decided that you would compare the machines on the basis of original cost, upkeep, touch, and special features important to the work (although not necessarily in that order).

Before starting your interviews, you made a study of the use of type-writers in Illinois Auto's offices. You found that only experienced secretaries were employed and that they typed almost constantly for 40 hours a week. The work included letters with varied margins, stencils, memos with many carbons, and tables and price lists that required turning 8½- by 11-inch sheets sideways.

The salesmen who demonstrated the four machines to you each had some gadgets to point out; but when you tried the machines, you saw that the gadgets had little importance for your purposes. Only Regal had a store and repair shop in each town where there is an Illinois Auto Store.

The UBM machine, the second choice of Illinois Auto secretaries and secretaries in general, does the neatest work and is fairly durable; but the price is $575, and the machines are hard to repair, making upkeep expensive. The Remingwood, priced at $528, is the most durable, and it has an indicator to show inexperienced typists how much space is left on the page. But its touch is so heavy that it is even more tiring than the Over-wood, priced at $532. Touch is the main reason secretaries put Regal first and UBM second. The three independent repairmen you talked to agreed that Regal machines require more frequent adjustment and repair but that they are so constructed that repair is easy, parts seldom have to be re-placed, and bills on them are usually low.

Use your imagination as the source of any further details you want, so long as you do not imagine anything contrary to what is said or implied here. For example, you may attribute the information to any of the possible sources cited, and you may want detailed statistics to support the general-izations given here.

Write your report, including title page, letter of transmittal, table of contents, synopsis (which may be interwoven in the transmittal letter), and body (introduction, text, conclusions and recommendations). You may use appendixes if you need them.

3. As an assistant to Mr. Robert Boyd, president of Factseekers, Inc., you have been directed to analyze the following SMSA statistics gathered from the most recent editions of *Statistical Abstract of the United States* and *County Business Patterns* on the economies of (two cities named by your instructor) to determine which economy would be more likely to withstand a recession (or fluctuation in the business cycle). He requests that a report of your findings be on his desk (in memo form) no later than a week from today.

Employees on nonagricultural payrolls		
Total (most recent two years)	*City A*	*City B*
Percent of total (most recent year) in:		
Manufacturing		
Wholesale and retail trade		
Services		
Transportation and public utilities		
Contract construction		
Finance, insurance, and real estate		
Government		
Total work force		
Most recent two years available		
Unemployment (annual average)		
Most recent two years available		
Percent of total work force		

Secure dollar figures for the two most recent years available on retail trade (sales and payroll), selected services (receipts and payroll), wholesale trade (sales and percent merchant wholesalers), manufactures (value added, total number of establishments, percent with 20 or more employees, total employees, annual payroll; give percents for dollar value added by (and percent of total employment in) food and kindred products, chemicals and allied products, printing and publishing, machinery, electrical equipment and supplies, transportation equipment, textile mill products, apparel and other textile products, lumber and wood products, paper and allied products.

Secure data for most recent year available for the following.

Retail trade

Sales (dollars)
Payroll entire year (dollars)

Selected services

Receipts (dollars)
Payroll entire year (dollars)

Wholesale trade

Sales total (dollars)
    Percent merchant wholesalers

Manufactures

Establishments
    Total number
    Percent with 20 or more employees
Employees, annual average (thousands)
Payroll, entire year (dollars)

Value added, adjusted (dollars)
  Food and kindred products (percent)
  Chemicals and allied products (percent)
  Printing and publishing (percent)
  Machinery, except electrical (percent)
  Electrical equipment and supplies (percent)
  Transportation equipment (percent)
Manufacturing-Employment
Food and kindred products
Chemical and allied products
Printing and publishing
Machinery, except electrical
Electrical equipment and supplies
Transportation equipment
Textile mill products
Apparel and other textile products
Lumber and wood products
Paper and allied products
Total employed

4. As advertising manager of *Tempo,* you have encountered some difficulty in getting the advertising of manufacturers of products appealing primarily to women because many of them think of *Tempo* as a man's magazine. Some recent research you've done shows that 87 percent of the subscribers are men; but most of them have wives, and in your national interview survey you found that 1.8 million men and 1.5 million women read at least part of the magazine weekly. Further analysis of the 1,600 interviews led to the following table:

Department	Number of women readers for each 100 men
Art	128
Books	120
Business	59
Canada	75
Cinema	122
Education	97
International	74
Letters	97
Medicine	93
Music	117
National Affairs	80
People	103
Press	78
Religion	102
Science	73
Sports	55
Theater	114

Write the study as a short report which you will mail to two groups: (*a*) advertisers who have products appealing primarily to women (to keep them convinced that their advertising is in a good medium) and (*b*) other manufacturers who should be but aren't advertising with you. Some of these have been reported by your salesmen as turning them down because the magazine is a man's magazine. Others—you don't know why.

5. The biggest chain grocery in your locality is having quite a problem nationally with various forms of larceny—$8 million of losses last year through customer shoplifting, employee theft, etc. The management therefore issued a memo directing the manager of each store to study his situation and institute needed changes. (If you need another memo situation, here's one.)

The local manager, under whom you work, tossed the directive memo (and thus the ball) to you. You are to confer with him for any information he already has, to study the layout and procedures by on-the-spot observation and questioning, and to propose (for his consideration) the things to be done to reduce losses.

The job may or may not include a memo or other set of directions to all store employees on just what to do when they know or suspect that larceny or pilferage is going on. This could be a separate memo assignment, requiring a good knowledge of the law and/or law enforcement procedures —perhaps a talk with some police officers.

6. A certain professor has class and other records on 1,137 of his students over the past five years: honor points (4.0 maximum), attitudes toward class attendance, and whether or not on academic probation. Since one of his biggest courses is often required of students on probation (a concentrated, individually adapted course to correct weaknesses in reading, listening, speaking, and writing), only 8 percent of his total students had a 3.3 or better average, and not one of these admitted any objection to being forced to attend class. Of the 31 percent who were on academic probation, 81 percent strongly objected to being forced to attend class. ("Forced" means application of the university's present system of checking on attendance: An instructor sends a warning note any time attendance is unsatisfactory to him; after that, he may send a *drop* note to the registrar for further absences, and the student is automatically dropped from the course.) Many of the professor's students said they wished more instructors demanded class attendance as he did: 12 percent.

Last year, two sections (53 students) of the professor's report-writing course interviewed all students they could find leaving the campus for the weekend five weekends in succession (hitchhikers and others). No student objected to the simple questioning. Results:

a) Of the 309 cases studied, 83 percent proved to be repeaters; that is, they left the campus at least two of the five weekends.

b) A surprising 92 percent were taking textbooks with them.

c) Of the 309, 59 percent admitted to being on academic probation.

Not counted elsewhere are these figures on lecture attendance (in a lecture-discussion course where the professor gives the lecture):

A .... 6.6 percent absenteeism
B .... 8.4 percent absenteeism
D .... 9.7 percent absenteeism
E .... 17.0 percent absenteeism

Write the report for the professor to the vice president for academic affairs. At a recent faculty meeting he said he had a committee considering revision of the regulations on probation, attendance, etc.

7. A recent study of its readers (*Profile of Subscribers to the National Edition of Time*) shows: median age, 39.3; household income, $14,904; children, 1.5; majority own home worth an average $27,235; 76 percent, washing machine; 30 percent, electric carving knives; 38 percent, garbage disposal; 50 percent, two or more cars (67 percent bought new); 79 percent, college attendance; 31 percent, postgraduate work; 67 percent of heads of families (not students or retirees) hold managerial or professional jobs; 94 percent, life insurance (average $43,613); 67 percent own stocks and/or bonds; total family liquid assets average $37,441; 52 percent, one or more FM stereos; 71 percent attend theater; 58 percent, home power tools; 77 percent, record collections; 90 percent of families took trips last year (27 percent out of the country); 75 percent swim for recreation; 40 percent each golf and bowl; 34 percent, members of country or sports clubs; 74 percent entertained guests at home within two weeks before interviews; 81 percent serve liquor (Scotch, gin, bourbon, vodka preferred).

As a study in adaptation, analyze these figures *in relation to* a careful analysis of the current issue of the magazine and point out to the managing editor where he's going wrong in both style and content.

8. Assume that you received the memo mentioned in Case 31 (p. 640), that you've completed the investigation authorized, and that you're now ready to write the report. Write it.

9. As director of the placement bureau at your school, you have been asked by the dean to submit a short report by (date) to be distributed to department chairmen on the status of employment and starting salaries of commerce graduates using the bureau for the past four semesters. He feels that departments would be interested in: (1) What are most of our majors employed in as compared with overall employment of graduates? (2) How does the salary of our majors compare with the overall average salary? (3) Do our majors use the bureau?

Since you ask all graduates using the bureau to report on job placement, you have the available statistics. Thus you are ready to prepare a short report (with introduction, body, terminal—using appropriate style and statistical display).

College of Commerce and Business Administration
May, August, January (most recent year)

Total number reporting 431
Total number of graduates 664 = 64.9 percent

Average monthly salary $704.00
Number of individual interviews 3367
Number of students interviewing 485

Status of employment	Accounting	Business law	Business statistics	Economics	Finance	GB†	Manage-ment	Marketing	OA‡	Totals	Percent
Industry	4	3	1	1	19	14	23	37	1	104	24.1%
Government	4	0	0	0	2	0	1	0	0	7	1.6
CPA firms	22	0	0	0	0	0	0	0	0	22	5.1
Banks	0	0	0	0	6	0	1	1	0	9	2.0
Family	2	0	0	0	3	4	1	0	0	10	2.3
Self-employed	0	0	0	0	1	0	0	1	0	1	.3
State institutions	3	0	0	0	1	1	0	1	2	8	1.8
Military	7	11	5	1	13	16	23	30	1	107	24.8
Continuing education	6	22	3	4	13	9	8	21	0	86	20.0
Unemployed or undecided	8	4	1	0	9	19	15	17	4	77	18.0
Total number reporting	56	40	10	7	67	63	72	108	8	431	100.0
Total number by major	87	52	16	15	102	95	110	176	11	664	

Starting salaries

	Accounting	Business law	Business statistics	Economics	Finance	GB†	Manage-ment	Marketing	OA‡	Totals
Number reporting	33	2	1	2	27	13	26	2	2	144
Low	$500	$500	$1200	$600	$500	$500	$525	$450	$394	$394
High	925	650	1200	675	1000	1000	845	900	450	1200
Average	784	575	1200	637	661	687	723	677	422	704
Median	800	575	1200	637	650	680	740	650	422	700

† General Business
‡ Office Administration

College of Commerce and Business Administration
May (most recent year)

Total number reporting 207
Total number of graduates 314
BS degree level

Average monthly salary $724.00
Number of individual interviews 1284
Number of students interviewing 244

Status of employment	Accounting	Business law	Business statistics	Economics	Finance	GB†	Management	Marketing	OA‡	Totals	Percent
Industry	3	1	2	0	8	7	8	17	0	46	22.3%
Government	4	0	0	0	0	0	0	2	0	6	2.9
CPA firms	13	0	0	0	0	0	0	0	0	13	6.3
Banks	0	0	0	0	2	0	0	1	0	3	1.4
Family	0	0	0	0	0	3	1	1	0	5	2.4
Self-employed	0	0	0	0	1	2	0	0	0	3	1.4
State institutions	0	0	0	0	0	0	0	0	0	0	
Military	7	3	0	0	8	4	8	12	0	42	20.3
Continuing education	7	16	1	4	5	1	5	9	0	48	23.2
Unemployed or undecided	3	1	0	1	5	3	6	17	5	41	19.8
Total number reporting	37	21	3	5	29	20	28	59	5	207	100.0
Total number by major	50	27	4	8	46	35	42	93	9	314	

Starting salaries

	Accounting	Business law	Business statistics	Economics	Finance	GB†	Management	Marketing	OA‡	Totals	
Number reporting	19	1	1	0	8	6	9	17	0	61	
Low	$675	$650	$708.33	0	$500	$580	$600	$500	0	$500	
High	950	650	708.33	0	800	917	806	825	0	950	
Average	818.97	650	708.33	0	644	719	699	677	0	724	
Median	835	650	708.33	0	612	710	700	700	0	715	

† General Business
‡ Office Administration

10. To test the effects of its direct mail, as suggested in Chapter 9 on sales letters, the national advertiser where you work has employed a national fact-finding interview service (called Factseekers, Inc.). The cooperative manufacturer-retailer direct-mail campaign involved six monthly mailings, April through September, each clearly identifying local retailer, product, and manufacturer. Between 10 and 20 days after the last mailing, interviewers talked to people at 1,670 of the addresses in 12 cities of 60,000 or more (one city in each of the company's marketing divisions). Interviewers called at normal mail-delivery time, so as to talk with the person normally receiving the mail, and talked to 75 percent women and 25 percent men. In each city, interviewers attempted to have about 50 interviews in each of three separate retailers' neighborhoods.

The interviewers have tabulated their results and turned them in. As an employee in the research department, you have the job of presenting the facts and interpretations of facts in a report for the vice president in charge of advertising. Here are the findings along with some details of procedure.

To check the respondents' recognition, reading, and passing-on of the campaign pieces, interviewers first used only the last mailing (September) and masked retailer, product, and manufacturer identifications. Results: Seen by 966 or 57.8 percent of the 1,670; product identified by 83.7 percent of the 966, manufacturer identified by 79.8 percent, retailer by 64.8 percent, his location by 70.2 percent. Of the whole 1,670, 27.1 percent had read part of the September mailing, 18.4 percent at least a fifth of it. These 966 who remembered seeing the piece *knew* they had shown it to 427 others and *thought* they had to 292 more. Other findings show 50.4 percent of the husbands saw the mailing, and probably 20.5 percent more; and 90.1 percent of the husbands buy the product (not all this brand!), as do 47 percent of the wives.

Further findings were based on the whole campaign of six mailings, without identifications being masked. Of the 1,670, 77.2 percent remembered seeing at least one mailing: April, 41.3; May, 39.2; June (a mechanized pop-up), 44.4; July, 31.9; August, 34.9; September, 57.8. Of the 77.2 percent, 65.8 percent got a favorable impression of the retailer, 34.2 percent no particular impression. Of all the 1,670, 97 percent said they thought the advertising retailer could serve them satisfactorily, 0.3 percent said no, and 2.7 percent didn't know or didn't answer. More specifically:

	Saw none	Saw September only	Saw one or more, April–August	Saw September and one or more others
Favorable impression of retailer	34.5%	48.8%	59.5%	77.8%
No impression	53.5	41.5	35.6	16.2
Don't know	12.0	9.7	4.9	6.0

Favorable opinion of direct mail in general, 69.9 percent; unfavorable, 23.5 percent (7.8 percent pay no attention to it, 5.1 percent no comment, 3 percent don't have time, 2.9 percent waste of time and money, 1.7 percent throw away unread). More specifically:

	Saw none	Saw September only	Saw one or more, April–August	Saw September and one or more others
Favorable to direct mail ..	44%	57%	72%	84%
Unfavorable	41	30	25	13
Don't know	15	13	3	3

Reasons for buying where they do: Like retailer personally, 44.6 percent; convenient location, 37.4 percent; good service, 34 percent; like product (not all this advertiser's), 21.3 percent.

11. As vice president of marketing for Black's Boutique, you have received the following memo from Marion Morris, president:

Factseekers, Inc., has recommended (name of city supplied by your instructor) as the next market for a new branch of Black's. On the basis of available statistics on retail trade—especially trade from women's clothing, specialty stores, and furriers—should we locate in the central business district (CBD) or the standard metropolitan statistical area (SMSA)? Please submit a report to me by (date supplied by your instructor).

Using the three latest census publication figures, *Census of Business: Major Retail Centers* in (name of state supplied by your instructor), and the *Survey of Buying Power,* for the corresponding years, gather the following data:

		Stores and sales						
		SMSA			CBD		City	
Retail stores		19xx	19xx	19xx	19xx	19xx	19xx	19xx
Total number								
sales (in thousands)								
Apparel and accessory stores								
Total number								
sales (in thousands)								
Women's clothing, specialty stores, furriers								
Total number								
sales (in thousands)								
Women's ready-to-wear								
Total number								
sales (in thousands)								

Percent change in sales (two most recently dated sources)

	SMSA	CBD	City
Retail stores			
Apparel and accessory			
Women's clothing,			
specialty, furriers			
Women's ready-to-wear			

Percent distribution of sales of all retail stores

Apparel and accessory			
Women's clothing,			
specialty, furriers			
Women's ready-to-wear			

CBD sales as percent of City

	SMSA
All retail stores	
Apparel and accessory	
Women's clothing,	
specialty, furriers	
women's ready-to-wear	

Analyze these statistics (and any other you think pertinent) and write a short report in the form your instructor directs answering Mr. Morris' question about the CBD location.

12. The owners of the Luthrie-Garner Nursery, Mobile (Paul Luthrie and William Garner), have asked you, the office manager, to submit a report analyzing demand over the past few years.

You've gone through the sales records of the past four years to see what sells the best as a guide to what to plant the most of, what to reduce, and maybe even what to discontinue. Classifications are hard to set up; for instance, there's no way to tell what kinds of roses are in most frequent demand—but at average sales of $2, it's a safe bet that not many prize rosebushes are sold. But you've worked out the classifications, the number of bushes sold for the last four years, and the average sale of each variety.

Your records show that you average about 5 percent replacements; that is, about 5 out of every 100 plants sold have to be replaced under the terms of your replacement policy: replacement at one-half price if the plant dies within the first year. Your profit margin is about 50 percent.

Study the figures for what they imply in the way of increasing or decreasing demand for particular types and for the relative profitability of the various items. Then make recommendations about next year's stock.

Submit the report to the owners in attractive, readable form. Use a title page as a cover, a letter of transmittal which is also synopsis, and the analysis itself.

Gross sales of shrubbery sold by the Luthrie-Garner Nursery in the last four years

	Four years ago	Three years ago	Two years ago	Last year	Average sale
Abelia	2,896	2,980	4,422	4,460	$ 2.25
Ashfodi Juniper	136	144	202	235	3.00
Azalea	2,940	3,672	6,440	8,756	6.00
Berkman Arborvitae	146	105	137	165	3.50
Boxwood	126	262	344	423	18.00
Camellias	2,888	3,070	4,175	5,480	12.00
Cherry Laurel	174	198	234	256	9.00
Dogwood	81	76	143	166	4.00
Gardenia	1,178	1,239	1,897	1,976	9.00
Ilex Bullata	602	875	1,092	1,160	4.50
Ilex Burfordi	247	288	370	406	6.00
Ilex Rotundifolia	1,786	1,930	2,706	2,816	3.00
Irish Juniper	176	189	259	278	3.00
Ligustrum	2,982	2,646	4,562	4,250	4.50
Nandina	3,364	3,544	3,782	3,802	3.00
Pfitzer Juniper	2,078	2,108	2,986	3,208	2.50
Photinia Glabra	472	381	277	199	2.00
Roses	7,271	7,492	8,792	9,879	2.00
Sargent Barberry	601	507	488	462	3.00
Spirea	192	160	107	126	2.50
Spirea Thunbergia	148	164	92	86	3.00
Yellow Jasmine	296	243	203	194	4.00
Total	30,780	32,270	43,710	48,783	

13. One of the projects you've inherited as director of educational research for the American Association of Collegiate Schools of Business (AACSB) is that of college teacher recruitment and training. Your committee of cooperating university professors of business administration (at Alabama, Indiana, Illinois, Michigan, Minnesota, Kansas, Ohio State, Pennsylvania State, Texas, and Wisconsin) administered your questionnaire to 1,260 juniors, seniors, and graduates at the 10 institutions. Prior to that, you tested your tentative questionnaire on representative students at Wade State University and revised the "free response" questions twice in an attempt to get accurate indications of students' attitudes toward college or university teaching as a career.

Following are questions and tabulated answers which your research assistant has placed on your desk as a basis for writing a report intended for your readers-members of the AACSB, other college administrators, professional associations (accounting, marketing, management), and foundations.

a) Have you ever talked with anyone about the advantages and disadvantages of a career as a collegiate teacher of business administration?
   196 Yes

b) What do you consider to be the advantages of collegiate teaching of business administration as a career?

	Number of times mentioned
Prestige	441
Opportunity to help others	412
Continual learning	252
Short hours	240
Long vacations	226
Regularity of income	156
Absence of pressure	138

	Number of times mentioned
Pleasant duties	129
Desirable associates	128
Research opportunities	125
Consulting opportunities	124
Stimulating intellectual environment	118
Pride in doing significant work	110
Stability of job	93
Independence in carrying out duties	62
Freedom of thought	40

c) What do you consider the disadvantages of collegiate teaching of business administration as a career?

	Number of times mentioned
Pay too low	879
Monotonous, dull duties	213
Industry pays more	188
Promotions too slow	157
Limited room at the top	131
Teachers become too theoretical and impractical	130
Training period too long	128
Inadequate retirement benefits	122
Advanced degree programs too difficult	118
Decreasing demand for teachers	103
Teachers lose drive and originality	62
Teachers not appreciated by society	58
Ability and pay not correlated	52
Restricted expression	48
Restricted personal life	39

d) As a whole, would you favorably consider collegiate teaching of business administration as a career?

781 No   303 Don't know   176 Yes

e) Do you intend to teach business administration at collegiate levels?

1,058 No   177 Don't know   25 Yes

f) Do you think you have enough information about college teachers' training, duties, responsibilities, and rewards (tangible and intangible) to answer questions b and c intelligently?

567 No   569 Yes

Plan the report for final distribution with a title page, letter of transmittal, contents page, and the analysis itself (introduction, survey findings and what they establish as well as imply, and a terminal section summarizing the most significant findings together with appropriate conclusions and recommendations).

14. In charge of the placement bureau at Bugan University, Indianapolis, Morton Fields, director, decided to find out what personnel managers prefer in letters of application from college graduates. So he asked you, director of the research bureau, if you would help him out. After joint consultation with the head of the department of communications, the head of the vocational guidance department, and the head of statistics, you prepared and sent the following questionnaire to 500 personnel managers in Indiana, Illinois, Ohio, Michigan, and Pennsylvania. The replies of the 324 who returned the questionnaire are tabulated below. From this material prepare a short analytical report for Fields which will help him when he talks to applicants. Copies will also be available in school libraries. Submit the report to Fields with cover, title page, letter of transmittal, which is also an epitome, table of contents, and the analysis itself.

1. Which of the following do you prefer from an applicant?
   - 9 Application letter only
   - 86 Application letter and data sheet (or résumé)
   - 106 Application letter with placement office credentials sent separately
   - 123 Application letter and data sheet with placement office credentials forwarded separately

2. Which of the following is more important to you in selecting an applicant:
   - 55 Application letter
   - 37 Data sheet
   - 232 Both equal in importance

3. *a*) Do you object to a duplicated letter of application?
   234 Yes   90 No

   b) When considering several applicants for a job, do you eliminate those who send you a duplicated letter of application?
   143 Yes   181 No

4. *a*) Do you object to a mimeographed data sheet?
   76 Yes   248 No

   b) Do you object to a commercially printed data sheet?
   48 Yes   276 No

   c) When considering several applicants for a position, do you eliminate those who send you either of the following:

Mimeographed data sheet	22 Yes	302 No
Commercially printed data sheet	17 Yes	307 No

5. Which of the following do you prefer?

   123 Applicant's letter addressed to you by name, followed by your title

    85 Applicant's letter addressed to "Personnel Manager"

   116 No preference

6. What is your reaction to the following kinds of enclosures with the application?

   Return-addressed postal card

    29 Favorable   207 Unfavorable   88 Neutral

   Return-addressed stamped envelope

   214 Favorable   71 Unfavorable   39 Neutral

7. *a*) What is your reaction to an applicant's sending you a follow-up letter within a month after he has mailed you his application letter and data sheet?

    252 Good   10 Annoying   62 Neutral

  b) If your answer to the above question is "Good," why do you favor a follow-up? (More than one reason allowed.)

     73 Shows persistence

    178 Indicates interest

    220 Lets me know he is still available

8. In selecting inexperienced employees, which of the following backgrounds do you prefer? Please rank on a 1–2–3–4 basis (highest rank = 1).

  a) Applicant who participated in many extracurricular activities and maintained a passing grade in his studies

    (1) 37, (2) 74, (3) 114, (4) 99

  b) Applicant who participated in several extracurricular activities and maintained above-average grades in his studies

    (1) 102, (2) 124, (3) 79, (4) 19

  c) Applicant who helped pay his own way through school and maintained above-average grades in his studies

    (1) 164, (2) 106, (3) 36, (4) 18

  d) Applicant who participated in no extracurricular activities and maintained honor grades in his studies

    (1) 13, (2) 13, (3) 66, (4) 232

9. On many data sheets or application letters the applicant lists several specific references—usually under a caption labeled "References."

  a) When do you check these references?

    187 Before the interview

    120 After the interview

     17 Do not check

  b) Do you want this list of references included on the application?

    260 Yes   16 No   48 Immaterial

  c) If your answer to the above question is yes:

    (1) How many references do you prefer? Please encircle your choice.

       (1) 0, (2) 16, (3) 193, (4) 72, (5) 43

    (2) What types of references do you prefer? (Check as many as you desire.)

      314 Previous employers

37 High school teachers

25 Dean of the college

252 College instructors of related courses

193 (Former) supervisors

Other (please add) character references (banker, doctor, minister, etc.) 44

10. Many college students have worked part time while attending school. Do you want to know about these jobs, whether they are related or not?

298 Yes   26 No

11. Many college students have worked full time during summers. Do you want to know about these jobs, whether they are related or not?

306 Yes   18 No

12. Do you want personal details? (Age, physical condition, organizations/memberships, hobbies, etc.)

312 Yes   10 No   2 Immaterial

13. If answer to 12 is yes, where?

37 Application letter   256 Data sheet (or résumé)   19 Immaterial

APPENDIXES

appendix A | The communication process and semantic principles

The communication process

WHETHER YOU ARE talking or writing, listening or reading, you are doing one half (sending or receiving) of the two-way process of communication.

Essential to this process are symbols—usually words. (We are not concerned here with smoke signals, smiles, gestures, winks, and other forms of nonverbal communication.) When a person has an idea he wishes to convey to somebody else, he cannot just hand over the idea; he necessarily uses symbols of some kind. In oral communication, these are sounds; written, they become words and figures. The first step in communication, then, is the sender's formulating his ideas into symbols.

These sounds or written symbols do not communicate, however, until they are transmitted by some channel from the sender to the receiver.

Then, to complete the communication process, the receiver has to interpret these symbols back into an idea in essentially the same way the sender had to formulate the idea into symbols.

This simple-sounding three-step process of symbolizing, transmitting, and interpreting nevertheless involves many possibilities of breakdown of communication. If the person with the idea or concept has not learned to talk or is mute, or his would-be receiver is deaf, they obviously cannot communicate orally. But these are problems for the speech and hearing therapists. If he does not know how to write, or his receiver to read, they cannot use written symbols. But these are problems for the teachers of young children. Similarly, we leave to the Postal Service and the electrical engineers in telephone, telegraph, radio, and TV companies the manifold problems of transmitting symbols from sender to receiver with a minimum of interference (called "noise" by communications specialists).

But if the person with an idea has not learned the English language (a system of symbols) well enough for the expression of his idea according to the system, or if his receiver cannot interpret according to the system, they cannot communicate effectively—and they are our problem.

These two steps of formulating concepts into meaningful, standard symbols (frequently referred to as encoding) and interpreting the symbols (decoding) are the two major points of communication breakdown. Since we are concerned primarily with writing (one form of the initiating phase of communication), we deal mostly with encoding, but many of the causes of communication breakdown involve decoding too.

Some basic semantic principles[1]

Fundamental to communication is this general principle: *The symbols used must stand for essentially the same thing in the minds of the sender and the receiver.*

Just as our money is a medium of exchange for goods and services, our language has developed as a medium of exchange for ideas. Although the unit values of both may change with time and circumstances, at a given time and in a given set of circumstances the values of both are pretty well set. You therefore cannot pay a bill for 35 cents by offering a quarter, and you cannot convey the idea of localism by offering the word *colloquialism.* Good diction—choice of the proper word to represent the sender's idea—is thus a minimum essential in oral or written communication.

The diction problem is complicated by the fact that the sender's chosen words must also be in the receiver's vocabulary. You can't use perfectly good Greek to communicate to a person who knows only English. You can't use the highly technical language of medicine, law, engineering, insurance, or accounting to communicate with people who don't know the terms. They're all Greek to the nonspecialist. If you want to communicate, then, you must estimate your receiver's vocabulary and adapt your own accordingly. In general, you are justified in using unusual words or the special language of any field only if you're sure all your receivers know the terms or you explain them as you go along.

------

[1] The bibliography of semantics is extensive, and the books vary greatly in difficulty. If you want to read further on the subject, we suggest that you see the following books in the order listed: David K. Berlo, *The Process of Communication: An Introduction,* Holt, Rinehart & Winston, Inc., New York, 1960. William V. Haney, *Communication: Patterns and Incidents,* Richard D. Irwin, Inc., Homewood, Ill., 1960. Bess Sondel, *The Humanity of Words: A Primer of Semantics,* World Publishing Co., Cleveland, 1958. Stuart Chase, *Power of Words,* Harcourt, Brace, New York, 1953. Stephen Ullman, *Semantics: An Introduction to the Science of Meaning,* Barnes & Noble, Inc., New York, 1962. Irving J. Lee, *Handling Barriers in Communication,* Harper & Bros., New York, 1957. S. I. Hayakawa, *Language in Thought and Action,* Harcourt, Brace, New York, 1964. John L. Austin, *How to Do Things with Words,* Harvard University Press, Cambridge, 1962. Alfred Korzybski, *Science and Sanity,* Institute of General Semantics, Lakeville, Conn., 1948. Ragnar Rommetviet, *Words, Meanings, and Messages,* Academic Press, New York, 1968.

Even words which properly name a broad group of things for both sender and receiver, however, may still not reproduce in the mind of the receiver the sender's specific concept. If you write *machine* while thinking *typewriter,* your reader is likely to miss your intent by envisioning a calculator, a mimeograph, or some other machine. To communicate well, then, a sender must use words specific enough for the necessary precision.

Even then, words alone are far from the whole of this system of symbols we call the English language; the way they're put together, punctuated, and sometimes even spelled can make a vast difference. A bear does not have a bare skin. To a reader who follows the English system of placing modifiers as close as possible to the things they modify, "Only three men passed the first screening" does not mean the same as "Three men passed the first screening only." To the reader who knows anything about the punctuation of essential and nonessential clauses, "The prices which are higher than those last year for the same items are simply too high" does not mean the same as "The prices, which are higher than those last year for the same items, are simply too high." To get the right idea, the reader has to assume that the writer didn't know how to handle participles when he wrote, "Having hung by the heels in the 30-degree temperature overnight, we found the venison made an excellent breakfast." That writer tried to pass a lead nickel in our medium of exchange, the English language. He needs to learn the fundamental principle: The symbols used must stand for essentially the same thing in the minds of the sender and the receiver.

Here are eight specific principles that might be considered subheads of the general principle.

1. *A statement is never the whole story.* Even in reporting the simplest event, you omit some details which another reporter might well have told. Usually you report only on the macroscopic level, omitting additional details that could be added if you made microscopic or submicroscopic examinations of all the objects involved. But you also omit much of the macroscopic. Even if you think you cover the standard *who, where, when, why, what,* and *how,* another reporter could easily add more details and more specifics on each of them. By way of illustration, consider how infrequently you see, in other reports, certain details that are standard in police reports of traffic accidents: mental and physical condition of the driver(s), weather conditions, condition of the roadway, etc.

Whether you are sending or receiving the facts and arguments in a court case, in a report leading to a multimillion-dollar decision, in a sales letter, or in some other communication, you do not have the whole story. Even the witness who takes an oath to tell the truth, the whole truth, and nothing but the truth, never does; to additional questions, he could always tell more. Even an application letter of ten pages does not tell the whole life story of the applicant.

This concept of inevitable incompleteness—often called "abstracting" and defined as calling attention to some details while neglecting others—is basic in the thinking of semanticists. The International Society for General Semantics has therefore titled its journal *ETC.*, thus stressing Korzybski's suggestion that writers use the abbreviation as a reminder and warning that their statements are incomplete.

The importance of the incompleteness concept stems from the dangers of ignoring it—the "allness" fallacy. If you consider only parts of a whole and judge the whole, you're in danger of the logical fallacy of hasty generalization and unsound conclusions like those of the six blind men who each described an elephant after feeling only one part. If you forget that you do not have all the facts, you are in danger of closing your mind to other facts and points of view. You may think of your way as the only way. You thus act on the basis of preconception and may become unteachable, intolerant, dogmatic, and arrogant. Recognizing that you never have the whole story, on the other hand, helps to keep you open-minded, tolerant, and humble. That's one of the values of travel and of a broad education: to open the mind and replace the provincialism of the person who knows only a small area. The Italians have a proverb which makes the point: *Assai sa chi sa che non sa,* freely translated as "He knows a lot who knows that he doesn't know."

2. *Perception involves both the perceived and the perceiver.* Since you are never telling or considering the whole story, you are *selecting,* from all things that might be or have been said, *those which seem to you important.* What you say about a thing or how you react to it, then, often depends as much on you as on what the thing really is.

Both your judgment of what is important to select and your conclusions based on selected facts are influenced by the kind of person you are. And you are what you are (different from anybody else) because of different inherited traits and different experiences. Your special interests, values, tastes, and attitudes will naturally cause what you say about a thing or how you react to a statement to differ from what anybody else would say or how he would react. In effect, you are a special filter. Another filter (person) with different characteristics would filter out different things. Hence neither you nor he can be strictly objective. When we claim to be objective, we are deluding ourselves—and others if they believe us. And when we expect others to be objective or to see things exactly as we do, we are simply being unrealistic. Constant recognition of this point will help to keep you reasonably tolerant of people who disagree a bit.

A famous French movie aptly illustrates the point that the background of a person influences his decision—sometimes more than the factual evidence. The movie gives a life history (selected, of course) of each juror in an important trial and shows how the different backgrounds produced different votes in the jury room, even though all jurors had heard and seen exactly the same evidence. Other illustrations may be more readily available in newspaper accounts of court decisions determined by the prejudices of the judges, or even in different grades for equally good schoolwork because of teacher favoritism or the teacher's special background, attitudes, and emphases.

Thorough recognition of the point—that in terms of the other fellow's background and point of view he may be just as nearly right as you are in terms of yours—can go a long way toward preventing disagreements by making you cautious about using *is* dogmatically. When you use *is* to connect a noun and adjective ("Harry Smith is honest"), you are saying that the quality of honesty belongs to or exists in Smith. This predicate-adjective construction, using what some semanticists call the *"is* of predication," actually misrepresents reality and seems dogmatic to another person who disagrees because he either knows different facts about Smith or defines honesty differently. If you remember that your thinking about Smith is influenced by what you know about him (not *all* the facts) *and* by what honesty means to you (probably somewhat different from what it means to the other fellow), you are more likely to say, less dogmatically, "Harry Smith seems to me . . ."—and to avoid an argument or even a fight.

Two subpoints about the perceiver and the perceived deserve special attention.

a) By the psychological principle of projection, we are inclined to attribute to others our own characteristics and feelings. People who pay their bills are inclined to assume that others will too. The reverse is also true. A credit man—and anybody else who wants to avoid being duped—needs to realize that his views of things depend heavily on the kind of person he is and that others may have different views. The wise credit man will use the statistician's rather than the psychologist's meaning of *projection:* He will get information about a credit applicant's past reputation for paying bills, project the trend line, and decide to approve or disapprove the application according to where the projection points.

b) Psychologists also tell us that we are inclined to resist the unpleasant. Facts and ideas that go contrary to our preconceptions, wishful thinkings, and other selfish interests are among the unpleasant things we must face because they provoke us to change our comfortable old ways. A semantically sound person will therefore try to avoid the comfortable but anti-semantic idea in "Don't confuse me with facts; my mind's made up."

3. *Statements or actions based on whims, feelings, imaginings, preconceptions, customs, traditions, and platitudes are questionable.* Although you never get all the relevant facts, and although you can never be strictly objective in evaluating those you do get, you should get what facts you can and evaluate them as objectively as you can. You need not give up and use the excuse "all or nothing." Ignoring observable facts will almost certainly lead you into conflict with reality. And when you go too far "out of touch with reality," as the psychiatrists say, you base action on emotion instead of reason, and you go to the bughouse.

A reasonable approach to problem solving involves two beginning questions: (*a*) What are the facts? (*b*) How do you know? Because of the importance of instantaneous response in some simple situations, we have certain reflex mechanisms (for blinking the eyes, sneezing, etc.) that do not involve thinking. But you are courting real trouble if you make reflexlike responses to complex situations. Fortunately, as situations become more complex, the allowable time for decision becomes greater, and the reactions become voluntary. A reasonable person will use some of that time to collect and consider at least some of the significant facts. As some semanticists say, he will look at the territory before drawing a map; he will be extensionally instead of intensionally oriented. That is, he will look outside his own skin for some facts instead of relying wholly on his internal feelings and cogitations. To do otherwise is to act on prejudices, preconceptions, and whims.

While considering the collected data, you need to ask, "How do you know that this information is reliable?" Many platitudes, prejudices, customs, and the like are based on assumptions that simply do not line up with reality. Even "well-established" teachings of science are often discarded after the discovery of new evidence by such men as Harvey, Pasteur, and Reed. The atom that could not be split, according to "authoritative" books not many years ago, has been split. More recently, discoveries in outer space are bringing into question many of the "established" principles meteorologists have followed for years. (Perhaps we can look forward to more reliable weather forecasts.)

If scientists—who generally pride themselves on being careful in collecting data and in drawing conclusions, and who usually have good equipment—can be so wrong and so dogmatic as they have been on some of these things, should we all not learn the lesson of humility and caution? Should we not all be careful about the adequacy and the reliability of what appears to be information, and about the validity of our conclusions? Surely we should all see the dangers of accepting information from old books. And the disagreements among "authorities" in almost every field should warn us to question authoritative statements or at least to check them as best we can against our own experience. Even then, reasonable humility would seem to warn that we rarely "prove" anything well enough to justify saying such and such *is true*.

Incidentally, our best modern scientists have just about learned their lessons. They now admit that they usually deal with probabilities rather than certainties.

If the careful research methods and conclusion making of scientists still lead to questionable results and probable truths, what of the statements of people who do not bother to get the facts at all and, without thinking or checking, act on the bases of prejudices, preconceptions, whims, etc.? A semanticist would at least warn you to take what they say with a few grains of semantic salt.

4. *Facts, inferences, and value judgments are not the same thing.* If you

have ever heard a court trial, you have probably heard a judge order some testimony stricken from the record because the witness was stating his opinions or conclusions (inferences) rather than restricting himself to what he had seen, heard, felt, etc. (sense data). The fact that our legal procedures do not allow inferences as evidence unless the inferences are made by experts reflects society's faith in sense data and its lack of faith in inferences unless made by people specially qualified to make them. Most of us would do well to be more skeptical of the mouthings of people who have not bothered to get the facts—and especially of nonexperts talking on professional topics.

You see why when you consider the nature of sense data, inferences, and value judgments. Sense data usually approach certainty, inferences vary all the way from near certainty to slight probability (usually depending mainly on how many verifiable facts form the basis for them), and value judgments are nearly always debatable. For example, you see a good friend in a men's store on December 20. She tells you that she wants to buy a tie for her husband Joe and asks your help in selecting a pretty one. After she disapproves three ties you suggest and then you disapprove three she is considering, you leave her to make her own choice because you see that the two of you don't agree on what is a nice tie (value judgments). On December 27 you see Joe wearing a tie that seems to be new and looks like one of the three Jane suggested and you disapproved. More courteously than sincerely, you say, "That is a pretty tie Jane bought you." (Note the dogmatic *is*, discussed in Item 2 above.) Joe says that he hates to be so disagreeable, but he thinks it's ugly and Jane didn't buy it. You see that your value judgment matches Joe's better than Jane's; and when Joe tells you that a friend gave him the tie, you see that you took a calculated risk with your inference—and lost. (Note that to make this decision, you have to assume that Joe is telling the truth.)

Both the general experience of almost any adult and the results of many tests show rather convincingly that two or more eyewitnesses of an event often disagree considerably on what happened. Nevertheless, people generally agree with the courts in trusting "factual reporting" more than inferences. Apparently the reason lies in Item 2 above: Sense data are believed to be more reliable than inferences, which are too likely to get distorted in being filtered through the personality of the one drawing the inferences.

Not even the courts rule out inferences completely, however. Judges make them, and jurors' votes are pure inferences. As a matter of practicality, we make and act on inferences all the time. We have to. We cannot always know with the near certainty of sense data; many times we have to act on inferences and thus take calculated risks. Even calculated risks, however, are based on *some* data and are safer than wild guesses or hunches.

The danger in inferences is not in acting on them but in acting on them *as if* they were completely reliable. By recognizing the risks we are taking when acting on inferences, or even on hunches, we can reduce the danger considerably because we will not be so surprised by otherwise unexpected turns of events.

To avoid deluding ourselves and others with whom we communicate, then, we will do well to remind ourselves and forewarn others of the *bases* on which our statements rest. A statement, like a ladder, is no more secure than its foundation. As communicators, we owe ourselves and others the clear indication of which statements are based on verifiable fact or on sense data, which are inferences (along with the verifiable data on which they are based), and which statements are value judgments. Our readers and listeners have a right to know about the foundations if they are going to risk their necks on our ladders.

Still, we need not make ourselves as ridiculous as the skeptical farmer who remarked, "At least it is black on this side," when he was asked to observe that black sheep in the pasture. He did seem a bit ridiculous, but he was no sucker.

5. *No two things are exactly alike.* Even things so much alike that they appear identical to the naked eye always reveal differences under close inspection. To be absolutely precise in naming things would require a different word or other symbol for each. Obviously, such precision is impractical—and unnecessary for most purposes.

General words, naming whole groups of things similar in one or more aspects that concern us, help us in classifications. Thus we can save words and time by talking about, or otherwise treating, somewhat similar things collectively instead of individually. If what we say or do with the group applies equally well to all members of the group, we operate efficiently.

Trouble arises quickly, however, when we group things on the basis of a few similarities and then act as if all things in the group were identical in all ways. Such a situation exists when colleges try to treat all freshmen alike because all are first-year students, ignoring the great variety of interests and abilities in the individuals.

Some ugly results of ignoring differences and stressing similarities are faulty categorizing (or labeling or pigeonholing) and faulty analogy making. Thus we get the unsound, unyielding, and prejudicial stereotyping so often seen in fiction. Not all cowboys, politicians, professors, businessmen, delinquent credit customers, Russians, or blacks are alike—although they may have some similarities that justify the grouping *for a particular purpose.* No one of the groupings is sound for *all* purposes, however, because each group involves differing individuals. Sound thinking requires recognition of the differences and variation of one's attitudes toward and treatment of the individuals accordingly.

As a communicator, you can do several things to help solve the problem. For one thing, you can *use symbols (usually words) that are specific enough for your purposes.* When you do mean your statement to apply equally to a number of somewhat similar things (perhaps all new customers), be efficient and use the group name instead of handling each separately; but surely you should not lump together for similar handling as "delinquent accounts" the good customer who got behind because of a temporary misfortune and the marginal risk who tried to skip by moving and leaving no address. And if what you say applies only to typewriters, don't say machines. If it applies only to portables, don't say typewriters. If it applies only to Royal portables, don't just say portables.

Accepting the premise of uniqueness, and recognizing the fallacy of identity, some semanticists recommend using the "which index." To distinguish which individual they are referring to in a group name, they suggest using subscript numbers after the name, $typewriter_1$ being different from $typewriter_2$. Carried to extremes, this system is as impractical as the limitless vocabulary necessary to give each individual thing a name; but used in moderation, it can help. In either case a little use of it will remind you of an important point: If significant differences exist in the group named, make clear which members of the groups you are talking about. Usually this means using a more specific name or otherwise limiting the group to where your statement is valid. "Businessmen who do such and such things are unethical" is quite different from "Businessmen are unethical."

For another thing, you can *consider significant differences along with similarities.* Analogies, similes, and other metaphors pointing to the similarities between two things help greatly in explanations. Indeed, they become almost necessary, because teaching and learning involve explanation of the unknown in terms of the known. Dictionaries explain words in terms of other words presumably known to the dictionary user. You often hear and read explanations in terms of a football game, which you presumably understand. Because you know English verbs generally go like *stay, stayed, stayed,* you can usually form the past tense and the past participle of a verb you have just learned. But if the new verb is *think,* the analogy misleads you.

That misleading analogy points to three warnings about using analogies to make them helpful rather than harmful.

a) Since no two things are exactly alike, no analogy can be complete. Although *stay* and *think* are both English verbs, they belong to different classes. Although we speak of synonyms, they are alike only in some ways and are not always interchangeable.

b) Because two or more things always have some differences even when they are largely similar, an analogy never proves anything. The truth may slip through one of the holes that make the difference between the two "analogous" things. Stock-market and weather forecasters often predict certain futures because those results followed similar conditions in the past. But forecasters are often wrong because they have failed to consider significant differences in seemingly similar conditions.

c) In using analogies, you must be sure your reader understands the supposedly known side of your analogy. Otherwise, you are in the position of one explaining a Russian word in Chinese terms to a person who knows neither language.

6. *Some either-or, black-white classifications are legitimate, but most are not.* The question is whether your two-part classifications are mutually exclusive. A person is either married or he is not; there is no middle ground; no one can be both married and not married at the same time. But you cannot say with equal validity that the same person is tall, intelligent, honest, and the like. Where do you draw the line between intelligent and not intelligent, honest and not honest?

You are being true to reality when you use either-or, black-white, two-valued logic for mutually exclusive things—things that cannot both exist at the same time. But most things are continua, with gradations, shadings, or degrees between the extremes. For them you need a "how-much index." Applying black-white logic to them ignores the gray. It is similar to the false dilemma in logic. And like the false dilemma, it is used especially by the unthinking, the intolerant, and the shysters among us. The results are delusions of self and others, intolerance, and hard feelings if not fights. The person who thinks of himself categorically as a success or a failure, for example, will almost certainly become arrogant or unhappy. The professor who speaks of his students' papers as the accurate and the interesting implies (probably incorrectly) that the accurate papers are dull and the interesting ones are inaccurate (as if accuracy and interest were mutually exclusive), and that all are therefore bad. He probably has drawn an inaccurate "map of the territory," as some semanticists would say, and probably has incurred the enmity of most of his students.

As a communicator, you can do several things to avoid the undesirable consequences of two-valued thinking. First, you must recognize the difference between legitimate (mutually exclusive) two-pole classifications and continua. Then you can use the readily available facilities of English to show the proper gradations in continua. English contains not only somewhat similar nouns of varying degrees of specificity and strength but a large supply of adjectives and adverbs with similar variations. Moreover, the adjectives and adverbs have three standard degrees of comparison like *good, better, best* and *speedily, more speedily,* and *most speedily.* If you still feel the need for better indication of the degree of grayness in a continuum, you can always *add* specific details, as in "Quickly (3.2 seconds) the operator turned the heavy (5-ton) crane around and . . . ."

7. *Things change significantly with time.* Nature works as a dynamic process. As part of nature, Joe Smith today is not exactly the same as Joe Smith yesterday, much less 10 years ago. Significant aspects of a present situation may not have existed in the past and may not continue in the future. To be true to reality, you need to consider the date in connection with statements sent or received. Some semanticists refer to this principle as the

necessity for the "when index." Ignoring it produces what some call the "frozen evaluation."

Most universities recognize the point in readmitting students, after specified periods of time, who were dropped for poor scholarship or infraction of rules. Most homes would run more smoothly if parents would recognize that their teen-agers are no longer babies. Ex-convicts would find readjustment to normal living much easier if their neighbors would at least give them a chance to show whether they have changed instead of pinning permanent labels on them. Many blue laws on statute books should be rescinded. We may as well get used to reinterpretations of the Constitution —and to changed usages and new dictionaries of English. Our language is not static. Fighting new English textbooks and new dictionaries (which do not make but merely record current usage) is more futile than fighting city hall; it's fighting the whole country. One can better spend his time considering the changing values of the dollar before investing too heavily in things like government bonds and endowment insurance payable in fixed amounts 10 or 20 years later. Surely a credit man should know that the facts which force him to refuse a requested credit arrangement may change in a few months—and should hold open the possibility of reconsidering them. And speakers, writers, listeners, and readers would all be better communicators if they considered more carefully the *time* in connection with many statements.

8. *Words are not identical to the objects they represent.* They are symbols of concepts that exist only in the mind. They do not have meanings themselves but only the power to represent or evoke meanings in our minds.

Concrete objects react on our various senses to give us our concepts of those things. We then use words to represent those concepts. Only the physical objects are real; our concepts and the symbols (words) to represent them are the first and second levels of abstraction in the "ladder of abstraction" or "structural differential" which semanticists talk about. We can then go on and on up the ladder of abstraction through a series of inferential labels or descriptions, each concerned with the preceding level of abstraction.

In this scheme, clearly the names we give are not the things themselves —even names that have referents (concrete, tangible objects to which they refer). If you question this statement, try eating the word *pie* the next time you get hungry for something sweet. Or since a word is to its referent as a map is to its territory, just take a walk on your map the next time you want to take a trip. As Korzybski repeatedly explains, our words merely represent the world of events and things outside our skins but are never the real things. Ogden and Richards (*The Meaning of Meaning,* Harcourt, Brace, New York, 1930, p. 11) present the symbolic nature of language as a triangle, the three points representing referent, thought, and symbol.

This semantic principle of the symbolic nature of language points to these suggestions for better communication:

a) Insofar as possible, use words with real physical objects or actions as referents, and make them specific enough to call to the receiver's mind the particular referent you want him to consider. If your receiver has seen or touched the kind of thing you are talking about, he is much more likely to get the concepts you want to convey about it than if you talk in generalities or talk about abstractions (concepts like loyalty and honesty that do not exist in the physical world but only in the mind). Even when your word has a referent, avoid equating the word with the physical object (for which it is only a symbol) or with some facet of it: "Russia *is* the Berlin Wall" or "Communism *is*. . . ."

b) Especially in reading and listening, try to look behind the words and envision the things and ideas the words represent. You can remember the thought much easier than all the exact words used to represent it. And in taking notes or answering questions about what you've heard or read, present the concepts in your own words except for key words and phrases. If you concentrate on words, you'll likely learn the words and repeat them parrotlike without understanding the thought they were intended to convey. Instead, concentrate on "What does *he* mean by those words?"

c) Although you cannot avoid the use of some abstract words (which have no referents in the physical world), try to keep them to a minimum. Then consider the context in which they are used. If you have described several actions a man has taken and then you commend him for his *integrity*, the context makes clear what you mean by the otherwise abstract word *integrity*. That's the way abstract words are used best: as summarizing words.

Listening and reading

Speaking and writing are forms of the initiating phase of communication. Listening and reading are forms of the receiving phase. Considerable skill in each is vital for a literate individual in today's civilization.

Most training in schools is devoted to writing, reading, and—to a lesser extent—speaking. Yet from the time we start to learn, and as long as we continue to learn, we spend at least as much communicating time in listening as we do on all the other three. As we advance and become more proficient in and dependent on reading, many of us, unless we consciously strive to do otherwise, steadily deteriorate in listening efficiency.

But how much easier we can make our learning and living if we are conscious of the fact that listening (to TV, radio, lectures, sermons, interviews, conferences, directives, conversations, etc.) accounts for about three times as much of our communication time as reading does!

The task of listening.[2]   Neither good reading nor good listening is easy.

----

[2] See Ralph G. Nichols and Leonard A. Stevens, *Are You Listening?* McGraw-Hill Book Co., Inc., New York, 1957, 235 pp.; Ralph G. Nichols and Thomas R. Lewis, *Listening and Speaking,* William C. Brown Co., Dubuque, 1954, 250 pp. Both these publications contain extensive bibliographies.

Both require training, either supervised or self-disciplined. Of the two activities, listening is the more demanding and the more difficult for most of us. The written word is always there for the reader to go back to. The spoken word, once uttered, is gone unless stored in the reader's mind (a job that most of us do not perform well). The reader can proceed at his own speed; the listener must adapt to the pace of the speaker. And from early childhood we are taught a greater respect for the printed word than for the spoken one. With but a few quite recent exceptions, schools have emphasized reading far more than listening. As a result, although we are far from being good readers, most of us are deplorably worse listeners.

Through good listening we can certainly broaden our knowledge on many subjects; we can frequently secure information that is not available any other way; we can improve our own speaking; we can save ourselves time. Then, too, good listening has a therapeutic value for both listener and speaker: Good listeners make a good speaker better, and this in turn is a direct benefit to the listeners.

Listening takes time, certainly. It requires patience, even courage, to listen to the things we don't want to hear—for example, that we are wrong. Conversely, attentive listening can often win an argument by making the speaker careful about his "facts" and phrasing.

Although the statement may strike you as obvious, learning to be a good reader does not make you a good listener any more than learning to be a good listener makes you a good reader. Several differences in the two communicating processes help to explain why. Not only are the styles different (greater variety in sentence length and style, much more use of phrases, more personal references, more informality, more repetitions, and more adaptations in oral than in written). The role of the nonverbal is even more significant. A speaker's gestures, facial expressions, pitch of voice, inflections, rhythm and speed, and pronunciation constantly affect the final message received by his listeners.

The reader uses his eyes alone. The listener uses his eyes and ears. This concentration of effort is no easy matter to be taken for granted. It can be immensely rewarding, however.

Although in what we shall term "everyday living" you will listen and learn in interviews, lectures, conferences, and conversation, the following suggestions are concerned primarily with listening to speeches and lectures.

Identify the subject and plan. Most speakers will deliver planned talks organized in the traditional pattern of introduction, thesis, body, and conclusion.

Many excellent speakers will tell a story, or quote from some well-known authority or publication, or say something startling first to secure your favorable attention. Such a beginning may be appropriate, even germane, but rarely is it of the essence. Many excellent lecturers dispense with the irrelevant beginning and start immediately with genuine subject matter, and wisely so.

The essential point for concentration is when the speaker announces what he is going to talk about; he may also point out why; and often he will announce his plan of presentation. If you are not tuned in for his thesis statement, you are going to have difficulty following what he says. If you can also get his general plan from the first, you will be able to follow his development more easily.

Stay tuned in.   The body of the speech (the longest part) includes all the points that support the speaker's fundamental proposition or thesis. For evidence, he may use statistics, testimony, or stories, to name some.

He may present his points and the evidence supporting them in *deductive* order (he usually will if his purpose is only to inform). This is, stated very simply, generalization followed by supporting material. If his purpose is to persuade, he will likely follow an *inductive* order (generalization after evidence).

Obviously, this is the part on which you should exercise your powers of concentration and your critical faculties. The questions of completeness (omissions and slanting), validity, appropriateness, and recency are significant here.

You will find this part easier to follow (and more interesting to you) if, when possible, you check the speaker's announced plan of presentation against what he delivers and stay on the alert for transitions—those statements signaling a change of point. The points or principles (the *ideas*) the speaker establishes reveal the blueprint of his plan and establish the final structure. The *facts* supporting the principles are subheads.

If the speaker announces no plan, try to anticipate what he is going to say. If your guess proves to be right, you'll feel pleasure—and probably reveal it in an empathic circuit response to the speaker. And if you're wrong? Never mind, you'll have concentrated better and benefited from the mental exercise of comparison and contrast.

This anticipating process will not cause you to miss out on anything significant: The mind can function (receive and decode) at a pace about four times faster than the average speaker will deliver (transmit after encoding).

Good speakers (and good writers) will build up their points or principles step by step so that the conclusion suggests itself before it is announced. In an informative speech the conclusion is often very short. It may be no more than a quick recap of the main points and a brief statement of how the thesis (or subject or speech) is significant to the audience. The conclusion of the persuasive speech may be a little longer. The persuasive speaker may not reveal his stand until this time. In addition to establishing his real objective, he may use strong argument. Question. Challenge. But reserve judgment until you've had the time to sift and revaluate—to review and rebuild.

When you're the trapped victim of a speaker who indulges in harangue, cajoling, or bombast, tune out; you're entitled to stop listening.

Be sensible; control your note-taking.   The temptation to apply pencil or pen to paper and start to record a speaker's words verbatim is one that is too great for many listeners to overcome—unfortunately. This kind of note-taking causes even the experienced listener to lose many of the significant ideas, to become confused, and eventually to become so frustrated that he gives up on note-taking—and usually on listening also.

Most speakers and lecturers (including teachers) agree that good listeners (including students) take good notes. They also agree that those who take good notes listen a lot and write a little. Possibly the best piece of advice we can give you is to keep your notes brief and clear during listening (complete thoughts for major points; just words and short phrases for supporting details). You can expand and review later.

Rarely does an introduction merit recording. Even the thesis is better not written down when it is first stated—although you certainly want to have it clearly in mind when the speaker launches into his main points and evidence. (Write it down after the completed speech.) Even the brief outline or plan (if the speaker gives you one) is better recorded point by point as you go along rather than at the time the speaker first announces it, just before going into his first major point. In listening, try to jot down ideas, not facts and illustrations.

The careful distinction between fact and idea leads a listener to one system of note-taking that is economical and efficient. Divide your paper into two columns, one for facts, the other for principles. You'll have difficulty determining which is which sometimes. But the effort will help you to concentrate and will provide enough useful reminders for later review. You'll have more entries in your facts column than in your principles column. If you have to slight the recording of one, slight the facts; concentrate on the principles.

An even less time-consuming system of note-taking is that of précis writing. (The words *abstract* and *summary,* even *synopsis* and *epitome,* mean essentially the same.) Stated very simply, this means to listen extensively, then write rapidly. Most speakers will state a generalization followed by supporting details (or the reverse) and then, by a clearly indicated transition, signal the completion of that point and the approach of another. During this time, jot down a sentence or two stating in your own words the idea or principle the speaker has attempted to establish. Then resume listening until he states the next generalization.

Certainly, as a good listener, you will always write a précis of the conclusion and of the thesis or fundamental proposition (the latter preferably after the speaker has finished).

The sooner you can review your notes after the speech, the better. Of course, as you listened, you should have mentally questioned for completeness, adequacy and appropriateness, authenticity, recency, and omission of data. An even more fruitful time to do this is shortly after the talk in a review of notes, supplementing and rebuilding, questioning, searching for negative evidence, and finally arriving at an evaluation.

As a good listener, you want to strive to understand each main point made by your speaker. If you're too preoccupied with proving him wrong, you won't get his message. Withhold your judgments and decisions until after you have reviewed his main ideas and thesis.

Avoid the main stumbling blocks to good listening. Without the wish and the will to, you won't profit from anyone's suggestions. Our pointing out some common failings may help you to improve, however.

To begin with, accept the fact that most of us much prefer to be heard than to keep silent and lend an attentive ear and mind. Listening is hard work demanding patience, an open mind, a considerate—even charitable—mind. Most of us much prefer to consider our own individual interests and air what is on our own minds. The temptation to tune out and escape to reverie or daydreaming is ever with us.

And so we are prone to pretend attention when our minds are not receiving any ideas being transmitted. No speaker with much experience is easily fooled by the head nodder, the glassy-eyed starer, the marbleized "thinker." Such audience characters are only fooling themselves. They are no more interested in listening than the foot tapper, the pen flipper, the book slammer, etc. If you fall in one of these classes, wake up—and learn.

Another stumbling block (founded on very superficial attitudes) is undue attention to the speaker's appearance, voice, or speech characteristics. A word is only a symbol, not reality; a man's appearance is only his outward shell, not an indicator of his mind; speech is only the vehicle, not the idea. Although we all like to be personable people and do respond in almost motor fashion more to good-looking people than to those who are not, we need to remember that Steinmetz was a deformed man, almost a dwarf. One of the most brilliant lectures at a recent medical meeting was delivered by a man whose hands, head, and face (because of an uncorrectable breakdown of his nerve system) trembled and twitched almost convulsively. These are extremes, yes; but the principle is the same. Don't shut yourself off from learning because of a person's physiognomy, size, dress, or voice characteristics. He may have a lot to contribute.

All too often we are guilty of abruptly rejecting or dismissing a speaker and his subject because we consider them dull or difficult. Very few "uninteresting" speeches are devoid of something useful. Remember that the "dull" speaker is probably doing just what his assignment was—to give you facts and ideas—and that he refuses to insult your intelligence, or take pay under false pretenses, by entertaining you instead. Be selfish: Take for yourself what is meaningful and useful. Furthermore, if the speaker really is wrong, remember that you can often learn by observing what not to do! As for rejecting the difficult discourse, remember that this can become a pattern of progressive mental deterioration. The more you do it, the flabbier and more superficial your mind becomes. The only suggestions we can make are continually renewed determination to "hear the man out" and a planned effort to tackle uninteresting as well as difficult material.

Another stumbling block is the tendency of listeners to let physical surroundings distract them. Airplanes, buses, trains, thunder, and other outside noises are sometimes loud, and rarely can the listener do anything about them. But they are noises that most of us readily ignore when we want to (during a favorite TV program, for instance). Many physical circumstances you can control as an individual. Windows and doors close as well as open. Heating mechanisms turn off as well as on. Wraps certainly can be removed as well as put on. If you as an individual can't control the distraction, enlist the aid of the speaker; he'll probably appreciate your report. Even if listeners and speakers are trapped and can't move to a more favorable place, at least they will be alerted to the fact that both will have to exert extra effort to concentrate on effective sending and receiving of the message.

One more point, which is a reminder of something already said: In your listening, concentrate on principles, not detailed facts presented in support of principles. Emphasis on facts makes you lose principles, which are the most significant parts of speeches; emphasis on principles makes you not only get the principles or ideas but also helps you remember many of the facts that support them.

Good listening saves the listener time and money—in academic, social, and professional roles.

Efficient reading. Unless you are an exception, you have had much more specific training in reading than in listening. Besides, much of what was said about listening in the preceding section also applies to reading. We shall therefore discuss this form of the receiving phase of communication in much less detail than the listening form just covered.

If you are reading only for pleasure, you can relax and be almost passive as you proceed at whatever pace you please. If you are not satisfied with your reading pace, you may want to enroll for one of the reading-improvement courses offered by many schools and counseling services or clinics. The aim of these courses is to increase the reader's rate and comprehension. If no such work or counseling is available to you, you may want to read some of the excellent books on the subject.[3]

---

[3] We suggest that you start with these books in this order (some of them have bibliographies to direct you further): (*a*) Mortimer J. Adler, *How to Read a Book*, Simon and Schuster, Inc., New York, 1940; (*b*) Walter Hill and William Eller, *Power in Reading Skills*, Wadsworth Publishing Co., Inc., Belmont, Calif., 1964; (*c*) A. L. Raygor and D. M. Wark, *Systems for Study*, McGraw-Hill Book Co., New York, 1970; G. A. Gladstein, *Individualized Study*, Rand McNally, Chicago, 1967; and William W. Farquhar et al., *Learning to Study*, Ronald Press Co., New York, 1960; (*d*) Luella Cole, *Students' Guide to Efficient Study*, Holt, Rinehart & Winston, Inc., New York, 1960; (*e*) Walter Pauk, *How to Study in College*, Houghton Mifflin Co., Boston, 1962; (*f*) Francis P. Robinson, *Effective Study*, Harper & Bros., New York, 1961; (*g*) George D. Spache and Paul C. Berg, *The Art of Efficient Reading*, Macmillan Co., New York, 1966; (*h*) Arthur S. McDonald and George H. Zimmy, *The Art of Good Reading*, Bobbs-Merrill Co., Inc., Indianapolis, 1963; (*i*) James I. Brown, *Efficient Reading*, D. C. Heath & Co., Boston, 1962; (*j*) Horace Judson, *The Techniques of Reading*, Harcourt, Brace, New York, 1963; (*k*) Paul D. Leedy,

If you are reading for information and instruction (as opposed to pleasure or entertainment), you can profit even more from such courses and books. The following brief suggestions give you only the main points of some of these books.

When you read an informative publication (book, section, chapter, or article):

1. Understand the scope and limitations of the subject as evidenced in the title and often in a subtitle, the preface, introductory comments, and footnote explanations.

2. Determine as closely as you can the primary purpose, which may be only implied. Phrase it in your own words.

3. Take advantage of mechanical aids (indentions, paragraphing, outline symbols, change of type, etc.) and transitions as you read through the article, section, or chapter the first time *rapidly.* Don't ponder over phrases or even whole sentences; don't look up definitions. *Read through and read fast!*

4. When you've finished, try to recall as much as you can. Check the theme or central idea you have formulated against the author's expression of it either in the ending or in the beginning.

5. Reread the material paragraph by paragraph. (The first rapid reading will decrease your reading time at this stage, and much that was foggy the first time will be clear.) If you own the material (but not in library materials, please!), underscore key words and topic sentences (which do not necessarily appear in every paragraph but often do at the beginning or end). Indicate which paragraphs belong together. Paraphrase in the margins the main ideas.

Then

1. If you are reasonably certain of the meaning of a word from the context, you are probably safe in not looking it up. Otherwise, look it up and pencil the appropriate definition in the margin.

2. When the article is fairly short and not formally organized, you're probably better off simply to write a short précis.

3. When the article or chapter is formally organized, you may want to write a formal outline. Such outlining is another step in remembering and is a vital necessity if you need to submit an oral or a written report. This will be fairly fast for you if you have followed the preceding suggestions.

These suggestions apply if you want or need to do more than record and possibly transmit what some author wrote. If you want or need to evaluate, you will have to answer such questions as the following:

1. About the author:
    a) Who is he?

Read with Speed and Precision, McGraw-Hill Book Co., Inc., New York, 1963; (*l*) M. J. Maxwell, *Skimming and Scanning Improvement,* McGraw-Hill Book Co., New York, 1969; and Paul C. Berg, et al., *Skimming and Scanning,* Educational Developmental Laboratories, Huntington, N.Y., 1962; (*m*) A. L. Raygor and G. B. Schick, *Reading at Efficient Rates,* McGraw-Hill Book Co., New York, 1970.

    b) What is his position or status?
    c) Is he a recognized authority?
    d) Is he unbiased, or does he have an ax to grind?

2. About the treatment:
    a) Are generalizations supported by evidence?
        (1) Is evidence secondary or primary?
        (2) If evidence is primary, does the author's research method appear sound?
        (3) Is there ample evidence?
    b) Is coverage of major points adequate, or are there significant omissions?
    c) What is the announced or apparent intended audience? Is treatment adapted to this audience?

You may want to add to this list. Certainly it is not intended to be exhaustive.

And remember, no speaker or writer is infallible. A printed statement may mean nothing more than that the statement is in print.

Speaking

Speaking is one form of the initiating or transmitting phase of communication (the other, of course, is writing, with which the greatest part of this book is concerned). This treatment of speaking is brief because we have pointed out in the sections on listening some of the basic considerations affecting speakers and speeches and because this book is *not* intended for use in speech development. So many excellent books on the subject are available that we shall not even suggest any.

Certainly successful speeches are characterized by centrality of theme, adequate and reliable facts, coherent and compact organization, clarity and vividness of phrasing, and other stylistic considerations which are also characteristics of good writing.

Although a speaker is relieved of the necessity for observing the conventions of punctuation and spelling, he must assume responsibility for indisputable pronunciation. He also has a greater responsibility for clear, unmistakable labeling of parts (transitions, topic ideas) because his listener has no opportunity to ask for repetition of a point—unless he is in conversation. A writer knows (although he should not rely on that knowledge) that a reader can, if absolutely necessary, go back and reread passages which are not immediately clear. A listener (except in conversation) must understand the first time or not at all.

Precise pronunciation (necessary in speaking) will help you to eliminate many spelling errors when you write. The principles of good organization you learn in becoming a good speaker will carry over to make you a better writer—and vice versa. And since you talk (not necessarily make a speech) much more frequently than you write, you will write more clearly, effectively, and economically *if you make a constant effort also to speak that way*. Unfortunately, however, most of us merely converse; we do not plan and deliver speeches. And many of us do not practice precision and economy of speech or grammatically acceptable language in our daily conversations. Our bad speech habits, no less than our good, are inclined to show up in our writing too.

But you can plan and even write out an excellent paper which is a miserable speech unless you take advantage of the assistance available to you from speech specialists. You will be a better speaker for being a better writer. However, training and practice in writing are no substitute for training and practice in speaking. For the technical details of speaking (articulation, pronunciation, voice control, gestures, audience approach, type of speech), nothing supplants a qualified speech instructor (or coach) and/or a thorough, specialized book.

appendix B | Letters and the law*

BECAUSE THE LAWS of the 50 states and the federal government vary somewhat and are continually changing, the specific details of the law as applied to letters are too voluminous to treat here—and generalizations are dangerous. Yet enough similarity exists on certain points to justify the following statements of special significance to letter writers.

Responsibility and rights of possession and publication

The law of responsibility for a letter is fairly clear. The first name after the body of the letter is responsible. The writer's name alone at the end makes him responsible, whether on plain paper or on a company letterhead. The letterhead makes no difference. For an employee to avoid personal liability on letters and contracts he signs with proper authority of the employer, therefore, the employer's name must precede the agent's (employee's) signature.

If the letter is about company business the writer is authorized to handle as the company's agent, and he signs with his title, he is responsible; but he can in turn pass that responsibility on to the company under his agency agreement.

To avoid this two-step process of putting responsibility where it belongs, he can type the company name (preferably in solid capitals) a double space below the complimentary close and a quadruple space above his typed name and title, with his signature in the large space between. This arrangement makes the company directly responsible for company business a writer is authorized to handle—but of course, not for the writer's personal business or unauthorized company business.

Because the company name defeats some of the attempts of salesmen to set up a feeling of personal relationship between themselves and their prospects, they often sign their letters without the company name. Conversely, putting in the company name may give the reader an additional

---

* Special thanks go to Mr. James J. Cavanaugh, formerly of the business law staff, Michigan State University, for a careful and helpful reading of this appendix.

feeling of security in dealing with an established company instead of the individual who signs the letter. The end legal effect is the same.

Regardless of who is responsible for a letter, he retains publication rights to it. The addressee who receives it has every right to keep it; but without the consent of the responsible sender, he does not have the right to publish it.

Legal aspects of buying and selling by mail

In writing sales promotion letters, inquiries and replies about goods and services for sale, orders, and acknowledgments of orders, writers need to keep in mind what constitutes a *contract*—to be sure of forming one when desired and otherwise avoiding one.

When buyer and seller agree on a legally enforceable arrangement calling for one to act in certain ways in return for the other's acting as specified, we say they form a *contract*.

The required actions must be legal. Two people cannot make a contract to rob a bank or kill somebody, for example.

The phrase "in return for" means that an exchange of value—"consideration," the lawyers call it—is necessarily stated or implied. Hence many contracts which might otherwise leave a question include a phrase something like "in return for $1 and other valuable consideration" or "for value received."

And agreement is essential—or, as it is sometimes stated, "a meeting of the minds." If the terms are indefinite, unclear, or misunderstood, no contract is formed. The basic elements, then, are an *offer* and an *acceptance*.

An *offer* must be reasonably definite to provide agreement. In general, it needs to be fairly clear by explicit statement or reasonable implication in answer to *who, what, when, where,* and *why*. That is, the two or more parties involved must be clear. What each agrees to do, or refrain from doing, has to be specific. In terms of goods for sale, not only the general class of goods but a fairly clear understanding of the quality, price, and number is necessary. The time the offer goes into effect and ends must be reasonably clear, by explicit statement or by implication. Where the actions are to take place is also often necessary to a valid contract. The consideration is the answer to the *why*.

A catalog listing, advertisement, or sales promotion letter is not ordinarily an offer to sell because it is usually not specific enough to answer adequately the five W questions. Although it may identify the prospective seller and describe the goods and give the price, it ordinarily does not indicate the number of items (another part of the *what*), and the *when* and *where* may not be clear enough. Simply quoting prices is not an offer.

Certainly most inquiries about products for sale do not complete contracts, both because the cataloging or advertising of the goods was not a specific offer to sell and because the inquiry is usually not an acceptance, or even an offer to buy. Hence even a specific order for goods does not usually complete a contract. More likely it has to be considered the offer, which the seller can accept or reject.

An offer by mail becomes effective when received and stands to the end of any stated time or until withdrawn, rejected, or accepted—or for a reasonable time in view of the nature of the product and the circumstances. In the absence of any statement about the duration of the offer or the amount available, an offer to sell fresh fruit at the orchard, for example, would probably hold only so long as the supply lasts; but an offer to sell the orchard would last considerably longer. An offer can be withdrawn any time before acceptance, but the withdrawal has to be received to become effective.

Assuming that a valid offer has been made by mail, a letter accepting it must agree to all the terms exactly, or else it forms no contract. Thus a simple acknowledgment of receipt of an order does not complete a contract. The acknowledgment must adequately identify the order and agree to act as the offer (order) specifies. Any change in terms *required* by the receiver of an offer rejects the original offer and makes a counteroffer. The original offerer can then reject it or, to form a contract, accept it. A proposal to buy half a farm offered for sale is not an acceptance but a counteroffer. That does not mean, however, that the receiver of an offer cannot accept its terms exactly and then ask for modifications—prices, delivery schedules, quality, or the like. He forms a contract by accepting the original terms. If the original offerer agrees to the requested change, he rescinds the original contract and substitutes the new one by mutual consent.

Until recently, unless the offerer had said that the contract depended on his receiving the acceptance, a properly addressed and stamped acceptance of a mailed offer became effective when posted. Thus it could not be rescinded without mutual consent, even if a faster message attempting to rescind arrived before the mailed acceptance. The assumption was that the letter was beyond the control of the acceptor. Postal regulations providing for the recovery of a mailed letter now make that assumption and the law doubtful. Because of that possibility, revocation of an acceptance by other means may also be possible; but in general, an acceptance is effective when mailed.

Warranties relate closely to contracts, in that a buyer can bring civil suit to recover for nonperformance, or to force performance, on the basis of either stated or implied warranties. Of course, any stated warranty is a part of the contract. But in the absence of any statement to the contrary, a seller warrants by implication that he has clear title to the product sold and that it will perform the usual functions for which such products are sold. To avoid these implied warranties, a seller must be very specific; a general statement that no warranties apply if not stated does not absolve him of responsibility. For this reason, detailed denials of warranty often appear on the containers of such things as insecticides. Furthermore, if an orderer specifies the use he intends to make of a product, leaving the seller to send the appropriate thing, the seller sending the product implies warranty that the product is suitable for the specified purpose. For example, if a farmer orders a pump and says he wants it to pump water for his stock from his 100-foot well, he has a legal claim against the seller who sends a shallow-well pump; a shallow-well pump will not bring water up from that depth.

Fraud in selling by mail—intentional misrepresentation of a product to the buyer for the purpose of inducing him to buy—not only subjects the seller to civil suit by the injured buyer to recover damages sustained; it also opens the possibility of criminal prosecution by the state (and by the Postal Service for use of the mails to defraud).

The law of exchanging information

Any contractual relationship in connection with the sale of goods used to be between the buyer and the seller. Therefore, information that a manufacturer distributed about his goods to consumers who bought from retailers was not a matter of contract. Thus the injured consumer had no recourse against the manufacturer in terms of contract law. Today, however, this privity of contract no longer holds in cases about food and drugs, and probably not in other cases where most of the information about a product as inducement to purchase comes from the manufacturer directly to the consumer. The reasoning is that the dealer is the manufacturer's agent in this special sense or that the consumer is a third-party beneficiary of the manufacturer-dealer contract or that the warranty runs with the goods.

If the manufacturer intentionally misleads the consumer, however, the consumer always could and still can recover any damages in *tort* law on the basis of deceit or fraud.

Similarly, a person seeking information about other persons (credit or job applicants, for example) may sustain *tort* action for damages against an informer who intentionally or carelessly misleads him to his detriment. The informer obligates himself to the inquirer to take reasonable precautions for accuracy of information and to avoid intentional deceit.

A letter writer who gives information about one person to other persons also has obligations to the state and to the person who is the subject of the report. Failure to meet the obligations subjects the informer to possible charges of *libel*—publication of defamatory statements about another person which damage that person. "Publication" in this special sense means merely giving the damaging statements to one or more other persons, or negligently allowing other persons to see them. For this reason, duns for past-due accounts and letters conveying unfavorable information about people should go only in sealed envelopes addressed so that they are seen only by the debtors and other people specially privileged (as explained later) to see them.

The state assumes that the informer will be fair-minded (show good faith rather than malicious intent). Hence good faith is usually a complete defense against criminal libel charges, although truth is not if malice is present. Both good faith and truth always provide complete defense.

Civil libel suit brought by the injured person for damage to his business or profession, however, is different. The informer obligates himself to tell the truth. In most legal jurisdictions truth is a complete defense against civil libel suit for damages, no matter how damaging or malicious the information may be. Where it is not, truth and absence of malicious intent are, although good faith alone is not.

Apparently for the purpose of facilitating the exchange of important business information, the law gives an informer considerable benefit of doubt and applies the principle of *privilege*. That is, a writer is said to be *privileged* if sending *requested* information in good faith to someone for the purpose of helping him to protect an interest (a prospective employer or creditor, for example, who could suffer considerable loss if he deals with an unworthy man). The information need not be absolutely true, provided the writer has been reasonably careful to get the facts, for the privileged informer to be invulnerable to civil libel suit. One who requests information about a third party normally expects the informer to answer "to the best of your knowledge" and to include some opinion. If the informer volunteers the information, is reckless with the truth, or shows malice, however, he loses privilege as a defense.

In collection letters, for example, a writer disgusted with a troublesome debtor may maliciously try to get even with the debtor by making true but damaging statements about him to others who have no interest to protect. He thus provides the basis for criminal libel charges. If some of the statements are untrue, he also throws himself open to civil libel suit for damages—without benefit of privilege because the information is going to people who have not requested it to protect an interest.

Credit organizations that provide requested information about credit risks to members immediately faced with credit applications are probably protected by privilege; but if an organization distributes the information to all members, including those without immediate need or request for it, and thus forms a kind of blacklist, privilege probably does not apply.

A letter writer requesting personal information should therefore show that he has an interest to protect and promise to keep the information confidential except for the particular use—to help the informer protect himself against libel suit. The informer should show that the information is requested, be reasonably careful to tell the truth and avoid any malice, and ask that the information be confidential.

Recent legislation, however, has limited the meaning of "confidential" to give certain new protection to the person being refused credit, insurance, or employment on the basis of reports received about him. Formerly, even he had no legal means of finding out what was said about him, by whom, or to whom. Now he can get the otherwise "confidential" information.

The Fair Credit Reporting Act (which became effective in April, 1971) gives you the right, on request, to

—see the information in your file (except medical), including the sources;

—get the names of all who have received reports on you;

—have any inaccurate or out-of-date information (usually more than seven years old) removed, new information added (including your own statement up to about a hundred words), and have the changes reported to all who have received erroneous reports on you (about employment within two years; about credit within six months).

Though the act applies especially to the approximately 2,500 credit bureaus in the U.S., its basic principles probably apply to the individual letter writer who gives information about job and credit applicants. The courts have not yet clarified the act in application to many specific situations.

Motivation by extortion

In collection letters—and others trying to induce a reader to act in a certain way—writers sometimes resort to threats not in due process of law to force the desired action beneficial to themselves. In so doing, they become guilty of *extortion*, a criminal offense in all state and federal jurisdictions. The due process of law for enforcing a contract (including the payment of contracted debts) is civil suit. If a writer threatens such a suit, he is on safe legal ground, although he may lose the reader's goodwill; but if he threatens physical violence ("I'll beat you up") or criminal charges ("I'll report you for income tax evasion"), he is going beyond due process and is subject to criminal prosecution for extortion.

The same threatening letters—if they wilfully use abusive language to incite fear, confusion, or humiliation—also subject the senders to civil liability in tort law. The older cases usually allowed recovery only where physical harm resulted, but recent cases are supporting recovery where substantial mental anguish and emotional disturbance result even without actual physical infirmity.

appendix C | Pointers to good dictation

[To your secretary you may dictate; to your customer, never.]

SINCE MOST business letters are dictated to a secretary or a machine, anybody who needs to send out many letters also needs to learn how to dictate them.[1] Fortunately the learning job is easy and quick—with a little intelligence, a little study, and a little practice—although a person who refuses to give it any study can and usually does make a mess.

To help those willing to learn, we append these pointers—drawn from years of experience on both ends of the dictation job and from the suggestions of various dictating-machine manufacturers.

As with many procedures, getting ready is the biggest and most important part; so don't skip the next section and jump into the fire of the actual dictating.

Before you dictate

1. *Be sure you know how to compose good letters of various kinds.* You won't gain much by learning how to do a good job of dictating unless you first know what a good letter is. Certainly skill in dictating is not going to make a bad message into a good letter. And improved efficiency in getting out bad messages is no virtue. So unless you're sure you know how to compose a good message—with appropriate style, tone, psychology, degree of persuasion, and organization—forget about dictating for the moment and take a good course in letter writing, or at least read Chapters 2–4 in this book.

Once you know how to compose good letters, you may profitably proceed to learn how to dictate as a means of getting your good messages on paper efficiently.

---

[1] For efficiency in wording, we'll confine our suggestions to dictating letters, the most frequent use of dictation, although most of the pointers apply equally to dictating reports and other messages.

2. *Acquaint yourself thoroughly with your helpers.*

a) If you're going to use a dictating machine, you need to know more about it than where the on-off switch is. Once you get it, it's your baby; you'd better learn how to give it a change. At least you need to know how to interpret its cries for a change—of tape, belt, disc, or roll—before it makes a real mess by ceasing to record in the middle of your dictation.

Each of many available models has its own peculiarities too. And many dictating machines have great flexibility, a surprising number of conveniences for the man who knows which button to push for what. Trying to use one without learning its ways is being like the old man who never used his car radio, heater, air conditioner, cigarette lighter, windshield washer, or turn signals because he didn't know what all those buttons and knobs were for.

Surely you don't expect us to tell you specifically how your machine works—and all the dozens of its competitors—only to have the information outdated by the next model. The best sources of information about it are the user's manual and the salesman.

b) Whether you use a machine or not, a secretary (or stenographer or typist, if you like) has to do the transcribing—and she's a special model too. Nevertheless, you two are a team that had better learn to work together.[2] You've probably seen the cartoon of the two mules tied together and each trying to get to a different haystack. They got what they wanted only by learning to cooperate. So with you two; you will beget letters better by learning to work in unison, or at least cooperatively.

Most secretaries have some pride (deserved or not) that will be hurt by your dictating things they know well and thus implying that they don't. Some know capitalization, paragraphing, punctuation, and spelling. You aren't being efficient or tactful if you dictate these things to such secretaries, but you're being foolish if you don't to those who need help. Failing to dictate such things when needed also hurts their pride.

We don't agree with the wag (or fool) who said you have to keep beating a secretary down to show her you're the boss, her superior. Unless you have given her a chance and found her inept, we don't even think you should dictate every simple little letter. She should be able to handle such things herself.

Of course, if she is no good but thinks she is, cowing her is one way to get rid of her. But if she is capable, recognizing her assets appeals to her pride and induces cooperation. She will then gladly show what she can do, perhaps reducing your dictation load by half—and perhaps doing her half better. We've seen many secretaries frustrated by having to type the poor letters of their bosses and resentful of no chance to make suggestions or write letters themselves.

---

[2] We recognize that the increasing use of network dictating by telephone to pools of machines and typists reduces the significance of some things said here (while raising other problems), but the main principles are the same.

The cooperation of your secretary is so important to you that we think you should even size up her personality and at least to some extent act accordingly. Some girls are sensitive and jittery. Minimize your boisterousness, impetuousness, and even rafter-rattling throat clearings, which only make things worse. Some secretaries want to be efficient and will resent the inefficiencies of intermittent dictation throughout the day or any hemming and hawing, calling for numerous corrections, long-winded telephone interruptions, or calling for filed information while you should be dictating —and while their work piles up.

Some secretaries are conservative and will resent off-color jokes and stories, flirtations, and facetiousness; others may get distracting ideas. Either way, your dictation efficiency suffers. If efficient dictation is your goal, you need to know your secretary and act accordingly.

3. *Be prepared to start talking* by the time you have turned on a dictating machine or secretary and allowed for the warm-up; that is, prepare in advance what you're going to say. Have in your head, or before you, decisions to be given, facts you'll need, and letters to be answered, with at least markings of points to be covered and questions to be answered—and have your thoughts organized. For difficult, long, and important letters, you may need outlines—maybe even topic sentences for paragraphs. You may enjoy the show of your secretary's bobbing up and down to get things from the files during a dictation session, but the session is inefficient and she won't enjoy the show—unless she's a show-off.

4. *Stop thinking about other things and get on with the job at hand.* You can better avoid making interruptive appointments and receiving disruptive telephone calls if you set aside a certain time each day for dictation. At best, you will have enough such interruptions, and enough need to get out something on the spur of the moment during the rest of the day, to keep your secretary adequately frustrated.

While you dictate

1. *Relax and speak clearly,* piping your voice into the appropriately distanced microphone on the machine or girl. Don't slur, don't mumble, don't pace, and don't talk too fast or too slow, too loud or too low, or with great variation in volume or speed. Nervousness is contagious. Sounds are directional. The best distance from machine mikes is about three inches. (The best distance from a secretary will vary.) Cigars, pipes, and cigarettes are not particularly good megaphones to help your words come out loud and clear. And your smoke screen is more likely to put a haze on your words than to filter out any aberrant sounds. At best, you probably talk with enough mush in your mouth without the help of chewing gum.

2. *Before dictating the copy, dictate the format:* what it is (letter, memo, telegram), kind of paper and postage, number of copies, and anything else the typist needs to know to avoid going wrong. Unless you do, she may use

letter form on the company's letterhead with one carbon, only to learn later that it was to have been a memo on plain paper with four carbons. She won't appreciate your misleading her and making her do double duty—maybe half of it after 5 o'clock.

3. *Dictate capitalization, punctuation, paragraphing, and spelling* according to your secretary's needs, erring on the safe side and including the unusual, regardless. Certainly you will need to spell out all words the sounds of which do not clearly indicate their spelling (confusing pairs like *accept* and *except* and all proper nouns naming people, places, and products unless obvious or well known). A dictated "innuendo" once came out "in your window," caught by the dictator in reading before signing. But this one, not caught because the dictator did not read before signing, caused real trouble for a while before it was cleared up: In replying to sales information about a line of products, a dictator said, "I know your line. When you say XXX . . . , I think a more accurate statement would be . . . ." The typist wrote, "I know you're lying when you say XXX will . . . . I think a more accurate statement would be . . . ."

4. *Try to minimize the need for corrections* (preplanning is the best way), but make necessary ones promptly. Otherwise, you may forget or mislead the girl in going so far wrong as to be beyond correction.

5. *Turn off the recorder during unavoidable interruptions* to keep confusing irrelevancies (which can be embarrassing) from getting into your letters. And if the interruption is a private affair, the recorder here includes the secretary. Some girls tattle to the company grapevine.

❀   ❀   ❀   ❀

Dictators are inclined to become careless. To slap their careless hands, the stenographic department head of one firm using network dictation by telephone to a steno pool designed the following form. You might well use it as a kind of checklist for dictation (at least the mechanical part of actual dictation).

Dictator _____ Department _____
We had difficulty in transcribing the attached dictation for the reason(s) checked. We would like to get out your work just the way you want it. Will you help us by attention to these details?

_____Number not shown	_____Dictation indistinct
_____Carbons not indicated	_____Dictation too _____ fast,
_____Corrections not marked	_____slow
_____Length of letters not specified	_____Voice too low, _____ espe-
_____Stationery not indicated	cially at sentence ends
_____Enclosures not indicated	_____No paragraphing indicated
_____Unusual names not spelled	_____Punctuation not clear from
	context

_____Letters needed for names and addresses omitted from dictation
_____First words not on cylinder—too short warm-up

_____Dictation ran off cylinder (or tape)—watch for warning signal
_____Dictated over defective recording device
_____Letters sent for addresses not cross-referenced with dictation

Remarks: _____
_____

After you dictate

1. *Shut up after dismissing the secretary or turning off the machine.*

2. *Read and sign the letters* that are all right when they come back to you. Remember that you, not your machine or secretary, are responsible for the letters you send out.

3. *Thank your secretary* for the good work she did, including improvements made. Deserved thanks go a long way in developing cooperation.

4. *Ask for corrections* of other letters as needed, diplomatically teaching your secretary not to repeat any errors she has made and consulting with her about the most efficient way to correct yours and hers. She will appreciate light pencil notations, instead of heavy ink ones that look angry and require retyping of the page even though she might have been able to make the necessary correction simply.

| # Concise writer's handbook

THIS ALPHABETICAL LIST of short, easy-to-remember symbols will save a teacher's time in marking papers and will help students wanting brief explanations of errors frequently found in business writing.

The symbols are easy to remember because they are nearly all abbreviations of already familiar grading terms. Even the few abstract, unalphabetized ones at the end are mostly standard proofreader's marks.

The list includes everything teachers and students of business writing are likely to need for correcting the English in their papers. Although it is much more concise than the usual English handbook, it omits only those points college students already know or don't need to know. Selection was based on 30 years of experience in observing the good and the unacceptable in the writing of college students.

The explanations of points of grammar and usage are based solidly on the studies of linguists—the true authorities.

A, an   Use *a* as the indefinite article if the following word begins with a consonant sound (including the now pronounced *h* in *hotel* and *historical*—and combined consonant and vowel sounds, as in *European, usage, unit,* and *eulogy*); use *an* if the next word begins with a vowel sound, including words beginning with silent *h* (*hour, honor, honest*).

Ab   Before using an abbreviation, make sure that it is appropriate, understood, and correct in form (including the capitalization, spacing, and punctuation). Ordinarily, dates and states are not abbreviated (except that the Postal Service is working on a complete system of abbreviations for states on envelope addresses—adapting to electronic mail sorting). Mr., Mrs., Dr., A.M., P.M., c.o.d., f.o.b., and e.o.m. are commonly abbreviated. Chemical symbols, certain engineering terms, and certain footnote references are preferably abbreviated when the reader will understand. Check your dictionary if in doubt about an abbreviation.

Accuracy   Get facts, names, addresses, and statements right. If your statement may be misinterpreted, restate it so that it has only one clear meaning.

Adapt to your reader's interests, reading ability, and experience. A message that seems to be written for somebody else, or for nobody in particular, will be less effective than one which seems to fit the reader. See p. 62.

Agreement of subjects with their verbs and of pronouns with their antecedents is essential to clear, inconspicuous writing. For each kind of agreement, the following points apply: (*a*) Don't be confused by other words that come between the two that are supposed to agree.   (*b*) Collective nouns take singular verbs and pronouns when the action is unified group action but plurals when the action is that of various individuals.   (*c*) In an either-or situation, with one noun singular and one plural, verbs and pronouns agree with the closer noun.

1. Notice that the first sentence about agreement is an illustration of the first point: *agreement* (singular) is the subject of the verb *is*; but between them is a prepositional phrase with four plurals. As other illustrations, consider

   —Selection of topics *is* based on the reader's knowledge and interests.
   —Government programs help make more food available to the consumer but *cost* a great deal of money.
   —Lee also tells how important the arrangement of the records offices *is*.

   Part, series, type, and other words usually followed by plural phrases are frequently pitfalls to the unwary writer:

   —The greatest part of his investments *is* in real estate.
   —A series of bank loans *has* enabled the firm to stay in business.

2. *Any, anyone, each, every, everyone, everybody, either,* and *neither* all point to singular verbs (and pronouns), except when the choice next to the verb or pronoun in an either-or situation is plural:

   —Any of the men in the group *is* expected to give some of *his* time to helping the group when asked.

—Either board members or the president *has* power to act on the point.

—Neither the mayor nor the council members *are* allowed to use city-owned automobiles in transacting *their* own business.

3. Two separate singular subjects combined by *and* require a plural verb and pronoun; but when combined by *besides, either-or, together with,* or *as well as,* they take a singular:

—The honorary president and leader of this group *is* Mr. Anderson.

—Mr. Weeks and his secretary *do* the work in the central office.

—Considerable knowledge, as well as care, *is* necessary in good writing.

4. Be sure your pronouns agree in number and gender with their antecedents (words they stand for).

—The benefits a student gets from studying the practical psychology, writing skills, and ways of business in good courses like letter writing and report writing will help *him* throughout *his* life.

—The company plans to move *its* main operations closer to *its* major source of raw materials.

5. Relative clauses beginning with *who, that,* or *which* require verbs agreeing with the antecedents:

—The manager is one of those *persons who* expect unquestioning loyalty.

—The actions in the life of any animal which *interest* a biologist are those concerned with food, shelter, protection from enemies, and procreation.

6. Plural-sounding collective subjects take singular verbs and pronouns when the action is that of the group but plural verbs when the action is that of various individuals:

—The board *is* having a long meeting.

—The board *have* been arguing and disagreeing on that point for months.

—Twenty-five dollars *is* a reasonable price in view of. . . .

—The faculty *are* allowed almost complete freedom in the conduct of *their* classes while the administration *plays its* part by providing the facilities, general policy, and record keeping (the collective faculty acting as individuals, the administration acting as a group).

Avoid using a collective as both singular and plural:

—The company *is* located in Chicago, but *its* (not *their*) products are sold all over the country.

7. Beware of letting the complement tempt you to make the verb agree with it instead of the subject:

—Our main difficulty *was* errors in billing.
—The biggest cost item *is* employees' salaries and wages.

In most such situations, however, rewriting would be better to avoid equating a subject with a predicate noun of different number.

8. Certain words deserve careful attention because their form is an uncertain or misleading indication of their number:

—The meaning of the whole context determines the number of *any, all, more, most, some,* and *none.*
—*Acoustics, economics, genetics, linguistics, mathematics, news, physics,* and *semantics* are all singular despite their look and sound; *deer* and *fish* are both singular and plural; and *mice,* like *men,* is a plural word despite the singular smell.

Ambiguous—more than one possible meaning and hence not clear. Usually the temporary confusion can be cleared up (1) by correcting a faulty pronoun reference (see **Ref**) or (2) by rewording to straighten out a modifier so that it can modify only what you intend (see **Mod**).

—He took over the management of the business from his father when he was 55. (When his father reached 55, Carl took over management of the business.)
—We agreed when we signed the papers that you would pay $100. (When we signed the papers, we agreed that you would pay $100 *or* We agreed that you would pay $100 when we signed the papers.)

And is a strong coordinating conjunction—one of the most useful and most troublesome of words.

1. It should be used only to connect (in the sense of addition) things of similar quality and grammatical form. Used otherwise, it produces faulty coordination between an independent and a dependent clause, misparallelism, or sentence disuntiy. See **Sub, Para,** and **Unit.**

—The plans call for a new four-story building, and which will cost $4.5 million. (Omit *and;* it can't connect an independent clause to a dependent one.) See **Coh.**

—In this course you learn the ways of the business world, the principles of practical psychology, and to write better. (The infinitive *to write* is not parallel with the nouns *ways* and *principles.* Make them all the same form before connecting them by *and.*) See **Para.**

—We feel sure that the saw will serve you well, and we appreciate your order. (The two ideas are not closely enough related to appear in the same sentence—probably not even in the same paragraph.) See **Unit.**

2. *And* is properly the most-used connective, but don't overuse it to connect a series of independent clauses into a long, stringy sentence. If the clauses deserve equal emphasis, they can be made separate sentences. If not, the weaker ones should be subordinated. See **Sub.**

—The consultant first talked with the executives about their letter-writing problems *and* then he took a sample of 1,000 carbon copies *and* he classified them into two groups *and* 45 percent of them were for situations that could just as well have been handled by forms. (After talking with the executives about their letter-writing problems, the consultant classified a sample of 1,000 carbon copies from the files. He found that 45 percent of them were for situations that could just as well . . . .)

3. *And* may be used as a sentence beginning only if you want to emphasize it.

4. *And* is not proper before *etc.;* the *et* (*et cetera*) means *and.*

5. *And* may be used with *or* (and/or), except in formal writing, to mean either one or both of two possibilities.

Ap The appearance of a letter, as of a person, should be pleasant but unobtrusive and should suggest that the writer is competent, accurate, neat, and alert. It requires a good grade of paper, proper spacing, typing with a reasonably fresh ribbon, and clean type without messy erasures or glaring errors. Check Chapter 1.

Apostrophes (usually considered with punctuation, although they belong with spelling) should be used in

1. Possessives (except *its* and the personal pronouns): before *s* in

singulars (*man's*); after the *s* in plurals if the *s* or *z* sound was added to make the word plural (*ladies'* but *women's*).

2. Contractions: to mark the omission of a letter (*isn't, doesn't, it's*—meaning "it is," quite different from the possessive *its*).

3. Plurals of symbols: figures (illegible *8's*), letters of the alphabet (one *o* and two *m's*), and words written about as words (too many *and's* and *but's*).

Appropriateness to the situation is an important test of good English. Is your statement too slangy, colloquial, or formal for the occasion? See **Adap** and p. 45 for a discussion of levels of usage.

Assign   Follow the facts and directions in the assignment. Although you are expected to fill in with necessary details of your own invention, you are not to go contrary to the facts or the spirit of the problem; and you are to make only reasonable assumptions.

Authorization letter. See the reports checklist (p. 569).

Courtesy could be improved here. See p. 75.

Capitalization is pretty well standardized except that newspapers set their own practices and hence are not guides for other writing.

1. Capitalize the names of specific things, including the titles of people, but not general words. For instance, you capitalize the name of any specific college, university, or department; but you write

    —A university education may well cost $12,000, regardless of the department in which one studies.
    —L. W. Wilson, president of the University of . . . .
    —When President Wilson came . . . .

    You capitalize any specific course, room, lake, river, building, etc., but not the general words. So you might write that you are

    —Taking Economics 215, majoring in engineering, but right now going to a history class in the Liberal Arts Building, after stopping in to see a professor in Room 115.

    Next summer you may

    —Fish mostly in Portage Lake and some in the Ausable River, although I prefer river to lake fishing.

    Of course, you capitalize *English, French, German*—all the languages, because they derive from the names of countries.

2. In titles of books and articles, capitalize the first word and all others except articles (*a, an, the*), prepositions (like *of, to, in, on, for*), and conjunctions (like *and, but, or, nor, although*)— unless you use solid capitals.

3. Capitalize the seasons (spring, summer) only when they are personified (rare except in poetry).

4. Capitalize sections of the country (the South, the East Coast) but not directions (east, west).

5. Capitalize people's titles (*Mr., Mrs., Miss, Dr., Colonel, Professor, Judge, Governor, President*) and terms of family relations (*Uncle Jim*) when used before names but only to show unusual respect when used in place of or after names:

   —Yes, Son, ...
   —The Senator then went . . . .
   —After Mother had seen . . . .

6. Capitalize the first word after a colon only if it starts a complete sentence. (In an itemized listing, you may capitalize the first word of items even though they are incomplete sentences.)

7. The abbreviation of *number* (No.) and certain others are always capitalized. Many, however, are not, and some may go either way. In case of doubt, see a good dictionary.

Cardinal numbers (*one, two, three; 6, 7, 9*) are preferable to ordinals (*first, second, third; 1st, 2d, 3d, 4th,* or *2nd, 3rd*) in dates except in very formal invitations and legal documents, or when the day is separated from the month. As a general rule, use the form that would be pronounced if read aloud. Since the simple ordinal forms may be either adjectives or adverbs, they need no *-ly* endings, ever.

   —On October 7 . . . ; sometime in November—probably about the 7th.

Case is no particular problem with English nouns. One form serves for all cases except the possessive (genitive), and the only real problem there is remembering correct use of the apostrophe (see **Apos**). For pronouns:

1. Use the nominative case (*I, we, he, she, they, who*) for the subject of a verb (other than an infinitive) and for the complement of a linking verb (any form of *to be* except the infinitive with a subject).

2. Use the objective case (*me, us, him, her, them, whom*) as the object of a verb or preposition and as the subject or object of an

infinitive (except *to be* without a subject). In informal speaking and writing, however, *who* is often used (and acceptable) as the object of a preposition unless it immediately follows the preposition, especially if it is in the usual subject position:

—*Who* was the letter addressed to?

3. Use the possessive case to show possession and to serve as the subject of a gerund (a verb form ending in -*ing* and used as a noun):

—*His* accusing me of dishonesty . . . .
—*My* thinking that a . . . .

4. The case of an appositive (an immediately following, and usually parenthetical, explanation like this) is that of the thing explained.

5. Watch case particularly after *than* and *as* and in compounds with a name and a personal pronoun:

—He is better informed on the subject than I (*am informed* implied).
—I am a more cautious man than he (*is* understood).
—He is not so cautious as I (*am* understood).
—Virginia and she went . . . (subject) *or* She and Virginia went . . . .
—I am to pick up Virginia and her . . . (object of verb).
—He told the story to Virginia and her (object of preposition) *or* He told the story to her and Virginia.

CB Comma blunders—also called comma faults and comma splices—are serious errors. See **P2** and **SOS2**.

CF Comma faults—also called comma blunders and comma splices—are serious errors. See **P2** and **SOS2**.

Choppy, jerky, short sentences are slow and awkward. Usually the trouble is (1) incoherence (the sentences don't follow each other naturally—see **Coh**); (2) poor control of emphasis (all the ideas in independent clauses, although of different importance—see **Sub**); or (3) lack of variety (all the sentences of the same pattern, usually all beginning with the subject or nearly the same length—see **Var**). Try combining several of the sentences, subordinating the less important ideas, and stressing the important ones in the independent clauses.

Cl Immediate clearness is a fundamental of good writing. Make sure your reader can get your meaning quickly and easily. Usually a statement that is not immediately clear requires fuller explanation, more exact wording, or recasting of a faulty, ambiguous, or involved construction.

Coherence—that quality of writing which shows the reader the relationships of the ideas—is essential to clear, quick, and easy reading. It comes best from a logical sequence of ideas expressed with heavy emphasis on the important ones and less on the related but less important ones, and with any necessary conjunctions to show what relationships exist. The worst kind of incoherence comes from putting apparently unrelated ideas together in the same sentence or paragraph. Be especially careful not to connect unrelated thoughts, or ideas of different importance, with *and*.

1. Plan what you want to say so that your ideas fall in a natural sequence. Sometimes a topic sentence can help hold together several otherwise seemingly unrelated ideas. For example, if you begin with "Three factors deserve special consideration," the three following sentences or paragraphs all seem related in being tied to the topic statement.

2. Be sure your ideas have the proper relative emphasis. (See **Emp** and **Sub.**) Ideas deserving emphasis should be in independent clauses (groups of words that can stand as whole sentences). If two or more of these ideas are closely related and deserve equal emphasis, they can be put together in one sentence (compound). Ideas deserving less emphasis should be put in dependent clauses. (Since a dependent clause cannot stand alone as a sentence, it has to be attached to the independent clause most closely related in thought—making a complex sentence.)

3. Check carefully to see whether you need transitional words or phrases to help the natural sequence and sentence type show the proper relationship of your ideas. If so, see **Conj** and **Tr**, and consider the following words and others of somewhat similar meaning to select the one which fits your purpose best:

     —and ... moreover, besides, in addition, also, furthermore
     —but ... however, nevertheless, yet, still, although, while
     —either-or ... neither-nor, else, whether
     —therefore ... consequently, hence, as a result, accordingly, so, ergo
     —because ... since, as, for, the reason is
     —then ... after that, afterward, later, subsequently
     —meanwhile ... during, simultaneously, concurrently, while
     —before ... preceding, previously, prior to
     —if ... provided, assuming, in case, unless

Conciseness (which is not necessarily brevity) depends on leaving out the irrelevant, leaving unsaid what you can adequately imply (see **Imp**), and cutting out deadwood. See pp. 31 ff. for explanation and illustration of techniques.

Confidence in yourself, in your decisions, and in your success in obtaining the action you request will go a long way toward getting acceptance of your proposals; but you need to avoid overconfidence or presumptuousness. In an application letter, for example, the writer who is too meek or modest hurts his chances, but so does the fellow who is too cocky or aggressive. In phrasing the decision to refuse an adjustment, a writer needs to explain adequately and then assume that his decision will be acceptable. In making recommendations, usually the writer is not justified in commanding, but he needs to word them with as much confidence as the facts and the reader-writer relationship will allow. In the endings of C–plan letters the request for action should be stated with success consciousness (p. 67) but not with presumption. Words like **if, hope,** and **trust** indicate doubt—a lack of confidence.

> —*If* you want to buy an X, just . . . . (After your sales presentation, assume that he does and tell him how: "Just fill out the handy order form and mail it today, and you can have your X within . . . .")
>
> —We *trust* this arrangement will be satisfactory. (Too much doubt. If you've explained adequately, assume acceptability of your decision.)
>
> —When may I have an interview? (Presumptuous. The question seems to leave no alternative as to whether, the only question being when. Better: "Please tell me a time when I may come to talk with you more fully about . . . .")

Conjunctions connect ideas to show the kind of relationship that exists. See **Coh** and **Tr**.

1. Unless the relationship is already clear, put in the necessary conjunction.

2. Be sure the one you use reflects accurately the relationship you intend. (See the list under **Coh** for groups of somewhat similar connectives with different shades of meaning.)

3. Guard particularly against using *but* when no contrast is intended, and against using either *but* or *and* to connect things unless they are of the same grammatical structure (noun with noun, verb with verb, etc.).

4. Before using *therefore, because,* or any of the other similar words, make sure that a true cause-and-effect relationship really exists.

Connotations—the overtones or related meanings of words—are often as important as the denotations, or dictionary meanings. Be sure that the words you use are appropriate in connotations as well as in denotations. Consider, for example, the connotations in the following pairs: *cheap, inexpensive; secondhand, used; complaint department, customer service department; basement store, thrift store.*

Copying from the assignment or from other people produces writing that doesn't sound like you. Put your ideas in your own words. You won't learn much about writing by copying the phrasing of illustrations in the text. Read them for ideas, approaches, and psychology; then express your ideas in your own phrasing.

Correlatives (*either-or, both-and, not only—but*) require parallel elements. See **Para.**

—Either letters or reports (not *report writing*) may involve this point.
—Both men and women (not *females*) . . . .
—You are expected not only to write correctly but to write effectively (not *but should write effectively*).

Cpr   Comparisons require special attention to these points:

1. The things compared must be comparable. Usually the trouble is omission of necessary phrases like *that of, that on, other,* or *else.*

—The markup on Schick shavers is higher than *that on* Remingtons. (You can't omit *that on* or you'll be comparing the height of a Remington—measured in inches—with the markup on Schicks—a percentage.)
—Frank Mosteller sells more Fuller brushes than any *other* salesman. (Without *other*, the statement is illogical if Frank is a salesman; he can't sell more than he himself sells.)

2. Incomplete comparisons mean nothing; complete them.

—You get more miles per dollar with XXX. (More than with what?)
—This material has a higher percentage of wool. (Higher than what?)

3. Be sure to use the correct form of comparison words. Compari-

sons involving two things are usually shown by adding *-er* (the comparative) to the simple form (*cold, slow*). Those involving more than two usually require the *-est* (or superlative) form (*coldest, slowest*). For words of three syllables or more—and for many with two and some with only one—the better form is *more* plus the simple form (for the comparative) or *most* plus the simple form (for the superlative): *more frequently, most hopeful.* Some words may be used either way: *oftener* or *more often; oftenest* or *most often.* Attention to the sound of the expression is usually a sufficient guide to native speakers of English. When in doubt, see the dictionary.

4. Watch these idioms: Complete the *as much as* phrase and use *to* after *compare* when pointing out similarities only, *with* when pointing out any differences:

—Price increases may be worth as much *as,* if not more than, the dividends on a common stock purchase.
—Comparison of X *to* Y shows that they involve the same principles.
—Comparison of sales letters *with* application letters shows that they are quite similar but that they have minor differences.

5. Certain words (*unique, empty,* and *final,* for example) are logically absolutes and hence cannot take either comparative or superlative forms.

CS Comma splice—a serious error. Except when they are in series or are short and parallel, two or more independent clauses must be separated by a period, a comma and a coordinating conjunction, or a semicolon (which may or may not be followed by a transitional phrase like *that is* or by one of the conjunctive adverbs). See **SOS2** and **P2**.

CSP Select a central selling point and give it the major emphasis by position and full development. Scattering your shots over too many points leaves the major ones weak. See **Emp** and **Dev.**

Diction Use a more suitable word. The big test, of course, is whether the word conveys your thought accurately, including its connotations. Consider whether your words will be understood easily; whether they give a sharp, vivid picture by being natural and fresh instead of pompous, jargonistic, or trite; whether they give a specific, concrete meaning instead of a fuzzy or dull concept because they are general or abstract; and whether they are appropriately informal, formal, standard, technical, or nontechnical—

according to the topic and reader. Watch especially the following often-confused pairs: *accept, except; adapt, adopt; affect, effect; almost, most; amount, number; already, all ready; all right, "alright"* (no such word); *altogether, all together; are, our; beside, besides; between, among; capital, capitol; fewer, less; formerly, formally; imply, infer; it's, its; loose, lose; moral, morale; oral, verbal; personal, personnel; principal, principle; than, then; there, their; too, to, two.*

Date   Be sure to put a date on all letters and reports (except possibly ephemera). Any papers worthy of going into files need dates. Dates should be written in the standard form (*November 2, 1971*) unless you have good reason to do otherwise. Your most likely good reasons could be: (1) You are in the armed services, where the form *2 November 1971* is used; or (2) you're writing a formal notice, where everything is spelled out; or (3) you're writing an informal note and may well use the form *11/2/71*. Modern business writing usually does not abbreviate months and does not use the ordinal forms. See **Card.**

Deadwood phrases add nothing to the meaning but take writing and reading time. See **Conc** and the list of frequent deadwood expressions on p. 34.

Develop your point more thoroughly with more explanation, definition, specific details, classifications, comparisons, or examples to make it clearer, more interesting, more convincing, or more emphatic. See **Spec.**

Directness saves words, speeds up reading, and makes your ideas clearer. Don't waste words by beginning too far back in the background of the subject, by stating what the reader already knows, or by expressing what will be clearly implied if you begin with the key thought. Write direct, active-voice sentences beginning with the important word as the subject. The expletives "It is . . ." and "There are . . ." are indirect, passive, and wordy (see **Exp**).

Dng   Dangling modifier. See **Mod.**

Documentation—telling your sources—is necessary when you use the ideas of others. See pp. 516 ff. for discussion and illustration. Also see the reports checklist (p. 566).

Emphasis should be divided among your ideas according to their relative importance.

1. When you state important ideas, give them deserved emphasis by one or more of the following methods: putting them in the emphatic beginning or ending position of your letter or paragraph, putting them in independent clauses, developing them thoroughly (including intentional repetition), phrasing them in active voice, and perhaps underscoring them or writing them in solid capitals (or a different color). See p. 30 for fuller explanation.

2. When you have negative, unimportant, already known, or other ideas that don't deserve emphasis, avoid overemphasizing them. Some useful methods are putting them in unemphatic middle positions, putting them in dependent clauses or phrases, and giving them brief mention or just implying them. Particularly objectionable is overemphasis on things the reader obviously knows and on things that are (or can be) adequately implied. The first insults the reader's intelligence, and both waste words:

   —Spring is just around the corner. You'll be needing . . . . (With spring just around the corner, you'll . . . .)
   —On October 3 you asked me to write a report on . . . . I have finished it and am . . . . (Here is the report requested in your letter of October 3 . . . .)
   —I have your letter of April 20 in which you ask for quotations on X. I am glad to give you our prices. Our present prices on X are . . . . (Just omit the first two sentences. They're implied in the third.)

Transitional words like *and, but,* and *however* usually do not deserve the emphasis they would get at the beginning of a sentence; and prepositions usually do not deserve end-of-sentence emphasis. Indeed, this is the only legitimate reason for objection to such words in these positions.

3. When writing about two or more things of differing importance, word the discussion to emphasize the proper one(s), as explained in 1 and 2.

Etc., an abbreviation of Latin *et cetera,* meaning *and so forth,* should not be used unless the reader will have a good idea of how to fill out the incomplete list (as in "Please take even-numbered seats 2, 4, 6, etc."). Otherwise, it can mean only "Reader, you guess what else I mean to include," and this does not communicate. Because *etc.* is an abbreviation, it takes a period; but because it is anglicized, it need not be italicized (or underscored in typed copy). In no case should you write "and etc."; *et* means *and.*

Expletives (*it is, there are*) nearly always make your writing unnecessarily wordy, weak, and passive. They usually result from a misguided attempt to write an impersonal style. In general, you should
avoid them, although sometimes they may help to soften a
command or avoid presumptuousness in a recommendation:

> —It was thought that you would prefer . . . . (I thought you
> would . . . .)
> —There are four important factors involved. These are: . . . .
> (The four important factors are . . . .)
> —It will be necessary to have your . . . . ("You must send . . ."
> might be too commanding.)

Fast movement that gets to the point quickly—without cumbersome detail or explicit statement of ideas that should be implied—is desirable when your message will be accepted readily; but if you need
to persuade the reader either to accept an unpleasant decision or
to take action the reader is reluctant to take, you have to build up
your case adequately before starting the key point. Stating the bad
news before adequate justifying reasons, or requesting an action
before showing enough reader benefits to motivate that action, is
therefore marked **Fast**, meaning "You got here too fast."

Figures are better than words (except at the beginning of a sentence) for
serial, telephone, page, chapter, chart, catalog, and street numbers;
for money, dimensions, and dates and time (except in formal announcements); for all quantities when several are close together
(but not adjoining) in a sentence or paragraph; and for other isolated quantities requiring more than two words. (As an acceptable
replacement for the two-word rule, your teacher may authorize
this: Use figures if the quantity is above ten.)

1. If a quantity comes at the first of a sentence, write it in words or
   recast the sentence.

2. When a sentence involves two different series of quantities, use
   figures for one and words for the other; if more than two, use a
   table.

   > —On the qualifying exam, ten percent of the applicants scored
   > 90–100, thirty percent 80–89, ...
   > —Please make six 2″ x 3″ black-and-white prints and three
   > 5″ x 7″.

3. The old longhand practice of stating quantities twice—in one
   form followed parenthetically by the other form—is unnecessary
   and undesirable in type or print, although it is still sometimes

used in legal documents, and always in checks, for double certainty and security.

4. Except in dates, street numbers, and serial numbers, use a comma between groups of three digits, counting from the right.

5. Except in tables involving some cents, periods and zeros after money quantities are wasted typing and reading.

6. Two-word quantities between 20 and 100 require the hyphen (twenty-six).

7. Cardinal numbers (*1, 2, 3, 4, etc.*), are preferable to ordinals (*1st, 2d, 3d, 4th*) in dates except when the day is separated from the month. See **Card** and **Date.**

8. Since ordinals are either adjectives or adverbs, an *-ly* ending is never necessary.

Fragments (phrases or subordinate clauses posing as sentences) are serious errors except when perfectly clear and intentional—as they usually are when used by professional writers for special effects. But they are like dynamite in the hands of the unskilled. Beware! Attach them to the independent clauses to which they belong (see **P3**) or change their wording to make them the complete, independent sentences they pretend to be.

—The latter being the better way. (This is a phrase fragment which should be attached by comma to the preceding sentence. Or you could simply change *being* to *is.*)
—One job in revising any paper is checking for and correcting any fragments. Which is easy to do. (The second "sentence" is a dependent clause and hence a fragment unless attached—by a comma—to the preceding.)

Fusing two independent clauses into one sentence (called a run-on) without benefit of a semicolon, or a connective word and a comma or semicolon, shows serious lack of sentence sense. The remedy is to use a period or—if the two really belong in the same sentence—to provide the right punctuation and any necessary connecting word. See **SOS2, P1,** and **P2.**

—Some people go to college because they have nothing else to do others have a serious purpose. (Put a period or semicolon before *others,* or use a comma and *but.*)
—Thirteen people boarded the plan in Jacksonville most of them were going to New York or Philadelphia. (Put a period or semicolon after *Jacksonville*—or, another way that is some-

times better, put a comma there and subordinate the second clause by taking out *were*.)

Gobbledygook is big-wordy, roundabout, long-winded, or stuffed-shirt language. Characteristically it shows two or more of those traits and comes in long sentences and paragraphs. Avoid it like poison; it works against both clarity and ease of reading.

Graphic devices of various kinds can often supplement words to make the information clearer, easier, or more interesting. Use them where they will help, but only if they will; make them big enough and detailed enough (but no bigger or more detailed than necessary) for your purpose; and be sure you use the most appropriate kind (line, bar, or pie chart; drawing, map, or photograph, for example). See the reports checklist (p. 562).

Gw   Goodwill, the fourth basic requirement of a business letter, is lacking or poorly handled here. See Chapter 4.

Introduction   See the reports checklist (p. 563).

Idiomatic usage—the natural, customary, accepted way of saying certain things—is correct that way simply because that is the way we say it, although it may defy grammatical analysis and rules. Idioms are so numerous and varied that they cannot be fully explained here. Usually, however, an error in idiom is use of the wrong preposition. Consider *possibility of, possible to, necessity of, need for,* and *ability to*. See **Prep.**

Imply rather than express the idea, to save words or avoid overemphasis. See **Emp** and pp. 31–33.

Italic print, indicated by underscoring in typewritten and handwritten copy, is used to emphasize occasional words; to mark the title of a book or journal; to mark a word, letter, or figure used as an illustration or typographical unit (instead of for its meaning); and to indicate an unanglicized foreign-language expression used in English context.

—Italics are *preferably not* used for titles of *parts,* such as the title of an article in a journal or a chapter in a book. Quotation marks are preferable for that purpose.
—Chapter 2, "The Second Test of a Good Letter," stresses clear, natural style and general linguistic *savoir faire.*
—*Convenience* and *questionnaire* are often misspelled.
—Use of fewer *I*'s and more *you*'s would improve many letters.

Jargon is fuzzy or inappropriate writing attributable to pompousness, circumlocution, deadwood, abstractness, big words, technical terms (written to nontechnical readers), or hackneyed expressions. It is the opposite of simple, natural, clear writing. Avoid it.

Juxtapose (put side by side) facts and ideas that the reader needs to consider together. For instance, wholesale and retail prices need to be seen together (with the difference and percentage of markup figured) if they are to mean as much as they should to the retailer being asked to stock the product.

K   Awkwardness in expression calls attention to itself, and it may confuse the reader. Reconstruct your sentence or change word order for a more natural flow.

lc   Lower case needed here, instead of capital. See **Cap.**

Logic   Avoid statements which will not stand the test of logic or for which the logic is not readily clear. Perhaps you need to supply a missing step in the logic. Maybe you need to state your idea more precisely. Or maybe you need to complete a comparison to make it logical. (If the last, see **Cpr** for fuller explanation.)

Mechanics   See the reports checklist (p. 570).

Modifiers should be placed in the sentence where they fit most naturally and make the meaning clearest. To avoid awkwardness and write clearly, you have to make sure that each modifier relates clearly to the thing it is supposed to modify. As a general rule, the two should be as close together as natural sentence construction will allow.

1. Participles (usually phrases including a verb form ending in *-ing* or *-ed,* and usually at the beginning of a sentence) require careful attention lest you relate them to the wrong word (or nothing at all).

    —Smelling of liquor, I arrested the driver. (The officer did not intend to say that he himself had been drinking.)
    —After soaking in the prepared mixture over night, I set the specimen up to dry for two days. (The scientist didn't mean what he said.)

These errors are commonly called "misrelated modifiers" or "dangling participles." Infinitives can dangle the same way:

    —To enjoy the longest, most dependable service, the motor must be tuned up about every 100 hours of operation. (The motor cannot enjoy dependable service.)

—In order to assist you in collecting for damages, it will be necessary to fill out a company blank. (The two infinitives dangle because they are not related to any doers of the actions indicated.)

But absolute phrases (a noun plus a participle) and participles, gerunds, and infinitives naming an accepted truth rather than the action of any person or thing do not need to relate to any subject:

—The sun having set, the fish began to bite.
—All things considered, Steve is the better man.
—Counting all costs, the little X is not an inexpensive car.
—To judge from results, that was an effective method.

2. *Only, almost,* and *nearly* are tricky words. Watch where you put them. Consider the varied meanings from placing *only* at different spots in "I can approve payment of a $30 adjustment."

3. A so-called "split" infinitive (putting a modifier between *to* and a verb) is usually undesirable because it is usually awkward; but if it is clear and natural, you'll do better to go ahead and split the infinitive rather than write an awkward sentence trying to avoid doing so.

4. Be sure to use the correct form of modifier. Adjectives modify nouns and pronouns; adverbs modify verbs, adjectives, and other adverbs. Most adverbs end in *-ly,* but some don't. See **WF.**

Monotonous See **Var.**

Mood The usual indicative and imperative moods (for normal statements and commands) give almost nobody trouble. But be careful with the subjective or conditional mood for verbs after commands and wishes, and for uncertainties or conditions contrary to fact (especially in formal writing). See **Sub.**

Natural writing avoids triteness, awkwardness, and pomposity. Clichés, trite and hackneyed expressions, and jargon suggest that a writer is not thinking about his subject and his reader; awkwardness suggests carelessness; and big words and pomposity suggest that the writer is trying to make an impression. He probably will—in the wrong way. Really big men think through what they want to say and put it simply, smoothly, and naturally. Although you cannot write exactly as you talk, you should try to write with the same freedom, ease, simplicity, and smoothness of your talk. See p. 36.

Negative in letter writing is defined as anything unpleasant to your reader. Since you want his goodwill, you should avoid the negative when you can, and subordinate it when you can't avoid it. Insofar as possible, stress the positive by telling what you have done, can do, will do, or want done instead of their negative opposites. See p. 65; and for methods of subordinating, see p. 30, **Emp,** and **Sub.**

Organization   See p. 506 and the reports checklist (p. 560).

Objectivity   Use of emotional or feverish words (especially if extensive) suggests a prejudiced rather than an objective view of the situation and therefore causes the reader to lose faith in the writer— especially a report writer. See pp. 510 and 520.

Obvious statements—when they are unnecessary as bases for other statements—at least waste words; and when they are put in independent clauses, they show poor control of emphasis and may insult the reader's intelligence. When you need to state an obvious fact as the basis for something else, put it in a dependent clause and use the independent clause for the new idea. (See **Emp** and **Sub.**)

> —New York is America's biggest city. Therefore . . . . (Since New York is America's biggest city, ...)

Omission of a word or necessary idea. Make your statements both grammatically and logically complete. See **Tele, Log,** and **Cpr.**

1. Conciseness is certainly a desirable quality in letters and reports, but it should not go so far as to push you into telegraphic style—omission of subjects, connective words, and articles:

   > —Please send check $123 for shipment April 1.

2. Unless the same verb form or preposition applies appropriately in a double construction, use the necessary two:

   > —His interest *in* and hard work *on* accounting have. . . .
   > —He should have *sold* earlier, and perhaps will now *sell*, since the market trend is clearer.
   > —The product *is* new and prospective buyers *are* numerous.

Outlining   See p. 506 and the reports checklist topic "Organization" (p. 560).

Punctuation which follows the conventions of written English (and is therefore understood by most readers) is a helpful device for both reader and writer in communicating clearly, quickly, and easily. But when it goes contrary to the understood conventions, it does not help and may even confuse. You should not try to use even good punctuation, however, as a crutch for bad writing. Heavy punctuation cannot make a bad sentence into a good one; the need for it suggests revising the sentence rather than trying to punctuate the involved statement. The best style is so direct and simple that it requires little punctuation except periods at the ends of sentences. Still, you cannot write much without need for some internal punctuation. Here are the conventions most commonly violated:

P1 Use a comma between two independent clauses connected by *and, but, or,* or *nor* if no other commas are in the sentence; but be sure you are connecting two clauses rather than a compound subject, verb, or object.

> —You may buy the regular Whiz mixer at $18.75, but I think you would find the Super Whiz much more satisfactory. (Two clauses.)
> —We make two grades of Whiz mixers and sell both at prices lower than those of our competitors' products. (Compound verb; one subject.)

Be sure, too, that you don't use obtrusive commas before the first or after the last item in a series or between a subject and its verb, a verb and its object, or a noun and its adjective. Also, you do not usually need a comma after a transitional word, but you may use one to emphasize.

P2 The semicolon is a pivotal mark; avoid using it between expressions unless they are of equal grammatical structure (usually two independent clauses or two items in a complex series). Use a semicolon between two independent clauses unless connected by *and, but, or,* or *nor;* and even then, use a semicolon if the sentence already has a comma in it (as in this one). Typical weaker connectives requiring the semicolon between two independent clauses are *therefore, so, moreover, hence, still, accordingly, nevertheless, furthermore, consequently,* and *however.* When these words are used as simple connectors not between two independent clauses, however (as right here), they are set off by a pair of commas unless they fit so smoothly into the sentence that they require no marks.

> —Jets made airline maintenance men relearn their jobs; the jet manual is twice as thick as the old one for prop planes. (No connective.)
> —The preceding sentence could be made into two, of course; but because the ideas are closely related, it is better as one.

(Commas elsewhere require semicolon before even a strong conjunction.)

—Good letter writing requires proper punctuation; therefore you must know how to use the semicolon. (Weak connective.)

—The proper style for letters is simpler and less involved than for most other writing, however, and therefore does not require very complex punctuation procedures. (*However* is a simple transition, *not used* between two clauses here and *not* close-knit into the phrasing the way *therefore* is; so it is set off by commas while *therefore* goes unmarked. Note, too, that the weak connective *so* requires the semicolon because it connects two clauses.)

P3   Use a comma after all first-of-sentence dependent clauses, long phrases, or other phrases containing any form of a verb. But when these forms or appositives or transitional words appear elsewhere in a sentence, use commas only with nonrestrictive (nonessential) ones. (Nonrestrictive statements add descriptive detail about an already identified word and are not necessary to the logic or grammatical completeness of the sentence; restrictive ones define, limit, or identify and are necessary to convey the intended meaning or complete the sentence. If, on reading aloud, you naturally pause and inflect your voice, the statement is nonrestrictive and requires the comma(s).

—Because the dependent clause comes at the beginning, we have to use a comma in this sentence.

—We do not need a comma in a complex sentence if the dependent part comes at the end or in the middle and restricts the meaning the way this one does.

—Having illustrated the two points about dependent clauses at the beginning and restrictive clauses elsewhere in the sentence, we now use this sentence to illustrate the use of a comma after a long phrase at the first of a sentence. (Because it includes a verb form, it would require a comma even if it were short, like "Having illustrated the point, we now leave the topic.")

—The three points already illustrated, which are certainly important, are no more important than the point about using commas to set off nonrestrictive clauses anywhere, which this sentence illustrates. (In fact, it illustrates twice: Both the *which* clauses could be omitted; they are nonrestrictive because they merely give added information unnecessary to either the meaning or the grammar of the basic sentence.)

Sometimes you need a comma to prevent misreading—especially after a gerund, participle, or infinitive—but sometimes anyway:

—In the office, files had been emptied all over the floor.
—By shooting, the man attracted the attention of the rescue party.
—Thinking that, he was unwilling to listen to reason.
—Seeing the foreman's unwillingness to help, the men gave up.

P4 Be sure to put in both commas—or dashes or parentheses—around a parenthetical expression in the middle of a structure. Direct addresses ("Yes, Mr. Thomas, you may . . .") and appositives (restatements like this one that follow immediately to explain a term) are typical examples. But, like clauses, some appositives are restrictive or so closely related that they require no punctuation, while others are nonrestrictive or so loosely related that they do.

—His starting point that good punctuation is a matter of following the conventions has not been stressed enough.
—His second point, the importance of writing letters so smoothly and naturally that they require little internal punctuation, would preclude most punctuation problems.
—General Motors opened a new plant in Akron, Ohio, in November, 1965, to produce certain auto parts.

P5 Use commas to separate coordinate adjectives. As two tests for coordinacy, see if you can put *and* between the adjectives or invert their order without producing awkwardness. If so, they are coordinate and require a comma.

—Proper punctuation can help greatly in writing a clear, easy-to-read style.
—Fairly heavy white paper is best for letterheads.

P6 The comma is the usual punctuation between items in a series (preferably including one before the *and* with the last item, because it is sometimes necessary for clearness and is always correct). But if any item except the last has a comma within it, use semicolons at all points between items. (Suggestion: If only one of a series requires an internal comma, consider putting it last and using commas between the items.)

—Make your writing clear, quick, and easy to read.
—Use commas between independent clauses connected by *and, but, or,* or *nor;* semicolons between independent clauses with other connectives or no connecting words; commas for dependent clauses and verbal or long phrases at the beginnings of sentences, for nonrestrictive ones elsewhere, and for simple series; and semicolons for complex series like the one in this sentence.

P7   Dashes, commas, and parentheses are all used in pairs around parenthetical expressions that interrupt the main part of the sentence. The choice depends on the desired emphasis and on the other punctuation. Two dashes (called "bridge dashes") emphasize most, commas less, and parentheses least of all. If the parenthetical part contains internal parentheses, dashes have to be used around it; if it contains commas, dashes or parentheses have to be used around it. (Of course, only a pair of parentheses can be used around a whole sentence which gives explanations, relatively unimportant additional detail, or side information not germane to the trend of the discussion, as this sentence does. In that case the period comes inside the closing parenthesis, although it comes outside otherwise.) A single dash—made on the typewriter preferably by two hyphens without spacing before, between, or after but also by one hyphen with spacing before and after—may be used to mark an abrupt change in the trend of a sentence or to precede an added statement summarizing, contrasting, or explaining the first part. In this second function, it is commonly called the "pickup dash."

—Your main weaknesses in writing—misspelling, faulty punctuation, and incoherence—should be corrected before you write letters.

—Errors in spelling, punctuation, or coherence—these all mar an otherwise good letter.

—A letter writer must avoid the common errors in writing—misspelling, bad punctuation, and incoherence. (Of course, the colon could replace the dash here; but ordinarily it should not unless the preceding statement is a formal introduction, usually indicated by the word *following*, or unless it is an introduction to an itemized list.)

P8   Hyphenate two or more words (unless the first ends in *-ly*) used to make a compound adjective modifying a following noun or pronoun.

—fast-selling product, wrinkle-resistant material, long-wearing soles, never-to-be-forgotten experience

Note that the point usually does not apply when the adjectives follow the noun.

—The material is highly wrinkle resistant and long wearing.

Certainly it does not apply when the adjectives modify the noun separately. See **P5**.

—These slacks are made of a hard, durable material.

Nor should the compound-adjective principle be applied to various other compounds: *extracurricular, classroom,* and *textbook,* for example. For such words, unless you know for sure, the only safe guide is the dictionary.

The compound-adjective principle does apply, however, to double compounds made with one element in common, where the "suspension hyphen" follows the first: three- and five-pound cans; only light- and middle-weight boxers.

The hyphen also marks the break in a word at the end of a line. See **Syl.**

Other less-frequent uses of the hyphen include (1) spelling of fractions (*three-fourths*) and two-word quantities between 20 and 100, and (2) prefixing words or syllables to names (*post-Hitler* Germany), to other words beginning with the same vowel as the end of the prefix (*re-entry, pre-established*), or to any word that might otherwise be confusing (*re-collect,* not *recollect; re-cover* not *recover*).

P9 Quotation marks are used primarily for short, exact quotations of other people's words and for titles of *parts* of publications, such as magazine and newspaper stories or book chapters. (The titles of journals and books should be italicized—underlined in typed copy —or written in solid capitals. See **Ital** and **Cap.**) If a quotation is more than two or three lines long, you should indent it from each side, single-space it, and omit quotation marks. You should not use quotation marks around a paraphrasing, but only for exact quotation.

Usually you should avoid using expressions so slangy as to require quotation marks; if an expression is inappropriate without the quotes, you'd better find a different word.

When closing quotation marks and other marks seem to come at the same place, the standard *American* practice is as follows: Place commas or periods *inside* the closing quotes; place semi-colons or colons *outside;* and place question or exclamation marks inside or outside depending on whether they are part of the quotation.

P10 The colon is either an anticipating or a separating mark. As an anticipator, it is used after introductory lead-ins to explanations or quotations, especially if the lead-in includes such formalizing terms as the word *following* or if the explanation is itemized or lengthy.

—The X Company's ink was even redder: its third-quarter loss of . . . .

—Three main benefits deserve your attention: . . . . (Enumeration follows.)

—On the use of the colon, Perrin says: . . . . (Long quotation follows.)

Because the colon is also a separating mark, however—used to separate hours from minutes and volume numbers from pages, for example—it should not be used as an anticipating mark when the lead-in phrasing fits well as an integral part of a short, informal statement. Summey calls this the "obtrusive colon."

—The three main advantages are (colon would be obtrusive here) speed, economy, and convenience.

—Perrin reports that (no colon; not even a comma) "*Will* has practically replaced *shall* in. . . ."

Almost invariably words like *namely, that is, for example,* and *as follows* are wasted (and browbeating) when used with a colon. The introductory phrasing and the colon adequately anticipate without these words.

—We have several reasons for changing: namely the . . . (Omit *namely.*)

—We had several reasons for changing. These reasons are: . . . . (This is worse. Omit *These reasons are;* put the colon after *changing.*)

Although practice varies, usually you should capitalize the first word after a colon only if it begins a complete sentence; but if itemizations follow, you may capitalize even though each item depends on the introductory statement for completeness.

The same idea applies to the end punctuation of items following a colon. If the items make complete sentences, put a period after each; but if all are to be considered one sentence, use comma or semicolon at the end of each (except the last, of course) as in other series—or you may use no end punctuation.

P11 Underlining in typed or handwritten copy calls for italic type when printed. Its main uses are to mark titles of books and journals, to emphasize, and to indicate unanglicized words. In copy not to be printed, it should be used also for any heading not written in solid capitals. Otherwise, the heading, which is really a title for the copy over which it stands, does not stand out sufficiently. (A printer would make it stand out by using big or boldface type.)

Type underlining is preferably continuous, rather than broken by individual words, because it is easier both to type and to read that way.

P12 Besides its well-known use at the end of a question, the question mark may be used in parentheses immediately following a statement or spelling about which the writer is uncertain and unable to determine. Obviously, it should not be used as an excuse for laziness; but if you have only heard a difficult name, for example, and have to write to that person, you'd better use the mark than unconcernedly misspell the name.

A question mark should not be used after indirect questions or commands softened by question form.

—We need to know what your decision is. (Indirect question.)
—Will you please ask the girl in your office to change my mailing address. (Softened command.)

Paragraphs in letters and reports are the same as in other writing—unified and coherent developments of topics—except that they tend to be more compressed and shorter for easier readability. (The symbol ¶ may be used to replace **Par.**)

1. Keep your paragraphs reasonably short. Long ones are discouragingly hard to read. Especially the first and last paragraphs of letters should be short (rarely more than three or four lines). Elsewhere, if a paragraph runs to more than about eight lines, you should consider breaking it up for easier readability. Usually you can find a good place. Certainly you should ignore any idea that a paragraph has to be more than one sentence. Often one sentence can say all that you need to say on a topic.

2. But develop your paragraphs adequately to clarify and support your points—by explanation, detail, facts and figures, or illustrations and examples.

3. Make each paragraph unified and coherent by taking out elements irrelevant to the topic, by organizing carefully, and by showing the interrelationship of the ideas. Consider these means: (*a*) beginning with a topic sentence and/or ending with a summary, (*b*) using the same key word or a synonym for it, and (*c*) using a connecting word or phrase such as those listed under **Coh.**

4. Show the relation of the paragraph to the preceding (by following logical sequence, carrying over key ideas, and/or using transitional words) and to the purpose of the whole paper or section (by pointing out the significance and/or by using transitional words or sentences).

—Paragraph unity also includes. . . . (*Also* means some of the explanation has preceded.)

—Carrying over key words and using transitional words are both means of providing unity between paragraphs as well as within them. (As *well as* means we've discussed unity *in* paragraphs and now will discuss it *between* them.)

5. **Par** with **No** before it means "No new paragraph needed here because you are still on the same topic and within reasonable paragraph length."

Parallelism means using the same kind of grammatical structure for ideas that are used coordinately, as in pairs, series (including lists), comparisons, and outlines. These structures state or imply relationships usually indicated by *and, but,* or *or* and hence should relate only full sentences to full sentences, nouns to nouns, verbs to verbs, active voice to active voice, plural to plural—indeed *any* grammatical form only to the same grammatical form in the related part. Watch for parallelism with *not only . . . but also, as well as, larger, less expensive,* and the like. (See p. 508, Item 5, for parallelism in outlines.)

—One of the duties of the airline hostess is to offer customers magazines, pillows, and hang their coats. (Two plural nouns and a verb improperly connected by the coordinating conjunction *and.*)
—The No-Skid knee guard is long wearing, washable, and stays in position. (Two adjectives connected by *and* to a verb.)
—John Coleman is 39, married, and a native. (Two adjectives and a noun.)
—If we fair each side of the arc, we produce a more practical airfoil section and an increase in performance is attained. (Active voice related to passive. Rewrite the last part as "increase the performance.")
—The next step is baking or catalyzation ("baking or catalyzing").
—Swimming is better exercise than to walk. (A gerund compared with an infinitive.)

Parallelism in pairs, series, and comparisons is largely a question of logic; you can add together and compare only like things. See **Log.**

Passive voice (in which the subject receives rather than does the action indicated by the verb) is usually wordy, awkward, and weak. Most of your sentences should therefore use the active voice. It makes important words (usually persons or products in letters) the subjects and objects of your verbs, as they should be.

Writers often use passive constructions trying to avoid *I* and *We* as the subject. If you feel that you must avoid them to prevent monotony of sentence pattern, you should see p. 38 instead of resorting to the passive. If you feel that you must avoid them to increase objectivity, you are working under a false impression; you can be just as biased without them. But you can avoid the first person and the passive at the same time, as explained in the first illustration below.

Still, you may find appropriate use for passives to meet a thesis director's or company executive's requirement that you write impersonally, to avoid a direct accusation, to put emphasis on something other than the doer of the action, or to weaken an otherwise rankling command or recommendation.

—Your Long-Flight skis were shipped this morning by our mailing department. (Can be made active and impersonal as "Two Long-Flight skis are on their way; they left the mailing department this morning.")

—The subject has been considered from the following viewpoints: . . . . (The requirement of impersonal style may justify the passive here.)

—The mower apparently has not been oiled adequately. (Avoids accusing the user.)

—The Wembley has been in great demand among the buying public for years. (The passive puts emphasis on the product rather than on the people demanding it.)

—Careful attention should be given to . . . . (Weakens a possibly rankling command.)

—It is recommended that . . . . (Weakens and avoids egotism in a recommendation.)

PD Psychological description (interpreting facts and physical features of a product in terms of reader benefits) is the real heart of selling. Unless your reader readily makes the interpretation himself, pure physical description is ineffective in selling. So when you name a physical feature of a product you're selling, show the reader what it means in terms of benefits to him. (See pp. 339–40.)

—The Bostonian Sporty shoe has Neolite soles and triple-stitched welt construction. (The Neolite soles and triple-stitched welt construction cause the Bostonian Sporty to last long and keep your feet dry.)

Personalized messages written for and adapted to specific readers are more effective than mass broadcasts. What seems to be for everybody has less interest to anybody. Even form letters should be worded to give each reader the feeling that the message is directed to him. Expressions such as "Those of you who . . ." and "If you are one who . . ." give just the opposite impression. (See p. 63.)

Plan your letter more appropriately for the circumstances as an A, B, or C plan. (See p. 55.)

Pompous Try to express the thought simply, not to impress the reader.

Pr Follow more generally acceptable business practice.

PR Personal references (names of people or pronouns referring to them) not only help to keep the reader in the picture and produce the you-attitude (**YA**); they help to avoid the passive (**Pas**), to make your writing specific and concrete instead of general and abstract (**Spec**), and to make your writing easier and more interesting to read. Naming or referring to persons—Flesch suggests at least 6 percent of your words—is an important element in readability.

Prepositions indicate relationships within a sentence.

1. Be sure to use the right one for your construction. Some words require certain prepositions; others vary prepositions for different meanings. See **Id.**

   —ability *to;* agree *to, with,* or *in;* compare *to* (for similarities only) or *with* (for likenesses and differences); different *from.*

2. When you use two words that require different prepositions, use both:

   —Because of your interest *in* and aptitude *for.* . . .

3. Don't use many of the .45-caliber group prepositions (*according to, in regard to, by means of, in connection with, on the part of*) for squirrel-size ideas or your prepositions will "bulk too large," as Perrin says.

PV Insofar as possible, keep the same point of view in a sentence, a paragraph, or a whole letter. Make only logically necessary shifts, and let your reader know by providing the necessary transitional words. Watch carefully for shifts in time, location, and those whose eyes you seem to be looking through. For effective you-attitude, look through the reader's eyes whenever possible. See **YA.**

R Bring your reader into the picture early and don't forget him later. He is the most important person involved with your letter. See **Per, PR, PV,** and **YA.**

Redundancy includes not only useless repetition but wasting words saying things that are obvious or clearly implied. Avoid it.

Ref The references of your pronouns must be immediately certain and clear to your reader—not ambiguous, too far away or merely implied. Except for the few indefinite pronouns (*one, everybody, anybody,* and *it* referring to the weather), a pronoun confuses or distracts a reader unless it refers clearly to a preceding noun or pronoun and agrees with it in number and gender. *Each, every, any,* and their combinations *anybody* and *everybody* are considered singulars requiring singular verbs and pronouns; but see **Agr** for further explanation of agreement.

1. Often the trouble with a pronoun reference is that the antecedent is just too far away. Repeat the antecedent or change the word order so that the reader knows immediately what the antecedent is.

2. Guard particularly against *this, that, which, it,* and *they* making vague reference to ideas of whole preceding clauses instead of clear, one-word antecedents.

   —Dayton adopted the plan in 1914 and has kept it ever since, which is a good example of the success of the council-manager form of government. (What does *which* refer to?)
   —After reading a book about television engineering, the young man wanted to be one of them. (One of what? Only implied.)

3. Of the relative pronouns, *who* usually refers only to persons, *that* to persons or things, and *which* to things, including animals and collections of persons such as boards and committees.

4. *That* usually introduces restrictive clauses (not requiring commas) and *which* usually introduces nonrestrictive ones (requiring commas).

5. Don't use the same pronoun with different meanings in the same sentence:

   —The directions say that it is up to the owner to change the filter whenever it needs it.

Repetition of words or ideas seems wordy and monotonous unless it serves a justified purpose. Restatement of important ideas deserving emphasis is often desirable; but even then, the restatement usually should be in somewhat different words to avoid monotony.

Resale material—reassuring a customer that his choice of goods and/or firm was a good one—not only shows your service attitude (**SA**); it helps keep incomplete orders and delayed shipments on the books, rebuilds reader confidence when used in adjustments, and serves as a basic idea in collections. Look it up in the Index and read about it in connection with the particular type of letter involved.

Style See Chapter 2 and (especially for reports) pp. 512–31 and the reports checklist (p. 564).

SA A service attitude—showing a genuine desire to give the reader the kinds and quality of goods and services he wants, favorable prices, and various conveniences, plus unselfish reassurance of appreciation for his business—can go a long way toward overcoming any feelings he may have that you are indifferent. Your basic techniques are to interweave into your letters some sales promotion material (**SPM**) and resale talk (**Res**). See p. 82.

SC Show more success consciousness. See page 67 and **Conf.**

Selfish interest is assumed by both reader and writer, but it does not help your cause and therefore is best not mentioned. Your reader is more interested in his own benefit and will be persuaded only if you show him what's in the situation for him. See **YA** and p. 59.

Shifting of tense (time), voice (active-passive), mood (indicative, imperative, subjunctive), or person (first, second, third) should be avoided unless the logic of the situation dictates otherwise.

Simplify Needlessly big words or involved sentences are hard to read.

Sincerity is essential if you are to be believed. Don't pretend or overstate your case. See p. 79.

Slow movement is desirable in a B–plan letter where you must reason calmly with the reader to justify the unpleasant point you are preparing to present (see **Fast**); otherwise, it is objectionable.

1. Don't use too many words before getting to an important point. Starting too far back in the background, giving too many details, or saying things that should be implied are the most frequent faults.

2. Don't use too many short, choppy sentences and thus slow up a message that should move fast.

SOS   Serious errors in sentence organization and structure justify the distress signal.

1. Don't present a phrase or dependent clause as a sentence. Usually correction requires only attaching the dependent element to the preceding or following sentence (on which it depends).

—In answer to your request concerning what the company is like, what has been accomplished, and the future prospects. Here is the information I have been able to acquire. (Replace the period with a comma.)

2. Don't use a comma—or no punctuation at all—between two independent clauses unless a strong conjunction (*and, but, or,* or *nor*) is there. The error is not basically one of punctuation (as discussed in **P**1 and **P**2) but the more serious failure to recognize what a sentence is. You need a period if the two statements are not so closely related that they ought to be in the same sentence, or a semicolon if they are.

—The credit business is big business some people estimate that it is as much as 86 percent of American business. (Period needed before *some*).

—Running two sentences together without punctuation is about the worst error a writer can make, however it is little worse than using a comma where a semicolon is required, as in this sentence. See **P**2.

3. Don't put words together in unnatural, confusing relationships that the reader has to ponder to get the intended meaning. (See **K** and **Mod.**)

—Just because you want to sell I don't want right now to buy. (The fact that you want to sell is insufficient reason for me to buy right now.)

4. Don't put ideas together with connectives that falsely represent their relationship. See **Coh, Conj,** and **Unit.**

Spelling error   Here are some tips on spelling and a list of words frequently misspelled in business writing.

1. *Ie* or *ei*: When pronounced like *ee,* write *ie* except after *c* or in *either, neither, leisure, seize,* and *weird* (*achieve, believe; receive, deceive, perceive*). When pronounced otherwise, write

ei (as in *freight, height, forfeit*) except in *die, lie, pie, tie, vie,* and *science.*

2. Double a final single consonant preceded by a single vowel (*a, e, i, o, u*) in an accented syllable when you add a suffix (*-ing, -ed, -er*) beginning with a vowel (*plan, planning; shop, shopping*). Note that if the word already ends in two consonants, or one preceded by two vowels, you do not double the last consonant (*holding, helping; daubing, seeded*). Note, too, that the consonant usually is not doubled unless in an accented syllable (*benefit, benefited; refer, referred, references*).

3. Drop a final, unpronounced *e* preceded by a consonant when you add a suffix beginning with a vowel (*hope, hoping; owe, owing*); but retain the *e* after *c* or *g* unless the suffix begins with one of the front vowels, *i* or *e* (*noticeable, changeable, changing, reduced*).

4. Change final *y* to *i* and add *es* for the plural if a consonant precedes the *y* (*ally, allies; tally, tallies*); otherwise, just add *s* (*valley, valleys*).

5. Add *'s* for the possessive of all singulars and of plurals which do not end in *s* (*man's, men's, lady's*); add only apostrophe for *s*-ending plurals (*ladies', Davises', students'*).

6. Hyphenate fractions (nine-tenths) and double-word quantities between 20 and 100 (*twenty-one, thirty-two, forty-four, ninety-eight*).

7. Get somebody to pronounce for you while you try to spell the following words commonly misspelled in business. Then study those you miss (along with others which give you trouble, from whatever source) until you are sure of them.

accidentally	benefited	environment
accommodate	category	equipped
accurate	choose (chose)	exaggerate
achievement	comparative	excellence
acquaintance	conscientious	existence
acquire	conscious	experience
affect (influence)	consensus	explanation
all right	consistent	forty
among	convenience	government
analyze	decision	grammar
apparent	definitely	guarantee
argument	description	height
attorneys	disastrous	imagine
beginning	effect (result)	immediately
believe	embarrass	incidentally

interest	possession	referring
interpret	practical	repetition
it's (its)	precede	sense
laboratory	preferred	separate
led	prejudiced	stationary
lose (loose)	prepare	stationery
maintenance	principal	succeed
moral (morale)	principle	surprise
mortgage	privilege	than (then)
necessary	probably	their (there)
noticeable	proceed	thorough
occasionally	procedure	transferred
occurrence	prominent	tries
offered	psychology	too (to, two)
omitted	pursue	undoubtedly
original	quantity	unnecessary
paid	questionnaire	until
passed (past)	realize	using (useful)
perform	receive	varies
personal	recommend	whether (weather)
personnel	referent	writing (written)

Specific wording, like sharpness of a photograph, helps the reader get a clear idea; general words give only a hazy view. /

1. If you are inclined to use the general word for a class of things, consider the advantages of giving the specific kind in that class (machine—mower; office equipment—files, desks, chairs, and typewriters; employees—salesmen, janitors, secretaries, and others).

2. Another kind of specificness is giving supporting details, illustrations, examples, and full explanations for general statements made. If you use generalities to gain conciseness in topic and summarizing statements, be sure to provide necessary supporting explanations or further details; otherwise, your unsupported statements will not be accepted.

3. Still another important kind of specificness is giving the evidences of abstract qualities you may use. If you are inclined to say that something is a bargain, an outstanding offer, of the highest quality, revolutionary, best, ideal, or economical, give the concrete evidences for these qualities instead of the abstract words. In an application letter, if you want to convey the idea that you are intelligent, industrious, honest, dependable, and sociable, give the evidence and let the reader draw his conclusions; you will sound too cocky if you apply these words to yourself, and your reader will not believe them anyway, unless you give the supporting concrete facts.

SPM Sales promotion material (when appropriate and unselfish) not only shows a service attitude (see **SA**) and produces some additional sales; it helps to take the sting out of early collection letters and provides a pleasant ending for essentially bad-news letters, provided that the situation is not too seriously negative. See p. 84.

Subordinate Don't overstress negative ideas, facts known to the reader, or insignificant points. If you must say them, put them in the middle of the paragraph or letter, devote little space to them, and/or put them in dependent clauses or phrases. Since dependent clauses are particularly useful in subordinating, here are some of the main beginning words that make clauses dependent: *after, although, as, because, before, if, since, though, till, unless, until, when, where, while.*

Subjunctive mood is complex; but nearly all the problems with it in business writing can be solved if you remember these statements: (1) *Were* is the form for present tense, regardless of person (first, second, or third); *be* is the auxiliary form (to be used with present and past participles). (2) Use the subjunctive for conditions contrary to fact (including unachieved wishes) and after commands.

—If he *were* better trained in. . . . (Present tense, third person, contrary to fact.)
—The manager directs that these topics *be discussed* thoroughly. . . . (Past participle with *be;* follows command.)
—"Let it *be* so ordered," the chairman intoned.
—I wish it *were* possible to approve all requests.
—If it *were* the only possibility, ...

SW Shall-will; should-would. General usage differs so much from formal usage of *shall* and *will* that formal practice sounds unnecessarily stiff in most letters and reports. In general usage (which is usually appropriate for business writing), *will* has almost completely replaced *shall*, although formal usage still calls for *shall* with the first person and *will* with other persons to indicate the simple future, and for the reverse to indicate firm promise or determination.

More important for business writers is the distinction between the simple futures and their conditional forms, *should* and *would*. Using the simple future sometimes seems presumptuous.

—I will (or *shall,* if you want to be formal about it) appreciate your giving me your answer by November 20 so that . . . . (*Would,* in place of *will,* removes the presumption that the reader will answer, by using the conditional mood and saying, in effect, "*If* you will answer . . . I will appreciate it.")

Synopsis   See p. 539 and the reports checklist (p. 568).

Syl   Divide words at the ends of lines only at syllable breaks, and then only if each part has at least two letters and is pronounceable. If in doubt about where to divide a word, check the dictionary.

Terminal section (of a report). See the reports checklist (p. 567).

Tabulate or itemize when you have lots of figures to present or a series of distinct points to make. Itemization will make you think more sharply and state your ideas more precisely and concisely. Thus you produce clearer, quicker reading and more emphasis.

Telegraphic style (omitting subjects, connective words, and articles, as in telegrams and newspaper headlines) is not acceptable practice in letters and reports.

Ten   Watch the tense (time indicated by your verbs) for appropriateness in the individual verb and logic in the sequence of verbs. Do not shift tenses unless the logic of the situation requires. Normally you use the present, past, or future according to the time of the action you are reporting; but use the present for statements that were true in the past, are true now, and will be true later. Any statement you might make about what a book *says* fits the conditions. (See the reports checklist, p. 565, Item 12, for tense in reports.)

> —The law of supply and demand *means* . . . .
> —The 1969 edition *says* . . . .

The tense of the key verb in an independent clause governs a sentence. So the tenses of other verbs or verbals indicate time relative to the time of the main verb:

> —I will do it as soon as I am able (a future and relative present).
> —I had hoped that I would be able to go (a past perfect and relative future).

Tone   Watch out for a tone of distrust, indifference, undue humility, flattery, condescension, preachiness, bragging, anger, accusation, sarcasm, curtness, effusiveness, and exaggeration. See p. 71.

Since salutations and complimentary closes are the first and last indications of your feelings about the formality of your relationship to your reader, be sure they represent those feelings accurately. See Chapter 1.

TL   Transmittal letter. See the reports checklist (p. 569).

Transitions between sentences in a paragraph and between paragraphs must show the relationship. Your best method is use of a thread of logic that will hold your thoughts together like beads on a string. When the logical thread does not make the relationship clear, however, you need to do so by repeating a key word or idea from the preceding, or by using a connecting word or phrase that shows the relationship. See **Coh** and **Unit**.

Trite expressions (a form of **Jargon**) are usually overused and hence worn-out figures of speech that dull your writing. The remedy is to state your idea simply in natural, normal English or to use an original figure of speech.

Unity (of sentences, paragraphs, or whole pieces of writing) requires that you show how each statement fits in or belongs (is not irrelevant). Applied to a sentence or paragraph, **Unit** means that the statement seems irrelevant or that the several ideas are not closely enough related to be in the one sentence or paragraph. When applied to a whole letter or report, it means that the content seems so varied as to lack a central theme and should be put in two or more separate papers. Often, however, the writer sees relationships that justify putting things together as he has, and his fault is in not showing the reader the relationships—an error of coherence (see **Coh**).

> —Please put your answers in ink and have your signature witnessed by two people. One of our envelopes is enclosed for your convenience. (The envelope is not a convenience in doing what is requested in the first sentence. The two unrelated ideas should not be in the same paragraph. Adding "in returning your answers" would help.)

Usage refers to the appropriateness of the language to the situation. A passage or expression marked with the symbol may be too formal and stiff, literary, flashy, or highbrow; or too slangy, familiar, crude, or lowbrow. The normal, natural English of educated people conducting their everyday affairs is neither formal nor illiterate, but informal and natural. That's what you should use for most letters and reports.

Variety (of diction and of sentence pattern, type, and length) is necessary to avoid monotony, which puts readers to sleep. Achieving variety should be a part of the revision process, however, and should not distract your thoughts from saying what you want to say in writing a first draft. In your revision, see that you haven't begun too many successive sentences the same way (especially not with *I* or *we*). If you have repeated yourself, cut out the repetition unless you need it for emphasis, and then change the wording if the two statements of the same idea are close together.

The usual English sentence pattern is subject-verb-complement; in revision, vary the pattern to avoid a dull sameness. (Page 38 lists various kinds of sentence beginnings.)

Good style also requires variety in sentence type. Some of your sentences should be simple (one independent clause); some should be compound (two independent clauses stating two closely related ideas of nearly equal importance); and some should be complex (at least one independent clause and one or more dependent, all expressing related ideas but of unequal importance). Especially to be avoided are too many successive simple sentences for ideas not deserving equal emphasis or too many compound sentences connected by *and*. (See **Sub.**)

Although most of your sentences should be relatively short (averaging 15–20 words for easy readability), you will produce a monotonous choppiness if all your sentences are in that range. See

Sim and **Chop,** and revise accordingly.

W Wordy.

WF Word forms. As you know, many words change forms slightly according to their use in the sentence. Be sure you use the right form for the purpose.

1. Verbs change according to what we call their principal parts. Here are some of the troublesome or unusual ones.

Present Tense	Past Tense	Present Participle	Past Participle
I begin	I began	beginning	have or had begun
blow	blew	blowing	blown
choose	chose	choosing	chosen
forget	forgot	forgetting	forgot
lay	laid	laying	laid
lead	led	leading	led
lend	lent	lending	lent
lie (recline)	lay	lying	lain
pay	paid	paying	paid
prove	proved	proving	proved
set	set	setting	set
sit	sat	sitting	sat
throw	threw	throwing	thrown
wear	wore	wearing	worn
write	wrote	writing	written

2. Adjective and adverb forms are sometimes confused. Determine whether the word modifies a noun or pronoun (for the adjective form) or a verb, adjective, or adverb (for the adverb form). Most, but not all, adverbs are the same as adjectives with *-ly* added; but *-ly* added to a noun makes it an adjective (*manly* qualities, *wifely* duties).

Usually modifiers after verbs modify them and are adverbs, but not so after linking verbs (all forms of *to be, become, seem*) and those indicating actions of your senses—*feels, sounds, tastes, smells, looks.*

—June-bloom Temple oranges usually taste good (not *well*), feel soft (not *softly*), smell sweet (not *sweetly*), and look horrible (not *horribly*).

The idea is that the predicate word really describes the subject (a noun), not the verb. Of course, if the modifier truly describes the action, even in these same verbs, it is an adverb:

—A good driver looks carefully to right and left before entering an unprotected intersection.
—Doctor, please feel gently of this sore spot; much pressure hurts.
—I feel bad today after working too late last night (although usage now seems to condone *badly*).

3. Not only must pronouns agree with the words they refer to (see **Agr**), but they must be in the proper form (see **Case**) for their use in the sentence. Most of the troubles are cleared up in this one sentence: Use the nominative case (*I, we, he, she, they, who*) as the subject of a verb or the complement after any form of the verb *to be;* use the objective case (*me, us, him, her, them, whom*) as the object (receiving rather than doing the action) of an active-voice verb or the object of a preposition. Be especially careful to make the second of a compound object of a preposition in the objective case:

—He said that the story was a big secret, but he told it to Betty and *me.*

In informal writing and speaking, you may go contrary to the general rule and use *who* at the beginning of a sentence (because that is "subject territory"), even though its function in the sentence calls for *whom.*

—Who would you consider the better authority on a point like this, a linguist like Fries or somebody else?
—Who did you tell? Who did you buy that for?

4. Be on guard against any of the following illiterate forms (mostly

the result of bad pronunciation): "He is prejudice" (*prejudiced*). "He is bias" (*biased*), "usta" or "use to" (*used to*), "had of" (*had*), "would of" (*would have*), "most all" (*almost all*), "a savings of" (*a saving of*).

5. Use comparative forms (*former, latter, better, more, faster,* and the like) only when referring to two things; use the superlative form (*best, most, fastest*) only when referring to three or more. See **Cpr.**

6. Distinguish between the often confused pairs: *may be, maybe; some time, sometime; all ready, already; with regards to, in regard to; its, it's; your, you're.* See **D.**

7. Use the possessive form for the subject of a gerund (a present participle used as a noun ("We appreciate *your notifying* . . .).

Wordy   See pp. 32 ff.

YA   You-attitude. The you-attitude is certainly one of the three most important points about letter writing. People do things for their own benefit, not yours. If you want to persuade them to act, you have to show them the advantages to themselves. Both your reader and you know that you're interested in yourself. Trying to deny that fact would be insincere and disbelieved. But you need not put your selfish interests in the letter; the fact that you want something is no reason for the reader to act. The benefits he gets are. Show them to him. See **Self** and p. 59.

To show the reader what is in the situation for him, you have to visualize his way of life and show how your proposal fits in. See **Adap.**

Although using more *you*'s than *I*'s or *we*'s may help, it is no assurance that your letter has the you-attitude.

X   Obvious error. Proofread carefully and correct such errors.

∿   Invert the order or sequence of words or ideas.

⊃   Close up the unnecessary space.

¶   New paragraph needed.

1. Paragraphs in letters and reports are the same as in other writing—unified developments of topics—except that they tend to be more compressed and shorter for easier readability. Especially the first and last paragraphs of letters should be short (rarely more than three or four lines). Elsewhere, if a paragraph runs to more than about eight lines, you should consider breaking it up for easier readability.

2. Develop your paragraphs adequately to support your points—by further explanation, detail, facts and figures, or illustrations and examples.

3. But avoid putting unrelated things in the same paragraph. See **Unit** and pp. 40, 42 for tips on paragraph construction.

Additional space needed here.

γ or 6 Delete (take out); unnecessary.

↑←→↓ Move in the direction pointed.

Index

Index

A

A-plan letters: basic plan of, 55; in inquiries, 110 ff.; in replies, 117 ff.; in acknowledgments, 141 ff.; in credit approvals, 146 ff.; in adjustments, 153 ff.

Abbreviations, 692

Abstract: words, 36, 515 (6); of report, 539. *See* Synopsis

Accepting a job, 471

Accuracy, of wording, punctuation, grammar, 42, 48

Accusations: as element of tone, 76; avoiding, 254, 267

Acknowledgments: standard, 141; of incomplete orders, 267; back-order, 270; declining orders, 273; selling substitutes, 275; combination, 281

Action endings: according to purpose, 68; elements of, 128 ff.; choice of, 129, 271, 278; in sales letters, 344, 350; in applications, 461, 469

Active versus passive voice, 35, 515 (5), 719

Adaptation: as a principle of persuasion, 62 ff.; in invited sales, 131 (6); in sales, 342, 350; in collections, 393 (4); of qualifications to job, 435; in reports, 513; as a principle of communication, 662

Address: inside, 18; of envelope, 26

Adjustment: approvals, 157 ff.; analysis and classification, 158; refusals, 253; compromises, 257, 260

Àgreement: of subject and verb, 693; of pronoun and antecedent, 693

Analysis: of adjustments, 158; of product, 339; of sales prospects, 341; of self, 430; of employers, 433; of report problems, 493

Analytical reports: importance, nature, and classes, 487; preparation of, 493 ff.; analysis and illustration, 532 ff.; short, 606 ff.

Anger, 76

Annual reports: as information about jobs, 434; history and nature of, 604

Apologies: in adjustments, 160; versus reasons, 249

Apostrophes, 696

Appeals: in requests, 318; in selling, 342; in collection, 393, 400

Appearance: as requirement of good letter, 12; effect on courtesy, 79

Appendix, in reports, 558

Applications: for credit, 113, 326; for jobs, 429 ff., 453 ff.; following up, 467; telescoped, 475

Appreciation: implication of, 61; versus "thanks in advance," 116 (4); for order, 142; for claims, 161; letters of, 225

Appropriateness: of stationery, 12; of language, 45; of sales promotion, 86

Approval: of credit, 146; of adjustments, 157

Attention: lines, 24; in requests, 59; in sales letters, 345 ff.; in applications, 454

Attitudes: you, 59; in relation to goodwill, 70 ff.; service, 82; of indifference, 141; of adjusters, 159; in collections, 389, 390; in applications, 435

Authorization, letter of, 534, 569

B

B-plan letters: theory and plan of, 56; in replies, 246; in adjustments, 253 ff.; in credit refusals, 259, 262; in acknowledgments, 267 ff.

Back-order acknowledgment, 270

Backtracking, in collections, 399

Bad-news letters, 56, 246 ff.

Balance of personalities, effect on tone, 71

Bases of credit, 146, 148

Beginnings: of sentences, for variety, 38; in inquiries, 110 ff.; of favorable replies, 117; of invited sales, 124; of unfavorable letters, 246; for requests, 319 ff.;

737

This book has been set in 10 and 9 point Caledonia, leaded 2 points. Part numbers and titles are in 14 and 24 point Helvetica. Chapter numbers and titles are in 12 and 18 point Helvetica. The size of the type page is 27 by 46½ picas.